Ethics in Banking

INDIAN INSTITUTE OF BANKING & FINANCE

Revised and updated by Mr. Atul Kumar, Former Chief Ethics Officer, SBI and Vetted by Dr. Asha Prasuna, Professor of Economics & International Finance, K J Somaiya Institute of Management, Mumbai

Edition : 2024

Price : ₹ 980

Published by :
Taxmann Publications (P.) Ltd.

Sales & Marketing :
59/32, New Rohtak Road, New Delhi-110 005 India
Phone : +91-11-45562222
Website : www.taxmann.com
E-mail : sales@taxmann.com

Mumbai
35, Bodke Building, Ground Floor M.G. Road,
Opp. Railway Station, Mulund (W), Mumbai - 400 080
Mob. +91-9322247686, 9619668669, 7045453844/45/51
E-mail : sales.mumbai@taxmann.com; nileshbhanushali@taxmann.com

Regd. Office :
21/35, West Punjabi Bagh, New Delhi-110 026 India

Printed at :
Tan Prints (India) Pvt. Ltd.
44 Km. Mile Stone, National Highway, Rohtak Road,
Village Rohad, Distt. Jhajjar (Haryana) India
E-mail : sales@tanprints.com

FOREWORD

ETHICS is the ROAD to WEALTH and GOODWILL (Kural: 31 —Thiruvalluvar)

There is nothing in this world except ethics which would bring both reputation and wealth together; therefore, ethical principle in business is essential.

The above couplet written 2000 years ago by Thiruvalluvar in his notable literary work Thirukkural guides human beings to lead a moral, ethical and useful life. Many research scholars have highlighted the relevance of the poet's couplets on business ethics even in today's contemporary business leadership including banking.

Banking is the backbone of any economy. It fuels growth, development and progress, ushering in immense responsibility not only in terms of managing financial transactions but also extending its responsibility towards the society at large by building trust and accountability. The reputation and confidence of public are closely connected with the honest, fair, transparent and ethical transactions of banks and other financial intermediaries.

Banks are economic and social institutions. They serve customers' needs at right place, right price and quality. Banks need to nurture a culture of ethical leadership which should conform to legal and professional standards of conduct. While being mindful of productivity and profitability, banks are advised to adhere to the highest standards of ethical principles like, honesty, integrity, accountability, fairness in dealing and social responsibility. The consequences of unethical practices may lead to loss of trust and reputation, criminal prosecution and regulatory actions.

FOREWORD

Considering the growing importance of ethics in banking and financial institutions, the Institute introduced a course on Ethics in Banking to help understand the various aspects of ethics and application of ethical principles to business. The revised book delves into some deeper aspects of business ethics through relevant case studies, the different ethical dimensions, environmental ethics, ethical issues of corruption, bribery, white-collar crimes etc. alongside latest developments pertaining to Fintech, ESG, Digital India Act etc.

We acknowledge the professional expertise of Mr. Atul Kumar, former Chief Ethics Officer, SBI, for updating and enriching the book and comprehensively covering all facets of the subject.

We hope that the book will be useful not only to the bankers but to all those interested in the subject.

Suggestions for improving the book are welcome.

Mumbai
2024

Biswa Ketan Das
Chief Executive Officer

RECOMMENDED READING

The Institute has prepared comprehensive courseware in the form of study kits to facilitate preparation for the examination without intervention of the teacher. An attempt has been made to cover fully the syllabus prescribed for each module/subject and the presentation of topics may not always be in the same sequence as given in the syllabus.

Candidates are also expected to take note of all the latest developments relating to the subject covered in the syllabus by referring to Financial Papers, Economic Journals, Latest Books and Publications in the subjects concerned.

SYLLABUS

MODULE A - UNDERSTANDING ETHICS

Introduction to Ethics: An Overview; Ethics, Business Ethics & Banking: An Integrated Perspective; Banking and Normative Ethics in Management; Ethics, Financial Services and Regulation.

MODULE B - DIFFERENT OPERATIONAL LEVELS OF ETHICS IN BANKING

Ethics at the Individual Level; Ethics at the Organisational Level; Ethical Dimensions-Marketing; Ethical Dimensions-Employees; Ethics, Corporate Social responsibility and ESG.

MODULE C - WORKPLACE ETHICS AND AN ETHICAL ORGANISATION

Work Ethic and the Workplace; Building an Ethical Organisation; Banking Ethics: Changing Dynamics.

MODULE D - WIDER ASPECTS OF ETHICS IN PRACTICE

Corporate Governance and Ethical Dimensions; Environmental Ethics; Ethics and Globalisation; Ethical issues of Corruption, Bribery and White-Collar Crime; Ethics: A Holistic Approach.

CHAPTER-HEADS

CONTENTS

UNIT 2

ETHICS, BUSINESS ETHICS AND BANKING: AN INTEGRATED PERSPECTIVE

PAGE

UNIT 3

BANKING AND NORMATIVE ETHICS IN MANAGEMENT

UNIT 4

ETHICS, FINANCIAL SERVICES AND REGULATION

MODULE B: DIFFERENT OPERATIONAL LEVELS OF ETHICS IN BANKING

UNIT 5

ETHICS AT THE INDIVIDUAL LEVEL

MODULE C: WORKPLACE ETHICS AND AN ETHICAL ORGANISATION

UNIT 10
WORK ETHICS AND THE WORKPLACE

PAGE

UNIT 11

BUILDING AN ETHICAL ORGANIZATION

PAGE

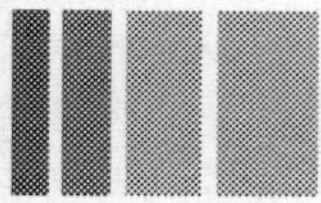

MODULE D: WIDER ASPECTS OF ETHICS IN PRACTICE

UNIT 13
CORPORATE GOVERNANCE AND ETHICAL DIMENSIONS

CONTENTS

PAGE

UNIT 14
ENVIRONMENTAL ETHICS

UNIT 15
ETHICS AND GLOBALIZATION

UNIT 16

ETHICAL ISSUES OF CORRUPTION, BRIBERY AND WHITE-COLLAR CRIME

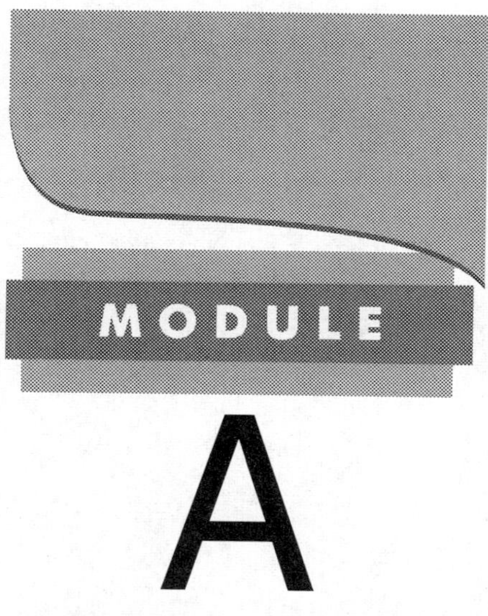

A

UNDERSTANDING ETHICS

1 UNIT

Introduction to Ethics: An Overview

1.1 Learning Objectives

1.2 Concept & Evolution of Ethics

1.3 Dimensions of Ethics: Personal, Professional and Managerial

1.4 Ethics and Human Interface: Essence, Determinants and Consequences of Ethics in Human Actions

1.5 Need of Ethics in Governance: Objectives, Scope, Types: Transactional, Participatory and Recognition

1.6 Ethics and Concept of Welfare State

1.7 Ethics, Religion and Law

1.8 Let Us Sum Up

1.9 Key Words

1.10 Check Your Progress

1.11 Exercise Your Ethics Muscle

Case 1: The Equifax Data Breach

Case 2: Helping the Students

1

UNIT

Introduction to Ethics: An Overview

1.1 LEARNING OBJECTIVES

In this unit, we will try to understand the meaning and concept of ethics and how ethics became an inevitable part of our social system. To maintain good governance in a social system, ethics builds and promotes trust amongst citizens. Ethical code of conduct and individual moral principles help in differentiating good from bad, which encourages ethical practices at personal, professional and managerial levels. Various theories suggest that ethics helps in finding solution to dilemma like "What should I do?" both in work and life situations. We also discuss how ethics lays the foundation of welfare state, which plays a vital role in building a society by focusing on the wellbeing of its citizens. Although religion inculcates morals and values at individual level, however, there is a difference between being ethical and being religious. Also, we see how and why laws are formulated in a society or a country by keeping in mind right and wrong behaviors.

1.2 CONCEPT AND EVOLUTION OF ETHICS

While going to office in the morning, should we stop to help a stranger who seems to be in trouble? Should we tell the billing boy at the shop that he has given us more change than was due? Should we submit an academic paper at the university that a friend who specializes in the subject has written to get better grades in the final examination? Should we donate a little portion of our hard earned money to educate one or two children from the poor families? Should we ignore or tell our supervisor if we suddenly come to know about a colleague who is indulging in some fraudulent activity at the workplace and is a good friend? Should we report the matter to higher-ups in case we come across in our office someone doing misappropriation of the organization's money? Should we escalate to the higher-ups that your immediate superior is pressurizing you to sanction poor quality loans in order to achieve the budgetary targets? We all face such ethical choices every day of our life. Ethics examines the various ways in which we try to answer those questions in our own lives. Ethics tells us what it means to be a good or bad person and how should we decide as to which actions are right or wrong?

Meaning of Ethics: The word 'Ethics' is derived from the ancient Greek word 'ethikos' meaning 'relating to character'. 'Ethikos' has its roots in 'ethos', a term that refers to character or moral nature. In this sense, at a broad level, ethics deals with the study and practice of the standards of human behaviour, specifically the determination of right and wrong behaviours. In other words, ethics involves principles of human conduct or human actions. These human actions must serve a purpose, which constitute part or whole of the moral agent's intention in doing what he or she does. As discussed in the opening para, we all know that at the individual level, at the level of a family, community, religion, society and the international fraternity, each day, there are dozens or even hundreds of issues that make one think whether the situation, one gets to know through the media or personal encounter, is (ethically) acceptable or otherwise. Likewise, should we remain indifferent, if we come across a nearby clinic conducting gender-detection tests on pregnant women and resorting to termination of one gender as per the liking of the customers? Or for that matter, should we use too much of air-conditioning and excessive use of motor cars using fuels like petrol/diesel if we can afford? Let us also take certain broader purposes of life that are related to the issues as raised above:

- Why should we live having born on this planet?
- How should we lead our lives?
- Should we pursue our personal pleasures or happiness or is there any other thing/s we require to care for?
- Is it acceptable to us if we have abundant money and wealth whereas several persons in our neighbourhood starve each day?

Can we escape such questions, if we reflect on how we should live? Perhaps not, as these are fundamental and vital questions. At the same time, it is also important what answers we come up with for these questions, for it matters what we intend to do with our lives on this planet. Ethics attempts to address such concerns of human life both conceptually and practically. Citing the words

of the English moral philosopher Bernard Williams, 'ethics is an autonomous concept and addresses the very broad question, how one should live?' According to Thomas J Higgins, the author of 'Man As Man: The Science and Art of Ethics'-'Ethics is the art of human living and its results should be ease in being good men in every circumstances.' If we think over all these expressions, we shall find their genesis in the famous argument of Aristotle that 'a life lived in line with the virtues is the best life for any human being. This is the happy and fulfilled life, the life that allows us to flourish and realize all our capacities.' Setting down the same meaning in terms of means and ends, Thomas Garrett, the ethicist, also defines ethics is the science of judging specifically human ends and relationship of means of those ends. In some way, it is also the art of controlling means so that they will serve specifically human needs.

Thus, it can be stated that ethics continuously makes a systematic enquiry to learn:

(*a*) What are the standards of morality of people?

(*b*) Why those are the standards of morality?

(*c*) How people practice these standards?

This means that ethics is not simply an emotional expression such as "be good" and "do good". It is a rational analysis and conclusion about the fundamental element, that decides good or bad and right or wrong behaviour. For that very reason, ethics grows into a discipline that examines our standards of behaviour or the standards of collective behaviors of a society. In the words of renowned ethicist, Manuel G. Velasquez, "It asks how these standards apply to your life and whether these standards are reasonable or unreasonable - that is, whether they are supported by good reasons or poor ones. What do these standards imply for the situations in which I find myself? Do these standards really make sense? What are the reasons for or against these standards? Why should I continue to believe in them? What can be said in their favor and what can be said against them? Are they really reasonable for me to hold? Are their implications in this or that particular situation reasonable?"

When we start out asking such kind of questions about our own behavior or the behavior of our group or society, we begin thinking ethically. Most errors in ethics come from ignoring one or more of these questions. Deepak Parekh, the Chairman of HDFC, puts the whole idea in a very simple way when he says that ethics is simply to 'not do something that one would be ashamed of, if it becomes public.' What Mr. Deepak Parekh is stating is being echoed since thousands of years as we can observe in the definition of ethics given by Epicuras, a famous Greek philosopher, who says that ethics is the one which deals with 'the things to be sought and things to be avoided with ways of life and with the telos (Telos means the chief aim of life).

The Objectives of Ethics

The word ethics has a broad-spectrum and individual ethics cannot be completely isolated from ethics in society or a country. The evolution of society led to evolution of individual morals and a certain code of conduct. That is, how an individual should behave and is able to distinguish between the good behavior and bad behavior. The moral system of a society prescribes that certain behaviors like helping others, speaking truth, keeping one's promises, etc. are good. At the same time, it proscribes certain behaviors such as lying, cheating, stealing, harming others, etc. as bad. Such common standards of behavior or conduct are not only necessary but also required for continued survival and well-being of a society. As such, morality deals with right and wrong conduct along with good or bad character while ethics clarifies the concept of right and wrong with fitting justifications. Ethics provides reasons to define and distinguish what is right, what is wrong and what ought to be. Thus, ethics is moral values in action. To put it differently, ethics is a system of moral principles and attitudes that guides us to live our lives according to a standard of "right" or "wrong" behavior - in a morally correct, fair and just way. For example, we all play a number of roles in our lives: son or daughter, brother or sister, husband or wife, parent, employee or employer, student, friend, neighbor, citizen and so on. Each of these role places certain expectations on us and obligations towards those who relate to us in that particular role. A student has an obligation to attend class, to study and not to cheat; an employee has an obligation do her job well; a spouse has an obligation to be loyal and supportive and likewise. Most of the times, we keep on navigating these roles successfully but sometimes situations occur which cause conflicts between our different obligations. When this happens, it becomes hard to decide what the right thing to do is. To take the case of one student who is expected to attend classes and hand in assignments on time, but

a family emergency comes up and he is required to support the family member in need. If he cannot do the both at the same time, how should he decide which has a priority. In such situations of conflict, ethics helps us evaluate different obligations and make a decision that is fair, just and the morally correct. The below-given box plots the objectives of ethics diagrammatically:

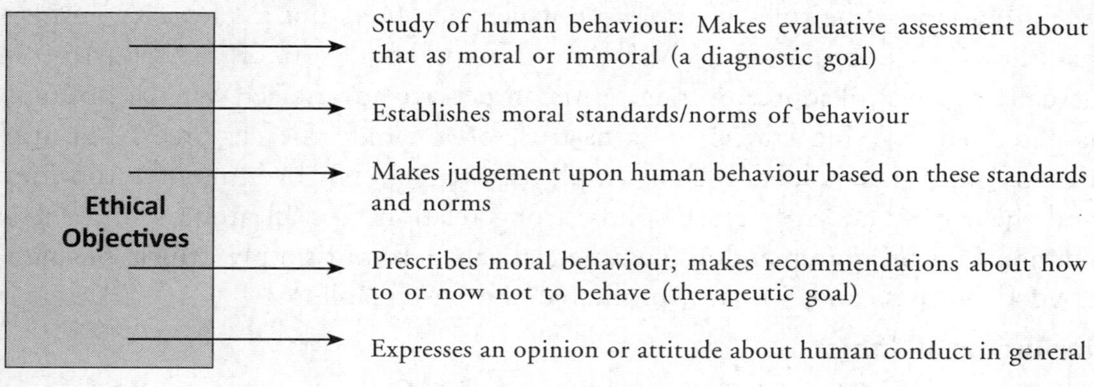

OBJECTIVES OF ETHICS

Ethics in Business: The purpose of business is to make money, if it does not, it will have failed in its primary objective. If it does make money but does it in an unethical fashion, it will be in breach of social system that permits and fosters its commercial activity. It is the aim of teaching ethics to constantly make the point that the purpose of business is to make money and to make it without compromising on principles. Thus, ethics is equally pertinent for individuals, as well as business. Integration of ethics with business is essential as every business operates within the society and it cannot disassociate itself from the people working within and outside the organization. We all might be familiar with the 18th Century economist Adam Smith's parable that market is an "invisible hand" which moves goods and services to those individuals who value them more. For example, a farmer 'who has harvested more corn than he can possibly eat sells some of the corn for money that he then uses to buy a much-needed pair of shoes. On the other hand, the shoemaker, who has manufactured more shoes that he can possibly wear, sells a pair to the farmer for money he can then use to buy some of farmer's corn for dinner. Both the farmer and shoemaker have made money and both feel they have been left better off. The world is a better place for their self-interested exchange. Each party has not only benefitted himself, but someone else as well.' In this way, 'ethics in business ensures that business is doing well by doing good, rather than doing well by doing harm.' Still, the biggest barrier in the introduction of ethics in the business is that it is sometimes considered as a luxury, which a business may find it difficult to adhere to on account of intensifying competitive pressures in the short run. It is normal to think how one can compete against others successfully when one obeys the rules of the game while the others don't? However, history has shown that, acting ethically, far from being some sort of costly luxury, is actually a powerful source of long term competitive advantage. When a business is perceived as being ethical, it earns trust of not only the customers but also that of other stakeholders such as employees, regulators, government authorities and the society at large. Trust builds strong relationships all around, and these relationships bring tremendous commercial value. To put simply, ethical business is good business and, in turn, profitable and sustainable too.

Evolution of Ethics

All humans as rational beings attempt to grow. If the individuals are allowed to practice whatever they believe, then there could be violence. Hence, a set of norms have evolved over centuries to bring orderly growth in the society. For achieving the growth, the society requires peace and coexistence, which is not very easy to achieve by itself.

Frequent fights, conflicts and even full-fledged wars gave people of most countries in the world the realization that we need to be civilized. Only then peace is possible. Peace ensures us to plan and utilize our energies and ideas in the desired manner, which alone will give us lasting prosperity.

Instead of kings or emperors in the olden days, a democratically elected government as a political institution, which remains accountable to its judiciary through a Constitution and to its people for greater acceptability and appreciation of governance and also for better chances to win elections, is considered a better form of political system.

States started encouraging certain behaviours of individuals in their jurisdiction and discouraged or punished some other behaviours which were broadly agreed in a given period of time as unacceptable and was believed that these actions will not help the society at large.

India's society, for example is one of the most complex ones in the world even for a seasoned sociologist to fully comprehend, leave aside persons with science,

engineering, pharmacy, biotechnology, IT, etc. branches. Some of the salient features of India's society are:

- ◆ Patriarchal and strongly hierarchal.
- ◆ Dominant caste system (especially in rural India) has made Indians very rank and status oriented.
- ◆ The people of India can be found in traditional (even orthodox), modern and almost Western segments. Value systems, among the people in the three segments, also vary accordingly.
- ◆ India is a pluralistic (multi-religious, multi-ethnic, multi-lingual) society.
- ◆ Social events (like marriage, child-birth, death) are accorded extreme importance.

With the democracy, the following features are pursued. These become the characteristics of a typical democratic society:

- ◆ Democratic governance
- ◆ Citizens can freely elect the government of their choice through secret ballot without any threats or coercion.
- ◆ Political system allowing fair political competition (overseen by a constitutional body like the Election Commission) and tolerance among the political parties.
- ◆ Press and media have freedom to report (expose and criticize) government actions.
- ◆ Respect for the fundamental rights and all basic human rights.
- ◆ Respect for the Rule of law.
- ◆ Citizen participation and citizen-oriented development.

With a political party (or a coalition of parties) in power, Cabinet prepares some Acts and get them passed by the Parliament. Administrative rules are formulated by the various departments. Besides these, there can be a regulatory body created to supervise and guide some critical areas like banking, insurance, capital markets, civil aviation, telecommunications, pension funds, etc. These regulatory bodies can also have their own sector-specific Acts and guidelines, circulars, standards, etc.

These Acts, rules and guidelines are never static but are amended as per the changes witnessed in the society from time-to-time.

Dynamic and rapid changes in the society are taken care by the systems created by the society in which State plays a prime role. Changes in the society can be on account of various changes in education, beliefs, technology, accessibility of information through the Internet, etc.

Citizens influence their elected representatives in formulating and getting enacted the laws that are consistent with their value or importance they attach to something. All of us value something or the other. We value that certain basic education is must whether or not a child's parents are able to afford for the same. Likewise, primary health, pollution-free environment, silent surroundings during some hours of the night till dawn, etc. There would be laws formulated suiting the mood of the citizens in a particular context, which may be enacted. If need be, after some years of implementing these laws, there can be amendments in the existing law or a new law may be formulated by incorporating necessary changes.

These Acts and administrative rules (like eligibility and qualifications to a post, pay, benefits, confirmation, promotion, retirement or termination, etc.) help society to utilise its human, financial and material resources efficiently with some intended manner ensured by the authority.

Ethics theories begin with ancient Greek philosophers (Sophists, Socrates, Socratic schools, Plato, Aristotle, Epicurus, Stoics) and after recovered by early English positivists, has been the main topic of discussions in the medieval times in Europe. As the scholastic doctrines are by-passed (therefore Christian Ethics is not a scientific term anymore), we come to the illuminated times after the Medieval, and continue with Hobbes, the Father of Modern Ethics. This type of ethics is known by two logical methods; criticism and comparison.

After Hobbes, English and German schools of ethics have been differentiated. These led to English Intuitionist (naturalists) followed by Utilitarian against Kantian ethics. Throughout the 19th Century these ideas have been discussed very fiercely throughout Europe. Then Comte, Darwin, and finally Spencer followed by Green came in, who set the evolution concept into physical sciences as well as the development of ethics. So, at the beginning of 20th century Ethics was more with evolutionary concepts but still divided between Utilitarians (teleology) and Kantians (deontology).

1.3 DIMENSIONS OF ETHICS: PERSONAL, PROFESSIONAL AND MANAGERIAL

Personal Dimension: Ethics provides the guiding principles, which affect the behaviour of an individual. Certain predetermined code of conduct helps an individual in determining how to behave in a particular situation. The following are few such situations:

- Doing personal work during office hours (such as searching on the Internet for deciding brand of a mobile phone for self or family member, etc.)
- Taking credit for others' work
- Doing homework of the children at office as a routine
- Claiming the medical reimbursement even through medicines were never purchased
- Using office photocopying for personal works
- Using the personal details of bank customers for personal benefit and mileage

The decisions taken by an individual in the above situation reflect his/her personal ethics. An individual may or may not be aware of this fact but every decision that is made embeds a moral element. It is important for individuals to realize that how everyday choices can shape their personal ethics in the long term. Here, it is to be understood that personal values have a significant influence on decision-making, ethical or otherwise. People act in accordance with what is important to them or what do they value most. We will discuss about personal ethics in detail in the subsequent Unit-5.

Professional Dimension

The idea of 'profession' originated in the medieval period. At that time, only three occupations *viz.* law, medicine and divinity were recognized as professions because these occupations required formal, standardized and intellectual training. Over the years, the idea has become more inclusive and today professions are those occupations that 'offers effective expert assistance to society' which : (*i*) require extensive training, (*ii*) have a significant intellectual component, (*iii*) provides an important service to society, (*iv*) are organized into associations and (*v*) articulate technical and ethical standards of competent professional practice.

Being professional, thus, means one is required to follow certain pre-defined standards or principles or a code of conduct in one's practice.

Certain values that are essential for a professional are – responsibility, respect, fairness and honesty.

Professionals need to be **Responsible**; that is, they should take ownership of decisions made or actions taken or inability to make decisions or take actions.

Professional must **Respect** themselves and show a high regard to resources entrusted to them, which includes people, money, reputation, the safety of others, and natural or environmental resources. Respect engenders trust, confidence, and performance excellence by fostering mutual cooperation-an environment where diverse perspectives and views are encouraged and valued.

Professionals must practice **Fairness**, and be transparent in decision-making and act impartially and objectively. A professional's conduct must be free from favouritism, prejudice, and competing self-interest. Professional must practice equality in providing access to vital information and providing equal opportunities to qualifying ones.

Lastly, **Honesty** is non-negotiable for professionals. Honesty aids understanding truth and acting truthfully in communicating and conduct. Professionals must engage with all stakeholders truthfully and timely at all times. Only then they can become trustworthy by developing the trust of those whom they serve. Trust is not only fundamental to effective and successful professional practice but also an obligation to honor the fiduciary commitments attached with the particular profession. Thus, a professional is expected to exhibit 'an intrinsic knowledge of the difference between right and wrong, show the courage to act upon that knowledge with empathy and respect for others, and the environment.'

Let's try to understand the professional ethics through one practical scenario. Imagine that you are a lecturer at a central university. You are very popular amongst your students. They adore you as you are very helpful and friendly. You personally know all of your students. One day, during an examination, you see that one of your favorite students is cheating and you feel upset. He is a good student, inquisitive and bright and keeps on coming to you for guidance on the subject. You know that he has lost his father recently and, as a result, he is distracted from studies. You can stop him from cheating but then he would fail

in the exam. You can also ignore his cheating. However, the university's policy against cheating is very strict and categorical. It has zero tolerance for cheating. It also prescribes that the faculty members can exercise no discretion in case of cheating. The Dean is very firm on that the cheating cases should be dealt with ruthlessly and must result either in suspension for a semester or in expulsion.

Now, the questions for reflection are (i) What should you do as a professional? (*ii*) What considerations should form the basis of a decision in the given situation? (*iii*) In case you decide to ignore the cheating, whether that would be a responsible action on your part as a lecturer? Would that be fair and free from favoritism? (*iv*) Does the fact of death of the father of the student mitigate the wrong of his cheating? Would that be a right thing to do as a professional?

If we think through the various ethical questions underpinning the given scenario in an objective manner, we could arrive at adequate clarity on what a professional is truly expected to be.

Cost of Healthcare is Hidden Here!

Healthcare may be understood as the maintenance or improvement of health *via* the prevention, diagnosis, and treatment of disease, illness, injury, and other physical and mental impairments in human beings. General Practitioners, Clinics, Hospitals are engaged in taking care of the health of people on a continuous basis. Medicine is a valuable profession and societies, world over, offer a great reverence to medical practitioners for their tireless and humane efforts in treating the patients throughout their long careers.

Let us examine a recent incident in some prominent city of India in the healthcare sector, which is relevant to our comprehension of the professional ethics.

A girl child under the age of 10 was admitted to a private hospital in an Indian city for treatment of ordinary viral infection and fever. The hospital stay was for about for two weeks. The child could not survive. Doctors or hospitals may only try their best to treat the patient, they will not guarantee recovery of all patients. Some complications may arise and patient may not get cured or worse, patient may not survive. But the doctors and hospitals must act ethically with all patients at all times.

The lengthy medical bill, provided at the time of leaving the hospital, contained all details of the medicines used, cost of consulting by several specialist doctors, etc. which was prohibitively high. Though the parents cleared the bill, there is a serious doubt for any person in this country that an ordinary viral infection and associated treatment cost so much. The total bill was close to 14 years of per capita income of an average Indian.

While the Union Government and the State Government where the hospital was located ordered for an enquiry, there are some ethical issues and some serious governance issues of the hospital under discussion here.

Firstly, why is there no transparency in the cost of the treatment? The patient's parents were not indicated anything at the likely bill that they may have to clear for the treatment. Secondly, medicines that were available outside the hospital premises in the pharmacy outlets were not allowed for the patient, and the same medicines with exactly same ingredients were used costing 700 to 800% more per dose. Thirdly, the statement by the hospital was that high-end or state-of-the-art equipment was used as a life-support system to the patient. But the parents of the patient were never informed of the expenses they require to shell out towards the treatment. Are services like healthcare, in the private sector, being misused to the extent of making unjustifiable amount of profits? This is certainly an ethical issue. Also, it is not known whether or not hospitals of repute have in place medically-qualified Boards of Directors to oversee such matters, and how is it that they are not taking corrective steps to curb such unethical practices that seriously impair the reputation of the hospital.

Managerial Dimension - In business, ethics deals with the question whether specific business practices are acceptable. In case of managers, business ethics helps in arriving at ethical decision during complex situations. For example - in a sales presentation to a client, should a sales person omit facts about a product's poor safety records? While auditing a company, should an accountant report inaccuracies discovered by him or her? Such situations put professionals in dilemma, since there is no universally accepted approach to resolve these issues.

In a business environment with intense competition, ethical attitude of managers is of vital importance for a successful organization. Managers must acknowledge their role in shaping organizational ethics and seize this opportunity to create a climate that can strengthen the relationship and reputations on which their companies' success depends. It is difficult to separate ethics from competition.

No society can continue to be successful if it is based on cheating, theft and unfaithfulness.

Relationship of the organization to the employee, is a critical aspect of business ethics. It involves recognizing the humanity and rights of individuals, promoting fairness and justice and creating a positive and supportive workplace culture. Organization that prioritize ethical considerations in their interactions with employees tend to foster a healthier, more engaged and more productive work environment.

Ethical considerations also depend on employee relationship with the organization. Their commitment to the well-being and development within the workplace depends on the organizational culture and increased employee engagement.

Stakeholders, which include individuals, groups, entities having interest in the organization and its operations, encompass transparency, fairness and accountability. Organizations can contribute more sustainable, responsible and mutually beneficial business environment.

A manager needs to establish ethical practices not only within an organization (by caring for its employees) but with external stakeholders (customers, investors, lenders, Government etc.) as well. Linda Trevino, the business ethicist, says that the 'ethics for the managers is being a combination of a moral person and a moral manager. Being a moral person rests on a combination of key traits such as integrity, honesty, and trustworthiness while being a moral manager means that a manager needs to serve as an example of ethical conduct for others in his or her duties. It also means communicating openly, explicitly, and frequently about ethics and values.'

Conflicts of values may arise when different ethical principles, cultural norms, organizational values come into tension. When managers face conflicts of values in decision making, it can be challenging that requires careful consideration and ethical judgment. Utilizing Ethical frameworks through consultation and advisories of ethics committees are some of the strategies to be considered.

Principles or rules that govern Employee behaviour are outlined in Organization's code of conduct, which sets standards on expected behaviour and ethical conduct within the workplace. Managers behaviour with integrity and honesty are always lead by example.

It is important to note that firms that adopt and commit itself to ethical practice benefit in several ways. The examples of leading business firms in India like Tata group, Infosys, Wipro, etc. were the first few beginners in the area of corporate governance. These firms have always treated employees as partners in business by giving them recognition for their work and ownership in the form of shareholding in the company. This has resulted in creating committed and honest employees and in turn better productivity.

Many studies have shown that ethical practices make a firm more profitable in the long run, though in the short run they may seem to lose money. Ethical practices bring significant benefits in terms of enhanced reputation. In modern times, reputation has come to be regarded as a company's most important asset - an asset that is extremely difficult to rebuild, should it be lost.

Therefore, a manager should always be sensitive of the fact that every decision that he or she takes has multifarious effects for multiple stakeholders. It may affect people or the organisation. It may affect the environment or other stakeholders at large. A manager must take those direct or indirect effects and impacts into consideration at the time of making decisions. If he or she does so consistently, ethics shall move to the core of management practice, and thereby lead to a quantum jump in the reputation and brand equity of the particular bank or company.

Ethical Decision-making vs. Commercial Orientation

In some parts of Africa and Latin America, river blindness is a serious and agonizing disease and over 18 million people are affected. According to the US National Centre for Biotechnology Information, following are some of the details on the disease:

- About 125 million people world-wide are estimated at risk of onchocerciasis, and, of these, 96% are in Africa.
- Of the 37 countries where the disease is endemic, 30 are in sub-Saharan Africa, 6 are in America and 1 in the Arabian Peninsula.
- A total of 18 million people are infected with the disease, of whom 99% live in Africa and at least one million are either blind or severely visually disabled. To these, are added each year an estimated 40,000 new blind.

As per the World Health Organisation, river blindness or Onchocerciasis "is an eye and skin disease caused by a worm (filaria) known scientifically as Onchocerca volvulus. It is transmitted to humans through the bite of a blackfly (simulium species). These flies breed in fast-flowing streams and rivers, increasing the risk of blindness to individuals living nearby, hence the commonly known name of "river blindness". Within the human body, the adult female worm (macrofilaria) produces thousands of baby or larval worms (microfilariae) which migrate in the skin and the eye".

One US based renowned pharmaceutical company felt that it may not be ethical to leave the rural people with extremely low incomes to suffer from this disease and their company must do something to save them from this disease. However, in the late 1970s when the company scientists were contemplating to help the poor people of Africa, this pharmaceutical company was not making any human version of the drug which it was inclined to use to cure this river blindness problem.

The company's CEO was convinced that even though other pharmaceutical companies in the US or other developed countries, which were making millions of dollars of profit a year, remained indifferent in this regard, his company must do something on humanitarian grounds. Funds worth US$100 million were apportioned towards this as part of the medical research and large-scale clinical testing required to develop a version of the drug for humans. The company was sure not to recover anything out of the money spent on this cause. Still the company went ahead in producing the drug and got the clinical tests cleared finally after seven long years.

The medicine developed was such that a single pill of the new drug, taken once a year, would eradicate all traces of the parasite from the human body that caused river blindness and prevent new infections. The company sought the help of the leading world organisations in the healthcare and prominent governments to come forward to support this cause by making use of their existing distribution networks to freely give away the medicine to the patients, which was declined by them. This pharmaceutical manufacturing company went ahead on its own to distribute the drug free of cost to the patients of Africa.

When enquired the motive of the company's investment decision and efforts into researching, developing, manufacturing, and distributing a drug that made no money, a top official responded saying once the company suspected that one of its animal drugs might cure a severe human disease that was ravaging people, the only ethical choice was to develop it.

This company has later become one of the most respected and trusted pharmaceutical companies in that part of the world (Africa and Latin America), and a good amount of sales are contributed by the region after about 35-40 years now.

The said case purshes or enables us to think on the relationship between ethical decision-making and commercial objectives. This is wrong to think that there is an inherent conflict between ethical decision making and the 'self-interested pursuit of profit'. On the contrary, ethical behavior of a corporate brings in goodwill and reputation which amplifies 'it's opportunities for profit' as already explained in detail under the heading 'Ethics in Business'.

1.4 ETHICS AND HUMAN INTERFACE: ESSENCE, DETERMINANTS AND CONSEQUENCES OF ETHICS IN HUMAN ACTIONS

Ethics is the study and evaluation of human conduct in the light of moral principles, which may be seen as the standard of conduct or duty of an individual or as a social obligation. We may analyze it as a system of accepted beliefs, morals and values, which influences human behaviour. However, ethics is not synonym to values or morals. Ethics is known as moral philosophy and as a science of morality. Ethics can be described as a science that examines the general principles for determining the true worth of the ultimate ends of human conduct.

According to Mackenzie, ethics is the study of what is right or good in human conduct. It is a moral philosophy that studies the evolution of concepts, such as right or wrong behaviour. William Lillie describes, ethics is a normative science of the conduct of human beings living in societies which judges this conduct to be right or wrong, good and bad.

Determinants of Human actions: Human behaviour whether correct or incorrect is judged in the light of the motive and actions carried out by him/ her. Ethics can be classified as general and special. Ethics that develops principles pertaining to the morality of human actions is general ethics. While application of principles, developed in general ethics to people's conduct towards themselves, other human beings, society and the state, is special ethics. Special ethics is also known as applied ethics. Hence, for any individual, values and judgments play a critical role whenever he or she is making ethical decisions.

Principles and values collectively contribute to ethical behaviour and guide individuals in making decisions. Specific principles and values may vary based on cultural, philosophical and personal perspectives.

Consequences of ethics in human actions: Ethics significantly focuses on human behaviour, which is driven by human actions. Human actions form a base in defining law in a country - whether an act is legal or illegal. Ethics is concerned with human actions that are deliberate - that is—

(1) It was done voluntarily

(2) It was done with some knowledge

(3) Such actions were freely done.

Human actions are subject to scrutiny, if the action were carried under factors such as—

(1) Ignorance or lack of knowledge

(2) Passion

(3) Under the influence of Fear

(4) Action influenced by Violence

(5) Actions performed out of habit or voluntariness

(6) Temperament

(7) Pathological states

Protection for those who secure others

Each day a common man in the village, town or city of India is feeling a sense of security. Thanks to the security personnel guarding the country's borders and other police and its various divisions who constantly take care of the people inside the territory. It is the minimum responsibility of the society in turn to take care of their security against some violent mobs, extremists or terrorists.

About a decade ago, a prominent city in India was attacked by a group of highly motivated and trained terrorists. The attack came as a bolt from the blue. Being a city and having got its own specialist police officers who were trained to deal with such attacks, a team of senior officers got into the action. They gathered some preliminary information and prepared a plan of action and went to implement the same.

Suddenly, the terrorists overpowered and killed all the three specialist officers though they were wearing (as per the standard procedure) bulletproof vests. This was something paradoxical as to how bullets may enter and kill a person wearing a specially designed protection.

There were allegations that the procurement process did not follow the standards prescribed by the Government of India's agency. As per one of the standards relating to the size of the vests to be effective in case of a need, a bulletproof vest should stretch from neck to the groin. As against this, the jacket, as seen in a video frame of the terror attacks widely covered by many media, indicated that a major portion of the officers' upper chest lay exposed.

While these vests were ordered apparently around six years prior to the attacks, the team involved in checking quality, selecting the vendor firm, negotiating for price, etc. may not have foreseen the ramifications or consequences of their omission (assuming no *quid pro quo* took place for buying sub-standard materials). But the loss of three highly-trained personnel suffered by the State Police and the emotional loss to all the three families is an irreparable damage. Could it have been less bad (such as the officers not losing their lives but escape with minor injuries on legs/arms etc., which is not likely to be fatal)?

A point that emerges here (or in similar such cases) is that as an employee, each person is expected to do his/her job with a greater involvement and commitment and not as a mere compliance. If there is any let up in the commitment level while discharging the duty (be it in case of a building occupancy certificate, fire certificate, fitness certificate for elevator, etc.), the person issuing the certificate is not only treated as having low on work ethic but is clearly not ethical in the work. Accepting some money to flout the norms is certainly illegal.

Hence, what is expected here is that the society (here through the police department) must ensure that those protecting a city or the borders of the nation, or keeping traffic in order, etc. must be protected against their own lives and health. This is the minimum that the society can offer to their services.

1.5 NEED OF ETHICS IN GOVERNANCE: OBJECTIVES, SCOPE, TYPES: TRANSACTIONAL, PARTICIPATORY & RECOGNITION

Ethics is the vital and fundamental component of good governance, since it has significant potential to influence public trust in all types of government systems. Good governance refers to the processes for constituting and implementing decisions. It is not about making 'correct' decisions, but about the best possible process for making those decisions.

Good decision-making processes, and therefore good governance, share several characteristics. All have a positive effect on various aspects of governance including consultation policies and practices, meeting procedures, service quality protocols, councillor and officer conduct, role clarification and good working relationships.

Integrity is a fundamental value that holds significance across various domains, including Individual, Political and Social contexts.

- Individual integrity refers to the consistency between values, principles and actions, which involves honesty, loyalty and commitment to ethical behaviour.
- Political Integrity involves transparency, accountability, trustworthy and efficiency.
- Social integrity relates to inclusivity, justice, respect for other, tolerance and transparency.

Hereunder, let us try to know some key characteristics of good corporate governance:

Accountability – Being accountable is the fundamental requirement of good governance. Any governance system has an obligation to report, explain and be answerable for the consequences of decisions it has made on behalf of the organization or community it represents.

Transparency – The decision-making process should be understandable and easy to follow by the people. In other words, people should be able to evidently figure out the reason and process in which decisions are made – that is what information, advice and consultation, decision makers considered, and which legislative requirements (when relevant) they followed.

Conflict of Interest – In a scenario when a professional's primary judgment or decision-making may be influenced due to his secondary activities or roles, the person must stay away from performing that task and ideally assign it to others. Examples in this context could be a judge taking up a case of person who is known to him and had helped him economically in the past. If he is required to give a judgment, there could be a doubt or perceived public opinion that the judge may not have acted with complete professional conscience or morality. Similarly, in another case, a surgeon became a promoter of a corporate hospital and he wants to conduct the surgeries on patients, which he was doing quite eminently in the past with high success rate. Patients may perceive that the promoter doctor has a dual role of earning profits for the hospital from each surgery besides performing the procedure effectively. It may be better if he stays away from conducting active surgeries, excepting giving professional guidance to other surgeons where necessary.

Follow the Rule of law – Decisions are consistent with relevant legislation or common law and are within the powers of legislative authorities.

Equitability and Inclusiveness – Welfare of the people whether in a nation or a community is based upon its members feeling that the governance system has considered their wellbeing in the decision-making process. This means that all groups should have opportunities to participate in the process, particularly the most vulnerable ones. At the organizational level also, there needs to be a fair opportunity to be given to all deserving employees in terms of serving a particular task and it is incorrect to keep assigning some tasks only to select few based on some personal preferences.

Effectiveness and Efficiency – A good governance system ensures that implementation of decision processes should be such that it makes the best use of the available people, resources and time to ensure the best possible results for their community or organization.

Participation – Anyone affected by or interested in a decision should have the opportunity to participate in the process for making that decision. This can happen in several ways – community or organizational members may be provided with information, asked for their opinion, given the opportunity to make recommendations or in some cases, be part of the actual decision-making process.

Ethics Types: Transactional, Participatory and Recognition

Transactional ethics refers to the following ethical considerations while dealing with others through different social transactions. This type of ethics is based on two specific moral principles:

1. Principle of honesty
2. Principle of reciprocity

One is expected to remain honest and reciprocal to other's rights in the domain of transactional ethics. From governance perspective, this ethics is needed for smooth functioning of social relations in their various forms.

Participatory ethics is a superior kind of ethics and aims at producing more distant but common good for all. This is based on two specific moral principles:

1. Principle of Decency
2. Principle of Enunciation

Participatory ethics is about collaboration and the shape of solidarity in an age of individualism. From the governance perspective, it is the ethics of civil society and essential for efficacy of governance. This ethics also inspires a corporation to rise above its legal entity and take seriously its corporate citizenship.

Recognition ethics refers to solving the conflicting situations through correct recognition of the situation with empathy or by understanding the problems of others as human beings. This ethics is in fact about asymmetrical relations. This is about the rights of interest of the one generating a duty for another. It is primarily based on the recognition of the worth, dignity and rights of each and every human being. Recognition ethics clarifies and supports this type of discussion by applying the principles of transactional and participatory ethics and other moral convictions that are considered appropriate. From the governance standpoint, it provides a psychological and moral foundation for the evolution and development of a welfare state.

(*Source:* Dr. K. Govinda Bhat in 'Ethics and Governance'; Himalaya Publishing House; www.himpub.com)

Ethics are classified as under

(*A*) Descriptive Ethics – Descriptive ethics is the scientific description of what ethics is. It explains what people think is right. It presents sound logic and reasoning for every ethical behaviour. Also known as comparative ethics, it is the study of people's beliefs about moral standards. These moral standards can be applied to human action to judge their moral character, that is, whether they are right or wrong.

Descriptive ethics mainly aims at understanding and elaborating the moral beliefs and practices, since such principles are built and governed by social, economic, and geographic environments. It attempts to describe and explain moral action, moral decision-making, and moral phenomena. Looking for answers to questions like – "What are the most important influences or causes for individuals behaving ethically or unethically?" is descriptive or explanatory in nature.

For instance – there are several standards to measure weight, such as grams, kilo, pounds, etc., similarly, there are several standards to judge an action, whether it is right or wrong.

(*B*) **Normative Ethics** – This form of ethics is concerned with determining how one ought to act in a moral sense in a collective group or a community. Traditionally, a normative ethical system is an ordered set of moral principles of conduct or a direction by referencing to which, along with the addition of factual knowledge one can determine, in any situation of choice, what a person ought to do or ought not to do. Normative ethical systems provide us sound moral principles to defend our moral judgments. To illustrate – certain way of behaving, which is acceptable or unacceptable in the social system as good or bad such as dishonesty, lying, cheating, bribery, etc. When it comes to deciding a course of action, normative ethics helps an individual to answer a question like "What should I do?"

The normative ethical system is based on two popular theories developed by researchers, namely – **Utilitarianism** and **Ethical formalism**. Well-known philosophers Jeremy Bentham and John Stuart Mill propounded the Utilitarianism theory – which suggests that for an action, to be good or bad, is determined by the results it brings. German Philosopher Immanuel Kant propounded Ethical Formalism; where in, right conduct performed by an individual is out of moral duty or law. Utilitarianism is a teleological ethical system (also called the consequential ethics) and ethical formalism is a deontological ethical system (also called as non-consequential ethics).

(*C*) **Metaethics** – It is the intellectual study of meaning, methods and the language of ethics. Metaethics is the scientific study of the concepts of ethics in itself. It explains what is the meaning of 'good or bad' and 'right or wrong'. Metaethics is a study of the universal principles that regulate appropriate and inappropriate human actions. Unlike descriptive ethics and normative ethics, which describes and decides the moral code of conduct, metaethics is the study of morality itself. It involves second-order or formal questions as against the first-order or substantive questions answered by normative ethics.

For instance – Behavioral questions like "what we mean by being benevolent?" or "why being honest is good?" or "what is goodness?" are addressed by metaethics.

PRODUCT RECALL: AN OPTION ONLY FOR COMPANIES

In spite of maximum possible care taken by companies or organizations, sometimes they end up producing and selling some defective products in the national or international markets. Once a company gets convinced that the defect is serious enough and may endanger the reputation of the company or result into equally costly legal hassles such as slapping crores of rupees as penalties by courts, the better recourse is recalling and requesting the buyers to get the replacement done free of cost. Some companies may give newspaper advertisements, send emails to the customers or call up over phone to intimate the problem and steps to be taken to get this rectified.

Many companies of national and international repute were found having used product recall as a method to shield the loss-financial or reputational or both. This only helps the company maintain the patronage of the existing customers rather than shifting their loyalty to other companies' products.

Business schools train each year tens of thousands of prospective managers for companies, service-based organisations or consulting firms. In one of the business schools, after the yearly review of academic and placement activities was done, the management learnt (from preserved video footage) that a good proportion of a batch of students resorted to malpractice in the end term examination, that too in the subject relating to Professional and Business Ethics.

There were deliberations between the Dean of Academics and Examinations and the Head of Placements on the proposed action to be taken against the students who resorted to such an unethical act. Finally, the business school authorities decided not to write or inform the companies and organizations, which recruited a couple of dozens of these students, about the incident. The reason they had was that the recruiters have no clue of the incident, and that they fully got satisfied with the candidates' scores and performance in the interviews. Having voluntarily selected based on students' performance, why should the business school become a party to spoil the careers which they managed themselves.

However, some of the employees in the institute became unhappy with this decision. Though they did not raise this point in writing with the management, they wondered how come such vital aspect be covered up by the business school. It is the trust factor between the recruiters and educational institutions which gets many recruiters to the management institutes for campus recruitment each year. If the trust gets lost, the placements may suffer and may even affect the enrolment. It (action to hide students' unethical behavior) may pay dividends to the institute in the current year, but in the long run, it may prove to be a costly mistake. Also, some staff and students wondered what if these students behave in the same unethical manner in their workplace also.

1.6 ETHICS AND CONCEPT OF WELFARE STATE

The philosophy of ***Welfare State*** refers to the government where the state plays a key role in the protection and promotion of economic and social well-being of its citizens. A welfare state is based on the principles of equality of opportunity, equitable distribution of wealth and public responsibility for those unable to avail themselves of the minimal provisions of a good life.

A welfare state provides social equality to all its citizens. By social equality we mean a state where discrimination on the grounds of caste, colour, creed, sex religion and language are absence. Social equality gives everyone equal status and opportunities.

The ultimate objective of a society is to achieve excellence in all aspects; thus, for development of moral framework of the welfare state, a state needs to incorporate hierarchy of values; right-justice, virtue-excellence, good-efficiency. For establishment of a stable society, justice must be a priority amongst other moral values. To protect the interest of different members of society a Law

enforcing authorities must create governing guidelines/laws regulating businesses as well, such as – regulation of competition, protection of consumer interest, protection of employee interest (equity and safety at work place), and corporate governance and disclosure norms.

A welfare state is required to be built on strong moral principles. This provides strong foundation to a state and places it on a strong growth trajectory. India is a democratic republic, where every citizen has certain rights and duties. Rights and duties go hand in hand. Every citizen of a nation is abided by law.

However, on the flip side, a welfare state has certain drawbacks, for instance it can also create social dependencies and discrimination in the society.

Minimum Wage: A Good or Bad Idea?

In India, the National Minimum Wage has been considered at various forums in the past. However, State and Union Governments are not unanimous on the need of a National Minimum Wage, though the Minimum Wages Act was passed in 1948. As socio-economic conditions vary from state to state, region to region as also from industry to industry due to different geographical, topographical and agro-climatic factors, there cannot be uniform minimum wages.

The seventh pay commission recommended about 600 rupees per day as the minimum wage for persons working in the government and in select private organisations for employees holding posts which bear a scale of pay with prescribed increments and allowances. The pay commission recommendations do not, normally, cover tenure-based or contractual appointments.

India is a mixed economy, in the sense, that barring certain sectors reserved exclusively by the government or private sector, there are quite a few sectors where the public and private sectors operate separately with a healthy competition between the two. Manufacturing, Education, banking, insurance, healthcare, telecommunications, transport, power, etc. are some of the prominent sectors in which private and public investments are made.

There are two ways of looking at the minimum wages. Minimum wage protects the workers particularly in the private sector for a fair compensation for their work. Trade unions help in ensuring this through their negotiations with the managements. However, the industrialists or promoters view wages as a cost, and are generally not willing to commit for future wages unless they know about their profits, which are unknown at any given point in time for predicting the future.

As the policy makers of the states in India and even their international counterparts are seriously competing with one another in attracting industries both within the country and from outside, those firms where the trade unions press or insist for payment of minimum wages, the managements of select private firms may wish to relocate to other states/country of their choice if the wages prove to be a contentious and unviable issue. It may not be in the interest of individual workers if they believe in the philosophy of the trade unions beyond a limit. Instead of protecting their wages, they may end up losing the jobs, which are not easily obtainable in a situation wherein automation and labour-saving methods of production are being adopted rapidly by the employers ranging from agriculture to construction to manufacturing and many other fields:

- Are trade unions ethical or unethical in pressing for implementation of minimum wages for their fraternity?
- If there is inflation, and prices of essential items and overall living costs keep rising, what is the way out for the workers without being influenced by the trade unions for minimum wages?
- Should managements be obsessive (and more than that ethical) only on earning more profits if one of the prime stakeholders, namely the workers, remain unhappy with low wages?

1.7 ETHICS, RELIGION AND LAW

Ethics and Religion

India is a vast country where all its citizens have faith in different belief systems. Various faith systems are Hinduism, Jainism, Islam, Buddhism, and Sikhism, etc. Each belief system inculcates certain values in an individual who follows a particular faith. Sometimes ethics is identified with religion, since all the religions advocate high ethical standards.

Religion can set higher ethical standards and can also provide intense motivation for ethical behaviour. According to Kant, religion is based upon ethics and the

existence of God is due to the existence of ethics. Kant believes that bliss invariably accompanies virtue. Likewise, in Sanskrit, Dharma means the moral order of the universe. However, religion and ethics cannot be graded as synonymous. This leads to an assumption that a religious person is moral and a non-religious person is immoral. This can be true to a certain extent, however, there are people who do not follow a faith system but are aware about the morality of their actions.

The benefits of worshiping God in ethics, vary widely among different religious and philosophical traditions. Some may find ethical guidance, community support and personal fulfilment in their religious practices. Individuals who do not follow a particular faith may derive ethical principles from secular philosophies, humanism and other such sources.

Justification of values are multifaceted that involves, emotional, cultural and ethical considerations, such as Rational justification, Empirical Justification, Pragmatic justification and Spiritual justification.

Although a certain school of philosophy (Descartes, Locke, Paley and others) suggests that morality should be based on religion as it preaches good deed and sins. Moreover, in a society people act morally because their moral sense is based upon reason and there is a social approval for that kind of behaviour.

Ethics, Ethical Code of Conduct and Law

The legal system of a country is based on its customs, which also form the basis of ethics in a society. Ethics and law share a strong relationship in any country. Laws in a country are created to protect innocent law-abiding citizen from unethical conduct of immoral citizens. Breach of ethical code of conduct also involves legal breach. For example, it is a moral duty of a business to pay its taxes to the government; dividend payment to its shareholders and interest payment/repayment of bank loans. Ethics differentiates between right and wrong, which is also the underlying premise of law. As a result, ethics and law become two mutually complementary tools for governing human conduct so as to make it more socially acceptable. Both are required for wellbeing of individual as well as society. For example, sitting on a metro seat reserved for women is both unethical and illegal. It would be easy to understand the relationship between ethics and the law through the following diagram.

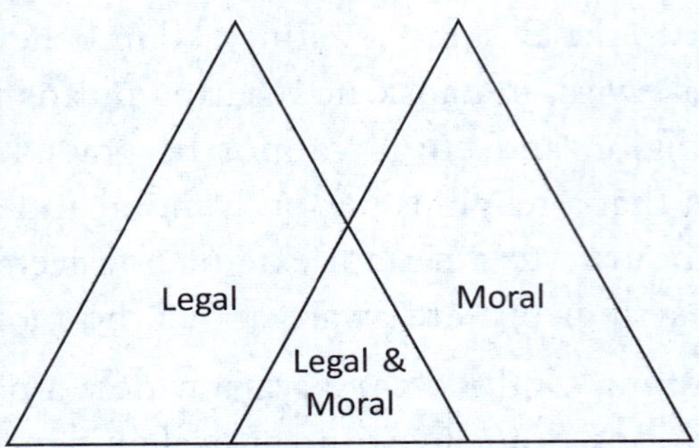

Most people believe that law-abiding behavior is also ethical behavior. This is not correct as there is an overlap between what's legal and what's ethical. Though ethical codes and law are interrelated, yet there are limits to the law. If one betrays a confidence or tells a lie, one is not acting illegally but unethically. The law cannot make people honest, caring or fair. However, many standards of conduct are agreed upon by society and not codified in law. For example, having an affair with someone who reports to you might be legal, but it is considered unethical in most companies. Racial discrimination has always been highly unethical but it was legal in the United States for a long time. Thus, the sphere of ethics extends well beyond the law to include ethical standards that the law does not address.

Individuals can be ethical without being religious and *vice versa*. Ethics and religion are distinct but interconnected aspects of human life, and people can derive their ethical principles from various sources, not solely based on religious beliefs.

Legislative approval to certain ethical codes makes them binding. However, using a single ethical principle might create a conflicting situation when several principals seem to apply and we have to weigh them to find out which one is best to apply. This is called the **pluralist approach.** Many philosophers ridiculed the Pluralist approach, as it does not provide us any uniform basis for distributive justice. Thus arises the need to search for general theory of justice in economic distribution. Three such theories are - **Utilitarian, Libertarian and Rawlsian.**

1.8 LET US SUM UP

Ethics deals with the study and practice of the moral principles or standards of human behaviour, which helps distinguishing between right and wrong. Ethics

involves principles of human conduct or human actions. And integration of ethics with business is essential as every business operates within the society and it cannot disassociate itself from the people working within the organization and outside the society. Dimensions of Ethics ranges from personal to professional to managerial. Every professional has to imbibe certain qualities like being responsible, respecting others, be honest, practice fairness etc. Ethics also plays a vital role in corporate governance. Ethics are classified as Descriptive Ethics, Normative Ethics and Meta Ethics. The ethics extends beyond the law to include those standards which are not addressed by law.

1.9 KEY WORDS

Morals and values, Fairness, Honesty, Responsibility, respect, Telos, Ethics for Managers, Human actions, Conflict of Interest, Transactional Ethics, Participatory Ethics, Recognition Ethics, Descriptive Ethics, Normative Ethics, Meta Ethics, Utilitarianism, Ethical Formalism, Pluralist Approach.

1.10 CHECK YOUR PROGRESS

1. Ethics deals with study and practice of the ____________ of human behaviour, which helps distinguishing between right and wrong.
   (*a*) Differences
   (*b*) Similarities
   (*c*) Deficiencies
   (*d*) Moral principles
2. Which one of the following is a significant moral issue that one needs to keep in mind with regards to responsibility towards environment?
   (*a*) Excessive and unnecessary use of car
   (*b*) Buying a new car
   (*c*) Replacing car interiors
   (*d*) Disposing off the car on an online site

3. Frequent fights, conflicts and even full-fledged wars gave people of most countries in the world the realization that we need to be ____________.
   (*a*) Civilized
   (*b*) Educated
   (*c*) Wealthy
   (*d*) Militarily equipped
4. Which of the following is NOT a characteristic of India's society?
   (*a*) Patriarchal and strongly hierarchal
   (*b*) Dominant caste system has made Indians very rank and status oriented
   (*c*) Social events are accorded extreme importance
   (*d*) Need a lot of "elbow room"; people like personal space around them
5. Professional practicing equality in providing access to vital information and providing equal opportunities to qualifying ones comes under
   (*a*) Sincerity
   (*b*) Responsibility
   (*c*) Fairness
   (*d*) Honest
6. Companies frequently recall their defective products because it may otherwise lead to
   (*a*) Losing current market share
   (*b*) May lose projected revenue for current financial year
   (*c*) Endangering the reputation of the company or equally costly legal hassles
   (*d*) Face low inventory for running financial year
7. Which of these concepts relates to utilitarianism?
   (*a*) consequences
   (*b*) actions

(*c*) character

(*d*) duty

ANSWERS

1. (*d*)	2. (*a*)	3. (*a*)	4. (*d*)	5. (*c*)	6. (*c*)	7. (*a*)

1.11 EXERCISE YOUR ETHICS MUSCLE

Case 1: The Equifax Data Breach

Equifax is a major global credit reporting agency. On September 7, 2017, the company announced a data breach that exposed the personal data of approximately 147 million US citizens and its share fell nearly 14 percent. The hackers had accessed the company servers between mid-May to late July. However, before the public announcement, the company executives sold off nearly $2 million of their company stock and booked profits in potential violation of insider trading rules. To compensate the customers and clients, the company offered free credit monitoring and identity-theft protection. After one week of the public announcement, company's Chief Information Officer and Chief of Security retired. Within a couple of days, the CEO also resigned. Equifax denied any wrongdoing. Federal investigation and class action suits were filed against the company for the data breach. A federal court approved a class action settlement and the settlement is effective even today and customers are getting paid as a part of data breach settlement.

Issues to Reflect:

(*a*) Whether the action of the executives of the company was legally compliant and ethically, correct?

(*b*) What did the company executive do which they were not supposed to do?

(*c*) What did the company executives not do which they should have done?

(*d*) Whether the data breach and the subsequent behaviour of the company executives would have impacted the future growth of the company?

(*e*) Do you agree that the freebees offered by the company to compensate the affected customers were adequate?

(*f*) What could have been the best course of action for the company and its executives after the data hack came to their knowledge?

Case 2: 'Helping' the Students

You teach in a junior school. You have come out of a staff meeting just now wherein the principal has made it clear that the teachers whose class-rooms do not score well, will lose their jobs. You need this job desperately as your mother is sick and you need money for her medical treatment which is expensive. The board exams start after two weeks. You are upset as you know that your students, mostly from weaker sections of society, are not well-prepared and wouldn't score good marks. One of your colleague suggests that there is nothing to worry as you can walk around the examination hall and help the students on difficult questions. Other teachers will do the same.

Issues to Reflect:

(*a*) Do you think that your colleague has suggested a good solution for your problem? If yes, then why?

(*b*) What is your priority? Responsibility of mother's medical treatment or responsibility as a professional when everyone else is going to help their students?

(*c*) There is nothing morally wrong in a tad helping the students as they don't come from the privileged classes and are studying amidst several adversities. Isn't that a win-win situation for all?

(*d*) What is the right thing to do in the given situation as a teaching professional? Evaluate ethically?

2

UNIT

Ethics, Business Ethics and Banking: An Integrated Perspective

2 UNIT

Ethics, Business Ethics and Banking: An Integrated Perspective

2.1 LEARNING OBJECTIVES

This unit throws light on concept of ethics and values, and also differentiates between Business Ethics and Values. It tries to split the myths regarding Business Ethics from reality. We have focused on principles and practices of Business Ethics, which are helpful in running a successful business. We have also explained what ethical crisis in business is and how it can be prevented and how an organization can overcome such situations by following ethical practices and maintaining the resilience of the business. Ethical practices are extremely important for banking industry which is the backbone of every economy. The Banking sector functions on one of the key principles of ethics, *viz.* trustworthiness. Therefore, for the banking professionals also, it is significantly important to be honest, responsible and also have excellent leadership qualities. In the end, we have highlighted few vital case studies where failure to abide by the ethical code of conduct led to a turmoil which massively affected the global economy.

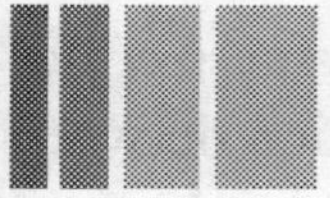

2.2 ETHICS AND BUSINESS VALUES: MYTH AND REALITY

Business values are an informal term and explain the core principles or standards that guide the way business is done. Values sum up what your business stands for and what makes it special.

Business ethics has been defined as established principles and standards that guide behaviour in the world of business. Investors, employees, customers, interest groups, and legal system, and the community often determine whether a specific action is right or wrong, ethical or unethical. Although these groups are not necessarily right, their judgments influence society's acceptance or rejection of a business and its activities.

Business ethics in a broad sense also inquires about the most appropriate or just designs for firms, markets regulations and political oversight in a democratic society and a globalized economy.

Difference between Business Ethics and Business Values

Business Ethics	Business Values
Ethics refers to the guidelines for conduct, that address questions about morality	Value is defined as the principles and ideals, which help them in making judgment of what is more important.
Moral principle system	Induces thinking
What is morally correct or incorrect in the given situation?	What we want to do or achieve?
Magnitude of rightness or wrongness of one's options.	It explains the level of significance.

Myths vs. Reality

In an organization, business ethics aids in prioritizing moral values in the firm and also ensures behaviours are aligned with those values. Yet, myths about business ethics keep thriving. Some of these myths either arise from general skepticism pertaining to the concept of ethics or from limited or elementary opinions about ethical dilemmas:

1. Myths say that business ethics modifies peoples' behaviours – they cease to be what they are, which comes in way of realization of their full potential. However, in reality, business ethics is all about managing values and conflict resolution. Moreover, conflict management is what business ethics stresses the most upon. However, there could be some conflict between individual and organizational ethics, which can be eased out.
2. It is also a belief in many organizations that most of their human resources are already ethical and therefore they would not need to be trained upon. This is a highly mistaken view. In reality, when managers have to face complex ethical dilemmas, they often find it hard to resolve the same because there is a conflict of principles that varies among differing interests. To act ethically is difficult and complex. Even good character

on its own cannot equip people to face the complex ethical dilemmas. Therefore, organizational ethics will challenge the choices that are equally logical and help the managers to navigate the grey areas.

3. Another myth suggests that business ethics is the privilege of philosophers and theologians. It is also said that there is no such predetermined term as business ethics that can determine how organizations should go about their routine activities. It is considered as a fad with no realistic application. The majority of this can be attributed to lack of interest and involvement of business managers in the process of ethical decision-making. The fact is, business ethics is not a fad. It has a lot to do with the daily operations of an organisation.
4. There is nothing novel about business ethics is also said regularly. It is considered to be something that only affirms what we all already know and what we naturally aspire for. However, proponents of this view ignore that business ethics safeguards the interest of the stakeholders, the overall society and those employees who are working at the bottom of the pyramid. Functioning of an organization cannot be in a programmed manner. An organization cannot try to ensure that there is no violation of a certain code of conduct in the absence of ethics and values.
5. Business ethics is all about good guys sermonizing to the bad guys. Those who promote ethical behaviour by and large claim to have higher moral ground and often feel distressed about the dismal condition of leadership of a troubled organisation. It is true that good managers might make wrong decisions in a scenario that is full of skepticism and apprehensions. Such situations are common and could be due to exogenous factors. Management of ethics at any organization requires contribution of all the individuals working together and also helping everyone to adhere to ethical course of action through ambiguous and stressful ethical dilemmas.
6. Ethics cannot be managed, is another myth that surrounds business ethics, which is not the case. The reality is that it can be totally managed. Neuroscientists say that the brain structures are malleable, which means that we can improve our moral functioning throughout our life spans. As such, businesses can manage their ethics by training their employees to recognize the ethical challenges in their daily work life and by providing

them with frameworks for thinking about ethical issues in the background of their unique nature of business activities. However, at times, priorities of an organization can also be indicative of the ethics followed in the organization. For example, a sale-oriented organization is expected to be aggressive in nature, while a service-oriented organization is bound to be different as it is into the business of hospitality.

7. Business ethics are often deemed as social responsibility. However, the two are not similar. Moreover, corporate social responsibility is only one aspect of the overall business ethics. Corporate social responsibility is regarded as in itself managing business dealings and interface with the society; it does not deal with ethics at the workplace. However, both fall under the continuum of business ethics.

Here, one should remain mindful of the fact that the business ethics exists in the sphere of aspiration where, as neatly articulated by James S. Bowman and Jonathan P. West (Public Service Ethics: Individual and Institutional Responsibilities), "one's reach exceeds one's grasp – the gap between the "is" and the "ought". Ethical quandaries are both hauntingly unavoidable and maddeningly intractable."

2.3 BUSINESS ETHICS, DEFINITION PRINCIPLES AND PRACTICES

In 1776, Adam Smith quoted "People of the same trade seldom meet together, even for merriment and diversion, but the conversation ends in a conspiracy against the public, or in some contrivance to raise prices". According to him, in a capitalist economy, both customer and industry co-exists for the benefit of each other. Ethics involves both internal stakeholders (employees) as well as the external stakeholders (investors, lenders, and customers). Ethics in business also spreads out to inter-corporate relationships. An organization must protect the interest of its internal and external stakeholders, and therefore arises the need to have a proper corporate governance system in place.

Business is a part of society and business firms' function within the society, thus affecting everyday human life. Consequently, a business organization cannot estrange itself from the notion and principles of good and bad that are formed by human society. Also, an organization cannot contain its liability or disregard from its responsibility towards the society. To function successfully, an

organization needs to engage in ethical dealing with its clients, setting standards for its employees and dealing with ethnicity amongst the employees.

Values and Ethics in Business:

Respect	Mutual respect between Business owner/employees/customers
Fairness	Treating each customer equal, each employee with fairness, justly without discrimination.
Honesty	Being truthfulness and upholding honesty contributes to building trust among stakeholders.
Integrity	Ethical principles and moral values with integrity is the fundamental value in business ethics.
Transparency	Openness, clarity and honesty in communication and business operations.
Loyalty	Individual and organizational loyalty build value to long term relationships.
Accountability	Adherence to clear policies and standards, accountability in business, reporting and whistleblower protections build trusts among stakeholders.
Trustworthiness	Promotes reliability, dependability, consistency in business. Ethical dilemmas may test trustworthiness of individual and organizations.

Business is a part of Society

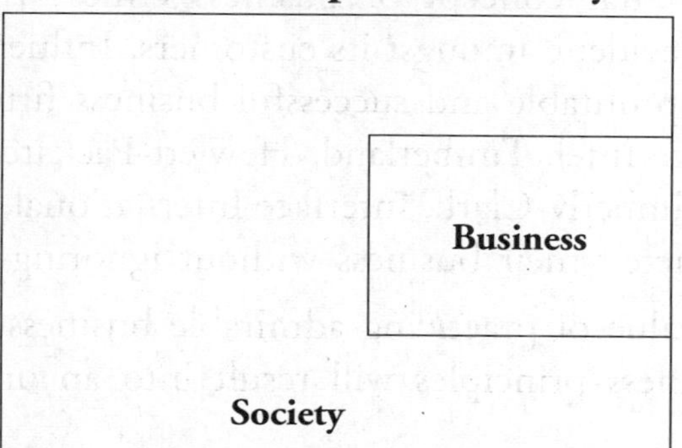

For a business, ethics covers each and every aspect of business and applies to all decision-making and operational activities. Thirukkural, authored by Thiruvalluvar comprising of short poems and the most popular literature of Tamil Nadu, deals with ethical code of conduct in its first part. This ancient literature, comprising of short poems, has its relevance even today about business ethics in the modern context of leadership. He considers ethics as a road to wealth and goodwill. C.S.V. Murthy in his book-'Business Ethics: Text & Cases' highlights one more relevant aspect – On numerable occasions, businesses face ethical questions in which a balance has to be found between the different and often conflicting rights and interests of the parties involved. In this sense, it can also be said that the weighing of rights and interests, at stake, in determinate circumstances, constitutes the common domain of business ethics."

Principles of Business Ethics

Being ethical is of utmost importance for business in present times. Any organization following dubious and unethical business practices might experience failures in long-term, which in turn would tarnish the reputation of business. Every organization needs to have a standard code of ethics. Thus, ethics is a discipline, which should be developed meticulously and practiced persistently.

Principles of ethics are universal and also applicable to businesses. They express the highest level of generality of standards and acts as the first reference point. Principles represent the supreme aspirational level of ethical behaviour. The principles gathered hereunder might be preferred in a modified form.

From the very beginning, a firm must recognize the significance of business ethics as a tool for attainment of firms' desired results. When a small business inculcates a fundamental concept of business ethics within its policies and guidelines, it will be evident amongst its customers. Influence of strong business ethics will lead to a profitable and successful business firm as has happened in case of companies like Intel, Timberland, Hewlett-Packard, Cisco Systems, Levi Strauss, Patagonia, Kimberly-Clark, Interface International, and Starbucks Coffee etc. who have conducted their business without ignoring ethics.

By recognizing the value of practicing admirable business ethics, and following the undernoted business principles will result into an unprecedented business success:

1. **Dignity**: The most important principle of ethics is to treat each other with utmost respect regardless of difference, which is treating each individual as an end rather than as a means to an end. In case of employment, people should be treated as an end in themselves instead of treating them as a means to an end. For a business, it is of utmost importance to always treat others with professional respect and courtesy irrespective of any type

of divergence in any aspect. Similarly, while dealing with customers, a business's ultimate objective should not be only profit making but also the customers' interest. Courtesy is a major element of dignity and it is essential to treat people with courtesy. Good manners or ethical behaviour has become a vital attribute rather than just a necessary course of action.

2. **Fairness**: Fairness is about displaying concern with actions, processes, and consequences that are morally right, honourable and equitable. The primary advantage of fairness is that it establishes moral standards for decisions that affect others. However, on the flip side, misuse of power or authority, imbalances a relationship in any organization.

   A practicing fairness is committed to equal distribution of justice and treats all individuals equally. There are three aspects to this perspective. One is that everyone gets equal share (simple equality), the second is that people get shares according to their contribution (commercial equitability), the third is that people get share according to need (the socialist model).

   Fairness in competition provides level playing field to all the firms in the industry. The company should not conspire with anyone to lessen fair competition or engage in anti-competitive practices such as price-fixing or bid rigging.

3. **Honesty**: Honesty means being truthful and straightforward. It is an attribute that is largely linked to an individual rather than a situation. Integrity is also linked to honesty. To have integrity is to have consistency of honesty that is, being honest in one situation is generalized to all situations so that a person of integrity does not wear the hat of honesty in one forum and hat of dishonesty in another. The attributes one would expect of a person of integrity are those of being honest (not deceitful) and consistency of such behaviour. Honesty in business practices always rewards the businesses, as it is helpful in building foundations of trust with employees, customers and other stakeholders. A firm needs to be truthful in various situations such as publishing financials to investors, filing tax returns, marketing its products and services etc. For the customers, a business should pledge to offer good quality products and services. For the investors, if a business reports its earnings truthfully, investors, and financiers will express confidence in the business by offering funding

solutions to the firm. *Honest practices* also inspire employees' in building the foundation of trust amongst colleagues, and they are motivated to drive the business forwards working together. An organization engaged in unethical practice and adhering to cheating, lying, stealing and deception will have to bear the negative impact.

4. **Openness:** The concept of openness is that things should be as they are supposed to be, and not concealed in some casuistically manner. That is not concealing that which should be revealed. Even when it is not possible for a firm to reveal vital information, there is openness about the reason for non-disclosure.
5. **Reputation/goodwill:** Goodwill is one of the most important assets of a business, and also one of the most difficult to rebuild should it be lost. Business should work on building a good reputation, along with high morale for its staff. The business should not engage in any conduct that might impair the respect of the business and in case of a crisis situation business should take necessary corrective actions to correct or prevent inappropriate conduct of others. Good reputation or goodwill helps in resolving many problems and also has material value.
6. **Prudence**: It is the ability of a business to make right decision, which is gained over a period of time from experiences and knowledge. Business requires prudence to exercise a degree of judgment that makes the situation no worse, but rather improves the circumstances. In business terms, one could imagine a case in which a company is required to be prudent in nearly every aspect of business operations – inventory procurement, hiring staff, product/services offering to customers, capacity expansion etc.
7. **Concern for Others**: *Social Responsibility*: Every business takes birth, survives and grows with the consent and co-operation of the society. Since the business is an integral part of the society, it makes the business morally responsible towards the society, which is also viewed as an inherent obligation of a business towards the society. A socially responsible business builds a better quality of life by harmonizing organizational actions with society's wants. Thus, a business will have to function in such a way that it will acquire the desired economic gains and at the same time will

accomplish the social benefits also. A business firm will have to fulfil its responsibility towards both internal groups – stakeholders (investors protection) and employees (staff welfare and protection) and external groups – that includes the consumers and the community as a whole. There are several studies that find a positive relationship between socially responsible behavior and business profitability. As Manuel Velasquez says "there are good reasons to think that businesses are shortsighted when they fail to take the ethical aspects of their activities into consideration."

Gandhiji's philosophy of 'Trusteeship' as a moral-foundation for business

Gandhiji advocated 'trusteeship' as a moral starting point for individuals in position of wealth. He envisaged trusteeship as a system wherein individual capitalist considers that part of his wealth – which is in excess of his needs – as being held in trust for the larger good of society and also acts accordingly. Gandhi ji further explained that riches should not be expropriated by the use of force, but by making an appeal to the basic principle of reason and love. By this way the capitalist should be convinced that the wealth in their hands is the fruit of hard work, toil, efforts and sacrifice of the workers and other sections of the society. Thus, they should not treat this wealth as their own possession but should realize and accept that it's the right of other people too with whose consent, cooperation and contribution its creation and growth has been possible. The capitalist, therefore, should act as trustees. They should be morally encouraged to act as trustees. One ethicist in recent times, Peter Singer has strongly espoused a similar view that 'in the world as it is now, I can see no escape from the conclusion that each of us with wealth surplus to his or her essential needs should be giving most of it to the people suffering from poverty so dire as to be life threatening.'

Gandhian philosophy of trusteeship has its origin in "Bhagwat Gita", which tells about 'Aparigraha' (non-possession) and 'Nishkam Karmyoga' (selfless work). Gandhiji's trustees are presumed to act upon two noble principles of selfless work and non-possession. They have to create, preserve and increase wealth without expecting the enjoyment of wealth. They should not think of themselves as the owner of this wealth.

Gandhiji was of the opinion that, in an industry, both the labour and management are equal partners. One supplies the workers and another supplies the capital.

Both these elements separately cannot make anything useful and fruitful. Labour and capital combined together produce the wealth and bring prosperity to the society. Labour and management are thus cotrustees of the business enterprise. Both have to work in harmony and maintain peaceful coexistence.

In a wider sense, Gandhiji's philosophy of "trusteeship" takes in both labour and capital as cotrustees and provides a generic dynamic process for translating the principles of business ethics into a cherished social reality.

Business Ethics Practices in India – *Corporate Governance* – Ethics as a concept in the Indian business evolved during the 1980s, following rise of corrupt business practices. Major unethical issues were also on rise such as bribery, deceptive advertising, price collusion, product safety and environment conservation. Business confidence also started to decline.

Directors of a firm are responsible for creating wealth and happiness for all the stakeholders of an organization and improvising by using corporate governance. It is the duty of directors to avoid ethical misconduct in their director role and also to provide leadership in decisions to prevent ethical misconduct in the organization. To remove the opportunity for employees to make unethical decisions, most companies have developed formal systems of accountability, oversight, and control-known as corporate governance.

In India, with the introduction of SEBI in 1992 and addition of clause 49 (listing agreements) in 2005, business ethics gained the centre stage of business operations. Several other Committees have been set up over the past 25 years, the latest of them has been the Uday Kotak Committee set up by SEBI, most of whose recommendations were accepted in 2018.

2.4 IS BUSINESS ETHICS AN OXYMORON?

Many times a question arises that how can business be ethical in practices and still remain successful too. Do business and ethics mix well?

The perception that business and ethics are at odds is based on a view that comprehends business as the sole pursuit of self-interest and ethics as involving the consideration of others at the cost of self-interest. Obviously, there is a clash between these two objectives and that is why business and ethics don't mix well.

This view utterly flawed as a business management approach. It ignores the basic need for trust and cooperation in the larger socio-economic environment in which businesses operate and have interconnected dependencies. No business can serve only itself. Every business needs some amount of honesty, trust and consideration for others. For example, if a business is honest with customers and looks out for their interests, it will establish long-term relationships that create customer satisfaction, and lead to more sales and profitability over the course of time.

In fact, business ethics appears to be a contradiction only when we think that the sole purpose of business is the pursuit of profit and that as ethics is concerned with right means and ends, it will slow up this exclusive pursuit. Unless we reframe our view on the purpose of business, we can't envisage any meaningful relationship between the business and ethics. According to the ethicist, Ronald Duska, 'a well-founded purpose legitimates an institution. The function and purpose of the corporation must be viewed from a societal perspective. From society's point of view, the function and purpose of a corporation is not maximization of profits for individuals, but the creation of goods and services to make the members of the society more fulfilled, and not at the expense of those in need. Society invented business to serve its needs, to help its members to flourish. Business, from a societal perspective, was not invented to allow some individuals to prosper at the expense of others.' Peter Drucker has also the similar thoughts : "To know what a business is, we have to start with its purpose. Its purpose must lie outside of the business itself. In fact, it must lie in society since business enterprise is an organ of society". Drucker further adds, "Profit is not the explanation, cause or rationale of business behavior business decisions, but rather the test of their validity".

As we have seen in the case of the pharma company which ethically handed the issue of river blindness (resulting in short term financial losses but huge long-term gains) in the first chapter of this book under the heading. "Ethical decision-making v. Commercial orientation", that although businesses mostly choose profits over ethics whenever there is a conflict between the two, that, however, is not a sustainable approach from a long term profitability point of view.

Nevertheless, on certain occasions, a business might have to adhere to practices that are unpopular and sometimes unethical. For instance, layoffs might negatively affect many people, however it is not an immoral act. Also, closing down a manufacturing unit or hiving off unprofitable businesses is essential in certain situations for the survival of a business. In such cases, an ethical organization would compensate the redundant staff and will also assist them in finding new jobs to earn living. Thus, doing the rightful thing might be very costly for a business as compared to an unethical business. However, it proves beneficial in the long run and also provides significant competitive advantage over the company that does not act ethically.

On the flip side, issues like bribery, corruption, theft, fraud, and malicious marketing policies, insider-trading are unquestionably wrongful acts. Thus, an ethical company needs to eliminate such practices within itself and build strong ethical business standards.

In several cases the need for business ethics arises out of moral crisis. In recent past, the shift to business ethics was also witnessed subsequent to increased distrust in business. The change witnessed in the business and society relationship is occurring owing to integration of ethics in business. For instance, after a significant number of entry-level cars failed the collision test in India, many car manufacturers have now stopped manufacturing cars without the airbags.

Therefore, we can conclude that a business manager's ultimate objective is to create value for business and build trust with the society. This is the reason that business ethics is not an oxymoron in any sense and good ethics is good business.

2.5 ETHICAL FOUNDATION OF BANKING: FINANCE DEPENDS ON TRUST

Banks play a vital role in a country's economy by contributing close to 65% of the total financial market in India. Banks perform an array of services for the society which includes accepting deposits, lending money, payment assistance, investment services, electronic money transfers etc. Like every other business, banking is based on being just and truthful in its relationship with employees, regulators, investors and customers. Banks have obligations to meet the expectation of such diverse stakeholders which necessitates that a high level of integrity informs and nurtures these relationships.

Therefore, success of banking business is dependent on various moral codes of conduct like truthfulness, honesty, integrity, fairness, transparency etc. Moral code of conduct is the behavior that does not violate the interest of others and also does not intensify a grave situation.

Need and importance of Ethics in Banking – Similar to any other type of business, ethics in banking is an echo of the ethical norms that are pervasive in society. Ethics is moral dependability, punctuality of fulfilling obligations and honouring the terms of contracts. Thus, ethics creates credibility for the banks.

Banks need to deliver high quality services to its customers, which are driven by high ethical standards, and therefore maintain the same in its work culture, management and also with the quality of its employees. Banks can only work well when the public trust them.

Ethics help in dealing with dilemmas – Any banking business however well-placed, at times, it may have to confront moral dilemmas in their regular course of business. Banks have to deal with complex dilemmas in decision making, which is not about distinguishing between right and wrong, but between right versus less right. Thus, a Bank needs to adhere to a set of strong moral principles, which helps its employees in navigating through the obstacle of ethical choices, while making important decisions.

Guards Reputation/Goodwill – This is a two-pronged process. First, banks' ethical practices aid in safeguarding depositor's interest, thus, maintaining the stability of the system and preserving the reputation of the bank. Second, employees adhering to ethical practices prevent the breaches of law and corrupt activities. Besides this, it will also protect stakeholders' interest and enhance the banks' competitiveness and brand image.

Helps avoid risk – A well-defined code of ethics followed by the superiors will ensure that the bank at all times maintain high ethical standards and have preventive and corrective measures against unethical practices by any of the staff members. This will refrain the staff members from committing an offence with the temptation of a gratification. This could be approving unqualified loan application, granting credit at unjustifiable terms and delaying the process of loan application deliberately, etc. Thus, ethics helps accelerating the pace of decision-making and in doing so, wards off the risk of adverse reputation for a bank.

Principles of ethical banking

Banks are dependent on people to carry out its business who are reflection of the ethical standards it follows. Therefore, it is important for banking professionals to know what is expected from them and also help them to avoid temptations and pressures. Principles of ethics in banking business provide a guideline to the banking professional, which helps them in dealing with ethical issues.

Banks are responsible not only towards its customers, but also its employees, investors, community, and Government. The first and the foremost principle of ethical banking is Trust. Money being an integral part of the economy and a standard medium of exchange across the world, the whole banking system is dependent on trust of the society:

- **Principle of Trust** – Trust is the confidence in quality or attribute of a person or a thing. It also includes truth of a statement. It includes both trustfulness and trustworthiness. In business, trust always means trustworthiness – which is established by trustfulness. It inspires customers, investors, regulators and lenders to feel confident in an individual, a product or an organization. When trust is reciprocated, it is mutual between the two participants.

- Trust is identified as a vital factor in successful leadership and management. Mutual trust has significant importance for successful functioning of any business system. In present times, when vital and substantial deals are often undertaken over the phone, in the absence of witnesses, nevertheless the relationship between the two participants is often dictated by the resilient principle of mutual trust. It is also important that none of the partners in a business relationship should feel cheated. Trustworthiness is a broad term as it lays the foundation of the banking system.

The other principles of banking include:

- Principle of **Integrity** – Is very important for business ethics and moral behaviour. This principle means that there is no intention to treat the business partner in an immoral way, whether it refers to deception, theft or some other undesirable way of treating a business partner. It helps build trust that any bank needs to thrive.

- Principle of **Neutrality** – Should not differentiate among its employees and customers and refrain from any kind of biased behaviour. A Bank's success depends on the rule of 'respect all human beings'. Banks should honour all their commitments and obligations towards its customers.
- Principle of **Reliability** – Banks should provide information to its customers that is understandable, clear and accurate while performing their services and operations. It should perform customer service in minimum time frame and impeccably without a glitch.
- Principle of **Transparency** – Banks should keep its customers clearly updated about their rights and obligations and all aspects of the products and services offered to them. Also, Banks' must assess the customers' financial capacity, status and needs before offering them a particular product or service suitable to their requirement and profile. Transparency is also important in banks' dealings with other stakeholders such as shareholders, regulators, employees and the communities at large.

Banking consists of an array of activities that involves the handling of other people's money. The welfare of everyone depends on the safe deployment of these funds. As the bankers deal with a large volume of activities with the other people's money and billions of banking transactions take place every day, there always linger temptations to obtain financial gains at the cost of others. It is therefore important that every banker irrespective of role, follows the principles of banking and conducts himself or herself in accordance therewith.

With digitization continuing to sweep the banking industry not only in India but the world over, internal structures, roles and decision-making patterns are undergoing transformation. This is a paradigm shift in banking practices and raising different kinds of ethical concerns. Traditional standards of conduct that are designed for human interactions are getting challenged. In this interconnected digital environment, ethics again sits as the centerpiece to bring in and strengthen the much - needed trust, by defining the moral principles for carrying out digital interactions amongst various stakeholders particularly employees, customers and third parties.

2.6 ETHICAL FOUNDATION OF BEING A PROFESSIONAL

Professionals have a certain set of acquired skills and specific qualifications. For a professional, the most valuable virtue is ethical decision-making with moral judgment. Professionals have to prescribe standards for themselves, but they are accountable to the overall society.

Duties of a professional include - Integrity in dealing, Honesty in actions along with being truthful, Humane values, Thoughtfulness in decision-making, Objectiveness in actions, Responsibility towards employer and customer and Leadership qualities at the workplace:

- Professionals must possess knowledge of law and comply with all applicable laws and regulations of the government, even in the event of conflict. Professionals should disassociate themselves from violation of laws or rules and regulations.
- Professionals must take reasonable care and judgment in maintaining their independence and objectivity in their activities. Accepting gifts, benefits, compensation etc. will compromise their independence and objectivity.
- Professionals must not engage in any conduct of dishonesty, deceit, fraud, or an action, which might affect their reputation and integrity.
- Professionals must not make any misrepresentation regarding the product or service they are offering, which might be misleading to others.

Professionalism in Banking – The image and reputation of a bank as well as people's confidence in a bank depends heavily on the behaviour of its employees, their ability to interact and show attention to their co-workers and clients. Therefore, a banking professional is also expected to act in a certain way and, like any other professional, observe the conduct norms such as integrity in dealings, honesty in actions, thoughtfulness in decision-making etc. However, unlike other professions, banking deals with money. This unique nature of core activity can easily lead to greed and result in misconduct, looking to the fact that individuals who are handling and supervising the banking activities are humans like us. According to Boatright ('Finance in Ethics'), "ethical misconduct is not always a matter of bad people doing bad things, but often of good people who stumble unwittingly into wrong doing."

In this context, professionalism becomes the foremost quality needed for a banker. Not only for adhering to the norms of conduct and doing right things for gaining trust of customers (and building long term business relationships) but also for safeguarding the reputation of the organization, protecting confidentiality of customer information, making appropriated disclosures and finally earning the trust of other stakeholders as well. Trust is a function of consistent professional conduct and without trust, banking practice would not be in a position to bring in the desired outcomes. A banking professional therefore must be "effectively trustworthy" and for that purpose he or she has to develop 'the virtues necessary to build credibility amongst those they serve.'

What Would You Do?

X works in a bank and a perk of the job is zero charges for issuance of a draft in personal name. One close friend M, who is always looking for a bargain, approaches him in the bank one day and asks for issuance of a draft for himself in the X's name.

Reflections:

- How should X handle this situation and why?
- Would it matter if the person in the situation were someone closer to you, perhaps a brother or sister? If so, why?

Ethical issue for professionals

Strong moral values help professionals in crisis situation. It helps them in coming up with suitable solutions when they are facing ethical dilemmas. Practicing high ethical standards are essential elements of professionalism.

An ethical dilemma for profession is a situation, which requires an individual to choose among actions that may need evaluation as just or unjust.

Dilemma arises either due to conflict among personal/organizational values or conflict with the social values. For instance, conflict of interest could be due to (*a*) an issue that might impair their independence and objectivity or (*b*) priority of transaction, for example customer over employer or (*c*) monetary benefits received following completion of a deal.

2.7 BANKING ETHICS IN GLOBAL CONTEXT: ENRON AND ITS LESSONS

Enron was the major gas pipeline company in United States of America. The company capitalized on the opportunities by the privatization of natural gas and electricity in United States of America. It became one of the major conglomerates in the development, construction and operation of power plants, pipelines and other energy-related projects all over the world. By financial year 2000, Enron became the seventh largest Fortune 500 Company with revenue of $100 bn. The company's management and top executives were extremely aggressive in achieving higher business growth and were running the company old-styles. Authorities were centralized in the hands of few and also suffered poor managerial accountability. The top executive also carried a prideful attitude.

The crisis situation

Soon after Enron gained recognition as the leading energy trading company, the problems at Enron started to reveal, as one of the senior executives at the company highlighted the issue with accounting discrepancies, inflated financial statements, frauds and other unethical practices been followed by Enron. The Whistle blower indicated that a large amount of liabilities were managed in an off-the-book entity by creating a special purpose vehicle (SPV), which was backed by the Enron's stocks. CEO of the company resigned knowing that the ship is sinking and also sold his shareholding in the company.

Towards the end of 2001, large amount of borrowing became due, and the company could not make repayments. In due course, Enron filed for bankruptcy. Its stock price, which was hovering at $90 in August 2000, plunged to $0 by December 2001.

There was a significant impact on the auditor's reputation and following the Enron scam, the auditors to the company, Arthur Anderson, also lost their professional credibility which also impacted their clientele.

Reasons for the crisis

Highly ambitious promoters targeted to achieve fast pace growth for the business. Significant and rapid diversification of business was undertaken from a gas distribution company to an energy major and further venturing into a non-core business like broadband network and bandwidth trading company.

Learnings from the case

- Unethical accounting policies along with misrepresentation of financial statements cannot be used to accomplish higher aspirations. Also, tremendous performance pressure on the employees to achieve higher business goals will only result in wrongful practices in business dealings.
- The companies should avoid unfair practices and poor transparency in the business dealings. Only good corporate strategies will help achieve success in the long run.
- Precrisis preventive measure by way of regular audits can help nip the problem at the very beginning. However, poor ethical literacy, at the organizational level and lack of awareness amongst employees leads to concerns of higher proportions in future.

2.8 GLOBAL FINANCIAL CRISIS AND FEW CASE STUDIES

The financial crisis of 2007-08, which is also called the Global Financial Crisis (GFC) is considered as the worst financial crisis after the great depression of 1930. It became evident only in September 2008, when major banks in the United States of America ended up in an immense financial upheaval.

What really happened?

It all started a decade back before the actual crisis became evident in 2008. Real estate as an investment avenue became very lucrative in America as the property prices were on an upward trajectory.

Lower interest rates gave a thrust to the demand for mortgage loans. Fannie Mae and Freddie Mac were the two quasi-public corporations that were so focused on growth at any cost, that they abandoned any element of prudent risk management.

Large amount of mortgage loans was the key ingredient to the financial crisis of 2008 which jacked up the real estate prices in America. This further encouraged the homeowners to borrow more against their home, and banks were also lending to a large number of high-risk families or subprime (those who find difficulty in meeting their obligation) borrowers.

These loans were pooled together and securitized as asset-backed securities and sold to hedge funds, banks and financial institutions. Soon these subprime mortgages started to default subsequently leading to financial crisis and a melt down across the world economies.

How unethical practices triggered the crisis

The global financial crisis had an ethical dimension too. Many researchers investigated the causality of GFC, and concluded that – failure to adhere by the principles of ethics coupled with absence of transparency were few of the purported reasons that caused the global financial crisis of 2008. Jes Villa also finds the same cause for the failure of the banks in his book (Ethics in Banking) when he states that 'the American evidence indicates an ethical failure, which was demonstrated through irresponsible lending, a lack of concern for the plight of borrowers and a lack of transparency.'

In addition, the crisis was an illustration of failure of corporate governance and risk management at many systemically important financial institutions. Further, the implied guarantee by the US Federal government created a moral hazard and contributed to a glut of risky lending:

- Firstly, the mortgage brokers whose ultimate objective was business acquisition and building a loan book. However, they were never bothered about the quality (*i.e.*, creditworthiness) of borrowers they were targeting.
- Secondly, even the banks wanted to build their mortgage books aggressively and therefore did not hold the loan applications coming to them. Not only that, they also sold the pool of loans to other banks and financial institutions, despite knowing the fact that they were subprime.
- Lastly and most importantly, top-rating agencies also gave a biased rating following conflict of interest, and were not genuine. They played a critical role in the marking of risky mortgage – backed securities. For instance – Lehman Brothers' continued to enjoy an "investment grade" rating even after it had filed for bankruptcy protection. Later, the bonds which enjoyed the "triple A" rating, were downgraded to junk towards the end of crisis and as a result top investment banks like Bear and Sterns, Lehman Brothers and Merrill Lynch vanished. This raised a question on the integrity and transparency of the practices followed in such credit rating agencies.

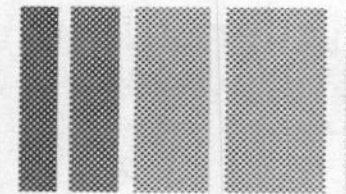

2.9 BANKING ETHICS IN INDIAN CONTEXT: SATYAM AND ITS LESSONS

The Satyam Case

Company Background – The Indian IT major announced acquisition of significant stake in an infrastructure development company and a real estate company. Shareholders rejected the proposal and the stake acquisition plans were called off. However, this incident raised question about the corporate governance practices followed at the company. Leading clients ended their contract with the company, which was followed by resignation by independent director and sell of stake in open market by key stakeholders.

What went wrong – A whistle-blower alerted one of the board members about financial misrepresentation of fraud at the company, which resulted in, resignation of merchant bankers followed by external auditors. It was discovered that the corporate governance mechanism was weak in monitoring the action, policy and decision-making at the company.

Independent Directors' role was ambiguous; they could not discover the fraud and manipulation at the company. They even ignored the significant amount of cash component in the books of the company. Even the auditors ignored the financial irregularities. No transparency was maintained in financial disclosures and financial statements of the company. Even the cash and balance at bank was fake and never existed.

Learnings from the case study:

- Regular scans of inaccuracies must be carried out by companies. Every fraud starts small and investigation of even a small discrepancy can save a company from a larger misfortune.
- Reputation is adversely affected, not only a company's but for the whole industry. After the crisis became public, all the other players were placed under scrutiny by the regulators and skepticism also developed among the investor groups.
- There is a need for strong corporate governance practices across industries. Also, selection of top managers and executives must be done carefully, individuals with high level of credibility and credentials will always bring high moral values and standards to the organization. CEO duality can

also influence the unvarying checks, which are essential for regular audits and timely monitoring the misappropriation and frauds.

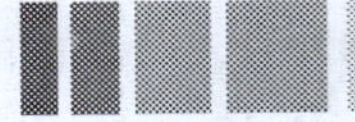

2.10 INDIAN CASE STUDIES

A bank that went bust

Background – Private Sector bank with state-of-the art technology was one of the earliest private sector banks in India. And opened first branch in Secunderabad in Andhra Pradesh. The bank collected Rs. 1 bn in deposits on the first day of its operations and reached a deposit of Rs. 27 bn in a span of 3 years. After a flying start, the bank landed in to a loan trouble of Rs. 15 bn Also, it failed to maintain the minimum statutory capital requirements. Banking regulatory body issued moratorium for the bank's operations, but later extended the period of moratorium. During this period, the bank was only allowed certain specific payments or orders and withdrawals were not allowed from the ATMs, which left about 80,000 customers in a risk of losing their money.

This was followed by promoters selling their stake in the bank and making a complete exit. Both RBI and SEBI probed the bank, and the findings were shocking. The promoters were close allies of the individuals involved in insider trading and were part of stock market scam. Accounts were also misrepresented and the capital of the bank was completely wiped out. Capital Adequacy Ratio (CAR) had also turned negative. Therefore, RBI had advised infusion of fresh capital in the Bank.

Exposure to capital markets comprised a significant portion of the bank's loans, which was significantly higher than the prescribed limit for exposure. Therefore, when the capital market collapsed, the value of investments held as collateral, plunged drastically, which resulted into nil recoverable value from the securities.

The regulator played a major role, in resolving the biggest crisis in banking industry. RBI advised a merger with another public sector bank to protect the interest of its employees and large number of customers.

Failure of Punjab and Maharashtra Cooperative (PMC) Bank

This was one of top bank frauds that took place in the country in the year 2019. PMC bank was a multi-state scheduled primary cooperative bank with its area of operations spread over seven states *viz.*, Andhra Pradesh, Delhi, Goa,

Gujarat, Karnataka, Madhya Pradesh and Maharashtra. The bank had a network of 137 branches. In the early weeks of September 2019, the RBI started to look into the matters of the bank after receiving a whistleblowing complaint that the PMC bank was undertaking fraudulent activities which involved even the bank's board of management. There was truth in the whistleblowing complaint and, on September 23, 2019, RBI placed restrictions on PMC Bank and took control of the bank's operations.

The reason as given by the regulator for the drastic step was 'on account of major financial irregularities, failure of internal control and systems of the bank and wrong/under reporting of its exposure. The bank had created fictitious accounts to hide over Rs. 4,300 crore loans to the firm which was on the verge of bankruptcy at that time. The bank had covered up 44 fake and problematic loans, and Housing Development and Infrastructure Ltd. (HDIL) was one of these accounts. 73% of the bank's Rs. 8,800 crores loan book was tied to just this one borrower group. Later, it transpired that Joy Thomas, the former Managing Director of PMC Bank, allegedly cheated the bank board, auditors, the government, and the RBI for many years by concealing the faulty loan records of Rs. 6,500 crores to HDIL, a Mumbai Based real estate firm. Thomas reportedly said that he concealed the information to safeguard the reputation of the bank.

A number of people were taken into custody in the money laundering and fraud case including the joint general manager of PMC bank, former board director of PMC Bank, Chairman and Managing Director of HDIL, and 2 former directors of RBI. The main accused Daljit Singh, the board director, was arrested from Bihar when he was trying to flee for Canada through Nepal. Daljit Singh had cleared the loans to HDIL leading to crisis in the bank. Reportedly, 15 staff members of the bank were found to be associated with the fraud and the law enforcement agencies are in the process of initiating action again them.

In this case, one of the most important point from the perspective of ethics is the letter of Joy Thomas, the former MD of the bank, addressed to the RBI where he states the reason for his concealment of facts that "as the loans outstanding were huge and if these were classified as NPA, it would have affected the profitability of the bank and the bank would have faced regulatory action from RBI also. Further, this would have created reputational risk for the bank. As the HDIL group had a good track record of clearing their dues with certain delays, we continued to report all the accounts as standard accounts." Further, while interacting with the reporters, Thomas said that 'Whatever has happened is not a fraud. No body has run away with the money without providing security, it is a technical matter which could have been managed better." This statement is an indicator of the mindset that has little or no regard for the meaningful regulatory compliance and is also wilfully blind to the serious unethicality of his words or deeds.

It would be interesting to note that the PMC bank had a declared mission 'to emerge as a strong, vibrant, most preferred premier cooperative bank, committed to excellence in serving the customers, and augmenting the stakeholders value through concern, care and competence.' The bank had also won 'Best Bank Award' by State Cooperative Banking Associations, and recognition for 'work ethics oriented to depositors' service by the All-India Bank Depositors Association etc. (Based on various newspaper and internet reports)

Reasons for failure – The key reason in both the cases was ethical collapse. The massive irregularities were caused by unethical and irresponsible practices of the promoters, board directors and the senior management. In the first case, promoters have colluded with the stock scam perpetrators ignoring the interests of other stakeholders and in the second one, not only the board and senior management but also the middle and junior level employees in the bank have collectively compromised their integrity by resorting to unlawful practices and financial misrepresentation.

Lessons learnt -

- **Unethical practices followed by the staff** – Special favors were given to a specific customer, without evaluating his ability to service the borrowings.
- **Assuming, that things will not change and everything will remain constant, overlooked the potential risks involved.**
- **Violation of principle of trust** – Poor corporate governance followed by the promoters' group and board directors. None of the promoters or board director was worried about the interest of the customers who trusted in the bank and deposited their money with bank.

2.11 LET US SUM UP

The unit explains the difference between Business Ethics and Business Values. Banking is based on trust. It is therefore vital that banks follow ethical practices to maintain the trust of its stakeholders. The principles of ethical banking have been outlined and explained through few Indian and global case studies.

2.12 KEY WORDS

Business values, Business ethics, Myths v. reality, Principles of Business ethics, Ethics in banking and Principles, Trust and Ethics, Professionalism, Enron Case, Global Financial crisis, Satyam Case, PMC Case.

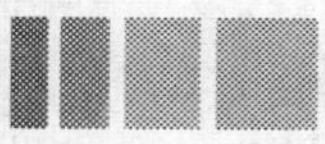

2.13 CHECK YOUR PROGRESS

1. Which one of the following statements is true?
   (*a*) Business ethics modifies people's behavior.
   (*b*) Objective of ethics is managing values and conflict resolution.
   (*c*) Business ethics and corporate social responsibilities are the same.
   (*d*) Ethics cannot be managed.
2. Which one of the following is not a principle of ethics?
   (*a*) Fairness
   (*b*) Dignity
   (*c*) Goodwill
   (*d*) Remaining conscious for profits at all costs
3. Whistle blower protection Act............, in India, protects people who provide information about wrongdoing.
   (*a*) 2009
   (*b*) 2010
   (*c*) 2005
   (*d*) 2011

4. Which one of the following is NOT included in a standard banking code of conduct?
   - (*a*) Profitability
   - (*b*) Neutrality
   - (*c*) Reliability
   - (*d*) Integrity
5. Business Ethics is helpful in
   - (*a*) Dealing with dilemma
   - (*b*) Guards' reputation
   - (*c*) Helps in avoiding future risk
   - (*d*) All the above
6. The US-based natural gas and electricity company, ENRON, by financial year 2000 with revenue of $100bn, became the
   - (*a*) 21st largest Fortune 500 Company
   - (*b*) 74th largest Fortune 500 Company
   - (*c*) 9th largest Fortune 500 Company
   - (*d*) 7th largest Fortune 500 Company

ANSWERS

1. (*b*)	2. (*d*)	3. (*d*)	4. (*a*)	5. (*d*)	6. (*d*)

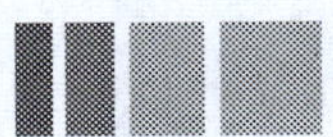

2.14 EXERCISE YOUR ETHICS MUSCLE

Case 3: What Would You Choose ?

You have graduated from a good business school. There are two job offers on your hands. The first company is a bank known to be a place where honesty and hard work are highly valued with a lot of focus on employee wellbeing. The bank has been taking several ESG initiatives and encourages its employees to

participate and contribute to social and environmental causes. The second job opportunity is with a marquee hedge fund where culture is highly competitive and intensely profit-oriented along with long workhours every day. It's a much-coveted job. Moreover, working in this hedge fund will provide opportunities to travel abroad and explore jobs in Europe and USA as well in future. The second job offers 25 percent more salary per year.

Issues to Reflect:

(*a*) Of the two job offers, which one would you accept and why?

(*b*) What is more important to you? Money or a fulfilling work environment?

(*c*) What is better? Being a workaholic and facing burn-out in the long term or having work-life balance and enjoying a healthy life?

(*d*) Do you think that your choice shows what kind of human being you are?

Case 4: Lives or Morals?

An Aircraft manufacturer has invested huge amount of money in designing and building a new carrier airplane. The global company is facing financial constraints on account of high deployment of funds for this new product. Its order book is not satisfactory and if it does not sell few planes soon, it will have to shut down some part of its operations in Philippines. Doing that will put thousands of local workers out of job. The action will jeopardize the livelihood of the workers and create social unrest in the town in which they live and the factory is based. The Philippines factory is the flagship facility of the company and if the present existential crisis is not resolved, the company might have to exit the country with insurmountable financial losses in its books. The CEO of the company has been trying to induce the government of a country in a large purchase. His marketing head tells him that one of the key governmental ministers authorized to close the deal is heavily in debt because of gambling. He quietly contacts that minister and offers him one million USD in cash if a contract to purchase 6 planes from his company is awarded. The contract is awarded once the money is paid.

Issues to Reflect:

(*a*) Is it correct to pay illicit money to protect the jobs of workers and thereby averting misery for their families?

(*b*) Which is more important? High ground of morals or the reality of basic human survival?

(*c*) Is it correct for the company to resolve its acute financial crisis by resorting to unfair means? Is this the only way out?

(*d*) What is your assessment of the CEO's personal ethics based on his action in this highly conflicting situation?

3 UNIT

Banking and Normative Ethics in Management

3 UNIT

Banking and Normative Ethics in Management

3.1 LEARNING OBJECTIVES

This Unit throws light on the various ethical theories. It aims to develop understanding of virtue ethics, utilitarianism, rights and justice. We have also explained Kant's theory of non-consequentialism theory. The Unit briefly explains relations and differences between morality and ethics, morality and self-interest and the concept of enlightened self-interest. Ethical decision-making for any business has been explained along with key features of the Indian ethos for management. The relationship between Normative ethics and applied ethics are discussed.

3.2 ETHICAL THEORIES

Normative ethics is a branch of philosophy that develop moral theories about how people should behave. The three main areas of normative ethics are meta-ethics, applied ethics and descriptive ethics. Meta-ethics looks at the nature of moral language and what kinds of things can be called good or bad. Applied ethics looks at ethical issues that arise in particular professions, such as medicine or engineering. In other words, applied ethics is more specific than normative ethics. Normative theories seek to provide action guides. There is only one ultimate criterion of moral conduct, single rule or set of principles, either we establish a single principle against which we judge or a set of foundational principles.

Let us attempt to learn some of the Normative theories relating to ethics.

These are:

Virtue (theory of) Ethics, Utilitarianism, Rights Theory, Justice Theory, Rawlsian Theory, Duty Ethics and the Deontological Theory.

(*a*) Virtue Ethics

The root of the virtue theory lies in the works of great philosophers like Plato and Aristotle. The approach to ethics in which human nature is characterized by the objective of ethical thinking is called virtue ethics. The most vital objective for ethical thinking is *being good*. Virtue Ethics is also categorized as teleological theory, which is governed by the ultimate objective to be achieved and not by the rules.

Virtue theory is a character-based theory that looks for the role-played by one's character in the process of decision-making and how that decision will affect the character of that particular individual.

Virtue ethics primarily emphasizes on the role of one's character and the virtue that one's character personifies for determination or evaluation of ethical behaviour. Virtue ethics theory places emphasis on being good or right rather than doing good or right. In virtue ethics, morality sprouts from the identity and/or character of the individual, rather than being a response of the actions (or consequences) of the individual.

Therefore, possessing these virtues is what makes one moral and one's action is a mere reflection of one's inner morality.

Virtues are established and developed on the basis of—

Virtue can be acquired – It is called the intellectual virtue or wisdom – it is that quality of mind and character that promotes intellectual flourishing and critical thinking based on curiosity. It can also be acquired by habit.

Virtue by morals – This was explained by Aristotle as traits of an individual's character. It can be an individual's passion to be good and perform good actions.

Components of virtue

Habit – Virtues have to be developed, as they cannot be acquired at once. Thus, when virtues become habit – they are more reliable and consistent. Once virtues become habit and practiced as a daily routine, they are strongly embedded in one's character.

Thoughtfulness to reasons – Virtue implicates evoking certain matters as practical reason, which will motivate people and also steer their actions. For instance, seeing someone's vulnerability as a reason to help him or her and not taking his or her advantage; or evoking value of truth as reason to conduct business honestly.

Emotions and attitude – Virtue also comprises of sentiments associated with certain actions performed. Say, you feel happy to perform a virtuous deed, or you are attracted to other virtuous people. The malicious behaviour of your friends and family makes you sad. This is contrary to Kant's argument on virtue ethics, which says that it is the individual's desire to do the right thing that tend to make someone more virtuous.

Natural Inclination to Act Well – To a virtuous person, virtuous actions come naturally. Rather virtue is incorporated in one's character and it comes naturally. Thus, there is no need to battle contrary desires. It is spontaneous expression of one's innermost desires.

Phronesis: Phronesis is more specifically a type of wisdom relevant to practical things. It is an individual's ability to evaluate the situation correctly, which will be supportive in making choices wisely, and it also encourages practical virtue. Wisdom cannot be inherited or passed on as customs; it requires knowledge and life experience. It helps solve conflicts between the virtues (or moral rules). It only supplements mere "natural virtue": it perfects (is a check on) the spontaneous component.

Limitations of virtues—

- Difficulty in establishing the nature of virtues mainly because different individuals, cultures and societies have different opinions.
- The virtue ethics is considered as self-centered as its main concern is the agent's own character, while morality should be concerned about how our actions can affect others.

Virtue theory, thus, has its roots in the Greek philosophical tradition, whose followers sought to learn how to live a flourishing life through study, teaching, and practice. The cardinal virtues to be practiced were courage, self-control, justice, and wisdom. Socrates was often cited as a sage and a role model, whose conduct in life was held in high regard.

Virtue Ethics

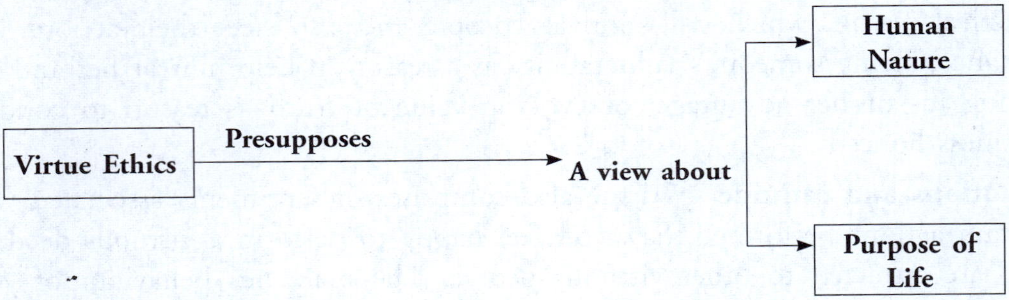

Virtue Ethics → Presupposes → A view about → Human Nature; Purpose of Life

Virtue ethics in business

The pluralism of virtue gives the business manager an affirmative character and institute the very best of integrity of character. The virtue ethics perspective to business can be summed up as follows.

- Individual virtue and integrity count, but good corporate ethics programs encourage individual virtue and integrity.
- By the employee's role in the organization, these virtues associated with appropriate conduct form a good person.
- The ultimate objective is fulfilment of demands of the society along with the public good and to be rewarded in one's career.
- The well-being of the community coupled with individual fineness because of the social cognizance and public spirit of every individual.

Over the years, it is being seen globally that the most respected and admired companies are also among those that had the highest profit margins. Being socially cognizant, going green, having good governance and taking a personal interest in employee happiness levels adds to the bottom line. Consumers want to use companies that follow virtue ethics in their business and care for others and environment. Many unethical companies have gone bankrupt. However, those companies that 'avoided the "quick buck," risky and unethical investments, and other unethical business practices often flourished.' In the present times, customers' feedback on the social media sites has become so powerful that it can simply damage an organization's prospects who ignores the public good as has we have recently seen in the case of the failure of one US bank.

Example of virtue ethics theory: Lack of courage leads to cowardice, where an individual may fail to confront necessary challenges or face danger when it is

ethically required. At the same time, excessive courage can lead to recklessness, who takes unnecessary risks without proper consideration of consequences. A virtuous person displaces courage in a balanced way, neither recklessly endangering themselves nor avoiding necessary risks.

(*b*) Utilitarianism

John Miller's theory of utilitarianism suggests that for any action to be right or wrong is dependent on the outcome of choosing that action over other actions with a different outcome. Also a right action must promote happiness.

In literal meaning, utilitarianism is based on the concept of utility, which means usefulness. Thus, when utilitarianism is applied to actions and conduct, it should be useful in bringing about desirable or good results.

Another philosopher Paul Taylor has described utilitarianism as an end and not as a means to achieve something in life.

For example, defense preparedness of a nation is not an end in itself but only a means to ensure protection to people of a society.

Types of Utilitarianism

- **Hedonistic Utilitarianism** – Suggests that happiness, pleasure, peace, and fulfilment are intrinsically valuable and they are not the means but they are ends in themselves. Whereas, suffering and pain are intrinsically invaluable.
- **Eudemonistic Utilitarianism** – As explained by Aristotle, eudaimonia means living well and doing well and happiness is the highest good. He also suggested that Eudaimonia *i.e. happiness or wellbeing* can be achieved through *Virtue.*
- **Agathistic Utilitarianism** – Suggests that goodness cannot be defined in terms of either pleasure or happiness; rather it is a unique and identifiable property of things.

Application of Utilitarianism – by act or by rule.

From applicability perspective, utilitarianism is generally found in two forms – in a particular action or in general rules. This is also called as **act *utilitarianism or rule utilitarianism*.**

Act Utilitarianism

Act utilitarianism is the basic version of utilitarianism. It says that we must find out what are the consequences of a particular act in order to know whether it is right or wrong. Principle of utility is applied directly under the act utilitarianism to each alternative act in a situation of choice. The right act is then defined as the one that has greater utility than any other alternative act. It also suggests that we must ponder over the consequences of a certain action in a certain type of situation – what will be the impact on those people who will be affected by that particular act. Suppose, if a particular act brings total good for the people as compared to any other alternative action, then that action is considered as the right action and it should be performed.

Act utilitarianism is criticized for the following reasons.

1. It is difficult to attain full knowledge and there is certainty of consequences of someone's actions.
2. Also, it is possible to justify immoral acts using the act utilitarianism concept.

Is it right to press the switch to avoid the deaths of the five workmen?

You are at the wheel of a runaway trolley quickly approaching a fork in the tracks. On the tracks to the left is a group of five railway workmen. On the tracks to the right is a single railway workman. If you do nothing, the trolley will proceed to the left, causing the deaths of the five workmen. The only way to avoid the deaths of these workmen is to hit a switch on your dashboard that will cause the trolley to proceed to the right, causing the death of the single workman.

Rule utilitarianism

Rule Utilitarianism articulates that for an action to be right, it should conform to valid rules of conduct, and if rules are violated, it is considered as wrong. Principles of utility help determine the validity of the rules. Valid rule of conduct is the rule that either leads to obtain the maximum good for maximum people or inhibits people or abstain actions which produces pain. Therefore, a valid rule of conduct should be to produce happiness or avoid pain. Right action and wrong action are then defined as following or breaking the valid rule of conduct.

Rule-utilitarianism is criticized on following grounds:

- Rule utilitarianism irrationally worships the rule-based action where as in certain cases good actions could be performed by violating the rule.
- The rule utilitarianism will collapse with the act utilitarianism if rules factor in maximum possible exceptions or flexibility in a moral code of conduct.
- Rule utilitarianism avoids the weaknesses associated with act utilitarianism and thus it cannot support the right answers to crucial moral problems. Also, it does not acknowledge the importance of justice and rights.

Is it right to push one person off the footbridge to save lives of the five workmen?

A runaway trolley is heading down the tracks towards five workmen who will be killed if the trolley continues on its present course. You are on a footbridge over the tracks, in between the approaching trolley and the five workmen. Next to you on this footbridge is a stranger who happens to be very large. The only way to save the lives of the five workmen is to push this stranger off the bridge and onto the tracks below, where his large body will stop the trolley. The stranger will die if you do this, but the five workmen will be saved:

Questions:

- Is it acceptable to push the stranger on to the tracks in order to save the five workmen?
- Would your answer be different if you knew for certain that the large stranger had previously completed a prison sentence for murdering someone?

If we think over the situations given in the above two boxes, these two superficially seeming to be similar situations will turn out to be different in their dilemmas. But if a question is asked what is the difference between the situations, we are sometimes confused and can't exactly point out what it is.

How did you respond to each of the dilemmas in previous boxes? What is the difference in the dilemmas posed by the situations?

In such cases, to arrive at a reasoned answer through the utilitarian approach, the following lines of reasoning as suggested by S. Manikutti in his book 'Being Ethical' can be depended upon:

1. What are the options available to me?
2. In each option, who is affected? Positively? Negatively? By how much?
3. If I add up the net consequences under each option, which option gives the best overall outcome?
4. We can select that option.

Criticism of Utilitarianism

1. Since a utilitarian tries to maximize the happiness by evaluating the likely results of an action, comparing and measuring happiness amongst different individuals is significantly complicated. Moreover, if for comparison purpose, happiness of two different people is quantified, it will be difficult to make the calculations accurately. Thus, Utilitarianism is criticized for not being really workable.
2. According to utilitarianism, the results of an action, and not the character of an action, decide moral worth of an action. An action becomes objectionable only when it fails to produce maximum happiness or relatively less happiness than other alternative courses of action. However, certain wrong and immoral actions might also produce good results. However, morality is not only concerned with the end – result, which is say – happiness, how it is achieved is also equally important. In such situation, utilitarianism is criticized for behaving blindly in permitting actions, which may be immoral, but produce maximum happiness.
3. Utilitarianism is criticized for being concerned only about the production of happiness, and not being concerned about the distribution of happiness. An action, which has produced significant happiness for one person, is considered moral despite the fact that it has caused a lot of distress for others. Therefore, happiness of one individual is sacrificed for the happiness of another, which is explained as unjust or unfair. Such actions are imposition of injustice between individuals. Justice, herein, means equal and fair distribution of satisfaction.

> By stealing from the rich and giving to the poor. Robin Hood might be considered to have been a utilitarian.
>
> Whether you agree with this statement or not?

Example: In a scenario where there are five patients in critical condition, each requiring a different organ transplant to survive. All the five patient would die without organ transplant. In such circumstances, whether one healthy person willing to donate his organs required to save all the five patients at the cost of his life is justified or not under Utilitarianism.

Utilitarianism at an organizational level

Moral standards for decision-making for any organization is critical in nature and is subject to thoughtful quest and analysis. For an organization, profit making or any other economic activity cannot be used as moral justification for any decision-making. Hence, to guide the policies and proficient decision making, an organization requires theories like Utilitarianism as the standard for moral decision-making:

- Utilitarianism has the capacity to provide a clear, logical, rational, and straightforward, basis for formulation and evaluation of organizational policies, which guides the decision action and behaviour. A good organizational policy should promote general welfare. Utilitarianism does not suggest blind acceptance of rules, rather it suggests assessing and testing the worth of the policies, in maximizing the happiness for maximum people.
- Utilitarian standards emphasize and explain its objectivity and attractiveness of conflict-resolution. Conflicts arising from self-interest are more complicated and cannot be resolved by egoism. Utilitarianism is concerned with the overall happiness of maximum people and not merely the wellbeing of the agent. This stimulates moral decision-making in an organization beyond self-interest, by evaluating their action as means to achieve the ends.
- Utilitarianism encourages executives of an organization to evaluate the consequences of decisions made by them pertaining to policies and actions – whether they are right or wrong. It guides the decision – maker to customize their decisions to suit the complex business situations. Hence,

utilitarianism aids the managers in making decisions that are realistic, workable and ethically appropriate.

Did You Know What is 'Auto-Icon'?

Jeremy Bentham was the father of utilitarianism. He made a seemingly bizarre request for the disposition of his body after his death. He donated half his estate to London University, a public university open to all and offering a secular curriculum, unusual for the times. Bentham also mandated that his dead body be preserved for medical instruction and later placed on display in what he called an "auto-icon," or self-image. Bentham's body has been on display ever since. Bentham adhered to his convictions even after his death.

(*c*) Rights Theory

Ethics involves a moral code of conduct which helps develop understating for right action and wrong action, *i.e.* what people should do and what people should not do. This theory of ethics pertaining to Rights is explained as – something that an individual claims or is entitled to have. Rights are primarily focused on the actions of an individual or the actions of others towards him/her. Therefore, an individual holds freedom to act in a certain way and he/she can also expect a conduct of a certain form from others. Hence, rights allow a person freedom to pursue certain actions without interference from others. Certain vital features of the rights are:

- One individual must respect the rights of another.
- Rights let people act as equals.
- Rights will let moral justification of an individual's actions.

Rights can be classified as follows:

Legal Rights – Such rights are derived from the legal system, but law does not create them. The legal system of a country merely recognizes and protects such rights. For instance, every citizen of India has a right to fair trial in the court of law.

Natural Rights – These rights belong to the individual himself and the society cannot take these rights away from the individual, nor can it be surrendered, like the right to live, liberty and being happy.

Human Rights or Moral Rights – These rights are based on ethical standards. They are also known as fundamental moral rights. Such rights emerge from specific roles or specific relationships or situations. Such as – an employee has rights to fair and equal treatment in an organization, like induction, appraisal etc. Moral rights that are not dependent on relationship, role or situation are human rights. Human rights are universal and equal for all. We have these human rights purely on the basis of humanity and are protected by law. Some of the widely accepted human rights are as follows:

- Right to life
- Right to freedom
- Right to health and medical care
- Right to education and knowledge
- Right to worship
- Right to security
- Right to work and receive a living wage
- Civil Rights
- Minorities' Rights
- Women's Rights
- Elder People's Rights
- Privacy Right
- Non-smokers' Rights
- Smokers' Rights
- Fetal Rights
- Embryo Rights
- Victims' Rights

Human rights are further classified as negative rights and positive rights.

Negative rights – Right to have freedom from outside interferences or non-interference, that is, one person will not interfere in the rights of another.

Positive rights – Rights which reflect the vital interest that people have in receiving certain benefits. It is just like rights to wellbeing, this can also be explained as – it is a moral duty of one person to assist another in perusing his/her rights.

Limitations of the rights theory:

- Rights theory eliminates the view of assessing the result of actions.
- Rights express moral rights and individual's view, and not view of the society. Does not look at the number of people who benefit from limiting another person's rights. For example – Right to freedom of speech and expression will stand in India even if a person expresses a dissenting view.

Example of rights theory of ethics: A controversial speaker is invited to give a talk on a public gathering. The views expressed by the speaker are offensive which could lead to wild spread protests. Right to freedom of speech is considered a fundamental and inherent right and that the speaker's opinion is valued above potential discomfort or disagreement to some sections. Those emphasize the right to be free from offensive or harmful speech argue that cancelling the event would protect the potential harm. Hence, principle of individual rights takes precedence and ethical decisions are based on upholding even some find disagreeable.

(*d*) Justice theory

The Justice theory looks at the balance of benefits and burdens equally distributed among the members of a group or society. Greek philosopher Plato was of the opinion that just men build a perfect and harmonious society.

Justice is also a result of application of rules, policies, or laws that apply to a society. When someone is mistreated or deprived of his or her rights, Justice Theory often asks a question like does a decision or behaviour show fairness and impartiality? Hence, the concept of Justice is related to our notions of fairness, equality, desert and rights. Since justice means being fair to all individuals, justice and fairness are synonymous.

Justice is of vital importance when it comes to economic justice in the society, which is also called the *Distributive Justice.* Distributive justice refers to equal and fair distribution of benefits and burdens, based on principles of pure equality, merits, needs and social contribution or efforts. These principles are opposite to one other and pull us in different directions, therefore, when several principles are applied and weighed to find the most suitable one – it is called the pluralist approach.

Utilitarian view of distributive justice – Justice Theory holds the view that just action is the right action, therefore, in certain cases; actions resulting from justice may override utilitarian results. The utilitarian view considers justice as just with the maximization of good for the society. John Stuart Mills was of the opinion that the wide gap between labour and capitalist should be gradually suspended and that there should be fair distribution of profits with the workers and increase in participation in the management. This is a must to achieve the economic justice in a society and reduce the economic disparity. This will help in maximization of happiness in the society. Income disparity is considered as unjust and unfair.

Libertarian view of the distributive justice – This theory suggests that justice is concerned with protecting the liberty of people, and that people should have the freedom of making choices. It considers the interference with other peoples' freedom as unjust.

For libertarianism – personal liberty is of prime importance, which is opposite stance to utilitarianism. Utilitarianism restricts individual liberty and interferes in making personal choices, if such action leads to maximization of social happiness. It supports liberty that means non-interference. Here, Government needs to follow minimal interference. Thus, Government should protect citizens against wrong action, while on the other hand should provide freedom of choice. Also, in performing economic activity, libertarians support laissez-faire, that is, all buying, selling and all other exchange activities should be free from Government interference.

(*e*) Rawlsian Theory of Justice

This Theory is a modern alternative to utilitarianism. Rawls rejected the idea of reducing justice to a matter of society-utility. In his opinion, justice is a social concept and that it is associated with fairness and moral equality of individuals.

According to him, justice has two principles, which is explained below:

1. Provision of a guarantee of certain familiar and fundamental liberties to each person.
2. To justify economic and social inequalities only if they benefit the least advantaged members of the society.

Rawls is of the opinion that primary focus of the justice should be on social structure and not on the transactions between individuals. Thus, he criticized the entitlement theory. According to him, Utilitarianism may permit unfair distribution on benefits and burdens.

(f) Duty Ethics

Duty means what a person is ought to do, which is why duty is an obligation that an individual has to perform irrespective of his or her situation. Kantian approach to morality insists on performance of duty for its own sake. To be moral, good thoughts are not enough but good actions are also required. Human being have an intellectual understanding regarding their duty but also have an innate urge to perform their duties. The prime and basic moral duty of every citizen in a society is to protect and respect the rights of others. Indian philosophy also propounds that the whole of our life has only one principle, which is to perform our duty.

(g) Deontological Theory

Deontological ethics is the belief that moral laws guide people's action, and that these moral laws are universal and are cited as the foundation for most of the laws. This theory rejects consequences as a standard for morality; rather it focuses on performing duty to a moral code. And it also opines duty to be the only intrinsic good.

Deontology requires a commitment to ethical act. Individuals should adhere to independent moral rules or duties; motives behind certain actions are right or wrong instead of focusing on results. This theory is based on duty. Duty to a social contract means obedience to rules consensually agreed to and democratically amended. The word deontological itself takes its roots from the Greek word "deon" which means duty.

Unlike utilitarians, deontologists argue that there are some things that we should not do, even to maximize utility. Deontological philosophies regard certain behaviour as inherently right and the determination of this rightness focuses on the individual actor, and not society. Thus, these perspectives are sometimes referred to as non-consequentialist as their ethics is based on the respect for other persons. For example, bribery is wrong by its very nature regardless of its consequences.

Similar to utilitarianism, deontologists are also divided into those who focus on moral rules and those who focus on the nature of the acts themselves.

Rule Deontologist believes that submission to general moral principles helps in determining ethicalness. Deontological philosophies use reason and logic to formulate rules and behaviour. Rule deontology is determined between the basic rights of the individual and the set of rules governing conduct.

Act deontologist; in contrast, hold that actions are the proper basis to judge morality or ethicalness. Act deontology requires that a person uses equity, fairness and impartiality when making and enforcing decisions. For act deontologists, rules serve only as guidelines with past experiences weighing more heavily than rules upon the decision-making process.

Example: Not taking credit for something you have not done. It would be wrong to take credit when your team produces a great result. Making sure everyone is treated fairly, regardless of their race, religion, or gender. If a Company is hiring new employees, it would be wrong to discriminate against any particular group of people.

Types of deontological theory

The following two types exist in the Deontological Theory:

i. **Agent-centred** - It focuses on safeguarding an individual's moral record as unblemished at any cost and deals largely with the actions performed by an individual. For an agent-centred deontologist, the morality is stringently personal. Popular example of this theory is ***Divine command theory*** – which says, "A person or action is good/bad if and only if God said so".

ii. **Patient-centred** - This is quite opposite of Agent-centred deontology. It focuses on protracting an individual's right – such as freedom of speech and on respecting the rights of others.

Criticism of Deontological theory

Deontology is often disapproved for its support of dogmatic obedience at the expense of the original intent of the rules. Many a times, duty can pilot people to do extremely irrational or immoral things; on the other hand, consequentialism is far less likely to.

3.3 META-ETHICS, ETHICS AND APPLIED ETHICS

Ethics is defined as the study of the principles of human conduct or human actions. These actions must serve a purpose, which constitutes part or the whole of the moral agents' intentions in doing what he or she does. Ethics is about the way we behave and the value that we hold.

Ethical-decision making is considered a peculiar human activity due to our ability to reason, to rationalize and to analyse what we do to see ourselves as part of a social group and in the modern world, as a member of society at large. The moral agent is a feature of all rational moral discourse.

Meta ethics is the conceptual analysis of why we should be concerned with ethics. Meta-ethical theories or fundamental ethics are the overarching principles and perspectives arising from the conceptual analysis of ethical questions. Western Meta ethics theories sit behind applied ethical approaches.

Applied ethics are normative ethics, which aim to guide conduct; the analysis of specific practical issues using ethical discourse and meta-ethical theories. However, the distinctions between pure and applied ethics are somewhat artificial, as the application of ethics has always flowed from a particular conceptual viewpoint.

- **Normative ethics**: How moral values should be determined.
  (What do individuals think is right?)
- **Descriptive ethics**: What morals are actually followed or adhered to.
  (How should individuals act?) Ex: Heinz Dilemma
- **Meta-ethics**: The fundamental nature of ethics, including whether it has an objective justification, how individuals determine for themselves what societal norms to follow.
  (What does it mean to be "right"?)
- **Prescriptive ethics:** Which defends and recommends concepts of right and wrong action. (Is this action wright or wrong?)
- **Applied ethics:** Application of ethical principles and moral theories to real-life issues. (Is it ethical to allow medical aid in dying?)

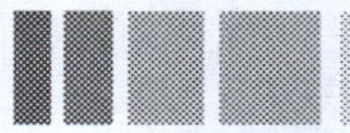

3.4 ETHICS AND MORALITY - WHAT'S THE DIFFERENCE?

Morality Definition

Morality is the belief system of a society, culture or religion. It is the values an individual has and it helps differentiate 'right' from 'wrong'. Morals are standard rules created by society, it is for an individual to decide what is right and follow morals. For example - speak truth, being loyal, should not steal, be patient etc.

In certain cases, being morally correct might not mean that it is objectively right and therefore sometimes an action may be morally correct but it might not be correct legally or *vice versa*.

There is, of course, an extensive theoretical background to speculation about ethical rules. The best known principle being that of the 'golden rule' (do to others as you would have them do unto you). In order for such a principle to be acceptable, it should be of universal application across every conceivable situation.

Morality and Etiquette

Several times morality is confused with etiquettes, and they are considered as same. However, etiquette refers to a typical code or courtesy. It can be explained as the prescription for the socially accepted behaviours. For example, saying 'thank you' and 'please' or 'excuse me' are the ways to show one's modesty and courtesy. Etiquettes are described as manners, which are necessary for a civilized and polite behaviour. However, if an individual violates these norms, he or she is considered ill-mannered or uncivilized or impolite but he or she is not immoral or unethical. As an exception, violation of etiquettes may have certain moral implications at times.

Morality and Religion

Another misconception regarding morality says that morality and religion are synonymous to each other. This leads to a conclusion that a person who is religious is moral and who is non-religious is immoral. Although it is true that religion integrates certain values, principles, moral rules and duties, it is not realistic and logical that non-believer in religion is unethical and immoral. It is also believed that religion influences morality positively and helps people understand good or bad and right or wrong where as a wrong interpretation of religion can create confusions. Hence, religion and morality have similar objectives of development of good character and being the heart of good human beings and good society.

Customary morality and Reflective Morality

Societies have their own moral standards or culture, and people living in these societies accept and follow these moral beliefs blindly. Such morality, which is based on customs, is called customary or conventional and passed from one generation to the next. Therefore, one who follows ***customary moralities*** finds it difficult to support its culture with rational arguments and also deny other moralities and reject all moral ideas. Thus arises the need for *moral maturity*, which requires an individual to be open-minded about his moral beliefs and support them with valid rationale.

Reflective morality

Reflective morality is that stage of moral development, where an individual frames moral judgment on the grounds of reflective evaluation of principles and examines the facts pertaining to human life carefully. Since the situations and dynamics of the world around us keeps changing, the conventional morality is not capable to address the conflicts between law and customs. Hence, reflective morality encourages critical evaluation of the norms of customary morality. Complete morality is – when an individual recognizes the right or chooses the good, freely devotes himself heartily to its fulfilment and seeks a progressive social development in which every member of society shall share.

Ethical relativism

Ethical relativism is the belief that what is right in one group or society can be morally incorrect in another culture or society. Ethical relativism suggests that rightness of an act and goodness of a person is dependent on the interpretation of a particular social group and therefore it may vary according to time, place and opinions of people. The ethical relativism theory concluded that morality is subjective and there is no universal standard to which people can appeal. The theory is criticized for the only reason that certain moral standards that are adopted by one society may not be acceptable to another society.

Difference between morals and ethics

1. Morals are general guidelines framed by the society, like respect your elders. While ethics is application of these guidelines to a particular situation.
2. Morals are prescribed by society, culture or religion; whereas Ethics that governs an individual's life, is chosen by an individual himself.
3. Morals are largely related with principles of right and wrong. On other hand, ethics emphasizes more on right and wrong conduct.

4. Morals usually differ from society to society and culture to culture. As opposed to Ethics, which remains identical, irrespective of any culture, religion or society.
5. Morals do not have any business applicability, while Ethics is broadly pertinent in the business as business ethics.

Ethics expresses morals in actions. Every individual has certain principles that guide him throughout his life in coping with possible unfavourable situations. This is called Ethics. On the contrary, morals are not the unbending rules, however they are the rules, which are considered as right by a majority of people. That is the reason people widely accept them and this is what differentiates morals from ethics.

Consider a defense lawyer. A defense lawyer may find murder immoral as per his personal moral code. However, ethics requires that lawyers defend their accused client to the best of their ability, even if they know that their client is most likely guilty. If lawyers do not want to adhere to this ethical principle, then they should leave the legal profession. Else, they stand to damage the ethics of their profession. This is a fundamental concept within any public service system, that ethics must trump personal morals for the greater good of maintaining the integrity of a system.

3.5 KANT AND NON-CONSEQUENTIALISM IN AN ORGANIZATIONAL CONTEXT

Immanuel Kant was a German philosopher, who propounded non-consequential approach to ethics. He said that results do not decide the worth of an action but it is determined on the basis of its underlying characteristic. He also believed in *good intentions,* because good intentions result into good actions.

Kant's theory suggests that the rightness or wrongness of action does not depend on their consequences but on whether they fulfil our duty. According to Kant, there was a supreme principle or morality, which was referred as categorical imperative. Kant says that an organization should frame moral rules for decision-making, which should not depend on either circumstances or results or individuals. The rules should be applicable to everybody and should not have any exception. This will effectively develop awareness across the organization that certain actions are wrong regardless of consequences or situation or people involved.

Also, Kant's approach had a humanistic dimension, as his approach emphasized on considering humanity as ends and not as a means. This is essential directive for business organization in today's context, as improved profitability remains the prime focus of management.

Kant's view

Reason	Is Final authority for	Morality

Non-consequentialism is a normative theory, which denies that the rightness or wrongness of our conduct is determined solely by the goodness or badness of the consequence of our acts or of the rules to which those acts conform. Hence, Non-consequentialism is the normative ethical theory that is not detached from consequences, as it is an attempt to figure out what people should do or whether their existing moral behaviour is judicious.

Kant's Theory in an organizational context

1. The categorical imperative provides a solid standard for the formulation of rules applicable to any business circumstances.
2. Kant emphasized the absolute value and dignity of individuals.
3. Kant stresses the importance of acting on the basis of right intentions.

Criticism of Kant's ethics

- Kant's ethics is too extreme in so far as it excludes emotion from moral decision-making and makes duty paramount.
- Kant fails to distinguish between excluding oneself from a rule and qualifying a rule on the basis of exceptions.
- It is not always clear when people are treated as ends and merely as means.

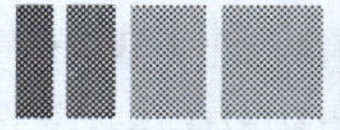

3.6 MORAL PRINCIPLES AND SELF INTEREST

In philosophy, relationship between self-interest and morality is perpetual and also at the centre of moral theory. The same was debated in Plato's Republic – whether living morally was in the best interest of an individual.

Self-interest generally refers to focus on needs and desire (interest) of the self. Many philosophical, psychological and economic theories analyzed the role of self-interest in motivating human actions.

Kant believed that a person must follow morality anyway, even if it is not in a person's best interest.

Egoism theory of Self-interest

This theory advocates individual's self-interest as its guiding principle. It states that an action is good if it produces results to maximize a person's self-interest. It associates morality with self-interest. An act is morally right if and only if it promotes long-term interest of an agent, which can be a single person or a group. Egoism has also been classified as Personal egoism, individual egoism and universal egoism. An individual ethical egoist would hold that all people should do whatever benefits "my" (the individual) self-interest; a personal ethical egoist would hold that he or she should act in his or her self-interest, but would make no claims about what anyone else ought to do. A universal ethical egoist would argue that everyone should act in ways that are in their self-interest.

Ethical egoism differs from psychological egoism, which asserts that one can only act in their own self-interest. Ethical egoism also differs from rational egoism; it considers that it is judicious to act in one's self-interest. Therefore, ethical egoism believes that actions whose consequences will benefit the doer can be considered ethical in this sense.

Categorical Imperative is the central philosophical concept in deontological moral philosophy, which is defined as a way of evaluating moral actions, and makes moral judgments.

Moralities are system of principles whose acceptance by everyone as over-ruling the dictates of self-interest is in the interest of everyone alike, though the rule of morality is not of course identical with following self-interest.

Conflict between self-interest and morality

Self-sacrifice does not necessarily involve conflict between morality and self-interest. And while making a sacrifice, a person does not necessarily harm his/her self-interest. A person's well-being is not the reason for action or source of value, thus people may reasonably care about his or her own well-being.

Enlightened self-interest

If human beings did not have an inherent will to protect themselves and further their own interests, they would not survive. According to enlightened self-interest, an action is morally acceptable if it benefits an individual or organization without intentionally harming others, and the benefits counterbalance the harm. If an individual operates with the win-lose attitude, then he/she cannot work in partnership with anybody.

Criticism of egoism- Egoism, as a moral theory, faces several objections and strong criticism as egoism can directly and indirectly support selfishness, which cannot be considered as a virtue in one's life. Selfishness has always been considered as an immoral behaviour.

Egoism is also criticized to be a form of hedonism. Hedonism is explained as pleasure is the only good. Egoistic hedonism thus states that we are not under obligation to pursue anything but our own greatest happiness. But happiness is largely dependent on relationships with others in the society and without the society one will be alienated if we are thoroughly unscrupulous and selfish.

3.7 MORAL DECISION-MAKING: TOWARDS A SYNTHESIS

Decision-making is a process of choosing good over bad alternatives. Individuals are shaped by the choices they make. Every moral choice an individual makes reveals the kind of person he/she is and it also forms the kind of person we become.

It is important to note that while making decisions on certain occasions, good choices may seem so evident that we pursue them without much deliberation. While sometimes, the good choices may not be that obvious, and one must consider all the significant aspects attached to it. For instance—

1. Decision-making circumstance.
2. Possible consequences short-term and long-term.
3. Guidance of other people.
4. Guidance of the moral norms, which form our values.

The results of an ethical decision are often uncertain; no one can always tell us whether we have made the right decision. It is difficult to agree on normative

judgments pertaining to what is ethical; which is why scholars developed descriptive models of business ethics that focuses on regularities in decision-making and the different phenomena that interest in a dynamic environment to produce predictable pattern of behaviour. Situations often arise in which people differ on the applicable moral standards. For example, if we consider a situation in which a man whose family is starving becomes desperate and breaks into a grocery store and steals few items of food. What moral standard should we apply on his action? One school of thought would tend to condone his theft out of a sense of compassion for his suffering family. Another school of thought will take a stringent view of morality and adhere to absolute ethical standards and condemn the act of theft. They will say that a theft is a theft irrespective of the thief's personal adverse circumstances. They are rigid moralists who apply strict moral standards in judging this act of theft. Even the great philosopher, Immanuel Kant would also apply rigid ethical rules in such cases.

Moral decision-making always presents such conflicts. Taking one more example, supposing that a doctor has only a single dose of a life-saving injection, and two patients in need of injection are brought to him. To whom shall he administer the injection? What principle can regulate his choice of whom to save? We have taken these two examples to show that commonly accepted ethical standards fail to provide guidance to moral agents in some situations and a defined framework for the purpose is needed.

Leadership Style is the key influencing factor while making such decisions in an organization. Leadership primarily impacts various aspects of organizational behaviour, which includes acceptance and adherence to organizational values and standard code of conduct.

Strong leaders need a mix of knowledge and experience to make decisions. They must have the right kind of moral integrity. Integrity should possess the quality of transparency. Although it is challenging to make a right decision, a leader must keep in mind his clients, employees, shareholders and the surrounding communities at the time of making a decision. An ethical leader should be:

- A person of strong character
- Passionate to do righteous act
- Proactive

- Considerate about stakeholders' interest
- A role model for the organizational values
- Transparent and involve actively in the decision-making of an organization.
- Competent enough to take holistic view of ethical culture in his organization.

Need for moral decision-making

Moral decision-making results in arriving at ethical decisions, which in turn helps in resolving ethical dilemmas. It is important to understand why do we need to make decisions more carefully:

- This is mainly because in certain situations choices before us involve conflicting values.
- Uncertainty about the consequences and impact of the decisions.
- Pressures from peers also play a significant role in impacting moral decision-making.
- Last but not the least, a decision may have some probable negative consequences.

3.8 INDIAN ETHICAL TRADITION

Indian ethical traditions have been one of the greatest foundations of moral beliefs in world philosophy. Early Greece, Europe, Asia, and the New World are also influenced by Indian ethical vision.

Indian system of ethics is very vast and rich. It has always believed that ethical theories are practically applicable. This application of ethical principles in practical life is a characteristic feature of Indian ethical traditions – there are principles we ought to follow but if some principle, theory or standard is impossible to be followed, then we ought not to try to follow it. This knowledge when applied in business for the benefit of both, society and business, is known as Indian Ethos in Management. Being a behavioural science, managements have to be culture specific. The basis for Indian ethics comes from Indian culture and also religion, as India is a country whose culture has its roots in religion. Thus, it does draw its lessons from the religions of the land – be it Hinduism, Buddhism, or any other.

The salient ideas and thoughts of Indian Ethos for Management revealed by our ancient scriptures are:

1. Every individual has substantial intellect and potential energy because each soul is a reflection of almighty.
2. Work is a kind of worship of the Lord Human being can approach God by honestly doing one's duty.
3. Work should be done as a sense of duty without anticipating rewards. This selfless work is always liked and blessed by God.
4. All work provides an opportunity to serve the humanity and by this one can get salvation.
5. When all of us unite and join hands to work together and live together – peace prosperity and pleasure grows and stays in the society permanently.
6. Honour people not simply by offering them material rewards but by showing respect to their ever-present divinity within.
7. One who recognizes the fact that all individuals are alike and care for them in the same way he cares for himself is a truly knowledgeable person. Therefore, learn to empathise.
8. He who works with calm and even mind can produce superior outcomes.
9. As we think, so we succeed, so we become. Attention to means ensures the end. One should always think positively and constructively.
10. Success comes to those who dare to act and do good things to all others.
11. Let us strive and work hard to make the universe sacred, beautiful and good to live in.
12. Be trustful. Be dutiful.

Principles of Indian Ethos in management are applicable universally. Indian ethos is helpful in developing an effective and holistic approach to management, which will ensure all over growth in productivity, marketing and profitability. This in turn helps in synchronization of public and private benefits and encourage individuals to lead an enriched quality of life together with worldly achievements. The best form of management has to be holistic and driven by values, which is the main objective of Indian ethos.

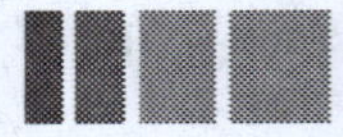

3.9 LET US SUM UP

Theories of ethics like Rights Theory, Justice Theory, Rawlsian Theory, Kant Theory, Deontological Theory have been discussed. Ethical-decision making is a peculiar human activity that reasons out, rationalizes and analyses our doing as part of a social group and society at large. The difference between Ethics and Morality has also been discussed.

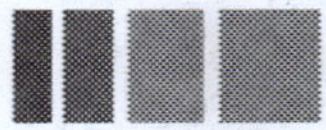

3.10 KEY WORDS

Character, rule utilitarianism, moral right, self-interest, Indian ethos.

3.11 CHECK YOUR PROGRESS

1. Rights theory classify rights as ------.
   (*a*) Legal rights
   (*b*) Natural rights
   (*c*) Moral rights
   (*d*) All of the above
2. Reflective morality means ------.
   (*a*) Morality based on customs.
   (*b*) Morality passed on over generations.
   (*c*) Morality based on reflective evaluation of principles
   (*d*) All of the above.
3. Which of the following statement is not true about virtue?
   (*a*) Virtue can be acquired
   (*b*) Virtue can be habits
   (*c*) Virtue develops through moral
   (*d*) Virtue is by birth
4. Kant's non-consequentialism is a ------.
   (*a*) Normative theory about good intentions
   (*b*) Meta ethics

(*c*) Importance to consequences of an action

(*d*) None of the above

5. Utilitarianism is classified as:

(*a*) Eudaimonistic Utilitarianism

(*b*) Hedonistic Utilitarianism

(*c*) Agathistic Utilitarianism

(*d*) All of the above

ANSWERS

1. (*d*)	2. (*c*)	3. (*d*)	4. (*a*)	5. (*d*)

3.12 EXERCISE YOUR ETHICS MUSCLE

Case 5: The Burning Building

Assume you approach a burning building and hear voices coming from both ends, each seeking help. Assume the fire is burning so rapidly you only have time to go to one or the other end of the building. Initially, you hear multiple voices at one end and a sole voice at the other end.

(An example of conflict between a consequences approach and a principles approach)

Issues to reflect:

(*a*) Which way do you go? And why?

(*b*) Now include some additional information. The sole voice is that of your daughter (father, mother, etc.). Or, the sole voice is that of a Nobel laureate who is close to finding a cure for cancer?

(*c*) Do you still choose to go to the end with multiple voices (will that even do the greatest good for society)?

(*d*) What will be the different approaches? What will you do?

(*Source:* Suggested by Stuart Youngblood, emeritus professor of management at Texas Christian University in Fort Worth, as he uses this example in his ethics class)

Case 6: Ransom or no Ransom

While passing through Somalia waters, one ship was hijacked by pirates and its crew was taken hostage by them. The pirates asked the owner of the shipping company to pay a hefty ransom for release of ship and crew. They also threatened that every crew member would be killed if the ransom were not paid. The owner of the shipping company had to decide whether to pay ransom to pirates who were holding his ship and its crew hostage.

(This is another example of conflict between a consequences approach and a principles approach)

Issues to reflect:

This business owner acknowledged that paying the ransom would reinforce the pirates' behavior and would likely lead to more kidnappings and hostage, an outcome that is clearly to the detriment of society overall. However, having considered this, he nevertheless concluded that he would pay the ransom because he felt strongly that his primary responsibility as an employer was to his people. His values of respect for human life and compassion for the employees' families were more important to him in this situation than the potential longer-term broader harm to society.

(*a*) Do you agree with the views of the owner of the shipping company?

(*b*) What are the values at play in this situation?

(Scenario is adopted from 'Managing Business Ethics: Straight Talk About How to do Right' by Linda K Trevino and Katherine E Nelson)

Case 7: As You Sow, So Shall You Reap

After the merger, the new CEO has joined. You are working as HR Head in the organization. The company is under severe financial stress. To reduce expenses, CEO asks you to sack half of the staff. You complete the task. This action generates a lot of hue and cry from all quarters and the CEO receives a lot of criticism. The CEO holds you responsible and asks you too to leave.

Issues to reflect:

(*a*) What are the organizational, pragmatic and normative dimensions involved in the scenario?

(*b*) Is there happened a breach of ethics? If so, what is it and on who is responsible for it?

(*c*) Whether it was ethical for you to follow the instruction of your CEO? If yes, then why?

(*d*) 'What goes around, comes around'. Do you agree?

4

UNIT

Ethics, Financial Services and Regulation

4 UNIT

Ethics, Financial Services and Regulation

4.1 LEARNING OBJECTIVES

The digitization of financial system and banking is making the sector prone to newer risks of scams and frauds. With inter-linkage of the global financial system, the sector has potential of deeper crises. There has been a pronounced trend amongst various governments, central bankers and regulators to design policy that will prevent certain risks in financial institutions. However, many times we have witnessed that many changes in policies are reactive in nature or steps initiated post-event. However, Indian regulators have been relatively proactive in the area of policy responses. Also, regulation and policy cannot be the sole solution. There is growing recognition of the need for a culture change: a need for ethics to have an increasing role in finance. To establish greater ethics in finance, it must be recognized that this is critical to those employed in finance functions and it must be understood that growth in economies must be sustainable and long term.

This unit attempts to offer to the readers the following:

- Provide a regulatory structure of the India's financial sector
- Familiarise some regulatory bodies in financial sector and their roles
- Broad depiction of the RBI's supervision of banks
- Review some recent developments in Indian monetary and banking sector
- Taking a note of ethics in financial regulation and its effectiveness

4.2 INDIAN BANKING AND REGULATION: DEVELOPMENTS: PAST, PRESENT AND FUTURE

The Indian banking sector is regulated by the Reserve Bank of India Act, 1934 (RBI Act) and the Banking Regulation Act, 1949 (BR Act). RBI, being the central bank, keeps issuing guidelines, notifications and policy statements from time to time to regulate the banking sector. Regulation of FX flows, cross border transactions of Indian Corporate and banks is regulated under Foreign Exchange Management Act, 1999 (FEMA).

Indian banking sector is primarily divided into public sector banks (ownership rests with the Government) and private sector banks (owned by private enterprises). Both public and private sector banks have presence outside India and are represented by foreign branches and representative offices. Banks in India can primarily be classified as:

- Scheduled commercial banks (*i.e.*, commercial banks performing all banking functions);
- Cooperative banks (set up by cooperative societies for providing financing to small borrowers);
- Regional Rural Banks (RRBs) (for providing credit to rural and agricultural areas); and
- In 2015, RBI has introduced specialized banks such as payments banks and small finance banks to perform only limited banking functions.

At present, the Indian banking system consists of 12 public sector banks, 22 private sector banks, 46 foreign banks, 56 regional rural banks, 1485 urban cooperative banks and 9600 rural cooperative banks, 11 small finance banks and 6 payment banks apart from cooperative credit institutions. The key statutes and regulations that govern the banking industry in India and particularly scheduled commercial banks are as follows:

RBI Act, 1934

The Reserve Bank of India was established on April 1, 1935 in accordance with the provisions of the Reserve Bank of India Act, 1934.

The Preamble of the Reserve Bank of India describes the basic functions of the Reserve Bank as:

> "To regulate the issue of Bank notes and keeping of reserves with a view to securing monetary stability in India and generally to operate the currency and credit system of the country to its advantage, to have a modern monetary policy framework to meet the challenge of an increasingly complex economy, to maintain price stability while keeping in mind the objective of growth."

Banking Regulation Act, 1949

The Banking Regulation Act, 1949 provides a framework for supervision and regulation of all banks. It also gives the RBI the power to grant licenses to banks and regulate their business operations.

FEMA

FEMA is the primary exchange control legislation in India. FEMA and the rules, made thereunder, regulate cross-border activities of banks. These are administered by the RBI.

Other key statutes

The other key statutes include:

- The Negotiable Instruments Act, 1881;
- The Recovery of Debts Due to Banks and Financial Institutions Act, 1993;
- The Bankers Books Evidence Act, 1891;
- The Payment and Settlement Systems Act, 2007;
- The Securitizations and Reconstruction of Financial Assets and Enforcement of Security Interest Act, 2002;
- The Banking Ombudsman Scheme, 2006; and
- The Bankruptcy and Insolvency Code, 2016.

Public sector banks are regulated by the BR Act and the statute pursuant to which they have been nationalized and constituted. These include:

- banks constituted under the Banking Companies (Acquisition and Transfer of Undertakings) Act, 1970 or the Banking Companies (Acquisition and Transfer of Undertaking) Act, 1980; and
- the State Bank of India and subsidiaries and affiliates of the State Bank of India constituted and regulated by the State Bank of India Act, 1955 and the State Bank of India (Subsidiary Banks) Act, 1959 respectively.

Regulatory Authorities

Reserve Bank of India (RBI)

The primary bank regulator in India is the Reserve Bank of India (RBI). The RBI has wide-ranging powers to regulate the financial sector. These include prescribing norms for setting up of bank and issue licensees to bank. Apart from regulation of banking activities, RBI also regularly guides banks on corporate governance, prudential norms and conditions for structuring of various banking products and services. Its other functions include, among other things:

- Announce monetary policy and guiding for interest rates, inflation, credit growth etc.
- Regulation of money, liquidity, foreign exchange, Government securities (G-Sec) markets and financial derivatives.
- Debt and cash management for the Government.
- Payment and settlement systems.
- Currency management and country's external reserves.

  The RBI has been actively involved in framing regulations to address the dynamic changes in the banking sector in India.

  India has several other financial sector regulators, including the:
- Securities & Exchange Board of India (SEBI), which is the regulatory authority for the securities market in India.
- Insurance Regulatory and Development Authority of India (IRDAI), which regulates the insurance sector.
- Pension Fund Regulatory and Development Authority (PFRDA), which promotes, develops and regulates pension sector.

The RBI often liaises closely with SEBI, IRDAI and where required, other financial sector regulators, to regulate banking activities which interact with other financial activities.

The Central Government, in particular the Ministry of Finance, also supervises and legislates on he functioning of banks and financial institutions. Acting through its Department of Financial Services, it:

- Monitors banking operations.
- Prescribes norms for the operation and functioning of public sector banks.
- Examines legislative measures for recovery of bank debts and establishes judicial mechanisms for this purpose.

How Banks are supervised by RBI?

The RBI supervises the Indian banking system through various methods such as on-site audit, off-site surveillance and reviewing regulatory filings made by the banks.

Every quarter, the RBI conducts an audit of financial inspection of the banks' books of account, loan and advances, balance sheet and investments. This is in addition to statutory audit that is required every year. RBI's surveillance division regularly supervises banking operations of every bank. On suspicion of any untoward transaction, RBI issues supervisory directions to banks highlighting the major areas of concern. Based on such alert as well as recommendations and report of concurrent audits, banks are then required to draw up an action plan and implement corrective measures to comply with the remark and inspection findings.

The RBI also monitors compliance on an ongoing basis by requiring banks to submit detailed information periodically under an off-site surveillance and monitoring system. Based on this, the RBI analyses the financial health of banks between two on-site inspections and identifies banks that show financial deterioration thereby requiring closer supervision.

Additionally, the RBI conducts:

- Quarterly discussions with the banks' executives on issues emanating from analysis of off-site surveillance, status of compliance with annual inspection findings and new products introduced by banks.
- Half-yearly meetings with the chief executive officers of the banking groups identified as financial conglomerates.

The ever-changing financial landscape of the country and advent of Information Technology has posed newer challenges for the banks as well as its regulator and supervisor. Banks being the engine of growth for the Indian economy, quickly adopted to this changed reality of competitive environment and resorted to various new practices to maintain their bottom line. The adoption of new business models without adequate risk management and weakness in internal controls and processes at times resulted in weakening of the underwriting standards and led to an explosion of non-performing assets in the banking sector during the previous decade. The adverse developments in a few regulated entities in the past exposed some fault lines, primarily in terms of inadequate governance, inappropriate business model and weak internal assurance functions. RBI, therefore, undertook a review of its approach towards supervision as well as the existing practices in Supervised Entities (SEs) to identify the root causes for these gaps. Accordingly, the supervisory approach was reworked out in recent period to bring more focus on addressing these weakness.

Today, the RBI focuses more to supervise weaker banks displaying financial and systemic weaknesses through the measures such as quarterly monitoring visits to banks, appointment of monitoring officers and direct monitoring of problem areas in housekeeping. RBI has also taken several steps to improve the rigour and efficacy of on-site and off-site monitoring processes. For example, the annual inspection process adopts a calibrated approach now, focus areas get identified in advance, risk-based scoping is ensured, inspections are completed in time-bound manner and quality of the review process has become stronger. Recently, it is being observed that supervisory communication has turned sharper and more focussed with clear outline of time-bound Risk Mitigation Plans (RMPs) to be implemented by the entities, among others. Direct engagements with the senior management of the regulated entities have increased and are intense. It is to be noted that RBI enjoys a wide mandate as the regulator of the banks, NBFCs and payment systems, regulator of the money, forex, government securities and credit markets; and also, as the lender-of-the-last resort. This is a unique combination of responsibilities and combines monetary policy with macroprudential regulation and micro-prudential supervision. This combination allows the RBI to exploit the synergies across various dimensions. The conceptual underpinnings of financial stability, as it evolved post-GFC, now entails preserving and nurturing a well-functioning financial architecture which includes not just the banks but also other financial institutions along with efficient and secure payment and settlement systems.

Regulatory developments and recent trends

Enhancing and refining the regulatory framework is a continuous process across the world. In India too, maintaining financial stability and resilience of its financial entities has been one of the uppermost objectives of the Reserve Bank's regulatory and supervisory approach. For example, to meet the COVID-19 pandemic related shocks, RBI asked all banks, large non-deposit taking NBFCs and all deposit-taking NBFCs to assess the impact of COVID-19 on their balance sheet, asset quality, liquidity, profitability and capital adequacy and work out possible mitigation measures including capital planning, capital raising and contingency liquidity planning, among others. This was to ensure that any pandemic related pressure on the balance sheets of banks in terms of non-performing assets, leading to erosion of capital, might be proactively managed. Building buffers and raising capital by banks – both in the public and private sector – was crucial not only to ensure credit flow but also to build resilience in the financial system.

In the last few years, the Reserve Bank has initiated a series of actions for unification of its supervisory approach, building specialization, capacity and skills in supervision etc. as mentioned below:

- In order to ensure a unified and systemic approach, a unified Department of Supervision (DoS) was created bringing all SEs, namely, Scheduled Commercial Banks, NBFCs and UCBs under one umbrella. Unification of supervisory functions has reduced the supervisory arbitrage and information asymmetries across SEs and addressed the complexities arising from their inter-connectedness. This will also help in the holistic understanding of systemic risks.
- A risk-based supervision framework focusing on know your customer (KYC)/anti money laundering (AML) risk has been created in line with global practices.
- A system for early identification of vulnerabilities to facilitate timely and proactive action is in place now. Early Warning Systems and supervisory Stress Testing have been made an integral part of prudential supervision.
- Advances in data analytics is being deployed to offsite returns so as to provide sharper and more comprehensive inputs to the onsite supervisory teams.
- Usage of Data and Analytical tools for offsite supervision in a variety of ways to aid in policy formulation, identify incipient stress, ascertain status of borrowers across lenders and check compliance to regulatory stipulations, among others.
- Data dump analysis is much more extensively used as part of transaction testing exercise. Many thematic assessments are being regularly carried out to identify system-wide issues and assess 'conduct' practices for taking corrective actions.

- Bank-wise as well as system-wide supervisory stress testing adds a forward-looking dimension for identification of vulnerable areas.
- In addition to Central Repository of Information on Large Credits (CRILC) and Central Fraud Registry (CFR), the data capabilities of RBI are in the process of being further upgraded through the revamped data warehouse, *viz.* the Centralized Information Management System (CIMS). It will encompass tools and applications for AI-ML data visualization and big data analytics.
- For continuous engagement with SEs, a web-based and an end-to-end workflow automation system has been developed. It has various functionalities including inspection, compliance and incident reporting for cyber security, etc. with a built-in remediation workflow, time tracking, notifications and alerts, Management Information System (MIS) reports and dashboards. This is being launched shortly.
- Supervisory specialization is being reinforced by way of creating specialized divisions for risk-based supervision of KYC/AML risk, data analytics, cyber security and IT examinations, among others.
- A Supervisory Action Framework has also been put in place which provides for graded early supervisory action depending on the frequency and severity of breaches identified.
- Fintech initiatives are being embraced in the form of innovative technologies for regulation (RegTech) and supervision (SupTech).
- With the proliferation of digital banking, cyber security has become an extremely important area of supervisory concern. To address this concern, the Reserve Bank has developed a model-based framework for assessing cyber risk in banks using various risk indicators, risk incidents, VA/PT, etc. Cyber drills are conducted based on hypothetical scenarios. Several Advisories and Alerts are issued on various cyber threats. Measures to build better awareness of cyber risks in supervised entities are continuing.
- The Digital Payment Security Control Guidelines were issued recently by RBI to set up a robust governance structure and implement common minimum standards of security controls. While a lot is being done in the cyber security space, but these risks are continuously evolving in the

dynamic environment we operate in and hence there should be constant vigil and continuous enhancements of IT systems.

- A separate College of Supervisors (CoS) has been set-up which is conducting extensive training programs in different areas.

The thrust of the Reserve Bank's supervision presently is more on root causes of vulnerabilities rather than dealing with symptoms.

Strengthening Sound Governance and Internal Controls in Banks:

RBI has been continuously pushing for strengthening of sound governance and internal controls in the commercial banks with special emphasis on:

i. **Risk culture**: As banks are in the business of taking risks, sound risk culture lies at the heart of every decision that they take. In alignment with global developments, Reserve Bank too has made risk culture and business model analysis as part of its supervisory assessment. The focus has been to ensure that entities put in place a well-defined risk appetite framework and business decision making is broadly in alignment with their risk appetite and risk bearing capacity.

ii. **Strengthening the assurance function**: To ensure effective functioning of internal assurance functions in its financial entities, RBI has issued revised guidance for concurrent, internal, as well as external audits in banks. The guidelines are expected to ensure that these audits act as an effective early warning, give greater clarity on supervisory expectations, avoid conflict of interest, provide sufficient authority/resources/independence to these functions, among others.

iii. **Compliance function**: The compliance function in a bank is an integral part of corporate governance, as it can affect the bank's reputation with its shareholders, customers, employees and the markets. The recent guidance by the Reserve Bank on compliance function casts responsibility of the compliance culture and management of compliance risk explicitly upon the Board. The guidance advises banks on laying down a Board-approved compliance policy, well-defined selection process for Chief Compliance Officer (CCO), a fixed tenure to CCOs and requisite authority. Reserve Bank would expect that the standards of regulatory compliance will see considerable improvement going ahead.

The demonetization announced by the government in the November 2016 essentially also paved way for far more participation of digital banking and cashless economy. The trend post demonetization clearly indicates that there has been a strong push towards digital transactions over cash payments and a significant increase in the use of mobile wallets, online payments systems and cashless transactions has been observed. With the exponential growth of digitization and online commerce in India, the Reserve Bank has also directed its policy efforts to put in place a state-of-the-art national payments infrastructure, while ensuring a safe, secure, efficient, cost-effective and robust payments ecosystem.

The Insolvency and Bankruptcy (IBC) Code, 2016

The Insolvency and Bankruptcy Code passed on May 5, 2016 by Lok Sabha and 11 May, 2016 by Rajya Sabha is to overhaul the existing framework dealing with insolvency of corporates, individuals, partnerships and other entities. The Bill received President's nod and was published and notified in Gazette on May 28, 2016. It paves the way for much needed reforms to tackle the NPA issue in the banking sector. The idea of this code is to make sure time-bound resolution of stressed assets and significantly improve the debt-recovering mechanism.

Key Highlights

Corporate Debtors: To initiate an insolvency process for corporate NPAs, the default should be at least Rs. 1,00,000. The Code proposes two independent stages:

- Insolvency Resolution Process, during which financial creditors assess the viability to continue the business of the defaulter and what all options are available for the revival and rescue of the business.
- Liquidation, when the creditor assesses that the business has no revival chance and there is no other credible option to rescue the business.

The earlier laws were inefficient and many defaulters abused those leniencies. This newly drafted IBC has not only strengthened the power of the lender but has also led to efficient resolution of NPA issues. However, IBC is an evolving law in the country and amendment ordinances have also been promulgated to further facilitate ease of resolving insolvency in India.

Regulation of Other Systemically Important Financial Institutions (SIFIs): NBFCs

The RBI *vide* its master direction updated upto November 2023, has introduced four scale-based layers for regulating NBFCs as (*i*) Base layer, (*ii*) Middle layer, (*iii*) Upper layer and (*iv*) Top layer. All NBFCs will be bucketed and regulated under one of these layers depending on the exposures.

The RBI Act also recognizes non-banking financial companies (NBFCs), which are registered with the RBI. NBFCs are companies undertaking financial activities but not regulated as banks. NBFCs undertake a range of activities such as investment, hire-purchase, leasing, factoring and lending, subject to the RBI Act and RBI regulations specifically for NBFCs. Under the powers provided under the RBI Act, RBI also issues directions, guidelines, and circulars in relation to activities, operations, prudential norms and other related aspects of NBFC operations. Over the years, NBFCs have come a long way in terms of their scale and diversity of operations. They now play a critical role in financial intermediation and promoting inclusive growth by providing last-mile access of financial services to meet the diversified financial needs of less-banked customers. The segment has grown so rapidly that a few of the large NBFCs have become comparable in size to some of the private sector banks. The sector has also seen advent of many non-traditional players leveraging technology to adopt tech-based innovative business models. The regulatory approach of the Reserve Bank has adapted to the increase in complexity of the entities within the NBFC sector as well as the growing significance of NBFCs within the financial sector. For example, considering the recent turmoil some NBFCs had to face because of liquidity stress, the criticality of sound liquidity risk management by NBFCs has been reinforced with the introduction of the liquidity risk management framework for NBFCs with asset size above Rs. 100 crore. However, the core principles of NBFCs regulation have remained intact *i.e.*, (a) protection of depositors (in case of deposit-accepting companies) and customers. (*b*) preserving financial stability. Nonetheless, NBFC regulation has undergone certain changes in recent years, which are fundamental in their effect:

- First and foremost, Government owned NBFCs (which account for more than one-third of the sector) have been brought under the purview of prudential regulation since May 2018.

- Secondly, ensuring good corporate governance in NBFCs has become a top priority. To ensure Good governance, appropriate filtering mechanisms have been put in place to allow only the genuine and able promoters to start the business of NBFCs. Scrutiny on 'fit and proper' criterion has been strengthened.
- Extension of the scheme of ombudsman to the NBFC sector has been done to ensure that their customers get fair treatment and avenues for grievance redressal.

Fintech regulation

It is now well recognized that non-banking financial sector would be a fertile ground for technology-based experimentation in financial products and services. Accordingly, regulations have sought to create a conducive environment in this regard. For example, the timely introduction of guidelines for P2P lending platforms has ensured orderly growth of the segment anchored in high standards of prudence. Those have made lending platforms a neutral meeting place for lenders and borrowers and keeping them insulated from handling of funds involved in the underlying transactions.

Further, the ecosystem created under the Account Aggregator (AA) framework is yet another example of proactive regulation in the technology-intense activities. The AA framework has ushered in the required framework for safe, secure and consent-based sharing of information on financial assets of a customer. The critical regulatory aspect to be noted here is that the Account Aggregator does not store or view the data passing through it, thereby leaving no scope for any perverse incentive to abuse/misuse the financial data.

Although significant regulatory steps have been taken already in the FinTech, the dynamic nature of the FinTech focused NBFCs keeps throwing up new challenges. The NBFC sector has been in the forefront in adopting innovative fintech-led delivery of products and services which are transforming the way one can imagine access to and interaction with these services. The advance technological solutions such as Big Data Analytics and Artificial Intelligence are being adopted by a large number of players to extend credit in an efficient manner over digital platforms.

The Reserve Bank has been on the forefront of creating an enabling environment for growth of digital technology for new financial products and services. In fact,

in the non-banking space, the RBI has been ahead of the curve and has come out with regulations for new products and services when the industry itself was at nascent stage. Peer to Peer (P2P) lending, Account Aggregator (AA), and credit intermediation over "only digital platform" are case in point where the regulations have helped the industry to grow in a systematic and robust manner. While making regulation for the future in FinTech area, orderly growth and customer protection and data security will remain the guiding principles for the RBI.

Other regulatory changes

The RBI revised the regulatory framework under the principles of proportionality for Core Investment Companies (CICs) with transparency and disclosures being the focus of the revised regulations. Taking over the regulation of Housing Finance Companies (HFCs) is yet another significant move.

Setting up of Fintech Repository

In order to gather appropriate information/nature of activities on Fintech entities and its ecosystem to the regulators and other stakeholders, a repository is setup which will aid in designing appropriate policy regulations. The Repository will be operationalized by Reserve Bank Innovation Hub in April 2024.

The key regulatory challenges are as follows

Main source of risks for the banking systems emanates from unethical practice and behaviour of individuals. Such kind of practices might be greed of an individual officer or systematic misselling of financial products. Over the years, the regulatory policies, compliances and overall framework is becoming much stricter. Such stricter compliance has reduced the risk but not completely eliminated it. In addition, developments in AI/ML, robotics and chat advisory, digitalization, Distributed Ledger Technology (DLT), quant computing, cloud arrangements, data analytics, new ways of remote working, etc. are giving benefits but also generating new risks. Climate change, KYC/AML, cyber security, virtual currencies as well as increasing reliance on outsourcing are some of the other major challenges that will need to be addressed in the years ahead. We shall discuss below a few of these challenges in detail:

Controlling the asset quality

One of the biggest challenges that the banking system may have to face again in future the issue of stressed assets/NPAs. The earlier phase of high NPAs was tough and has since been over. However, with the current aggressive focus of the banks on retail lending book, it is difficult to rule out the possibility of stress building in these portfolios after three or four years. No doubt, regulatory supervision is an ongoing activity and much closer now and the underwriting standards have also significantly improved across the banks, yet it is hard to change the lending behavior which is a human activity and contains potential behavioral risks. In a high interest rate scenario, such risks have the propensities to become more pronounced from a lending perspective. Further, all of us have realized or experienced that in the post pandemic world, digital lending has grown exponentially including in India leading to both an increase in scale and velocity of credit. However, at the same time it has also given rise to a host of business conduct issues. This poses a regulatory dilemma as the Regulator then needs to play a balancing act in weighing the benefits brought in by innovative business models on one side and emerging business conduct and regulatory concerns on the other side. An attempt has been made by the Reserve Bank to address this issue through issuing principle-based guidelines on digital lending.

Payment Banks/Payment Wallets/Payments and Settlements

Post-demonetization and after the pandemic the financial sector have witnessed significant jump in digitized transactions. The payment banks and payment wallets are becoming more and more popular. The ease of using such models for payment and transfer of money through smart phones have drastically increased the volume. This digitisation has surely led to financial inclusion as anyone using smart phone anywhere in the country is joining the organized banking system of the country.

However, this is a very new and dynamic sector which is still evolving. RBI is very careful in granting new licences and taking necessary steps to fit these segments along with main banks in the overall regulatory framework. As these payment banks and wallets increase their footprints across the country, challenge will come for RBI to consistently monitor their activities, have proper checks and balances in place in terms of reporting and regulatory compliance. Further, increase in digital payments and its users also brings to the fore potential risks pertaining to cyber security, data privacy and operational resilience. Regulatory challenge is to ensure that suitable risk mitigation measures are in place for the associated threats.

A related area that is creating challenge for regulators is outsourcing arrangements of PSOs with their vendors. Ensuring that (*i*) service level agreements with vendors meet minimum prescribed standards, (*ii*) all such agreements contain the PSOs' right to conduct audit of the service provider, (*iii*) good governance and prudent risk management processes, (*iv*) maintaining robust IT infrastructure with cyber resilience; and (*v*) putting in place responsive grievance redress mechanism. At times, some PSOs display unwillingness to comply with regulatory instructions, citing various reasons like cost of carrying out system-level changes. In this digital age, there is a necessity to constantly upgrade the systems so as to remain relevant and increase efficiency. Legacy systems must be updated to bring them in line with changing realities. While any system may be presumed to be resilient and safe, a single bad experience of the customer with digital payments may drive him away to other channels or modes of payments. Another challenge for the regulators is the formation of Self-Regulatory Organisations (SROs) for PSOs.

FinTech Sector

India has the third largest FinTech ecosystem in the world. While regulation can play a supporting role, FinTechs themselves have to ensure the balance between innovation and risks arising therefrom. Therefore, from the FinTech sector perspective, self-regulation can be a useful tool for setting and enforcing rules and standards. The regulators have to manage this challenge going forward. Role of such an SRO can include setting the standards for conduct as well as acting as a bridge between the sector and regulators who have to implement the objective of protecting the interest of customer and promoting high level of governance standard in FinTech entities. It is essential for the FinTechs to keep customers at the center of their innovation and follow high standards of good governance as part of culture. The RBI has to introduce a culture of refraining from mis-selling or imprudent lending in FinTechs. For the sustainable development of the sector, it is essential that FinTechs inculcate the values of accountability, fairness, transparency and independence.

Fast Changing Technology

The rapidly changing technologies have challenged the way banks have been operated traditionally. With App-based banking facilities that all the banks are offering today, the sustainability of the existing physical infrastructure in terms of branch networks/ATMs, etc. is in question today. In fact, Artificial

Intelligence (AI) is also making rapid progress into banking sector. Some of the banks are already testing the Robotic interface at branches to communicate with the customers. As we have already mentioned in the introductory para, fast developments in AI/ML, robotics and chat advisory, digitalisation, Distributed Ledger Technology (DLT), quant computing and cloud arrangements etc. are giving rise to newer regulatory challenges. While on the one hand, technological innovation further the objective of improving access of financial products to the members of public, on the other, they present challenges in front of the regulator to recalibrate regulatory interventions to achieve the objective of consumer protection and financial stability.

Emergence of Cryptocurrencies

Cryptocurrencies are the latest challenge for the regulator. In India, RBI and Finance Ministry have already noticed that they do not recognize Cryptocurrencies in India and it is not legal tender. Globally there is hardly any consensus on recognition and legality of Cryptocurrencies. Japan has recognized it but China has banned the same. Although USA has not made it legal but many exchanges in USA has allowed the trading in cryptocurrencies.

Cryptocurrencies are typically global products whose defining characteristic is that they are outside official control and they cannot be regulated by country-specific regulators. These should be reason enough to treat them with caution. We have also seen that cryptocurrencies are not amenable to definition as a currency, asset or commodity; they have no underlying cash flows, they have no intrinsic value; that they are akin to Ponzi Schemes, and may even be worse. These should be reason enough to keep them away from the formal financial system. Additionally, they undermine financial integrity, especially the KYC regime and AML/CFT regulations and at least potentially facilitate anti-social activities. More substantially, they can (and if allowed most likely will) wreck the currency system, the monetary authority, the banking system, and in general Government's ability to control the economy. They threaten the financial sovereignty of a country and make it susceptible to strategic manipulation by private corporates creating these currencies or governments that control them. All these factors have led RBI to the conclusion that banning crypto-currency is perhaps the most advisable choice open to India.

Introduction of fiat currency - Central Bank Digital Currency (CBDC)

The rapid inroads of crypto-currencies over the past years which had no intrinsic value has challenged the money flow. These virtual currency disturbs and de-centralise the traditional financial system. The CBDC is a digital form of currency notes issued by central banks across the globe. The key motivations for issue of CBDC are specific to each country's unique requirements.

The RBI defines CBDC as the legal tender issued by a central bank in a digital form which is akin to sovereign paper currency exchangeable a par with the existing currency and shall be accepted as a medium of payment, legal tender. CBDCs are classified as Retail and Wholesale.

Wholesale CBDC is designed for restricted access to select financial institutions and Retail for rest others.

The main goal of CBDCs is to provide businesses and consumers with privacy, transferability, convenience, accessibility, and financial security. It also reduces cost of maintenance, reduce cross-border transaction costs, and provide hose who currently use alternative money-transfer methods with lower-cost options.

Cyber security

As discussed earlier in the section dealing with the regulatory changes, cyber security has become an extremely important area of supervisory concern. This is an area where challenges will keep on happening and the regulator will have to exercise close supervision on the regulated entities so that adequate awareness of cyber risks is created in their organizations and all possible measures are implemented to minimize such risks with the understand that cyber security is shared responsibility across the business units and also embedded in various business processes, with the overarching goal of building a culture of resilience.

Transition to a Low-Carbon Economy

Another emerging challenge for the regulators is making finance available for transitioning to a low carbon economy. The Indian Government has already committed to reduce the total projected carbon emissions from now till 2030 by one billion tonnes, reduce carbon intensity of the economy by more than 45 per cent by 2030, and achieve 'Net Zero' emissions by the year 2070. As a central bank, RBI has a responsibility to promote sustainable economic growth which includes transition to a low-carbon economy through Banks which can play an essential role in financing the transition to a low-carbon economy by channelising finance to sustainable and green projects as well as by developing new financial products that incentivise green initiatives.

Summing up, it has to recognized that for regulatory challenges in a developing country like India, given the high rate of technology adoption, keeping pace with market innovations will keep on emerging. Regulating such a dynamic financial sector can be very aptly questions". (Source: RBI.org)

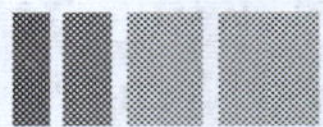

4.3 ETHICAL FOUNDATION OF FINANCIAL REGULATION

The most challenging aspects for any bank or financial institution is to create an internal value system that in itself encourages ethical behaviour in all individuals. As we have observed the risk of fraud or scams emanates from impropriety or unethical behaviour of individuals. No bank or financial institution today can probably guarantee or assure regulatory authority or society at large that their organization is scam-free or fraud-free. However, it must have an inbuilt system which alerts and gives early detection of any scam or fraud.

Post-2008 financial crises, that hit the US financial system and had a ripple effect across the entire globe, the regulators of all the countries have tightened the compliance and disclosure requirements.

Let us take the example of the Letter of Undertaking (LoU) scam that hit the Indian banking system in February 2018. As far as regulatory requirements, the bank was subjected to all kinds of internal, concurrent and statutory audit. These audits are in addition to normal disclosure a bank has to make based on various RBI guidelines. Even after such stringent disclosure and compliance, this particular "LoU Scam" went on for more than 6 years. This kind of scam again brings the focus on the "Ethical" behaviour of the officers/staff involved in the bank.

For regulator, it is difficult to draft any policy to regulate individual's behaviour as it is a very subjective matter. However, there are certain criteria that one needs to keep in mind while dealing with regulation on ethical aspects.

One can take a leaf from SEBI guidelines on Code of Conduct and Ethical Behaviour of Financial Intermediaries. These guidelines, in a way, clearly identify

the acts or omissions which are regarded as "Unethical" and as an intermediary, such kinds of acts or omissions shall always be avoided.

Ethics is about moral principles. Codes of ethics are general standards which have to be uniformly followed by everyone engaged in the same profession.

Code of Conduct is enforceable while codes of ethics are standards which have to be followed voluntarily by members in the interest of their clients as well as their own.

Code of ethics is required:

- To define acceptable behaviours
- To promote high standards of practice
- To provide benchmark for members to use self-evaluation
- To establish a framework for professional behaviour and responsibilities
- As a vehicle for occupational identity
- As a mark of occupational maturity

Code of Ethics is:

- Codes of ethics of integrity
- Codes of ethics of objectivity
- Codes of ethics of competence
- Codes of ethics of fairness
- Codes of ethics of confidentiality
- Codes of ethics of professionalism
- Codes of ethics of diligence
- Codes of ethics of compliance

Code of conduct for finance professionals:

- Compliance with law and policies of the organization
- Personal integrity
- Ethical decision making
- Avoiding conflicts of interest
- Managerial responsibilities

- External conduct
- Information confidentiality
- As a regulator, building these codes may not be a big challenge but the critical part is how an organization like a bank can deal with the same internally?

A bank interacts with internal and external forces. An internal force is the individuals, the workforce and the external force is the society at large. However, over period of time, the organization structure, internal ecosystem and environment shapes up the overall working of the organization. While dealing with the regulations, the organization might be adhering to the required compliances and disclosures but internally adherence to the self-discipline becomes more challenging.

4.4 REGULATORY PERSPECTIVE: THE LIMITATIONS OF COMPLIANCE

As mentioned earlier, although the banks adhere to the compliance, the work culture and ethical behaviour of the workforce plays much significant role. The ethical behaviour becomes much more critical and to a certain extent puts limitation in meeting the compliance. Research into behavioural psychology has made it clear that effectiveness of compliance can be enhanced by affecting both the behaviour of individuals and the organisational environment. Decisions are made by people rather than by organisations, although the structures, systems, objectives, culture and incentives that operate within organisations can affect the decisions made by the people who work in them.

To address this behavioural aspect, it is important to understand that while compliance means obeying the law, ethics is the intent to observe the spirit of the law, in other words, it is the expressed intent to do what is right. Therefore, any compliance program that strongly emphasizes both ethics and compliance will be more beneficial in terms of achieving the optimum regulatory compliance. In reality, organizations that follow both the letter and the spirit of the law by taking a "values-based" approach to ethics and compliance may have an advantage in the marketplace. Such an approach requires senior executives to understand clearly the culture and compliance controls that exist at all levels of their organizations. Banks should position ethics and compliance programs as a responsibility of each employee and a respected part of the organizational culture, not just a "thou shall not" obligation. Bank's senior executives and board members must adhere to the code of ethics and compliance policies in the same way that all other employees must Below are some of the issues that put limitations in meeting the best standards while meeting the regulatory compliance:

- Asset Quality: The major reason for the poor asset quality amongst PSU banks is the poor due diligence and credit appraisal. Although the RBI has set well established guidelines while sanctioning and disbursing credit facilities and the banks also have their internal guidelines and policies for taking exposure on any corporate and individuals, yet it is still observed that many time these established parameters and guidelines are flouted or bypassed. Such instance happens due to personal greed and unethical behaviour of individuals/officers. For example, the demonetization guidelines were simple and clear yet during demonetization drive, many lapses on the part of the dealing officials were noticed in meeting the guidelines of depositing and withdrawals of money from some of the branches of banks.
- Internal fraud and irregularities pose biggest limitation to adherence to regulatory compliance. The LoU scam is the example of how few officers of the bank manipulated the SWIFT transactions of the banks and helped few corporates to siphon of funds from the bank. Such kind of behaviour straight away puts lot of limitation on the regulatory guidelines. The banks are open to all kinds of internal, external and statutory audits. But the officer involved in the scam worked around such regulations and were able to bypass the audit trails of fraud transactions. What is more alarming is that such unauthorized transactions continued for a period of over 5-6 years. It clearly indicates that stricter compliance has limitations if the officer involved in meeting this compliance is the weak link.
- Window dressing of books every quarter-end or year-end leads to showing books better than actually they are. Many times, structured products and, derivative transactions are treated as "Off Balance sheet' items. These might be contingent liabilities but with potential to become actual liability. Again, the "LoUs" given by a large public sector bank in India were off-balance sheet items which later crystallized into a liability of over Rs. 12,000 Crs for the bank.

- Mis-selling of products is a big challenge. In order to maximize the commission income and to meet the stiff targets, mis-selling of various financial products and structured products is rampant in banking industry. Here again the greed of the officers involved becomes critical. Apart from selling financial products, many times various FX product derivatives or structured currency hedging products are sold to corporates without proper disclosure of risk involved and inbuilt fees. This kind of practices has potential to have adverse impact on financially illiterate customers or individuals who do not understand the complex structure of such financial products.
- Even after the rigorous KYC norms, many lapses are found in basic information of the Banks' clients. The AML act is very strict but still adherence to it at banks need stronger supervision.

All the above issues can be suitably addressed if there is a fundamental belief across the organization that people who practice good business ethics are more successful than people who don't. The challenge here is to reinforce this belief by demonstrating it – in words and in actions – if compliance has to be truly effective and sustainable. Otherwise, a weak compliance is an indication of the relative failure of the internal governance which devalues the regulatory instruments and their intent.

It is also seen that the banks keep on adding layers of controls for strengthening the efficacy of compliance. As a result, an unwieldy system of overlapping controls gets created that does not address the root cause of issues. Further, arising issues are approached one at a time and in insolation. Remedial efforts are also inadequately measured and tracked. The status quo approach of compliance does not allow for an integrated view across the enterprise. Regulated entities need to shift to a model of sustainable compliance through their ethics and compliance programs for laying the foundation for an effective internal control environment in which issues are not just reacted to the root causes are identified and regulations are translated into operational requirements amongst a workforce that believes in doing the right thing.

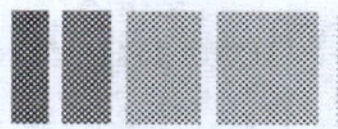

4.5 HOW EFFECTIVE IS REGULATION?

Post-financial crises of 2008, there has been significant changes across various regulations, disclosure requirements, building Chinese walls across various business segments within the organization, capping salaries/bonuses of bankers etc.

Even in India, post the rise in NPAs in the last decade the Insolvency Bankruptcy code has been introduced. Effectiveness of any regulation is dependent on the institutions and organization who comply to the same not only in the form but also in the substance. Eventually these institutions and organizations are run by individuals. Their adherence to these regulations, their work ethos and code of conduct finally decide the effectiveness of the regulations.

Below are some of the ways to make regulations more effective:

- Many times, ethical behaviour is a matter of judgment. Organization should develop an internal guideline and appraisal system which periodically evaluates the decision taken in light of such guidelines. The officers involved in decision making should take decision by putting themselves in fiduciary position. Such appraisal and evaluation can help institutions to follow established code of conduct and ethics.
- Have proper incentive and bonus structure in place. Most of the scam and frauds are result of greed. A proper transparent guideline in terms of pay packages of the work force will help put in place proper checks and balances.
- It is important to understand for the institution that it is the image, reputation and brand of the organization that should always stay clean. All the business decisions must be taken with long term implications on these intangibles of the organization. In the end, there is no substitute to "Self-Regulation". A well-established internal system and transparent work environment will go a long way in effective regulations.

4.6 THE COLLAPSE OF SILICON VALLEY BANK AND WHY WE NEED STRONG REGULATION?

SVB was founded in 1983 and was the 16th largest U.S. bank before its collapse. It was a regional bank and reckoned as quite trendsetting because it was among early banks to set focus on financing and banking for venture capital-backed startup companies, mostly technology companies. Based in Silicon Valley, SVB had assets totaling $209 billion at the end of 2022, according to the Federal Deposit Insurance Corporation (FDIC). In December, 2022, 56 percent of its loans were to VCs and PEs secured by their limited partners. SVB was a preferred bank for the tech sector because they supported startup companies that not all banks would accept due to higher risks.

The pandemic in 2020 was a hot market for tech companies as consumers spent big money on digital services and electronics. Tech companies mostly startups had a large influx of cash and SVB's services were needed during this time to hold their cash for business expenses, such as payroll etc. The bank invested much of these deposits as banks typically do in long-term U.S. treasuries and agency mortgage-backed securities. When the Federal Reserve hiked interest rates in 2022 to combat inflation, SVB's bond portfolio started to drop. SVB would have recovered its capital if they could hold those bonds until their maturity date. In 2021, the bank shifted to long-term securities such as treasuries for more yield, and they did not protect their liabilities with short-term investments for quick liquidations.

When economic factors hit the tech sector, many bank customers withdrew money as venture capital started drying up. SVB didn't have the cash on hand to liquidate these deposits because they were tied up in long-term investments. They started selling their bonds at a significant loss, which caused distress to customers and investors. When SVB announced their $1.75 billion capital raising on March 6, people became alarmed that the bank was short on capital. Word spread quickly on social media accounts such as Twitter and WhatsApp inducing panic that the bank didn't have enough funds. Customers started to withdraw money in waves. SVB's stock plummeted by 60% on March 7, 2023 after its capital raising announcement. Within 48 hours after disclosing the sale of assets, the bank collapsed. California regulators shut the bank down on March 8 and placed SVB under the FDIC.

On March 26, 2023, FDIC announced First Citizens Bank will purchase Silicon Valley Bank and assume the majority of its deposits and loans. The FDIC also estimated that the SVB failure cost nearly $20 billion.

Reasons for the Collapse:

The collapse of Silicon Valley Bank is the largest bank failure in the United States since the global financial crisis. The bank's vulnerability was the result of

- having a high proportion of uninsured deposits and a large proportion of deposits invested in hold-to-maturity (HTM) securities.
- lack of diversification

- depositors were also pulling out money for better deployment as rates started moving up; something that the US hadn't seen in decades.
- and a classic bank run, where many customers withdrew their deposits simultaneously due to fears of the bank's solvency.

The fall of SVB is a classic case of asset liability mismatch concerns which manifested into solvency issues for the bank. Only one other large bank – Signature Bank – had this combination of a high proportion of uninsured deposits and deposits invested in loans and HTM securities. On Friday, Signature Bank customers spooked by the sudden collapse of Silicon Valley Bank withdrew more than $10 billion in deposits. That run on deposits quickly led to the third-largest bank failure in U.S. history. Regulators announced late Sunday that Signature was being taken over to protect its depositors and the stability of the U.S. financial system.

Signature Bank, which was shuttered by US authorities was facing a criminal probe before it was seized by regulators. The bank was being investigated by US prosecutors in association with crypto clients Investigators from the US Justice Department in Washington and Manhattan were examining whether the failed bank took necessary steps to detect potential money laundering by its clients. The bank was being scrutinized by the Securities and Exchange Commission (SEC) too. US authorities are examining the collapse of SVB for misconduct by officers, including whether stock sales by executives violated trading rules, The probes, which are in early stages, are being handled by prosecutors in the Justice Department's fraud section, the US Attorney's Office for the Northern District of California and the SEC, Separate probes are in their preliminary phases. Shares in SVB Financial Group, which formerly owned the bank, fell 60% last week and have been stopped from trading since Friday. The investigations are also examining stock sales that SVB Financial's officers made days before the bank failed. Multiple federal authorities have launched investigations into the fall of Silicon Valley Bank, the second-largest bank failure in U.S. history, as lawmakers and officials point fingers over who and what to blame for the collapse. The separate probes from federal authorities, which were reported by a number of outlets, will examine the background of the event, including the actions of bank executives in the days leading up to the failure. The Federal Reserve is also reviewing the bank failure.

In addition to Silicon Valley Bank and Signature Bank, Credit Suisse was also facing solvency issues and UBS agreed to buyout Credit Suisse for $3 billion Swiss francs (or $3.25 billion) in a government-brokered deal on March 19. On March 14, Moody's Investor Service put six regional banks on review for credit rating downgrades, including Comerica Bank, First Republic Bank, Intrust Financial, UMB Financial, Western Alliance Bancorporation and Zions Corp. The reasons for these ratings include high unrealized losses and large amounts of deposits not covered by FDIC. These are issues that also impacted SVB. (Inputs from Amanda Hettler' piece on 'The Silicon Valley Bank Collapse: WhatIs.com) The entire saga of the SVB's meteoric rise and fall serves as a reminder that a strong, ongoing regulation is a non-negotiable for the financial sector. The US regulators missed the bus in the case and realizing now that it is difficult to make an assessment that an institution doesn't pose a risk to the system because of its size or that is easier to supervise. Many of the guardrails erected after the 2008 crisis have since been dismantled-at the behest of banks like SVB. Before becoming the second-largest bank to fail in US history, SVB had spent close to a million dollars in a five-year period lobbying for the deregulatory policies that ultimately created the conditions for its downfall. There is a news report from Reuters in the ET dated 29th April, 2023 that the Federal Reserve is planning to revamp of bank oversight after the fall of SVB. Fed issued a detailed and scathing assessment on 28th April of its failure to identify problems and push for fixes at Silicon Valley Bank before the US lender's collapse and promised tougher supervision and stricter rules for banks. Fed statement says that supervision of California-based bank was inadequate and regulatory standards were too low. Needless to say, that a strong regulation is a precondition for the financial stability of banking industry and whenever the regulatory standards are lowered, mishaps like SVB failure are bound to happen.

4.7 ETHICS AND REGULATION: DIGITAL TRUST IN A DIGITAL PARADIGM

The pace with which technology and digitization is changing the dynamics for banking sector is extremely fast. With introduction of payment banks, payment wallet, online transfer etc. the need for physical presence of branch or infrastructure is no longer a constraint. Anyone with a smart phone can initiate any transfer

or payments sitting anywhere. In the light of such advancement, regulation also needs to match the pace of this changing operational environment.

The regulatory and supervisory pace of digitization sets the limits within which all the desired innovations have to fit. This requires a breadth of vision on the part of all concerned, both public authorities and the private sector, which could exploit these opportunities, overcoming the obstacles that currently exist.

There are projects that do not fit easily into the existing regulatory framework, meaning they face an uncertainty which is either delaying projects (awaiting the approval of the authorities) or blocking them before their launch onto the market to avoid regulatory risks, because of the legal uncertainty and lack of trust being generated. The Cryptocurrencies are one such class which ereis termed as illegal and not been recognized by the regulators, but the popularity and ownership of Cryptocurrency is increasing consistently. This particular space will see lot of action from regulators, not only in India but the world over.

The solution is to adopt a holistic approach to seek a balance between the promotion of the new digital value propositions and protection against the risks involved.

The emergence of "Fintech" players essentially sets the new road map for the operations and digital environment for finance and banking space. These are high risk enterprises coming up with innovations and constantly challenging the historical way of doing business.

Digital Trust

One important role of financial regulation is to promote trust. Trust plays a key role in the formation and function of financial markets primary reason for the importance of trust is that financial systems are inherently unstable. There is a maturity mismatch inherent in the functioning of a financial market. Lenders cannot both provide long-term contracts and receive liquidity. Borrowers cannot both provide liquidity and receive long-term contracts. For example, in the simplest case banks have illiquid or long-term assets (loans) and liquid liabilities (deposits). Failures of Silicon Valley and Signature Banks as discussed in the previous section have shown it.

However, in the digitized environment of banking – where digital technologies support and mediate virtually all economic transactions, social connections and institutions. Nature of trust itself is undergoing a change and earning Digital trust has become a necessity in this new digital paradigm of financial services.

Digital trust is individuals' expectation that digital technologies and services – and the organizations providing them will protect all stakeholders' interests and uphold societal expectations and values. The shared goals or values that inform the concept of digital trust are (*i*) Security and reliability, (*ii*) Accountability and oversight, (*iii*) Inclusive, ethical and responsible use. There are dimensions of Cybersecurity, Safety, Transparency, Interoperability, Auditability, Redressability, Fairness & Privacy against which the trustworthiness of digital technologies can be operationalized and evaluated. For effective implementation of the digital trust principles, leaders have to play an important role in preparing their organizations to make the choice for digital trust through every step of the technology life cycle. Earning digital trust is a responsibility shared by banks, companies, governments, civil society and all individuals. For example, privacy, for individuals, is the expectation of control over or confidentiality of their personal or personally identifiable information. For banks, privacy is the meeting of this expectation through the design and manifestation of data processing that facilitates individual autonomy through notice and control over the collection, use and sharing of personal information. It effectuates inclusive, ethical and responsible data use – or digital dignity – by ensuring that personal data is collected and processed for legitimate purpose(s) (*e.g.*, consent, contractual necessity, public interest, etc.). Thus, only by deciding and acting for digital trust can leaders and organizations meet their obligations to society and individuals in future.

Globalization and business ethics: Globalization has led to rise in branching out of companies in various countries. Ethical business standards have to be rooted with integrity and applicable values. The relationship between business ethics and globalization refers to the manner in which the concept and its application to business operations can benefit from the practice of proper business ethics.

Relationship between ethics and regulations:

Ethics refers to the principles, values, and moral guidelines that govern individuals' and organizations' behaviour which involves making decisions based on a sense of right and wrong	Regulations are rules and laws established by governments or governing bodies to guide and control conduct. They are often created to ensure public welfare, safety and fairness

Ethics provides a broader framework for decision-making based on principles and values.	Regulations are often created in response to identified risks or issues.
It aims to foster moral behaviour and integrity beyond legal requirements.	Regulations are specific rules mandated by authorities to address particular issues, ensure compliance to maintain order in society.
Ethical behaviour is largely internal and relies on individuals' personal values, conscience, and the ethical culture within an organization.	Compliance with regulations is externally enforced by legal authorities. Violations may lead to legal consequences penalties, or sanctions.

Whether complementary or in conflict with each other: It could be complementary and at times in conflict. Ethical behaviour often involves complying with legal requirements, and regulations may codify certain ethical standards. In a dynamic nature, ethical standards can evolve more rapidly that regulations. There may be situations where regulations have not caught up with emerging ethical concerns.

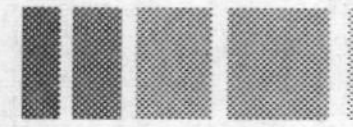

4.8 LET US SUM UP

The finance regulatory bodies in India are RBI, SEBI, IRDA, PFRDA, who regulate different aspects of the financial sector. Regulation has witnessed several micro-prudential changes in the recent times with the adoption of a unified and systemic approach by bringing all SEs, namely, Scheduled Commercial Banks, NBFCs and UCBs under one supervisory umbrella. RBI has also strengthened its offsite and onsite monitoring tools through increased use of data analytics models. Failure of two banks in US has reemphasized the importance of effective regulation. Regulation needs to adopt a value-based approach in its implementation to be truly effective. Digital trust is emerging as a new goal post in the fast-changing digital paradigm of financial services.

4.9 KEY WORDS

Supervisory directions, Non-performing assets, Insolvency and Bankruptcy Code, Financial Resolution and Deposit Insurance Bill, Risk Culture, Assurance function, Account Aggregators, Cryptocurrencies, Cyber Security, Digital Trust,

Interoperability, Silicon Valley Bank, Asset-Liability Mismatch, Federal Deposit Insurance Corporation (FDIC), Central Repository of Information on Large Credits (CRILC), Central Fraud Registry (CFR), Data Analytics.

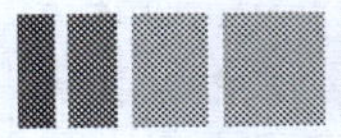

4.10 CHECK YOUR PROGRESS

1. The Preamble of the RBI Act, 1934 has all except which one of the following?
   (*a*) to regulate the issue of Bank notes and keeping of reserves with a view to securing monetary stability in India.
   (*b*) to ensure that Indian commercial banks perform their assigned activities with highest ethical standards.
   (*c*) to have a modern monetary policy framework to meet the challenge of an increasingly complex economy.
   (*d*) to maintain price stability while keeping in mind the objective of growth.
2. Indian Banking System today has
   (*a*) 20 public sector banks
   (*b*) 18 public sector banks
   (*c*) 12 public sector banks,
   (*d*) 14 public sector banks
3. The Insolvency and Bankruptcy (IBC) Code, 2016 was passed by Lok Sabha, Rajya Sabha, received the nod of the President and was notified. All took place in
   (*a*) May 2016
   (*b*) November 2016
   (*c*) May 2017
   (*d*) November 2017
4. In a bank, cyber security is the responsibility of
   (*a*) MD and Senior Management
   (*b*) Board of Directors

(*c*) All Employees

(*d*) All of the above

5. The main aim of financial regulation in India is to

(*a*) Protect banks

(*b*) Protect customers

(*c*) Protect businesses

(*d*) Protect financial stability

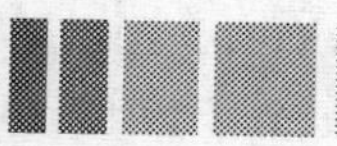

ANSWERS

1. (*b*)	2. (*c*)	3. (*a*)	4. (*d*)	5. (*d*)

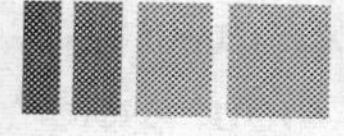

4.11 EXERCISE YOUR ETHICS MUSCLE

Case 8: Robinhood

In June 2020, 20 years old Kearns committed suicide believing he had racked up more than $700,000 in losses by trading options using Robinhood's investing app. Kearns had no source of income and he was able to get assigned almost a million dollars' worth of leverage through the investment app. A note left by Kearns to his family read. "There was no intention to be assigned this much and take this much risk, and I only thought that I was risking the money that I actually owned." Earlier, Robinhood was at the center of a "meme stocks" craze, where amateur investors, egging each other on *via* social media, inflated the price of previously flat stocks like GameStop and AMC Entertainment Holdings. Thereafter, the Financial Industry Regulatory Authority (FINRA) ordered Robinhood Financial to pay a record $70 million in penalties for the "widespread and significant harm". Robinhood customers suffered for receiving "false or misleading information" from the firm. After some time in November, Robinhood faced a data breach that exposed the email addresses or names of approximately seven million of its customers when a customer support employee fell victim to a social engineering attack.

Issues to reflect:

(*a*) Should digital engagement practices of such fintechs not be regulated?

(*b*) Whether the trading platform of Robinhood was getting operated responsibly?

(*c*) What are the ethical implications from the Robinhood's perspective here?

(*d*) What is your assessment of the internal controls and governance processes at play in Robinhood?

Case 9: Archegos Debacle

U.S. hedge fund Archegos Capital Management suffered a meltdown in March, reportedly losing \$8 billion in less than two weeks after entering several high-risk derivatives transactions that ultimately backfired. A consequential massive stock sell-off caused \$5.5 billion in losses for Credit Suisse as one of its largest lenders. The bank had an additional \$10 billion in funds tied to U.K.-based Greensill Capital, which filed for bankruptcy protection in March after investors walked away from the supply chain financing firm over concerns about risky loans that soured. Swiss authorities announced in April an examination into the bank's activities and its exposure to both the Archegos and Greensill collapses. An independent report into Archegos commissioned by Credit Suisse exposed "significant" risk management deficiencies, including a lack of accountability for risk failures, acute risks that were systematically ignored; and a cultural unwillingness to engage in challenging discussions or escalate matters posing grave economic and reputational risk. In April, 2022, the Securities and Exchange Commission charged the owner of Archegos Capital Management, LP (Archegos), & Archegos's Chief Financial Officer, Patrick Halligan; Head Trader, William Tomita; and Chief Risk Officer, Scott Becker with orchestrating a fraudulent scheme that resulted in billions of dollars in losses.

Issues to reflect:

(*a*) Do you think that compliance failures always result from intentional misconduct?

(*b*) What is the role of poor corporate governance in the fall of Archegos?

(*c*) The failure of risk management was central to the Archegos collapse. What is your assessment of the risk culture at Credit Suisse as inferred from this event?

(*d*) Those who do not learn from history are doomed to repeat it. Archegos episode reasserts it. Do you agree?

(*e*) Excessive focus on maximizing short-term profits results in overlooking the apparent red flags. Do you agree?

MODULE

B

DIFFERENT OPERATIONAL LEVELS OF ETHICS IN BANKING

5

UNIT

Ethics at the Individual Level

5 UNIT

Ethics at the Individual Level

5.1 LEARNING OBJECTIVES

Understanding the concepts like values, norms, and beliefs and their significance for both individuals and businesses. We have defined core values and explained how identifying, communicating and alignment of values of an individual and that of an organization can help resolve conflicts. Personal value system establishes morality and governs personal ethics. A person working in an organization needs to align his personal ethics and values with that of the enterprise. The Golden rule fits well in an enterprise as it best defines the organizational behavior. Mismatch between individual ethics and business ethics leads to ethical dilemma. For an organization, resolution of ethical dilemma is vital to accomplish its business goals on a sustainable basis.

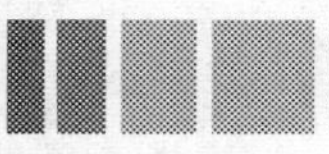

5.2 VALUES, NORMS, BELIEFS AND THEIR ROLE

Values

Values are a concept of the desirable behavior, or an internalized standard or principle, which evaluates – what is embraced by an individual. Since values describe what is desirable, it must be desirable for all and not for a selected few. Something that is good for all can be considered as truly good. Such a concepts and standards are relatively few and determine or influence an individual's evaluation of many objectives encountered in everyday life. Values are tinted with moral hues entailing individuals' judgment pertaining to good, right or desirable. Thus, values are our measures or standards for making a judgment regarding right and wrong things. Also, the true values must have a universal command and acceptability.

Values are internalized as our core beliefs, this is because we live in a world full of values and since our childhood, where we are continuously and consistently taught certain values by our parents', family members, teachers', etc. along with the rest of the society. Values are derived from norms present in our society and culture. Therefore, we continue to learn these values even with a subconscious mind and they are imbibed in our personality and become an integral part of our actions and thoughts. Our individual perceptions also influence our attitudes, which guide our behavior, impact our interests and preferences and complement considerably in development of our personality. Thus, whatever we think and act is always in synchronization with our value system. In other words, **values become the essential driving force behind our thoughts and actions through the following aspects of a multi-tier cognitive process**:

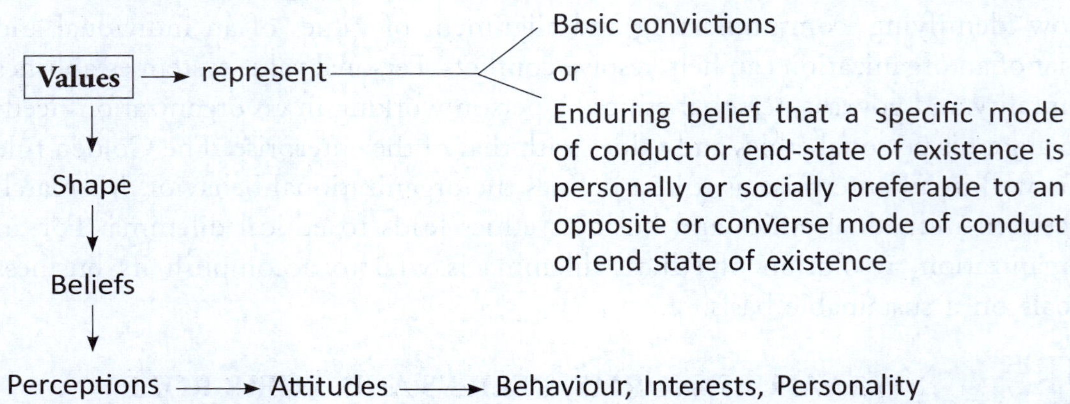

Characteristics of Values

Values have following salient features:

- **Values provide standards of competence and morality**. The value-system of an individual serves as the basis for his or her moral principles.
- **Values are not large in number** and we have a few selective values. These selective values decide and determine our concept of virtuous life.
- **Values outdo specific objects situation or persons**: **values act as a measure**. This measure of evaluation is applicable to all, irrespective of persons, situations or objects. For example, honestly if taken up as a value, then any kind of dishonest behaviour by any person in any situation at any time becomes intolerable.

- **Values are relatively perpetual and resilient to change.** Values describe the concept of an ideal for the individual. It describes what ought to be. And as such values are relatively stable and permanent. Values are in the form of strong beliefs in respect of ideal situations in life. And such strong beliefs are so deep rooted in individuals and societies that they are very difficult to alter or eliminate. This does not mean that change in values never happen. Change in values also happen over time. However, the process of change is gradual and comparatively lengthier. Sometimes, the value systems undergo a change as a result of a social crisis.
- **Values are at the core of a personality.** Values are the powerful force steering decisions and actions that direct human behaviour. As we have seen that whatever we decide and do is always compatible with our value system. Values contain moral elements and provide for us a list of dos and don'ts. They tell us what is permissible and what is not on the basis of standard for good, right and desirable.
- **Values carry a judgmental element.** This judgment of desirable is subjective as well as objective. They are subjective as they describe an experience, which is personal. At the same time, values are objective because they exist for all persons and through proper training such judgments can be brought to a common standard.
- **Values have content along with strength and distinctive features.** As such values are central to the core of a person, many a time we distinguish two persons from one another on the basis of their value-systems and concept of values. Values are central to individual personality. Values make each individual distinctive on the basis of thoughts and responsiveness. As values are judgments of what should be; they describe our ideals and moral standards. This belief in principles and standards influence an individual's over-all behaviour and also guides his or her actions across various situations for attainment of objectives. Values are key element to our ethical perceptions. An individual's moral standards emerge from the value system.

Values are classified as

- **Terminal Value** – A terminal value is an ultimate goal, which we desire to achieve in our lifetimes. These values are desirable state of existence.

It is enduring belief that a certain end-state of existence is worth striving for and attaining.

- **Instrumental Values** – It is a tool or means for acquiring a terminal value. Thus, instrumental values are, in the simplest words, the modes of behaviour. They are helpful in activating terminal values, which are desired end-states. Instrumental values are the core values and permanent in nature, they form the personal characteristic of an individual. Some examples of instrumental values are being polite, obedient, and maintaining self-control.

Norms

Norms are expectations of proper behaviour and not the requirements of that behaviour. Norms are the ways an individual expects all the people to act in a given situation. They are inconsistent but universal. Norms are not published, therefore, may not be obeyed and cannot be made obligatory except by sanctions of a group who use penalties as condemnation or exclusion.

Norms are informal guidelines about pertaining to behaviour and actions, which are considered normal (what is correct and incorrect) social behaviour in a particular group or social unit. Norms form the prejudice of collective expectations that members of a community have from one another and it also plays a key role in social control and social harmony by exerting a pressure on the individual to conform.

Even though norms influence every aspect of our lives, including what we value, our approaches towards things, and how we behave, we are many a times unaware that we are getting influenced at all.

Beliefs

Beliefs in the ethical code are standards of thoughts. Beliefs are criteria of intangible thought that does not necessarily evoke action. It may stimulate or force certain pursuit in the environment that corresponds with one to behave in a certain manner.

Beliefs are among the most primitive and central of mental constructs and yet there is little agreement as to what they are or how they should be constructed. They are basic to our understanding of a wide range of central phenomena in the modern psychology. For example, our beliefs are the key constituents of

our personalities and senses of individuality, and our expressions of beliefs often define us to others. Many of our reactions to others are based on our beliefs and perceptions of others. Besides this, sometimes it is impossible to understand beliefs like – racism, prejudice, religion and national conflicts without considering disagreement in basic belief systems.

Values are core ideas about how people should live and the ends they should seek. They are shared by a majority of people within a community or society. They are simply expressed generalities, often no more than single words such as peace and honesty. As they are very broad, they do not give guidance on how particular things should be evaluated.

Attitudes, like values, are evaluations of whether something is good or bad. But unlike values they are evaluations of particular things, issues, people, places or whatever. Attitudes, because they relate to specific circumstances, are more changeable than values.

Role of norms, beliefs and values in management

A corporate culture is a set of values, beliefs, norms and goals and ways of solving problems, which is shared by the employees of an organization. Over the period of time, shareholders view company as an independent organization who has a mind of its own. Another important component of an organization is the ethical culture. It is the ethical culture that represents the ethical principles of the organization as a whole, by also incorporating the corporate policies on ethics and views of its management leadership on ethical issues. Ethical culture of an organization also exhibits the influence of its co-workers and opportunities for unethical behaviour.

The more ethical employees are perceived to be in an organization culture, the less likely they are to make unethical decisions. Corporate culture and ethical culture are closely linked to each other and facilitates ethical decisions within the organization. Also, ethical values embodied in an organization culture are positively related to employee's commitment to the enterprise and their sense that they fit into the organization. These findings suggest that organizations should develop and promote ethical values to enhance employees' commitment to the enterprise and their sense that they fit into the organization.

5.3 CORE VALUES: THE VALUE OF A VALUE

Core values are the fundamental beliefs of a person or organization. These guiding principles dictate behaviour and can help people understand the difference between right and wrong. Core values also help companies to determine if they are on the right path and fulfilling their objectives by creating an unwavering guide.

An organization's values are based on human values and thus to effectively handle the human side of a business organization, it is important to develop an exhaustive understanding of the normative value system emerging from traditional philosophical thinking of the society. We should understand the value system of individuals and organizations and then develop a suitable practice based on alignment of the both. This is management by values.

In an organization, managing by values has three basic elements: identifying core values, communicating core values and aligning values and practices.

Identification of core values – The core values provide the necessary realization to organizations about the purpose and cause of their existence and action. By corporate values, the enterprises know what they stand for and what principles they should follow. Once the values and mission of the organization are clear, its management practices can be evaluated objectively and easily. An organization can protect its survival as well as its distinctiveness in the most competitive business world only by developing its core values and identifying and following them consistently in all its decisions and actions.

Every organization must have a set of core values, which are referred to as the Business or Corporate values. The below mentioned are the few of core values practiced by Fortune 500 companies across the world:

- Customer service
- Employee care
- Quality
- Ethics
- Integrity
- Growth and Stability
- Innovation

- Flexibility
- Social Responsibility

Communicating core values – A company should effectively and properly communicate its core values to all the stakeholders, specifically to its employees. The employees should know completely, what the company stands for, what is its mission and core values, what are the dos and don'ts in the company. What is the right conduct from the company point of view? This provides direction and guidance for them for decision-making and actions. Simply identifying the core values is not enough, in addition, they should be canvassed and communicated to all stakeholders so that everybody will become aware about the same and try to respect them and avoid causing contradictions.

Aligning values and practices – In order to make management by values successful, there is a need to put the core values into actual practice. There must be an alignment between values and practice. If this is not done, then the values will remain merely as a wish list. So, there should not be any gap between the values and behaviour. The organization and its people must walk its talk. The misalignment between values and practices results into development of double standards and creation of energy drain that sabotages the productive behaviour.

Managerial Values:

As decision-makers, managers have more opportunities than others to set an ethical tone for the organization. They are the key people who actions are observed and followed by the other employees in the organization.

- **Pragmatic:** Pragmatic is pertaining to public business or skilled in affairs (Individual has an evaluative framework that is primarily guided by success – failure considerations *e.g.* Will a certain course of action work or not? How successful or unsuccessful? Is it apt?).
- **Moralistic** (Ethical – moral code) : Evaluative frame work consisting of ethical considerations influencing behaviour towards actions and decisions, judged to be 'right' and away from those judged to be wrong.
- **Affective** (feeling) : Suggest an evaluate framework guided by hedonism – one behaves in ways that increase pleasure and decrease pain. Hedonism is the doctrine that tells happiness is the highest good.
- **Combination** of the above.

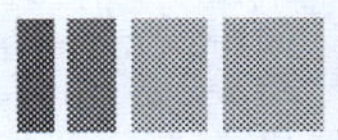

5.4 MORALITY AND PERSONAL VALUES

Morality

Morals are one's guiding principles. Morals are those principles that have internalized automatic response to the situations. They are part of who we are and our unique personality. Moral standards are first absorbed as a child through family friends and various social influences.

Different moral standards emerge from the different value systems which people and society hold. Moral standards include the norms we have about the kinds of actions we believe are morally right and wrong and also the values we place on the kind of objectives we believe are morally good and morally bad.

Values are at the heart of all kinds of morality. Morality is the standard that an individual or a group has about what is right and wrong; or good and evil. Moral standards are expressed as 'Honesty is the best policy'. Moral norms are expressed as general rules or statements: – 'Always tell the truth'. Moral Values are expressed as statements describing objects or features of objects that have worth like – 'Honesty is good' and 'Anger is bad'.

Personal Values

Individual values-system is like a fingerprint. It is unique in case of each individual. Because it is in the form of a combination of different instrumental and terminal values. And this combination varies from person to person. Therefore, in the context of an organization when different business managers come across similar ethical dilemma, their interpretation of the situation and responsive actions may differ significantly.

Personal values provide an internal reference for what is good, beneficial, important, useful, beautiful, desirable and constructive. Values generate behaviour and influence the choices made by an individual. They are values precisely because they are valuable to the particular person.

Values may help common human problems for survival by comparative rankings of value, the results of which provide answers to questions of why people do what they do and in what order they choose to do them. Moral, religious and personal values, when held rigidly, may also give rise to conflicts that result from a clash between differing ways the world would view it.

Personal values denote a sense of right or wrong, good or bad and other judgmental criteria based on our strong sense of what the ideal ought to be.

Personal values serve five purposes in organizations

- Values serve as standards of behaviour.
- Guidelines for decision-making and conflict – resolution.
- Values affect our thoughts and actions.
- It influences the perception and motivation of employees.
- It also has strong influence on behaviour and attitude.

It is to be kept into the sight that personal values are essential elements that a person uses to act with a certain amount of coherence in the different areas of life. For instance, if one has loyalty as a personal value, it will be carried over to the personal, social, and professional areas–being loyal to one's wife, friends or organization, respectively. If an individual wants to be coherent and consistent with what he or she thinks, says, and does, 'the individual must also show this coherence of values in all levels of life, though different contexts may seem to call for different values'. In this way, the personal values should cover in a transversal way the different fields of personal conduct, from family, friends to professional life. Personal values are like a glue between the different facets of the person. Just as cement is necessary to join one brick to another and build a solid building, personal values are the cement of one's life. Without them, personal building can be built but the risk of collapse is much greater.

According to the ethicist, Carlos María Moreno Pérez, "The personal values that people choose, materialized in action, have consequences not only for the immediate environment of the person but also for the person himself or herself. Personal values, if they are more than just good intentions and are indeed embodied in the person, make the person. The identity of the person is closely tied to his or her personal values. In the heart of the person are the values that give sense to the person. Therefore, personal values are also tied to the sense that the person wants to give to his or her life and aims. This is because personal values guide the behavior and actions of the person. Personal values help the person to live life to the fullest, with purpose, according to the aims that he or she pursues and the rules that he or she follows. The daily fulfilment of these will give the person a calm spirit due to the coherence between his or her personal values and actions to be undertaken and when faced with adversities, the necessary calmness to face difficulties that may arise."

5.5 VALUE – CONFLICT: HOW SHOULD I LIVE?

Moral code of conduct is developed on the grounds of individual value-systems. The moral code guides and directs a person's decisions and action in his/her personal life along with work life. Likewise, every organization also has its own corporate culture, which is a set of values, beliefs, goals, norms and ways of solving problems that its employees have. Our own moral code defines what is of value to us in life and therefore, identifies part of who we are.

Values are equally important in an organization and they are based on the following rationale:

- Values energize people as they motivate people.
- Values motivate people to work collectively as a group.
- Values are like ever-receding or never-ending goals. The higher the values, more the energy and effort required to achieve and sustain them. The more you pursue them, the greater the energy they release and put into action.
- Quality of performance on every job, every activity and every act can be accurately assessed in terms of values.
- Those companies that have assigned highest rating to the implementation of their key corporate values have also reported the highest levels of revenue growth and profitability in their respective industries.
- Improving corporate performance on a single value can virtually transform the way a company functions.

Value – conflict in an organization

Value differences and conflicts are caused by two discrete, perceived or actual, incompatible belief systems. Values are beliefs that people use to give meaning to their lives. Values explain what is "good" or "bad," "right" or "wrong," "just" or "unjust." Differing values need not cause conflict. For instance, if any discrepancy occurs between the individual values and corporate culture, then the friction between the individual and organization where he works is inevitable.

Values are considered as the common characteristics of both individuals and organizations. The extent to which personal values match with the values prevailing in an organization is considered to be an indicator of perfect "fit" between the organization and the individual. This concept of person-organization fit focuses on how the constituents and sculpting of an individual's values, when compared with the organizational values prevalent in an organization, affect the individual's approach and behaviour. Many philosophers have suggested that an appropriate personal-organizational fit enhances employees' job satisfaction in organizations.

On the other hand, an individual with low levels of work-related interests and attributes may possess personal values that are contrasting with the value system of the organization. In another situation, a person, who decides not to join an organization because it involves certain dishonest actions, has honesty as a personal value when doing business. Joining such an organization would contradict the individual's personal values. In such situations, conflict is created due to a friction between personal values and organizational values. Nevertheless, the positive effect of personal-organization fit on job satisfaction has been well highlighted, still the contradictory function of personal-organizational value conflicts on job satisfaction remained a fundamental question to many philosophers of organizational behaviors.

Building high levels of alignment between personal values and those of the organization is a great challenge. There are many initiatives that would promote this, but the most effective method is to ensure that values constitute a valid feature of the organization and that leaders at all levels actively, visibly and consistently live the values.

To conclude, aligning (existing) company values with (existing) personal values is difficult, however, by articulating and sharing one common vision for the organization, allows an employee to focus on the core values and grow the company in one agreed upon direction.

The Win-Win Decision

You direct the real estate department of a major retail clothing chain. Your primary responsibility is choosing sites for new stores as the company expands. When selecting sites, you use a grading system based on such factors as the average income of area residents, the cost of land, surrounding businesses, and access to local highways and mass transit. Your firm wants to add an outlet in a mid-sized city in a new territory. Your sister owns one of the proposed sites under consideration. When you grade the possible locations, hers is the only one that earns an A. The other two sites come in at B and C grade respectively. You decide to recommend your sister's property since it received the highest rating. You do not think you need to notify your supervisors that a relative owns this parcel of land. After all, this appears to be a win-win decision, one that benefits the company and your family. However, you decide to take a couple of days to reflect on your choice before submitting your report.

Should you stay with your initial decision to recommend the property without revealing that you are related to the owner?

[*Source: Adapted from Goldman 5. M. (2008), Temptations in the office: Ethical choices and legal obligations. Westport, CT: Praeger, Ch. 5*]

5.6 PERSONAL ETHICS & BUSINESS ETHICS: INDIVIDUAL INTEGRITY & RESPONSIBILITY

Personal ethics – Personal ethics is a class of philosophy that governs an individual's beliefs about morality and correct and incorrect behaviours. Personal ethics is the basic standards and values that influence interaction among individuals. This is usually distinguished from business ethics or legal ethics, since such branches of ethics come from outside organizations or governments, not the individual's conscience.

Business ethics – Business ethics can be explained as either written or unwritten codes of guidelines and values that influence the decisions and actions within a company. In the business world, the organization's culture sets standards for determining the difference between good and bad decision-making and behaviour.

Ethics, which concerns with right and wrong conduct, is totally dependent upon the value-system. Good ethics may be good business in majority of the cases. When the crisis comes, when ethics conflicts with the firm's interest, any ethics program that has not already faced up to this possibility is doomed to fail because it will undercut the rationale of the program itself. In business as in all other human endeavors, we must be prepared to pay the cost of unethical behaviour. So also, in the developing an ethical code of conduct in an organization, it must

define the guidelines for its stakeholders carefully so that it aligns the personal ethics with business ethics.

This value system and moral code guides and directs the individuals' decision and actions in his/her personal life as well as work life. Similarly, every organization too has its own corporate values, culture and goals. If any discrepancy occurs between the individual values and corporate culture; then the friction between the individual employees may value freedom and autonomy whereas the corporation gives importance to rule-bound hierarchy – oriented conduct. An individual employee may strongly favor initiative, innovation and creativity whereas the organization consistently may emphasize conformity, obedience and sincere followership. The organization may have profit motive and the individual employee may be always thinking beyond the material gains. In all such situations, the probability of conflict between the personal ethics and the business ethics are likely to increase.

From a broader perspective, it is the ethical responsibility of a business to become more active partner in dealing with social concerns. Rather than being a part of problem, a business must creatively find ways to become a part of solutions. Enterprises should not isolate themselves from participating in solving problems, leaving it up to others to find the answers and to tell them what not to do.

Conflict between Personal ethics and Business ethics

The organization's ethical dilemmas are often resolved and decisions taken by committees and formal and informal group and not by an individual. Moreover, the decisions that are taken are based on business goals and exclude individual goals. Ethical clashes or dilemmas may arise in several situations like:

1. The individual ethics may clash with the group ethics predominant in the organization.
2. The individual ethics of a single powerful person in the organization may be predominant in the organization. If that individual is ethical and works for the good of all the shareholders, it results in positive outcome but if that person is unethical, it may result in negative impact on the organization.
3. In some cases, employees may be taught to ignore an issue, which he or she thinks is unethical.

Although it is important to resolve these ethical dilemmas, the answer is not to compromise and go along with management or the group on business ethics issues. Open discussion of ethical issues with honesty are important to successful ethical decision-making.

We believe that most companies and business people try to make ethical decisions. However, because there is so much difference between individuals, ethical conflict is inevitable.

There are no easy answers for resolving ethical conflicts and sometimes resolving an ethical issue is a close call. One thing, however is certain that if we understand how ethical decisions making is followed in organization, our awareness and ability to tackle such decisions is enhanced and we are then in a position to take better, more informed decisions and resolve ethical conflicts more effectively.

Individual Integrity and Responsibility

Integrity is explained as firm adherence to a code of values. For an Individual or for a Business, Integrity is the quality or state of being complete or undivided. In other words, it means being true to our values and ourselves and also keeping our commitments not only towards others but to ourselves also. In the individual value – set, Integrity is the core value, which makes an individual complete or undivided. It also gives us power to accomplish greater task.

When an individual/business fails to keep his commitment, he gets out of integrity. Therefore, without integrity, we are incomplete, or divided. Also, without integrity, it isn't possible for him/her to act powerfully in a situation.

For restoration of integrity, it is essential that an individual/firm first acknowledge that he/they have failed to keep a commitment, however, no alibis is required here. Second step for restoration is completing the commitment – either by recommitting or by altering the commitment.

Why is it important to restore integrity? This is mainly because it gives you the ability to powerfully deal with not only specific situations but also in other areas of one's life.

When an individual is working with an organization, his commitment to fulfil his responsibilities is of upmost importance. Besides, an individual should be honest – first to himself and then to others, which is the prerequisite for keeping his or her commitment and also others commitments to us.

Individual Responsibility

Responsibility is defined as a moral, legal or mental accountability. This makes an individual a cause of doing something with a motive or an agent of some action.

An individual's responsibility is taking on accountability for our personal situation. Suppose if an organization declares that we are responsible for what we do and what we have, who we are and for all the conversations we have and situation we are in. Therefore, individual responsibility is the commitment one makes to himself for being an agent in the world, *i.e.* the cause of who we are and what we have.

For an individual, it is important to be responsible for himself, as thereafter he does not need to blame anyone or feel guilty about it. Hence, what has happened and generated so far is already created and thus should be accepted. In case, you are not satisfied with it, one can always recreate it.

When we fail to take responsibility or onus of a situation, we look for an alibi and give explanations for non-fulfilment of results. It is concluded that the situation was not under control and the results were impacted by uncontrollable factors. However, whenever an individual is working in a business organization as a team, the responsibility of the teams' failure to perform lies on the whole of the team.

A manager needs to be supportive towards his team members, and also assist them if need be. Also, a manager must give the team members equal opportunity to contribute.

It is important to note that since everyone on a team is responsible for achieving team goals, there can be no finger pointing. In case a responsibility isn't fulfilled, the manager is required to take action to meet the obligation.

However, if someone promised to do something and didn't do it, manager must convey that his or her approach is not suitable for the team. This is not about someone being right or wrong, good or bad. It's about whether we've produced the result as promised.

Apologies are not essential. Often, the first thing we do is apologizing when we've missed a commitment. Simply apologize – the most important thing is to declare what you're committed to. So, recommit to do whatever you didn't do (by a specific date and time) or else let your teammates know that you aren't going to do it!

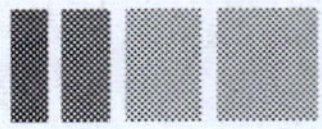

5.7 THE GOLDEN RULE

The moral principle known as the 'The Golden Rule' has been espoused by many humanists, which otherwise is also known as the ethic of reciprocity. Reciprocity is an interchange of giving and receiving in social relationships. Reciprocity occurs when an action that has effect upon another is reciprocated with an action that has an approximately equal effect upon the other. In other words, it is the return of small favours that are almost equal in value.

The Golden rules suggests that people should aspire to treat each other as they would like to be treated themselves – with tolerance, consideration and compassion. It suggests that one should treat inferiors, as you would want superiors to treat you.

The Golden Rule is liked by many philosophers due to its universality; because it is resulting from human sentiments and past experience and it also entails people to think from the perspective of others and tries to envisage how the other person might feel and think. For purpose of moral decision-making, this is a modest and transparent default position. The Jewish and Christian traditions refer **The Ten Commandments** which is one of the earliest recorded codes of conduct or ethical commands as found in the Bible:

- Honour your father and your mother
- You shall not kill
- You shall not commit adultery
- You shall not steal
- You shall not bear false witness against your neighbours
- You shall not covet your neighbor's house. You shall not covet your neighbor's wife, nor his male or female slave, nor his ox or ass, nor anything else that belongs to him.

This golden rule is common to every religion and culture with minor variations as we can see below:

Christianity: "Whatever you want men to do to you, do also to them."

Islam: "No one of you is a believer until he loves for his neighbor what he loves for himself."

Judaism: "What is hateful to you, do not do to your fellow man. This is the entire Law; all the rest is commentary."

Buddhism: "Hurt not others with that which pains yourself."

Hinduism: "This is the sum of duty; do naught unto others what you would not have them do unto you."

Zoroastrianism: "Whatever is disagreeable to yourself, do not do unto others."

Confucianism: "What you do not want done to yourself, do not do to others."

Bahai: "And if thine eyes be turned towards justice, choose thou for thy neighbor that which thou choosest for thyself."

Jainism: "A man should wander about treating all creatures as he himself would be treated."

Yoruba Proverb (Nigeria): "One going to take a pointed stick to pinch a baby bird should first try it on himself to feel how it hurts."

There are three Golden rules of ethics, which establish the foundation of human moral values. These rules have remained essentially unchallenged over centuries together, which is why they are applicable universally. They are as follows:

i. Do not do anything to others something, which, if done to you can cause harm to you.

ii. Everything you want others to do to you, you should do to others.

iii. Do not do to others that you do not wish them to do to you.

These golden rules should be always kept in focus while developing and identifying core values. Many times, what we take as a value, may not be that much valuable. These golden rules provide us a screening test for finding out the validity of what we decide as core values. John Maxwell writes that – 'It's the closest thing to a universal guideline for ethics a person can find. There are really only two important points when it comes to ethics. The first is a standard to follow. The second is the will to follow it.' The Josephson Institute of Ethics, a nonpartisan, non-profit organization that exists to improve the ethical quality of society, states it well when they say, 'Ethics is about how we meet the challenge of doing the right thing when that will cost more than we want to pay. There are two aspects to ethics: The first involves the ability to discern right from wrong, good from evil, and propriety from impropriety. The second involves the commitment to do what is right, good and proper. Ethics entails action; it is not just a topic to mull or debate.' Even if we apply the golden rule in an organizational context, it is good for employees, it is good for customers and it is good for management.

What Does Confucian Ethics Tell Us?

Chinese philosopher Confucius emphasized creating an ethical society based on human interaction rather than the belief in an after-life. Although the philosophy of Confucius doesn't deny the existence of God or an afterlife, Confucius held that humans are incapable of knowing or understanding such things, so they should focus on creating an ideal society in this life. According to Confucianism, correct behavior is more about developing the greater good than acting in one's own self-interests. Self-interest isn't inherently bad, but Confucius and his followers considered acting for the good of society to be the more righteous path. The Confucian theory of ethics also teaches that circumstances can determine what's ethical and what isn't. So, although lying may be unethical in most situations, it can be ethical when doing so serves the greater good when a lie can prevent a murder, for example. In business, Confucian ethics are similar to the Golden Rule. In one translation of his works, Confucius is credited with saying:

> "What one does not wish for oneself, one ought not to do to anyone else; what one recognizes as desirable for oneself, one ought to be willing to grant to others."

However, the flipside of the Golden Rule in real life is that not everyone thinks like you, acts like you, or believes in the same principles that you do. If you live your life on the assumption that your pursuit of an ethical ideal will match others' ethical ideals could make you upset. For example, if you were the type of person who values honesty in your personal value system, and you found a wallet on the sidewalk, you would try to return it to its rightful owner. However, if you lost your own wallet, could you automatically expect that the person who found it would make the same effort to return it to you? Nevertheless, the most important feature of The Golden Rule is that, it cannot be claimed by any one philosophy or religion; undeniably, the communities that

have evolved successfully being influenced by its use as a benchmark through which conflict can be resolved. Throughout the ages, many philosophers like Confucius, Immanuel Kant and spiritual traditions have promoted one or other version of it.

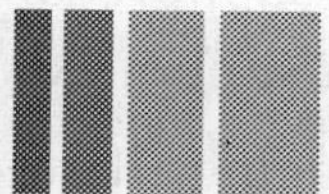

5.8 UNDERSTANDING RIGHT AND WRONG: DOING THE RIGHT THING

Morality is the system through which we determine right and wrong conduct. Right actions are those which take into account the rules that define our duty and rights of others. Individual's passion to do right is the bond that holds ethical concepts together. Leaders tend to develop this quality relatively early while others develop it over time through experience, reason or spiritual growth. They often state familiar point of views for doing right – to prevent the society from disintegrating and also relieve all human suffering, to advance human prosperity, to unravel conflicts of interest fairly and logically, to praise the good and punish the guilty or just because something is the right thing to do. Having a passion to do right indicate a personal characteristic of not only recognizing the importance of ethical behaviour but also the willingness to face challenges and make tough choices. It is also a core responsibility that we cannot shirk in any circumstances.

Crisis in Australian cricket over the ball-tampering scandal

The incident generated a high level of moral indignation which far outweighs the nature of the transgression of ball tampering. Smith and ex-vice-captain David Warner were given one-year bans and Bancroft was suspended for nine months by Cricket Australia. Smith and Bancroft were banned from captaining Australia for two years and Warner will not be considered for leadership positions in the future. This episode has three ethically disquieting elements: premeditation (Smith admitted the "leadership group" openly discussed ways to get the ball moving laterally), 'passing the buck' (Bancroft is the least experienced member of the team) and context (the incident occurred during a fractious, ill-tempered series).

Don't you think that the episode is an example of the failure of individual as well as collective ethics? Also, consider the enormous loss of reputation that was caused to the Australian cricket as a result of the cheating.

5.9 ETHICAL REASONING AND REAL-WORLD APPLICATION

Ethical reasoning is the process of recognizing, which decisions require ethical judgments, determining potential reasonable course of action, finding support for potential course of action and then selecting the course of action best supported.

Ethical reasoning has the same basic structures that underlie all reasoning. If we are to reason well ethically, we must learn to identify and assess our use in ethical reasoning of these basic intellectual structures. Here is the basic idea: whenever we think, we think for a purpose within a point of view, based on assumptions leading to implications and consequences. We use ideas and theories to interpret data, facts, and experiences in order to answer questions, solve problems, and resolve issues. In other words, all thinking has following ingredients:

- **General purpose** – Firstly, an individual is trying to determine the ethical goals or an objective that he or she is trying to achieve.
- **Raise questions** – The key ethical question a person is trying to answer, that is identification of issues he or she is facing and then formulating key ethical question embedded in the issues, keeping in mind the relevant point of views.
- **Use information** – One must identify the information, collect all the data and facts, which will enable a person to understand and consider the requirement of evidences or observations relevant to others. Individual's own experiences also helps in developing suitable reasons.
- **Utilizes concepts** – The key ethical concepts and principles that would assist in developing a thought process. Identification of ethical definitions, theories, models etc. that is applicable for reasoning through the issues.
- **Makes assumption** – The main assumptions or pre-suppositions used in reasoning in the ethical issue. Assumptions should also be justified for reasoning. Assumptions must also be evaluated from the perspective of understanding the ethical issues along with available alternatives.
- **Embodies a point of view** – It is frame of reference or perspective of looking at ethical issues in case of complex ethical issues. An individual will have to consider a situation from different orientations and also see it from the perspective of the way the world would view it.

- **Draw inferences** – Drawing inferences or conclusion on the basis of certain reasons for the ethical issues. Also, it is essential to enquire if there is any other option available and considering most reasonable solution amongst them.
- **Generates implications** – Next step is to view the implications of the conclusions drawn. Evaluating conclusions from the perspective of implications or alternative consequences, which follows logically.

Through our understanding of these elements, we can better analyze ethical reasoning. We can target our ethical purposes. We can formulate our ethical questions in various ways to identify the question that best embodies the issue. We can determine whether we have the information we need to solve the ethical problem. We can identify the inferences we are making and consider alternative inferences or conclusions. We can figure out the ethical concepts and principles we are using to reason through the issue. We can check our assumptions before coming to conclusions. We can determine whether more than one ethical viewpoint needs to be considered. And, we can follow out the ethical implications of our decisions.

Theory of Moral Judgment

Lawrence Kohlberg, who explained that moral judgment is based on the concept of objectivity, justice and fairness, developed a framework for moral judgment that presents the argument that we develop a reasoning process over time, moving through six distinct stages (classified into three levels of moral development) as we are exposed to major influences in our lives.

Level 1: Preconventional. At this lowest level of moral development, a person's response to a perception of right and wrong is initially directly linked to the expectation of punishment or reward.

- Stage 1: Obedience and punishment orientation. A person is focused on avoidance of punishment and deference to power and authority, that is, something is right or wrong because a recognized authority figure says it is.
- Stage 2: Individualism, instrumentalism and exchange. As a more organized and advanced form of Stage 1, a person is focused on satisfying his or her own needs, that is, something is right or wrong because it helps the person get what he or she wants or needs.

Level 2: Conventional. At this level, a person continues to become aware of broader influences outside of the family.

- Stage 3: "Good boy/nice girl" orientation. At this stage, a person is focused on meeting the expectations of family members, that is, something is right or wrong because it pleases those family members. Stereotypical behavior is recognized, and conformity to that behavior develops.
- Stage 4: Law-and-order orientation. At this stage, a person is increasingly aware of his or her membership in a society and the existence of codes of behavior, that is, something is right or wrong because codes of legal, religious, or social behavior dictate it.

Level 3: Post conventional. At this highest level of ethical reasoning, a person makes a clear effort to define principles and moral values that reflect an individual value system rather than simply reflecting the group position.

- Stage 5: Social contract legalistic orientation. At this stage, a person is focused on individual rights and the development of standards based on critical examination, that is, something is right or wrong because it has withstood scrutiny by the society in which the principle is accepted.
- Stage 6: Universal ethical principle orientation. At this stage, a person is focused on self-chosen ethical principles that are found to be comprehensive and consistent, that is, something is right or wrong because it reflects that person's individual value system and the conscious choices he or she makes in life. While Kohlberg always believed in the existence of Stage 6, he was never able to find enough research subjects to prove the long-term stability of this stage.

Kohlberg's framework offers us a clearer view into the process of ethical reasoning-that is, that someone can arrive at a decision, in this case the resolution of an ethical dilemma-on the basis of a moral rationale that is built on the cumulative experience of his or her life. Kohlberg also believed that a person could not move or jump beyond the next stage of his or her six stages. It would be impossible, he argued, for a person to comprehend the moral issues and dilemmas at a level so far beyond his or her life experience and education.

Application of Business Ethics

- **Ethics of human resource management** – Human resource management is that branch of the management where ethics is significantly important since it is concerned with human issues, such as health and safety at work place, skill enhancement and development, compensation and overall employee-employer relationship.
- **Ethics of sales and marketing** – Ethics in marketing is a philosophy that promotes honesty, fairness and responsibility in all sales and marketing activities performed by an enterprise. Since advertising is a mode of communication, therefore it should not be misleading and manipulative. It needs to create a balance between self-interest and social responsibility.
- **Ethics of production** – Manufacturing ethically is holistic approach of business that includes focus on well-being of consumer and society as a whole. Business needs to provide its customers best quality products, and should not compromise, to achieve cost efficiencies. Production process and technology should also be updated to match administered standards.
- **Ethics of finance** – Professionals in financial services business have to serve both their customers and company with honesty and integrity. They must avoid conflict of interest and provide information to its customers in full-accurate, fair, timely and understandable manner. Professionals must also respect the confidentiality of information they obtain during the course of business and should not use it for personal advantage.

5.10 ETHICAL DILEMMAS: RESOLVING ETHICAL ISSUES

Everyone wishes to always follow the right conduct. When we have a choice between the right and wrong, an individual will certainly choose the right alternative. When actions are overtly right or wrong, it is easier to make choices. For example, to choose between lie and truth, arrogance and modesty, violence and peace or selfishness and sacrifice can be relatively simple job. Since we can categorize the behaviour alternative, specifically as right and wrong.

However, in real life we come across several situations where it is difficult to differentiate and categorize the rival actions as right and wrong. Both contending actions seem to be right from an alternative perspective. After-effects of this are dilemma. When both contending actions contain some kind of moral elements and both such actions therefore, appear to be ethically right; the situation results into an ethical dilemma.

Thus, an ethical dilemma occurs when there is a clash between the two rights. It is not disagreement between right and wrong. But it is a conflict amongst two equally right moral perspectives. As such, to the decision maker, the problem is how to decide which right is more right than the other right. For example, if a particular product division of a company has become unprofitable. Should the manager suggest for the closure of that unit? If the unit is continued, losses will mount up and perhaps this unit will become a burden on other units. If the unit is closed, the people working in that unit will lose their jobs. Under such circumstances any of the rival actions seems as right. Dilemmas are more complex when law, religion or any moral theory does not have guidelines for its solution.

A bigger ethical dilemma is faced by organization when there is conflict between economic goals or economic performance and social performance. When the organization has to allocate resources for economic and social goals and decide its priorities, this dilemma becomes more complicated and acute.

An ethical dilemma exists when one is faced with having to a make choice among following alternatives:

1. Significant value – conflicts among differing interests.
2. Real alternatives that is equally justifiable.
3. Significant consequences on stakeholders in situation.

Resolving dilemmas

Ethical dilemmas are required to be thought about and analyzed in a broader perspective. Then, the situation will not be regarded simply as a win-lose situation. Then, the decision-maker identifies and understands the multiple alternative solution-options. Ethical dilemma can be better resolved with use of ingenious thinking and different decision-alternatives are considered. People mostly analyze the problem from a win-lose position. This restricts their reasoning process and influences them to make narrow evaluative judgments. On the other hand, we can create a win-win situation also. But for this purpose, we have to think in an

ingenious manner. We have to make a complete and comprehensive understanding of the problem-situation in the most objective and factual way. Ethical dilemmas are appropriately resolved by searching out innovative solutions.

Steps for dealing with ethical dilemma are as follows:

- Acknowledge that there is a moral issue.
- Ascertain the people who will be affected by the decision. Also, determine your role.
- Gather the facts about sequence of occurrence of events. Because the more facts we know, we can better comprehend the situation.
- Ascertain your test for right versus wrong. How would you define the problem, if you were to stand on the other side of the fence.
- Ascertain the test for right versus right theory, for example trust *v.* loyalty, justice *v.* mercy, etc.
- Apply the resolution principle. Work through all three approaches to resolve the dilemma, namely:
  - Thinking based on end-do whatever produces the greatest good for maximum people.
  - Rule based thinking-follow the rule strictly.
  - Carebased thinking-treat others with love and compassion. Do to others, what you would like the do to you.
- Your approach must look reasonable and persuasive.
- Investigate, if there is any third way out of the situation.
- Make decision and take action.
- Revisit and reflect on the decision.

Managers should respond to dilemma and try to resolve them. One approach is that the personal traits and characteristics of the manager has an influence on the response of the manager to ethical dilemma. However, it is not the personal characteristics of the individuals, which alone affects his/her response to ethical dilemmas, but there are certain organizational factors also which influence the manager's response to ethical problem solving. Thus, factors influencing the management of dilemma can be broadly classified into two categories such as organizational factors and individual factors.

Following are the organizational factors:

- The company policies, rules, work-procedures and systems.
- The organizational culture and shared values.
- The organizational structure, authority-orientation and hierarchy in the organization.
- The attitude of top management towards ethical problem-solving and the precedents the top management has developed in this respect.

If the company has a clear policy relating to ethical issues, the confusion relating to choice of decision – alternatives is less. For example, if the company policy explicitly prohibits giving bribes, kickback and gifts to get business; the manager has then a precise direction for ethical decision-making.

The individual factors, which affect the management of ethical dilemmas and ethical decision-making in organization, are as follows:

- The manager's perception of the job – narrow perception.
- The personal background and characteristic of the manager influence his/her approach to ethical problems.
- The personal value system and code of ethics of the manager, which defines what is right or wrong.

Sometimes, in reality, the "answer" to an ethical dilemma is often the lesser of two evils. It is unrealistic to assume that there will always be a perfect answer. Then, it becomes more a question of whether or not you can arrive at an outcome you can live with. Joseph L. Badaracco Jr.'s book 'Defining Moments' captures this notion of living with an outcome in a discussion of "sleep-test ethics":

"The sleep test is supposed to tell people whether or not they have made a morally sound decision. In its literal version, a person who has made the right choice can sleep soundly afterward; someone who has made the wrong choice cannot. Defined less literally and more broadly, sleep-test ethics rests on a single, fundamental belief: that we should rely on our personal insights, feelings, and instincts when we face a difficult problem. Defined this way, sleep test ethics is the ethics of intuition. It advises us to follow our hearts, particularly when our minds are confused. It says that, if something continues to gnaw at us, it probably should."

5.11 A FRAMEWORK FOR ETHICAL DECISION-MAKING

We have tried to understand in the previous paras how we may face difficult ethical situations in our work life. However, it is important for us to recognize the ethical elements that are embedded in our daily activities in the bank. Our decisions have implications on the bank's revenues, cost, profitability, etc. and would sometimes naturally attract everyone's attention. It is, therefore, imperative, for the employees to not only remain ethical while making such decisions, but ensure that they are perceived by all others also – internally or externally – as ethical in their decision-making. Towards that end, it is desirable that we should have some decision-making guidelines that can help us make better ethical choices both individually and collectively. With this purpose, we shall examine a few existing ethical decision-making framework in subsequent paras.

Traditionally, ethical decision-making has involved weighing of four factors as under:

- The desired outcome of a decision
- The means used to achieve the desired outcome
- The motivation behind the decision
- The possible consequences of decision

In this framework, if even a single factor is not acceptable, the decision is unethical. However, in modern times, the ethical decision-making especially for the bankers has become more complex. It also has to include other dimensions in terms of the effect of a particular decision on the other stakeholders like customers, colleagues, organization, investors and public at large. Therefore, a comprehensive lens for making ethical decisions is required to help us avoid decision-making blunders.

Josephson Institute of Ethics has developed a 'Character-Based Decision-making Model' that can be applied to general decision-making, many common problems and during ethical dilemmas. It involves three steps:

1. All decisions must take into account and reflect a concern for the interests and well-being of all affected individuals ('stakeholders'): The underlying principle here is the Golden Rule-help when you can, avoid harm when you can.

2. Ethical values and principles always take precedence over non-ethical ones: Ethical values are morally superior to non-ethical ones. When faced with a clear choice between such values, the ethical person should always choose to follow ethical principles. Perceiving the difference between ethical and non-ethical values can be difficult. This situation often occurs when people perceive a clash between what they want or 'need' and ethical principles that might deny these desires. If some rationalization begins to occur, this situation is probably present.
3. It is ethically proper to violate an ethical principle only when it is clearly necessary to advance another true ethical principle which, according to the decision-maker's conscience will, produce the great balance of good in the long run.

Some decisions will require you to prioritize and to choose between competing ethical values and principles when it is clearly necessary to do so because the only viable options require the sacrifice of one ethical value over another ethical value. When this is the case, the decision maker should act in a way that will create the greatest amount of good and the least amount of harm to the greatest number of people.

(*Source:* https://blink.ucsd.edu & Josephson Institute of Ethics)

However, we feel that step-by-step procedures can ensure that a manager identifies and defines a problem, assesses the available options, thinks about the implications of the choices, and arrives at a decision by applying ethical principles. In this direction, Harvard Ethics Professor, Lynn Paine offers a four-part 'moral compass' approach for guiding the ethical decision-making. The goal of the compass is to ensure that ethical considerations are factored into every organizational decision. Lynn suggests four frames or lenses for the purpose. Each frame highlights certain elements of the situation so that they can be carefully examined and thought of. Taken together, the lenses make it easier to evaluate the ethical content of even routine decisions:

1. Purpose – Will this action serve a worthwhile purpose?
2. Principle – Is this action consistent with relevant principles?
3. People – Does this action respect the legitimate claims of the people likely to be affected?

4. Power – Do we have power to take this decision?

   (*Source:* Organizational Ethics: A Practical Approach by Craig E Johnson)

   We are of the view that if we add three more under mentioned lenses to the Lynn's model, the decision-making would become even more easier.

5. Prescription – Does the action violate any of the Bank's policy, regulation or law?

6. Public – Can I share the action with media tomorrow?

7. Person – Am I setting a good example for others?

These are simple and effective tools to integrate ethical aspects in daily decision-making and reframe an ethics-laden situation in which all parties can benefit- that is, a win-win situation for everyone. Nevertheless, it is not as important which decision-making framework is applied as the fact that our approach to the decision-making should be thorough and systematic within the organization.

5.12 LET US SUM UP

Values, norms, belief and their role/significance for individual and business are explained. Values-desirable behaviour for all-perpetual in nature-provides standards of competence and morality. Values are further classified as terminal value, *i.e.*, an ultimate goal and instrument values, *i.e.*, tool or means for acquiring terminal value. Norms are expectations whereas beliefs are standards of thoughts. Organizations need to identify its core values, communicate with stakeholder and ensure aligning them in all their decisions and actions. Moral norms are expressed as general rules or statements while personal values provide an internal reference for what is good, beneficial, important, useful, desirable and constructive. Philosophy that governs an individual's beliefs about morality and correct and incorrect behaviours comes under personal ethics. Business ethics are either written or unwritten codes of guidelines and values that influence the decisions/actions of an organization. Golden rules of ethics always be kept in focus while developing and identifying core values within an organization. Clash between two rights leads to ethical dilemma. It is not disagreement between right and wrong. Ethical dilemma can be better resolved with use of ingenious thinking. Putting in place a framework for ethical decision making is desirable for an organization.

5.13 KEY WORDS

Norms, beliefs, core values, value conflict, personal ethics, resolving ethical dilemmas.

5.14 CHECK YOUR PROGRESS

1. Managing by values in an organization has few basic elements, which is:
   (*a*) Identifying core values
   (*b*) Communicating core values
   (*c*) Aligning values and practices
   (*d*) All of the above
2. Which of the following is not a feature of value:
   (*a*) Values provide standards of competence and morality
   (*b*) Values are very large in number
   (*c*) Values are relatively temporary and vulnerable to change
   (*d*) None of the above
3. The Golden Rule says:
   (*a*) Don't react to others
   (*b*) Do as you want others to do to you
   (*c*) Do as you wish to behave
   (*d*) None of the above
4. Corporate culture is explained as
   (*a*) Set of values, beliefs, goals & norms
   (*b*) Ways of looking at problems
   (*c*) Maximizing profitability
   (*d*) Targeting bigger market share

5. Ethical dilemma occurs when:
   (*a*) There is clash between the two rights
   (*b*) Conflict between right and less right
   (*c*) Disagreement between right and wrong
   (*d*) All of the above
6. Integrity is the core value, which:
   (*a*) Makes an individual complete
   (*b*) Make an individual partial
   (*c*) Make an individual extensive
   (*d*) None of the above

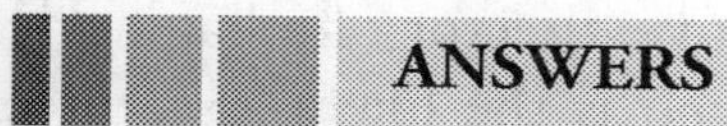

ANSWERS

1. (*d*)	2. (*a*)	3. (*b*)	4. (*a*)	5. (*a*)	6. (*a*)

5.15 EXERCISE YOUR ETHICS MUSCLE

Case 10: Would I? Should I?

You are driving a government vehicle on the most direct route to a late morning meeting in another town. You pass within a block of a store holding a personal package for you. You need that package urgently. Your service rules prohibit the use of official vehicles for the personal purpose. For efficiency's sake, do you stop by to pick it up?

Issues to reflect:

(*a*) Yes. It's a highly trivial matter with no connection to ethics or no ethics. It's outrageous to bring any moral color here.

(*b*) Yes. No one is aware that en route I will do the personal errand.

(*c*) No. I will drive my personal car to the store tomorrow to pick the package.

(*d*) What are the ethical, legal, and pragmatic considerations implicit in the situation?

Is it an ethical dilemma or a relatively simple choice between right versus wrong?

Case 11: Sweet Pill or a Bitter One?

An irresponsible and disagreeable employee is looking for a job in some private bank? To get rid of this person, do you agree to provide a positive reference?

Issues to reflect:

(*a*) If yes, then what are your reasons for providing a positive reference?

(*b*) Would it be truthful and responsible to write a good reference in the matter?

(*c*) What are the conflicting claims or ethical values at play in the situation?

(*d*) What is the right thing to do in the situation?

Case 12: Truth or Half-Truth?

You are working as an executive assistant to the executive director of a bank. He has asked you about the antecedents of the person who is the likely appointee to the position of Head (Human Resources) in the bank. The said person, very friendly with you, is a very smart guy but quite weak in his knees. You are aware of an old case of sexual harassment against him which was later closed due to withdrawal of complaint by the affected woman officer. As per the grapevine, the woman officer was pressurized to withdraw the complaint through coercive means. There are around 35 women officers working in the HR Department of Central Office. The executive director has recently joined the bank and not aware of any such past history or personal weakness in the character of the said person. Would you apprise your executive director truthfully or avoid to share the unsavory event?

Issues to reflect:

(*a*) Yes. I would be truthful truth with the executive director. But why?

(*b*) No. It's an old, closed case. Everyone should be given a second chance in life. Your reasons for this choice?

(*c*) What is the right course of action in the situation?

(*d*) What are the aspects of personal values, personal ethics and organizational ethics embedded in the situation?

6 UNIT

Ethics at the Organizational Level

6 UNIT

Ethics at the Organizational Level

6.1 LEARNING OBJECTIVES

The objective of this unit is to elucidate ethical dimensions in respect of customers, Marketing and Employees. It also provides an overview of ethical practices for MSME customers and ethical dilemmas in marketing and advertising. It explains as to how one needs to handle ethical dimensions for employees. Some of the case studies are also discussed so as to bring in practical orientation.

6.2 BUSINESS ETHICS AND CUSTOMERS

Customer being the back-bone of the banking business, it is essential that both parties, *i.e.,* bank and customer understand all ethical dimensions in conducting the banking activities. Customers can be of various types including individuals (salaried, retired, high networth individuals, semi-literate or illiterate), Hindu Undivided Family (HUF), Firms, Companies, Trusts, Clubs, Local authorities, Co-operative societies, Non-resident Indians, etc. Customers open different types of accounts and conduct their banking activities with the banks.

Ethical dimension refers to the conduct of business in line with the prescribed code of conduct of the respective profession. For example, 'Fair Practices Code for Lenders' is introduced by Reserve Bank of India, the regulator, lays down the processes of conducting ethical business practices while giving loans. Likewise, to ensure transparency in the digital lending process, RBI has come up with guidelines on digital lending, which *inter alia* require regulated entities to provide a Key Fact Statement or KFS to the borrower before the execution of the contract. The KFS shall mandatorily contain details of the Annual Percentage Rate of interest, the recovery mechanism, the grievance redress officer designated specifically to deal with digital lending/ FinTech related matters and the look-up period. Any fees or charges, including penal charges, which are not mentioned in the KFS cannot be charged by the Regulated Entity to the borrower at any stage during the tenor of the loan.

The guidelines also envisage that a borrower shall be given an explicit option to exit digital loan by paying the principal and the proportionate interest without any penalty during a look-up period. With an aim of ensuring ethical conduct in the context of rapidly digitizing banking service delivery platforms, RBI has recently set up a high-level Committee for "Review of Customer Service Standards in RBI Regulated Entities", chaired by Shri B P Kanungo, former Deputy Governor of RBI. The committee will examine and review the state of customer service in the regulated entities as well as adequacy of customer service regulations and suggest measures to improve these aspects. One of the key terms of reference of the committee is to review the emerging and evolving needs of the customer service landscape, especially in the context of evolving digital and electronic financial products and suggest suitable regulatory measures.

Starting from the account opening to the end of closing the account, the life-cycle of a customer relationship with any bank is to be covered by the Code of Ethics laid down by the management of the Bank in line with the regulatory framework.

Business ethics refers to honesty, integrity, loyalty, correctness, care, respect for others, respect for law, concern for excellence, leadership, reputation and responsibility.

Consequences of unethical behaviour can lead to:

- Affecting fame and reputation of the bank
- Disappearance of the Bank
- Losing clients and business partners
- Wasting resources to hide unethical behaviour
- Cheating customers with unfair practices/pricing
- Dishonest/misleading advertising
- Breach confidentiality of customers/clients

Ethical business with customers refers to Respect, Honesty, Transparency, Responsibility, Trust, Fairness, Compassion and Privacy. When businesses uphold these ethical principles, customers benefit from a positive and trustworthy

experience. They are more likely to feel valued, respected and appreciated, leading to increased customer loyalty, positive word of mouth.

In the recent past, it can be observed that there has been an increasing gap between customer expectations *vis-à-vis* the banking services. Indian banking which was administered with social and developmental objectives has transformed into modern banking in line with liberalization, privatization and globalization. Post-2008 global financial crisis, regulatory measures helped in regaining customers confidence. However, instances of ethical problems and dilemmas continue to shake the customer confidence. Ethical issues like mis-selling, lack of transparency in pricing, disproportionate service charges, very high penal rates, strong-arm tactics by some recovery agents etc. are still being reported against the bankers. Incidents of digital frauds and cheating through phishing, vishing, fake links and websites, remote access apps, etc. are cause for concern.

Bank provides services to meet a customer's financial and non-financial needs and as such it is essential to understand the customer, his requirements and expectations. The customer needs can be explicit or implicit that require to be addressed with speed, timeliness, accuracy, courtesy and concern. There has been a paradigm shift in the manner of interaction between customers and the banks in recent years. Financial services are now available 24 × 7 × 365 on omnichannel basis. The spectrum of products and services has speedily expanded to internet and mobile banking, electronic funds transfer, UPI, Aadhaar eKYC, Bharat Bill Payment System (BBPS), QR Scan & Pay, digital prepaid instruments, etc. Even as the financial landscape evolves and transforms, the underlying principles for good customer service and customer protection namely, transparency, fair pricing, honest dealings, responsible business conduct, protection of consumer data and privacy, etc. continue to be relevant.

Ethical dilemma exists in providing banking services to the customer during various phases. For instance, opening an account, the KYC norms have been adhered to or not, charging the interest on different products and services, disbursement of loans and advances as per the process and need of the customer, carrying out due diligence in credit proposals, monitoring the accounts for timely repayment and proper implementation of provisioning norms, etc. At every stage, the bank staff should follow the ethical principles not withstanding any outside or inside pressures. Staff must refer to the Law or Code of Ethics or internal guidelines if a dilemma exists. One should not misguide or sell the products which is not in line with the customer's need/profile or risk appetite.

Ethical consumerism reflects to consumer driven approach to purchasing goods and services that considers the social, environmental and ethical impacts of products. Ethical consumerism involves aligning purchasing decisions with personal values and principles. They prioritize factors such as environmental sustainability, fair labour practices, animal welfare and social justice. By making intentional and ethical purchasing decisions, it contributes to sustainable, socially responsible and environmentally conscious marketplace.

6.3 ETHICAL CONSIDERATIONS AND MANAGING CUSTOMER RELATIONSHIPS

Customer relationship in the context of banking involves customer acquisition, customer orientation, customer education, customer service, handling customers, customer retention, customer complaints/grievances, and public relations as well. Ethical considerations begin with every stage of managing a customer. One should not entertain customers based on their affinity with caste, religion or economic status in the society. Interface with vulnerable segments, such as senior citizens and weaker sections, should be done with due sensitivity. Bank staff should be trained in such a way that they understand the adverse impact of one dissatisfied customer that can create a negative image for the bank. Moreover, they should be made to understand that banking implies a fiduciary duty on their part. It is not simply a commercial activity and he or she is morally obliged to put the customer's best interests first, even if the customer is unable to put them into words. In doing so, the banker must eliminate any asymmetry of understanding.

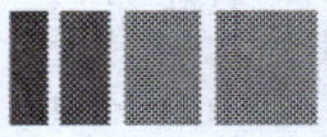

6.4 QUALITY AND PRICING OF PRODUCTS

Banks provide both products and services to the individual customers as well as non-individual customers, *i.e.,* firms, companies, etc. As far as the products are concerned, these can be divided as wholesale, international and retail banking products. Wholesale banking refers to bank dealing with manufacturing and business enterprises including multinational companies, financial institutions and public sector undertakings. In India, this is also known as commercial banking

or corporate banking. Wholesale banking products include providing financial assistance in the form of trade finance, forex, project finance, working capital loans, term loans, derivative products, bill/invoice discounting and accepting bulk deposits, etc. Banks also provide ancillary services like merchant banking, cash management services and advisory services. In other words, wholesale banking products include deposits, insurance, investment and providing service for securities selling and purchasing through demat accounts.

Retail products include both deposit and loan products. Deposit products are in the nature of savings bank account, recurring deposit account, current account, term deposit account, zero balance account and senior citizen deposit account. Retail loan products include home loans to residents and non-resident customers, auto loans, consumer loans, personal loans, educational loans, credit cards, debit cards, lockers, mutual fund, depository and investment advisory services, payment services and insurance products.

Banks has different distribution channels like call centers, ATMs, Branches, Internet banking self-help Kiosks for printing passbook or depositing cash. In recent times, most of the banks have launched their mobile apps for providing the banking and other financial services such as YONO of SBI, VYOM of Union Bank of India, PNB1 from PNB, IndusMobile from IndusInd Bank to name a few.

Quality and pricing of Products

With respect to the quality of products, one can observe that standardization of wholesale and retail banking products has taken place in line with the guidelines and processes issued by the regulator. The service delivery quality varies from bank to bank depending on various factors. However, with the increased competition, most of the banks are ensuring that the commitment given to the customers in terms of service delivery are being adhered to. To retain customers and also to attract new customers, Banks have to maintain good quality consistently.

With regard to pricing of products, RBI has given flexibility to banks to price assets and liability products based on the bank's costing, availability of IT enabled infrastructure, risk appetite, broad guidelines prescribed by the regulator, etc. One can observe minor differences in pricing of the products and services being offered by different banks. That can be due to different strategies they adopt to acquire customers.

6.5 PROTECTING CUSTOMERS' RIGHTS: CONFIDENTIALITY OF INFORMATION ETC.

Confidentiality of information of the customer both in wholesale and retail banking has become a major challenge for Banks along with ethical aspects of customer relationship management such as fairness of treatment and transparency etc. Every bank should recognize its responsibility to meet its customers' expectations with regard to privacy, confidentiality and security of their personal information that resides with the bank. Accordingly, the Reserve Bank of India (RBI) has a formalized Charter of Customer Rights that outlines customers' rights. The charter gives RBI legislative powers to step in and take action against the errant bank. This has been done to safeguard customers' banking rights at all times. The main tenets of the charter are as under:

Right to Fair Treatment

Every banking customer has a right to get fair treatment from his or her financial institution. The bank cannot discriminate against on grounds such as sex, age, religion, caste, sexual orientation, and physical ability. However, there are some exceptions to fair treatment rights. Banks can use their discretion to offer differential interest rates or products to certain customers. A common example is interest rates on fixed deposits. Banks often offer better interest rates to senior citizens. They also offer competitive interest rates to women on various loan products.

Right to Transparency

A customers has a right to transparency. Banks have a diktat that they need to be absolutely honest and transparent in all their dealings with their customer. Hence, they need to be upfront and disclose all information to the customer. For example, if anyone invests in an equity product with bank, they need to honestly tell you the product's price, market performance and all the risks involved. Moreover, they need to tell all of this in simple and clear language. All contracts need to be drafted so that a common person can easily understand. It is the bank's responsibility to ensure effective communication. If there is something that a customer doesn't understand and ask them, it is their duty to explain the same to as clearly as possible. As the charter says, any features that can be disadvantageous to a customer, should be made known to him or her.

Right to Suitability

Customers also have a right to suitability. This right ensures that banks don't sell products and services that are not suitable for a particular customer. Mis-selling is a common complaint in the banking industry. Despite several regulations, there have been instances where customers are sold wrong products to meet internal targets or get higher commissions. These products may or may not suit a particular customer's unique needs. This Charter makes it difficult to palm off unsuitable products to unsuspecting customers. It has made it mandatory for banks to sell products only after keeping the customers' unique needs, financial circumstances, and life goals in mind.

Right to Privacy

Privacy is another of customers' fundamental banking rights. All the personal information a customer shares with bank, like Aadhaar card, PAN card, salary slips or income, phone number, email ID, investment information, must be heavily protected. They have to ensure that such information does not fall into the wrong hands, whereby customers are affected or inconvenienced. For example, they cannot sell or pass on your information to telemarketers for cross-selling or even use the same data themselves to pitch products to you. They have to remain ethical at all times. Banks are required to keep all customer information confidential unless a customer explicitly permits them to use his data or they are required by the law to disclose the same.

Right to Grievance Redressal and Compensation

Despite all the rules mentioned above that banks have to follow, there are chances that things could go wrong. In such circumstances, customers have the right to grievance redressal and compensation. The charter explicitly says that banks are accountable for their own products and third-party products they sell, such as insurance. If they fail to adhere to these basic norms, they have to bear the brunt. To ensure customers are aware of their grievance redressal rights, banks have to communicate the policy for compensation. In their policy, banks have to clearly state the rights of customers if and when such an event occurs.

As we can sense that the above charter is guided by ethics since often questions arise about the duties and obligation of banking service providers to customers as well as the rights of the customers in that regard.

Ethics and the Vulnerable

One of the basic tenets of ethics is the principle of equity. The exploitation of the vulnerable is a particular expression of the breach of that principle. We do not admire those who take sweets from children, who misuse monopolistic power, attempt to negate the doctrine of the separation of political powers or criminals who attack soft targets (such as the aged and the frail). It is the imbalance of power, the unevenness of the contest that offends our sense of ethics. Retail customers of banking services are especially vulnerable more so in a country like ours since the providers of these services typically have great powers that can be easily abused. They have also strong incentive to do so. For their part, customers vary greatly in their financial knowledge and sophistication and given the importance of financial services in our lives, everyone should be able to utilize them without fear of being abused. Although the regulators provide customers with considerable protection, no bank can survive without trust and loyalty of their customers. Ethical treatment of customers goes beyond what regulation demands. For example, every bank has a policy that delineates comprehensively the customers rights but in reality these rights are violated day-in-day out as we gather from the number of complaints filed under the Integrated Ombudsman Scheme of RBI. In fact, bankers must determine what is ethical in their treatment of customers and how to implement ethical standards through their practices and policies.

6.6 CODE OF BANK'S COMMITMENT TO MICRO AND SMALL ENTERPRISES

Micro and Small enterprises play a significant role as clients for all the banks including scheduled, private or joint sector banks. MSMED Act of 2006 provided protection to MSEs in terms of dealing with the banks for their financial needs. Code of Bank's commitment to MSEs has been brought out to set minimum standards of banking practices while dealing with the Bank. This code provides detailed description of the process and explains how to deal with MSE customers in day-to-day operations and also in times of difficulty.

This Code envisages to:

- Provide easy access to credit through various banking services efficiently.

- Effectively communicate with the MSE to understand the business and promote cordial relationship.
- Ensure quick response to the MSE banking needs.
- Foster confidence in banking system.

This Code covers Micro and Small Enterprises as defined by the MSMED Act 2006 that are involved in manufacturing, processing, production, or providing services. The products and services offered by the Bank include: loans, credits, discounting, credit facility, over draft, cheque and bill purchase/discounting, letter of credit, non-fund based guarantees, foreign exchange services, third party insurance services, factoring services, merchant services, etc.

Bank's key commitments to MSEs are:

- To act fairly and reasonably in dealing with MSEs.
- To help them to understand various banking products and services.
- To provide timely updates on SMEs accounts through various channels.
- To deal with promptness and sympathetic in case of any mistakes from both the sides.
- To maintain confidentiality of SME personal and business information.
- To provide a copy of the Code to all customers.
- To follow non-discriminatory policy and practices.
- To provide information on interest rates, fees and charges, and changes in them from time to time.
- To provide information about various incentives provided by the government in terms of credit guarantee schemes and rehabilitation process.
- To hold meetings with MSE customers to exchange views, feedback and address any grievances.
- To provide standardized application forms for various products and services.
- To make you understand the credit assessment process and documents required to be submitted for credit appraisal.
- To convey properly the reasons for rejection of an application.
- To maintain central registry of records of the MSEs.

- To monitor post disbursement on an on-going basis.
- Timely alerts on status of your account turning into NPA.
- To provide non-fund-based activities like LCs, insurance and other bill discounting services.
- To advise sympathetically in case of any financial difficulties.
- To help sick units in restructuring and one-time settlement process.
- To help in securitization of loans/dues if required.
- To collect dues and security repossession as per the guidelines of the Bank policy.

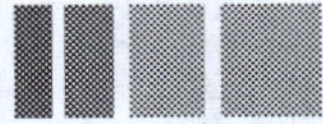

6.7 CASE STUDIES: INDIAN CONTEXT

Customer Service – Loan recovery

One of the fast-growing private sector banks engaged a third-party agency for ensuring follow-up of the retail segment loans. The Agency started operating on behalf of the bank.

One of the customers complained that he is getting an e-mail informing delay in payment of EMI and penalty thereon. The actual name of the bank's customer (borrower in this case) was different and was wrongly captured for some similar name in the database and hence this issue cropped up. When the recipient of the mail (whom the third-party believed as bank's customer) lodged complained about it through the grievance redressal process, the bank initially sent an auto-reply saying that the complaint will be addressed in 48 hours. The complainant gets a reply from the bank that the issue got resolved with necessary correction in their database. However, after 5 months again, the same EMI overdue mail started coming to the non-customer. The person had no other choice but to take it up to the higher authorities to resolve.

- Why is the mistake which was claimed in-writing as having got rectified is occurring again?
- Do you feel it may be due to the inefficiency of staff members? Or it may be due to lack of verification and updating of the database from time to time?

- How extended columns with customer names along with surnames, name of father/husband and other details may enhance the quality and reliability of the database?

Unsolicited Guidance at the Bank Branch

Mr. RK is a highly qualified person in the finance field and is working in a metropolitan city in India. He maintains a salary account with a private sector bank. While he has his salary account in a place closer to his office, he prefers to visit the nearest branch that had come up about 3 years ago closer to his residence.

RK gets a decent salary and he depends very less on his salary, as he also gets rental income from inherited properties (3 houses and 2 mini resorts) located at a popular tourist attraction. Being a person with good amount of financial knowledge, he keeps on transferring proceeds from his salary account depending upon his convenience and market conditions in select financial markets.

A staff by name BR kept on reminding RK to use part of his low interest earning savings for investing in select mutual funds. RK somehow managed to ignore the staff's advice and moves out of the branch each time saying he was busy on that day.

It is nearly 18 months now, RK is reluctant to visit the branch closer to his residence and does online banking to the extent he can manage. Else, he is preferring to take an hour permission to visit a rather crowded branch closer to the city center where his office is located. He shared his experience with his colleagues.

- Is the branch helping the customers at large by its guidance?
- Is RK overreacting to sporadic help being offered by BR at the branch closer to his residence?

Before we close this module, we shall like to present a scenario from the other side of the counter for an understanding that although customers' rights are of paramount importance but sometimes customers are so rude that they create a challenge for the employees to offer a good service. In bank branches, all of us would have likely come across such misbehaving customers. Such situations can also put the employees' rights at risk as is evident from the incident narrated in the box below:

Is the Customer Always Right?

At an independently owned Pizza Hut franchise in Oklahoma, two regular customers made sexually offensive remarks to a female employee named Lockard. She then told her boss she did not like waiting on them. Next day, these customers again entered the restaurant, and her boss instructed lockard to wait on them. She did, but this time the customers became physically abusive. Although it is the employee's duty to provide good customer service but that does not mean accepting harassment. Lockard sued her employer, the owner of the franchise, for failing to take her complaints seriously and for making her continue to suffer sexual harassment and assault by customers. The jury ruled in her favour, awarding her $360,000, and an appeals court upheld the judgment.

Reflections:

- How far should an employee be expected to go in the name of customer service?
- Just as every employee should treat customers with respect, so is every employer not ethically-and often legally-obligated to safeguard the employees on the job?

[Adapted from: LOCKARD, Plaintiff-Appellee, *v.* PIZZA HUT, INC., a corporation, doing business as Pizza Hut; A & M Food Services, Inc., a corporation, doing business as Pizza Hut, Defendants-Appellants. US Ct. App. Tenth Circuit (1998).]

In situations like the Pizza Hut case as above, the best solution lies in the approach that both the employee and the management should come forward and work together.

6.8 LET US SUM UP

Ethical dimension in respect of customers refer to the conduct of business during life-cycle of a customer within the Bank in line with the Code of Commitment to Customers and MSMEs, besides the procedures/standards laid down by the regulator and the Bank. Important aspects of the Code among others include informing customers about interest rates, service charges and changes therein,

maintaining confidentiality of data/information, adhering to time norms, addressing complaints, etc.

6.9 KEY WORDS

Types of customers, Customer relationship, Customers' rights, Commitment to customers.

6.10 CHECK YOUR PROGRESS

1. Consequences of unethical behaviour of bank leads to:
   (*a*) Affecting fame and reputation of the bank
   (*b*) Disappearance of the Bank
   (*c*) Losing clients and business partners
   (*d*) All of the above
2. Which of the following is unethical behaviour of an employee?
   (*a*) Honesty
   (*b*) Integrity
   (*c*) False promises
   (*d*) Respect for others
3. As per the code of ethics for customers, they should not be discriminated based on:
   (*a*) Affinity with caste
   (*b*) Religion
   (*c*) Economic status in the society
   (*d*) All of the above
4. Bank's commitment to MSMEs relates to:
   (*a*) Provide easy access to credit through various banking services efficiently
   (*b*) Ensure quick response to the MSE banking needs

(*c*) Foster confidence in banking system

(*d*) All of the above

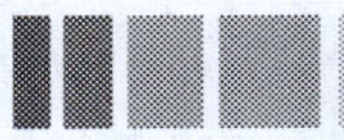

ANSWERS

1. (*d*)	2. (*c*)	3. (*d*)	4. (*d*)

6.11 EXERCISE YOUR ETHICS MUSCLE

Case 13: The LIBOR Scandal

On June 27, 2012, as part of a U.S. Department of Justice Investigation, Barclays Bank, a multinational financial services and banking firm headquartered in London, admitted to manipulating and reporting fraudulent interest rates used in international financial markets and was fined more than $450 million dollars (U.S.) by both U.K. and U.S. regulators. Evidence showed that Barclays had regularly manipulated the LIBOR (London InterBank Offered Rate) since at least 2005, in order both to profit from large trades and to falsely portray the bank as financially stronger than it was. The LIBOR is the rate at which major London banks report that they are able to borrow. This rate then serves as the benchmark at which interest rates are set for countless other loans, ranging from credit cards to mortgages and interbank loans. It also acts as a measure of market confidence in the bank, if a bank must pay a higher rate to borrow than others do, then markets must have less confidence in the institution's financial strength.

The LIBOR is established in a surprisingly simple manner. Each morning at 11 A.M. London time, members of the British Bankers Association (BBA) report to the financial reporting firm of Thomson Reuters the rates at which they would expect to pay for loans from other banks. Discarding the highest and lowest quartiles, Thomson Reuters then calculates a daily average, which becomes the daily LIBOR benchmark. Within an hour, Thomson Reuters publicizes this average worldwide, along with all of the individual rates reported to them. This benchmark is then used to settle short-term interest rates as well as futures and options contracts. By one estimate, the LIBOR is used to set interest rates for global financial transactions worth more than $500 trillion. The individual rates also provide an indirect measure of the financial health of each reporting institution, the lower their rates, the stronger their financial position. Evidence shows that as early as 2007, before the major financial collapse of Lehman Brothers and the economic meltdown that followed, regulators in both the United States and the United Kingdom were aware of allegations that Barclays was underreporting their rates. In the early days of the 2008 financial collapse, the Wall Street Journal published a series of articles questioning the integrity of LIBOR reporting and suggested that banks were intentionally misreporting rates to strengthen public perception of their financial health.

Internal documents and e-mails showed that traders, compliance officers and senior management at Barclays were aware of and approved the underreporting. An e-mail sent from a Barclays employee to his supervisor in 2007 said: "My worry is that we are being seen to be contributing patently false rates. We are therefore being dishonest by definition and are at risk of damaging our reputation in the market and with the regulators. Can we discuss urgently please?" Evidence also showed that Barclays employees were in regular communication with traders who would explicitly ask that Barclays report specific higher or lower rates in order to benefit their trades. For example, Derivative traders, who would stand to gain or lose millions of dollars depending on the rate, would communicate directly with their Barclays banking contacts and request that certain rates be reported. The tone of their communication demonstrates the familiarity that existed between these parties: "Dude. I owe you big time!... I'm opening a bottle of Bollinger," wrote one trader to his Barclays contact. "Pls set 3m Libor as high as possible today," wrote another.

Investigations into the LIBOR scandal showed widespread intentional fraud among many individual employees and executives at Barclays. But from the earliest days of the scandal, allegations were being made that other banks were equally involved. While admitting guilt, Barclays denied that they were the only bank involved in misreporting data. In a conversation between a senior executive at Barclays' and a representative of the British banking Administration, which was reported by the U.S. investigation, the Barclays employee defended the bank, saying "We're clean, but we're dirty-clean, rather than clean-clean." The BBA representative responded: "No one's clean-clean." By the end of August 2012, the investigation had spread to include allegations of fraudulent LIBOR reporting by HSBC and Royal Bank of Scotland, the two other largest banks in the United Kingdom, as well as more than a dozen other international banks.

Issues to reflect:

(*a*) What ethical issues are involved in this case?

(*b*) Who are the stakeholders in this case? Who would be hurt by rate fixing?

(*c*) What responsibilities did senior executives at Barclays have to prevent fraud in circumstances.

(*d*) If the LIBOR scandal is as widespread as the investigations suggest, are there ethical issues involved in this case that are different from those that would be involved if only Barclays was guilty? What are they?

(*e*) Who is responsible for the ethical integrity of such institutional practices as the LIBOR?

(*f*) Is anyone at fault for this fraud other than the individuals involved in reporting false information?

(*g*) From customers' rights perspective, what are the ethical dimensions that are in-built in the case?

Case 14: Refund or Replace?

The organization, of which you are the Head (Customer Service and Relationship), has been receiving complaints persistently from the public that one of your products is defective and does not meet its advertised features properly. Therefore, they want their money should be refunded, but your policy is to just replace the faulty goods. The customers are not agreeable for the replacement as they no longer trust your company products. Your policy is however designed to maximize the company's profit. Replacement is cheaper and easier than refunding.

Issues to reflect:

(*a*) What are the ethical issues at play in this scenario?

(*b*) What is more important? To earn customers' confidence or maximize the company's profit?

(*c*) What is the most ethical course of action in the case?

(*d*) Hypothetically speaking, if the same situation happens in a bank in respect of an insurance product, how can one balance the customer satisfaction against the business imperatives?

7 UNIT

Ethical Dimensions: Marketing

7 UNIT

Ethical Dimensions : Marketing

7.1 LEARNING OBJECTIVES

This section tries to elucidate marketing – related ethical dimensions. Various dilemmas faced in ethical marketing and ethical and unethical marketing practices are explained. It also covers competition and fair play and RBI's Code of Fair Practices.

7.2 EMERGING ETHICAL PROBLEMS IN MARKETING MIX

With the advent of information technology and consistent innovations, the landscape of all activities, including marketing of banking and financial services, has undergone tremendous changes. Mobile banking and online banking have provided a complete new model of service delivery mechanism reducing the need for the customer to go to the branch for any of the banking transactions. The customer communication from the traditional mode is now converted to e-mails, messages and phone banking. Marketing of bank products and services also has transformed into digital mode with each bank promoting digital marketing compared to print advertisements and television or media-based advertisements. The question is what is the right mix of marketing in terms of digital and print media, what could be the resources spent on these marketing activities, how are they impacting the sales and revenues of the bank and whether ethical principles are followed in the process of marketing the products and services.

The term *marketing* usually refers to promoting or selling of products or services. It is also considered as advertising or promoting a product or service through newspapers, radio, television, signboard, etc., which is sponsored by the promoter company/bank. The concept is much broader starting from what to produce, for whom to produce and for how much to sell or what is the value-creation in the process of production or delivering a service to the ultimate customer. Marketing is a wider concept and practice that involves clearly and fully understanding customer needs, creating product, ensuring that customer chooses to buy the product or service, and servicing in a way that makes the product or service successful. Virtually all aspects of marketing from the development of a new product to pricing, promotion and sales raise critical ethical questions that do not always have an easy answer.

Traditional marketing has been replaced by modern marketing that consists of social media and digital media marketing. Modern marketing has been facilitated with the increased channels of communication with the customer and providing a varied experience of choosing quality products from across the local and global markets. With the increase in the investments in market research by the companies/banks to understand the changing needs and expectations of customers through surveys, companies are able to better focus on the geographies and specific target customers for their products and services. Globalization also helped companies to offer a bouquet of products and services from various tie-ups with foreign partners, franchises, different modes of inventory management and strategic alliances.

Banking services marketing is closely associated with clear understanding of customer segments and their financial needs in case of retail banking, while wholesale or corporate banking, refers to marketing of various products and services to the MSEs and large corporates. Marketing of banking services thus comprises of increased offerings of new products and services to the existing clients and also to new clients.

From time to time, banks need to assess both current and potential financial needs, and be able to offer different products and services to suit customers. Marketing helps the bank to achieve its social and commercial objectives. Bank tries to fulfil social objectives serving the lower strata of population through priority banking and agriculture-related loans and advances to small and micro enterprises. To be profitable, the bank has to focus on target market segments and customer base.

Social media and digital marketing has become popular in India too with most of the Banks investing in various technology platforms to promote this type of marketing. For instance, at micro level, if a Bank wants to expand its education loan portfolio, it may use the social medium Facebook that provides database to the bank to target its education product sales to a particular university student at a metro city. The bank can select a university and a specific age group in the ad target option and approach him/her.

E-mail marketing also has been used by the bank for its existing customers to keep them engaged with the information on new products and services and providing quarterly statements of transactions.

Another social media marketing option banks are using is of search engine marketing/optimization, a tool provided by the Google called (SEO, SEM). These tools help companies to go for online advertisement and, based on their specific choice, they pay to the search engine company Google to ensure that the product or service of their company comes at the top when any prospective customer searches for information about any product or service.

These online search engine tools have become more popular with the increased availability of various online products and services companies provide discount offers and also spend budgets in attracting the online customers as this has become cost-effective compared to traditional mode of marketing and selling products and services.

Some of the platforms even provide comparison of prices of a single product or service with that of all competitors by giving complete analysis of features, benefits, differentiating factors, customer reviews, etc. This will help prospective customer to decide from a wide range of products and services available based on his personal choice and affordability.

It can be observed that many Banks have outsourced marketing activities to Direct Selling Agents (DSAs)/Direct Marketing Agents (DMAs). Minimum standards code has been set forth for implementation of various marketing activities by these agents. Do's and Don'ts have also been clearly specified both in terms of product features and also customer services including recovery process. In spite of these efforts, it appears that these two agencies did not work up to the expectations of either of the Bank or the customers due to various reasons.

Business Correspondents (BCs) have been appointed by banks to promote banking services in places where no branch of the bank is available. Banks have opted this model due to thin population in these locations and opening of full-fledged branch may not be a viable option. This module enables the banks to expand their reach to unbanked areas and also reach to its customers in a cost-effective manner. They collect information of the customer and do counselling, collect application forms, provide information of banking products and services to framers and support them in getting processed their loan applications, government incentives besides undertaking activities associated with deposits, etc. It has been observed that the staff of BCs sometimes indulge in high pressure sales tactics and try to manipulate the customers to buy the products they are marketing. RBI has also expressed serious concern over the unethical marketing practices of such third-party marketers. Therefore, the banks should be careful that the staff of such BCs are regularly trained in respect of the provisions of the Fair Practices Code and also about the broad ethical considerations relating to marketing so that any misselling or other unethical activity on account of the lack of awareness may be avoided. It is pertinent see the relevant RBI guidelines in this regard: "Regulated Entities (REs) are responsible for the actions of their service providers including Recovery Agents. It has been observed that the agents employed by REs have been deviating from the extant instructions governing the outsourcing of financial services. In view of concerns arising from the activities of these agents, it is advised that the REs shall strictly ensure that they or their agents do not resort to intimidation or harassment of any kind, either verbal or physical, against any person in their debt collection efforts, including acts intended to humiliate publicly or intrude upon the privacy of the debtors' family members, referees and friends, sending inappropriate messages either on mobile or through social media, making threatening and/or anonymous calls, persistently 1 calling the borrower and/or calling the borrower before 8:00 A.M. and after 7:00 P.M. for recovery of overdue loans, making false and misleading representations."

Ethical dilemmas in marketing mix

Given the different channels of marketing mix, it is difficult and complex to choose one or use a combination. Also, the traditional marketing mix was developed keeping in mind the manufacturing products. Banking services are based on customer expectations and perceptions that cannot be standardized in terms of quality and hence requires careful picking up of right marketing mix.

Ethical marketing is aimed at promoting honesty, fairness and responsibility in advertising based on a set of laid down guidelines to ensure that the right communication is taking place. In practice, it is necessary that Banks use fair practices to compete with each other. Ethical dilemmas arise while providing after – sales service to the customer. During the sales, one may promise some benefits of the product and does not provide any service after the sales. Customer while in need may want to liquidate his fixed deposit, transfer funds with urgency or any other information or service, but the request is not honored by the bank staff. Then, the customer feels very disappointed and may spread negative feedback about the Bank.

If the banker is not able to provide the required service to the customer, he has to explain the customer well in advance what to expect and what not so that customer is clear. Many of the disputes arise due to service charges levied on various banking services.

The idea of free service for some time and then gradually charging for each and every service without clear communication or making aware of the charge to the customer amounts to unethical behaviour. The bank staff should not have an ethical dilemma that if he reveals all the information, customer may not take the service and in a rush to sell the service he should not hide the implicit charges. Establishing mutual goodwill and trust with customers is very important to achieve the business development. In the urge to retain and expand customer base due to increasing competition, the bank staff should not indulge in unfair practices of seeking personal information of the customers from third parties, bribing the customers to open multiple accounts or use banking services like credit cards and personal loans, etc. Educating the customer on products and services will help the bank in improving its customer base. However, ethical dilemma comes in when the bank's staff intentionally force customer to purchase the product or service for achieving their own sales targets associated with financial/non-financial incentives.

7.3 UNETHICAL MARKETING PRACTICES IN INDIA

Unethical marketing practices can be observed in cases of managers having negative personality traits that prompt self-interested manipulation in inter-personal relationships and may lead to unethical behaviour. These persons are also adaptive individuals who tailor their behaviour to the immediate context and feel constrained to manoeuvre selfishly in tightly-structured work environments. Discussing the ethical dilemmas based on person – situation interaction perspective, one can analyse whether managerial ethical leadership buffers the negative influence of negative personality traits of some of the employees' ethical work intention. Principles of ethical marketing refers to having fairness, transparency honesty, accountability and responsibility besides others.

In Indian banking industry, increased competition especially in the past two decades since late – 1990s and high operational costs put pressure on top management to sustain business growth on one hand and profitability on the other. Sometimes, unethical practices are being undertaken by some of the employees and management personnel as well in pursuit of higher incentives.

Are You Doing the Right Thing?

You are working for a prestigious NBFC. You have just been recruited last month through campus placement after doing your MBA. For last two weeks, you have been meeting the prospective clients, successfully marketing the mutual fund products by telling them about the best options available as well as about what suit them. One day, you are called by your boss to discuss your performance. It is unusual in case of a new recruit. After the meeting, it is clear to you that your boss wants that all products should be pushed aggressively notwithstanding the fact what is a safer option for the customer. You are aware that the proper thing to do is to offer a safer option but you don't want to antagonize your boss. You start marketing all products to the customers assuring them that there is low risk and that their money is safe.

Aggressive mis-selling of banking products like interest rate and foreign exchange derivatives, to small and medium enterprises without making them aware of the inherent risks involved, have caused losses not only to the businesses but also to the Bank as most of such loans became non-performing assets. Of late, there have also been ethical concerns with the marketing of credit cards as the quick delinquencies in the segment are on a rise. Like any other financial product, the cards should be made available to the customers with full, accurate, disclosure of relevant information without any guile or subtle manipulation. Following the ethical principle of transparency, the terms regarding late fees, interest rates, service charges etc. should be clearly disclosed in a language and manner that is easily understandable by the card applicants.

Education loans are another example where the loans have been disbursed even when the economic cycles were in downturn and employability of students was

very low as per some recent credible Indian industry association surveys. This has led to a non-performing portfolio of education loans. When placement opportunities are low with stagnant or declining salaries, the burden of education loan becomes huge.

There are instances of mis-selling of third party products by banks often, in Insurance and Mutual Funds products, without proper disclosures and not being empathetic to the customers' needs and requirements. They often resort to pressure selling tactics with hidden commissions and charges being levied.

Another instance of unethical marketing practices relates to the product called Loan Against Property (LAP). Here also, when the real estate price cycle is upward, valuations were astronomical and loans were disbursed. After sometime, when the prices started falling, it led to pile up of huge Non-Performing Assets (NPAs) in this segment.

SME sector also faced similar situation, wherein also huge NPAs were added due to global slowdown and technological disruptions.

7.4 ETHICAL DILEMMAS IN MARKETING

Principles of ethical marketing:

- Give credit where it is due
- Quantify performance and appraisal
- Treat your customers as human
- Own up your mistake
- Employ and empower people with knowledge and skill

Marketing requires thorough understanding of customer need, economic and business cycle, appraisal and due diligence standards. The dilemma arises when a Bank's appraising staff compromises on the process for selfish motives and reject or accept the proposal. It is expected that intentionally the staff should not indulge in any unethical behaviour and follow the laid down process and principles. They should never allow self-interest to morph into greed and selfishness. Sometimes a faulty reward system can induce unethical practices of marketing. It should always be kept into mind that professional duty towards customers is not overshadowed by any kind of perverse incentivization. Competitive pressures are always there in the market but the same should never be allowed to come into any conflict with ethical considerations of marketing. When in dilemma, they should seek opinion of senior management or the compliance and legal officers but not take unilateral decision with manipulative intention.

American Marketing Association (AMA) has prepared a code of ethics to provide guidelines for ethical conduct in marketing. In essence, it says that marketers shall uphold and advance the integrity, honour and dignity of the marketing profession, by being honest in serving the customers, clients, employees, suppliers, distributors and the public. The three ethical principles advocated by AMA are:

1. Do not harm: Consciously avoid harmful actions or omissions
2. Foster trust in marketing system: Strive for transparency and fairness in marketing ecosystem.
3. Embrace ethical values: Embrace core values such as, honesty, responsibility, equity, transparency and citizenship.

We as bankers can take a leaf or two from this AMA code while marketing the banking products. In India also, the Loyola Centre for Business Ethics and Corporate Governance has formulated a written code of ethical marketing practices.

7.5 GROUPING THE MARKET AUDIENCE

When Banks are dealing with many customer segments and using various marketing mix and distribution and delivery channels, it becomes a difficult task to group market audience. However, based on the past experience and also the banks' presence in terms of geography or clusters, it needs to have clear guidelines in terms of how to group audience and conduct a target marketing of their products and services. It can be on the basis of North, South, East and West regions, state-wise segmentation or branch-wise segmentation or it could be based on clusters where it has large chunk of business. However, the segmentation process should be without any bias or discrimination.

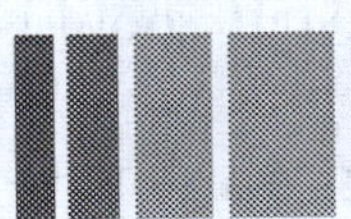

7.6 ETHICS IN ADVERTISING AND PRODUCT PROMOTION

Banks are expected to follow the laid down ethical framework in advertising and promoting their products and services. Ethics in advertising refers to:

- Conveying the information of product or service clearly.

- Information that helps customer's buying decision.
- Advertisement should contain true and honest information of the product or service.
- Advertisement should not be deceptive.
- Advertisement should not exploit emotions.
- Advertisement should respect human values.
- Advertisement should not be irresponsible in its portrayal of women and minorities.
- Advertisement should not create ambiguities in the mind of customers.
- Advertisement should avoid trade puffing and exaggerations.

What Would You Do?

You are marketing head in a bank. You have to choose between three ad campaigns proposed by the shortlisted company. The first (*a*) is a soft sell, honest information campaign. The second (*b*) uses highly emotional appeals and exaggerate the product's benefits. "The third (*c*) involves a noisy, irritating commercial that is sure to gain audience attention. The *ad* company has carried out the Pre-tests which indicate that the campaigns are effective in the following order (*c*), (*b*) and (*a*).

7.7 COMPETING FAIRLY

Competition – Fair or unfair?

In order to compete with close rivals, it may be observed that few banks try all trick measures to get *inside information* on their competitors. It can be in the form of—

a. recruiting key personnel from the competitor so as to get inside information of products, services and technology about the competitor besides acquiring talent.

b. calling to the competitor under the guise of a new customer and seeking information about products or services.

Competition needs to be based on fair play and based on products and services each one can offer. The core strengths of the bank become its differentiating factor and attracts customers/clients and retains them in the long-run. Fair procedures and practices and level of service delivery commitment are the key factors that attract customers. Unfair or unethical practices may give temporary benefits but are prone to have negative consequences in the long-term.

Here, it is useful to understand the difference between the terms 'ethical practice' and 'unethical practice'. Most of the people think of these terms as being opposite but conceptually these are two different constructs. An 'unethical practice' is which in a marketing exchange alters the entitlement of either the buyer or the seller in such a way that is at the expense of the other. For instance, few banks market the loan at a slightly lesser rate of interest to attract the business but make up for the loss through other charges such as administrative charges or higher processing charges. This is an unethical marketing practice as it offers a pseudo benefit to the customer and violates the good faith under which the transaction has taken place. Any action of the bankers that in some sense takes advantage of the customers' good faith should be considered as unethical. As compared to the term 'unethical practice' the concept of 'ethical practice' is much wider in meaning. In this connection, we can consider the case of the pharma company, discussed in the earlier units of this courseware, which could have chosen not to manufacture and distribute Mectizan medicine free of cost to alleviate the sufferings of millions of poor people. In that case, the company would not have committed any unethical practice but by distributing the medicine free for the disease of river blindness, the company has adopted a highly 'ethical practice' and demonstrated a strong sense of social responsibility.

7.8 NORMATIVE MARKETING ETHICS

Organization culture plays an important role in building ethical capacity and ethical thinking in marketing. On one hand, the active engagement of top leadership is crucial for fostering an organization culture that values ethics, on the other ethics must become a part of the marketing planning process since the first stage. For example, one way for ethical marketing can be to instil reasonable ethical values and develop moral standards in the culture of the organization is by using the culturally established values of an average family as a guide in determining what its reaction to society ought to be. That is to say, a marketer must make and market only those products he/she would feel comfortable and

safe when his/her own family uses them. Ethics in marketing can be improved if one could deliberate on what virtues are. For example, thinking how the customers are being affected by each product is a good start.

Marketers should not market products that retard character or virtue development. Consider the TV ad of Parle G biscuits that shows a young boy from the spectators signaling to a chess player a move that the player interprets as the winning one, but which results in a loss. The subsequent scene shows the player spying the young boy shaking hands with the opponent player and obviously is left feeling cheated. The caption shows the boy to be a genius. Ethical slips made by the brand are obvious: it shows deception and cunning as the measures of genius. Ethical capacity is fostered when one has a caring orientation, a desire to be responsive to the interests of those likely to be affected. For instance, a marketer has an obligation to consider whether a consumer can take an informed choice; this means understanding whether the consumer has such capability, information, and choice. Marketers must promote consumers interests even without a market pressure to do so. Marketing children and underprivileged rural sections of the society has to be carefully done.

The norms indicated above are not exhaustive at all. However, they set the stage to discuss marketing a broader context. We shall hereinafter examine this subject in detail.

7.9 RBI'S FAIR PRACTICES CODE

RBI issued Fair Practices Code for Lenders on May 5th 2003, which was made applicable to all scheduled commercial banks and financial institutions excluding RRBs and LABs. Brief of the applicable guidelines include:

- Application of loans for their processing with all details of fee charges and conditions.
- Banks/financial institutions should give receipt of loan application.
- Bank/financial institutions should process the loan application within a reasonable period.
- Loan disbursement process.
- Monitoring process and recovery mechanism and clauses.

Detailed circular is given as annexure in the end of this chapter.

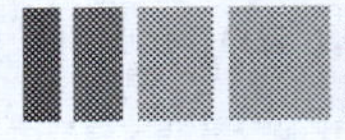

7.10 LET US SUM UP

Technological innovations have changed the method of marketing of banking and financial products and services. In addition, banks also make use of channels like Business Correspondent to reach out to customers in non-banked areas. Banks currently deploy multiple modes of marketing including face-to-face dialogue with the customers, electronic/social media and BC channels. Ethical marketing through these channels aim at promoting honesty, fairness and responsibility based on a set of laid down guidelines to ensure that the right communication takes place. Unethical marketing practices such as mis-selling, etc. and eliciting inside information on competitors through various unethical means are also observed.

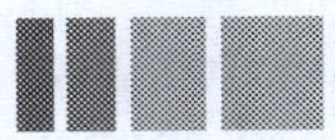

7.11 KEY WORDS

Ethical dilemmas in marketing, Aggressive mis-selling, Correct marketing mix, Direct Marketing Agents (DMA), American Marketing Association (AMA), Fair Practices Code, Ethical Practice, Unethical Practice, Normative Marketing.

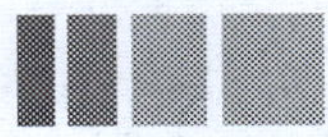

7.12 CHECK YOUR PROGRESS

1. In Indian context, marketing of banking products and services does not include:
   (*a*) Direct selling
   (*b*) Social media
   (*c*) Selling through franchise
   (*d*) Print media
2. Which is the unethical practice in marketing of bank products or services?
   (*a*) Aggressive selling with discounts to select customers
   (*b*) Selling products without explaining underlying risks
   (*c*) Not understanding customer's current or potential need
   (*d*) All of the above

3. Marketing mix should include:
   (*a*) Assess the geography of reach of marketing campaign
   (*b*) Combination of print and social media
   (*c*) Creating awareness in local languages
   (*d*) All of the above
4. Ethical dilemmas in marketing occurs when:
   (*a*) Understand the economic and business cycles
   (*b*) Prepare projections of customer data on sales, revenues expense
   (*c*) Following due diligence properly
   (*d*) Reject or approve proposals with selfish motive
5. As part of the Fair Practices Code for the Lenders, in the case of small borrowers seeking loans up to Rs. 2 lakhs, the lenders:
   (*a*) Should convey in writing, the main reason/reasons which, in the opinion of the bank after due consideration, have led to rejection of the loan applications within stipulated time.
   (*b*) Need not convey anything in writing for rejection.
   (*c*) May, at their own discretion, convey orally the reason for rejection.
   (*d*) May give reason/reasons for rejection of the loan applications irrespective of application date at the end of the financial year.

ANSWERS

1. (*c*)	2. (*d*)	3. (*d*)	4. (*d*)	5. (*a*)

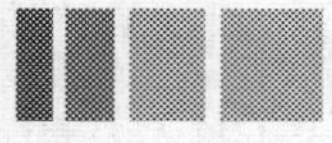

7.13 EXERCISE YOUR ETHICS MUSCLE

Case 15: Selling or Mis-selling

Ram and Shyam have worked in a public sector bank for 10 years. They are in the retail banking operations. When bank started focussing on cross-selling, both were involved in advising and selling insurance products to customers alongside mortgages and personal loans. There were incentives attached with the cross-selling budgets. So, they were very aggressive in their approach in selling such products. Today they are at a senior level and hold very different views about their all-out cross selling efforts in the earlier years. Ram has come across many customers lodging complaints against mis-selling of insurance policies. He now feels that it was wrong to sell such policies aggressively to all customers knowing well that the same offered little benefit to them. He is of the view that it was really unprofessional on his part to engage in selling the policies.

Shyam does not agree with Ram. He says that all the product features along with the product-deficiencies were explained to all customers who purchased the policies. For example, many customers cancelled their policies soon after few months when they realized the limitations of the cover. Shyam further says that the insurance policies served a genuine purpose for salary class customers by providing them cover against sickness, accident etc. Shyam is of the view that it was his professional duty to help achieve the bank's business goals.

Issues to reflect:

(*a*) Do you think that it is ethical for banks to market cross-selling products to all customers irrespective of their needs?

(*b*) Do you agree with Shyam or Ram and why?

(*c*) Should the insurance products not be sold to the appropriate persons as well?

(*d*) Mis-selling is an issue of personal ethics or the organizational ethics?

Case 16: Good Intentions Paved with Ruse

You are working as a branch manager of an agriculture branch. The branch has been provided with a jeep for visiting the villages of its catchment area for marketing and inspection purposes. The brakes of the jeep are defective and that is the reason you are selling this jeep and buying a new one for the branch. A person comes, inspects the vehicle and buys the it but you don't inform him that there is problem with the brakes. You think you are managing a better price for the bank by not sharing this information.

Issues to reflect

(*a*) What are the ethical considerations here?

(*b*) Is it appropriate on the part of the branch manager to not disclose the problem with the brakes?

(*c*) Who will be responsible if some accident takes place and the buyer along with few pedestrians are injured?

(*d*) What is your view about the personal ethics of the branch manager?

Enjoy the Blog – Transparency Fosters Trust

You wonder sometimes. What goes behind a seemingly normal song you keep humming. Well, after much thought what I could figure out was transparency. You pour your heart, your feelings. You burn midnight oil. And then there are those few lines, hummed by all. But only truly realised and appreciated by you. Now, connecting the dotted lines. I was conducting a P-Review. The summary of the Region left me red faced. Advances down by close to 25 cr. The culprit. One of my SME intensive branches. Seemed they lost a big account. The whole region impacted. So, the class will begin with Vaskar. CM of that branch. Controlling my raging emotions. As polite could be, asked him "What happened?"

"Sir, it was a good account. When booked few years ago, there were many concessions extended. Continued. In all the renewals. However, looking to the market, other banks' pricings. Our own concerns of the NIMs. Stress on optimum profitability for each cent deployed in credit. I felt that a call needed to be taken to rationalize the pricing. I met the customer. Shared my views. And advised that this renewal, there will be some hike in the pricing. He threatened to shift the account. For me, the easy option would have been to refer the whole matter to you. But I took a call, what I felt, in the best interests of the Bank, in line with market. Told him, openly and clearly that a Fully transparent Business is not a one-way street. We are always there to serve you. But you should also understand our genuine concerns.

Anyways, he got in touch with some other banks. The account was taken over by one of them. We have lost a business in short run. Trust me. Will try to compensate with another." There was an eerie silence. I was looking at Vaskar. Rest of my BMs were looking at me. Vaskar was looking at his file.

Well, had to look on the performances of other branches as well. Skipped to next branch. And next. Then looked at the watch.1.30 pm. Time for lunch. As Napoleon had said, an army cannot march on empty stomachs, we all dispersed. Assembled again in 45 minutes.

It was around 5.30 pm. Last branch. By 6.00 pm was done with that also. Before my closing comments to all. A round of tea. I requested a cup of coffee for me.

Took a sip. Closed my eyes. A long and tiring day. Opened my eyes. Well, my position looked changed. Trying to figure out my orientations, found, I was on Vaskar's seat. Where I was supposed to be seated, was my friend Aristotle, the famous philosopher. Smiling. He also took a sip. Seemed he had time travelled.

I looked around. There was no one. Only me and Aristotle. He said "As a RM, I understand your business concerns. I came here before your closing comments. Because, I sensed, for sake of business you might utter something that might compromise the value of second word of STEPS. Transparency. I have told you time and again. Living our values is not a one-time affair. These are sustained efforts. They enrich you, your family, your organisation and the communities you live in. And again, as told to you earlier, values are all encompassing. They do not differentiate between your personal and professional life. My advice. Don't be harsh on Vaskar. There is always a new day dawning. Brimming with opportunities." I looked down, Vaskar's folder. Next moment, orientations had changed. Aristotle had disappeared. I was where I was supposed to be seated. My team, waiting to hear me. With a pep talk. Closed the meeting.

Few days passed. Got a call. Vaskar. "Yes. What more have you lost now." I commented sarcastically. "No Sir. It's a piece of good news. The account we lost is back with us. And with it 2 more big value accounts, referred by the same customer."

"How come? "I enquired. "Sir, my being transparent was the initial reason for the customer to fish elsewhere. Seemed, he got lot of promises, but eventually realised that the platter was way empty on delivery. He was taken aback. He then realised. He had left a transparent eco-system of branch banking. However, he chose to come back. Bearing repeat processing charges, documentation fees etc. And the bonus Sir, during his discussions with his fellow businessman friends, banking elsewhere, he narrated the entire thing. So, Sir. The loss is made up. Two new takeovers in pipeline. Hopefully by next P-Review, the region will see a spurt of Rs. 40 cr in advances." Speech less, I congratulated Vaskar. Recalled Aristotle's advice. Buzzed for a cup of coffee. Was feeling much relaxed. So, started to hum one of my favourites. Heard a chorus. Startled, saw Aristotle, gripping his cup, also humming. So apart from coffee, he too had developed a taste for Kishore Da.

[*Source:* Courtesy: SBI….this blog was written by the then Chief Ethics Officer under the Blog series_ Coffee With Aristotle]

8 UNIT

Ethical Dimensions: Employees

8 UNIT

Ethical Dimensions: Employees

8.1 LEARNING OBJECTIVES

The objective of this section is to elucidate ethics relating to employees, Bank's obligations to third party vendors, misuse of official power, discrimination based on religion, race or gender, sexual harassment, issues relating to conflict of interest, accounting practices and role of employees in implementing the ethical principles.

To recap the concept of ethics in banking, there are two dimensions of ethics-internal and external. Internal ethics relates to honesty and integrity, transparency, corporate governance and well-being of employees. External ethics refers to cooperation with society, environmental – friendly practices, commitment to customers and fair and equitable treatment of customers.

Ethical dimensions of employees encompass person-situation interactions, unethical tendencies of employees for selfish motives, and role of managerial ethical leadership. Profit at any cost - a capitalist tendency-leads to selfish behaviour of adopting any means for short term gains. In an attempt to accomplish performance and get incentives based on traditional key performance indicators (KPIs) could be the root cause of the unethical behaviour of some of the employees both at top or bottom of the pyramid. The quantitative targets attached to the KPIs make employees just focus on the targets regardless of whether means used are ethical or unethical.

8.2 OBLIGATION TO BANK: OBLIGATIONS OF BANK

- Obligation to Honour Cheques: Provided all necessary conditions are met like sufficient balance in one's account, all necessary information filled, properly drawn, no legal sanction on bank otherwise to pay to/draw money from an account, etc., all banks are under statutory obligation to honour all bona fide cheques.

- Obligation to maintain secrecy: No bank should disclose details of account of the customer maintained with the bank to any third party. There are however exceptions to this, namely when the courts ask banks in their trials against the account holder in some legal issue or any enforcement agencies like the CBI or ACB for example request formally for a particular bribery, corruption, disproportionate assets case or any other matter, the banks may have to comply with such disclosures.
- Obligation to follow all financial instructions of customers: All banks are under obligation to honour the instructions issued by their customers such as payment of electricity bills, gas bills, payment of property tax, payments to a hotel booking or railway or air ticket purchases, etc.
- Obligation to honour vendors' claims if otherwise in order banks cannot pick and choose vendors to whom they honour and cannot refuse to any other bona fide vendor-domestic or foreign, including banks.
- Obligation to keep records in order: All banks at any point in time must be obliged to maintain fully updated records of customers, despite any amount of seasonal work-related pressures.
- Obligation to give notice before closing the Account: For any valid reason, a bank requires to close the account of a customer, it cannot do so unilaterally without consulting the account holder. Bank must give a reasonable notice to the customer and specify by tick-marking some of the standard or routine reason or give description if the reason is very specific to a customer.
- Besides the obligations towards the banks' customers, they also have got the obligation to follow all the laws, guidelines, directives and policies of the regulator - RBI.

Rights of a Bank

For fulfilling the obligations towards the customers, bankers enjoy the following rights:

- Right of General Lien: A general lien authorizes a bank to retain goods and securities till all the bank's claims against the customers are satisfied. A lien is an implied pledge such that if a default is made by the debtor, the bank, by giving a reasonable notice to the borrower, can sell and recover

the amount due to it. No other valuables, cash, etc. kept in lockers or fixed deposits etc. should be set off against the claim.

- Right to charge interest and commission: Bank has implied right to charge interest on loans and advances and commission on services rendered to the customer. Any upward revision in the variable interest rate-based loans for example housing loan, need not require prior consent of the borrower. The revised interest is charged and intimated to the customer by the bank.
- Closure of Account: The Bank has the right to close a customer's account if it is inoperative for the specified duration, provided it informs in writing to the customer to respond within a stipulated time. If the customer does not respond, the bank may close the account.

8.3 OBLIGATIONS TO THIRD PARTIES: FIDUCIARY RESPONSIBILITIES

When the bank is outsourcing any of its permitted functions to the third parties, it needs to have clear, transparent contracts and agreements with all terms & conditions incorporated. Especially in service contracts, the service level agreements (SLAs) have to be defined minutely and ensure that the third party do not cause an inconvenience to the bank customer.

(*a*) Obligations under the KYC for Regulated Entities:

As per the Master Direction issued by RBI on February 25, 2016 (which was updated as on April 20, 2018), known as the Reserve Bank of India (Know Your Customer (KYC)) Directions, 2016, the following are the directives issued for the Regulated Entities (REs refer to Banks, Asset Management Companies, Investment Managers/Advisors, Portfolio Managers, etc.):

For the purpose of verifying the identity of customers at the time of commencement of an account-based relationship, REs, shall at their option, rely on customer due diligence done by a third party, subject to the following conditions:

(*a*) Records or the information of the customer due diligence carried out by the third party is obtained within two days from the third party or from the Central KYC Records Registry.

(*b*) Adequate steps are taken by REs to satisfy themselves that copies of identification data and other relevant documentation relating to the customer due diligence requirements shall be made available from the third party upon request without delay.

(*c*) The third party is regulated, supervised or monitored for, and has measures in place for compliance with customer due diligence and record-keeping requirements in line with the requirements and obligations under the Prevention of Money Laundering (PML) Act.

(*d*) The third party shall not be based in a country or jurisdiction assessed as high risk.

(*e*) The ultimate responsibility for customer due diligence and undertaking enhanced due diligence measures, as applicable, will be with the RE.

These Directions further require that REs shall frame Customer Acceptance Policy. REs shall ensure that:

(*a*) No account is opened in anonymous or fictitious/benami name.

(*b*) No account is opened where the RE is unable to apply appropriate Customers Due Diligence (CDD) measures, either due to non-cooperation of the customer or non-reliability of the documents/information furnished by the customer.

(*c*) No transaction or account-based relationship is undertaken without following the CDD procedure.

(*d*) The mandatory information to be sought for KYC purpose while opening an account and during the periodic updation, is specified.

(*e*) 'Optional'/additional information, is obtained with the explicit consent of the customer after the account is opened.

(*f*) REs shall apply the CDD procedure at the Unique Customer Identification Code (UCIC) level. Thus, if an existing KYC compliant customer of a RE desires to open another account with the same RE, there shall be no need for a fresh CDD exercise.

(*g*) CDD Procedure is followed for all the joint account holders, while opening a joint account.

(*h*) Circumstances in which, a customer is permitted to act on behalf of another person/entity, is clearly spelt out.

(*i*) Suitable system is put in place to ensure that the identity of the customer does not match with any person or entity, whose name appears in the sanctions lists circulated by Reserve Bank of India.

The RBI Master Direction makes it very clear to the REs that Customer Acceptance Policy shall not result in denial of banking/financial facility to members of the general public, especially those, who are financially or socially disadvantaged.

(*b*) Obligations While Outsourcing Various Services:

Banks or other REs have been extensively leveraging Information Technology (IT) and IT enabled Services (ITeS) to support their business models, products and services offered to their customers. They also outsource substantial portion of their IT activities to third parties, which expose them to various risks. In order to ensure effective management of attendant risks, RBI has issued suitable regulatory guidelines on Outsourcing of IT Services on 10th April, 2023 through a Master Direction on Outsourcing of Information Technology Services.

Role of the Regulated Entity: Regulatory and Supervisory Requirements

(*a*) Outsourcing of any activity shall not diminish the regulated entity's (RE's) obligations as also of its Board and Senior Management, who shall be ultimately responsible for the outsourced activity. RE shall take steps to ensure that the service provider employs the same high standard of care in performing the services as would have been employed by the RE, if the same activity was not outsourced. REs shall not engage an IT service provider that would result in reputation of RE being compromised or weakened.

(*b*) Notwithstanding whether the service provider is located in India or abroad, the REs shall ensure that the outsourcing should neither impede nor interfere with the ability of the RE to effectively oversee and manage its activities. Further, the RE shall ensure that the outsourcing does not impede the RBI in carrying out its supervisory functions and objectives.

(*c*) REs shall ensure that the service provider, if not a group company, shall not be owned or controlled by any director, or key managerial personnel, or approver of the outsourcing arrangement of the RE, or their relatives. The terms 'control', 'director', 'key managerial personnel' and 'relative' have the same meaning as assigned under the Companies Act, 2013 and the Rules 6 framed thereunder from time to time. However, an exception to this requirement may be made with the approval of Board/Board level Committee, followed by appropriate disclosure, oversight and monitoring of such arrangements. The Board shall *inter-alia* ensure that there is no conflict of interest arising out of third-party engagements.

(*d*) Additional requirements pertaining to usage of cloud computing services and outsourcing of Security Operations Center (SOC) services are outlined in Appendix I and Appendix II, to the Master Direction.

Comprehensive Assessment of Need for Outsourcing and Attendant Risks:

REs shall evaluate the need for Outsourcing of IT Services based on comprehensive assessment of attendant benefits, risks and availability of commensurate processes to manage those risks. REs shall *inter-alia* consider: (*a*) determining the need for outsourcing based on criticality of activity to be outsourced; (*b*) determining expectations and outcome from outsourcing; (*c*) determining success factors and cost-benefit analysis; and (*d*) deciding the model for outsourcing.

Compliance with all Applicable Statutory and Regulatory Requirements

The RE shall consider all relevant laws, regulations, rules, guidelines and conditions of approval, licensing or registration, when performing its due diligence in relation to outsourcing of IT services.

Grievance Redressal Mechanism

(*a*) REs shall have a robust grievance redressal mechanism that shall not be compromised in any manner on account of outsourcing, *i.e.*, responsibility for redressal of customers' grievances related to outsourced services shall rest with the RE.

(*b*) Outsourcing arrangements shall not affect the rights of a customer against the RE, including the ability of the customer to obtain redressal as applicable under relevant laws.

Inventory of Outsourced Services

REs shall create an inventory of services provided by the service providers (including key entities involved in their supply chains). Further, REs shall map their dependency on third parties and periodically evaluate the information received from the service providers.

Governance Framework

An RE intending to outsource any of its IT activities shall put in place a comprehensive Board approved IT outsourcing policy. The policy shall incorporate, *inter alia*, the roles and responsibilities of the Board, Committees of the Board (if any) and Senior Management, IT function, business function as well as oversight and assurance functions in respect of outsourcing of IT services. It shall further cover the criteria for selection of such activities as well as service providers, parameters for defining material outsourcing based on the broad criteria, delegation of authority depending on risk and materiality, disaster recovery and business continuity plans, systems to monitor and review the operations of these activities and termination processes and exit strategies, including business continuity in the event of a third-party service provider exiting the outsourcing arrangement.

Role of the Board

The Board of the RE shall be responsible, *inter alia*, for:

(*a*) putting in place a framework for approval of IT outsourcing activities depending on risks and materiality.

(*b*) approving policies to evaluate the risks and materiality of all existing and prospective IT outsourcing arrangements.

(*c*) setting up suitable administrative framework of Senior Management for the purpose of these directions.

Role of the Senior Management

The Senior Management of the RE shall, *inter alia*, be responsible for:

(*a*) formulating IT outsourcing policies and procedures, evaluating the risks and materiality of all existing and prospective IT outsourcing arrangements based on the framework commensurate with the complexity, nature and scope, in line with the enterprise-wide risk management of the organisation approved by the Board and its implementation.

(*b*) prior evaluation of prospective IT outsourcing arrangements and periodic evaluation of the existing outsourcing arrangements covering the performance review, criticality and associated risks of all such arrangements based on the policy approved by the Board.

(*c*) identifying IT outsourcing risks as they arise, monitoring, mitigating, managing and reporting of such risks to the Board/Board Committee in a timely manner.

(*d*) ensuring that suitable business continuity plans based on realistic and probable disruptive scenarios, including exit of any third-party service provider, are in place and tested periodically.

(*e*) ensuring (*i*) effective oversight over third party for data confidentiality and (*ii*) appropriate redressal of customer grievances in a timely manner.

(*f*) ensuring an independent review and audit on a periodic basis for compliance with the legislations, regulations, Board-approved policy and performance standards and reporting the same to Board/Board Committee.

(*g*) creating essential capacity with required skillsets within the organisation for proper oversight of outsourced activities.

Role of IT Function

The responsibilities of the IT Function of the RE shall, *inter alia*, include:

(*a*) assisting the Senior Management in identifying, measuring, monitoring, mitigating and managing the level of IT outsourcing risk in the organization;

(*b*) ensuring that a central database of all IT outsourcing arrangements is maintained and is accessible for review by Board, Senior Management, Auditors and Supervisors;

(*c*) effectively monitor and supervise the outsourced activity to ensure that the service providers meet the laid down performance standards and provide uninterrupted services, report to the Senior Management; co-ordinate periodic due diligence and highlight concerns, if any and

(*d*) putting in place necessary documentation required for contractual agreements including service level management, monitoring of vendor operations, key risk indicators and classifying the vendors as per the determined risk.

Evaluation and Engagement of Service Providers

Due Diligence on Service Providers

(*a*) In considering or renewing an outsourcing of IT Services arrangements.

Risk Management Framework

(*a*) REs shall put in place a Risk Management framework for outsourcing of IT Services that shall comprehensively deal with the processes and responsibilities for identification, measurement, mitigation, management, and reporting of risks associated with outsourcing of IT Services arrangements.

(*b*) The risk assessments carried out by the REs shall be suitably documented with necessary approvals in line with the roles and responsibilities for the Board of Directors, Senior Management and IT Function. Such risk assessments shall be subject to internal and external quality assurance on a periodic basis as determined by the Board-approved policy.

(*c*) REs shall be responsible for the confidentiality and integrity of data and information pertaining to the customers that is available to the service provider.

(*d*) Access to data at RE's location/data center by service providers shall be on need-to-know basis, with appropriate controls to prevent security breaches and/or data misuse.

(*e*) Public confidence and customer trust in REs is a prerequisite for their stability and reputation. Hence, REs shall seek to ensure the preservation and protection of the security and confidentiality of customer information in the custody or possession of the service provider. Access to customer information by staff of the service provider shall be on need-to-know basis.

(*f*) In the event of multiple service provider relationships where two or more service providers collaborate to deliver an end-to-end solution, the RE remains responsible for understanding and monitoring the control environment of all service providers that have access to the RE's data, systems, records or resources.

(*g*) In instances where service provider acts as an outsourcing agent for multiple REs, care shall be taken to build adequate safeguards so that there is no combining of information, documents, records and assets.

(*h*) The RE shall ensure that cyber incidents are reported to the RE by the service provider without undue delay, so that the incident is reported by the RE to the RBI within 6 hours of detection by the TPSP.

(*i*) The REs shall review and monitor the control processes and security practices of the service provider to disclose security breaches. The REs shall immediately notify RBI in the event of breach of security and leakage of confidential customer related information. In these eventualities, REs shall adhere to the extant instructions issued by RBI from time to time on Incident Response and Recovery Management.

(*j*) Concentration Risk: REs shall effectively assess the impact of concentration risk posed by multiple outsourcings to the same service provider and/or the concentration risk posed by outsourcing critical or material functions to a limited number of service providers.

Business Continuity Plan and Disaster Recovery Plan

(*a*) REs shall require their service providers to develop and establish a robust framework for documenting, maintaining and testing Business Continuity Plan (BCP) and Disaster Recovery Plan (DRP) commensurate with the nature and scope of the outsourced activity as per extant instructions issued by RBI from time to time on BCP/DR requirements.

(*b*) In establishing a viable contingency plan, REs shall consider the availability of alternative service providers or the possibility of bringing the outsourced activity back in-house in an emergency and the costs, time and resources that would be involved. 5 As regards combining of data, it would suffice to comply with the following: A clear separation and isolation of data (RE and its customer specific data and information) to ensure that only the personnel as authorized by the RE is able to access data that belongs to them in a multitenant environment/architecture.

(*c*) In order to mitigate the risk of unexpected termination of the outsourcing agreement or insolvency/liquidation of the service provider, REs shall retain an appropriate level of control over their IT-outsourcing arrangement along with right to intervene, with appropriate measures to continue its business operations.

(*d*) REs shall ensure that service providers are able to isolate the REs' information, documents and records and other assets. This is to ensure that, in adverse conditions or termination of the contract, all documents, record of transactions and information with the service provider and assets of the

RE can be removed from the possession of the service provider or deleted, destroyed or rendered unusable.

Monitoring and Control of Outsourced Activities

(*a*) REs shall have in place a management structure to monitor and control its outsourced IT activities. This shall include (as applicable to the scope of Outsourcing of IT Services) but not limited to monitoring the performance, uptime of the systems and resources, service availability, adherence to SLA requirements, incident response mechanism, etc.

(*b*) RE shall conduct regular audits (as applicable to the scope of Outsourcing of IT Services) of service providers (including sub-contractors) with regard to the activity outsourced by it. Such audits may be conducted either by RE's internal auditors or external auditors appointed to act on RE's behalf.

(*c*) While outsourcing various IT services, more than one RE may be availing services from the same third-party service provider. In such scenarios, in lieu of conducting separate audits by individual REs of the common service provider, they may adopt pooled (shared) audit. This allows the relevant REs to either pool their audit resources or engage an independent third-party auditor to jointly audit a common service provider. However, in doing so, it shall be the responsibility of REs in ensuring that the audit requirements related to their respective contract with the service provider are met effectively.

(*d*) The audits shall assess the performance of the service provider, adequacy of the risk management practices adopted by the service provider, compliance with laws and regulations, etc. The frequency of the audit shall be determined based on the nature and extent of risk and impact to the RE from the outsourcing arrangements. Reports on the monitoring and control activities shall be reviewed periodically by the Senior Management and in case of any adverse development, the same shall be put up to the Board for information.

(*e*) REs, depending upon the risk assessment, may also rely upon globally recognized third-party certifications made available by the service provider in lieu of conducting independent audits. However, this shall not absolve REs of their responsibility in ensuring assurance on the controls and procedures required to safeguard data security (including availability of systems) at the service provider's end.

(*f*) The RE shall periodically review the financial and operational condition of the service provider to assess its ability to continue to meet its Outsourcing of IT Services obligations. RE shall adopt risk-based approach in defining the periodicity. Such due diligence reviews shall highlight any deterioration or breach in performance standards, confidentiality, and security, and in operational resilience preparedness.

(*g*) In the event of termination of the outsourcing agreement for any reason in cases where the service provider deals with the customers of the RE, the same shall be given due publicity by the RE so as to ensure that the customers stop dealing with the concerned service provider.

(*h*) REs shall ensure that the service provider grants unrestricted and effective access to:

(*i*) data related to the outsourced activities.

(*ii*) the relevant business premises of the service provider; subject to appropriate security protocols, for the purpose of effective oversight use by the REs, their auditors, regulators and other relevant Competent Authorities, as authorized under law.

[The detailed master direction RBI/2023-24/102 DoS.CO.CSITEG/SEC.1/31.01.015/2023-24 dated April 10, 2023, from which we have mentioned few important aspects above, can be accessed at the RBI's website.]

General Guidelines on Managing Risks and Code of Conduct in Outsourcing of Financial Services by banks

The world over, banks are increasingly using outsourcing as a means of both reducing cost and accessing specialist expertise, not available internally and achieving strategic aims. 'Outsourcing' may be defined as a bank's use of a third party (either an affiliated entity within a corporate group or an entity that is external to the corporate group) to perform activities on a continuing basis that would normally be undertaken by the bank itself, now or in the future.' 'Continuing basis' would include agreements for a limited period. In keeping with this international trend, it is observed, that banks in India too have been extensively outsourcing various activities. Needless to say, such outsourcing, results in banks being exposed to various risks as detailed in para hereafter. Further, the outsourcing activities are to be brought within regulatory purview and the interests of the customers have to be protected.

Typically outsourced financial services include applications processing (loan origination, credit card), document processing, marketing and research, supervision of loans, data processing and back office related activities etc.

Outsourcing brings in its wake, several risks. Some key risks in outsourcing may be Strategic Risk, Reputation Risk, Compliance Risk, Operational Risk, Legal Risk, Exit Strategy, Risk, Counter party Risk, Country Risk, Contractual Risk, Access Risk, Concentration and Systemic Risk. The failure of a service provider in providing a specified service, a breach in security/confidentiality, or non-compliance with legal and regulatory requirements by either the service provider or the outsourcing bank can lead to financial losses or loss of reputation for the bank and could also lead to systemic risks within the entire banking system in the country. It would therefore be imperative for the bank outsourcing its activities to ensure effective management of these risks. The guidelines are applicable to outsourcing arrangements entered into by a bank with a service provider located in India or elsewhere. The service provider may either be a member of the group/conglomerate to which the bank belongs, or an unrelated party. The underlying principles behind these guidelines are that the regulated entity should ensure that outsourcing arrangements neither diminish its ability to fulfil its obligations to customers and RBI nor impede effective supervision by RBI. Banks, therefore, have to take steps to ensure that the service provider employs the same high standard of care in performing the services as would be employed by the banks, if the activities were conducted within the banks and not outsourced. Accordingly, banks should not engage in outsourcing that would result in their internal control, business conduct or reputation being compromised or weakened.

Banks which desire to outsource financial services would not require prior approval from RBI whether the service provider is located in India or outside India. In regard to outsourced services relating to credit cards, RBI's detailed instructions contained in its circular on credit card activities vide DBOD. FSD. BC. 49/24.01.011/2005-06 dated 21st November 2005 would be applicable.

Activities that should not be Outsourced

Banks which choose to outsource financial services should however not outsource core management functions including Internal Audit, Compliance function and decision-making functions like determining compliance with KYC norms for opening deposit accounts, according sanction for loans (including retail loans) and management of investment portfolio.

Material Outsourcing

During annual financial inspections, RBI will review the implementation of these guidelines to assess the quality of related risk management systems particularly in respect of material outsourcing. Material outsourcing arrangements are those, which if disrupted, have the potential to significantly impact the business operations, reputation or profitability. Materiality of outsourcing would be based on:

- The level of importance to the bank of the activity being outsourced.
- The potential impact of the outsourcing on the bank on various parameters such as earnings, solvency, liquidity, funding capital and risk profile.
- The likely impact on the bank's reputation and brand value, and ability to achieve its business objectives, strategy and plans, should the service provider fail to perform the service.
- The cost of the outsourcing as a proportion of total operating costs of the bank.

The aggregate exposure to that particular service provider, in cases where the bank out sources various functions to the same service provider.

Bank's role and Regulatory and Supervisory requirements:

The outsourcing of any activity by bank does not diminish its obligations, and those of its Board and senior management, who have the ultimate responsibility for the outsourced activity. Banks would therefore be responsible for the actions of their service provider including Direct Sales Agents/Direct Marketing Agents and recovery agents and the confidentiality of information pertaining to the customers that is available with the service provider. Banks should retain ultimate control of the outsourced activity. It is imperative for the bank, when performing its due diligence in relation to outsourcing, to consider all relevant laws, regulations, guidelines and conditions of approval, licensing or registration.

Outsourcing arrangements should not affect the rights of a customer against the bank, including the ability of the customer to obtain redress as applicable under relevant laws. Since the customers are required to deal with the service providers in the process of dealing with the bank, banks should incorporate a clause in the product literature/brochures etc., stating that they may use the

services of agents in sales/marketing etc. of the products. The role of agents may be indicated in broad terms.

Outsourcing, whether the service provider is located in India or abroad should not impede or interfere with the ability of the bank to effectively oversee and manage its activities nor should it impede the Reserve Bank of India in carrying out its supervisory functions and objectives.

Banks need to have a robust grievance redressal mechanism, which in no way should be compromised on account of outsourcing.

The service provider if it is not a subsidiary of the bank should not be owned or controlled by any director or officer/employee of the bank or their relatives having the same meaning as assigned under Section 6 of the Companies Act, 1956.

Risk Management practices for outsourced Financial Services

Outsourcing Policy

A bank intending to outsource any of its financial activities should put in place a comprehensive outsourcing policy, approved by its board, which incorporates, *inter alia*, criteria for selection of such activities as well as service providers, parameters for defining material outsourcing based on the broad criteria indicated in para 3, delegation of authority depending on risks and materiality and systems to monitor and review the operations of these activities.

Role of the Board and Senior Management

The board of the bank, or a committee of the board to which powers have been delegated should be responsible *inter alia* for:

- Approving a framework to evaluate the risks and materiality of all existing and prospective outsourcing and the policies that apply to such arrangements.
- Laying down appropriate approval authorities for outsourcing depending on risks and materiality.
- Undertaking regular review of outsourcing strategies and arrangements for their continued relevance and safety and soundness.
- Deciding on business activities of a material nature to be outsourced and approving such arrangements.

Senior Management would be responsible for:

- Evaluating the risks and materiality of all existing and prospective outsourcing, based on the framework approved by the Board.
- Developing and implementing sound and prudent outsourcing policies and procedures commensurate with the nature, scope and complexity of the outsourcing.
- Reviewing periodically the effectiveness of policies and procedures.
- Communicating information pertaining to material outsourcing risks to the Board in a timely manner.
- Ensuring that contingency plans, based on realistic and probable disruptive scenarios, are in place and tested.
- Ensuring that there is independent review and audit for compliance with set policies.
- Undertaking periodic review of outsourcing arrangements to identify new material outsourcing risks as they arise.

Evaluation of the Risks

The key risks in outsourcing that need to be evaluated by the banks are:

(*a*) Strategic Risk – The service provider may conduct business on its own behalf, which is inconsistent with the overall strategic goals of the bank.

(*b*) Reputation Risk – Poor service from the service provider, its customer interaction not being consistent with the overall standards of the bank.

(*c*) Compliance Risk – Privacy, consumer and prudential laws not adequately complied with.

(*d*) Operational Risk – Arising due to technology failure, fraud, error, inadequate financial capacity to fulfil obligations and/or provide remedies.

(*e*) Legal Risk – Includes but is not limited to exposure to fines, penalties, or punitive damages resulting from supervisory actions, as well as private settlements due to omissions and commissions of the service provider.

(*f*) Exit Strategy Risk – This could arise from over-reliance on one firm, the loss of relevant skills in the bank itself preventing it from bringing the activity back in-house and contracts entered into wherein speedy exits would be prohibitively expensive.

(*g*) Counter party Risk – Due to inappropriate underwriting or credit assessments.

(*h*) Country Risk – Due to the political, social or legal climate creating added risk.

(*i*) Contractual Risk – Arising from whether or not the bank has the ability to enforce the contract.

(*j*) Concentration and Systemic Risk – Due to lack of control of individual banks over a service provider, more so when overall banking industry has considerable exposure to one service provider.

Evaluating the Capability of the Service Provider

In considering or renewing an outsourcing arrangement, appropriate due diligence should be performed to assess the capability of the service provider to comply with obligations in the outsourcing agreement. Due diligence should take into consideration qualitative and quantitative, financial, operational and reputational factors. Banks should consider whether the service providers' systems are compatible with their own and also whether their standards of performance including in the area of customer service are acceptable to it. Banks should also consider, while evaluating the capability of the service provider, issues relating to undue concentration of outsourcing arrangements with a single service provider. Where possible, the bank should obtain independent reviews and market feedback on the service provider to supplement its own findings.

Due diligence should involve an evaluation of all available information about the service provider, including but not limited to:

- Past experience and competence to implement and support the proposed activity over the contracted period.
- Financial soundness and ability to service commitments even under adverse conditions.
- Business reputation and culture, compliance, complaints and outstanding or potential litigation.
- Security and internal control, audit coverage, reporting and monitoring environment, Business continuity management.

- External factors like political, economic, social and legal environment of the jurisdiction in which the service provider operates and other events that may impact service performance.
- Ensuring due diligence by service provider of its employees.

The Outsourcing Agreement

The terms and conditions governing the contract between the bank and the service provider should be carefully defined in written agreements and vetted by bank's legal counsel on their legal effect and enforceability. Every such agreement should address the risks and risk mitigation strategies. The agreement should be sufficiently flexible to allow the bank to retain an appropriate level of control over the outsourcing and the right to intervene with appropriate measures to meet legal and regulatory obligations. The agreement should also bring out the nature of legal relationship between the parties – *i.e.* whether agent, principal or otherwise. Some of the key provisions of the contract would be:

- The contract should clearly define what activities are going to be outsourced including appropriate service and performance standards.
- The bank must ensure it has the ability to access all books, records and information relevant to the outsourced activity available with the service provider.
- The contract should provide for continuous monitoring and assessment by the bank of the service provider so that any necessary corrective measure can be taken immediately.
- A termination clause and minimum periods to execute a termination provision, if deemed necessary, should be included.
- Controls to ensure customer data confidentiality and service providers' liability in case of breach of security and leakage of confidential customer related information.
- Contingency plans to ensure business continuity.
- The contract should provide for the prior approval/consent by the bank of the use of subcontractors by the service provider for all or part of an outsourced activity.
- Provide the bank with the right to conduct audits on the service provider whether by its internal or external auditors, or by agents appointed to

act on its behalf and to obtain copies of any audit or review reports and findings made on the service provider in conjunction with the services performed for the bank.

- Outsourcing agreements should include clauses to allow the Reserve Bank of India or persons authorized by it to access the bank's documents, records of transactions, and other necessary information given to, stored or processed by the service provider within a reasonable time.
- Outsourcing agreement should also include clause to recognise the right of the Reserve Bank to cause an inspection to be made of a service provider of a bank and its books and account by one or more of its officers or employees or other persons.
- In cases where the controlling/head offices of foreign banks operating in India outsource the activities related to the Indian operations, the Agreement should include clauses to allow the RBI or persons authorized by it to access the bank's documents, records of transactions and other necessary information given or stored or processed by the service provider within a reasonable time as also clauses to recognise the right of RBI to cause an inspection to be made of a service provider and its books and accounts by one or more of its officers or employees or other persons.
- The outsourcing agreement should also provide that confidentiality of customer's information should be maintained even after the contract expires or gets terminated.
- The outsourcing agreement should provide for the preservation of documents and data by the service provider in accordance with the legal/regulatory obligation of the bank in this regard.

Confidentiality and Security

- Public confidence and customer trust in the bank is a prerequisite for the stability and reputation of the bank. Hence the bank should seek to ensure the preservation and protection of the security and confidentiality of customer information in the custody or possession of the service provider.
- Access to customer information by staff of the service provider should be on 'need to know' basis *i.e.*, limited to those areas where the information is required in order to perform the outsourced function.

- The bank should ensure that the service provider is able to isolate and clearly identify the bank's customer information, documents, records and assets to protect the confidentiality of the information. In instances, where service provider acts as an outsourcing agent for multiple banks, care should be taken to build strong safeguards so that there is no comingling of information/documents, records and assets.
- The bank should review and monitor the security practices and control processes of the service provider on a regular basis and require the service provider to disclose security breaches.
- The bank should immediately notify RBI in the event of any breach of security and leakage of confidential customer related information. In these eventualities, the bank would be liable to its customers for any damage.

Responsibilities of DSA/DMA/Recovery Agents

Code of conduct for Direct Sales Agents formulated by the Indian Banks' Association (IBA) could be used in formulating their own codes for Direct Sales Agents/Direct Marketing Agents/Recovery Agents. Banks should ensure that the Direct Sales Agents/Direct Marketing Agents/Recovery Agents are properly trained to handle with care and sensitivity, their responsibilities particularly aspects like soliciting customers, hours of calling, privacy of customer information and conveying the correct terms and conditions of the products on offer etc.

Recovery Agents should adhere to extant instructions on Fair Practices Code for lending (Circular DBOD. Leg. No. BC.104/09.07.007/2002-03 dated 5th May 2003) as also their own code for collection of dues. If the banks do not have their own code they should, at the minimum, adopt the Indian Banks Association's code for collection of dues and repossession of security. It is essential that the Recovery Agents refrain from action that could damage the integrity and reputation of the bank and that they observe strict customer confidentiality.

The bank and their agents should not resort to intimidation or harassment of any kind either verbal or physical against any person in their debt collection efforts, including acts intended to humiliate publicly or intrude the privacy of the debtors' family members, referees and friends, making threatening and anonymous calls or making false and misleading representations.

Business Continuity and Management of Disaster Recovery Plan

A bank should require its service providers to develop and establish a robust framework for documenting, maintaining and testing business continuity and recovery procedures. Banks need to ensure that the service provider periodically tests the Business Continuity and Recovery Plan and may also consider occasional joint testing and recovery exercises with its service provider.

In order to mitigate the risk of unexpected termination of the outsourcing agreement or liquidation of the service provider, banks should retain an appropriate level of control over their outsourcing and the right to intervene with appropriate measures to continue its business operations in such cases without incurring prohibitive expenses and without any break in the operations of the bank and its services to the customers.

In establishing a viable contingency plan, banks should consider the availability of alternative service providers or the possibility of bringing the outsourced activity back in-house in an emergency and the costs, time and resources that would be involved.

Outsourcing often leads to the sharing of facilities operated by the service provider. The bank should ensure that service providers are able to isolate the bank's information, documents and records, and other assets. This is to ensure that in adverse conditions, all documents, records of transactions and information given to the service provider and assets of the bank, can be removed from the possession of the service provider in order to continue its business operations, or deleted, destroyed or rendered unusable.

Monitoring and Control of Outsourced Activities

The bank should have in place a management structure to monitor and control its outsourcing activities. It should ensure that outsourcing agreements with the service provider contain provisions to address their monitoring and control of outsourced activities.

A central record of all material outsourcing that is readily accessible for review by the board and senior management of the bank should be maintained. The records should be updated promptly and half yearly reviews should be placed before the board.

Regular audits by either the internal auditors or external auditors of the bank should assess the adequacy of the risk management practices adopted in overseeing and managing the outsourcing arrangement, the bank's compliance with its risk management framework and the requirements of these guidelines.

Banks should at least on an annual basis, review the financial and operational condition of the service provider to assess its ability to continue to meet its outsourcing obligations. Such due diligence reviews, which can be based on all available information about the service provider should highlight any deterioration or breach in performance standards, confidentiality and security and in business continuity preparedness.

In the event of termination of the agreement for any reason, this should be publicized so as to ensure that the customers do not continue to entertain the service provider.

Redressal of Grievances related to Outsourced services

(*a*) Banks should constitute Grievance Redressal Machinery within the bank and give wide publicity about it through electronic and print media. The name and contact number of designated grievance redressal officer of the bank should be made known and widely publicised. The designated officer should ensure that genuine grievances of customers are redressed promptly without involving delay. It should be clearly indicated that banks' Grievance Redressal Machinery will also deal with the issue relating to services provided by the outsourced agency.

(*b*) Generally, a time limit of 30 days may be given to the customers for preferring their complaints/grievances. The grievance redressal procedure of the bank and the time frame fixed for responding to the complaints should be placed on the bank's website.

(*c*) If a complainant does not get satisfactory response from the bank within 60 days from the date of his lodging the complaint, he will have the option to approach the office of the concerned Banking Ombudsman for redressal of his grievance/s.

Reporting of transactions to FIU or other competent authorities

Banks would be responsible for making Currency Transactions Reports and Suspicious Transactions Reports to Financial Intelligence Unit (FIU) or any other competent authority in respect of the banks' customer related activities carried out by the service providers.

Centralised List of Outsourced Agents

If a service providers services are terminated by a bank, IBA would have to be informed with reasons for termination. IBA would be maintaining a caution list of such service providers for the entire banking industry for sharing among banks.

Off-shore outsourcing of Financial Services

The engagement of service providers in a foreign country exposes a bank to country risk – economic, social and political conditions and events in a foreign country that may adversely affect the bank. Such conditions and events could prevent the service provider from carrying out the terms of its agreement with the bank. To manage the country risk involved in such outsourcing activities, the bank should take into account and closely monitor government policies and political, social, economic and legal conditions in countries where the service provider is based, during the risk assessment process and on a continuous basis, and establish sound procedures for dealing with country risk problems. This includes having appropriate contingency and exit strategies. In principle, arrangements should only be entered into with parties operating in jurisdictions generally upholding confidentiality clauses and agreements. The governing law of the arrangement should also be clearly specified.

The activities outsourced outside India should be conducted in a manner so as not to hinder efforts to supervise or reconstruct the India activities of the bank in a timely manner. The outsourcing related to overseas operations of Indian banks would be governed by both, these guidelines and the host country guidelines. Where there are differences, the more stringent of the two would prevail. However, where there is any conflict, the host country guidelines would prevail.

Outsourcing within a Group/Conglomerate

The risk management practices expected to be adopted by a bank while outsourcing to a related party (*i.e.*, party within the Group/Conglomerate) would be identical to those specified in Para 5 of this guidelines.

Self-Assessment of Existing/Proposed Outsourcing Arrangements

Banks may conduct a self-assessment of their existing outsourcing agreements within a time bound plan and bring them in line with the above guidelines expeditiously.

[*Source:* BI/2006/167 DBOD.NO.BP. 40/21.04.158/2006-07 November 3, 2006]

Outsourcing of Financial Services – Responsibilities of regulated entities employing Recovery Agents

Regulated Entities (REs) have the ultimate responsibility for their outsourced activities and they are, therefore, responsible for the actions of their service providers including Recovery Agents (hereafter referred to as 'agents'). It has been observed that the agents employed by REs have been deviating from the extant instructions governing the outsourcing of financial services. In view of concerns arising from the activities of these agents, it is advised that the REs shall strictly ensure that they or their agents do not resort to intimidation or harassment of any kind, either verbal or physical, against any person in their debt collection efforts, including acts intended to humiliate publicly or intrude upon the privacy of the debtors' family members, referees and friends, sending inappropriate messages either on mobile or through social media, making threatening and/or anonymous calls, persistently 1 calling the borrower and/or calling the borrower before 8:00 a.m. and after 7:00 p.m. for recovery of overdue loans, making false and misleading representations, etc. [RBI/2022-23/108 DOR.ORG.REC.65/21.04.158/2022-23 August 12, 2022]

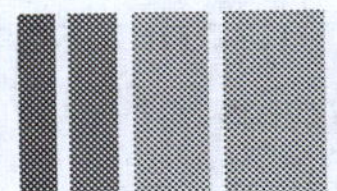

8.4 ABUSE OF OFFICIAL POSITION: INSIDER TRADING, PROPRIETARY DATA, BRIBES ETC.

Employees are advised to follow Code of Conduct laid down by the Bank. Abuse of official position for personal gains or providing gains to friends, family members and others with selfish motive amounts to violation of employee's obligation to the Bank. Examples of abuse of power can be:

a. Bank employee goes for a personal travel and claims reimbursement as official travel

b. Showing discrimination to the customers based on their proximity to the employee (his relatives, friends, etc. showing special preference)

c. Use of official resources for personal use

d. False claims beyond the fixed perquisites

Insider Trading

Employee-trading based on the internal information of the client which is not available to public amounts to insider trading. For instance, just before a specific bank account of a large company is going to become NPA and this information is still not announced officially by the bank. If an employee who is in possession of this information sells the stocks or advised friends to sell and get out of the stock, amounts to insider trading. Similarly, in another instance, if a news relating to regulatory approvals is not in favour of a company, an employee who possesses this information can sell the stocks and get profited by this information. We all are aware of the famous case of Rajat Gupta in relation to insider trading in which he was sentenced to imprisonment. In 2012, the prominent hedge fund manager Raj Rajaratnam was found guilty and sentenced to 11 years in prison in the same case for trades that netted him an alleged $60 million dollars in illicit profits.

Often, insider trading is said to be a victimless crime, the suggestion being that it does not in fact have any moral consequences because the extent of the damage (which often takes the form of lost income) is unknown, because it is unclear who suffers the damage, and/or because the supposed damage is shared among large numbers of people in very small amounts (although the benefit tends to be highly concentrated). Yet it poses some interesting ethical problems. The person who carries out the insider trading has an informational advantage that outsiders lack, but that does not make every insider trading transaction immoral or illegal. There are three key arguments against insider trading. First, it is or may be unfair for ordinary investors. Second, it hurts or may hurt a property right of the firm. Finally, it threatens the fiduciary relationship between the firm, its shareholders, and its employees. There is another reasoning that argues that insider trading can cause harm to the ordinary investors or to the market. Indian Regulator SEBI has issued Insider trading rules and consequences of violation of the rules and declarations required by the employees on a quarterly basis.

Examples of Insider Trading

- Senior executives of Silicon Valley Bank sell their shares after coming to know of the imminent big losses.
- The director of a company sells a stock after discovering that the company will be losing a big contract next month.
- The CEO's relative buys a company's shares after hearing from him that the company is negotiating a big deal with foreign buyer.

Insider Trading and Fiduciary Duty

One of the most famous cases of insider trading implicated Michael Milken, Dennis Levine and Martin Siegel, all executives of Drexel Burnham Lambert (DBL) and the company itself. Ivan Boesky, also accused, was an arbitrageur, an outside investor who bet on corporate takeovers and appeared to be able to uncannily anticipate takeover targets, buy their stock ahead of time and earn huge profits. Everyone wondered how. The answer was that he cheated. Boesky went to the source, the major investment banks, to get insider information. He paid Levine and Siegel to give him pre-take over details, an illegal action, and he profited enormously from nearly every major deal in the merger-crazy 1980s, including huge deals involving oil companies such as Texaco, Getty, Gulf, and Chevron. The SEC started to become suspicious after receiving a tip that someone was leaking information. Investigators discovered Levine's secret Swiss bank account, with all the money Boesky had paid him. Levine then gave up Boesky in a plea deal, the SEC started watching Boesky and subsequently caught Siegel and Milken. The penalties were the most severe ever given at the time. Milken, the biggest catch of all, agreed to pay $200 million in government fines, $400 million to investors who had been hurt by his actions and $500 million to DBL clients – for a grand total of $1.1 billion. He was sentenced to ten years in prison and banned for life from any involvement in the securities industry. Boesky received a prison sentence of 3.5 years, was fined $100 million, and was permanently barred from working with securities. Levine agreed to pay $11.5 million and $2 million more in back taxes; he too was given a lifetime ban and was sentenced to two years in prison. Milken and Levine violated their financial duties to their employer and the company's clients. Not only does insider trading create a public relations nightmare, it also subjects the company to legal liability. DBL ended up being held liable in civil lawsuits due to the actions of its employees, and it was also charged with violations of the Racketeer Influenced and Corrupt Organizations (RICO) Act) and ultimately failed, going bankrupt in 1990. (As a note of interest regarding the aftermath of all of this for Milken, he has tried to redeem his image since his incarceration. He resolutely advises others to avoid his criminal acts and has endowed some worthy causes in Los Angeles.)

This case raises a few critical questions for our consideration as bankers:

- Managements in banking & financial services must have stringent codes of professional behavior for employees to observe. Even given such a code, how should employees honor their fiduciary duty to safeguard the firm's assets and treat customers equitably?
- What mechanisms should be there for keeping employees in banking and other financial advising within the limits of the law and ethical behavior?
- This case dominated the headlines in the 1980s and all the accused were severely fined and received prison sentences. How do you think this case might be treated today?
- Should employees in the banking and other financial services be encouraged or even required to receive ethical certification from the professional associations? Why or why not?

[*Source:* Andrew Beattie, "Top 4 Most Scandalous Insider Trading Debacles," Investopedia, August 22, 2017. https://www.investopedia.com/ articles/stocks/09/ insider-trading.asp#ixzz56LjMgfhQ]

Proprietary data

Proprietary data refers to the information that is owned by an individual or organization, which is deemed important enough that it gives competitive advantage to that individual or organization. This data can be protected under copyright laws or patents or trade secrets. All employees are expected to keep confidentiality of the data relating to all stakeholders, customers, vendors, promoters, investors and others who are associated with the bank. Key strategies and sensitive data are to be kept confidential and should not be revealed to competitors through unfair means.

To stay competitive, organizations take serious measures to protect their sensitive data. Typically, organizations require anyone working with them to sign a contract that includes a non-disclosure agreement. This agreement binds third parties not to share any proprietary data they obtain through review and discussions of the sensitive data in question.

Bribes

Bribes refer to paying money or gift to a person with a motive of getting some favour done. Bank employees conduct various operations of credit appraisals, loan disbursements, monitoring, recovery, marketing of bank products and services. In their activities, taking or giving bribes both amount to unlawful activity and is punishable. Bank's service regulations provide details of dos and don'ts with respect to bribes. However, one can observe many cases have been filed and information in public domain states how some of the employees at senior positions misuse their power and indulge in taking bribes in various forms.

8.5 JOB DISCRIMINATION

Discrimination refers to unequal treatment. Discrimination is contrary to the basic principle of equality. Job discrimination refers to differentiating employees based on religion, sex or race. Right from the entry into the job, working conditions, emoluments and promotions, one can observe cases of discrimination in spite of the laid down rules and regulations that there should be no discrimination among employees. According to Prof. Manuel G Velasquez, 'to discriminate in employment is to make an adverse decision against employees based on their membership in a certain group'. Thus, discrimination in employment must involve three basic elements as discussed below.

1. It is a decision against one or more employees that is not based on the merits of the case.
2. The decision drives solely from racial reasons, sexual prejudice or some other kind of morally unjustified attitude against members of a class or group.
3. The decision has a harmful impact on the interests of the employees, perhaps costing them their jobs.

One can observe more law suits in global banks relating to the discrimination. However, one can observe various legal cases have been lodged by the employees seeking justice in Indian context as well.

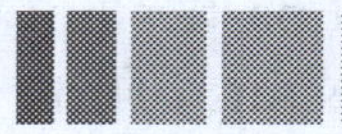

8.6 SEXUAL HARASSMENT

Indian banks have implemented robust system of handling the sexual harassment cases. One can observe increasing number of cases have been reported in the larger society in the recent years. This can be attributed to the transparency in dealing with cases and also awareness of the legal recourse amongst the employees.

As far as India's commercial banks are concerned, about two decades ago, the RBI (DBOD Department) notified all commercial banks in India on February 3, 1998 for implementation of the Guidelines given by the Hon'ble Supreme Court of India titled *Sexual Harassment in Work Places – Guidelines by Supreme Court to Prevent Such Harassment.*

RBI advised all the commercial banks (in the capacity of employers) stating that "as the onus for implementation of the guidelines lies solely on the employer, RBI urged the commercial banks to initiate immediate action to specifically ensure the following:

i. Bring to the notice of those working in your bank the definition of sexual harassment as laid down by the Supreme Court and its express prohibition.

ii. Take all necessary action to suitably modify the conduct rules governing the employees to ensure that these include the express prohibition of sexual harassment and provide for appropriate penalties against the offender.

iii. Take all steps necessary to ensure that appropriate work conditions are provided in respect of work, leisure, health and hygiene, to further ensure that there is no hostile environment towards women at work places and no woman employee has reasonable grounds to believe that she is disadvantaged in connection with her employment.

iv. Set up a mechanism in all bank to deal with complaints of sexual harassment.

The Guidelines and norms prescribed included the definition of sexual harassment and details as under:

For this purpose, sexual harassment includes such unwelcome sexually determined behaviour (whether directly or by implication) as:

(*a*) Physical contact

(*b*) A demand or request for sexual favours

(*c*) Sexually coloured remarks

(*d*) Showing pornography

(*e*) Any other unwelcome physical, verbal or non-verbal conduct of sexual nature

Where any of these Acts is committed in circumstances where under the victim of such conduct has a reasonable apprehension that in relation to the victim's employment or work whether she is drawing salary, or honorarium or voluntary, whether in government, public or private enterprise, such conduct can be humiliating and may constitute a health and safety problem. It is discriminatory for instance when the woman has reasonable grounds to believe that her objection would disadvantage her in connection with her employment or work including recruiting or promotion or when it creates a hostile work environment. Adverse consequences might be visited if the victim does not consent to the conduct in question or raises any objection thereto.

To avoid sexual misconduct or harassment cases, banks should take at least the following steps:

1. Establish a statement of policy naming someone in the bank as ultimately responsible for preventing harassment in the organization.
2. Establish a definition of sexual harassment that includes unwelcome advances, requests for sexual favors, and any other verbal, visual or physical conduct of a sexual nature; provides examples of each; and reminds employees the list of examples is not all-inclusive.
3. Establish a non-retaliation policy that protects complainants and witnesses.
4. Establish specific procedures for prevention of such practices at early stages. It is expected by law from the banks to train employees in accordance with the policy, measure their effects and ensure the policies are enforced.
5. Establish, enforce and encourage victims of sexual harassment to report the behavior to authorized individuals.
6. Establish a reporting procedure.
7. Make sure the company has timely reporting requirements to the proper authorities. Usually, there is a time limitation (ranging from six months to a year) to file a complaint for a formal administrative sexual charge.

Once these steps have been taken, a training program should identify and describe forms of sexual harassment and give examples, outline grievance procedures, explain how to use the procedures and discuss the importance of them, discuss the penalty for violation and train employees about the essential need for a workplace free from harassment, offensive conduct or intimidation. A corporation's training program should cover how to spot sexual harassment; how to investigate complaints, including proper documentation, what to do about observed sexual harassment, even when no complaint has been filed, how to keep the work environment as professional and non-hostile as possible, how to teach employees about the professional and legal consequences of sexual harassment and how to train management to understand follow-up procedures on sexual incidents.

8.7 MANAGING CONFLICT OF INTERESTS

A conflict of interest exists when an employee must choose whether to advance his or her own interests, those of the organization, or those of some other group. To avoid conflicts of interest, employees must be able to separate their private interests from their business dealings. The dictionary meaning of conflict of interest is "a situation in which a person is in a position to derive personal benefit from actions or decisions made in their official capacity". It is expected that the top management recognises such conflicts of interest and take some definite pre-emptive measures so that they do not result in inappropriate or adverse consequences on the banks and some or all stakeholders.

Some examples for conflict of interest are:

- A given bank and its client/clients
- Among the employees of a bank
- Employee of a bank and a client
- Between a given bank and one or more of its clients
- Provision of bank's services to two or more clients

Many of these conflicts can be resolved internally by the banks. Among options available to deal with the conflicts are:

- Identifying and preventing such conflicts to the extent feasible.
- Setting up an institutional controls and mechanisms within the accepted system and handle them as per the degree of potential risks of each of these conflicts such that the ones with highest risk are addressed first.
- Fuller disclosures to the parties concerned (affected) so that they become aware of the potential impact.

To illustrate, the three major bond rating agencies - Moody's, Standard & Poor and Fitch Rating had significant conflicts of interest during the global financial crisis. The agencies earned as much as three times more for grading complex products than for corporate bonds during the period. They also competed with each other for rating jobs, which contributed to lower rating standards. Additionally, the companies who wanted the ratings were the ones paying the agencies. Because the rating agencies were highly competitive, investment firms and banks would "shop" the different agencies for the best rating. There were clear and obvious conflicts of interest in the action of the rating agencies. An effective control over the conflict-of-interest issues requires that the banks should have a comprehensive policy on the management of conflict of interest. The policy should provide guidance in identifying circumstances which may give rise to conflicts of interest and may involve a risk of damage to customers', stakeholder's or bank's interests and also detail the arrangements which Bank has put in place to forestall or manage such conflicts of interests.

8.8 FAIR ACCOUNTING PRACTICES: RELATED PARTY TRANSACTIONS

Reserve Bank of India in its Master Circular dated July 2, 2012 instructed the scheduled commercial banks on their Disclosure in Financial Statements – Notes to Accounts. RBI in this Master Circular further clarified the banks that "in addition, disclosure requirements contained in "Master Circular – Prudential Guidelines on Capital Adequacy and Market Discipline – Implementation of the New Capital Adequacy Framework (NCAF)" will be applicable".

The following are two major aspects that can be considered in the context of fair accounting practices as per the July 2, 2012 circular of the RBI:

Minimum Disclosures

At a minimum, the items listed in the circular should be disclosed in the 'Notes to Accounts'. Banks are also encouraged to make more comprehensive disclosures than the minimum required under the circular if they become significant and aid in the understanding of the financial position and performance of the bank. The disclosure listed is intended only to supplement and not to replace, other disclosure requirements under relevant legislation or accounting and financial reporting standards. Where relevant, a bank should comply with such other disclosure requirements as applicable.

Summary of Significant Accounting Policies

Banks should disclose the accounting policies regarding key areas of operations at one place (under Schedule 17) along with Notes to Accounts in their financial statements. A suggestive list includes – Basis of Accounting, Transactions involving Foreign Exchange, Investments – Classification, Valuation, etc., Advances and Provisions thereon, Fixed Assets and Depreciation, Revenue Recognition, Employee Benefits, Provision for Taxation, Net Profit, etc.

Disclosure Requirements

In order to encourage market discipline, Reserve Bank has over the years developed a set of disclosure requirements which allow the market participants to assess key pieces of information on capital adequacy, risk exposures, risk assessment processes and key business parameters which provide a consistent and understandable disclosure framework that enhances comparability. Banks are also required to comply with the Accounting Standard 1 (AS 1) on Disclosure of Accounting Policies issued by the Institute of Chartered Accountants of India (ICAI). The enhanced disclosures have been achieved through revision of Balance Sheet and Profit & Loss Account of banks and enlarging the scope of disclosures to be made in "Notes to Accounts". In addition to the 16 detailed prescribed schedules to the balance sheet, banks are required to furnish the following information in the "Notes to Accounts".

Accounting Standard 18 – Related Party Disclosures

This Standard is applied in reporting related party relationships and transactions between a reporting enterprise and its related parties. The illustrative disclosure format recommended by the ICAI as a part of General Clarification (GC) 2/2002 has been suitably modified to suit banks. The illustrative format of disclosure by banks for the AS 18 is furnished below:

Accounting Standard 18 – Format for Related Party Disclosures

The manner of disclosures required by paragraphs 23 and 26 of AS 18 is illustrated below. It may be noted that the format is merely illustrative and is not exhaustive.

(Amount in Rs. crore)

Items/Related Party	Parent (as per ownership or control)	Subsidiaries	Associates/ Joint ventures	Key Management Personnel@	Relatives of Key Management Personnel	Total
Borrowings #						
Deposit#						
Placement of deposits #						
Advances #						
Investments#						
Non-funded commitments#						
Leasing/HP arrangements availed #						
Leasing/HP arrangements provided #						
Purchase of fixed assets						
Sale of fixed assets						
Interest paid						
Interest received						
Rendering of services *						
Receiving of services *						
Management contracts*						

Note: Where there is only one entity in any category of related party, banks need not disclose any details pertaining to that related party other than the relationship with that related party

* Contract services etc. and not services like remittance facilities, locker facilities etc.

@ Whole time directors of the Board and CEOs of the branches of foreign banks in India.

The outstanding at the year-end and the maximum during the year are to be disclosed.

Source: Reserve Bank of India: https://rbi.org.in/scripts/BS_ViewMasCirculardetails.aspx?id=7359#as18

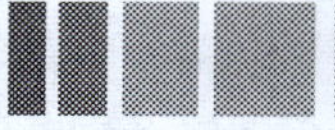

8.9 HRM ETHICS

Human Resource Management refers to designing and managing formal systems to optimally utilise the people as human resources. The typical responsibilities of management of human resources include staffing, compensation and benefits, defining and designing work, training and development, etc. The ethics of HRM revolve around those ethical issues arising out of the employer – employee relationship, such as the rights and duties owed between them. The most

important aspect imbuing this relationship is fair and equitable treatment of employees without any bias or discrimination. To achieve this fairness, HR executives should, apart from having an ethical conscience, follow a well-laid system of procedures that address the range of human resource issues in the pursuit of organizational justice. Further, it is being recognized these days by the HR experts that an ethical framework that informs HR practices with empathy and care is more relevant to manage the current intergenerational workforce in the banks. This means a shift in emphasis from formal systems to a more personalized approach. The sympathetic approach of human resources department with greater sensitivity to the individual needs of employees may lead to a greater satisfaction level amongst the employees. With satisfied employees in a bank, the bank tends to optimise their utilization with greater employee engagement. Banking is not solely a mechanical dealing with money. In fact, many treat it as a people's business. Unless the employees are satisfied with their conditions at work and compensation, recognition, promotion, etc., they are not fully motivated in performing their duties. This leads to a compromise of customer satisfaction, which would in turn affect the business for banks.

When the young talent with relevant qualifications is attracted into the public, private or foreign banks located in India, their retention depends not merely on the compensation but also on work environment, ethics, governance, scope to enhance knowledge, availability of state-of-the-art technology, human resource practices, etc. In the absence of nurturing of the talent, there is a danger of the talent migrating to the competitors. Hence, there needs to be fairness, non-discrimination and an unbiased approach in all the aspects of human resources engaged in the banking sector right from their selection, assigning of work, transfers, promotion, incentives, training, workplace ethics, relieving, etc.

HRM can play a proactive role in creating an ethical organization by checking unethical practices such as giving and receiving gifts, falsifying records to impress stock market analysts, official abuse, sexual harassment, cheating on expense accounts, lying about sick and casual leave, accepting bribes while giving loans etc. People pick up suitable hints and clues that tell them what kind of behaviour is acceptable and what is forbidden in an organization. This unarticulated understanding among employees, reinforced sometimes by codes of employees' behaviour, constitutes the ethical climate in the organization. It is that part of corporate culture that sets the ethical tone and forms the ethical conscience of the organization. Corporate culture and ethical climate can put pressure on employees to channel their actions in the directions desired by the company. To shape the organization's ethical conscience, HRM at all times should be guided by the highest principles of integrity and devotion to the welfare of the people.

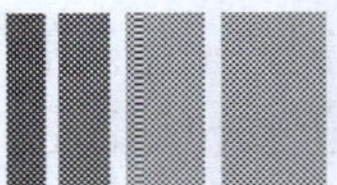

8.10 PRINCIPLES OF REPRESENTATION AND WORK ENVIRONMENT

A very well laid down process of representation of any concern or whistle blower policy helps employees to work fearlessly. Work environment that is based on ethical principles make employees more motivated and confident in delivering their duties and responsibilities. When any discrimination/dispute occurs between employees, an employee can represent his/her case to the superiors and get justice.

8.11 EMPLOYEES AS ETHICS AMBASSADORS & MANAGERS AS ETHICAL LEADERS

The ethical culture from the senior leadership percolates down in the bank. However, the employees do not personally know the senior leaders. They form their opinions based on what they come to know through others or when they listen to the top leaders. Therefore, the senior leadership should convey the importance of ethics in a variety of ways and in such a manner as to reach to every employee in the organisation. If senior managers talk about ethics regularly and also walk their talk without exception, they will develop a reputation for their ethical leadership. Leading by example, they shall become role models for others and the employees will take their cues from them. They will also practice ethics in letter & spirit and turn into ethics ambassadors in their own ways. Ethicists agree on the fact that 'integrity builds trust in senior management that is absolutely critical for high-performing organisations.' In this connection, please consider the following situation before we end this module:

> Shankar is an MBA from a prestigious institute. He specializes in Marketing and Advertising. He has just joined X Ad Agency. He is a competent and innovative person with outstanding performance during his stay at the MBA institute. Even then, he got this job with difficulty due to recession in the job market. He had somehow managed to find this job through a contact of his uncle. He is happy

working in the agency. One day, the chairman of the company wanted him to persuade a well-known newspaper in whatsoever manner to avoid reporting on a controversial corruption charge against him and instead write a favorable editorial. Shankar is not convinced that his chairman is clean in the case. When he contacted the newspaper, they were willing to oblige, if the company came out with a large size advertisement in his favor. Recently, Shankar's father died leaving his wife and three sisters on the verge of marriage with Shankar alone in a disastrous condition to help himself and his family.

In this situation,

- What should Shankar do?
- What would be your advice to Shankar to resolve this dilemmatic situation?
- Evaluate the dilemma from the perspectives of the ethics of senior leadership versus the individual ethics in an organizational setting.

8.12 LET US SUM UP

The chapter elucidates obligation to bank and obligations of bank towards customers, rights of a bank, obligations to third parties - fiduciary responsibilities, etc. KYC guidelines for banks. Rules relating to insider trading and abuse of official position are also discussed. Guidelines applicable to banks with regard to sexual harassment in work place are also detailed. Also includes disclosures in respect of fair accounting practices. HRM ethics refers to designing and managing formal systems to optimally utilize the people as human resources.

8.13 KEY WORDS

Obligations of banks, Obligations to third parties, Job discrimination, Sexual harassment, Managing conflict of interest, HRM Ethics, Fair accounting practices.

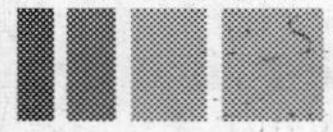

8.14 CHECK YOUR PROGRESS

1. Bank's obligations to customers include:
   (*a*) Maintain secrecy of the account
   (*b*) Honour cheques which fulfil the bank's rules

(*c*) Follow instructions given by the customer

(*d*) Closing customer account without prior information

2. Insider trading refers to:

(*a*) Employee making use of confidential information

(*b*) Passing on confidential information to relatives, friends

(*c*) Trading in the stock market without informing the bank

(*d*) All of the above

3. Job discrimination means Employee being denied opportunity based on:

(*a*) Race/Religion

(*b*) Caste

(*c*) Sex

(*d*) All of the above

4. Bank employees are expected not to accept bribes while:

(*a*) Credit appraisals & Loan disbursements

(*b*) Monitoring and recovery of loans

(*c*) Marketing of bank products and services

(*d*) All of the above

5. Under the Customer Acceptance Policy, which of the following is NOT true?

(*a*) No account is opened in anonymous or fictitious/benami name.

(*b*) No account is opened where the RE is unable to apply appropriate CDD measures, either due to non-cooperation of the customer or non-reliability of the documents/information furnished by the customer.

(*c*) No transaction or account-based relationship is undertaken without following the CDD procedure.

(*d*) The mandatory information to be sought for KYC purpose only once while opening an account.

6. As part of the Fair Practices Code for the Lenders, in the case of small borrowers seeking loans up to Rs. 2 lakhs, the lenders
   (*a*) Should convey in writing, the main reason/reasons which, in the opinion of the bank after due consideration, have led to rejection of the loan applications within stipulated time.
   (*b*) Need not convey anything in writing for rejection.
   (*c*) May, at their own discretion, convey orally the reason for rejection.
   (*d*) May give reason/reasons for rejection of the loan applications irrespective of application date at the end of the financial year.

ANSWERS

1. (*d*)	2. (*d*)	3. (*d*)	4. (*d*)	5. (*d*)	6. (*a*)

8.15 EXERCISE YOUR ETHICS MUSCLE

Case 17: To Do or Not to Do?

Your supervisor has asked you to inflate the annual review of one of your staff members who is not performing well.

Issues to reflect:

a. Should you go to your boss and explain that the employee has not performed well and good evaluation will reduce the credibility of the process and department in the eyes other staff members?

b. Should you refuse to fake the appraisal and stand firm? But that would harm the relationship with your boss.

c. Should you consult with some senior whom you respect to find a solution which does not compromise your personal integrity?

d. Is the issue worth fighting for? What would a person of integrity should do in the situation?

Case 18: To Share or Not?

Alka is a branch manager in Lord Krishna Bank. Her branch is in the outskirts of a small town. With a dedicated team of 10 staff members, she has always been achieving the yearly budgetary targets since she took over the charge 5 years ago. In view of declining profitability, Lord Krishna Bank is undergoing the process of cost rationalisation and planning to close few of its branches and lay off the staff. The local community likes the branch. However, CHRO of the bank has told her today in the strictest confidence that the branch is on a list of branch closures to be announced soon and that the closure will take effect within six months after that.

Mala, accountant of the branch and Alka's long-time friend, tells her during the lunchtime that she has decided to buy a larger flat as her son is growing and wants space. As Mala and her husband both are working, finances will not be an issue.

Issues to reflect:

a. Should Alka not tell Mala about the imminent closure of the branch?

b. Should Alka tell Mala about the closure of the branch and assure that she would look out for her and arrange some job in other bank?

c. Should Alka hint Mala that something is planned but she is not aware of the specifics?

d. Should Alka tell that Mala is on a potential redundancy list and she should defer her plan to buy a new flat?

Case 19: Are You a Good Employee and Colleague at Your Workplace?

Please take the following test to know how you are as an employee and colleague. Please be absolutely honest while responding.

[*Scoring:* 1 for (I never do) to 5 (nearly always do). Sum up your scores and generate a total to know where you stand. More the score, the better you are, as an employee and colleague.]

1. Help my colleagues in their work if they seek my help.
2. Always punctual in reporting at work in the morning and leaving in the evening.
3. I ignore if I see any of my colleagues working unethically.
4. I follow the bank's rules meticulously.
5. I tend to do what is required but not much more than that.

6. I don't go for long lunch breaks.
7. I am polite not only to seniors and peers but to juniors too.
8. I maintain appropriate confidentiality in the work-related matters.
9. I always say no to inappropriate requests.
10. I respect diversity in my organization.
11. I always inform in advance before applying for leave.
12. I make efforts to know people at work, get involved and make friends.
13. I tend to slack off when my boss is not in the office.
14. I don't care for branding and values of the bank. Senior management has to care for these.
15. I just go to work, do my job and then go home.
16. I dress up properly as I represent my bank's image while dealing with customers.
17. I continue to chat with colleagues even when the lunch break is over.
18. I demonstrate propriety while interacting with women colleagues.
19. I read content relevant for enhancing my job skills.
20. I never speak ill of my bank.

Issues to Reflect:

(*a*) Based on your score, what do you think of yourself as an employee and colleague?

(*b*) Think of the areas from the above list where you can improve upon and where you can not.

(*c*) Do you think that you overall are an ethical person?

(*d*) How would you rate yourself on your personal ethics on a scale of 10? Compare this score with the score you got from the above exercise.

9 UNIT

Ethics, Corporate Social Responsibility and ESG

9

UNIT

Ethics, Corporate Social Responsibility and ESG

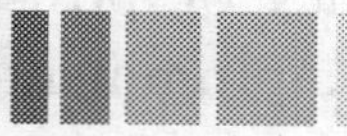

9.1 LEARNING OBJECTIVES

Today the concept of Corporate Social Responsibility (CSR) has achieved a lot of significance. Banks are lifeline of all these corporates. By virtue of banks' contribution towards the economy, country and society at large, it becomes more important for banks to make sure that their activities have positive socio-economic impact.

Although like manufacturing, banking sector *per se* does not cause any emission or pollution. But the financial service that they provide to the country can impact the overall economic and social environment of the country thereby it is important to understand the CSR in banking sector.

9.2 WHY SOCIAL RESPONSIBILITY OF BUSINESS: ROLE OF BANKING

Business firms in India are regulated and controlled through various acts. These make them to comply in various matters while carrying out their businesses. Although the same set of acts, rules, guidelines and norms do not become applicable to across-the-board businesses or organizations, one may broadly identify some of them as under:

- Workmen's Compensation Act, 1923
- Equal Remuneration Act, 1976
- The Payment of Bonus Act, 1965
- Employees Provident Fund and Misc. Provision Act, 1952
- The Payment of Gratuity Act, 1972
- Employees' State Insurance Act, 1948

- Industrial Disputes Act, 1947
- Product/service Standards
- Corporate Tax
- Companies Act, 2013
- Clause 49 of SEBI Corporate Governance guidelines for listed companies

Growth of Corporate Sector

India's industrial sector grew remarkably over the seven decades of post-independence period since 1947 till date. Today, the industry holds a prominent position in the Indian economy contributing about 30 percent of total gross value added in the country. Overall Gross Value Added (GVA) by the Industrial Sector, based on data available for the first half of the FY23, rose 3.7 per cent, which is higher than the average growth of 2.8 per cent achieved in H1 of the last decade. As per the data released by the National Statistical Office (NSO) under the Ministry of Statistics and Programme Implementation of Government of India, the provisional estimate for 2022-23 for the industry output stands at 63,20,816 crore (2011-12 prices), which accounts for almost 31% India's output for the year. Industry employs over 12.1 crore people. With nearly 53% of the output contributed by the services sector and 18.23% per cent by the agriculture sector for 2022-23. Output of India, there is an obligation moral or even legal for select companies after the passage of the Companies Act, 2013 making Corporate Social Responsibility mandatory for specified ones. India is the first country in the world to make Corporate Social Responsibility mandatory for the businesses.

Progress of the Social Indicators

As per the data released by the United Nations Development Programme (UNDP) for the year 2021-22 for India, the overall rank in terms of the Human Development Index (HDI) has slipped from 130 in the year 2020 to 132 in 2021. This is in line with a global fall in HDI scores in the wake of the **Covid-19** pandemic. India's HDI value stood at **0.633 in 2021-22,**which was lower than the world average of 0.732. The overall trend in the progress during last 30 years (1990-2020) reveals a marginal improvement.

The parameters used for the construction of the Index include Life expectancy at birth (years), Expected years of schooling (years), Gross National Income (GNI)

per capita (2011 PPP$), Inequality-adjusted HDI (IHDI), Gender Development Index (GDI), Multidimensional Poverty Index (MPI), Employment to population ratio (% ages 15 and older), Total Population (millions).

The rapid progress of the industrial and business sectors, during post-independence period and in particular during the post-reform period starting 1991, has presented the Indian corporate sector with opportunities to contribute to the communities in which they work and operate. As the government has some constraints in the form of a cap of the expenditure for welfare schemes due to passage of Fiscal Responsibility and Budget Management (FRBM) Act, corporates can play a major role to improve the human development and socio-economic conditions of the under privileged in the country.

Objectives of a Firm

There are two broad categories of objectives for a typical firm. These can be called

i. Economic Objectives

ii. Non-economic Objectives

Under the Economic Objectives, a firm's management focuses its attention on the following three major aspects:

(*a*) Higher efficiency in use of resources

(*b*) Profit maximization

(*c*) Raise shareholder's wealth (rise in stock price makes their investment to appreciate)

As far the Non-Economic Objectives are concerned, the following are broadly focused by the managements of firms:

(*a*) Good place for employees to work

(*b*) Provide good product/service to customers

(*c*) Act as a good citizen in the society

For an easy understanding, the above objectives of a business firm can be presented diagrammatically as under:

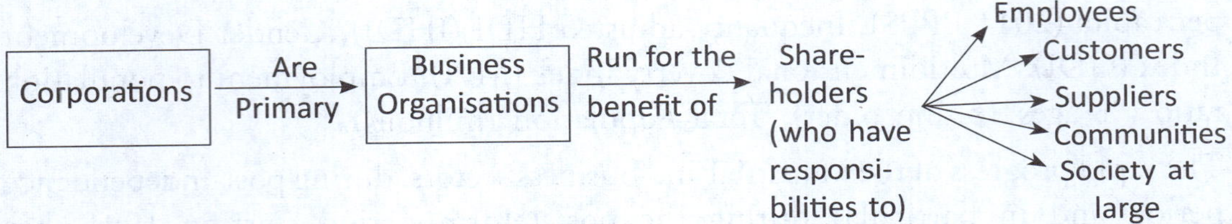

Role of Banking in CSR

Reserve Bank of India through its notification dated December 20, 2007 with the theme *Corporate Social Responsibility, Sustainable Development and Non-Financial Reporting-Role of Banks,* advised all scheduled commercial banks (excluding RRBs) that "the need for sustainable developmental efforts by financial institutions in India assumes urgency and banks, in particular, can help contribute to this effort by playing a meaningful role. In the circumstances, banks are advised to take note of the issues raised and consider using the same to put in place a suitable and appropriate plan of action towards helping the cause of sustainable development, with the approval of their Boards. In this context, particular reference is drawn to the IFC Principles on project finance (the Equator Principles) and carbon trading. Further, it will be advisable for the banks/Financial Institutions to keep themselves abreast of the developments on an on-going basis and dovetail/modify their strategies/plans, etc. in the light of such developments.

As part of an annexure, RBI advised the action points for the commercial banks in the context of CSR as under:

Indian Scenario: India acceded to the KP (Kyoto Protocol) in August, 2002. India is in a position to reap maximum benefits from the global carbon trade. According to estimates, India could emerge as one of the largest beneficiaries accounting for 31% of the world's total carbon trade which is expected to rake in at least 5-10 billion dollars over a period of time. India, being a developing country, is exempted from the requirements of adherence to the Kyoto Protocol. However, it can sell the Carbon Credit to the developed countries. The National Clean Development Mechanism (CDM) Authority receives projects for approval. Till February 2007, the National CDM Authority has approved 526 projects in the area of biomass-based cogeneration, energy efficiency, municipal solid waste, renewables such as wind, small hydro projects, etc. These projects would generate

357 million CERs by the year 2012, if all these projects get registered with the CDM Executive Board. The Ministry has started a project to sensitize and encourage States to take a lead. Initially, five states Andhra Pradesh, Rajasthan, Karnataka, Punjab and Maharashtra were given seed funding to set up their own CDM facilities. Most of the carbon credit consultants, including international players are planning to set up shop in India.

Plan of Action

- Environmental and social concerns have today become major considerations for determining the viability of a project. Environmental and social consequences have to be taken into account to ensure that a project is environmentally and socially sound and sustainable. The world over leading companies are beginning to build stakeholder trust and simultaneously improve their business performance by measuring and reporting on both financial and non-financial indicators related to such issues as environmental management, worker relations and social responsibility.
- In the financial sector too, there is a visible trend to promote environmentally and socially responsible lending and investment in emerging markets. Banks are beginning to recognize that they have a social responsibility to fulfil as they emerge from the shadow of traditional banking. Responsible banking is the new approach born out of the new market realities.
- Banking and finance's immediate environmental and social impacts are relatively low because most of those impacts are delivered through the activities of other businesses that rely on financial institutions – the businesses in a loan or investment portfolio. However, despite the relatively indirect nature of their environmental and social impacts, banks need to examine the effects of their lending and investment decisions.
- All business activities have some environmental and social impact that typically results from substandard environmental and social practices, including:

    i. over-use and wastage of natural resources;

    ii. environmental damage caused by continuing polluting activities;

    iii. persistent damage caused by past polluting practices;

iv. damage caused by accidents and mishaps;

v. use of environmentally sensitive materials.

- All these impacts have ramifications to business. The risks that such impacts create can be legal, financial and reputational and banks themselves are increasingly accountable for the effects their portfolios have on the environment and society. The costs that can be incurred by a business operating without regard to environmental and social issues include:

  i. pollution clean-up costs

  ii. fines

  iii. increased waste handling costs

  iv. costs from damaged assets with reduced value

  v. legal claims

  vi. regulatory delays

  vii. reduced public regard, and reduced sales.

  The risks that often get transferred to financial institutions include:

  i. increased loan defaults

  ii. decreased value of investment and loss of collateral due to decreased asset values

  iii. liability for damages arising from negligent investment advice

  iv. loss of reputation and standing as a result of association with polluting businesses.

- Incorporating environmental and social criteria into business decision-making can reduce the impacts of operating activities. Therefore, financial institutions that implement strategies incorporating environmental and social issues in lending and investment should be able to better assess, mitigate, document and monitor risks associated with financing and investment. Such strategies can be implemented by financial institutions by adopting the approach of sustainable development. The banking sector is of particular importance, as this sector is able to affect many projects and the development trends that result from them.

- There is much that banks can do to assist efforts to achieve sustainability. Internal efforts to make day-to-day operations cleaner, more efficient, and supportive of social structures can help. Integrating environmental and social issues into strategic operations is also important. In this way, financial institutions not only ensure that internal activity is sustainable, but they can also help financing itself become more sustainable. Sustainable finance places importance on the environmental and social consequences of projects and financial products, rather than just the economic impact. This can encompass incorporating environmental and social assessments into financial analysis, or developing products with an explicit environmental and social focus, such as Sustainable & Responsible Investment (SRI) funds. SRI is an investment strategy that identifies investment targets that carry net environmental and social benefits as well as provide financial growth.
- In order to be able to make an impact, banks need to integrate the concepts of Corporate Social Responsibility (CSR) and Sustainability with their business strategy. This can be done through:
    - (*i*) Commitment to Sustainability: Banks must expand their missions from ones that prioritize profit maximization to a vision of social and environmental sustainability.
    - (*ii*) Commitment to 'Do No Harm': Banks should commit to do no harm by preventing and minimizing the environmentally and/or socially detrimental impacts of their portfolios and their operations.
    - (*iii*) Commitment to Responsibility: Banks should bear full responsibility for the environmental and social impacts of their transactions.
    - (*iv*) Commitment to Accountability: Banks must be accountable to their stakeholders, particularly those that are affected by the activities and side effects of companies they finance.
    - (*v*) Commitment to Transparency: Banks must be transparent to stakeholders, not only through robust, regular and standardized disclosure, but also through being responsive to stakeholder needs for specialized information on banks' policies, procedures and transactions.
- Transparency in disclosures can be implemented by banks through Sustainability Reporting, a process for publicly disclosing an organization's

economic, environmental, and social performance. Through sustainability reporting, banks can report on progress against performance goals not only for economic achievements, but for environmental protection and social well-being. The Global Reporting Initiative (GRI) guidelines provide a generally accepted framework that can simplify report preparation and assessment, helping both reporters and report-users gain greater value from sustainability. The GRI is a long-term, multi-stakeholder, international process whose mission is to develop and disseminate globally applicable Sustainability Reporting Guidelines.

- As attention intensifies and focuses on the emerging philosophy of Responsible Banking, banks can make a positive impact on economic development by influencing environmental, social and ethical outcomes by integrating the principles of Corporate Social Responsibility and Sustainable Development and Sustainable Reporting with their business strategy. (Reserve Bank of India Notification-Section of the Enclosures)

Hence, it may be summarized that the RBI in Indian context has been making significant efforts to sensitize the commercial banks both public as well as private sector to remain aware of some global developments in financial and banking sector's commitments towards environment and enable investments that are environmentally sustainable and socially responsible. By ensuring these, banks would go a long way in achieving the goals of some of the national and international policies towards the CSR.

Need for CSR

It is now a widely acceptable norm that as corporates maximize their earnings and profits, they should remain highly sensitive to the needs of the society at large in which they operate. Banks are lifeline of all these corporates. Today banking sector is the biggest stakeholder in terms of providing finance for the operations of the companies across the country. By virtue of their contribution towards the economy, country and society at large, it becomes that much more important for banks to make sure that their activities have positive socio-economic impact. It is utmost important that the financial services and products that they offer provide benefits to the communities and society that they are serving.

Banks being an intermediary is at the core of all the financial transactions that happen in the economy. The kinds of risks that are attached to financial transactions are significant and have ripple effect across the entire financial system. With globalization and digitization, these risks are magnified and can move fairly quickly and can paralyze the financial system. Any bank failure will have impact on the entire economy.

The financial crisis in USA in 2008 is the prime example of how swiftly the sub-prime crises led to bankruptcy of banking behemoths. The carnage was not limited to USA but was felt across the globe as all countries fell in to the brief period of recession. The very recent "LoU" scam at a public sector bank in India is another eye opener for the entire banking system. Few handfuls of employees exploited the loopholes in the bank's system which resulted in undue favour and gain of few corporates and individuals.

Most of the time, risks to banking systems are caused by unethical practices. Such kind of practices might be greed of an individual officer or systematic mis-selling of financial products. The sub-prime crises are typical case study of how the financial institutions mis-sell financial products. The story of collapses keeps repeating itself. Banks need to therefore continually worry about the risks they face. Hence, risk becomes an underlying theme for banks as evident from the following:

- Technology and Digitization is taking over physical branch activities. With a significant portion of banking activity now being online and on the cloud, security risks are becoming prominent.
- Payment banks and Payment Wallets are increasingly used for smooth transfer of money and is leading to increase financial inclusion in the country. However, stringent checks and balances are critical to manage risk and provide a seamless service.
- The emergence of Cryptocurrencies is making financial market open to new challenges which were not in existence a couple of years back. These technologies are indeed disruptive technologies. The risk this development emanates is not known today but it would no doubt be significant in days to come.
- Customer data protection, data integrity and confidentiality are a critical ingredient of banking. Customer and society's well-being is at risk here.

- Banks need to be very careful of to whom and where they lend. Industries that are polluting or cause environmental degradation are prime cases where banks should exercise caution. Banks can play an effective role by binding these companies to targets for improving the environment.
- Anti-Money Laundering (AML), with terrorism financing is critical. Banks have to be sensitive to this issue and ensure that sufficient controls are in place. Lives could be at stake here. Also, it corrodes the financial system. From banking perspective as well, fines by regulators causes diminution of the shareholders' value.

From above, it is clear that apart from business and maximization of profit-oriented policies, banking system has rather more crucial role for overall well-being of the society.

9.3 MEANING, EVOLUTION AND TYPES OF CSR

There is no universally accepted definition of Corporate Social Responsibility (CSR). It is described as an instrument, a concept or even a business model that requires companies to apply a radical change in attitude. The latter assumes a paradigm shift in business, according to which there is more to a company than return on investment and maximization of profit. It is also a community of people, which operates in a social and natural environment, the environmental and social impacts of which must be considered (Szegedi, 2014).

One of the best known and most widely accepted definitions of CSR is by Carroll, who says that corporate social responsibility encompasses the economic, legal, ethical and discretionary (philanthropic) expectations that society has of organizations. The CSR pyramid distinguishes various layers of responsibilities. The foundation is economic responsibility. At the same time, however, companies also need to comply with legal norms. Ethical responsibility equals the obligation to conduct in a fair way and to do the right thing, going beyond mere compliance with rules. The ethical responsibility means the behaviors and norms that society expects business to follow from an ethical point of view. These ethical responsibilities extend to actions, decisions and practices that are beyond what is required by the law. Last category of responsibility is discretionary or philanthropic responsibility. Best examples of discretionary or philanthropic

responsibility are charitable, humanistic activities which business undertook to help society along with its own interests.

The idea of Corporate Social Responsibility (CSR) goes back to the early 20th century, when public discussions emerged in the United States about the role and social responsibilities of its large industrial corporations. Since then, the idea of CSR has evolved into a global doctrine on the interplay between business and society: at its core, CSR is commonly understood as a way for private companies to address social expectations by increasing their contributions to public goods in ways which are also profitable for their own business. Over the past two decades, this doctrine has favoured the emergence of new policies and practices on the part of companies, new public-private partnerships and various national and transnational 'soft' regulatory frameworks relying on incentives rather than legal obligations.

Over the years CSR has been also known as:

- Corporate conscience
- Corporate citizenship
- Social performance
- Sustainable Responsible Business/Responsible Business

According to United Nations Industrial Development Organization (UNIDO); "Corporate Social Responsibility is a management concept whereby companies integrate social and environmental concerns in their business operations and interactions with their stakeholders. CSR is generally understood as being the way through which a company achieves a balance of economic, environmental and social imperatives (Triple-Bottom-Line Approach), while at the same time addressing the expectations of shareholders and stakeholders. In this sense it is important to draw a distinction between CSR, which can be a strategic business management concept and charity, sponsorships or philanthropy. Even though the latter can also make a valuable contribution to poverty reduction, will directly enhance the reputation of a company and strengthen its brand, the concept of CSR clearly goes beyond that."

Simply, CSR pertains to what businesses do beyond profit making and obeying the law. The CSR pyramid distinguishes various layers of responsibilities.

- Ethical responsibility

- Legal responsibility
- Environmental responsibility
- Philanthropic responsibility

Ethical responsibility ensures to be ethical and obligation to do what is right. Legal responsibility involves obey the law and play by the rules of the game. Environmental responsibility involves being profitable and providing foundation to others. Philanthropic responsibility envisages being a good corporate citizen and improving quality of life.

What Do You Think?

Is it fair, sensible and/or ethical to ask, let alone expect, business organizations (or company executives) to take on the role of correcting the world's ills? How can organizations, established to fulfil a highly specific economic role, adopt the responsibility for enacting or at least contributing to roles that might be expected to be the responsibility of political parties and government?

Types of CSR activities for banks

CSR activity needs to be integrated with banking activity with both business and non-business activities. For instance, CSR activity integrated into banking involves:

- Developing financial literacy and awareness of financial education.
- Responsible, prudent lending and risk management practices.
- Fair and transparent banking and financial services and handling of customer complaints.
- Helping disadvantaged clients to use banking services, products for clients with special needs.
- Involvement and ethical treatment of stakeholders.
- Providing financial support to social enterprises.
- Financing environmental protection investments.
- Developing basic principles of financing sensitive sectors.
- Combating money laundering, corruption and terrorism.

CSR activities that are non-business include:

- Supporting disadvantaged social groups.
- Volunteering to improve the living environment.
- Supporting local communities.
- Supporting sports.
- Supporting NGOs.
- Supporting culture and arts.
- Providing jobs, appropriate working conditions and equal opportunities.

Below are the activities identified and notified in the Schedule VII of the Companies Act, 2013. However, this is not an exhaustive list as CSR activities include any such activities that will be notified from time to time:

- Contribution to Prime Minister Relief fund & such other funds
- Promotion of education
- Eradication of extreme poverty
- Gender equity
- Women empowerment
- Combating HIV & other diseases
- Reducing child mortality & improving maternal health
- Social business project & Environment sustainability
- Employment enhancing vocational skills

9.4 ASPECTS OF CSR

The following are the major aspects of evaluating whether or not the corporate social responsibility is taken up, implemented, monitored, reviewed and revised as per the needs of the society from time to time in a given context:

1. Responsibility
2. Accountability
3. Sustainability
4. Social Contract CSR Process

The following points provides some clarity on the steps to be adopted at a company's level in the context of chalking out a plan of action for CSR:

1. Developing a CSR Strategy and Policy
2. Operationalizing the institutional mechanism
3. Due diligence of the implementation partner
4. Project Development
5. Project approval
6. Finalising the arrangement with implementing agency
7. Progress monitoring and reporting
8. Impact measurement
9. Report consolidation and communication

Now let us try to understand each process mentioned in the above chart in detail:

Step 1: Developing a CSR strategy and Policy

The Companies Act, 2013 requires every company to put up its CSR policy in the public domain. The guidance provided in the Act and the draft rules on what constitutes a CSR policy are that it should:

- exclude normal business activities of the company;
- contain a list of the CSR projects or programmes which the company plans to undertake during the implementation year while specifying the annual report requirements, the draft rules go on to say that the company must provide;
- a brief outline of its CSR policy, including the statement of intent reflecting the ethos of the company, broad areas of CSR interest and an overview, of activities to be undertaken;
- a web-link to the CSR policy including 'the full list of projects, activities and programmes proposed to be undertaken by the company'. Since most of the development requires long-term commitments and their impact often takes a while to accrue, a good CSR practice requires that a company that is serious about its CSR should develop a long-term (three to five years) vision and strategy which is reviewed annually and the activities

and budgets are planned on an annual basis. The latter will comply with the CSR policy requirements of the Companies Act, 2013.

To avoid confusion regarding terms like policy, strategy, project and programme, a brief explanation has been provided here:

- CSR strategy refers to what the company expects to achieve in the next three to five years and incorporates the vision, mission and goals on a broader level. It also entails how it plans to achieve these in terms of organization and approach.
- CSR policy refers to what the company expects to achieve over the next year. This is aligned with the requirements of the Companies Act, 2013.
- Programme refers to a sector or an issue that the company proposes to address through its CSR. This can, for instance, be 'education of the girl child' or 'agriculture development'. Programmes will be clearly outlined in the company's CSR strategy.
- Programme goals will be achieved through a series of individual projects and, a project refers to a set of interventions, typically in a specific geography and addressing a specific stakeholder group, with a definite set of goals, beginning and end and a budget attached to it.
- Each project in turn will consist of a number of activities. All of which contribute towards the project goals.

Step 2: Operationalizing the institutional mechanism

In order for a corporate to gain the greatest leverage and a strategic advantage through the investment of intellectual and financial resources, they are required to select their implementation mechanism. In terms of implementation mechanism, a company has several options, which are permitted under the CSR draft rules:

- Self-execution through:
  - an in-house CSR department
  - a company foundation with execution capabilities
- Making grants to an independent implementation partner (which has a track record of at least three years).

- The grants can be made:
  - directly by an in-house CSR department
  - through the company's grant-making foundation

Step 3: Due diligence of the implementation partner

Due diligence refers to the process a company undertakes to determine the risks as well as the benefits of working with a potential implementation partner. This process has to be sufficiently robust to ensure that a company's implementation partners have the reputation, competence and integrity to deliver effective programmes on the ground.

It begins as soon as the discussions with the implementation partner suggest that there is *prima facie* interest of both parties to enter into a partnership. A detailed due-diligence is essential for large and long partnerships but may be brief for a relatively small or opportunistic partnership opportunity.

The due diligence process consists of five primary areas for investigation:

- competence of the implementation partner
- identity
- management
- accountability, transparency and financial capability

Step 4: Project development

The CSR strategy of a company will be implemented through a series of projects which will have definite beginnings, ends, expected outputs and outcomes as well as budgets associated with it. These projects may be of a short duration (a few months) or multi-year.

A company may choose to implement projects through its in-house teams or in partnership with other agencies or a combination of both. Whatever path it takes, it is important for the project to be developed clearly with distinct baselines, defined activities, 'monitorable' targets and budgets. In the case of multi-year projects, it is important to include a provision to undertake annual reviews which can form the basis to revise the project.

Step 5: Project approval

Every project, whether developed by the in-house team or an external agency, must be formally examined and approved. This is to ensure that each project is in line with the CSR strategy and policy, the monitoring indicators are clearly defined and relevant and there is an adequate budget available. Projects that go on for longer duration or demand a larger number of resources must be scrutinised more carefully than the others.

The CSR committee is ultimately the one responsible for every project. It can, however, choose to delegate authority to a project approval committee consisting of company staff and outside experts with clearly defined roles and responsibilities.

Step 6: Finalizing the arrangement with the implementing agency

While working with an external agency, it is very important to enter into a formal arrangement which is referred to here as a Memorandum of Understanding (MoU). It defines the roles, responsibilities, deliverables, commitments and consequences in case of any breach. This is essentially a formal acknowledgement that all the partners have voluntarily consented to work together to achieve an agreed outcome that requires each one to play their respective roles.

The term "MoU" is used more generically here to refer to the arrangements between partners which can range from a formal, legally enforceable contract on the one hand to a simple exchange of written documents on the other. However, what is important for the company to keep in mind is that it is entering into an arrangement with a partner, not a supplier and there is a greater sense of mutuality in this relationship.

It may also be noted that the "MoU" is relevant only if the project is being implemented by a legal entity other than the company's own CSR department. It must also be executed if the project is being implemented by the company foundation if it is a separate legal entity.

Step 7: Progress monitoring and reporting

Routine progress monitoring serves the following three important purposes:

- It highlights any slippages and helps to determine a corrective action that must be taken, if need be.
- It provides an excellent opportunity for learning: what worked and what did not. This can then be immediately applied to other projects.
- This is an essential part of the directors' report as per the CSR clause of the Companies Act, 2013.

To ensure objectivity, it is critical that the monitoring is done by someone other than the people directly engaged in the project implementation. In cases where the implementation is done by a partner or corporate foundation, this role can either be outsourced or played by the company's CSR department. In case the CSR department itself is implementing a project, then monitoring should either be outsourced to a third party or the department structure should include an independent monitoring cell. This decision should be taken by the CSR committee.

Step 8: Impact measurement

Impacts of the development projects typically take a while to manifest. For instance, a girl child education programme can show an increased enrolment and retention of girls and on a monthly basis, but further impacts such as improved learning levels will take at least a year. So, impact measurement studies have different objectives from project monitoring and typically have to be undertaken after providing sufficient time for them to manifest.

Impact measurement is often quite specialised and needs to be undertaken by an independent team with specific skills depending upon project design. For instance, if a girl child education programme has a strong component for mobilising communities, then the members of the evaluation team must not only understand education but also have knowledge of gender and the community in order to assess the impact.

There are several tools and frameworks for measuring impact. Each has its pros and cons depending upon the nature of interventions, time and budgets available for the study and the availability of people. Thus, selecting the impact measurement methodology is important.

Thus, impact studies have to be carefully planned in terms of team composition, timing and methodology. The process must be driven by the CSR committee which can delegate the day-to-day management of the process to an appropriate structure within the company.

Step 9: Report consolidation and Communication

Reporting and communication closes the loop between intent and achievement and is hence a crucial element of the CSR process. In the context of the companies

Act, 2013 this is also a mandatory requirement as it provides crucial inputs to preparing the Directors' Report.

Project-level reporting forms the base and hence getting it right is critical. Project reports have to be consolidated in programme related reports, aligned with the CSR policy stated by the company as a requirement under the Companies Act, 2013. The report has to conform to the requirements of CSR rules under the Companies Act, 2013 in terms of form and content as non-compliance attracts penalties. This report will also form a key input into the company's SEBI Business Responsibility Report and Sustainability Report. The CSR Committee may choose to go beyond the requirements of the Companies Act, 2013 and issue a stand-alone CSR Report.

Mandatory CSR Planning and Strategizing

The first step towards formalizing CSR projects in a corporate structure is the constitution of a CSR Committee as per the provisions contained in the Companies Act, 2013, clause 135. The CSR provisions within the Act is applicable to companies with an annual turnover of Rs. 1,000 Crs. and more, or a net worth of Rs. 500 Crs. and more, or a net profit of Rs. 5 Crs. and more.

The new rules, which have become applicable from the fiscal year 2014-15 onwards, also require companies to set-up a CSR Committee consisting of their board members, including at least one independent director. The act encourages companies to spend at least 2% of their average net profit in the previous three years on CSR activities. The net profit is defined as the profit before tax as per the books of account, excluding profits arising from branches outside India.

Role of the Board and CSR Committee

Based on the following three conditions, the companies need to create CSR Committee and the role of board has been spelt out clearly in the Act:

- Net worth > 500 crores INR
- Turnover > 1000 crores INR
- Net profit > 5 crores INR

Role of the Board include:

- Formation of CSR Committee
- Approve CSR Policy

- Ensure implementation of the activities under CSR
- Ensure 2% spend
- Disclose reasons for not spending (if applicable)

Role and Responsibilities of CSR Committee include:

- Three or more directors with at least one independent director
- Formulate and recommend a CSR policy to the Board
- Recommend activities and the amount of expenditure to be incurred
- Monitor CSR Policy from time to time

CSR Responsibility

In order to assist the businesses to adopt responsible governance practices, the Ministry of Corporate Affairs has prepared a set of voluntary guidelines which indicate some of the core elements that businesses need to focus on while conducting their affairs. These guidelines have been prepared after taking into account the governance challenges faced in our country as well as the expectations of the society.

Fundamental principle being that each business entity should formulate a CSR policy to guide its strategic planning and provide a roadmap for its CSR initiatives, which should be an integral part of overall business policy and aligned with its business goals. The policy should be framed with the participation of various level executives and should be approved by the board.

Core Elements as per the Guidelines:

Stakeholders

- The companies should respect the interests of, and be responsive towards all stakeholders, including shareholders, employees, customers, suppliers, project affected people, society at large, etc. and create value for all of them. They should develop mechanism to actively engage with all stakeholders, inform them of inherent risks and mitigate them where they occur.

Ethical Functioning

- Their governance systems should be underpinned by Ethics, Transparency and Accountability. They should not engage in business practices that are abusive, unfair, corrupt or anti-competitive.

Workers' rights

- Companies should provide a workplace environment that is safe, hygienic and humane and which upholds the dignity of employees. They should provide all employees with access to training and development of necessary skills for career advancement, on an equal and non-discriminatory basis.

Human rights

- Companies should respect human rights for all and avoid complicity with human rights abuses by them or by third party.

Environment

- Companies should take measures to check and prevent pollution; recycle, manage and reduce waste, should manage natural resources in a sustainable manner and ensure optimal use of resources like land and water, should proactively respond to the challenges of climate change by adopting cleaner production methods, promoting efficient use of energy and environment friendly technologies.

Social Development

- Depending upon their core competency and business interest, companies should undertake activities for economic and social development of communities and geographical areas, particularly in the vicinity of their operations. These could include: education, skill building for livelihood of people, health, cultural and social welfare, etc. particularly targeting at disadvantaged sections of society.

Of course, the success of CSR activities rests on the various benefits it brings on the table for bank or for any organization for that matter. With the implementation of Companies Act, 2013 requiring CSR to be a mandatory expenditure for the specified companies in India, there has been a remarkable progress in the area. During the previous year's till 2013, we saw only select companies spending at their discretion on areas of their discretion. However, with the implementation of a clear and focused set of areas (as detailed above in a chart detailing some of the CSR activities notified under Companies Act, 2013), the expenditure has been made by the companies on CSR in a well-directed manner.

For instance, as per the data displayed on the website of Ministry of Company Affairs of Government of India, for the financial year 2020-21, for 18012 companies for which CSR data were compiled which collectively contributed Rs. 25764.659 crore. Reliance Industries has made the single highest contribution at Rs. 922 crore for CSR spent in corporate sector while TCS is at 2nd place with a spend of Rs. 674 crore. Tata Sons and HDFC Bank have spent Rs. 545.83 crores and Rs. 534.03 crore respectively and stand at 3rd and 4th rank. There is an increasing trend in CSR spent over the years in the country. More than 9792 companies have spent more than the prescribed amounts whereas 3523 less than the prescribed amounts. At the same time, 3202 companies have spent zero amount on CSR during the year 2020-21. Maharashtra has been receiving the highest CSR contribution over the years. Notably, CSR in Kerala and Telangana has grown by more than 300% from 2015 to 2020. The remarkable growth of more than 200% can also be observed in Karnataka, Uttar Pradesh and Gujarat.

9.5 CSR: EXTENSION OF BUSINESS ETHICS

The Ethical Responsibility, as exhibited in pyramid above, is the most critical area in banking business. Ethical norms can be interpreted through conscience of an individual. It is more of a moral responsibility of the officer working in any financial institution. Any banking officer in a way is in fiduciary position while working or representing the bank or financial institution. For example, the motto of the London Stock Exchange "My word is my bond" embodies the basic ethical principles of honesty and sincerity, which together with trust,

are traditionally linked to the financial sector. The codes of ethics essentially include the basic principles of

- Integrity
- Respect
- Transparency
- Fair conduct and Diligence
- No conflict of interest
- Compliance to regulatory requirements

However, the above list is inclusive and not exhaustive. Although the fact that the most of the banks or financial institutions are compliant as per regulatory framework but mere compliance is not enough. The need to conduct the business in ethical way puts that much more responsibility on banks to cultivate and implement such business practices which goes beyond the rule books of regulatory bodies.

9.6 CSR & ESG AS A BUSINESS STRATEGY FOR SUSTAINABLE DEVELOPMENT

Sustainability (corporate sustainability) is derived from the concept of sustainable development which is defined by the Brundtland Commission as:

"Development that meets the needs of the present without compromising the ability of future generations to meet their own needs."

Corporate sustainability essentially refers to the role that companies can play in meeting the agenda of sustainable development and entails a balanced approach to economic progress, social progress and environmental stewardship.

Globally, the notion of CSR and sustainability seems to be converging, as is evident from the various definitions of CSR put forth by global organisations. The genesis of this convergence can be observed from the preamble to the recently released draft rules relating to the CSR clause within the Companies Act, 2013 which talks about stakeholders and integrating it with the social, environmental and economic objectives, all of which constitute the idea of a triple bottom line approach. It is also acknowledged in the Guidelines on Corporate Social Responsibility and Sustainability for Central Public Sector Enterprises issued by the DPE in April 2013. The new guidelines, which have replaced two existing separate guidelines on CSR and sustainable development, issued in 2010 and 2011 respectively, mentions the following:

"Since corporate social responsibility and sustainability are so closely entwined, it can be said that corporate social responsibility and sustainability is a company's commitment to its stakeholders to conduct business in an economically, socially and environmentally sustainable manner that is transparent and ethical."

CSR in India tends to focus on what is done with profits after they are made. On the other hand, sustainability is about factoring the social and environmental impacts of conducting business, that is, how profits are made. Hence, much of the Indian practice of CSR is an important component of sustainability or responsible business, which is a larger idea, a fact that is evident from various sustainability frameworks. An interesting case in point is the NVGs for social, environmental and economic responsibilities of business issued wherein the principle eight relating to inclusive development encompasses most of the aspects covered by the CSR clause of the Companies Act, 2013. However, the remaining eight principles relate to other aspects of the business.

Nonetheless, there are also subtle conceptual differences between CSR and Sustainability. CSR is used in order to assess what an organisation has done in the past and what their contribution to society has been whereas sustainability looks at the organisation from a future viewpoint assessing and planning the changes needed to secure its future impact and make the organisation more resilient by reducing waste, sustainable supply chains, developing new sustainable business strategies in order to grow, etc. and targeting the entire value chain represented by suppliers, business partners, shareholders up to the end use consumers. Both CSR and Sustainability focus on helping organisations to run in order to be ethically profitable by doing the right thing and helping them make a positive impact on those around them, rather than feeding the bottom-line linear economy.

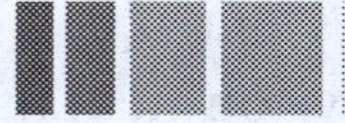

9.7 ESG (ENVIRONMENTAL, SOCIAL AND GOVERNANCE)

According to Gartner, Environmental, Social and Governance (ESG) refers to a collection of corporate performance evaluation criteria that assess the robustness of a company's governance mechanisms and its ability to effectively

manage its environmental and social impacts. Examples of ESG data include the quantification of a company's carbon emissions, water consumption or customer privacy breaches. Institutional investors, stock exchanges and boards increasingly use sustainability and social responsibility disclosure information to explore the relationship between a company's management of ESG risk factors and its business performance. Thus, ESG is a framework that helps stakeholders understand how an organization is managing risks and opportunities related to environmental, social and governance criteria (sometimes called ESG factors). ESG has changed how capital allocation decisions are made by many of the largest financial services firms and asset managers in the world.

Our world faces a number of global challenges: climate change, transitioning from a linear economy to a circular one, increasing inequality, balancing economic needs with societal needs. Investors, regulators, as well as consumers and employees are now increasingly demanding that companies should not only be good stewards of capital but also of natural and social capital and have the necessary governance framework in place to support this. More and more investors are incorporating ESG elements into their investment decision-making process, making ESG increasingly important from the perspective of securing capital, both debt and equity.

ESG receive a big push after the US Business Roundtable released a statement in August 2019 strongly affirming business's commitment to a broad range of stakeholders, including customers, employees, suppliers, communities, and, of course, shareholders. Another factor for the rising profile of ESG has been its alignment with the Sustainability Development Goals (SDGs). A major part of ESG growth has also been driven by the environmental component of ESG and responses to climate change. Further, Ukraine war and the ensuing human tragedy, as well as the cumulative geopolitical, economic and societal effects have also catalysed the importance of ESG. Of a piece with that emerging zeitgeist, ESG-oriented investing has experienced a meteoric rise. The acceleration has been driven by heightened social, governmental, and consumer attention on the broader impact of corporations, as well as by the investors and executives who realize that a strong ESG proposition can safeguard a company's long-term success. In other words, ESG performance is becoming a sort of sustainability credit rating for companies and their investors. It's not surprising that ESG is a worthwhile investing strategy right now. According to Reuters, capital totalling

US$649 billion flowed into ESG-linked funds in 2021. That's a record amount that more than doubles the investment seen in 2019.

Is there any difference between CSR, Sustainability & ESG?

A question might sometimes arise in the context of CSR, Sustainability and ESG as to whether there is a difference in these three concepts? 'Sustainability' is an overall, umbrella concept, whereas ESG and CSR are used to describe specific business models clear-cut corporate terms that do, nevertheless, involve sustainability in their DNA. In short, CSR is a company's framework of sustainability plans and responsible cultural influence, whereas ESG is the assessable outcome concerning a company's overall sustainability performance. One important difference between ESG and the CSR is the paradigm shift from a shareholder-centric philosophy to one that is undeniably focused on all stakeholders. As a result of the underlying philosophy, ESG is more integral to business and strategy as compared to CSR, but eventually both converge into sustainability in terms of outcomes.

However, ESG is the most emergent of the two, having shot up in popularity over the past few years. Sometimes it said that ESG is replacing CSR in view is increased popularity. To take one example, 'there has been a fivefold growth in internet searches for ESG since 2019, even as searches for "CSR" (corporate social responsibility), an earlier area of focus more reflective of corporate engagement than changes to a core business model, have declined'. Across industries, geographies, and company sizes, organizations have been allocating more resources toward improving ESG. More than 90 percent of S&P 500 companies now publish ESG reports in some form, as do approximately 70 per cent of Russell 1000 companies. In a number of jurisdictions, reporting ESG elements is either mandatory or under active consideration. In the United States, the Securities and Exchange Commission (SEC) is considering new rules that would require more detailed disclosure of climate-related risks and greenhouse-gas (GHG) emissions. Additional SEC regulations on other facets of ESG have also been proposed or are pending. In India also, SEBI has mandated a BRSR framework 2022-23. BRSR is an effective compliance and communication tool for a company's non-financial disclosures and is the next step in mandatory ESG reporting in India.

According to the World Economic Forum, CSR has evolved into ESG in the journey of corporate sustainability. This transition has been through three

fundamental changes. First, CSR and other precursor programmes are self-regulated practices and policies that capture a company's commitment to positive impact. While these CSR commitments are communicated widely through marketing messages, they lack quantifiable and comparable data to validate their outcomes. In ESG also, storytelling remains paramount but it's validated with specific metrics that gauge a company's holistic performance. The amount of transparency and specificity of the ESG metrics as well as incorporation of broader frameworks such as the Sustainable Development Goals (SDGs) bring a new layer of meaning. Let's take Diversity, Inclusion, and Equity (DEI) issues for example. While companies have championed DEI initiatives through symbolic gestures in the past, with ESG, DEI has come into the forefront.

Secondly, CSR programmes vary from company to company-each housing a variety of loosely connected activities ranging from philanthropic causes to employee volunteerism. Due to the varied topics and activities that fall under CSR, the oversight among these programmes is often siloed across the organization. ESG issues, on the other hand, are fundamentally intersectional. "E", "S" and "G" are not separate categories, but rather interconnected. Let's consider climate issues for example – ESG looks not only at an organization's environmental impact, but also the social justice issues around the disproportionate impact climate change has on low-income populations. This type of system-based programme requires an integrated approach to management where the entire leadership team, including the Board of Directors, takes ownership.

The final difference worth noting in the evolution to ESG is the motivation behind pursuing corporate sustainability. Traditionally, the argument used to get stakeholders on board to pursue CSR initiatives was the benefit of driving down business costs, such as lower energy consumption. Today, that narrative has profoundly changed. ESG acts as a strategic lever that drives new growth opportunities and enhances performance. In fact, according to a study by BlackRock, 81% of a globally representative selection of purpose-driven companies with better ESG profiles outperformed their counterparts in 2020, despite a market downturn. When done successfully, a bespoke ESG strategy is underpinned by the company's purpose and embedded deeply within the business operations. ESG considerations, now seen as a crucial component of corporate governance, are at the top of the agenda for key stakeholders – millennials are leading the charge on sustainable investing, and consumers and employees are increasingly looking for businesses that share their values.

There is also a movement towards global ESG reporting standards from both the business and regulatory communities that is expected to intensify. In fact, Bank of America & B of A Securities predicts $20 trillion in assets will flow into sustainable funds and strategies over the next two decades, nearly equalling the market value of the S&P 500 today.

Do You Agree?

The critics of ESG say that ESG efforts mostly are just "greenwashing," "purpose washing," or "woke washing" or "virtue signalling". One Edelman survey reported that nearly three out of four institutional investors do not trust companies to achieve their stated sustainability, ESG, or diversity, equity, and inclusion (DEI) commitments.

We can conclude, in words of McKinsey, that "Names will come and go (ESG itself arose after CSR, corporate engagement, and similar terms), and these undertakings are by nature difficult and can mature only after many iterations. But we believe that the importance of the underlying ideas has not peaked; indeed, the imperative for companies to earn their social license appears to be rising. Companies must approach externalities as a core strategic challenge, not only to help future-proof their organizations but to deliver meaningful impact over the long term."

9.8 EVOLUTION OF REPORTING OF CSR ACTIVITIES: (NINE PRINCIPLES OF NVG & GRI PRINCIPLES)

The new Act requires that the board of the company shall, after taking into account the recommendations made by the CSR committee, approve the CSR policy for the company and disclose its contents in their report and also publish the details on the company's official website, if any, in such manner as may be prescribed. If the company fails to spend the prescribed amount, the board, in its report, shall specify the reasons.

The other reporting requirement mandated by the government of India is by the SEBI which issued a circular on 13 August, 2012 mandating the top 100 listed companies to report their ESG (Environmental, Social and Governance)

initiatives. These are to be reported in the form of a Business Responsibility Reports (BRR) as a part of the annual report. SEBI has provided a template for filing the BRR in line with the NVG published by the Ministry of Corporate Affairs in July 2011. Provisions have also been made in the listing agreement to incorporate the submission of BRR by the relevant companies. The listing agreement also provides the format of the BRR. The BRR requires companies to report their performance on the nine National Voluntary Guidelines (NVG) principles. Other listed companies have also been encouraged by SEBI to voluntarily disclose information on their ESG performance in the BRR format. In Feb 2022, MCA has introduced an amendment in the reporting rules and now all companies regulated by MCA have to start furnishing a report on Corporate Social Responsibility (CSR) in Form CSR-2 to the Registrar for financial year 2020-21 and onwards.

CSR Bill, 2013

As per Indian Constitution, Sec. 135.

(1) Every company having net worth of Rs. 500 Crs. or more or turnover of RS. 1,000 Crs. or more or a net profit of Rs. 500 Crs. or more during any financial year shall constitute a Corporate Social Responsibility Committee of the Board consisting of three or more directors, out of which at least one director shall be an independent director.

(2) The Board's report under sub-section (3) of section 134 shall disclose the composition of the Corporate Social Responsibility Committee.

(3) The Corporate Social Responsibility Committee shall,

   (*a*) Formulate and recommend to the board, a Corporate Social Responsibility Policy which shall indicate the activities to be undertaken by the company as specified in Schedule VII;

   (*b*) Recommend the amount of expenditure to be incurred on the activities referred to in clause (a); and

   (*c*) Monitor the Corporate Social Responsibility Policy of the company from time to time.

(4) The Board of every company referred to in sub-section (1) shall,

   (*a*) After taking into account the recommendations made by the Corporate Social Responsibility Committee, approve the Corporate Social Responsibility Policy for the company and disclose contents of such

Policy in its report and also place it on the company's website, if any, in such manner as may be prescribed and

(*b*) Ensure that the activities as are included in Corporate Social Responsibility Policy of the company are undertaken by the company.

(5) The Board of every company referred to in sub-section (1), shall ensure that the company spends, in every financial year, at least two per cent of the average net profits of the company made during the three immediately preceding financial years, in pursuance of its Corporate Social Responsibility Policy.

Provided that the company shall give preference to the local area and areas around it where it operates, for spending the amount earmarked for Corporate Social Responsibility activities.

Provided further that if the company fails to spend such amount, the Board shall, in its report made under clause (*o*) of sub-section (3) of section 134, specify the reasons for not spending the amount.

Explanation —For the purposes of this section "average net profit" shall be calculated in accordance with the provisions of section 198.

CSR activities recognized under the Bill include: Eradicating extreme hunger and poverty; Promotion of education, Promoting gender equality and empowering women; Reducing child mortality and improving maternal health; Combating HIV, AIDS, Malaria and other diseases, Ensuring environmental sustainability; Imparting employment enhancing vocational skills; Social business projects; and Contribution to certain funds. The company is to give preference to local areas when formulating its CSR policy.

Other highlight of the CSR Bill, 2013

CSR Committee

Qualifying Companies required to form a CSR committee consisting of three (3) directors, at least one of whom has to be independent director

- Responsibility of the CSR committee
- To formulate and recommend a CSR policy to the board
- To recommend amount of expenditure to be incurred on CSR activities
- To monitor CSR policy of the Company from time to time

Director's Responsibility

- Approval of CSR policy recommended by the CSR committee
- Disclosure of the content of the policy on director's report and on the Company's website
- Ensuring that prescribed CSR activities are undertaken by the company
- Ensuring that a minimum of 2% of net average profit are spent on CSR activities
- Reporting CSR activities in the director's report

Consequences of non-compliance

For failure to spend prescribed amount on CSR activities: Disclosure to be made in the Directors' report under Section 134(3)(o) of the Act, specifying reasons for not spending the amount

- For failure to provide details on CSR policy in the Directors' Report as required under Section 134(3)(o): Company: Fine of not less than INR 50,000, and up to INR 25,00,000
- Every officer in default: Imprisonment for a term which may extend to 3 years or fine of not less than INR 50,000, and up to INR 5,00,000, or both

Format for the Annual Report on CSR Activities to be Included in the Board's Report

1	2	3	4	5	6	7	8
Sl. No.	**CSR project or activity identified**	**Sector in which the project is covered**	**Project or programs Local area or other. Specify the State and district where projects or programs were undertaken**	**Amount outlay (budget) project or program wise**	**Amount spent on the projects or programs. Sub-heads Direct expenditure on projects or programs Overheads**	**Cumulative expenditure upto the reporting period**	**Amount spent: Direct or through implementing agency**
1							
2							
3							
	TOTAL						

Source: *The Gazette of India: Extraordinary, dated February 28, 2014 by Ministry of Corporate Affairs, GoI*

SEBI Circular on CSR

SEBI, on 20th April, 2014 came out with a detailed circular on CSR norms for listed companies providing for stricter disclosures and protection of investor rights, including equitable treatment for minority and foreign shareholders.

The new rules, which would be effective from October 1, require companies to get shareholders' approval for related party transactions, establish whistle blower mechanism, elaborate disclosures on pay packages and have at least a woman director on their boards.

SEBI's norms issued in this circular were aligned with the new Companies Act and are aimed to encourage companies to "adopt best practices on corporate governance".

The capital market regulator has amended clauses 35B and 49 of the listing agreement. Now, under changed 35B norms, listed companies are required to provide the option of facility of e-voting to shareholders on all resolutions proposed to be passed at general meetings.

Under Clause 49, pertaining to corporate governance, listed entities have to get shareholders' nod for related party transactions. It would be effective prospectively from October 1 onwards.

"All existing material related party contracts or arrangements as on the date of this circular which are likely to continue beyond March 31, 2015 shall be placed for approval of the shareholders in the first general meeting subsequent to October 1, 2014," SEBI stated in the circular.

Besides, the market watchdog has come out with norms to ensure "equitable treatment of all shareholders including minority and foreign shareholders".

Apart from providing adequate and timely information to all shareholders, listed companies should also facilitate the exercise of voting rights by foreign shareholders.

"The company should devise an effective whistle blower mechanism enabling stakeholders, including individual employees and their representative bodies, to freely communicate their concerns about illegal or unethical practices," the circular said.

Thus, the gradual, chronological evolution of **CSR reporting in India** can be easily understood from the following boxes:

2009
National Voluntary Guidelines (NVGs)
MCA issued NVGs on corporate social responsibility

2012
Business Responsibility Report (BRR) SEBI mandates that the top 100 listed companies by market capitalisation to file BRR based on NVGs along with their annual reports

2014
Corporate Social Responsibility (CSR) CSR is mandated and CSR Rules come into force

2015
Extension to top 500 listed companies Requirement for filing BRR was extended to the top 500 listed companies by market capitalisation

2017
Integrated Reporting (IR) SEBI circular advised that Integrated Reporting may be adopted on a voluntary basis from FY 2017–18 by the top 500 companies which are required to prepare BRR

2019
National Guidelines on Responsible Business Conduct (NGRBC) NGRBC released in March 2019

2019
Extension to top 1000 listed companies Requirement for filing BRR was extended to the top 500 listed companies by market capitalisation

2021
Business Responsibility and Sustainability Report (BRSR) Introduction of BRSR in May 2021

Source: MCA, SEBI, Companies Act, 2013 1 https://www.sebi.gov.in/legal/circulars/may-2021/business-responsibility-and-sustainability-reporting-by-listed-entities_50096.htm

9.9 BUSINESS RESPONSIBILITY AND SUSTAINABILITY REPORTING (BRSR)

In May 2021, the SEBI announced new reporting requirements aligned with global environmental, social, and governance reporting standards known as the BRSR (SEBI, 2021). The BRSR is voluntary for the top 1000 listed companies, by market capitalization, for the financial year 2021-22 and mandatory for these companies from 2022-23. The detailed framework includes comprehensive background information, including basic details, information related to employees, subsidiaries and associates, transparency-related disclosures, and material issues. The second section includes disclosures about the nine principles and core elements, structures, policies, and processes. The third section has been revised comprehensively include essential and leadership disclosures aligned with international standards through extensive stakeholder deliberations and public consultation.

The BRSR is the latest prescribed format. The GRI has also issued a detailed document mapping the BRSR disclosures with the Standards. As the extent of the mandate increased, the nature and number of disclosures also increased. There were no disclosures prescribed in the CSR guidelines of 2009, while the 2021 guidelines propose a robust structure comprising materiality analysis, stakeholder engagement and topic-wise disclosures. Apart from revelations of the social and environmental impacts, there are sections on policies, processes, governance, leadership and oversight. Although assurance is not mandatory, it is one of the disclosures in the latest guidelines. The format includes a note in case of disclosures pertaining to waste, water and energy that the company should indicate if the data was assessed, evaluated or assured by an independent external agency. The implementation guidance has also become much more comprehensive. However, GRI standards remain more comprehensive than BRSR – in terms of implementation guidance and disclosures.

In BRSR, the reporting questionnaire is divided into three sections as shown in the figure below:

Section A: General disclosures: The section contains details of the listed entity, products/services, operations, employees, holding, subsidiary and associate companies (including joint ventures), CSR, transparency and disclosure compliance.

Section B: Management and Process disclosures: It contains questions related to policy and management processes, governance, leadership and oversight.

Section C: Principle-wise Performance disclosures: Companies are required to report upon KPIs in alignment with the nine principles of the NGRBC highlighted in the next figure. The section classifies KPIs into two sub-categories that companies are required to report upon:

Essential indicators (mandatory):

KPIs include data on training programmes conducted, environmental data on energy, emissions, water and waste, social impact generated by the company, etc.

Leadership indicators (voluntary): Companies are expected to comply with these indicators for better accountability and responsible purpose. Some of the KPIs include data on life cycle assessments (LCAs), details on conflict management policy, additional data on biodiversity, breakup of energy consumption, Scope 3 emissions and supply chain disclosures.

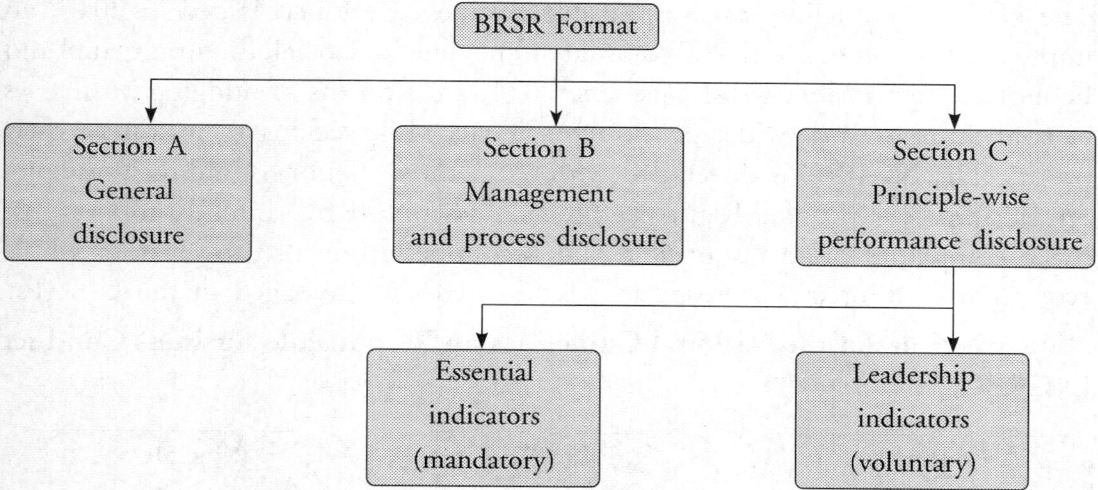

9.9.1 Nine principles under the National Voluntary Guidelines (NVGs)

The NVGs were introduced by the Government of India in 2011 and provide a set of principles and guidelines for businesses to follow in order to fulfil their social, environmental, and economic responsibilities. The guidelines are voluntary in nature, meaning that business are not legally obligated to follow them, but are encouraged to do so as part of their corporate social responsibility (CSR) efforts.

Principle 1 – Ethics, transparency and accountability

Principle 2 – Safe and sustainable goods and services

Principle 3 – Employees Well-Being

Principle 4 – Respect towards all stakeholders, especially the vulnerable/ marginalized

Principle 5 – Human rights

Principle 6 – Respect and efforts to restore the environment

Principle 7 – Responsible engagement in public and regulatory policy

Principle 8 – Inclusive growth and equitable development

Principle 9 – Value to the customers and consumers in a responsible manner

9.9.2 National Guidelines on Responsible Business Conduct (NGRBC)

The National guidelines on Responsible Business Conduct, issued in 2018, an improvement over the National Voluntary Guidelines on Social, Environmental and Economic Responsibilities of Business, 2011, are a means of nudging businesses to contribute towards wider development goals while seeking to maximize their profits. The NGBRC is dovetailed with the United Nations Guiding Principles on Business & Human Rights (UNGPs). The NGRBC intends to not just make companies more responsible and accountable but also to create a whole ecosystem to 'Protect 1', 'Respect 1' & 'Remedy' as envisaged in the UNGPs.

Nine principles of the National Guidelines on Responsible Business Conduct (NGRBC)

Principle 1	Principle 2	Principle 3
Businesses should conduct and govern themselves with integrity and in a manner that is ethical, transparent and accountable.	Businesses should provide goods and services in a manner that is sustainable and safe.	Businesses should respect and promote the well-being of all employees, including those in their value chains.
Principle 4	**Principle 5**	**Principle 6**
Businesses should respect the interests of and be responsive to all its stakeholders.	Businesses should respect and promote human rights.	Businesses should respect and make efforts to protect and restore the environment.
Principle 7	**Principle 8**	**Principle 9**
Businesses, when engaging in influencing public and regulatory policy, should do so in a manner that is responsible and transparent.	Businesses should promote inclusive growth and equitable development.	Businesses should engage with and provide value to their consumers in a responsible manner.

9.10 GREEN-WASHING

Green-washing term was coined by Jay Westerveld, a biologist and environmental activist. In 1986, when attacking the practices of certain hotels that place green cards in rooms cynically asking customers to re-use towels to save the planet, he used this term. It generally applies to individuals and companies that associate themselves to ethical causes or policies in order to improve their image and reputation. Green-washing is linked to the marketing and use of the media. Multinationals often take over companies and brands with a good green record to enhance their perception and to attract new consumers. According to the Terra Choice International, an environmental consultancy group based in Canada, there are 'seven sins' of green-washing. First, 'hidden trade-offs', which involve selecting a certain eco-friendly attribute over other or more significant concerns (*e.g.*, fossil fuel and nuclear industries). Second, claims that cannot be verified (no proof) or are extrapolated out of context. Third, using vague language such as 'all natural', 'chemical free' or 'non-toxic' – which is not necessarily 'green', as certain pollutants or toxins are found in nature. Fourth, using self-created labels, stamps or images to mislead consumers, including re-designing company logos to include green colors. Fifth, making irrelevant claims such as being free from internationally or industrywide banned substances free from irrelevant product testing; Sixth, creating compound words to soften the nature of the product such as 'green herbicides', 'organic-cigarettes', 'fuel-efficient 4 × 4 for the school run' or 'ecofriendly'. Lastly, seventh is lying by claiming or implying company-wide certifications when these have been awarded only to individual or niche products.

In this context, it would be insightful to mention one judgment of the Norwegian Consumer Ombudsman which stated that cars 'are neither green nor clean and cannot do anything good for the environment except less damage than others'. The Ombudsman, after consulting relevant stakeholders, examined the following statements used in advertisements by certain car manufacturers: Toyota Prius ('The world's most environmentally friendly car'); Opel ('Environmentally friendly engines'); Peugeot ('The powerful and environmentally friendly Hdi turbodiesel engine'); Suzuki ('The sales and environmental winner'); Smart ('Try out the world's most environmentally friendly and fun city car'); Toyota ('The world's cleanest diesel engines'); Saab ('environmentally friendly turbodiesel . . .');

Mitsubishi ('. . . environmentally friendly turbodiesel with particle filter'); Citroën ('Environmentally friendly diesel engine with particle filter'); and Fiat ('Environmentally friendly technology').The Ombudsman then issued a briefing letter stating that: It is impossible to show that a vehicle causes substantially less pressure on the environment than all other vehicles. On the basis of this we ask that expressions like "environmentally friendly", "green", "clean", "environment car", "natural" or similar are not used in the marketing of vehicles. This applies regardless of whether the environmental claims are used separately or with more detailed explanations in the marketing. In our assessment marketing of the "environmentally friendly because . . ." or "green because . . ." type would also give a misleading and incorrect picture of the vehicle's environmental properties and its effect on the environment. (For brukerombudet, Case No. 06/2449–6, Date: 03.09.07: 3). Few other groups such as Greenpeace, etc. working to reduce greenwashing. For example, they have developed campaigns such as 'Stop Greenwash', providing information for consumers and asking companies to 'clean up your act, not your image'. The focus of these groups is predominantly on the oil, automotive, electricity, coal, nuclear and foresting industries. They also provide examples and useful criteria for consumers to identify green-washing and for companies to avoid making 'unintentional' claims that could be considered green-washing.

9.11 FUTURE OF CSR IN INDIA

Corporate social responsibility (CSR) has become a crucial aspect of doing business in India. Also, there are several drivers and current trends in CSR in India today which look quite promising and present challenges as well as opportunities. Indian Companies Act and SEBI circulars have made it mandatory for the Companies to have sustainable CSR policies. The Ministry of Corporate Affairs (MCA) is responsible for enforcing CSR compliance in India. The MCA has established a CSR portal to track and monitor CSR activities undertaken by companies. The portal allows companies to upload their CSR reports and provides stakeholders with access to information on CSR activities. The MCA has also issued circulars and guidelines on CSR reporting to ensure that companies comply with the requirements. In addition to the MCA, other regulatory bodies such as the Securities and Exchange Board of India (SEBI)

and stock exchanges also play a role in enforcing CSR compliance. SEBI has mandated that listed companies must disclose the CSR activities in their annual reports on their websites. The National Stock Exchange and the Bombay Stock Exchange require listed companies to report on the CSR activities in a prescribed format. As a result, with an increasing focus on sustainability and environmental responsibility, companies are taking steps to reduce their carbon foot print, conserve natural resources and promote renewable energy. Another trend is emphases on education and skill development. Companies are investing in education and training program to improve the employability of youth and support skill development in rural areas.

There is potential for CSR to evolve in expand in India. One potential area of expansion is use of technology to enhance the impact of CSR activities. Technology can be used to increase access to education, healthcare, another basic services. It can also be used to track and monitor CSR activities, making it easier for stakeholders to hold companies accountable for their commitments. One challenge is the need to ensure that CSR activities are aligned with the United Nations sustainable development Goals (SDG's). Companies need to focus on addressing the most pressing social and environmental issues in a way that is sustainable and impactful. Another challenge is the need to improve quality and effectiveness of CSR activities. Companies need to ensure that their CSR activities are well designed, properly implemented and have a measurable impact. Additionally, collaboration between companies, civil society organizations, and the government can help to leverage resources, share expertise and increase the impact of CSR activities. Another opportunity is the potential for CSR to drive innovation and competitiveness. Companies that are committed to CSR can differentiate themselves in the market and attract customers and investors who value social and environmental responsibility.

As business organizations increasingly invest in CSR, it becomes critical to accurately examine the effects of these endeavors. In particular, business leaders should be able to rely on a coherent set of metrics to assess and prioritize the goals of different stakeholders – the ultimate beneficiaries of CSR programs – and to regularly evaluate progress made by the company in pursuing those goals.

Business organizations use CSR initiatives to build and strengthen relationships with multiple stakeholder groups. These groups may extend even beyond customers, suppliers and competitors to include investors, employees, members of the board of directors, local communities, regulators, media and financial markets. CSR activities affect a variety of different stakeholders, with potentially conflicting interests and goals. Company managers believe that CSR initiatives focusing on intermediate non-financial objectives with short-term negative cash flows may have a positive long-term effect on a firm's value.

For these reasons, measuring financial costs and benefits of CSR to a range of stakeholders is critical for companies to make strategic, systematic, informed and thoughtful decisions regarding their CSR initiatives going forward. CSR is not only a legal requirement but also a moral and ethical obligation for corporates operating in India. India's pledge to achieve net zero emissions by 2070 and the rapidly approaching deadline of the Sustainable Development Goals (SDGs) are driving policy changes to deal with climate change, biodiversity loss, impacts on vulnerable communities and other social problems. Businesses are significant stakeholders responsible for making an impact. In the last decade, the Union Government has issued various guidelines and frameworks to urge companies to measure and report their social and environmental impacts and strategies. Building an Indian society which is inclusive and equitable is a collective moral responsibility. Corporates must continue to engage in this developmental effort in a structured, socially sensitive and responsible way.

Further, in order to introduce the business case for CSR, let us look at the four-step approach as presented in the figure below:

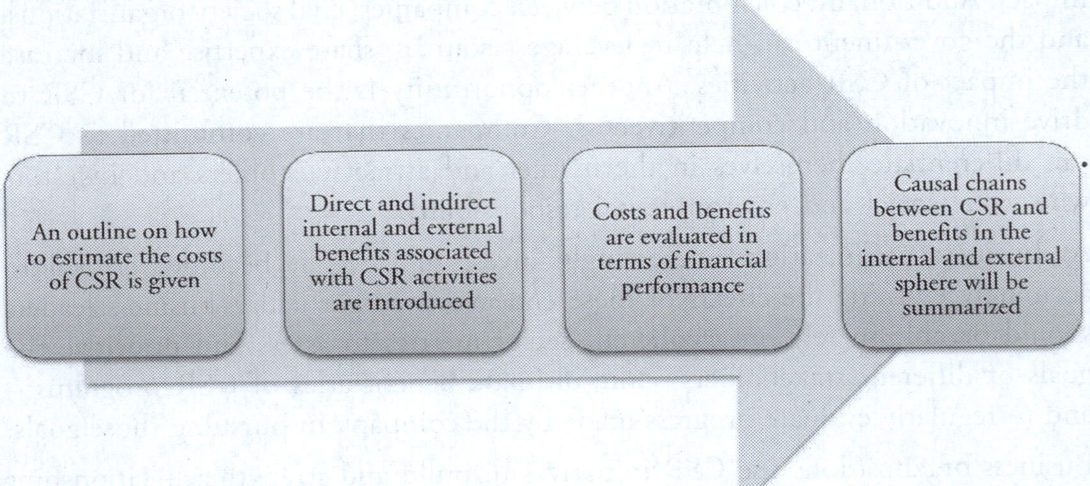

An outline on how to estimate the costs of CSR is given

Direct and indirect internal and external benefits associated with CSR activities are introduced

Costs and benefits are evaluated in terms of financial performance

Causal chains between CSR and benefits in the internal and external sphere will be summarized

9.12 BENEFITS OF CSR

Increasingly organizations like Infosys, the Tata Group of companies, The Body Shop, Starbucks etc. do make visible efforts to differentiate them from the rest on ethical pursuits. Socially responsible corporations are more likely to add an extra charm to their brands to get much needed competitive advantage for sustained organic growth in the present times. The greatest perceived benefit of practicing CSR and investing in social initiatives was seen as enhanced corporate image, goodwill and reputation.

A classic example of the long-term benefits of social responsibility was the Johnson & Johnson Tylenol incident in the 1980s, when several people died after ingesting Extra-Strength Tylenol capsules laced with the poison cyanide. To ensure the safety of its customers, Johnson & Johnson immediately recalled the product, an action that cost the firm millions of dollars in the short term. The company's production processes were never found defective. Customers rewarded Johnson & Johnson's responsible actions by continuing to buy its products, and in the long run the company. Once again became profitable.

Generally speaking, it is difficult to monetize benefits of CSR, as many benefits only get visible in the long run and are indirectly induced by positive changes through CSR. Nevertheless, CSR activities create direct effects on processes, governance and stakeholder relations of companies and these immediate changes again lead to indirect positive effects. Understanding the causal relationship between direct and indirect benefits from CSR helps us to trace improvements in competitiveness and financial performance of companies implementing CSR. There is no denying the fact that socially responsible business is good business, more so in this third decade of the 21st century.

For a quick overview on benefits of CSR, please refer to figure below:

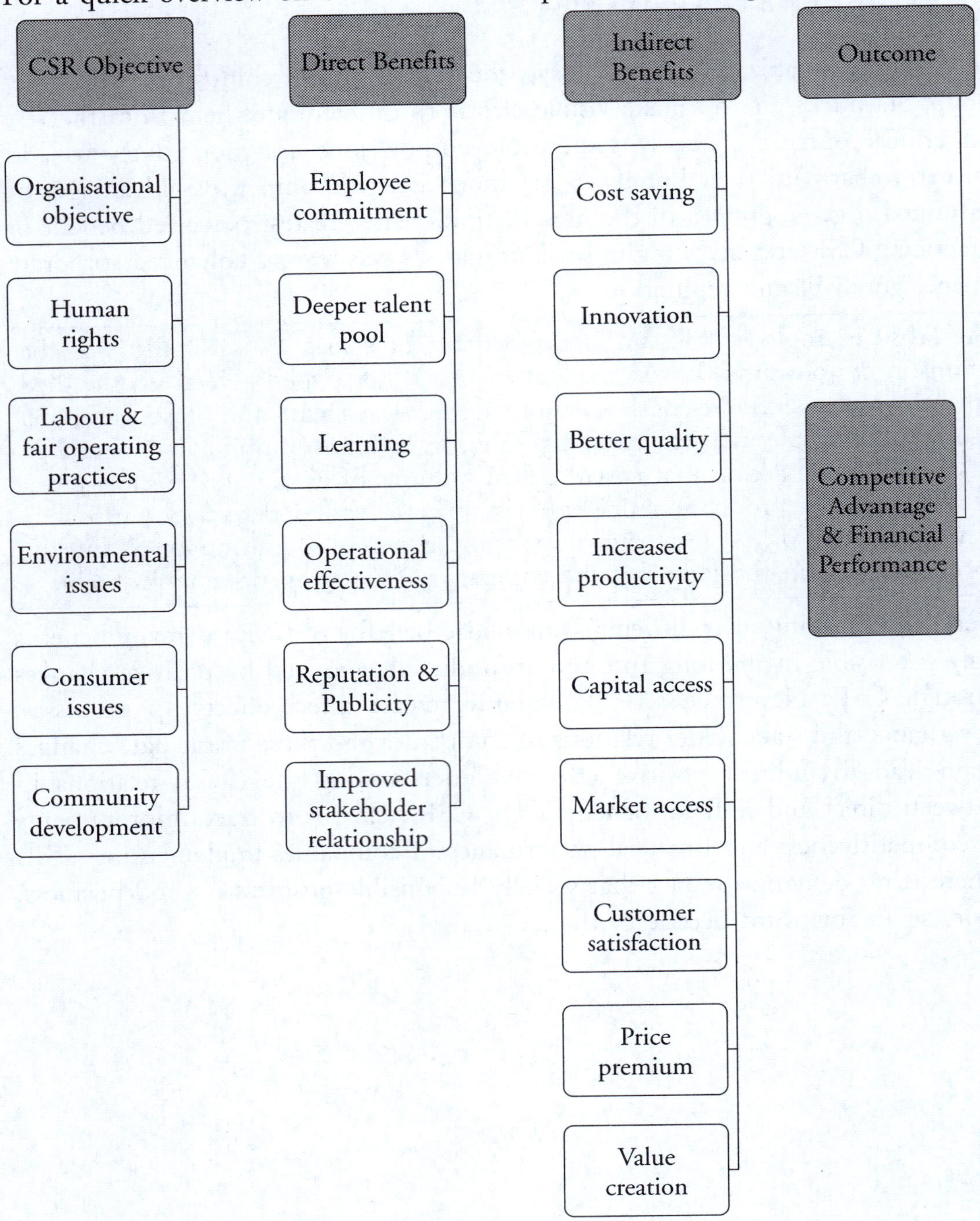

Benefits of ESG: How does ESG create value for companies?

Though at a basic level, the benefits of CSR and ESG are not much different. However, ESG, from a long-term success and resilience angle, provides companies better opportunity to evaluate their performance from an entirely different angle by increasing their bottom line by examining the following areas:

- Mitigating long-term risk: Companies that consider integrated reporting and assess ESG risks will have a more accurate assessment of any potential long-term risks. This helps them to make more informed decisions, ensuring they are better prepared for unexpected events or unexpected changes in the market.
- Improving operational efficiencies: By understanding what external factors could be impacting their operations, companies can improve efficiency and contribute to reduced costs in the long run.
- Reduced regulatory and legal interventions: A stronger external-value proposition can enable companies to achieve greater strategic freedom, easing regulatory pressure. In fact, in case after case across sectors and geographies, we've seen that strength in ESG helps reduce companies' risk of adverse government action.
- Employee productivity uplift: A strong ESG proposition can help companies attract and retain quality employees, enhance employee motivation by instilling a sense of purpose and increase productivity overall. Employee satisfaction is positively correlated with shareholder returns.
- Strengthening stakeholder engagement: Companies that embrace ESG efforts have strong relationships with stakeholders such as customers, employees, investors and the wider community. This is because they understand their impact on society and take responsibility for it.
- Creating new opportunities: Companies that are focused on ESG efforts can create new products, collaborations and business models that focus on sustainability and social impact. This leads to greater innovation, collaboration and growth potential.

There are several corporates who have created value through ESG efforts. For example, 3M has saved $2.2 billion since introducing its "pollution prevention pays" (3Ps) program, in 1975, preventing pollution up front by reformulating products, improving manufacturing processes, redesigning equipment and recycling and reusing waste from production. One major water utility, achieved cost savings of almost $180 million per year thanks to lean initiatives aimed at improving preventive maintenance, refining spare-part inventory management and tackling energy consumption and recovery from sludge. FedEx, for its part, aims to convert its entire 35,000-vehicle fleet to electric or hybrid engines. To date, 20 percent have been converted, which has already reduced fuel consumption by more than 50 million gallons. Thus, bankers should always keep in mind that a strong ESG proposition in their business and activities can create high value for them in a world where environmental, social and governmental concerns are becoming more urgent.

9.13 LET US SUM UP

The need for commercial banks to integrate the concept of Corporate Social Responsibility and Sustainability with their business strategy has been elaborately explained along with the Role and Responsibilities of the Board. CSR pyramid distinguishes various layers of responsibilities, *i.e.*, Ethical, Legal, Environmental and Philanthropic. CSR Guidelines forming part of the Companies Act, 2013 and SEBI Circular also notifies the activities and also regulatory provisions with regard to compliance and reporting at periodical intervals. The components of CSR Plan covering Developing a CSR Strategy and Policy, Operationalizing the Institutional Mechanism, Due Diligence of the Implementation Partner, Project Development and Approval, Implementation, Progress Monitoring and Reporting, Impact Measurement and Report Consolidation and Communication are discussed at length. The emerging issue of greenwashing has also been explained.

9.14 KEY WORDS

Human Development Index (HDI), Corporate Social Responsibility (CSR), Triple-Bottom-Line Approach, Mandatory CSR planning and strategizing, CSR Reporting in India, Greenwashing, Sustainability Development Goals (SDGs).

9.15 CHECK YOUR PROGRESS

1. The United Nations Development Programme (UNDP) considers Life expectancy at birth (years), Expected years of schooling (years), Gender Development Index, Multidimensional Poverty Index, among others, for the development of which of the following indices?
   (*a*) Human Development Index (HDI)
   (*b*) Gender Equality Index (GEI)
   (*c*) Life Quantity Index (LQI)
   (*d*) Education Effectiveness Index (EEI)
2. Which of the following is NOT a typical economic objective of a firm:
   (*a*) Higher efficiency in use of resources
   (*b*) Profit maximization
   (*c*) Raise shareholder's wealth (rise in stock price makes their investment to appreciate
   (*d*) Good place for employees to work
3. Over the years, corporate social responsibility is also known as all but NOT one of the following:
   (*a*) Corporate conscience
   (*b*) Corporate citizenship
   (*c*) Corporate membership
   (*d*) Sustainable responsible business
4. Identify one of the following which is NOT notified as a CSR activity by Ministry of Corporate affairs, GoI under the Companies Act, 2013:
   (*a*) Helping the Elderly people
   (*b*) Women Empowerment
   (*c*) Gender equity
   (*d*) Combating HIV & other diseases

5. As per the Ministry of Corporate Affairs data for the financial year 2015-16, for 5097 companies for which CSR data were compiled which collectively, 2691 companies had contributed positively to one or more CSR activities as notified by the government. On average each contributed company accounted for their CSR expenditure close to:
   (*a*) Rs. 1.5 crore
   (*b*) Rs. 3.6 crore
   (*c*) Rs. 8.5 crore
   (*d*) Rs. 12.2 crore
6. Government of India has mandated through a Gazette by notifying the *Format for the Annual Report on CSR Activities to be Included in the Board's Report* in early part of year—
   (*a*) 2014
   (*b*) 2011
   (*c*) 2013
   (*d*) 2016

ANSWERS

1. (*a*)	2. (*d*)	3. (*c*)	4. (*a*)	5. (*b*)	6. (*a*)

9.16 EXERCISE YOUR ETHICS MUSCLE

Case 20: Doing Good for Doing Well

1. Starbucks Coffee Company launched a $70 million initiative to help coffee farming communities around the world mitigate their climate change impacts and promote long-term crop stability. Starbucks transformed a 240-hectare farm located on the slopes of the Poas Volcano in Costa Rica into a global agronomy center, enabling the company to expand its Coffee and Farming Equity practices program (C.A.F.E.). Starbucks' chairman Howard Schultz said, "This investment, and the cumulative impact it will have when combined with programs we have put into place over the last

forty years, will support the resiliency of coffee farmers and their families as well as one million people that represent our collective coffee supply chain."

2. Joshua Shapiro visited three small villages in Uganda and was shocked by the unsafe cooking conditions he saw there. Kitchens were small, dark and unventilated. People could barely breathe. According to the World Health Organization, around 3 billion people cook and heat their homes using open fires and simple stoves burning wood, animal dung and crop waste for fuel. Shapiro, an engineer in Carnegie Mellon University's CREATE lab, began working on an idea and returned five years later as part of the Toyota's Ideas for good project to install a half-dozen hand-built, solar-powered ventilation systems to clear the air in the kitchens. Schapiro and his venture partner, Mike Taylor, assembled and installed an additional 25 systems during their second trip to Uganda and planned to construct hundreds more. These social entrepreneurs were funded by gifts and grants from various nonprofit organizations, corporations and individuals.

[Courtesy: *"Starbucks Expands $70 Million Ethical Sourcing Program with New Global Agronomy Center," Fort Mills Times, March 19, 2013, www.fortmilltimes.com. $"CMU Researchers Hope to Install Ventilation Systems to Remove Harmful Cooking Fumes," Pittsburgh Post-Gazette, July 8, 2017, www.post-gazette.com.]

Issues to Reflect:

(*a*) Are the efforts described above examples of social responsibility and citizenship practiced by a corporation and social entrepreneurs?

(*b*) Do they represent a successful merger of social and economic objectives?

(*c*) Should these programs be questioned as inappropriate uses of business assets – finances, personnel and products?

(*d*) Are these programmes really serving their purpose or just virtue signaling?

Case 21: The Greening (or Greenwashing) of Walmart

Can the world's largest company also be its most sustainable? Leaders at Walmart think so. Since 2006 Walmart has been engaged in an ambitious sustainability campaign. The company has pressured suppliers to reduce packaging (removing toilet roll cores and deodorant boxes, for example), set a goal of using 100%

electricity from renewable sources, installed water conservation technologies in its stores, kept the vast majority of its waste out of landfills and is well on its way to doubling its truck fleet's fuel efficiency. In one particularly bold move, the firm instituted a sustainability index. Walmart rates suppliers on their environmental impact in a variety of product categories, from best to worst. For example, the index measures the amount of fertilizer, chemicals and water used to produce ingredients for soup and beer. The performance of Walmart buyers is evaluated, in part, on how well their suppliers meet sustainability standards. Some environmental groups like the Earth Defense Fund and Act Now have partnered with Walmart, recognizing that its efforts to go green can have a significant impact because of the company's size and global reach. Walmart employs 2.2 million associates at 11,000 locations in 27 countries. In 2013, the multinational generated $473.1 billion in revenue. Its typical supercenter stocks 125,000-150,000 items.

Other environmentalists believe that Walmart is not going green but is engaged in "greenwashing." In greenwashing, companies make deceptive claims about their environmental efforts that cover up or "greenwash" their true environmental records. They tout their sustainability programs while continuing to despoil the planet. General Electric has been accused, for instance, of spending $90 million advertising its Eco imagination program while remaining one of the biggest polluters in the country and resisting efforts to make it clean up its waste sites.

Critics cite the following as evidence that Walmart is more about greenwashing than greening:

- Walmart derives less than 4% of its electricity from renewable sources despite its goal to reach 100%. Kohls and Whole Foods have already reached the 100% benchmark.
- The company relentlessly demands ever-lower prices from suppliers, who then supply shoddy products that wear out quickly, increasing the amount of stuff that ends up in landfills.
- Walmart's emission of greenhouse gases actually increased between 2005 and 2010, making it one of the biggest polluters in the United States.
- Walmart continues to gobble up land for new stores. In most cases it develops land that was previously unoccupied, threatening wildlife and

farm production. The company doesn't hesitate to abandon stores when it decides to open larger supercenters close by.

- The firm regularly contributes to anti environmental political candidates.

Is Walmart going green or merely greenwashing? Probably some of both. There is little doubt that the firm is committed to reducing waste and promoting more environmental sensitive practices in its stores and in its supply chain. However, at the same time, Walmart's business model makes achieving its sustainability objectives nearly impossible. Rapid expansion overwhelms environmental progress. For example, even though it reduced CO_2 emissions in existing stores, these savings were not enough to offset the CO_2 contributed by its new stores. Walmart's mission is to maintain its "Everyday Low Prices." Company leaders won't undertake some sustainability initiatives if the price is too high. The firm's use of renewable energy lags, in part, because it believes available sources are too expensive. According to the Walmart Canada CEO, the company would only consider raising prices on a few sustainable products: "Would we put our prices up [across the board?] No. Our raison d'être is to save people money."

Walmart faces some tough choices when it comes to sustainability. Many of its efforts like reducing fuel use and waste, are a natural fit for the firm because these initiatives help keep prices low and boost profits. However, more ambitious goals, like offering healthier food and recyclable small appliances and electronics, may mean higher prices and lower earnings. Company leaders will have to determine if they are willing to forgo short-term gains in order to leave the world a better place for generations to come.

Issues to Reflect:

(*a*) Do you think that Walmart is a good corporate citizen? Why or why not?

(*b*) Should environmental groups work with Walmart or against it?

(*c*) Do you think Walmart's business model makes it unlikely that it can become sustainable?

(*d*) Is Walmart going green or greenwashing? Why?

[SOURCE: Courtesy: Lambert (2010). Additional sources for this section are Cagle (2017) Fishman (2011 Camer 2013), Institute for Local Self-Reliance (2012): Kewalramani and Sabelson (2012) Kurtzleben (2012) MI November 8, 2011 November 18, 2011, February 2, 2012); Sacks (2007); Sheppard (2013) Walmart (2014)].

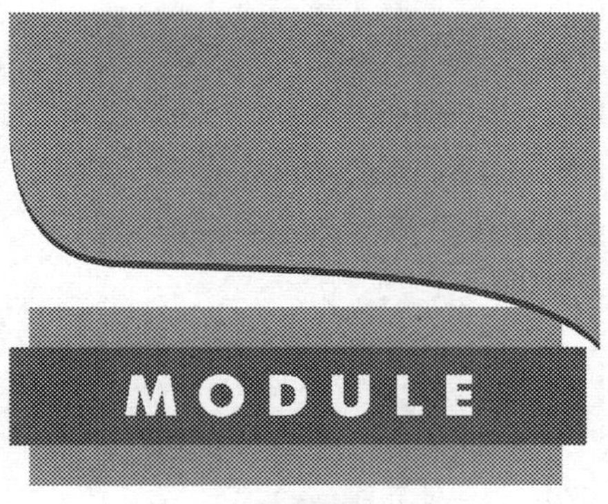

C

WORKPLACE ETHICS AND AN ETHICAL ORGANISATION

10 UNIT

Work Ethics and the Workplace

10 UNIT

Work Ethics and the Workplace

10.1 LEARNING OBJECTIVES

This unit attempts to familiarize the readers with the following:

- Meaning, identification and significance of work ethics
- Difference between work ethics and work ethic
- Importance of thinking beyond self-growth
- Ways of recognizing ethical workplaces
- Situational analysis for identifying causes of and solutions for unethical behavior
- Need for whistle blower policy, its role in good corporate governance and measures to protect all genuine complainants both in public sector and non-public sector banks in India

10.2 WHAT IS WORK ETHICS? SOMETHING BIGGER THAN THE SELF

Work Ethics

It is a rather tough question to deal with when someone is asked to identify whether or not some employee is following work ethics. Let us try to grasp what constitutes work ethics. Though work ethics does not have universally similar connotations across countries, religions, organizations, departments and so on, still there is a great amount of common agreement on the aspect called the work ethics.

This can be done by observing and analyzing how an individual employee feels about the job (and thereby the responsibilities and authority) and how he/she is engaged in with the current organization. How the person gets along with his subordinates and superiors in matters relating to execution of work, how he values the tasks associated with the job, the way he communicates with the external stakeholders, etc. also define an employee's work ethic. Whether one feels the sense of purpose and considers himself as part of the organization's larger vision and mission also is important in distinguishing the person with high work ethic from the rest. Some treat themselves as merely out-of-the-way or detached employees who, at a given point in time, are with a given organization and, eventually, would move to some other organization for a better designation or pay or comfort such as lesser commuting. This type of employees can be easily described as low on work ethic. Unless one clearly identifies through his belief, feelings, and actions with the given organization, one cannot be engaged in productive activities all through the work hours of a day and hence can be called low on work ethics.

Some of these characteristics of individuals are innate and some people believe that these characteristics cannot be developed through training or inculcated through any amount of sensitization or external motivation initiatives. However, the research conducted in this field tells us that hardened criminals also have been remarkably transformed over time when they were motivated through the right type of communication.

In the European Union, it has been witnessed in recent years that some countries like the Netherlands have a greater number of cells in the prisons developed by the country's law enforcement agencies, keeping in mind the trends in convictions of the criminals over time. However, the fair treatment and revered behavior by the jail authorities in dealing with the convicted prisoners and the influence of the preaching have resulted in a drastic reduction in the number of new convicts due to the falling crime rate. Here in India, there are select prisons called as model prisons where qualified police personnel with good image in their careers are posted to transform the criminals.

While not showing the required desirable qualities like work ethics cannot be compared with the crime or heinous offence, inappropriate behavior in the workplace causes difficulties, anguish to some customers and may result in reputation loss for the organization. Such behaviour is no less damaging than the effect of criminal behaviour by a few on the larger society. The silver lining, however, is that work ethic can be imparted into the employees with low commitment and low values at the workplace.

Something Bigger Than the Self

There is a hierarchy in which one needs to think about the purpose of one's life. The hierarchy can be as under:

- Oneself
- Family
- Community
- Religion
- Society at large
- Global causes (like peace, human rights, environment, etc.)

Self: Many a time, individuals remain busy with their personal and professional achievements. They keep revising some of their goals like salary, savings, standard of living, assets, promotion and reach a point when they realize that they had just ended the active part of their life. Even when they realize, they remain helpless due to the non-availability of energy to undertake some of the individual social obligations like helping others who may be requiring financial, emotional support from others.

Family: Members of the core family like spouse, sons or daughters' education, health, upbringing, etc. also take away significant part of one's time in life. The settlement of the offspring after acquisition of requisite qualifications and training is also undertaken by the parents themselves. There are other religious or moral obligations in India like selection of the better half for the son/daughter in which active engagement of parents is quite common. A typical marriage process involves time ranging from a few months to over a year. Fulfilment of these activities or obligations would involve a significant proportion of one's active life.

Community: As a person gets associated over decades with others in the community, more so in smaller towns and villages, there would be natural expectations for help or support from other members for their relatives. This social pressure builds up more on those who achieve significant positions in various occupations. This is where one has to be helpful, but at the same time, must remain ethically conscious not to go out of the way to bend and break the rules for helping members in the community. The help should be confined to motivating, financial assistance for buying books or receiving training to appear a competitive exam, sharing the publicly available information regarding the syllabus, date, fee and mailing address to submit the application offline/online, etc.

Religion: Those persons who have a faith in one religion may help rendering some free service in the place of worship of their choice and convenience. They may also participate in religious activities as a devotee/member of a trust of a religious body, etc. without any remuneration. However, these are purely personal matters and they need not canvass their religious service at the workplace. This should not be used to take mileage from seniors by facilitating comfortable visit to the sanctum sanctorum or taking care of the entire visit with special and differentiated treatment by using all their workplace clout, if any.

Society: Larger social issues like dealing with the underprivileged, physically challenged, mentally retarded and other backward members of the society, tribal development, rural poverty, rural unemployment, illiteracy, women oppression, etc. are some national-level challenges which cannot be expected to be tackled by the national government alone. Individuals who are reasonably settled in their work and personal lives, can give their contribution howsoever miniscule, to help achieve better results in this area. The difference in some of the developed and less developing countries in the context of solving social issues is that many like-minded individuals and others as volunteers take up the above social problems in groups or individually and try to contribute in their own way and within their means. In developing countries, individuals by and large treat social problems as issues that need to be solely handled by their Governments.

Global Causes: More than the national boundary are issues of global purview. These may include solving the environmental problems, international child trafficking, money laundering, ensuring sustainable development and global ethics, etc. These types of challenges require everyone to feel concerned about the current state of the global order and start working towards solving these challenges by making use of the existing laws and rules already put in place by various organizations including banking and financial sector. Under no circumstances, polluting industries or industries using outdated technologies be encouraged by bank loans, or banks should partner with those organizations which do not support sustainable development or use child labour (directly or indirectly) or honor those who do not disclose fully the KYC norms or details of all transactions, etc.

To sum up, the essence of the above explanation is that employees in a bank or other organizations are required to think beyond the salary, expected rise in pay after bipartite settlements/pay commissions, possibilities of promotion, transfers, retirement benefits, etc. These employment matters relating to oneself do not adequately and meaningfully engage all the employees all the time during their career of about 30-odd years. Given the life expectancy these days, there are professionals in our country who are active for over 60 years in a given field of their choice like legal, medicine, teaching, financial sector, education, etc. A career, at best, may give an opportunity for about 30-35 years. Once better realization sets in at an early stage, say by early or mid-30's on this theme that something bigger than the self, a person can surely rise above the narrow perceptions of self-growth and can certainly contribute to the growth of the society and even the world's prosperity and peace. What is required is the belief that it is not the designation or pay one achieves as an individual, but rather what impact he or she has caused in one's life that is remembered by the people. There are several examples in this regard.

Starting with Mahatma Gandhi, Martin Luther King, Mother Teresa, Abraham Lincoln, APJ Abdul Kalam, are some personalities who left a great impact on the people of India and the world at large due to their relentless efforts for the belief they had in the larger society. Likewise, a few other names we may recall include Sunder Lal Bahuguna for the cause of environment, Dr. Devi Prasad Shetty for his untiring efforts to make heart surgery affordable to poor patients from not only India but from many other countries.

Difference between Work Ethic & Work Ethics

We have by now understood what is work ethics. Sometimes a term 'work ethic' is also used in the banking industry. Most of the times both terms are employed to convey the same meaning but there is a minor difference between the exact meaning of these two terms. If a person works very hard and exhibits a great deal of pride in that work, that person is said to have a good "work ethic." These people tend to be loyal, dependable, self-motivated and satisfied workers. They believe that they have an obligation to work hard in order to provide for their families, contribute to the economic health of their community and achieve a level of success for their own self-esteem. The "work ethic" concept originated back in the early Protestant church, as part of the Reformation movement in Europe. People believed that God had given them each a talent, gift or skill (or maybe several skills) that they were expected to use to the best of their ability. To not use their god-given abilities in service to their fellow citizens was a form of sin and the "Reformationists" dedicated their entire lives to avoiding sin. They wanted to serve god and their fellow citizens with all their heart, thus fulfilling their purposes in life. Some aspects of this "work ethic" concept remain in our society today. The moral obligation that many people feel to engage in productive, demanding and appropriate work comes from these religious roots. In fact, our society sees this desire as a very good one. Organizations strive to hire workers who are dependable, persevering, perceptive, resourceful, self-initiating, adaptable, independent, collaborative, considerate, appreciative and dedicated. These attributes are considered by some to be the core elements of the modern work ethic needed for success and employability. Employers are pleased when their employees exhibit qualities of this "work ethic." The more of these qualities the worker exhibits, the better worker he or she is considered to be. So, the "work ethic" could be defined as the belief that one should work diligently, beyond minimum expectations, striving for excellence in every aspect of the labor. This modern understanding of work ethic has been significantly influenced by a conceptualization of work grounded in perfection, the goodness of labor and the necessity of hard work. With roots in the same religious belief system, the work ethics is usually thought of today as a set of moral standards for each trade, profession or job classification. For example, bankers would never disclose information about their customers to third parties barring few exceptions or psychologists would never disclose information about their clients outside of their professional duties. To do so would be a violation of their workplace ethics (or their moral/professional standards). In the same way, it is considered unethical to advertise a certain product as having certain qualities if it really doesn't. Medical care workers agree that they should do everything they can to save a patient in danger of dying. There are many, many other standards that workers within each occupation or profession try to live up to. These are workplace ethics (plural, with an "s"). The concept of work ethics tries to encompass many general ethical principles such as honesty, loyalty, confidentiality, accuracy, and open-mindedness etc. These are also the qualities that most employers hope their workers will possess. Every one of us practices workplace ethics. However, some of us practice it more conscientiously than others.

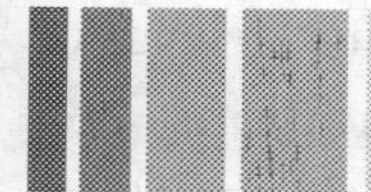

10.3 ETHICAL BEHAVIOUR AT THE WORKPLACE: BENEFITS

All those actions that are warranted and are highly appreciated not only by the internal management and colleagues of an organization but even by the outsiders like the stakeholders can be considered as ethical behavior. Each employee, howsoever new to a workplace or howsoever ordinarily qualified academically, would be in a position to realize whether his actions augur well for the organization or not. What one must consider is not to spend excess amount of time while dealing with routine transactions on the ethicality of each action. What is desirable is once the action is felt fully legal and within the service rules and does not violate a principle or guideline of an existing code of conduct, the manner in which it is done needs to be focused or reflected upon, once it is complete.

Hence, an acceptable ethical behaviour involves an employee's general set of beliefs, values and behavior that he/she shapes up for the regular day-to-day method of service delivery dealing with all categories of the customers and to the other co-employees of the own organization. Those customers, who are semi-literate or illiterate, who come to a bank/other organization requiring some help in filling up a form may be helped by the staff whenever there is an opportunity to do so. Those having minor deficiencies with the eyesight or hearing issues may be given some extra help. Other courtesies may also be extended in select cases while dealing with the customers with special challenges. Talking high about the organization, its policies, assuring of future help relating to the work, etc. are all counted under ethical behavior by the employees at the workplace. There could be instances when an employee gets annoyed with a suggestion or directions by the other colleagues. Such differences or disputes need not be attempted to be solved at that moment itself rather such matters may be resolved beyond the work hours. Customers will never appreciate such open quarrels/arguments among the employees in their presence. Also, all employees of a typical organization must remain extremely vigilant by not talking in the presence of others at the workplace or even outside in public places, when others can identify their organization from their talk about resorting to criticizing their work conditions, salary, promotion policies, governance system, etc. They can do so only when they have been given an opportunity by the designated superior official/top internal management in a particular context regarding grievance redressal or at special meetings called for to improve working conditions, etc. Also, directly approaching the members of the board of directors, writing to them anonymous/pseudonymous letters or mails is not an ethical behavior. Executing all the lawful instructions of all superior officers to whom an employee reports to constitutes ethical behavior, and violation of the same is an unethical action, which sometimes calls for stringent punishment after departmental enquiry.

10.4 RECOGNISING ETHICAL WORKPLACES

An ethical workplace can be identified easily by even ordinary persons who may not have any expertise in fields like organization theories, philosophy, law, communication, etc. The following are some of the ways and means to recognize an ethical workplace:

- Respectful treatment of all categories of customers by the front-office personnel.
- Employees' awareness of the business processes and quick and to-the-point clear answers to queries.
- Giving correct and authentic information to customers on matters like interest rates/premature withdrawals of term deposits, actual eligibility for insurance claim on assets like house/flat, etc.
- Guiding a person on a short visit for multi-currency travel card and whether to take fixed exchange rate or to go in for real-time exchange rate.
- Strict adherence to minimal prescribed documentation as prescribed by the regulator/internal management and not insisting for additional documents from the borrower.
- Appropriate attire befitting the profession of the employee, and it should provide comfort to all customers who need to speak to the employee.
- Acceptable body language of the employees at the workplace.
- High degree of energy level and commitment to work and going the extra mile to help customers.
- Confining to work-related talks and avoiding all other matters not relating to the work directly.

- No direct or indirect hints to customers to meet the employees outside the workplace for any favor or guidance to get a benefit.
- No expectations or acceptance of gifts/favors (irrespective of the amount).
- Fair and appropriate treatment given to all co-employees.
- Wherever necessary, parsing and defending the policies and decisions of the employer.
- A prominent display of the names of all the major officials of the organization's branch who are responsible for core activities for the benefit of the customers.
- Escalation details may also be displayed if there are major complaints/ service quality dissatisfaction.

10.5 UNETHICAL BEHAVIOURS: CAUSES AND REMEDIES

Causes

The major causes for unethical behavior at workplace are as follows:

- Non-availability of code of ethics manual
- Lack of fear of action
- Unrealistic targets
- Influence of co-employees
- Unprincipled leadership
- Means are not appreciated

Code of Ethics Manual: Some organizations, particularly those which are founded in recent years, keep planning for a formal code of conduct manual. This intent may also be expressed or even discussed in some meetings or informal get-togethers. However, it does not take the shape of developing and adopting the code of ethics. Hence, in its absence, some employees pretend ignorance and when get caught or asked for an informal explanation for a perceived unethical action, the employees concerned plead innocence.

Fear of Action: Employees may behave differently if they found the management treating unethical behavior extremely seriously. If some teammates are given strict punishment like stoppage of increment or delay in promotion (if not dismissal) on account of an unethical behavior established through properly conducted enquiry, other employees would not take chance of resorting to any unethical activities. In the absence of such visible action by the top management, there will be no fear element in the minds of employees. This would result in recurrence of many unethical activities in a given organization.

Unrealistic Targets: As competition keeps intensifying in financial or other sectors, the employees will continue to be pressurized to meet some unrealistic targets. For facing the ire of the reviewing manager/team of managers during appraisals, some employees find short cuts by claiming work which was never done or provide some inflated benefits of a financial product or hide riders or conditions to qualify insurance amount and so on. This is what can be seen in examination-related malpractices resorted to by some students even in university examinations, entrance tests or sports, etc. The underlying cause of all these wrong practices is the pressure (external or self-created) to achieve some unreasonably high targets on account of growing competition and trying to succeed somehow.

Influence of Co-employees: In some departments or even entire organizations, few of the employees may resort to corrupt or unethical behavior at workplace. They focus on personal work during office hours, leave workplace several times during the day and carry out some tasks with which their organization has no relationship. On the contrary, sometimes these employees by doing unconnected works outside their organization may bring ill repute to their own organization. This kind of behavior has a bearing on the new recruits, who will be learning the work from their superiors or colleagues. If some of the new recruits do not follow suit and start confining strictly to the assigned work and remain seated 8-10 hours inside office premises, they are belittled by such kind of employees. They do not extend their cooperation to those new recruits when their help is solicited in select cases.

Unprincipled Leadership: If the regulators or investigative agencies enquire top managements of an organization and media reports poorly about their involvement in select cases involving favors, the middle and junior level employees lose respect towards such leaders and their advice. The ethical conduct always flows from the top management and if the top management itself is under cloud, it would be difficult to establish ethics among the employees of the organization.

Means are not appreciated: Let us take two situations where a sales department is dealing with two employees in comparable position with similar experience. Of the two, one employee A has achieved lesser sales target but has not violated any ethical principle. His style of selling a product was well received. On the other hand, second employee, B, has achieved a greater sales target but only by using some unethical methods like making commitments that product development or after-sales service departments are not equipped to honor. If B is applauded and A is not encouraged, it will emit signals that the organization does not visibly believe in appreciating the ethicality of means to achieve the sales-targets. In such situation, employees will prefer to focus on ends only and it would be difficult to promote ethics amongst them.

Remedies

Many of the preventive or remedial measures have already been discussed earlier. The following can be tried as some of the remedies to rectify unethical behavior at workplace.

- Developing Ethics Manual.
- Starting conversations about ethics in the organization.
- Recognizing that senior and top management are a role model by definition, by their actions, and by their values.
- Assuming the responsibility for instilling ethical behavior.
- Frequent utilization of Ethics Manual.
- Training the staff in ethical behavior.
- Being consistent.
- Abiding by the laws of the land.
- Nipping of unethical behavior in the bud.
- Appreciation and Rewards for ethical behaviour.
- Encouragement of counter viewpoints and discussions in meetings.
- Care for reputation rather than results.

Some of the following situations gives a comprehension about some of the unethical practices at the workplace:

1. Abuse of the official email

2. Personal Habits
3. Data Leakage
4. Helping Friends in Social Decisions

Abuse of the official email

Like scores of talented and ambitious youngsters, Mr. RK had also appeared for a selection process of a private bank and after getting selected, started building his career. RK is not a person with high degree of passion to his role in the current employment where he just spent two years after his probation. He is now a regularized employee. This private bank gives a unique email ID to each employee who joins the bank, from the very first day, so as to enable them to meaningfully communicate with each other, seek information or data from others and improve the employee's overall productivity. While the senior management of the bank was receiving some complaints and grievances about RK at work from his colleagues, the management was not taking it very seriously for the past nearly two quarters.

One day on October 3, 2017, after three consecutive days of holidays to the bank, RK's colleague SS brought the printout of a copy of the mail sent by RK from his personal mail ID to the official mail of SS and 2 more members of his department and shown to their Vice President Mr. NT. The content of the mail was highly critical and ridiculed the functioning of select internal top management and even alleged "lack of basic knowledge and awareness on the part of the board members who announced bonus to the top most official". The mail wondered "how can Mr. X, who already is making so much diversion of bank's money for himself in most tactful manner which is known to at least a quarter of our bank staff by now, be rewarded in the form of a bonus for the bank's financial performance in the first half of the financial year instead of grilling him and replacing him with more suitable internal or external person. Our bank is still able to generate half yearly profit thanks to hundreds of honest and sincere staff, who got nothing in return after the board meeting".

This mail content was *prima facie* felt by Mr. NT as something that requires a punitive action on Mr. RK. NT decided to constitute a 3-member committee to enquire the matter and submit a report in 4 weeks. RK, SS and the two others who received the mail besides 6 other employees were requested to appear before the committee individually, which they did. RK tried to defend his action saying

every citizen has been granted freedom of speech and expression, which he simply exercised. RK admitted that he sent the mail and it was not the handwork of anyone else. The committee wanted Mr. RK to show what evidence he had got to prove the diversion of funds by the top official of the bank. RK reply was vague and unfounded. He replied: "I challenge that if you speak informally to 50 randomly-selected employees of this bank, no less than 45 to 47 would say they believe his manipulation of funds". But he never claimed for any evidence for this nor produced any credible details. The committee spent nearly 2 hours with RK asking over 100 questions, some of which were directly relating to the email issue, while others were aimed at understanding his seriousness in banking career, diligence, belief system, etc. Other members were given a hearing for about 20-30 minutes each and main focus was on the mail and how they felt about such behavior and accusation.

The committee recommended the most exemplary punishment so that others would refrain from repeating the same act in future. Management, upon receiving the enquiry committee report and recommendation, called Mr. RK and asked him to submit his resignation seeking to be relieved on personal reasons and that if he failed to do so in the next 3 working days, he would be terminated on the grounds of his unacceptable behavior and conduct at workplace. RK consulted some of his colleagues and relatives who had legal awareness. Based on the advice from the persons he consulted, RK quit the bank.

One of the suggestions given by the enquiry committee in its report was to incorporate the email etiquettes so that in future, the employer can be free from guilt if similar action needs to be initiated against someone else. Management of the bank promptly acted on this advice and the existing code of ethics was revised with a quarter by incorporating a half a page on this matter of email norms.

Personal Habits

Suddenly, there was a lunch-hour protest in a company by a group of employees protesting against the decision of their HR department to carryout routine checks for their employees to know whether or not they have alcoholism and smoking as habits. Medical examination, carried out by a local unit of a renowned pathological hospital chain, had been conducted and employees' personal habits were shared with the HR department, who in turn passed this employee-wise information of close to 200 employees to the insurance company, which was providing Group Mediclaim Service to the Company.

The reasoning by the employer is that the insurance companies need to spend huge medical expenses in reimbursing select employees of various clients covered under the Group Health Insurance schemes, including a few from the company under discussion here. Many of the fresh graduates and post-graduates, according to some members of the HR department who select aspirants from campuses each year, somehow restrain smoking and or drinking till such time they get into any organization of repute. Once the young employees settle down in a job, they start getting addicted to some habits that are not acceptable to insurance companies. Diseases like kidney failures, lung or throat cancer, for instance require huge sums to be reimbursed to the affected persons who insure their health subject to conditions. If these conditions are violated, the employee is at fault and cannot merely put the blame on the employer.

But the issue here is that why employer should be concerned with the social and personal lives of their employees. So long as the employees resist pursuing their habits at the workplace, the employer need not have any difficulty. The stance of the employer in this case is that even we have no pleasure troubling and disturbing our own employees provided the insurers permit or ignore this. When premium details are shared in intranet, others get to know their personal habits, which some feel is a matter of privacy. Given that the company has nearly 200 employees, the HR department does not vouch that there will be no leakage of information or data on premium amount. They nevertheless say that they guarantee neither the pathological lab that conducts tests nor the HR department releases the employees data containing separate columns about their being smokers/alcoholics/both and neither. The tussle goes on in this case.

Data Leakage

A prominent hotel provides discount to individuals who spend a select number of days in their chain of hotels across in India. This is a typical marketing scheme to encourage guests to patronize their hotel chain.

Mr. KRR likes a prominent Group of hotels, with which he developed some bonding way back 15 years ago. One day, he found to his utter dismay that his spouse got to know specific details about her husband's stay, type of food consumed, quantity and brands of alcoholic drinks consumed, details of places

covered during site-seeing in each stay at various places. She is also a working woman and incidentally stayed at one of the hotels owned by the same group. The means and modus of obtaining her spouse's information is, however, unknown.

Usually for want of convenience, guest rely on taking food from the same hotel's restaurant, travel by the same travel desk service. All this information is analyzed by the hotel's top management to retain esteemed clients, who can also provide them future business by recommending the hotel to their select friends or relatives.

While hotel authorities may initiate some action on the person who leaked the information about a guest (probably some more who are either unaware of such leakage or have ignored it saying they have nothing to hide and their family has immense confidence on their character and they share all information with the family), what if the person/s who worked for the central billing section or information technology may have left the hotel some months back.

One way of looking at the issue is complaining about the matter to the police and keep visiting the civil courts till the matter is disposed. Sometimes these cases may stretch years or even decades, as the courts have significant burden of pending cases of greater urgency. Another way to deal with this situation is to demand some compensation and settle the matter mutually between the hotel and the aggrieved guest. The third one is to stop visiting the hotel and inform as many friends and relatives as possible about his experience.

- If you were to suggest some measures for improving the situation at this chain of hotels, what suggestion/s do you have for the employees, internal management and members of the board of the hotel, which is a listed entity on two stock exchanges?
- Is lack of ethics involved here? If so, who is unethical and why?

Helping Friends in Social Decisions

Ms. BD is a studious student and just succeeded in joining as a probationary officer with a famous bank. She was helped by one of her classmates' mothers for whom BD has a very high regard. After getting the employment in the bank, both her batch-mate and her mother complimented BD. And, a few years lapsed with no contact between them. BD's batch-mate was more than just a classmate; she is a close friend for nearly four years of their engineering degree.

After nearly five years, suddenly Ms. BD gets a phone call after office hours for seeking a "small" help. BD batch-mate's mother was looking for some suitable bridegrooms for her daughter. Of the three shortlisted bridegrooms, two have their salary accounts with the same bank BD works for.

BD was requested to assess and report whether these two bridegrooms' debit and credit card details are normal or have some social flaws. Some of the payments made using the debit or credit card by typical youths may be for settling bills at bars, pubs, etc., which BD friend's mother was eager to know.

- How should BD deal with this situation? Should she flatly explain to the mother of her ex-class mate or help her?
- If bank authorities find BD sharing this specific information of one customer with others, it amounts to a serious breach of trust the customers have on the bank in terms of confidentiality of their financial details. Does it not violate the trust?
- There is of course no quid pro quo which Ms. BD gets in this entire episode. Can this still be justified?

10.6 CONDUCTING PERSONAL BUSINESS DURING OFFICE TIME

As organizations become large with more employees, some decentralization of work becomes necessary. Each individual employee cannot be monitored on a day-to-day and hour by hour basis. Many organizations, private or public, would review the tasks assigned to individual employees as part of the routine weekly meetings. Some basic preparatory work for the meetings would be sufficient for the experienced employees who may not be seriously involved in the assigned tasks throughout the week.

What makes some employees indulge in personal work? Many a time, it is not on account of only one reason. There can be several reasons behind such activities. Some of unrelated tasks performed by some employees at workplace could be:

- Taking up preparation/filing of tax-returns for self, spouse and relatives
- Taking up assignments for clients
- Searching and comparing the products for online shopping

- Guiding employees of small businesses owned by the employee
- Completing the school assignments for kids
- Working for other organizations on informally agreed assignments like feasibility reports

The reasons could be as under:

- Low work ethic and least respect for customers
- Greed to earn more money and popularity
- Unquestioned job security in select organization
- Not believing in family members' abilities and competencies in their own tasks
- Denial of deserving promotion making employees demotivated and distracted
- Management may not have given role-based adequate workload
- Unassertive reporting officer/management
- Fear on the part of management to face litigations in courts

10.7 TAKING CREDIT FOR OTHERS' WORK

This problem is often seen in many organizations, which demotivates even the sincere workers/employees. The root cause for this problem is inappropriate ways of mixing individual responsibilities with the so-called team work. There can be shared responsibility in case of some tasks while individuals are and should be made, capable of handling some tasks. The problem arises by amalgamating the individual tasks into the team-based work. Some of the employees in the team are inherently weak and incompetent while others are low on work ethic, who find out some ways and means to evade the assigned work. These employees who shirk assigned tasks as part of a team, study the pattern by which reviews are conducted in meetings. These employees go on making some rehearsed statements that convince the manager taking the review. Others who have genuinely worked will remain quiet or would have no option but to wait for their turn, which never comes in a routine meeting. The organization also may be aware of the silent performers but the meetings have a peculiar environment where sometimes basic principles of democracy (like freedom of expression, equality of opportunity, fairness, non-discrimination, etc.) are not honored.

Some employees are introvert, come with rural or economically humble background, may have had education in regional languages, lack public-speaking skill, lack articulation when it comes to express one's own work, etc. The other set of employees have a contrast in their background-extrovert, affluent socio-economic background, convent-educated, exposure to various international cultures, sociable, know how not to work hard and sincerely but only to claim others' work as their own. These two sets of employees coexist in a typical organization. It is the responsibility of the top management to factor in this aspect and value the work by appreciating and discounting the claims appropriately to neutralize the non-claims on one hand and false and inflated claims on the other.

Till such time the top management carries out meetings merely as a routine ritual or compliance exercise, just with a view to record the minutes of meeting, does not go into the depth of the involvement of each employee in the assigned task and ignores the need to improve the capabilities and skills of some of the employees, the scenario does not change. Some employees always want to evade the work and pretend during the meetings with their articulation, action and tactful behavior having worked hard and achieved a lot, which would convince the management about their capabilities.

Few Other Ethical Lapses: Abuse Official Position, Lying and Favoritism

Apart from the ethical issues as reflected through the situations and other discussions under earlier paras, there are few organization vices which also need our attention as follows:

Abuse of Official Position:

In banks, individuals are entrusted with positions and official power on the understanding that they will use their delegated power in a way that serves agreed upon common ends in agreed upon ways. However, abuse of this power and position is often made to indulge in unethical actions like taking uncalled for advantages from a prospective borrower who needs money or deploying subordinates for personal tasks. In one bank, a Chief Manager used to take free math's tuitions of his boss's son after the office hours out of the fear of transfer to a distant place. In such situations, individuals let their personal interests override the mandate's purpose by granting or seeking undue favours on account of their hierarchical position in the bank. Few seniors in banks have been found to verbally abuse their juniors for non-achieving the overambitious business targets in the filthiest possible language. Using excessive psychological coercion or using the threatening language to achieve the organizational goals is also a kind of abuse of power. Further, forcing juniors to pass on distorted information or deliberate untruths to regulators and other stakeholders is serious abuse of official position.

Lying: The legitimacy and performance of banks depend upon transparency and accountability to ensure that actions align with public interest. Lying or falsifying information threatens the core integrity of banking and leadership. Lying distorts the ability of the organization and managers to understand exactly what is occurring in the organization. If mistakes are covered up and not acknowledged, individuals cannot grow and learn and the organization can never grow in the long term.

Favoritism: Favoritism involves special treatment of few individuals disregarding the merit considerations. It damages equity and fairness and engenders disrespect. Internally, favoritism such as unearned promotions or benefits undermines competence, trust and legitimacy. At a cultural level people come to believe that professional excellence does not get rewarded, but going along with superiors' wishes regardless of content does.

10.8 ETHICAL LAPSES AND ORGANIZATIONAL CULTURE

The typical codes of conduct, guidelines and other regulatory guidance from time-to-time focus on preventing unethical practices by employees and staff of various organizations, which can broadly be classified for our understanding in this unit as financial organizations and others. There has to be constant tracking, monitoring, review, analysis and assessment of each individual, departmental, divisions, regions, zones and so on, which is a time-consuming and costly exercise. Also, more often the morale of employees and staff at workplace towards surveillance is not positive. It is considered more as invasive, interference and presumptive untrustworthiness on the part of the own employees of the organization by its senior management.

Should a peon wasting some of his office time talking pleasantries with a few customers in a branch be treated at par with frauds involving tens of thousands of crores of rupees of bank money? Yes, in an absolute sense, both are wrong deeds and cannot be overlooked. However, is it worth taking action on one or two such instances by watching a week-long video footage in a branch as compared to a few passwords and codes stolen from some colleague from the other? There must be more stringent (ideally fool-proof) controls for high-value frauds (which also originate from unethical individual behavior) and grade-wise segregation of unethical practices be declared and efforts made to deal with them appropriately.

Paul D Sweeny (2014) in his paper published in the journal 'Academy of Management Perspectives' quotes Schminke and others who used the service recovery literature in marketing as a possible platform for understanding recovery from ethical lapses. "Schminke and others looked at how firms fix customers' problems, recover their loyalty, and keep their business, and asked whether similar strategies could help regain employee trust following an ethical lapse. The service recovery literature also shed light on what is often called the recovery paradox. This occurs when, say, a passenger arriving in London finds that her luggage is missing. If the airline manages to pull out all the stops and find the bags in short order, the customer may end up feeling even greater loyalty to the firm and writing the airline President to describe how well she was treated. Schminke and his colleagues suggest an ethical recovery paradox may exist if firms go the extra mile to deal with an ethical violation in a highly effective way. Such actions could, therefore, restore and enhance employee confidence and support".

After covering two experiments conducted by Schminke, Sweeny makes some observations in the conclusion part of his brief article: "For example, would the results extend to organization members who do not directly witness the violation, but merely hear about it? Put another way, does just hearing about an ethical lapse and a positive response create the recovery paradox or do employees have to personally witness it? Another interesting question is, what makes for a high-quality recovery effort? What features are seen as dealing directly with the issue rather than patching over, or worse yet, ignoring problems? Likewise, how many chances does a firm get (and in what timeframe) to go the extra mile to make things right and realize an ethical recovery paradox?"

Part of the above situations can be related to some organizations and identify the ways and means to deal with them. Also, unless employees as complainants give a written complaint by giving specific details of an unethical incident, management need not take cognizance of the oral complaints on simply someone having heard of some unethical behavior. If the accused employee goes to seek judicial help, the organization's reputation could get diluted for simply defaming some employees (if accepted routinely, oral complaints could be resorted by some employees for settling inter-personal issues and may create a poor work culture filled with fear and suspicion among the colleagues).

As we have explored in the preceding discussions, building an ethical and high-performing culture is a high priority agenda for any leader in banks who needs to get ahead of the possible erosion of value-based performance in his or her organization. The ethical leader has a moral obligation to seek out, identify and address where the greatest pressures leading to unethical actions on individuals will occur and proactively buttress individuals, policy and structure to tackle them as a cultural premise. Unethical action usually occurs at an individual level, but such actions often indicate a culture of distorted values. This means unethical behavior can reflect badly designed structures, training or incentives or controls where demands of performance conflict with the need for professional ethics. Such unethical behaviour - as it is imbedded in culture - becomes both invisible and self-sustaining. Leaders need to pursue holistic responses to anticipate and address issues at the level of organizational culture as we see from the following figure as to what are the determinants of individual behaviour in an organization:

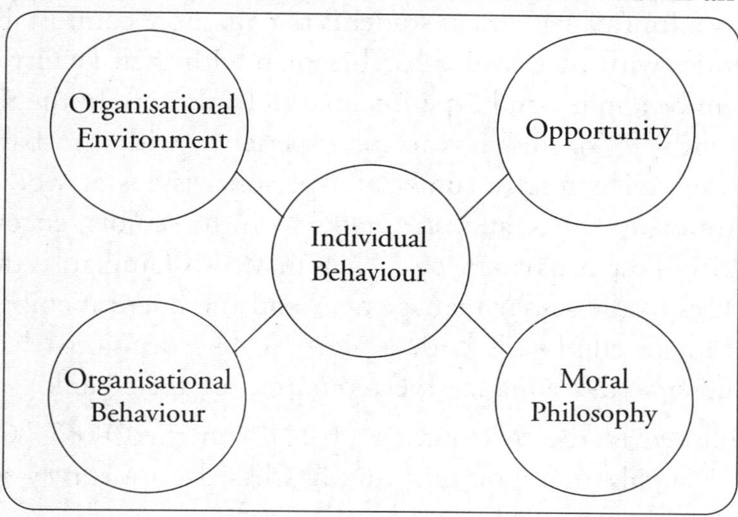

10.9 ETHICS OF A BANKER

A banker can be evaluated for the ethical commitment at three stages of his/her career:

i. at the initial stages up to first 5-7 years of taking up banking as career.

ii. at the middle management stage, typically after 7-15 years into banking sector.

iii. at the senior management level, normally after 15 years into banking service.

Banks need to groom an employee into an ethical professional in the first phase through adequate training and through informal interactions and as part of off-site get-togethers. As these employees form a good opinion about his/her career in banking (some might quit by trying civil services, Group I examinations for administrative careers, others for pursuing higher degrees including doctoral degrees to pursue careers in teaching/research), they cannot be left unengaged in the field of ethical behaviour. Such persons may be deployed as trainers and coaches, who may have lesser gap in age and seniority with the new recruits than the senior most officers of banks. Hence, the younger employees open up to these coaches and confide in them some of their dilemmas relating to ethics and may follow their advice more as a college senior guiding the previous batch students. Newly admitted batches of students remain more comfortable in seeking guidance on ethics with their senior batches than with their faculty or principal. This analogy can be applied and experimented in banks too. In the third category of employees with 15 or more years of experience with the banking sector, these persons can try to resolve some inter-personal issues at workplace, try to create an environment of free and open talks with the seniors, encourage openly employees with honest behaviour, etc. They may also familiarise the employees with the pressures of the senior management and the board members and guide all their subordinate employees with a view to take decisions that enable the top brass to preserve and enhance the reputation of their bank.

An article published in the first quarter of 2013 on the OECD Observer web site shows some highly disappointing findings based on a survey of bankers in 2012. The details are provided as under:

"Results from a survey of bank employees last year give little encouragement: at least one out of six respondents would be prepared to break the law with a little insider trading if it earned them US$10 million; a quarter of them have witnessed or have first-hand knowledge of misconduct; and nearly a third of them are convinced that getting ahead in banking requires unethical and even illegal, conduct."

They come from a 2012 survey, conducted in the US and the UK by Labaton Sucharow, a US legal firm which advocates for SEC (US Securities and Exchange Commission) whistle blowers. They show that despite reforms like the Dodd-Frank Act in the US-the biggest overhaul of the financial system since the Great Depression-or the Independent Banking Commission in the UK, the depth and sweep of misconduct remains astonishing.

There have been serious scandals too, such as when traders from 20 banks across three continents colluded to manipulate inter-bank lending rates-so-called LIBOR rates that determine what millions of people pay on their mortgages and the interest they receive on their savings. These events have undermined the already low confidence in the sector and in the way banks operate and are being regulated and supervised. In fact, as pointed out by a participant at a recent OECD financial roundtable organised to discuss the issues, too many actions by the financial sector have been destructive, even cynical, leading to negative returns for pension funds, misallocation of resources and scandals.

These beliefs and views among the respondents of banks in the survey are dangerous and self-destructive to them as well as may prove catastrophic to the banking sector as such. This trend needs to be reversed and, that too, on an urgent basis. Employees with highest ethical conduct never would fall prey to any amount of attractions of money, material and other forms of unacceptable inducements. The following are some of the major ethical qualities expected of a banker throughout his/her career.

1. Honesty and Integrity
2. Commitment to Customers
3. Confidentiality
4. Fair treatment

5. Transparency
6. Duty-mindedness

As the above ethical qualities are already discussed earlier, we can easily relate their role in shaping up ethical employees in the banking sector. However, nurturing of the above ethical qualities require the support of the practical principles of ethical power – purpose, patience, persistence, perspective and pride. These principles (proposed by Blanchard and Peale) are consistent with and integral to the basic competencies of managerial resourcefulness. These principles only can enable the managers to behave ethically and to consistently do what is right despite the various pressures so often inherent in a difficult situation.

Here it is to be kept in mind that efforts for shaping up ethical employees in the banks role modelling by seniors plays a great role. Several studies, guided by social learning theory, claim that role modelling by senior managers exerts great influence and is a very important characteristic for developing ethical conduct. Role modelling of ethical behaviour can 'trickle down' to lower levels of management. A 'moral manager' who is trustworthy, honest, reliable and credible has the greatest influence on the organizational culture. When asked," what is his job?", the chairman of Matsushita Electric said: 'To model love. I am the soul of this company. It is through me that our organization's values pass' (Blanchard and Peale, 1988: 89). Indeed, the leader creates the organization's moral environment, but it cannot be created by the fiat of the leader. The statements of the vision, mission, and policies, however numerous, well crafted, and articulated, are futile if the leader's actions and behaviour are inconsistent with these statements. Indeed, actions speak louder than words. What the leader does and values set the ethical tone and create the moral environment of the organization.

Once these efforts are made within a time-bound manner by all senior managements of banks in India and in rest of the world, say 3-5 years, the results mentioned in the OECD Survey as well as the negative perception building up in India owing to some recent unpleasant developments in select public and private commercial banks can certainly be reversed. After all, general public and the bank customers would never forget the service rendered by the banking sector in the past several decades to give them decent living standards and enabling the growth of businesses and industries to enviable positions.

10.10 WHISTLE BLOWING IN BANKS

The Concept of Whistle blowing

Whistle blowing involves calling public attention to the wrong doings in an organization, typically in order to avert harm. It can be defined as raising a concern about the wrong doing within an organization. The word whistle blower originates from 'whistle' as used by a referee to indicate an illegal or foul play. A whistle blower may be defined as a person who reveals the wrongdoings within an organization to the public or to those in positions of authority. He discloses information about misconduct in the workplace that he feels violates the law or endangers the welfare of others and speaks out with an intention to expose corruption or dangers to the public or the environment. He provides an early warning system that can alert their colleagues, employers or the public to danger or illegality before it is too late. Whistleblowing may be of two kinds: internal and external as shown under:

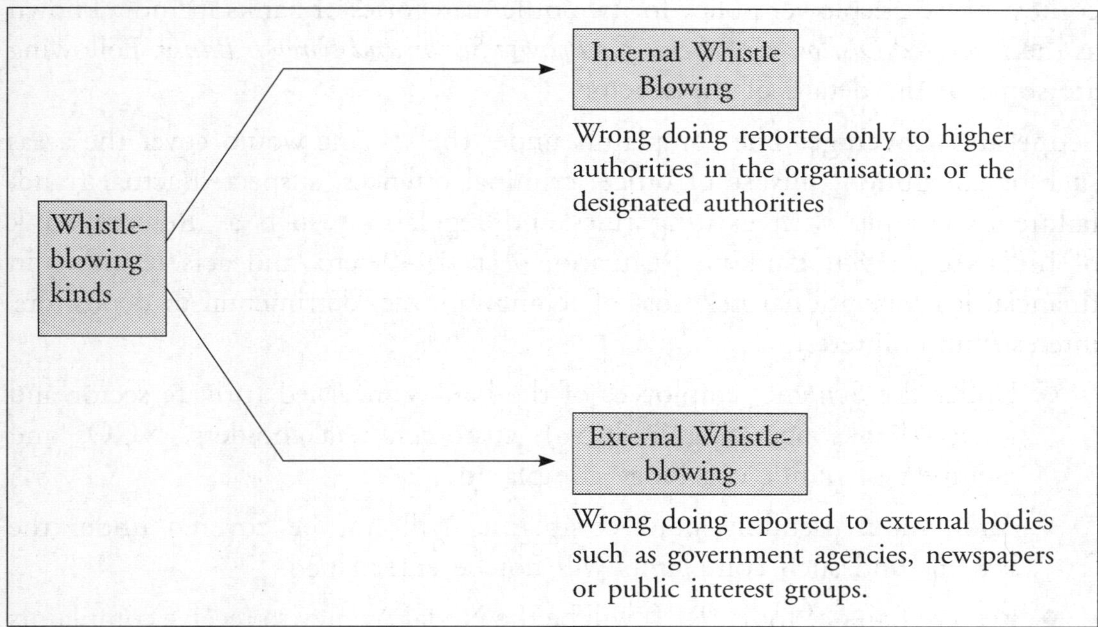

As can be seen from the figure above, internal whistle blowing is when an employee uses the internal channels for escalating the concerns. For example, through HR, internal hotline or any other similar whistle blowing channel. External whistle blowing is when an employee uses external channels such as regulators, government or media. This happens when an individual discovers a serious misconduct on the part of the organization itself or someone in position of power and feels that proper resolution of the issue will not be available through internal channels.

Whistleblowing Policies

Whistleblower policy for the public sector banks and the Reserve Bank of India has been brought under the purview of the Central Vigilance Commission (CVC) with effect from April 21, 2004. Within about three years, the other categories of banks such as private sector and foreign had also been asked to strengthen their whistleblower policy by protecting the complainant who wished to bring certain frauds or corruption or any other matter to the regulator adopting a laid down procedure.

Private and Foreign Sector Banks:

On April 18, 2007, the Reserve Bank of India brought out a scheme in the context of whistleblower policy for two other categories of banks in India known as the *Protected Disclosures Scheme for Private Sector and Foreign Banks.* Following are some of the details of the scheme:

Scope and Coverage: The complaints under the scheme would cover the areas such as corruption, misuse of office, criminal offences, suspected/actual fraud, failure to comply with existing rules and regulations such as Reserve Bank of India Act, 1934, Banking Regulation Act, 1949, etc. and acts resulting in financial loss/operational risk, loss of reputation, etc. detrimental to depositors' interest/public interest.

- Under the Scheme, employees of the bank concerned (private sector and foreign banks operating in India), customers, stakeholders, NGOs and members of public can lodge complaints.
- Anonymous/pseudonymous complaints will not be covered under the Scheme and such complaints will not be entertained.
- Reserve Bank of India (RBI) will be the Nodal Agency to receive complaints under the Scheme. RBI would keep the identity of the complainant secret, except in cases where complaint turns out to be vexatious or frivolous and action has to be initiated against the complainant as mentioned in the below point.

- The institution against which complaint has been made can take action against complainants in cases where motivated/vexatious complaints are made under the Scheme, after being advised by RBI. An opportunity of hearing will, however, be given by the concerned bank to the complainant before taking such action.
- Final action taken by RBI on the complaint will be intimated to the complainant.

Procedure for lodging the complaint under the Scheme: The complaint in a sealed envelope needs to superscribed as "Complaint under Protected Disclosures Scheme for Banks" and should be addressed to the Chief General Manager, Reserve Bank of India, Department of Banking Supervision, Fraud Monitoring Cell, Third Floor, World Trade Centre, Centre 1, Cuffe Parade, Mumbai 400005. Name, designation and address of complainant must be given in the covering note. Complaints may also be made in the email form. The complainant should ensure that the issue raised by him involves dishonest intention/moral angle. He should study all the relevant facts and understand their significance. He should also make an effort, if possible, to resolve the issue through internal channels in order to avoid making the complaint. The text of the complaint should be carefully drafted so as not to give any details or clue to complainant's identity. The details of the complaint should be specific and verifiable.

In order to protect the identity of the complainant, RBI will not issue any acknowledgement of receipt of the complaint and the complainants are advised not to enter into any further correspondence with the RBI in their own interest. RBI assures that, subject to the facts of the case being verifiable, it would take necessary action, as provided under the scheme. If any further clarification is required, RBI will get in touch with the complainant.

If the complaint is accompanied by particulars of the person making the complaint, the RBI shall take the following steps:

(*a*) If necessary, it would ascertain from the complainant whether he was the person who made the complaint or not.

(*b*) The identity of the complainant will not be revealed unless the complainant himself has made the details of the complaint either public or disclosed his identity to any other authority.

(*c*) If the identity of the complainant is concealed, RBI shall make discreet inquiries to ascertain if there is any basis for proceeding further with the complaint.

(*d*) Either as a result of the discreet enquiry or on the basis of complaint itself without any inquiry, if RBI is of the opinion that the matter requires to be investigated further, RBI may consider calling for the comments/response from the Chairman/Chief Executive Officer of the concerned bank.

(*e*) After obtaining the response of the concerned bank and/or on the basis of an independent scrutiny conducted/ordered by RBI, if RBI is of the opinion that the allegations are substantiated, the RBI shall recommend appropriate action to the concerned bank.

PSBs and RBI: Public Interest Disclosure and Protection of Informers (PIDPI) Resolution

The whistle blowing scheme for Public Sector Banks and RBI is known as Public Interest Disclosure and Protection of Informers Resolution (PIDPI). In 2004, the Government of India notified the Public Interest Disclosure and Protection of Informers Resolution (PIDPI) which gave the powers to the Central Vigilance Commission to act on complaints from whistleblowers. The PIDPI Resolution has the following main provisions:

(*a*) The Commission is authorized as the Designated Agency to receive written complaints or disclosure on any allegation of corruption or of misuse of office by any employee of the Central Government or of any corporation established by or under any Central Act, Government companies, societies or local authorities owned or controlled by the Central Government.

(*b*) Any public servant or a person including an NGO can make written disclosure to the designated agency except those referred in clauses (*a*) to (*d*) of Article 33 of Constitution.

(*c*) The designated agency may, if it deems fit, call for further information or particulars from the persons making the disclosure. If the complaint is anonymous, the designated agency shall not take any action in the matter.

(*d*) Anonymous complaints shall not be acted upon.

(*e*) The identity of the complainant will not be revealed unless the complainant himself has disclosed his identity.

(*f*) The Head of the Department/Organization to keep the identity of informant secret if he comes to know about it.

(*g*) The designated agency may call the comments/explanation of the Head of Department/Organisation on the disclosure made.

(*h*) The designated agency may seek the assistance of CBI or the police authorities to complete the investigation pursuant to the complaint received.

(*i*) The designated agency on finding the allegation of misuse of office or corruption substantive, shall recommend appropriate action to the concerned Department or Organisation.

(*j*) If the informant feels he is being victimized, he may make an application before the designated agency seeking redress in the matter. The designated agency may give suitable directions to the concerned public servant or the public authority.

(*k*) If on an application or on the basis of information gathered, the designated agency is of the opinion that the complainant or the witness need protection, it shall issue appropriate directions to the concerned Government authorities; and in the event of the identity of the informant being disclosed in spite of the designated agency's directions to the contrary, the designated agency is authorised to initiate appropriate action as per extant regulations against the person or agency making such disclosure.

The Chief Vigilance Officer of the Ministries or Departments of Government of India have been authorized to act as the designated Authority to receive written complaint or disclosure on any allegation of corruption or misuse of office by any public servant. The Central Vigilance Commission will supervise and monitor the complaints received by the designated authority.

Handling of Complaints Received under PIDPI Resolution

The Commission has the responsibility of keeping the identity of the complainant secret. Hence the Public Notice was issued by the Commission, informing the general public that any complaint, which is to be made under this Resolution should comply with the following conditions:

(*a*) The complaint should be in a closed/secured envelope.

(*b*) The envelope should be addressed to Secretary, Central Vigilance Commission and should be superscribed "Complaint under The Public Interest

Disclosure". If the envelope is not superscribed and closed, it will not be possible for the Commission to protect the complainant under the above Resolution and the complaint will be dealt with as per the normal complaint handling policy of the Commission. The complainant should give his/her name and address in the beginning or end of complaint or in an attached letter.

(*c*) Commission will not entertain anonymous/pseudonymous complaints.

(*d*) The text of the complaint should be carefully drafted so as not to give any details or clue as to the complainant's identity. However, the details of the complaint should be specific and verifiable.

(*e*) In order to protect identity of the person, the Commission will not issue any acknowledgement and the whistleblowers are advised not to enter into any further correspondence with the Commission in their own interest. The Commission assures that, subject to the facts of the case being verifiable it will take the necessary action, as provided under the Government of India Resolution mentioned above. The designated agency may, if it deems fit, call for further information or particulars from the persons making the disclosure. If the complaint is anonymous, the designated agency shall not take any action in the matter.

(*f*) The Commission can also take action against complainants making motivated/vexatious complaints under this resolution.

Certain categories of complaints received under PIDPI Resolution where it is not possible to maintain confidentiality about the identity of the complainants, are considered as Non-Public Interest Disclosure and Protection of Informers (Non-PIDPI) Complaints, but before processing such complaints, the identity of the complainant is masked, thus taking adequate safeguard in an attempt to maintain confidentiality about the complainant's identity. Some categories of complaints, which one similarly dealt with are as under:

(*i*) The complaint has been received in an open condition

(*ii*) The complaint has been addressed/endorsed to several authorities.

(*iii*) The issues raised in the complaint had earlier been taken up with other authorities.

(*iv*) The information has been sought/obtained under the provisions of RTI Act, by the complainant himself. The complainant had earlier taken up the issue with this Commission in the form of an ordinary complaint, under the Commission's Complaint Handling Policy.

(*v*) The complainant makes a complaint through email or seeks status/information regarding his earlier PIDPI Complaint by sending an email, thus making his identity public, which is violation of the guidelines issued by the Commission for making complaints under the provisions of PIDPI Resolution.

(*vi*) The complaint has been addressed/endorsed to many authorities of the Central Vigilance Commission, thus, disclosing his identity.

At present as per the procedure being followed in the Commission for handling complaints received from whistleblowers under PIDPI Resolution, it is important to know that in respect of those complaints which are considered fit for processing under PIDPI Resolution, a letter is sent to the complainant to obtain:

(*a*) confirmation as to whether he/she has made the complaint or not and

(*b*) a certificate that he/she has not made similar/identical allegation of corruption/misuse of office to any other authorities to qualify as a Whistle Blower complainant.

Prescribed time limit for receiving the confirmation and the certificate from the Complainant is 30 days from the date of receipt of Commission's letter by the complainant. In case of no response within the prescribed time limit, a reminder is issued, giving additional two weeks' time to the complainant for sending confirmation and the certificate to the Commission. If there is still no response from the complainant, the complaint is sent to the Branch concerned of the Commission for necessary action under Complaint Handling Policy of the Commission.

Protection to Whistle blowers

According to the PIDPI Resolution, following provisions have been made for protection of Whistle Blowers:

(*a*) If any person is aggrieved by any action on the ground that he is being victimized due to the fact that he had filed a complaint or disclosure, he may file an application before the designated agency (CVC) seeking redress in the matter, who shall take such action as deemed fit the designated agency may give suitable directions to the concerned public servant or the public authority as the case may be.

(*b*) Either on the application of the complainant, or on the basis of the information gathered, if the designated agency is of the opinion that either the complainant or the witnesses need protection, the designated agency shall issue appropriate directions to the concerned authorities.

(*c*) In the event of the identity of the informant being disclosed in spite of the designated agency's directions to the contrary, the designated agency is authorized to initiate appropriate action as per extant regulations against the person or agency making such disclosure.

Thus, with separate authorities supervising the complaints regarding the PSBs (the CVC and CBI) and the regulator RBI itself (for private and foreign banks), the whistle-blower policy mechanism is in place for about 15 years now. However, there appears to be some hesitation in the minds of some bank employees in reporting some matters of integrity and corruption to the CVC and the RBI. This inference can be arrived at based on the frequent and large-scale monetary fines imposed by the regulator on dozens of banks for non-compliance of KYC norms and some scandals reported in the media during the past few years. The reputation of the banking sector and the trust of the customers on banking are the two prime considerations here in the whistleblower policy.

What would you do?

If you come to know that few of your colleagues who are friendly to you are indulging in some serious malpractice and, if revealed, would lose jobs and their families would suffer, do you believe that you could undertake a whistleblowing act? What, if the non-escalation of the issue, if revealed, might result in similar action against you at a later date?

10.11 WHISTLE BLOWING: IT'S ETHICS AND ROLE IN CORPORATE GOVERNANCE

Whistle blowing is a characteristic of a healthy, self-aware and self-critical organization. Internal whistle blowing structures and plays an essential role in good corporate governance of banks. The model of corporate governance will

not be complete in the absence of whistle blowing mechanism. Enactment of several federal, state and other regulations in the area since 1960s testifies its significance for corporate governance. The past has witnessed many corporate scandals which were unraveled when an insider spoke or blew the whistle and not through an audit report or a regulatory investigation. For example, Sherron Watkins, who was one of the few people inside Enron who voiced concern about accounting five months before its collapse or Harry Templeton who challenged Robert Maxwell's plundering of the pension fund, better known as 'the Maxwell Saga' in the UK or Cynthia Cooper, the internal auditor and her subordinates who investigated unusual accounting entries at WorldCom's wireless division in early 2002. Later, Cooper's team figured out that the CFO's department had made $3.8 billion in questionable accounting entries that had the effect of inflating WorldCom's earnings. The CFO pleaded guilty to several crimes and testified against CEO Ebbers. CEO was convicted and sentenced for 25 years in prison; CFO got 5 years imprisonment due to his cooperation. The emergence of debacles like Enron, WorldCom, Satyam, etc. have given prominence to the concept of whistleblowing and has made it an inalienable component of corporate governance. However, in case the whistle blowing has to perform its function of a positive force in a bank, a culture has to be created in the organization that affirms the act of whistle blowing and sees the whistleblower 'as a witness, not as a complainant'. Unless this perception is built across the organization, a vital information gathering process through which troubles can be recognized in their initial stages and nipped will not add much value as the employees are well-positioned to uncover-and help control-wrong doings in the workplace will not come forward to speak up. The working of banks today has become so complex that detection of any transgression can easily be done only by the workforce. There is ample evidence on record to show that the whistleblowers are the single most important source for detecting and preventing organizational wrongdoings-more than any other channel such as audit, regulators or government.

For a whistleblower, the act of whistle blowing presents an ethical dilemma where the obligations that arise from the organizational and group loyalty often conflict with the inclination to blow the whistle. If the person has a strong sense of personal ethics, only then the larger good prevails over the smaller good and the act of whistle blowing occurs. In some cases, it has been argued that such actions were motivated by money or by the personal egos of "loose cannons" and "troublemakers" who challenge the policies and practices of their employers while claiming to act as the corporate conscience. In addition, whistleblowers are often severely criticized as informers, "sneaks," spies, or "squealers" who have in some way breached the trust and loyalty they owe to their employers. Nevertheless, whistleblowing is considered ethical if it results in saving an organization from causing serious and considerable harm to the public or consumers or break existing laws. If the employee is motivated by the opportunity for financial gain or media attention or that the employee is carrying out an individual vendetta against the person or the organization, then the legitimacy of the act of whistleblowing becomes questionable.

If whistleblowing helps an organization to eliminate internal malpractices and to project an image of an ethical organization, it will help it to build a reputation and establish credibility in the minds of the public. Moreover, when an organization has instilled in its employees a positive whistleblowing culture, it would be able 'to perform better by identifying, detecting and deterring unethical practices; create an environment to feed authentic information to managers to make meaningful decisions and to control risk; help communicate to stakeholders and regulators that the organization means not only good business but also good governance; reduce opportunities for anonymous and malicious leaks that would create very poor impression about the organization; and reduce the chance of legal claims against the organization'.

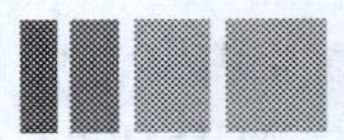

10.12 WHISTLE BLOWING LAW IN INDIA

Those officers and staff who attempted in the past to expose the corruption and wrongdoings by some unscrupulous employees or other stakeholders like contractors/operators empaneled with their organisation were killed or injured or faced life threats. Many incidents took place in public works of government of India, public sector enterprises and cooperatives and police departments to name a few.

Government of India and opposition parties in India have felt the need to stop the menace of attacks on the complainants and for passing a separate Act to protect the whistleblowers. The draft bill was introduced and referred to a Standing Committee in 2010. The Standing Committee submitted its report in 2011. It was introduced in about six months in end-2011 in Lok Sabha, which cleared the Bill. The Bill was later passed after just over 2 years by Rajya Sabha in February 2014. It received the President of India's assent in May 2014 and is in force for about 4 years now.

Whistleblowers Protection Act, 2014 provides a mechanism to investigate alleged corruption and misuse of power by public servants and also protect the complainant who exposes alleged wrongdoing in government bodies, projects and offices. The wrongdoing might take the form of fraud, corruption or mismanagement. The Act will, however, ensure punishment for false or frivolous complaints. The protection of genuine complainant is the responsibility of the CVC. The act lays down punishment up to two years in prison and a fine of up to Rs. 30,000 for false or frivolous complaint. The total penalty amount however cannot exceed Rs. 50,000. The penalty for revealing the identity of the complainant negligently or die to *mala fide* reasons is imprisonment up to 3 years and a fine up to Rs. 50,000. Any person aggrieved by the order of Central Vigilance Commission relating to imposition of penalty for not furnishing reports or revealing the identity of the complainant may file an appeal to the High Court within 60 days. Information related to national security has been kept out of the purview of the ACT. The Act is not applicable to J&K, the armed forces and the special protection groups mandated to provide security to the Prime Minister and former Prime Ministers, among others.

10.13 LET US SUM UP

Work ethics does not have universally similar connotations across countries, religions, organizations, departments but there is a great amount of common agreement on the aspect called the work ethic. It can be defined as the manner in which a person gets along with his subordinates and superiors in matters relating to execution of work, how he values the tasks associated with the job and the way he communicates with the external stakeholders. There is a hierarchy in which one needs to think about the purpose of one's life. All those actions that are warranted and are highly appreciated not only by the internal management and colleagues of an organization but even by the outsiders like the stakeholders can be considered as ethical behaviour. An ethical workplace can be identified easily by even ordinary persons who may not have any expertise in fields like organization theories, philosophy, law, communication, etc.

The major causes for unethical behaviour at workplace are as follows:

- Non-availability of Code of Ethics Manual
- Lack of fear of Action
- Unrealistic Targets
- Influence of Co-employees
- Unprincipled Leadership
- Means are not appreciated

Having an Ethics Manual in the organization and its effective implementation is the key to prevention of unethical practices and development of a great ethical culture in the organization.

Banks need to groom an employee into an ethical professional through adequate training and through informal interactions and as part of off-site get-togethers from the beginning of their career. Whistle blowing mechanism forms a critical component of corporate governance framework of a bank or for that matter any other organization. Whistleblower policy for the public sector banks and the Reserve Bank of India is known as PIDPI and is under the purview of the Central Vigilance Commission (CVC) with effect from April 21, 2004 and the Whistleblowers Protection Act, 2014 provides a mechanism to investigate alleged corruption and misuse of power by public servants and also protect the complainant who exposes alleged wrongdoing in government bodies, projects and offices.

10.14 KEY WORDS

Self, Work Ethic, Work Ethics Something bigger than the Self, Code of Ethics Manual, OECD Survey of bank employees, Favoritism, Major ethical qualities of a banker, Trickle-down, Internal Whistleblowing, External Whistleblowing, Whistleblower Policy of RBI, PIDPI, The Designated Authority.

10.15 CHECK YOUR PROGRESS

1. Unless one clearly identifies through his belief, feelings and actions with the given organization, one cannot be engaged in productive activities all through the work hours of a day, and hence can be called:

(*a*) Unethical at work

(*b*) low on work ethic

(*c*) Burden on the organization

(*d*) Misfit in the organization

2. If a banker strives towards *ensuring sustainable development,* which of the following hierarchies of 'bigger than self' can this be attributed?

(*a*) Community

(*b*) Religion

(*c*) Society at large

(*d*) Global causes

3. An acceptable ethical behaviour involves an employees' general set of beliefs, values and behaviour that he/she shapes up for the regular day-to-day method of service delivery dealing with

(*a*) Superior officers and board members

(*b*) All categories of the customers and to the other co-employees of the own organization

(*c*) Customers

(*d*) High Net worth Individuals

4. Of the following, which is NOT a cause for unethical behaviour of employees?

(*a*) Non-availability of Code of Ethics Manual

(*b*) Stringent regulatory requirements

(*c*) Lack of fear of Action

(*d*) Unrealistic Targets

5. Of the following, which one is NOT a remedy for unethical behaviour?

(*a*) Developing Ethics Manual

(*b*) Nip unethical behaviour in the bud

(*c*) Means are not appreciated

(*d*) Annual Performance Appraisals

6. Of the following, which does NOT amount to conducting personal work during business hours?
   (*a*) Searching and comparing the products for online shopping
   (*b*) Searching content and comparing corporate governance models to help the superior to deliver a speech in a bank's meeting
   (*c*) Guiding employees of small businesses owned by the employee
   (*d*) Completing the school assignments for kids
7. 'Taking credit for others' work' arises primarily because
   (*a*) Cadre-based work profiles are not created
   (*b*) The nature of work is such
   (*c*) Whatever be the contributions by individuals, superiors always give credit to select few
   (*d*) Amalgamation of the individual tasks into the team-based work
8. As per an article published in OECD Observer in 2013 based on a research survey, the proportion of respondents who believed that "getting ahead in banking requires unethical, and even illegal conduct" is:
   (*a*) One out of ten respondents
   (*b*) Two out of ten respondents
   (*c*) One out of six respondents
   (*d*) Two out of six respondents
9. Whistleblower Policy for the Public Sector Banks and the Reserve Bank of India has been brought under the purview of .... with effect from April 21, 2004:

(*a*) Serious Fraud Investigation Office (SFIO)
(*b*) Comptroller and Auditor General of India (CAG)
(*c*) Central Vigilance Commission (CVC)
(*d*) Chief Information Commissioner (CIC)

10. Reserve Bank of India brought out a scheme in the context of whistleblower policy called the *Protected Disclosures Scheme for Private Sector and Foreign Banks* on

(*a*) April 1, 2000

(*b*) April 1, 1991

(*c*) April 18, 2007

(*d*) April 18, 1995

ANSWERS

1. (*b*)	2. (*d*)	3. (*b*)	4. (*b*)	5. (*d*)	6. (*b*)	7. (*d*)	8. (*d*)	9. (*c*)	10. (*c*)

10.16 EXERCISE YOUR ETHICS MUSCLE

Case 22: Would You Help Your Colleague?

You are a senior manager in a bank. You report to a Deputy General Manager who is hardworking but not a good leader. He is also unpredictable and moody. He does not seek feedback or take it well when received. Last month, he initiated a major disciplinary action against a colleague of yours who attempted to correct his mistake during the course of preparation of presentation to be made before the General Manager. This has upset everyone working under him as they felt the individual was treated unfairly. He was trying to ensure that the work was done competently, while her boss wanted it done in an inferior manner. Your colleague has approached you to support him as a witness in defending him against the retaliatory action of the DGM. You feel that you should speak up for your colleague but are worried about the jeopardizing your relationship with the DGM.

Issues to reflect:

(*a*) What would you do?

(*b*) Is your participation actually needed? What is at stake here? Personal ethics or professional ethics or both?

(*c*) What is in the best interest of your DGM with whom you wish to maintain a good relationship?

(*d*) What is the right thing to do in the situation?

Case 23: Assess Your Workplace Ethics?

Think over the following statements. Indicate how you feel on each statement by writing a number in the blank before each statement:

[1.(Strongly disagree) 2. (Disagree) 3. (Not sure) 4. (Agree) 5. (Strongly agree)]

1. The sole purpose of banking is to grow and make profits.
2. I should do what is most convenient.
3. If you follow the law, you can't go wrong morally.
4. Ethics is an oxymoron in the competitive world of banking.
5. The lack of public confidence in the banking is not justified.
6. While applying for reimbursement of travel expenses, I can maximise it regardless to the extent of the actual expenses.
7. In office, I can do my personal works as I put in long hours here and otherwise have no time.
8. If it meant getting ahead. I would take credit for someone else's work.
9. I should do what I must to win.
10. If I made a mistake that could hurt the Bank. I would cover it up to avoid being reprimanded.
11. I will do whatever my boss asks me to do even if that is wrong. Else, my performance appraisal will get affected.
12. I would break a Bank's rule if my colleagues did.
13. I would not mind breaking a law to get a promotion as long as I did not get caught.
14. I would be willing to provide customers false information to get business.

Scoring: Once you have completed the exercise. Sum up your score and make an assessment of your ethicality as under:

(*a*) I am always ethical. (Score of 10)

(*b*) I am mostly ethical. (Score between 16-24)

(*c*) I am somewhat ethical. (Score between 25-35)

(*d*) I am seldom ethical. (Score between 35-40)

(*e*) I am never ethical. (Score of 40)

Issue to reflect:

(*a*) Looking at score, what do you think of yourself as an ethical person?

(*b*) Do you exhibit qualities of a strong work ethic?

(*c*) Do you practice good workplace ethics?

(*d*) If every one of your actions and attitudes could be seen on videotape and played back in front of your employer, would you be pleased or embarrassed? Would your boss be proud or disappointed? Or worse yet, would you be fired for some unethical act?

Case 24 : Olympus: Paying A Price for Doing What's Right?

At Olympus Corp., the Japanese camera and medical equipment manufacturer, unique whistleblowing occurred. The whistleblower was recently appointed Chief Executive Officer Michael Woodford. He was the former head of both UK and U.S. operations for Olympus, Woodford had benefited greatly from the tutelage and mentorship of Olympus Chairman Tsuyoshi Kikukawa. After taking over in 2011, as part of a regular review of Tokyo operations, Woodford began analyzing four separate acquisitions that Olympus had made between 2006 and 2009 costing Olympus $1 billion, but their assets had already been written down to just a fraction of that on the balance sheet. This indicated that the acquisitions were considered to be of no real value to the corporation. Further investigation revealed that all three companies were registered in the Caribbean tax haven Cayman Islands. In addition, all three companies were dissolved and closed shortly after being acquired by Olympus. The fourth company—a UK-based medical instruments company called Gyrus—was acquired for $2.2 billion in 2008. The purchase included a $687 million "transaction fee" to two investment bankers, with the funds going into a Cayman Islands account that was also closed shortly after the deal was concluded. Given that investment-banking fees typically amount to only 1 percent of the transaction, a fee of almost 33 percent was suspicious enough to warrant an independent audit, which the Olympus board had authorized in October 2009. The audit report subsequently declared that the company's directors had done nothing wrong. In one October 11, 2011 memo to Kikukawa, Woodford expressed his suspicions that a series of clear accounting irregularities had destroyed $1.3 billion of shareholder value in what he described as "a catalogue of calamitous errors and exceptionally poor judgment." The memo concluded with a call for Kikukawa to resign as chairman of Olympus Corp. Three days later, Kikukawa and his board of directors responded by firing Woodford from his position as CEO. Woodford's personal account of the days that followed his termination reads like a spy novel. Fearing for his life on the basis of a personal belief that the accounting scandal involved members of the yakuza – the Japanese mafia – Woodford left Japan for the United Kingdom very shortly afterward. It was later reported that Woodford was able to provide sufficient evidence to warrant investigation into his claims by the FBI, Scotland Yard's Serious Crime Unit and Tokyo's Securities and Exchange Surveillance Commission. After weeks of denials – and a disconcerting silence among Japan's regulators and mainstream media – the company was forced to concede in the face of incontrovertible evidence that it had misappropriated funds in order to hide investment losses dating back to the 1990s. Public promises were made to introduce a new Corporate Governance Committee and to release five years' worth of revised financial accounts. Kikukawa finally admitted to fraud and stepped down as chairman of Olympus. He along with two other Olympus executives, former executive vice president Hisashi Mori and former auditing officer Hideo Yamada, faced up to 10 years in jail for their roles in the scandal. In June 2012, Olympus announced that its board of directors had approved a settlement offer with Woodford of 1.2 billion yen ($15.4 million) for unfair dismissal, but the financial impact of the scandal was far from over. The stock price had plummeted by as much as 80 percent in the immediate post-scandal period, and in November 2012, the company announced that 48 mostly foreign institutional investors and pension funds had filed a lawsuit seeking 19.1 billion yen ($240 million) in compensation for investment losses resulting from the revelation of accounting irregularities.

In July 2013, all three former executives were given suspended sentences, serving no jail time for their roles in the accounting scandal. Kikukawa and Yamada were given three-year sentences and Mori a two-and-a-half-year sentence. Olympus Corp. was ordered to pay $7 million in fines for its role. In March 2016, Olympus agreed to pay $646 million to resolve FCPA charges that kickbacks were paid to U.S. doctors in the purchase of medical devices. A further $22.8 million was paid to resolve a DOJ criminal case involving bribes to health care providers in Latin America.

Issues to reflect:

1. What accounting irregularities did Michael Woodford uncover at Olympus?
2. How did the executive leadership respond to Woodford's revelations?
3. Critics argue that Woodford could have been more effective if he had taken a longer-term approach to addressing the accounting scandal, rather than the "showdown" approach he took with Kikukawa. Is that a fair assessment? Why or why not?
4. What are the moral obligations at play in the above case from a whistleblowing perspective?

[*Sources*: "The Olympus Scandal: Paying a Price for Doing What's Right," The Economist, November 24, 2012; Bill Powell, "A Rotten Picture at Olympus," Time, December 12, 2012, and "Scandal at Olympus: The CEO Who Knew Too Much," Time, October 28, 2011; Michael Woodford, Exposure: Inside the Olympus Scandal: How I Went from CEO to Whistleblower (London: Portfolio, November 2012); Yuri Kageyama, "Olympus Whistleblower Wins Millions in Settlement," Bloomberg Businessweek, June 8, 2012; "Olympus Investors Seek $240 Million Compensation," Associated Press, November 13, 2012; "Olympus Scandal: Former Executives Sentenced," BBC Business News, July 3, 2013; Pavel Alpeyev and Grace Huang, "Sony Agrees to Halve Its Olympus Stake with Sale to JPMorgan," Bloomberg News, April 1, 2015; and David Voreacos and John Tozzi, "Olympus Will Pay $646 Million to End Kickback, Bribe Probes," Bloomberg News, March 1, 2016]

11 UNIT

Building An Ethical Organization

11 UNIT

Building An Ethical Organization

11.1 LEARNING OBJECTIVES

The unit will explain the concept of building an ethical organization through various measures and guidelines. This unit will specifically enable one to understand:

- Institutionalizing ethics
- Building blocks in Ethics Management
- Success and failure of Code of Ethics
- Role of ethical leadership in determining organization culture and decision-making

11.2 INSTITUTIONALIZING ETHICS IN BANKS

Institutionalizing ethics in banks refers to creating a Code of Ethics and implementing the code in letter and spirit. It includes all activities of banks like sales and marketing, customer relationship, service delivery, credit management, regulatory compliance etc.

Some of the disturbing trends in non-adherence to ethical principles and laid down procedures have been witnessed in the past. In one case, the banking regulator Reserve Bank of India (RBI) imposed fines on some banks for violating KYC norms and other regulations in preventing money laundering. In certain other cases, loans were sanctioned/facilities extended to certain group of borrowers without adequate collaterals/margins.

Ethics, corporate governance and responsible financing are interlinked. In the cases mentioned above, certain checks & balances and safeguards which ought to have been followed were, however, not implemented on ground.

What is therefore required as a lasting solution for crafting and developing an organization into an ethically-bound or oriented entity is to inculcate ethics in every employee so that he/she retains this as part of his/her daily routine. No one then needs to remind, supervise, monitor, review on a daily/hourly basis using various online means as well as using closed-circuit cameras to oversee who is dealing with which clients or agents during the working hours. Mistrust creates the problem of unethical behaviour to take some innovative and non-detectible ways. What is needed, therefore, is to fully convince every employee about the merit and obligation to remain ethical throughout one's career.

Instead of giving routine speeches on importance of ethics during annual meets or other occasions of pride or phases of dishonour, it is always more useful and effective to incorporate an ethical code of conduct as part of the organization's policy so that every employee remembers and follows it without external advice or guidance. Some of the employees with enough seniority and known for their right moral character in the bank for several years can be requested to form part of the institutional building such that their conversations would have the greatest impact on newly joined employees. Another method can be calling some retired bankers of repute and other university teachers from India and abroad to provide some exclusive sessions on ethics as part of the executive education series for younger staff/management development programs.

The employees must be sensitized on the following aspects:

(*a*) Conflicts of Interest

Employees of banks and financial institutions should always avoid conflict-whether actual, potential or perceived – in their own personal interests or the interests of their immediate family, with the interests of the organization-bank or financial institution. Each organization may make it explicitly clear to its employees in this regard as to immediate family may include an employee's spouse, children, parents, in-laws, siblings, sons-in-law or daughters-in-law, brothers and sisters-in-law.

Employees should understand that conflicts of interest manifest themselves as conflicts of commitment or conflicts of obligation. An organizational conflict of interest is a situation in which a person has an interest that interferes with that person's ability to act in the interest of an organization when that person has an obligation to act in that organization's interest. Conflict of interest in banks can be defined as an employee's interest in his/

her role responsibility deviating from that of the bank or in other words, he/she is indulging in unethical behaviour for achieving self-interest.

However, conflicts of interest should not be collated with conflicting interests. Conflicting interests mean that those who are interested in a situation have different viewpoints and different things to gain from whichever action is taken but conflicts of interest refer to those dilemmas that force a person to choose between diametrically opposed interests, whether the interests are related to personal, employment or social affairs. Therefore, sensitization programmes should be designed with suitable examples to make employees comprehend subtle nuances of conflict of interest as this area is one major cause of unethical conducts in banks.

(*b*) Confidential information

Employees must maintain the confidentiality of information entrusted to them by their bank as employer or its customers, except when disclosure is authorized by a competent authority which the bank itself authorizes in-writing. Wherever feasible or when in doubt, the employees can better consult or verify with the officials of the legal department whether some specific information can be provided or not from the viewpoint of confidentiality. Many a time, someone claiming to be or (may be really related) the spouse or close family member asks a bank employee to mention the balance in their relative's account or the total fixed deposits outstanding. Under no circumstances, the bank staff is expected to disclose such information to others. Similarly, whether a cheque was issued in the name of an individual or a business entity also cannot be disclosed to anyone other than the account holder. Also, bankers may verify the identity in case of a doubt.

Keeping confidentiality of information possessed by the employee in his/her routine duties refers to not disclosing the sensitive information to the persons outside for personal benefits.

(*c*) Fair Dealing

It is expected that all employees conduct all dealings with their employer bank's customers and other stakeholders fairly and that, they function honestly and ethically. Sometimes, due to incentives in sale of select banking products, some employees may resort to concealing the risks and highlighting the benefits by inflating or quoting the exceptional returns provided by the financial product. Not all customers are financially well-versed in studying and evaluating various banking and financial products sold through banking counters.

Some customers who are ignorant of the specifications of a particular product may however invest in the same, solely based on the advice given by a bank staff. However, if the risk appetite of the bank customer is not adequately checked and only positive aspects get explained and the probable adverse factors are deliberately not divulged, it may lead to a wrong sentiment that such customers may develop on the bank itself. They may not remember the name or face of the employee who managed to sell these products for a good amount of sales incentive. But upon realizing after a few years that the investment had in fact caused a loss, such customers would canvass negatively about the bank. Mis-selling should be avoided at any cost as it creates a reputational risk for the bank concerned. Hence, banks will have to educate their staff to clearly explain to the customers all necessary details before selling any products involving risk.

Fair dealing means the employee must adhere to the ethical code of the bank in delivering his/her duties to the customer or stakeholder.

(*d*) Policy on Social Media

Many of the younger segments of the banks' employees spend time on social media [Facebook, WhatsApp, Twitter and so on and so forth] sharing some information with their friends who may, in turn, pass on the information almost instantly to several other groups. Banks may better specify some dos and don'ts on the type of information and comments that may not be expressed and which may have serious reputational risks or loss of confidence on account of the views and information shared on the social media. The likely punishments for such unethical behaviour of sharing sensitive information on social media, if established, can also be mentioned on the intranet of the banks. This would adequately caution employees from resorting to such comments on social media.

The increasing use of social media among the employees and its consequent impact has made it necessary to create guidelines for employees with regard to use of social media in order to regulate behaviour of employees

on social media so that they should not express views or opinions on behalf of the bank or in the official capacity of his position in the bank without taking approval from the competent authority or should create or promote any group, community or webpage which will use the name or logo/identifier of their bank or post anything on any social media platform or websites, things that would damage the reputation of the bank or any of its employees, among others.

Accordingly, all banks have come out with a social media code or policy that is to be adhered meticulously. All employees are mandatorily required to acknowledge the policy or code. In the event of any employee being found violating the Policy/Code, disciplinary proceedings will be initiated and penalties imposed. The Policy/Code shall also be applicable to all permanent and contractual employees. The social media Policy/Codes for employees state that an employee may create a social network profile in his/her real name but not by using any ID otherwise than the real name. The purpose of creating a social media policy or code is not to curtail the freedom of speech and expression while communicating staff's views/ opinion in social media blogs/sites. It is, however, desirable that all employees follow specific instructions/guidelines while communicating in social media in a more responsible and ethical way within the framework of the service rules/conditions.

Being a commercial organization, reputation is a key asset for banks. Therefore, employees should adhere to such Policy/Code by using social media tools responsibly so that their actions in anyway does not:

a. Breach their commitment on customer data secrecy

b. Cause loss of confidence to the stakeholders

c. Lead to noncompliance of the regulatory, judicial & bank's internal guidelines

d. Erode the bank's brand image

(*e*) Employee Relations

The top management of banks should make sure that all their employees adhere to the employment policies and practices of non-discrimination. No employee should discriminate others inside bank premises or outside during duty hours on the basis of sex, race, colour, religion, age, handicap, marital status, gender identity or expression or sexual orientation. All employees must be encouraged to conduct themselves in such a manner as to maintain a working environment free of discrimination of any kind.

How to induct new employees in a bank?

- **For the Fresher**

  Different banks adopt varying approaches to induct a fresher into their bank. The bank's own internal culture, experiences and collective wisdom may have evolved the induction processes to appropriately cater to their current and future requirements.

  The induction can be crisp and highly focused based on the new recruit's job profile or it can extend anywhere from 6 months in some banks to as extensive as up to 2 years in case of some other banks. When the candidates choose banking profession as their career, it is imperative that they understand their roles and responsibilities thoroughly in the formative years of their careers.

  In a one to two-week short training, basics of banking, banking products and services, details under the Know Your Customer (KYC) and some of the operational aspects can be familiarized and explained along with their ethical context.

  Some banks may insist that before they get into their banks, all eligible and prospective candidates (with suitable academic qualifications say a graduation with 55 per cent and age below 25 years, etc.) are required to complete a course from designated academic partner for a period of 12 months by covering various relevant aspects of banking including some case studies, etc. Upon successful completion of this course, these banks absorb them by giving suitable designations. This would save the bank's senior employees' time in frequently grooming the new recruits.

  A major public sector bank, on the other hand, has a 2 year long initial training which covers one-week development programme, across six weeks covering some core aspects of General Banking, Credit, Marketing, Investment Banking, Ethics & Compliance, Rural Banking and IT etc. Later, the trainee is expected to undergo

1.5 years of cross functional rotational programs across branches for a holistic grooming for a banking career.

Employee relations refers to the life cycle of an employee from the time he/she is recruited into an organization till he/she retires. Starting from inducting a fresher, ensuring that he/she undertakes induction training program on culture, non-discrimination, processes and policies, various activities of banks that support to perform his/her duties should be made known to the freshers.

- **For the Experienced**

At times, it is easier to groom or train a newly recruited bank staff or officer as he/she enters with no prior experience and therefore would be free from his/her own set of belief system on matters relating to banking.

It becomes relatively more challenging to groom a senior person who has some 7-10 years or more of banking experience. First, such experience may not be from one of India's commercial banks. The context and rules and regulations would then be entirely different. Second, there can be some variations in the regulation of foreign banks operating in India and that of the Indian commercial banks. Each organization has its own culture which may be different from the organizational culture of another organization. An individual who has worked for a sufficiently long time in an organization would have imbibed the organizational culture of that company/bank concerned. The past experience may sometimes act as an impediment rather than as a strength to the latter bank's advantage. What then is needed is to train such experienced employees with the new work environment and all modifications that may be needed to make them unlearn some of the previous methods and practices and become familiar with the new employer's needs. This can facilitate a smoother transition of the employees and they can turn out to be great assets. Also, banks may thoroughly do a background check of the experienced staff on aspects relating to integrity, honesty and professional values.

Handling experienced employee is very challenging, as there will be both positive and negative learnings from his/her previous experience. While the positive aspects can be used constructively in the current job, he/she needs to adapt to the new working environment and get aligned with the new processes instead of complaining about deviations of practices in the present organization as compared to the previous one.

(f) Sharing Bank's Own Experiences in ethical compromises

Some of the banks in private and public sectors have got a past history of ethical compromises. Not all such instances may have led to large scale scandals and scams. Hence, new recruits may benefit to differentiate between what is appropriate ethical conduct and what is not if banks share during their induction, some episodes of ethical compromises. It can be such that no specific information regarding the state, district, branch or higher levels and names of employee/s, date or amount need to be disclosed. Only sensitizing as to what went wrong by giving some situations in brief and asking the experienced employees to check where things went wrong. It may also be pertinent to find out from the newly joined experienced officers to come out with their way of averting such instances. If there is inability or general hesitation from the experienced new officers during the induction, senior trainers can share the ethical lapses in the situations during induction.

Sometimes, the past anecdotes in the form of dealing with ethical dilemmas can be documented and explained to the new joiners to ensure that the bank will not entertain compromise on ethics at any cost. The lessons, action taken in previous instances will work as a guideline and ensure that he/she will not intend to indulge in any unethical practices.

11.3 BUILDING BLOCKS IN ETHICS MANAGEMENT: AN ETHICS PROGRAMME

Any approach to be adopted while designing an ethics programme in a bank should be around a values-based cultural approach to ethics. This approach works best in practice because it keeps an ongoing attention to the key issues such as fair treatment of employees, rewards ethical conduct, shows concern

for external stakeholders and make efforts to ensure consistency between words and actions. Such ethics management programmes not only motivate employees to aspire to ethical conduct, produce highly committed employees who are aware of their ethical and compliance responsibilities and willing to report ethical violations to their superiors, but also hold them accountable for ethical violations. In this context, it will be useful to understand the seven Requirements for Due Diligence and an Effective Ethics & Compliance Program under the US Sentencing Guidelines framework:

- Establish standards and procedures to prevent and detect criminal conduct, which starts with a code of ethics or statement of values.
- Senior management must be knowledgeable about the compliance and ethics program as well as oversee its implementation and make reasonable efforts to ensure its effectiveness.
- Make reasonable efforts to exclude any individual who has committed an illegal act or engaged in other activities inconsistent with a compliance and ethics program from substantial authority in the organization.
- Periodically communicate the aspects of the compliance and ethics program to its members by conducting training programs and disseminating relevant information.
- Ensure that the program is followed by (1) monitoring and auditing activities to detect criminal conduct, (2) periodically evaluating its effectiveness and (3) employing systems that allow for anonymity or confidentiality if employees want to report criminal conduct without fear of retaliation. A common practice is a whistleblower hotline.
- Promote and enforce the program by offering incentives for performance in accordance with the program and instituting disciplinary measures for engaging in or failing to take reasonable steps to prevent/detect criminal conduct.
- Respond to criminal conduct and take steps to prevent future and similar offenses when criminal conduct has been detected.

US Department of Commerce has also outlined nine structural components of a business ethics programme that reflect global standards and best practices of responsible business conduct:

- Standards and procedures to guide member behaviour and foster reasonable stakeholder expectations.
- Adequate structures and systems that provide for authority, responsibility, accountability and sustainability.
- Communication of standards, procedures and expectations to the enterprise's members.
- Programs that monitor and audit member conduct.
- Encouragement of members to seek advice and report concerns.
- Due diligence in hiring, especially for sensitive positions in, for example, management, finance and accounting.
- Encouragement of members to follow standards and procedures.
- Appropriate responses when standards and procedures are violated.
- Regular evaluation of program effectiveness.

Though the Ethics & Compliance programme as suggested by the US Sentencing Commission is focused on developing strong internal controls for detecting illegal behaviour within organizations, it comprises all the elements of a good ethics management programme. Thus, building blocks in ethics management for a bank can be defined as:

- Top management commitment and involvement
- Policy framework: Policy or Codes
- Creation of the position of Chief Ethics Officer
- Training employees
- Implementing guidelines
- Review and monitoring
- Action taken in case of discrepancies

Top Management Commitment and Involvement

The role of top management is crucial to the way an organization does its business but this especially so in the case the ethical climate in the organization. An organization cannot be more ethical than its top management wants it to be. In their book, "Corporate Culture and Performance", Kotter and Heskett has so vividly explained that good leaders can change the course of their organizations:

"Visions and strategies were communicated with words – spoken simply, directly, and often and with deeds. They encouraged people to engage in a dialogue with them, not allowing the communication to flow in one direction only. In almost all cases, the leaders became living embodiments of the cultures they desired. The values and practices they wanted infused into their firms were on display in their daily behavior; in the questions they asked at meetings, in how they spent their time, in the decisions they made. These actions gave credibility to their words. The behavior made it clear to others that their speeches were serious. And successes, which seemed to result from that behavior, made it clear that the practices were sensible."

Unless the top management of the bank owns and actively support the ethics initiatives, the ethics management efforts can't succeed. According to Peters and Waterman in their classic book, 'In Search of Excellence'. "An effective leader must be the master of two ends of the spectrum: ideas at the highest level of abstraction and actions at the most mundane level of detail. The value shaping leader is concerned, on the one hand, with soaring, lofty visions that will generate excitement and enthusiasm. On the other hand, it seems the only way to instill enthusiasm is through scores of daily events." We have already explored the modalities of a normative leadership later in this unit and will briefly reiterate that for making success of an ethics programme, top leadership of the banks will have to (*i*) set high standards and articulate the same repeatedly in public and in private, (*ii*) be consistent in standards, (*iii*) act swiftly, firmly and fairly when someone violates the standards, (*iv*) insist on complete candor from direct reports and (*v*) remember that without supporting systems, corporate value statements are just collections of empty platitudes, to specify a few oughts. It is a fact that if ethics is poor at the top, such behaviour is copied down through the organization.

Policy Framework: Policy or Code

The organization's commitment to ethical behaviour must be documented in a code of ethics or ethics policy so that everyone in the organization formally knows what is the acceptable range of behaviours, actions and decisions within the bank. This is the most common ethics tool. A good policy framework for ethics promotion can capture what the organization understands ethical behavior to mean and establish a detailed guide to acceptable behaviors with stating policies for behaviour in specific situations. Such document should also incorporate punishments for violations of the policy. The code of ethics or policy should be applicable to employees, contractual employees, suppliers, senior management and board. The code of ethics or policy for bank is a kind of manual for managing a responsible business enterprise and should embody both business standards such as customer satisfaction, a high quality of products, safety and employee rights and values like mutual respect and politeness, trust, honesty and transparency. In order to put together a successful code of ethics or policy, McNamara (http://www.mapnp.org/library/ethics/ethxgde.htm) has offered highly useful guidelines as under:

1. **Review any values need to adhere to the relevant laws and regulations**; Review laws and regulations to which the organization must adhere. This ensures that the organization will not directly violate any laws.
2. **Define core values**: Identify three or four core ethical traits and values that are representative of your organization.
3. **Conduct SWOT analysis**: Identify what behaviors are needed to build on strengths, shore up weaknesses, take advantage of opportunities and guard against threats.
4. **Consider any top ethical values that might be prized by stakeholders**. For example, consider expectations of employees, clients/customers, suppliers, funders, members of the local community, etc.
5. **Determine important values**: From the above steps, determine the top five to ten ethical values which are high priorities in your organization. For example,
    (*a*) Trustworthiness: honesty, integrity, promise-keeping, loyalty
    (*b*) Respect: autonomy, privacy, dignity, courtesy, tolerance, acceptance
    (*c*) Responsibility: accountability, pursuit of excellence
    (*d*) Caring: compassion, consideration, giving, sharing, kindness, loving
    (*e*) Justice and fairness: procedural fairness, impartiality, consistency, equity, equality, due process
    (*f*) Civic virtue and citizenship: law abiding, community service, protection of environment.
6. **Compose the Code of Ethics**; In this step, it is important to associate with each value, two examples of behaviors which reflect the value. Include

here the wording that tells all employees they are expected to abide by the Code. Make clear that consequences will follow if the Code is not followed. Also, include the information letting them know whom they can talk to about any questions they have.

7. **Invite feedback:** The key members of the organization may review the Code and provide inputs.
8. **Communicate the new Code of Ethics**: Distribute the copy of Code to each employee and post it on the organization's intra site and website.
9. **Update the code at least once a year**. The most important aspect of codes is developing them, not the Code itself. Continued dialogue and reflection around ethical values produces ethical sensitivity and consensus. Therefore, it is required that the Code is revisited at least once a year.
10. **Remember** that no Code can include values and preferred behaviours for every possible ethical dilemma that might arise. The Code's goal is to focus on the top ethical values needed in your organization and to avoid potential ethical dilemmas that seem mostly likely to occur.

Creation of the Position of Chief Ethics Officer:

To implement the ethics programme properly in the organization, the responsibility of overseeing the ethics management should be assigned to an individual specifically appointed for this purpose. This is important as the task of incorporating and promoting ethical behaviour in the rank and file of an organization requires dedicated efforts. More than 35% of top Fortune 500 companies have established the position of chief ethics officer. State Bank of India had also created the position of chief ethics officer in the year 2017 and appointed one senior executive at the position. The duties of chief ethics officer may include to ensure that the organization adheres to code of ethics, an effective training programme is developed, the ethics communication processes are adequate, potential wrong doing in the organization are captured well in time and a strong reporting system is in place in the organization. The chief ethics officer can keep direct contact with the employees so that he may be able to give clear guidance on ethical issues and thus create a healthy ethical environment in the organization. He can also conduct employee pulse surveys annually to gauge the ethical climate in the organization with a view to assess the impact of ethics promotion efforts.

Training Employees

The ethics program is essentially useless unless all staff members are trained about what it is, how it works and their roles in it. Preparation and distribution of Code of Ethics/policy specifying the acceptable and non-acceptable standards of behaviour is a good starting point. However, the role of Code is limited only to provide guidance. The real test of an organization's code or policy comes when employees are presented with a potentially unethical situation and they to apply it in a live situation. At this point in time, an extensive training program to support the published code of ethics becomes so important. The subject of training employees has been explored in detail under subsequent sections in this unit, however, it should be ensured that during trainings, employees can work on:

- Recognizing the ethical issue.
- Discussing options for an appropriate response.
- Selecting the best option for the organization.

Efforts should be made to involve senior leadership of the organization in these training programmes as it is said that the best trainer is the behaviour of our leaders.

Implementing Guidelines:

To implement the ethics code or policy, creation of a conducive and enabling structure and system is a must. However, the following points must be kept into consideration to ensure the ethics management program is implemented in a meaningful fashion:

Recognize that managing ethics is a process.

Ethics is a matter of values and associated behaviours. Values are discerned through the process of ongoing reflection. Therefore, ethics programs may seem more process-oriented than most management practices. Managers tend to be skeptical of process-oriented activities and instead prefer processes focused on deliverables with measurements. However, experienced managers realize that the deliverables of standard management practices (planning, organizing, motivating, controlling) are only tangible representations of very process-oriented practices. For example, the process of strategic planning is much more important than the plan produced by the process. The same is true for ethics management. Ethics programs do produce deliverables, *e.g.*, codes, policies and procedures, meeting

minutes, authorization forms, newsletters, etc. However, the most important aspect from an ethics management program is the process of reflection and dialogue that produces these deliverables.

Ownership of Top Management

As already stated in the unit, top management must endorse and support the code and be seen to act in accord with it or it will be given only lip service by management and workers. It is critical that management "walk the talk," or the entire program will be a waste of time and money.

The bottom line of an ethics program is accomplishing preferred behaviors in the workplace. As with any management practice, the most important outcome is behaviors preferred by the organization. The best of ethical values and intentions are relatively meaningless unless they generate fair and just behaviors in the workplace. That's why practices that generate lists of ethical values, or codes of ethics, must also generate policies, procedures and training that translate those values to appropriate behaviors.

The best way to handle ethical dilemmas is to avoid their occurrence in the first place. That's why practices such as developing code of ethics or policy are so important. Their development sensitizes employees to ethical considerations and minimize the chances of unethical behaviour occurring in the first place.

Making ethics decisions in groups, and making-decisions public, as appropriate.

This usually produces better quality decisions by including diverse interests and perspectives and increases the credibility of the decision process and outcome by reducing suspicion of unfair bias.

Integrating ethics management with other management practices/policies & procedures

When developing the values statement during strategic planning, it is better to include ethical values preferred in the workplace. When developing human resources policies, it should be thought of what ethical values are to be most prominent in the organization's culture and accordingly policies should be designed to produce these behaviors.

There are numerous examples of how organizations manage values through use of policies and procedures. For example, we're most familiar with the value of social responsibility. To produce behavior aligned with this value, organizations often institute policies such as recycling waste, donating to local charities, or paying employees to participate in community events. In another example, a high value on responsiveness to customers might be implemented by instituting policies to return phone calls.

Using cross-functional teams when developing and implementing the ethics management program.

It's vital that the organization's employees feel a sense of participation and ownership in the program if they are to adhere to its ethical values. Therefore, include employees in developing and operating the program.

Establishing an ethics "hotline." This is a critical enabler for the implementation of ethics policy or code whereby the employees can report suspected unethical activities. Reinforcement of and compliance with the code should be furthered by mechanisms of encouragement, monitoring and facilitation of the reporting of wrongdoing. These issues should not be left to chance, else, the organization might miss an opportunity to head off a disaster or to accomplish an ethical performance objective implementation effort at times bring up certain issues regarding the interpretation of the code or policy guidelines.

Celebrate and rewarding the ethical behavior demonstrated by employees

With standards of behaviour specified in the code of ethics, along with the punishment served for failing to follow those standards, the threats of punishment must be balanced with promised rewards for successful behaviour. As such, examples of good ethical behavior should be celebrated in the bank's internal newsletter and prizes to be given to such employees. Employees who represent the standard of behaviour to which the code is committing should be recognized.

Review and monitoring

To have an effective corporate culture, not only do codes need constant upgrading under the watchful eye of chief ethics officer, but constant attention must also be given to improving training programs, measures and reports of performance, compliance and whistleblowing mechanisms. In addition, it is essential to have a formal external or internal review of the bank's culture, code and other mechanisms on a periodic basis. This is often referred to as an ethical audit and although it may be undertaken by the internal audit staff, an outside consulting service provides useful feedback. As stated earlier also, the most important aspect

of implementation process is continued dialogue and reflection around ethical values that produces ethical sensitivity and consensus.

Action taken in case of breaches/discrepancies:

An effective implementation requires that ethical breaches should be handled in a just, fair and demonstrative manner. In case of a seeming breach of the code, the first effort has to be to make a restitutional approach in an attempt to identify and resolve the problem. It is useful to express concern in a friendly and helpful way, drawing attention to the actions thought to be in breach and to the guiding principles. In circumstances where there is factual knowledge or reasonable grounds for believing that an ethical breach has occurred, it is time to take immediate action in terms of the applicable service rules or employment contract provisions after adopting a transparent disciplinary process before awarding any punishment.

Finally, it should be understood that it is unlikely that employees will see the merit of ethical behavior in regard to one area of operations if they believe management wants or is prepared to tolerate questionable behavior in other areas. Whistleblowers will not come forward, for example, unless there is a feeling of trust that they and the parties they accuse will be dealt with fairly and confidentially. Consequently, the development of a broadly based ethical culture within the company is an essential precursor for an effective code of conduct and *vice versa*.

11.4 GUIDANCE FOR TRADE-OFFS BETWEEN SHORT-TERM PROFIT AND LONG-TERM OBJECTIVES

If employees believe profit is to be earned at all costs, then unethical behavior based on short-term thinking can get the banks into trouble. Therefore, employees should be empowered to make correct decisions through creating focused sensitization on few of the following banking related issues involving such trade-offs:

- **Trade-off between personal loans *v.* priority loans**

  While banks have a moral obligation towards striving to earn profits through their loans, a judicious balance needs to be maintained between the high-interest yielding personal loans and priority sector loans. This is a tougher challenge more so in today's era as a bank's performance is judged based on the quarterly or yearly profits it earns. The bank's stock/ share price would then have a greater premium on the stock exchanges.

Guidelines covering advances to the priority sector, issued by Reserve Bank of India, cover advances to different segments namely: agriculture, MSME sector, export credit, education, housing, social infrastructure, renewable energy and others.

Personal loans include loan for one's wedding, house renovation, holiday or recreation, etc. There are varying amounts that banks can sanction depending on the borrower's creditworthiness.

As far as possible, employees of banks may try to adhere to the minimum prescribed target of priority sector lending at 40 per cent of the Adjusted Net Bank Credit or Credit Equivalent Amount of Off-Balance Sheet Exposure of their banks, whichever is higher. Over and above, a marginal percentage of the credit to such categories under the priority sector would help build the national economy rather than attempting to increase the share of personal loans or credit card, both of which maximize the bank's profitability but does not auger well in its long-term commitment of nation-building.

Banks have a trade-off between personal loans and priority sectors loans, as the former fetches higher profitability and the latter has a social cause to serve. Indian banking system was nationalized about 50 years back in 1969 and later in 1980 and also has the objective of providing liberal amount of credit to agriculture and MSMEs to support their livelihood. It is therefore the duty of each and every bank staff right from top to bottom to ensure that they implement the RBI guidelines of priority sector lending in letter and spirit.

- **Random Verification in select non-routine loan disbursal**

  It may not be feasible for the senior management of banks to verify every loan sanctioned and disbursed. However, a random scrutiny in case of select loan applications may prove to be useful to avert possible connivance of rare instances of bank employees with fraudsters posing as bonafide loan applicants. This would make all bank staff to remain vigilant before an internal or external audit unearths some loan-related irregularities.

Reviewing internal and external audits seriously for possible ethical deviations would go a long way in preventing frauds and malpractices.

While there has been a tremendous growth in the banking sector activity, it will be impossible to track each and every action of loan disbursals for their compliance to ethical standards. However, a random check will help to identify the problem in the beginning itself.

- **Personal Interest or Organizational Interest or Individualism *vs.* Collectivism**

  Individualism focuses on personal interest and achieving individual goals, whereas collectivism focuses on organizational interest and attaining team-based and organizational goals. Individualists abide by ethical standards to satisfy or protect their self-interests. Collectivists would comply with the organizational ethical standards. Employees should be sensitized to prioritize between the personal interest and organizational interest with a view to protecting their self-interest as well in the long term.

- **To speak up or not to speak up? Using Hotlines**

  Human nature suggests that not everyone is comfortable with reporting misconduct through channels suggested in the code of ethics. Many people would rather remain silent when reporting misconduct, often out of fear of retaliation, either through job loss or discrimination. This is an emotional trade-off and employees should be made aware of the benefits of speaking up as against the harms of remaining silent from the viewpoint of protecting the larger interest of the banks.

- **Productive conflict**

  It is important to differentiate between substantive conflict and affective (destructive) conflict, which is centered on the personal relationships between group members. Those caught in personality-based conflicts find themselves either trying to avoid the problem or when the conflict can't be ignored, escalating hostilities through name-calling, sarcasm, threats and verbally aggressive behaviors. This creates poisoned environment.

- **Group think**

  Social psychologist Irving Janis developed the term group think to describe the faulty thinking of groups that put unanimous agreement ahead of reasoned problem solving. Groups suffering from this symptom are both ineffective and unethical. They fail to (*a*) consider all alternatives, (*b*) gather additional information, (*c*) reexamine a course of action when it's not working, (*d*) carefully weigh risks, (*e*) work out contingency plans or (*f*) discuss important moral issues. The symptoms of group think are signs of overconfidence, close-mindedness and peer pressure. The risk of groupthink increases when teams made up of members from similar backgrounds are isolated from contact with other groups. The risks increase still further when group members are under stress (due to recent failure, for instance) and follow a leader who pushes one particular solution.

Avoiding the problem of groupthink is crucial for bankers as they come from similar professional backgrounds, work in silos and are often under stress to achieve the targets as the top management is pushing for the same.

- **Accepting or Not: Gifts & Entertainment?**

One of my friends was heading one of the state government offices. The office space was leased from a prominent real estate developer in the Mumbai. Each Diwali, the builder would send my friend one packet of expensive sweets along with a hamper of crackers. My friend liked the builder personally, although he would not count himself among the builder's personal friends. He did not want to offend the builder by refusing to accept the sweets when he was unsure himself about the propriety of such action. My friend routinely accepted the sweets and crackers and avoided ethical dilemmas in his own mind by simply distributing the sweets and crackers amongst the security guards of the building he lived. As the years progressed, my friend began to be concerned about whether he had taken the right action in accepting the first gift. He felt he could not stop accepting each year's gift since he had accepted it in preceding years. He also wondered if the other shoe would fall and the builder would come into his office one day expecting a favor that he would feel obligated to fulfill. After all, the builder had been giving and had been thanked for each gift. Eating the sweets and using the crackers with his family or distributing to others was my friend's choice. My friend's concern was that he was beginning to feel that he had unwittingly indebted himself to the builder.

Such situations are common in the bankers 'work life. Borrowers and other companies try to cultivate relationship by offering small gifts on festivals etc. to the bank officials working the credit related departments. But they have to be careful while accepting even a small gift from obligated companies to avoid any appearance of conflict in their decisions in the matters of those companies. As in our case, my friend, as a public servant, was obligated to avoid even the appearance of a conflict of interest between the best interests of the government and a private landlord. Loyalty to the government and responsible conduct in terms of guarding the public trust are important values. He simply could have asked himself the question: How would this look if it were to be printed on the front page of the newspaper? Most likely, he would have considered that it would appear to be a conflict of interest and the sweets etc. should not be accepted.

11.5 BEING ETHICAL IN AN UNETHICAL ENVIRONMENT

The behaviour of one's superiors is one of the greatest determinants of ethical (or unethical) behaviour. Since we are obliged to accept responsibility for our actions, we need to know how to be ethical in what may be an unethical environment. When an organization fails to provide such an ethical climate the employees may find themselves at risk of losing their job, morale may suffer, as may efficiency. An indication of trouble is when self-protective memos fly around the office and divert resources from what could have been more productive tasks. It is in these situations that we particularly need to know what are the protective devices for us to save the risk.

Self-empowerment in ethics may be achieved by resorting to a hierarchy of questions that the ethically troubled may use. The first question is – Am I mistaken? The supplementary questions are – Do I misunderstand the situation? Am I clear that this is an ethical issue? Do I have the relevant facts? The second question is – Do I want to do something about it? The answer may be No or one might want to remark and do the minimum (*e.g.*, let the ethical transgressor know that one knows, but do no more; or let the ethical transgressor know and say that the matter is being ignored on this occasion only). The third question is a doing question. Here one sets out to change the ethos. It may be that the reaction to a particular issue is to use that as a lever to promote ethics in general, but yielding on the particular case. As a strategy, this is good but here the flexibility is not on the principles of ethics but, rather, on retaining the commitment to principle, by applying continuous pressure to have ethical principles followed. Strong reward and encouragement for instances of ethical behavior, social approbation and due admiration are powerful tools. Criticism of a milder kind (unless for an outrageous transgression) is also commendable. A final way out and self-empowerment tool is blowing the whistle.

11.6 WHY A CODE OF ETHICS: CREATING THE ETHICAL IMPERATIVE

Code of Ethics broadly deals with possible behaviours and actions that could be harmful to the short- or long-term interests of the organization. A typical good Code of Ethics should be designed in such a way as to significantly motivate its employees and also its other stakeholders.

There should be enough clarity with explicitly spelt out consequences or actions of violations of the provisions of the Code. The language of the Code of Ethics should be simple to understand, concise and free from vagueness or interpretations. It should be easily accessible and widely communicated to all the employees of the organization at frequent intervals. It must be made to be followed by all.

Purpose

Four broad aspects can be identified to justify why banks need a separate Code of Ethics for their employees. These are:

1. Sensitizing their employees to their responsibilities
2. To display that bank values integrity
3. To avert innocent violations
4. To deal with habitual violators

Now, we shall dwell upon these objectives in detail:

1. **Sensitizing Employees to their Responsibility**

   One of the main purposes of developing and adhering to the Code of Ethics is to make all the employees to always remember that their organization carries out its business in a very responsible manner. Newly

inducted employees may have different belief systems and varied values that may not be accepted in highly ethical organizations. Hence, the Code of Ethics will exert a peer pressure on them from day-one of their joining so that organizations need not keep investing their valuable time on teaching them ethics on a day-to-day basis.

2. Displaying that Bank values Integrity

Since deposit holders (and borrowers who surrender original documents of high market value of the collateral property) keep their hard-earned money with the banks, it is but natural that the bank should not only practice the highest degree of ethical standards but it should also be perceived by all of them or whosoever cares that the bank really values ethical standards. Both existing and newly joined employees of a bank get an understanding of the bank's expectations from them through this Code of Ethics and in the process, an entire culture consistent with the bank's top management or the Board of Directors gets established in the shortest span of time.

3. Averting Innocent Violations

While in the training programmes, each bank adequately clarifies banking Acts and what constitutes a criminal misconduct, Code of Ethics primarily deals with matters like integrity, conflict of interest, honesty, transparency, etc. If not followed, this may tarnish the bank's reputation or may cause business loss. There can be a possibility whereby different employees having different socio-cultural backgrounds coming from a complex society of India may have varied beliefs about the same situation or action. Availability of the Code of Ethics brings all such employees on the same page as far as the standards and expectations and dos and don'ts are concerned. This would avert to a very large extent possible violations which otherwise would have happened out of innocent behaviour or due to ignorance or non-familiarity of the expected behaviour in a bank.

4. Dealing with Habitual Violators

Violations of the Code of Ethics carried out by a handful of errant employees of a bank can be adequate to tarnish the reputation of a bank. It needs to be documented as to who has violated which aspect of the Code in what context, where and on which date. Counselling or enquiry or inquiry committee observations also may be documented appropriately.

This would serve as a useful record to justify if bank management decides to discontinue such employees through termination and to take a stand in a court of law. Such violations, if not dealt with firmly, would send a wrong signal amongst other employees that Code of Conduct is merely a formality and no action would be taken even if it is violated. This is not the spirit with which a Code of Ethics is designed and developed. Ultimate utility of the Code lies in its embracing by all its employees in the right spirit, which makes the bank not merely following the ethics (besides relevant Acts, rules, and regulatory prescriptions) but it should also appear that the ethics is being practiced on all days by all its employees. In this context, it is helpful to understand that the Code of Ethics/Policy and Code of Conduct are not one and same thing, although both terms are sometimes used interchangeably. Code of Conduct is a statement of rules and has prohibitive nature while Code of Ethics is a statement of values and principles and define the purpose of an organization. It is aspirational in nature as shown in the figure below:

Difference between Code of Ethics *vs.* Code of Conduct

Code of Ethics	Code of Conduct
General	Specific
Values/principles	Prescriptions / directives
Judgement	Uniformity
Empowering	Enforceable statements of specific behaviors
Aspirational	Penalties for transgressions & appeal system

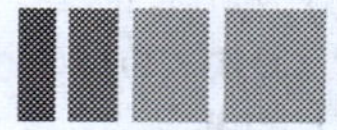

11.7 WHY CODES SUCCEED OR FAIL?

In case a bank, or any other organization for that matter, does not have one explicitly designed and developed Code of Ethics, the immediate task on hand would be to have one. Having put into place a Code of Ethics manual, the next responsibility of the top management is to make sure that the Code is taken seriously by all its employees. Whenever an employee of the same bank asks another or any outsider asks an employee of a bank "do you feel your Code of Ethics is useful or effective"? Unless the employee answers the question in affirmative, the bank cannot take the mere presence of a Code of Ethics as a

guarantee of ethical conduct of the bank's business. Answers that "it depends" or "I do not know" or "who knows" or even "I can comment about myself, but I cannot assure for the branch or entire bank" are all examples that there is something missing and the bank needs to enforce the Code more effectively.

It is not difficult to find reasons as to why a similar set of principles under the document with a title Code of Ethics may succeed in one organization but may fail in another. The following are some of the ideal conditions that contribute to the success of Code of Ethics:

1. Clear distinction between acceptable and unacceptable behaviours is stated.
2. Code is consistent with the mission of the bank.
3. Incentives and disincentives are given impartially to those adhering and violating the Code.
4. Top management or any designated cell within a bank takes into cognizance and involve themselves with all matters relating to the Code of Ethics seriously from time to time.

Organizations where a Code of Ethics might grossly and significantly fail to bring in any difference to the ethical working of the employees could be when:

1. Language used in Code of Ethics is very complex and ambiguous.
2. Code of Ethics commits for something that is very difficult for a bank to ensure.
3. Top management does not find time to periodically meet and take stock of the collated and reported information of employees violating Code of Ethics.
4. Management either remains biased or is perceived to be biased in dealing similar cases of Code violation and awarding different penalties.

11.8 THE ETHICS – PERFORMANCE LINKAGE

One of the perceived or even real limitations of the banking industry in India at the moment or as part of the post-liberalization era since 1990s has been the variation in the salary structure and incentives between the public sector and the private sector banks. The junior and officer-level banking employees of the public sector banks are on par with private sector banks at times better for comparable work efforts. However, the difference is more for the top management personnel of public and private sector banks as highlighted in the recent media discussions about the wide disparity between the salary of Chairman SBI and CEOs of private sector banks.

In this context, the Banks Board Bureau (BBB) has started working since April 2016 on a plan of developing a scheme of designing compensation package for the employees of public sector banks that become comparable with their private sector counterparts in India. With a view to attracting the best talent in the public sector banks, its Chairman observed that an adequate reward structure around ESOPs, performance-linked incentives and other benefits can be designed. Though the idea has been floated and under discussion since last 4/5 years but no tangible outcome has come out till date.

Views of Bank Unions

Some of the major policy decisions involving modification of the wage structure or terms of promotions, etc. are ideally required to be arrived at not merely by the decisions only by the top internal management or by the Boards of Directors of banks. Instead, the other major stakeholders, namely the staff and officers of banks, can also be taken into confidence. This would lead to a transparent mechanism and prove to have a smooth experience when such major policies are implemented.

Proper care needs to be taken when introducing performance-based incentives to ensure that they are not misused by the bank employees.

One needs to wait and watch how the proposed performance-based incentive structure would be implemented in the PSU banks by convincing the bank unions and other stakeholders. Nevertheless, this proposal has merits and is consistent with the rewards or incentives to be offered to bank employees based on their ethical behaviour and transparency in their decision-making process rather than merely accepting fixed grade-based pay for routine compliances.

11.9 ETHICS TRAINING: EFFECTIVENESS OF ETHICS TRAINING

Ethics is such a theme which needs to be given as a training theme to a person from banking, teaching and social service or any similar related or relevant

filed. Some of the bureaucrats (both from banking or pure civil services) who are known for their integrity and had earned about a decade to two decades or more impeccable image of enviable track record would be ideal resource persons.

Tainted persons (spread through informal channels or grapevine or covered by select media about the indulgence in questionable practices in recent past or even in early stages of career), howsoever articulate they might be in training sessions on ethics, can make little difference to convince the trainee officers of banking industry to inculcate ethics as part of their day-to-day activities. There would be a big acceptability issue among the participants in a training programme of a very short or medium tenure by such undistinguished persons who lack personal branding on ethical conduct.

As far as effectiveness of the ethics training is concerned, it is a slow process. Record of trainees from different regions and zones should be kept with the bank and the details of trainee officers who received training on ethics should be maintained, including the date or period of training as the case may be. Name of the resource person should also be available in records. If ideally none of the trainee has faced any ethics-related issue over first 3-5 years, probably that can be considered as an acceptable effect of training on the subject of ethics.

Incidents that get reported beyond a medium term cannot be firmly attributed to failure of ethics training, as the employee matures substantially over five years or more of regular service. Having passed through the daily grind of operations and execution of multiple tasks, in a normal scenario, the employee must be in a position to differentiate what constitutes ethical behaviour or otherwise in each scenario he/she comes across. In spite of the training, if a person is found involved in an unethical act, the blame cannot be attributed to poor quality of training of ethics undergone a few years ago. It is no exaggeration in this case to wrongly blame a primary school teacher (for his failure to teach morals or ethics) if a person passing out of a specific school does some unethical act on the verge of his/her retirement. Several other factors like friends, colleagues, superiors, media, society, etc. also have their influence on the value system of an employee.

Hence, only training in ethics has a value to the extent it removes all possible ambiguities, grey areas and doubts in the minds of a newly joined employee into a bank. Ethics training provides the distinction of ethical and unethical behaviour by narrating many examples of banking roles and highlighting the importance of ethical behaviour for personal benefit, benefits to customers, bank as employer and the society as a whole. The training on ethics need not be expected to reform or transform a misfit employee into a great banking professional. All trainee employees can be sensitized during the training that a great role awaits them to help build the economic and financial lives of the beneficiaries and they are directly and indirectly responsible to build the economy of India through their ethical behaviour on a daily basis throughout the long and meaningful careers.

11.10 CREATION OF ETHICS COMMITTEES

Creation of Ethics Committee needs to be done carefully for a bank. The head of the Committee can be a member of the top management who has ideally had a long experience with the same bank. A team of 10-12 other officers can be included in the team. Representation of all vital fields of banking such as marketing, operations and customer service, corporate and global banking, treasury, forex management, risk management, information technology, risk management, human resources department, retail assets, stressed assets resolution, etc. will be needed. The reason for forming a broader Ethics Committee is to enable at least one member having thorough domain expertise in a specific department where an unethical case has been referred to the Committee.

There can be a fixed term of 2-3 years for the members of the Ethics Committee. All cases can be documented and kept as confidential files. The bank can use these as future examples without giving the identity of the name of employee, committee members or head, branch and other specific details. A structured one or two-page brief case lets must be prepared as an integral task of the Ethics Committee members which can be approved by the top management for use as case studies in ethics in the bank's training programmes.

This Committee needs to examine various aspects of a case referred to it and make a recommendation based on a thorough evaluation of the incident from ethics point of view. Recommendations made by the Committee can be examined by the top management and suitable action may be initiated by explaining to the employee as to how his or her action was treated unethical and advising the employee not to repeat such actions and also the period for which such

employee may remain under close observation by the designated person/Ethics Committee.

Care must be taken while referring to the Ethics Committee some of the actions which are not having any ethical dilemma or dimension such as illegal activities, frauds, insubordination, etc.

11.11 ETHICAL LEADERSHIP: ROLE OF TOP MANAGEMENT AND BOARD IN CREATING AN ETHICAL CULTURE

It is the top management that has to have complete respect for an ethical culture in a bank as a whole. Hence, the top management can take out some time on a weekly basis to review the progress or maintenance of the highest ethical standards across all activities and departments and regions of the bank. If the internal senior most management takes ethics as yet another job along with their regular tasks, the outcome is a foregone conclusion. It is very difficult to control the widespread unethical practices, which may crop up when ethics is not given the required priority. Also, it may be too late to take action when a bank's reputation is severely tarnished due to an unethical act of an employee.

The Board of Directors may also be informed in writing that their bank takes ethics seriously not only on par with the business outcomes of the bank but rather, ethics being paramount and non-compromising. Unless the major stakeholders are serious about ethics, it is difficult to convince the members of a bank's board to take up ethics equally seriously as part of their regular quarterly agenda items. Also, the CEO of the bank and other executive directors of the bank must make sure that the Boards are briefed in writing about any major ethical lapse irrespective of the cadre of the employee committing it.

While trying to brief the Board of incidents involving unethical activities, banks should equally devote their time to identify, record and bring to the notice of the Board of Directors a few instances wherein select employees have exhibited extraordinary commitment to ethics beyond normal expectations. Such employees may be rewarded suitably with monetary incentives and speedy career progression. In order to rule out possible or perceived bias in doing so, the bank management may get such select cases ratified in Board meetings for motivating ethical behaviour amongst the staff.

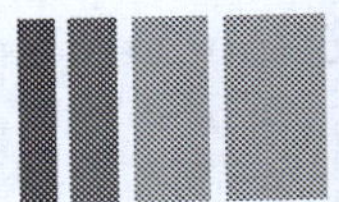

11.12 LEADERSHIP ETHICS: ETHICS IN ADMINISTRATIVE DECISION-MAKING

The leaders in a bank context or other commercial or even not-for-profit organizations are expected to set goals for themselves and subordinates and should persuade them to achieve the same within a predetermined timeframe. Leaders are expected to groom, motivate, guide, and monitor employees concerned while they carry out various tasks.

As far the leadership models to embrace ethics or otherwise is concerned, there are three broad types of models-immoral leadership, moral leadership and amoral leadership.

Immoral Leadership is a style of leadership wherein the person lacks ethical principles and takes a stance opposite to that of persons or individuals who are morally sound and principled. The reason is obvious, as such a person may want to capitalize on the position he/she has achieved and morally strong persons have nothing to offer except that they may have high regard towards principled leaders and probably refute the leaders who are immoral openly or tacitly.

Moral leadership is a style wherein the leader personally conforms to the highest standards of ethical behaviour. These standards may have been set during his/her tenure in the bank or any other organization. Such a moral leadership not only personally adheres to all ethical principles or codes sincerely. Such moral leaders also strongly encourage, defend, preserve and protect other subordinates who are demonstrating sound ethics. This is done by such leaders with a view to having ethics followed across the entire organization.

Amoral leadership is a third style of leadership wherein the leader does not intentionally consider or care for ethical factors. At the same time, such leader remains extremely casual or careless towards ethical considerations in business.

11.13 TOWARDS A NORMATIVE MODEL OF ETHICAL LEADERSHIP

In this unit, we have come across a number of themes, each of which says something about how leadership might be ethical. The common denominator, however, is that the moral sensitization seems to be a very good starting point

for ensuring ethical leadership in any organization. 'It is reasonable to assume that leaders who care about morality and who devote energy and resources to encouraging other people in their organizations to reflect on the moral implications of their actions, are more likely to lead ethically than those who do not.' Ethical engagement at all levels is an essential requirement given the impact of organizations on the lives of the people who work in them, on the lives of those who interact with them and on the many stakeholders who are affected by their actions. According to Joanne B. Ciulla, 'we live in a world where leaders frequently disappoint us. Meticulous biographers sometimes diminish the image of great leaders, such as Martin Luther King, Jr. and George Washington, by probing their moral shortcomings. It's difficult to have heroes in a world where every wart and wrinkle of a person's life is public. Ironically, the increase in information that we have about leaders has increased the confusion over the ethics of leadership. The more defective our leaders are, the greater our longing for highly ethical leaders.'

Ethical acts are based on moral principles that are universal because they incorporate fundamental values such as truth, fairness, courage and justice. All organizational members bear the responsibility to ensure that organizational objectives are achieved in a manner that is consistent with these ideals and serve their own welfare as well as the larger interests of society. However, the primary duty and responsibility for providing the proper direction and the high standards of performance rest chiefly with the organizational leader. Indeed, the leader is the soul of the organization. However, the conduct of senior management at companies such as Enron and WorldCom, along with the widespread economic malaise that followed the banking crisis of 2008, sometimes belies the idea that the people at the top have everyone's best interests at heart. So, if leadership is to play a part in actually making his or her organization a more ethically responsive place, then perhaps what is needed is a different kind of leadership – a leadership that is based on ethical principles – because the values that underlay an ethical corporate culture or culture of integrity cannot be effectively shared, implemented, nurtured, and monitored without effective ethical leadership. Without the right tone at the top, managers and employees will not subscribe to the organization's ethical values, believing instead that only short-term profit maximization matters as we will see in the case 23 in "Test Your Ethics Muscle" section.

Leaving employees to their own assumptions about a corporation's values is a very high-risk strategy for both the corporation and the employees themselves. Consequently, effective ethical leadership is becoming increasingly important to both banks and other companies. It must also be understood that, although ethical leadership should come from all persons in leadership positions, an ethical corporate culture cannot be created or sustained without strong, visible ethical leadership from the CEO and the board chair. The key to ethical leadership is visible effective action stemming from an ethical base. This kind of leadership will greatly reinforce the corporation's ethics program and its attempts to develop and maintain an ethical corporate culture. Without strong ethical leadership from executives and supervisors, attempts to develop and maintain an ethical corporate culture are doomed to mediocrity and probably failure. In summary, if ethical leaders genuinely want followers to learn appropriate behavior and to avoid counterproductive or unethical behavior, they must fully embody the intended vision and values and must not only believe in them but also communicate those beliefs in actions and exhortations. Only then can they provide the right tone at the top. Functionally, an ethical leader must do the following:

- Ensure that the vision and values of the organization are ethically sound.
- Identify with and support them.
- Communicate them.
- Ensure that the organization's ethical culture (code, training, decision-making, performance indicators, reward systems and monitoring system) supports its vision and values.
- Motivate other leaders and employees to adhere to them.
- Monitor and reward or penalize performance.

In order to best achieve these goals, a leader must be able to successfully influence other executives and supervisors as well as employees. Long-lasting influence is based on respect. Since their purpose is to influence ethical behaviour, ethical leaders cannot develop the necessary respect unless they present an ethical role model to be emulated. Research has shown that the following personality characteristics can have a direct effect on effective ethical leadership:

- Agreeableness – Are they altruistic, trusting, kind and cooperative? Are they approachable for discussion of concerns?

- Personal morality: Do they do the right things?
- Openness: Are they imaginative, curious, artistic and insightful?
- Extraversion: Are they active, assertive, energetic and outgoing?
- Conscientiousness: Are they dependable, responsible, dutiful and determined?
- Neuroticism: Are they anxious, hostile, impulsive or stressed? They should not be.

These are the characteristics, which can be summarized as integrity, trustworthiness, honesty, sincerity and forthrightness or candor and help win the trust and respect of the employees. Trust is vital in overcoming the natural thought that pervades organizations and reinforces the belief that a bank's purpose is to make profit at any cost. Organizational cynicism is also the reason why ethical leaders must visibly and audibly support their organization's ethical vision and values. In this connection, it is illustrative to read the opening address given by one Chairman of a very large bank in the country on the first day he took the charge of the institution:

"My dear colleagues,

After taking charge of this great institution, I, first of all, thank all my worthy and admirable predecessors who headed this bank and have made it what it is today. I also take this opportunity to express my special gratitude to my predecessor from whom I have taken over a sterling legacy and a host of path-breaking initiatives. This is a humbling moment for me and I really feel blessed to get the honour of leading a dedicated team of 2,68,705 associates, eager and keen to take forward the unmatched legacy of this bank.

We are a 211-year-old organization. We have relentlessly gone from strength to strength. We have faced challenges. We have enjoyed glories. But during all these long years, we have shone and continually preserved our position of being the Best Bank in the country. This fact gives huge satisfaction to each of us, who are committed to make a difference – each in his or her unique way.

The nation banks on us. We have always been the proud custodians of our people, their trust and their financial dreams. But let's face it, right now, the banking industry is passing through very tough times. This is happening world-wide. India has also not escaped the tremors. Despite our grit, fortitude, hard work and resilience, we also could not stay insulated from the unfavorable macro conditions, more so, in a highly interconnected world and economic environment.

But challenges inspire us. We are wired that way. Our history tells us this. The recent merger proves this. A few years ago, we were perceived as a traditional bank. Today we stand out as a technology – savvy, modern and forward-looking bank. Be it on the delivery channels, new cutting technologies, banking products and services and other less tapped customer segments, we are offering a slew of new age banking services to meet the financial needs of one and all Indians. This is our new persona. This is our ethos of optimism and inclusion. With this essential core of our strengths, I have no doubt that our bank will overcome the current challenges soon. Still, we should not forget that the crown position in the industry bequeaths greater responsibilities on us to push ourselves extra hard. In this background, I would like to share with you a few points which strike me on this occasion:

I read somewhere that a man without a smiling face must not open a shop. This is the finest expression of the spirit of a service organization that I have ever come across. A bank is as good as its frontline people. They are the face of the bank. They make what our brand stands for. Being polite to your customers is the best way to grow your community of loyal customers. Customers prefer to bank with the people who treat them well. We may have the best of products, technology, ambience, but if we are not courteous and polite to our customers, our business will not endure. We will not progress. Politeness is what builds a Great Bank.

We are living in a time when technology is changing the way we do banking. A hallmark of these technologies is that only a few realize at first, how transformative they will be, going forward. This situation brings us to confront the new challenge of assimilating technology in our operational culture. Bare adoption of digital platforms for delivery is not going to serve us. We need to educate and functionally update ourselves on the tech-front continually for providing easy-to-navigate and seamless digital services, especially for millennials and Gen-X customers. Only then will technology provide us with a sustainable, competitive advantage. Only then would we be able to efficiently deliver new-age banking for new India.

Each of our employees makes our backbone. We believe in the total welfare of our people, including their families, and form a life-long bond even when they are not actively serving us. We also care for the aspirations of our staff members by constantly trying to enrich their lives and job experiences. You will agree with me that a 'Healthy Mind in a Healthy Body' is applicable not only to individuals but also to organizations. While performance and productivity are non-negotiables, they are not achievable if the employees are not healthy and happy. We have been taking a number of new initiatives focused towards achieving a work-life balance for employees by introducing facilities like sabbatical and work-from-home and refining some of the existing ones. I urge all my colleagues to ensure that they and their co-workers pay attention to their health and maintain a proper work-life balance.

I strongly believe that ethics matters in a fiduciary setting like a commercial bank. Banking must stick to strong ethical standards. To ensure this, our conduct must be absolutely clean. But clean conduct requires that we follow the rules of governance and principles of strong ethics. We have always stood for the highest ethical standards in the country. We are the first in the Indian public sector to start an independent 'Ethics and Business Conduct Vertical' to weave our trademark ethos into our operational fabric. Today, there is also a severe trust deficit amongst the various stakeholders in the financial ecosystem. I believe that ethics is the only way out to bridge this gap. Therefore, I urge you all to promote moral and ethical grandeur unconditionally in your daily actions and decisions.

Let us keep in mind the values of STEPS, which stands for Strong Ethics; Transparent and High Standards of Corporate Governance; Empathy and Compassion for Colleagues, Customers and Communities around; Politeness in Dealing with Customers, Peers, Seniors and Junior Colleagues; and Sincerity. Let us ensure that this STEPS spirit passionately persists with us till the end.

I shall close by saying that I am proud to lead team and I wish that with the determined STEPS and untiring efforts of each of you, team will transform the bank making it a proxy for Grand and Divine India.

Thank you all."

We have removed the name of the bank from the above communication but it is worth noticing the powerful content of the communication, with moral commitment at its core – that makes a strong case for the primacy of ethical conduct as a banker not only in engaging with the external stakeholders but also while interacting with all colleagues whether seniors or peers or juniors. This is a live example of how the clear tone is set for a normative leadership right from the first day of coming at the helm. In the same vein, there was a chairman in a bank who despite being eligible travelled economy class and never accepted even a half kilogram of sweets from any of her customers or colleagues and sent her servant to buy sweets from the market so as to entertain guests on the festive occasions. We all know of Narayana Murthy of Infosys who travel economy class even after being one of the super most high net worth persons in India. As it is said that the behaviour of the leaders is the best training for the employees, such leaders provide role modelling of ethical leadership through their daily actions and behaviours.

Moral commitments are at the heart of ethical leadership and it engages with the organizational members in such a way that leaders and followers raise one another to higher levels of motivation and morality. Such leaders focus on terminal values such as liberty, equality and justice. These values mobilize and energize followers, create an agenda for action and appeal to larger audiences. Ethical leaders are driven by duty. They are guided by universal ethical principles, feel a sense of obligation to the group and treat followers with respect. They also empower others and focus on shared goals and objectives. "Ethical leaders engage in higher-level moral reasoning," writes Craig Johnson, demonstrate greater integrity, are more successful at leading organizational ethical turnarounds, encourage the development of positive ethical climates, institutionalize ethical practices and foster corporate social responsibility.

11.14 LET US SUM UP

Ethics needs to be followed not merely by a few in a bank or other organizations. One can state confidently that to get ethics institutionalized, all employees working at any given point in time must be sensitized about various aspects like conflict of interest, confidential *v.* public information, fairness, etc. so that they continue with ethical conduct throughout their employment tenure. Training in

ethics is to be treated as an important part of the employee induction process not merely for a fresher getting into a bank but even for an experienced banker who is joining a bank by leaving another bank. Creating and effectively functioning ethics programme and an ethics committee, regular training programmes in ethics and above all, leadership commitment to ethics are all essential factors that ensure building and sustaining ethical organizations.

11.15 KEY WORDS

Conflict of Interest, Confidential information, Employee Relations, Fair Dealing, Formal Code of Ethics, Policy on Social Media, Purpose of Code of Ethics, Code of Conduct, Leadership Models, Normative Model of Leadership, Extraversion, Neuroticism, Conscientiousness, Groupthink, Productive Conflict, Individualism, Collectivism, US Sentencing Guidelines.

11.16 CHECK YOUR PROGRESS

1. Which of the following are the reason/s for implementing banking Code of Ethics?
   (*a*) Sensitizing their employees of their responsibility,
   (*b*) To display that banks' value integrity,
   (*c*) To avert innocent violations,
   (*d*) All of the above
2. Code of Ethics at work refers to -----.
   (*a*) Confidentiality
   (*b*) Following laid down ethical policy framework
   (*c*) Conflict of interest
   (*d*) Intentional fraud
3. Leadership styles of implementing ethics at work include
   (*a*) Immoral leadership
   (*b*) Moral leadership

(*c*) Amoral leadership

(*d*) All of the above

4. Building blocks in ethics management can be defined as

(*a*) Policy framework

(*b*) Training employees & Implementing guidelines

(*c*) Review and monitoring

(*d*) All of the above

5. Sensitizing their employees to their responsibility can be done to ----.

(*a*) Display that banks value integrity,

(*b*) Avert innocent violations, and

(*c*) Deal with habitual violators

(*d*) Both (*a*) and (*b*)

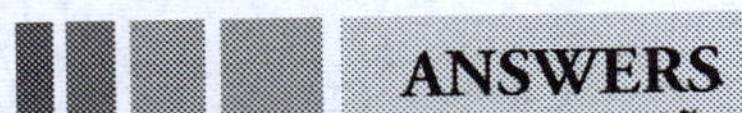

ANSWERS

1. (*d*)	2. (*b*)	3. (*d*)	4. (*d*)	5. (*d*)

11.17 EXERCISE YOUR ETHICS MUSCLE

Case 25: Wells Fargo: Sufferings from an Unethical Culture

Wells Fargo was recently ordered a fine of $3.7 billion by the Consumer Financial Protection Board (CFPB) of the US for legal violations across several of its largest product lines. The bank's illegal conduct led to billions of dollars in financial harm to its customers including loss of their vehicles and homes. The order says that the Wells Fargo's rinse-repeat cycle of violating the law has harmed millions of American families.

Wells Fargo is a global banking conglomerate with operations over 35 countries. It's the fourth largest bank in the US by asset-size and one of the largest by deposit-size and market capitalization. On September 9, 2016, the bank was fined $185 million for illegal banking practices caused by a faulty corporate culture where employee incentives motivated bank employees to cross-sell existing customers so that they would use at least 8 Wells Fargo products. This incentive pressure caused employees to open roughly 1.5 million bank accounts and create 565,000 credit cards that were not authorized by bank customers. When customers complained, the bank investigated, discovered the sham accounts and fired 5,300 employees, but not the executives in charge. They were scheduled to retire or continue working with significant stock options intact. Ultimately, pressure from regulators and the public forced the bank to refund about $2.6 million of inappropriately collected fees and two senior executives forfeited over $70 million in retirement allowances.

But that was not the full extent of what Wells Fargo ended up losing from its unethical culture. The bank, which had sailed through the subprime lending crisis in 2008 without needing a bailout because it had shown restraint in not participating in questionable practices, ended up in losing its reputation for clean, ethical dealings, the trust of its customers and the support of government regulators. Investigations brought out the other unsavory aspects of Wells Fargo's culture at that time such as that the employees who resisted illegal marketing tactics and/or reported them to an ethics hotline were fired for tardiness – even if they were only 2 minutes late. John Stumpf, the CEO, ignored a letter sent in 2007 referring to the illegal, fraudulent sales practices and warning "of professional and reputational damage, consumer fraud and shareholder lawsuits, coupled with regulator sanction". The bank's executives just ignored the employee complaints raising the issue of probable loss of customers' trust etc. despite knowing fully well that any bank's reputation is built on the basic cultural value of trust. Eve Stumpf initially failed to accept any responsibility for creating a culture where employees had to cheat, by creating fake accounts, just to keep their jobs. It was not until the Senate Banking Committee hearing that Stumpf admitted his responsibility for the failure. One of the more remarkable facets of the case is that the company has been aware of, since at least 2009, of the fraudulent cross-selling by employees. Stumpf was also aware of the wrongdoing by 2013 and the bank's board knew it since 2014. [Wells Fargo made less than $ 400,000 on its fraudulent cross selling. The reported fines and penalties are more than 295 million dollars excluding the latest $ 3.7 billion fine. The bank lost a market cap of over $ 6 billion.]

The Bank's reputation for integrity continues to be eroded as indicated by the latest fine by CFPB in December 22. The order states that "Wells Fargo is a repeat offender that has been the subject of multiple enforcement actions by the CFPB and other regulators for violations across its lines of business including faulty student loan servicing, mortgage kickbacks, fake accounts and harmful auto loan practices." The bank has a proud heritage but now seems to become the iconic case study of why the sustained promotion of ethical culture is a non-negotiable in a bank, more so in an uncertain moral time like ours.

Issues To Reflect:

(*a*) How come a legitimate, and beneficial business strategy like cross-selling turns into a high-risk, illegal activity? Examine the causative factors from the vantage point of an ethical culture?

(*b*) Who is primarily responsible for the Wells Fargo's continued problem? Its CEO, its employees or its senior management?

(*c*) Why a bank like Wells Fargo could get mired in such scandals? Excessive focus on business or lack of ethical bearings in the top management?

(*d*) What is your view on importance of whistleblowing as an early warning signal from the Wells Fargo saga?

(*e*) The case demonstrates that employees at all levels have a responsibility to keep the ship upright, from the CEO to senior management to the front-line employees. Do you agree?

(*f*) Please discuss this case with your colleagues for its valuable lessons to be learned to be an ethical banker.

Case 26: Lord Black and Hollinger International

Hollinger International Inc (HII) was a US-based global newspaper corporate. Hollinger Inc (HI) was a Canadian Company whose major asset was its interest in HII. HI owned 30.3 % of equity and 72.6% of the voting shares of HIL. Shares held by HI were super-voting shares carrying more votes per share than ordinary shares. This type of arrangement, which allows the control of a corporation with the ownership of less than a majority of the corporation's equity, is known as "multiple-voting rights" or "super-voting rights." The major shareholder of HI was Ravelston Corporation Limited (RCL) through Argus Corporation Limited (Argus). Lord Conrad Black, a high-profile business man,

was Chairman & CEO of HII. HII had been built up by Black over the years to own hundreds of newspapers, including the Chicago Sun-Times, the Daily Telegraph in London, the National Post in Toronto and the Jerusalem Post in Israel. In 2000, Black was knighted by Britain's Queen Elizabeth and accorded the title of Lord Black of Crossharbour and the right to sit in the British House of Lords. Lord Black exercised full control over the HII due to the unique shareholding structure and also over appointments to the board. All the directors of the Board were picked by Black.

Lord Black, in January 2004, made a deal, to sell the Daily Telegraph to the Barclay brothers. This deal was against the interests of the ordinary shareholders of HII and few non-interested board members challenged the deal and prevailed upon to set up a corporate review committee to scrutinize the deal. Lord Black reacted and used his controlling interest in the HII to change the company's by-laws. The new by-laws abolished the review committee and put practical constraints on the board's freedom to act. The matter went to court in Delaware and Lord Black lost the case. Thereafter, the board of HII started a detailed investigation through Richard Breeden, a former chairman of the American Securities and Exchange Commission (SEC), into the Lord Black's business affairs in relation to HII. The Breeden report accused Lord Black of 'fiduciary abuses and fraudulent acts'. The report said that Black had taken £223m from the company in a six-year period up to 2003 in the form of excessive management fees and expense claims. Lord Black challenged these claims and hired forensic accountants to work on his case. He argued that there was no misconduct and that all his actions were approved by the board.

One of the main accusations was that Lord Black and Mr. Radler, a former deputy Chairman, broke their fiduciary duties to the company's shareholders by causing HII to pay them unjustifiable management fees through Lord Black's private company RCL. This matter was the cause of Lord Black losing his position of CEO in 2003 when he was found to have overcharged for his services by $32m. Some of the fees were paid to shell companies registered in Barbados which does not tax dividends and charges only 2.5 per cent income tax. One particular device that was used by Black was non-compete payments that were made between 1999 and 2001. When Hollinger International wished to sell one of its publications, Black and his associates would demand a fee to sign a non-competition agreement with prospective purchasers which ensured that they would not enter the competition to buy the titles. The Breeden report considered this a conflict of interests because, as a board member of HII, Black had responsibilities to maximize the sale price of the company's assets. If these non-competition deals had not been made then the fee paid to Black (as compensation for not acquiring the assets) would most likely have gone to pay a higher purchase price to Hollinger International. The second main charge against Black made by the Breeden report was that Black and Radler and their families had used HII as a 'piggy bank'. The company paid for much of their living expenses, their housing expenses and their personal travel. Radler was given a private aircraft by the company, worth $11.6m and Black had a Gulfstream IV leased for him at a cost of $3m–$4m a year. The running costs of these aircraft between 2000 and 2003 were $23m. Two of the more high-profile items mentioned in the report were $43,000 spent by the company on Lady Black's birthday party and the $2,436 handbag she was given as a gift. KPMG, who were auditors for HII, HI and RCL, resigned as auditors in December 2003.

On November 17, 2005, Conrad Black and three other executives of HII were charged with eleven counts of fraud with regard to payments allegedly disguised as "noncompete fees" or in one case, a "management agreement breakup fee" and the misuse of corporate perks. The payments were alleged to be a self-dealing "series of either secret or misleading transactions involving sales of a series of various newspaper publishing groups in the United States and Canada." The sales involved several hundred newspapers and the alleged misdirection of over $80 million of the proceeds. There were a lot of people who didn't agree with the indictment and said that Conrad Black took the company, which was moribund and turned it into a powerful weapon for the values the conservatives believe in. He was a great proprietor, but more important, a great visionary. He and his wife should get their good name back and the sooner the better.

[Based on the Sources: Burt (2004), Hollinger international Inc. (n.d.), Investor Responsibility Research Centre (IRRC) (2004), Paris et al. (2004), Parker (2004), Rees-Mogg (2004), Rubin (2004), Observer (2004).]

Issues to Reflect

(*a*) Do you agree with the tone of leadership set by Lord Black in HII? Can you do an anatomy of his leadership from point of view of the organizational culture?

(*b*) How do you see Lord Black as an individual? A greedy one, a visionary or with great business acumen?

(*c*) What conflicts of interest may have been involved in Black's activities? Please list out.

(*d*) Conrad Black was the effective owner of HII. Was anything wrong on his part if he used HII to meet his living and other personal expenses?

(*e*) Have you ever manipulated your expenses or used organizational resources for personal benefits?

(*f*) What risk management practices would have prevented Black's potential conflicts from becoming harmful to the company?

12 UNIT

Banking Ethics: Changing Dynamics

12 UNIT

Banking Ethics: Changing Dynamics

12.1 LEARNING OBJECTIVES

Globalization has led to integration of economies as well as societies. The global connection through communication and technologies resulted in exchange of diverse cultural ideas and practices. This in turn has provided immense opportunities and potential to the Indian Banks to offer their services across borders. Having said that, this exponential changing dynamic of technology has also increased the complexity in the way banking and financial services are being offered. The business environment has become far too challenging and competitive with multiplying risk factors. In this section, we will highlight the risks and opportunities for the banking sector, offered by a changing dynamic in India & abroad.

12.2 ETHICS AND TECHNOLOGY

Role of Information Technology in Banking

In today's globalizing world, banking and financial services sector has been undergoing unprecedented changes and improvements with the increasing use of Information Technology (IT). This has resulted in the toughest competition amongst the various commercial banks and now it is no more a matter of *choice* for them, but a compulsion to use the state-of-the-art technology in their services for survival and growth.

Banking Operations are becoming increasingly customer-focused and, in a way, getting attuned to the ever-growing customers' preferences. Be it the highly educated and tech-savvy urban Indians or not so technology-familiar semi-urban or rural Indians, almost all bank customers today are used to taking the benefit of technology in their banking services.

Several mergers among banks have further intensified the competition among the banks. Banks are expected to remain equipped to offer to their clients access to several markets for different classes of financial instruments. Looking at the overall scenario and the factors responsible for the same, it could be said that one of the single-most important reasons for this change is attributed to the rise of Information Technology (IT).

IT has broadly been used under two different avenues in banking. One is communication and connectivity and the other is Business Process Reengineering (BPR). IT enables sophisticated product development, better market infrastructure, implementation of reliable techniques for control of risks and helps the financial intermediaries to reach geographically distant and diversified markets. IT has changed the contours of three major functions being performed by the banks *viz.* access to liquidity, transformation of assets and monitoring of risks. Further, IT and the communication networking systems have a crucial bearing on the efficiency of money, capital and foreign exchange markets.

Information Technology (IT) has brought about a significant change in the way organizations communicate and maintain relationships with their internal and external customers. In today's competitive scenario, banks are increasingly under pressure for margins and thereby look for solutions that not only provide the operational efficiency but also save costs. IT provides an economical or low-cost option for banks to be in constant touch with their customers thereby offering new ways of cultivating, nurturing and developing customer relationships. This, in turn, will lead to increased customer satisfaction and finally an increase in the profitability. Several IT-based tools and applications like the Internet, email, mobile phones, digital channels, etc. offer excellent opportunities for a cost-effective, personalized and interactive communication between the company and its customers. Using IT, customers can be provided with newsletters, reminders, interactive games, interactive training, etc.

Committees headed by Dr. C. Rangarajan, RBI's Committee on Mechanization in the Banking Industry (1984) and RBI's Committee on Computerization in Banks (1988) laid the foundation for large-scale introduction of IT in India's banking sector. Further, the Reserve Bank of India constituted a committee called 'Committee on Technology Issues relating to the Payments System, Cheque Clearing and Securities Settlement in the Banking Industry (1994)' under the Chairmanship of Shri W S Saraf. This Committee made a number

of recommendations that covered payment systems including Establishment of an Electronic Funds Transfer (EFT) system, introduction of Electronic Clearing Service Credit for low value repetitive transactions such as interest, dividend, salary, pension payments and an Electronic Debit Clearing for payments to utility companies. Large scale induction of computers and communication technology in service branches, etc. were also part of the recommendations.

The importance of technology in general and Information Technology in particular, has been realized over a period of time. It has been established that technology greatly helps in increasing the efficiency of operations, productivity and reduces cost. The banking sector also adopted technology in its pursuit for bringing about operational efficiency, cost reduction, increase productivity, responsiveness and aid financial inclusion. The banking industry was one of the very first to utilize Information technology back in the 1960s and has thus a record of influencing the development process through the technology.

The Reserve Bank of India, through its directives, has laid special emphasis on technology infusion in the day-to-day operations of banks. Since its first step towards adopting technology several years back, the banking sector has achieved several milestones and has several achievements to its credit in the last 2 decades. In today's context, almost all the banks and their branches are computerized with all of them having implemented the *Core Banking Solution.*

The advent of Internet and its ever-increasing penetration in India has also greatly aided and complemented the technological advances banks have made in recent times. As a matter of fact, most of the banks have built their "Online Banking" systems and made them accessible to tens of thousands of their customers, thereby taking an important step towards providing efficient services.

In today's context, almost all banks have reached the final stages of computerization and adoption of Core Banking Solutions. The focus has thus shifted to adoption of latest technologies in banking, revolving around analytics and business intelligence to enhance their Customer Relationship Management (CRM). Similarly, improving internal effectiveness includes Management Information Systems (MIS) and managing risks arising out of IT implementation are also key focus areas. With the advent of new technologies, a new era of disruption is being witnessed. Given the growing role of technology, data and network effects, there is a feeling among the banks that having an ethos of a technology company, while offering banking services, is the need of the hour. The speed with which technology is progressing, it can't be ruled out that what we have seen until now could be just the tip of the iceberg. For example, banks have started using Artificial Intelligence (AI) and Machine Learning (ML) to determine the creditworthiness of clients for small ticket loans by analysing data from a wide range of traditional and non-traditional data sources.

Technology thus has been the prime mover and enabler of banking business model evolution for the last forty years and banks have been automating, upgrading and industrializing their information technology to build a profitable, systemic risk resilient, and cyber-secure business franchise. The banking business model has evolved into what we can say as the Banking 4.0 with the development of technology. This has been the journey from the days of Banking 1.0 when the banking business model was enabled by a system of record on mainframe to Banking 2.0, when the banking business model was enabled by a system of record on fourth-generation language (4GL) technology (Core Banking), to Banking 3.0 when the banking business model was enabled by the provision of a consistent customer experience across the channels for self-serviced payments on omnichannel. Today banks have the digital process to deliver agile, scalable, and resilient business outcomes leveraging AI platform to deliver banking AI as a service. They deliver a digital experience to customers, partners and employees by industrializing its front and back offices which are then integrated. To illustrate, almost all banks in India have mobile banking apps today such as YONO from SBI, iMobile from ICICI, HDFC Mobile Banking from HDFC Bank, Axis Mobile from Axis Bank, PNB ONE from Punjab National Bank, CentMobile from Central Bank, KOTAK-81, BoB's etc. Quintessential features of all the mobile apps are payment systems, security, credit card handling, beneficiary handling, notifications, branch or ATM locator, AI-enabled chatbot and Bill payments systems, etc.

Role of Ethics in Technology

The last decade of the 20th Century and the nearly 2 decades of the 21st Century have witnessed a worldwide Information Technology revolution. Each second, some billions or more of the information and data gets captured and transmitted in public domains, while some of these data remain accessible to a few authorized persons. Some of these data captured by the bank may pertain to pure banking-related data (like opening or renewal of a term deposit, receipt of

interest, salary or rental income credited to one's account, etc.) and many others could be not directly related to banking but using bank's services in making payments (like air ticket booking, hotel payment, online payment of insurance premium, mutual fund investment, etc.).

When banks collect on a continuous basis all such customers' data and information and store and access it on a continuous basis, they have a primary moral obligation to ensure against data leaks and data misuse. Customers should have no doubt about the misuse or abuse of their information and data.

They must be assured by the banks that such capturing of data and information is being carried out in a fair and transparent manner so that anyone can have a sense of trust and faith in the banking system.

Many of the bank account holders on a regular basis receive unsolicited phone calls from resort operators, club houses, hotels, third party for airline operators, hospitals, fitness centers, etc. It is therefore, imperative that the banks' IT department personnel should be monitored to ensure that they do not capture and transmit bank customers' data to which they have access to various businesses for a reward. Such acts, even if done by a miniscule of the IT personnel of a bank, hold great potential to bring ill repute to the entire bank, besides legal risks. Banks' managements may carry out from time to time some orientation and sensitization training to these IT staff so that they are restrained to take away the bank customers' data and sell it in the market clandestinely. In spite of these trainings, if found guilty, such employees may be terminated as per the bank's service rules.

There is a constant competition among the financial services providers and the regulators. Two terms have been coined in recent years called the FinTech and the Regtech. FinTech refers to financial technology that describes an emerging financial services sector in the 21st Century.

A blend word of 'regulatory technology' that was created to address regulatory challenges in the financial services sector through innovative technology. Regtech consists of a group of companies that use technology to help businesses comply with regulations efficiently and inexpensively.

Institute for Development and Research in Banking Technology (IDRBT), established by RBI feels that "FinTech companies are accelerating at the pace of change and reshaping the financial services industry radically. Banks and financial institutions are realizing the value addition in adopting and/or adapting various FinTech innovations. Such collaborations present a great opportunity for banks and financial institutions not only to increase revenues, but also to bring about innovation to benefit the customers".

Report of the Working Group on FinTech and Digital Banking (Chairman Sudarshan Sen), which submitted its Report to RBI during February 2018 made several recommendations some of which are:

- There is a need to have a deeper understanding of various FinTech products and their interaction with the financial sector and, thereby, the implications on the financial system, before regulating this space.
- The regulatory actions may vary from "Disclosure" to "Light-Touch Regulation & Supervision" to a "Tight Regulation and Full-Fledged Supervision", depending on the risk implications.
- There is a need to develop a more detailed understanding of risks inherent in platform based FinTech.
- Various financial sector regulators to identify sector specific FinTech products and regulatory approaches.
- The adoption of digital channels to replace manual time-consuming processes to empower customers and/or workforce in insurance sector.
- Innovation labs may be established, including within insurance companies, to combine brand and product managers with technological and analytical resources.
- As and when any securities market FinTech products are introduced or emerge in the market, regulators may assess the product and see whether it can be monitored by way of registering them as an intermediary or through the activity regulations.
- Insurance companies may collaborate with "Insurtech" entities or start-ups to provide better customer experience in a cost-effective manner.
- Financial sector regulators need to engage with FinTech entities in order to chalk out appropriate regulatory response and with a view to re-align regulation and supervision in response to the changing environment.

- In order to identify and monitor the challenges associated with the development of major FinTech innovations and to assess respond to opportunities and risks arising for the financial system from these innovations, a 'dedicated organizational structure' within each regulator needs to be created.
- To provide an environment for developing FinTech innovations and testing of applications/APIs developed by banks and FinTech companies.
- Regulatory and legal reforms are essential to enable the sustained development of a digital financial industry for the future.
- Partnerships/engagements among regulators, existing industry players, clients and FinTech firms will enable the development of a more dynamic and robust financial services industry.
- Regulators may explore the use of RegTech that may facilitate the delivery of regulatory requirements more efficiently and effectively than existing capabilities.

12.3 DATA SECURITY, PRIVACY AND DIGITAL PERSONAL DATA PROTECTION BILL, 2022

As banking transactions are moving from offline to online on various digital platforms, the risks related to data security and privacy are that much more critical. Any lapse in the security can lead to catastrophic consequences and may well lead to failure of the bank. Hence the compliance related to data security and privacy has to be the top priority of top management and the internal audit team of any bank. As more and more technology is being outsourced to FinTech companies, banks need to have a very strict internal control system that need to make sure that the FinTech companies adhere to the established internal procedures and compliance of the bank.

As mentioned earlier, all such data security and privacy of banks is handled by the staff/people of the bank and the FinTech companies. Managing this risk is critical and the banks need to ensure that the staff/personnel have appropriate level of integrity, awareness and capability to ensure the compliance and privacy of banking data. Today data privacy rules vary from bank to bank and also geography to geography. There are no single standardized set of rules or procedures available from any regulator. So, it for each bank or financial institution to make sure that they develop strong internal awareness and capability to ensure data privacy at any point in time.

Reserve Bank of India provided "Guidelines on Information security, Electronic Banking, Technology Risk Management and Cyber Frauds" to all commercial banks. As part of these Guidelines, RBI has advised all commercial banks on data security as under:

i. Banks need to define and implement procedures to ensure the integrity and consistency of all data stored in electronic form, such as databases, data warehouses and data archives.

ii. A data security theory seeks to establish uniform risk-based requirements for the protection of data elements. To ensure that the protection is uniform within and outside of the institution, tools such as data classification and protection profiles can be used.

iii. Data classification and protection profiles are complex to implement when the network or storage is viewed as a utility. Because of that complexity, some institutions treat all information at that level as if it were of the highest sensitivity and implement encryption as a protective measure. The complexity in implementing data classification in other layers or in other aspects of an institution's operation may result in other risk mitigation procedures being used. Adequacy is a function of the extent of risk mitigation, and not the procedure or tool used to mitigate risk.

iv. Policies regarding media handling, disposal and transit should be implemented to enable the use of protection profiles and otherwise mitigate risks to data. If protection profiles are not used, the policies should accomplish the same goal as protection profiles, which is to deliver the same degree of residual risk without regard to whether the information is in transit or storage, who is directly controlling the data or where the storage may be.

v. There should be secure storage of media. Controls could include physical and environmental controls such as fire and flood protection, limiting access by means like physical locks, keypad, passwords, biometrics, etc., labelling, and logged access. Management should establish access controls to limit access to media, while ensuring that all employees have authorization to access the minimum data required to perform their responsibilities. More

sensitive information such as system documentation, application source code and production transaction data should have more extensive controls to guard against alteration (e.g., integrity checkers, cryptographic hashes). Furthermore, policies should minimize the distribution of sensitive information, including printouts that contain the information. Periodically, the security staff, audit staff and data owners should review authorization levels and distribution lists to ensure they remain appropriate and current.

vi. The storage of data in portable devices, such as laptops and PDAs, poses unique problems. Mitigation of those risks typically involves encryption of sensitive data, host provided access controls, etc.

vii. Banks need appropriate disposal procedures for both electronic and paper-based media. Contracts with third-party disposal firms should address acceptable disposal procedures. For computer media, data frequently remains on media after erasure. Since that data can be recovered, additional disposal techniques should be applied to sensitive data like physical destruction, overwriting data, degaussing etc.

viii. Banks should maintain the security of media while in transit or when shared with third parties. Policies should include contractual requirements that incorporate necessary risk-based controls, restrictions on the carriers used and procedures to verify the identity of couriers.

ix. Banks should encrypt customer account and transaction data which is transmitted, transported, delivered or couriered to external parties or other locations, taking into account all intermediate junctures and transit points from source to destination.

x. A few other aspects that also need to be considered include appropriate blocking, filtering and monitoring of electronic mechanisms like e-mail and printing and monitoring for unauthorized software and hardware like password cracking software, key loggers, wireless access points, etc.

xi. Concerns over the need to better control and protect sensitive information have given rise to a new set of solutions aimed at increasing an enterprise's ability to protect its information assets. These solutions vary in their capabilities and methodologies, but collectively they have been placed in a category known as Data Leak Prevention (DLP). It provides a comprehensive approach covering people, processes and systems that identify, monitor and protect data in use (e.g., endpoint actions), data in motion (e.g., network actions) and data at rest (e.g., data storage) through deep content inspection and with a centralized management framework. Most DLP solutions include a suite of technologies that facilitate three key objectives:

- Locate and catalogue sensitive information stored throughout the enterprise.
- Monitor and control the movement of sensitive information across enterprise networks.
- Monitor and control the movement of sensitive information on end-user systems.

Banks may consider such solutions, if required, after assessing their potential to improve data security.

Data Privacy

The RBI's Working Group mentioned above (February 2018) felt that "every FinTech company should invest in fraud prevention. Some studies show that it is easier to track frauds undertaken through electronic means than physical fraud. FinTech companies can use technology and analytics to prevent and predict frauds. The onus could be on the FinTech players to utilize their technological expertise, and assist/engage with regulators to draft appropriate guidelines to prevent fraud. There is dearth of coherent data protection and privacy law in the country and it is suggested to bring this to the notice of the financial sector regulators/Government".

Regulation around data privacy has been continuously trying to evolve over the years in India. The Ministry of Electronics and IT, Government of India, had constituted one 10-member panel headed by a retired Supreme Court judge, B.N. Srikrishna in August 2017 to develop a data protection framework for India. The Committee has submitted its report on data protection titled as 'A Free and Fair Digital Economy-Protecting Privacy, Empowering Indians' along with a draft Data Protection Bill on 27th July, 2018. The report identifies seven principles for the data protection laws. Technology agnosticism - data protection law must be flexible to include the changing technologies. Data minimization-data sought and processed should be minimal and as necessary.

Informed consent - consent is an expression of human autonomy; Accountability of data controller. Penalties for wrongful processing and Enforcement of data protection framework by a statutory authority.

It is considered as a welcome step towards securing the rights of the Indian citizens. It was the need of the hour that a comprehensive data protection and privacy framework should be put in place in a country where the second largest internet user base in the world exists. Recently, on 11th April, 2023, the Government of India has notified Supreme Court of India that a new law, namely the Digital Personal Data Protection Bill, 2022, to enforce individual privacy in online space is "ready". The key features of the bill are as under:

Digital Personal Data Protection Bill, 2022

The Bill will apply to the processing of digital personal data within India where such data is collected online or collected offline and is digitized. It will also apply to such processing outside India, if it is for offering goods or services or profiling individuals in India.

- Personal data may be processed only for a lawful purpose for which an individual has given consent. Consent may be deemed in certain cases.
- Data fiduciaries will be obligated to maintain the accuracy of data, keep data secure and delete data once its purpose has been met. "Data Fiduciary" is defined as any person who alone or in conjunction with other persons determines the purpose and means of processing of personal data.
- The Bill grants certain rights to individuals including the right to obtain information, seek correction and erasure and grievance redressal.
- The central government may exempt government agencies from the application of provisions of the Bill in the interest of specified grounds such as security of the state, public order and prevention of offences.
- The central government will establish the Data Protection Board of India to adjudicate non-compliance with the provisions of the Bill.

The proposed data Protection Board will be the cornerstone of India's data governance endeavours. It will function as an independent supervisory and adjudicating authority for all relevant stakeholders including the government.

Digital Personal Data Protection Act, 2023

The Digital Personal Data Protection Bill, after several years of debates, postponements and negotiations, was passed by the lower and upper houses of the Parliament, received the Presidential assent and came into effect on 11th August, 2023 as the Digital Personal Data Protection Act of India with its publication in the Official Gazette. As Gabriela Zanfir-Fortuna and Raktima Roy aptly explains in their blog namely 'The Digital Personal Data Protection Act of India Explained' that while the basic structure of the law is similar many other global laws like the GDPR and its contemporaries, India's approach has its differences, such as more limited grounds of processing, wide exemptions for government actors, regulatory powers for the government further specify the law and to exempt specific fiduciaries or classes of fiduciaries from key obligations, or no baked-in definition of heightened protection or special categories of data, and the rather unusual inclusion of powers for the Government to request access to information from fiduciaries, the Board and the" intermediaries" as well as to block access by the public to specific information in "computer resources." Finally, many details of the Act are still left to clarified once the data Protection Board of India is set up and further rules for the specification of the law are drafted and officially notified. (Source: The Future of Privacy Forum: httpss;// fpf.org>blog>the digital personal data protection.)'

Data Protection Laws in Other Nations

European Union Model:

- The General Data Protection Regulation focuses on a comprehensive data protection law for processing of personal data.
- In the EU, the right to privacy is enshrined as a fundamental right that seeks to protect an individual's dignity and her right over the data she generates.

US Model:

- There is no comprehensive set of privacy rights or principles in the US that, like the EU's GDPR, addresses the use, collection and disclosure of data.
- Instead, there is limited sector-specific regulation. The approach towards data protection is different for the public and private sectors.

- The activities and powers of the government *vis-a-vis* personal information are well-defined and addressed by broad legislation such as the Privacy Act, the Electronic Communications Privacy Act, etc.
- For the private sector, there are some sector-specific norms.

China Model:

- New Chinese laws on data privacy and security issued over the last 12 months include the Personal Information Protection Law (PIPL), which came into effect in November 2021. It gives Chinese data principals new rights as it seeks to prevent the misuse of personal data.
- The Data Security Law (DSL), which came into force in September 2021, requires business data to be categorized by levels of importance and puts new restrictions on cross-border transfers.

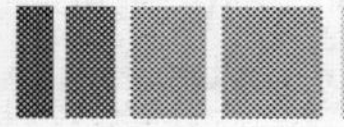

12.4 MANAGING DATA ETHICS

In our era data makes the world go round. It is the new oil. Accordingly, with an ever increasing prominence of data in the world, in the roles, rights and responsibilities are getting reorganized. However, the transition is also posing new ethical questions and data ethics is emerging as a serious challenge for the organizations including the banking sector. Data ethics can be defined as the data-related practices that seek to preserve the trust of users, patients, consumers, clients, employees and partners. In the data era, data ethics awareness' has become crucial for survival in a market where consumers progressively set the bar for earning their trust. Data ethics awareness is almost like the technology equivalent of corporate's environmental conscience which is essential for its survival, but also for the planet's welfare.

In one of the McKinney article on Data Ethics, the contributors, Alex Edquist, Liz Grennan, Sian Griffiths and Kayvaun Rowshankish state 'ethical lapses can occur when executives look only at the fidelity and utility of discrete data sets and don't consider the entire data pipeline. Where did the data come from? Can this vendor ensure that the subjects of the data gave their informed consent for use by third parties? Do any of the market data contain material non-public information? Such due diligence is key. One alternative data provider was charged with securities fraud for misrepresenting to trading firms how its data were derived. In that case, companies had provided confidential information about the performance of their apps to the data vendor, which did not aggregate and anonymize the data as promised. Ultimately, the vendor had to settle with the US Securities and Exchange Commission.'

As data is coming to be seen as an asset as well as a risk, organizations are implementing credible and clear transparency policies for data management to control the risks of data exhaust and unsustainable data practices. However, these processes are addressing the operational aspects of data management. Ethical aspects of data management are still not receiving their due attention systematically. This deficit has broad ramifications and responsibilities. 'If algorithms are trained with biased data sets or data sets are breached, sold without consent, or otherwise mishandled, for instance, companies can incur significant reputational and financial costs. Board members could even be held personally liable.'

Laws can tell what can be done but a data ethics framework can guide what should be done. Data ethics is the moral management of the human repercussions stemming from digital data developments. The proper management of data ethics risks can build the digital trust in customers. Digital trust is the foundation of banking relationships in a digital society. Trust is a prerequisite for the establishment of a digital relationship be it two people communicating with each other or between a business and a consumer. Studies show that consumers' digital trust is at its lowest when it comes to online shopping. Today, companies have cookie policies, privacy policies, data management policies and user terms of conditions for their data. But they need more than that. Digital ethics, in particular data ethics, is beginning to take up more and more of the public debate on digital tech's influence on society, economy and culture. Informed regulation is necessary, but it isn't the answer to all ethical dilemmas. The data-ethical companies are the ones that do more than simply comply with data protection legislation. They also uphold data-related ethics and values. This is because data ethics is becoming a part of a sustainable, trust-based data economy.

A data ethics strategy for the banks may comprise of components like establishing a framework that reflects a shared vision and mission for the bank's use of data, then communicating the same effectively inside and outside the organization, building a diverse data focused team, engaging champions from top leadership, assessing the effects of the algorithms and data used by them with test for bias

throughout the value chain and lastly, embedding the data principles throughout the operations. In the end, the entire strategy boils down to, changing the organizational culture. The stakes for the banks are high and if they fail to manage the data ethics risk, they will be losing their customers' trust and destroying value. (Inputs sourced from McKinsey's articles on data ethics and the book- Data Ethics: The New Competitive Advantage by Gry Hasselbalch & Pernille Tranberg.)

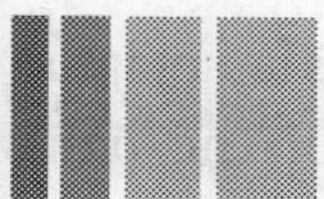

12.5 INTELLECTUAL PROPERTY RIGHTS, PATENTS AND PROPRIETARY RIGHTS

Intellectual property refers to creation of an asset by any individual or anyone using his or her creativity, innovation. Such intellectual property (IP) belongs to that individual and any unauthorized use of such IP is strictly prohibited under the applicable law of land. Some examples of IP are artistic works and symbols, innovative process, method, etc.

Intellectual property is divided into two categories:

- Intellectual Property includes patents for inventions, trademarks, industrial designs and geographical indications.
- Copyright covers literary works (such as novels, poems and plays), films, music, artistic works (e.g., drawings, paintings, photographs and sculptures) and architectural design.

Rights related to copyright include those of performing artists in their performances, producers of phonograms in their recordings and broadcasters in their radio and television programs.

Intellectual Property Rights (IPRs) are the formal mechanisms by which the asset or the property is established in intellectual assets. IPR allows its creator/innovator to use the IP for his or her own benefit and prohibits any third party to use such work. These rights are territorial by legal tradition, with each country or region establishing the terms under which it will define and protect such property. IPRs are a critical component of national business regulatory regimes.

What is a Patent?

A patent is an exclusive right granted for an invention a product or process that provides a new way of doing something, or that offers a new technical solution to a problem. A patent provides patent owners with protection for their inventions. Protection is granted for a limited period, generally 20 years.

Patents provide incentives to individuals by recognizing their creativity and offering the possibility of material reward for their marketable inventions. These incentives encourage innovation, which in turn enhances the quality of human life.

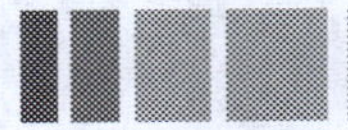

12.6 ETHICS OF INFORMATION SECURITY

As technology is taking over most of the banking activities, threats associated with the use of technology also need to be tackled. The IT team of the bank or financial institution in a way becomes the custodian of the information of its customers/dealings/activities. Hence, eventually their work conduct and ethical conduct becomes of paramount importance for the organization. Any failure on the part of the professionals handling the IT desk and data can result in severe leakages of the sensitive information, which can lead to huge losses for the banks, cause reputation risk and also result in expensive legal battles. There are various ethical issues involved in information technology but the same can be broadly categorized in four groups as follows:

i. **Accessibility**: It involves the right of accessing the required information as well as the true payment of charges to access the information.

ii. **Privacy**: It deals with the degree of privacy and dissemination of information about individual.

iii. **Property**: It talks about ownership and value of information.

iv. **Accuracy**: The information which is viable and being accessed is accurate and authentic. In the current scenario, the awareness towards ethical conduct has become very important with every technological advancement making it easy to access data and information and consequently resulting in the IT system becoming vulnerable to data theft or hacking. For any financial institution or bank, there needs to be a proper training program, orientation or at least refresher course for all the employees to make them understand the importance and criticality of ethical behaviour at all the time. This needs to be applied for not only those employees who are posted in the IT department of banks but even for those who are into basic operations jobs.

The following aspects relating to information security may be worth following by the employees:

- Making the employees (IT and non-IT) be aware of their professional obligations relating to the information security of the bank, customers and other stakeholders.
- Notifying from time to time the existing laws and crimes as and when the cyber laws get amended in the country or internationally (for off-shore transactions).
- Making the bank employees (especially the IT employees) aware of the patterns of IT attacks on bank customers/servers/other assets like ATMs, etc. and to familiarize the profiles of attackers and patterns of the thefts, *modus operandi*, if any.
- Developing cyber forensic expertise in the banks and nominating specialized team of IT employees of banks as investigators to receive training on most modern methods of investigating the attacks from specialized institutions in India or abroad and to make sure that more stringent shields are in place to avoid similar attacks in future.

In this context of creating employee awareness, the following Ten Commandments of Computer Ethics proposed by the Computer Ethics Institute in Washington, DC are insightful:

1. Thou shalt not use computer to harm other people.
2. Thou shalt not interfere with other people's computer work.
3. Thou shalt not snoop around in other people's computer files.
4. Thou shalt not use a computer to steal.
5. Thou shalt not use a computer to bear false witness.
6. Thou shalt not copy or use proprietary software for which you have not paid.
7. Thou shalt not use other people's computer resources without authorization or proper compensation.
8. Thou shalt not use other people's intellectual output.
9. Thou shalt think about the social consequences of the program you are writing or the system you are designing.

10. Thou shalt always use a computer in ways that demonstrate considerations and respect for your fellow humans.

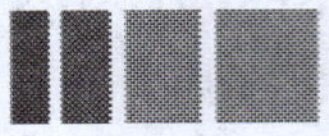

12.7 CYBER THREATS

Need for Cyber Security Awareness

Despite the Indian banking system having completed its process of computerization and online-ready transactions, a significant proportion of the customers of banks are still not adequately well-versed with the importance of cyber security. Banks are making their sincere efforts to educate and bring in awareness among their customers on the importance of memorizing their passwords. Firstly, setting the password itself is not taken seriously by many customers. There are four characteristics advised by typical IT personnel of banks while setting a password. The passwords are ideally to be:

- Personal
- Unique
- Secret
- Complex

Some of the most vulnerable passwords include: pass/1234/abcd/first four letters of customer's name/his or her year of birth/spouse/son/daughter's name/etc. These are most common and easy to crack by a fraudster. Customers also have the habit of using one common password everywhere for all banks and other online accesses say office PC, laptop, etc.

Whatever transaction one wishes to make in the Internet-based bank accounts, the ideal thing is to jot down what he/she wants to do in that particular login period. One cannot be thinking, consulting the members of family, etc., which could be inviting trouble whereby during the idle period, someone may gain access. Likewise, suspicious mails apparently sent by a bank seeking some debit card or credit card code or password by luring that it would enable one to gain some instant reward, etc. must not be responded or trusted. Likewise, responding to some calls on the registered mobile as well as SMS requesting customers to share sensitive information should be avoided.

Advanced technologies and digitized businesses have potential to increase cyber risk. Banks essentially deal with third parties funds and as such a stricter risk

management system is the need of the hour. Any failure to keep pace with the technology advancement can lead to heightened risk of cyber threat. Strict reliance on APIs, cloud computing and other new technologies facilitating interconnectivity with different outsourcing firms, which may not be subject to equivalent regulatory expectations, could potentially make the banking system more vulnerable to cyber threats and expose large volumes of sensitive data to potential breaches.

The banking fraud at the Central Bank of Bangladesh which is colloquially known as the Bangladesh Bank Cyber Heist in February 2016 highlighted the depth and range of cyber threats. The hackers fraudulently managed to gain entry into the server of the Central Bank and got millions of dollars transferred.

A survey by the BIS (Bank for International Settlements) has also identified that the highest number of FinTech service providers are in the payments, clearing and settlement category, followed by credit, deposit and capital-raising services. Within the payments category, retail payment services firms represented the majority, as compared with wholesale payment services providers. Like any other new developments, FinTech's also present a wide variety of risks. Banks should be aware of the risks and their implications before they develop their FinTech strategies. In one of his speeches, Shri T Rabi Sankar, Deputy Governor, RBI, has highlighted this issue - 'Fintech is transforming the financial landscape, the nature of regulation has to adjust. The sheer diversity in the functions performed by fintech firms, necessitates a widening of the regulatory perimeter. Cybersecurity risks are likely to overshadow financial risks for all.'

Today, customers have easy alternative for almost any banking service from transfer of funds, availing loans, payment of utility bills, etc. Any bank or FinTech firm which has better and efficient technology is able to use innovation more efficiently and deliver less expensive services that better meet customer expectations. However, this same technology comes with cyber risk. Everything online, data or information, today is open to cyber threat. The smart phone is prone to virus and potential hacking of the device. Banks need to consider their 'strategic options/risk' - when they collaborate with the risky technology for ease of doing business and maintaining their customers. A very strong internal cyber security team and internal checks and controls are important to detect/ deter any untoward incident.

Cyber Security Framework in Banks

Reserve Bank of India, through its notification dated June 2, 2016, advised all commercial banks in India to have in place a cyber-security policy with the approval of their Boards. RBI gave about 4 months' timeframe to the commercial banks to set up such cyber security policy and give a compliance confirmation to the RBI. RBI notification directed the commercial banks further on this aspect as under:

"In order to address the need for the entire bank to contribute to a cyber-safe environment, the Cyber Security Policy should be distinct and separate from the broader IT policy/IS Security policy so that it can highlight the risks from cyber threats and the measures to address/mitigate these risks.

The size, systems, technological complexity, digital products, stakeholders and threat perception vary from bank to bank and hence it is important to identify the inherent risks and the controls in place to adopt appropriate cyber-security framework. While identifying and assessing the inherent risks, banks are required to reckon the technologies adopted, alignment with business and regulatory requirements, connections established, delivery channels, online/mobile products, technology services, organizational culture and internal & external threats. Depending on the level of inherent risks, the banks are required to identify their riskiness as low, moderate, high and very high or adopt any other similar categorization. Riskiness of the business component also may be factored into while assessing the inherent risks. While evaluating the controls, Board oversight, policies, processes, cyber risk management architecture including experienced and qualified resources, training and culture, threat intelligence gathering arrangements, monitoring and analyzing the threat intelligence received *vis-à-vis* the situation obtaining in banks, information sharing arrangements (among peer banks, with IDRBT/RBI/CERT-In), preventive, detective and corrective cyber security controls, vendor management and incident management & response are to be outlined".

Thus, banks have to urgently strengthen their cyber defense, protect their customers, establish strong cyber-governance, collaborate more within the industry and with the regulator, develop advanced detection and surveillance capabilities and build cyber resilience with focus on extended ecosystem. This is an imperative

for them to drive productivity and innovation as also to remain sustainable. In addition, banks need to promote the following enabling measures:

- Create cyber threats awareness programs
- Take preventive steps
- Provide guidelines in simple form
- Engage state-of-the art IT security protection systems
- Build confidence in staff and customers

The RBI has recently initiated certain supervisory steps to deal with the emerging challenges in the area of cyber security. In this regard, the regulator has conducted Phishing Simulation exercises for select Supervised Entities (SEs) to assess their email security standards and cyber security preparedness. The process of conducting Cyber Reconnaissance exercises has also been set in motion this year. This will provide pre-emptive information on the cybersecurity risk vectors of the banks and other regulated entities. Besides, Cyber Drills which are conducted periodically have been further enhanced in terms of coverage and periodicity.

Cybersecurity Risk is Paramount

The CIA Triad is a well-known model for the development of security policies and procedures, to identify cybersecurity problem areas along with required solutions in the area of computer systems, data, information, infrastructure, network security, and others. The three letters in "CIA Triad" stand for Confidentiality, Integrity and Availability. It contains policies and procedures that are basis for a successful solution approach to protect information and adapts to changing threat event possibilities, to withstand and recover rapidly from cybercriminal attacks.

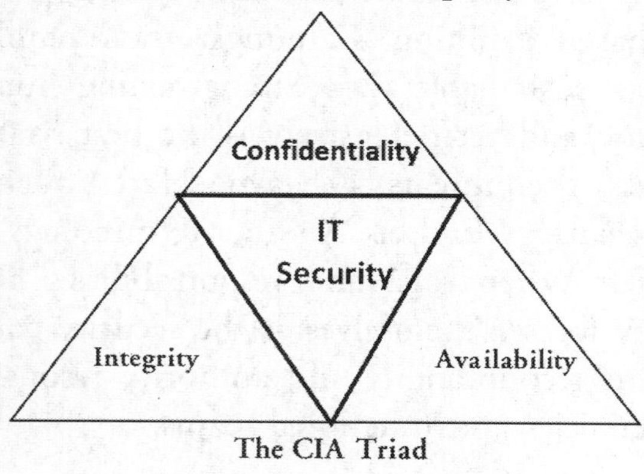

The CIA Triad

In the 2016, US's Federal Cybersecurity Research and Development Strategic Plan outlined a framework of four interdependent defensive capabilities:

- **Deter**: Ability to discourage malicious cyber-activities by increasing the cost to, diminishing the spoils of and increasing the risks and uncertainty of potential cyber attackers.
- **Protect**: Ability of components, systems, users, and critical Infrastructure to efficiently resist malicious cyber-activities and to ensure confidentiality, integrity, availability and accountability.
- **Detect**: Ability to efficiently detect and even anticipate cyber attackers' decisions and activities, given that perfect cybersecurity is not possible and that computer systems, networks, infrastructure resources and other should be assumed to be vulnerable to malicious cyber-activities.
- **Respond:** Ability of defenders, defenses and infrastructure to react dynamically to malicious cyber-activities by efficiently adapting to disruption, countering the malicious activities, recovering from damage, maintaining operations while completing restoration and adjusting to similar future activities.

Cyber security in banking sector encompasses many functionalities and protection standards that are constantly evolving. Each functional element contains the technologies, processes and policies that navigate, prevent and reduce risk exposure for the cybersecurity ecosystem. Many studies acknowledge that the dire need to concentrate on end-users' attitudes, beliefs and practices through a change in their mindset is warranted. Banks should focus their efforts on developing an adaptive cyber security mindset-a constant and vigilant mentality of situational awareness and risk-based thinking - amongst their employees to meet the cybersecurity risk in a sustainable way. Strengthening human firewalls where people think protection and act defensively is the best strategy for preparing a sound defence against cyber threats. Dewayne Hart underscores this point in his book- The Cybersecurity Mindset- 'Another terminology for human firewalls is a defensive mindset. When roles and responsibilities buy into the human firewall principle, they foresee themselves as the security culture. They envision an environment where accountability and authority resonate through working habits, goal-driven activities and functional teams.'

12.8 DIGITAL RIGHTS MANAGEMENT (DRM)

Indian banking has migrated over one generation since 1970 from the end of the day (EOD) to the Centralized Online Real-time Exchange or Core banking. Digitization involves conversion of information into a digital (*i.e.*, computer-readable) format, in which the information is organized into bits. Digitization has now become vital for gigantic data processing, storage and transmission instantly.

This rapid digitization is transforming the way basic human rights such as freedom of expression and access to information are exercised, protected and violated and are also leading to the challenge of recognition of new digital rights in terms of access and control of digital content. The law is therefore adapting to this new era with the development of digital rights and digital citizenship, allowing and regulating access to online information in a secure and transparent manner. Technological advances are constant and each brings with it the need for a new regulatory framework. The hyperconnectivity that 5G facilitates, the collection of data with devices from the Internet of Things, the analysis of the same with Big Data and the use of Edge Computing for processing, among others, generate the need to regulate this traffic of information, guaranteeing the digital rights of individuals.

Digital Rights means access and control of information that is in digital format. Digital Rights Management (DRM) involves enforcement of a security policy affecting use of digitally-encoded material specified by a content "owner" on computers not in the physical control of the content owner. Digital rights management is also known as information rights management, or enterprise rights management. As a technology, DRM is used to safeguard data over the application layer from illicit usage, using some form of encryption. Putting it simply, DRM technologies prevent unauthorized use by controlling access to and use of information. There are a variety of digital rights management (DRM) technologies employed by content owners to protect the integrity of the content itself.

Key elements of DRM are Licensing and Enforcement. These are narrated below:

- **Licensing:** It is the process of packaging and delivering protected bits with secured or unforgeable terms of usage ("digital license") useable only by authenticated user/environment.

- **Enforcement:** It is the process of ensuring that the use of the digital work adheres to enumerated use, privacy and operating restrictions stated in the digital license.

There are two categories of the content with which organizations dealing with DRM may be interested in - small and big rights management. While small rights comprise of protecting personal information of customers, their financial information, communication of the individual or corporate customers. Examples include web-content, protected information (access, its levels and length of access period) and centralized policy control.

The big rights management, on the other hand, deals with mass content such as books, audio, video or software, etc. Users may be asked to pay per view, etc. by the provide.

In order to secure their data effectively, banks have to leverage DRM technologies. This will require a multi-pronged approach to plug all potential loopholes and safeguard the 'crown jewels' of the organization. The first step in this approach is to have well-defined security policies that prescribe what information needs to be safeguarded and how it needs to be protected. Banks need to take a top-down approach to this, with the policies percolating from the CEO down to the lowest levels of the organization. A key factor is to ensure that the policies remain relevant to changing business needs and can be changed quickly to reflect new requirements. Solutions should automatically apply protection to reduce human error. Employee awareness about the latest cyber threats and protection methods is also important to ensuring security is properly enforced. The constantly evolving data security risks are a huge challenge for the security teams, but with the right policies and tools, they can secure their most critical information. A data-centric security strategy based on DRM that is flexible, dynamic and provides central visibility needs to be a key part of any security portfolio.

12.9 DIGITAL INDIA ACT, 2023

The Ministry of Electronics and Information Technology will soon come up with the Digital India Act, 2023 which will replace the Information Technology Act (IT Act) of 2000. The Indian parliament plans to implement the Digital

India Act alongside the Digital Personal Data Protection Bill, 2022, proposed in November 2022, where the two legislations will work in tandem with each other.

Need for a New Act

- Since the IT Act of 2000 was enacted, there have been many revisions and amendments (IT Act Amendment of 2008, IT Rules 2011) in attempts to define the digital space in which it regulates while trying to put more emphasis on the data handling policies. However, because the IT Act was originally designed only to protect e-commerce transactions and define cybercrime offenses, it did not deal with the nuances of the current cybersecurity landscape adequately nor did it address data privacy rights.
- Without a complete replacement of the governing digital laws, the IT Act would fail to keep up with the growing sophistication and rate of cyber-attacks.
- The new Digital India Act envisages to act as catalysts for Indian economy by enabling more innovation, more startups and at the same time protecting the citizens of India in terms of safety, trust and accountability.

Likely Provisions under Digital India Act, 2023

Freedom of Expression:

- Social media platform's own moderation policies may now be reduced to constitutional protections for freedom of expression and Fundamental speech rights. An October 2022 amendment to the IT Rules, 2021 says that platforms must respect users' free speech rights. Three Grievance Appellate Committees have therefore been established to take up content complaints by social media users.
- The following are now likely to be subsumed into the Digital India Act.

Online Safety:

- The Act will cover Artificial Intelligence (AI), Deepfakes, cybercrime, competition issues among internet platforms and data protection.
- The government put out a draft Digital Personal Data Protection Bill in 2022, which would be one of the four prongs of the Digital India Act, with the National Data Governance Policy and amendments to the Indian

Penal Code being others, along with rules formulated under the Digital India Act.

New Adjudicatory Mechanism:

A new "Adjudicatory Mechanism" for criminal and civil offenses committed online would come into place.

Safe Harbour:

- The government is reconsidering a key aspect of cyberspace — 'safe harbour', which is the principle that allows social media platforms to avoid liability for posts made by users.
- The term has been reined in recent years by regulations like the Information Technology (Intermediary Guidelines and Digital Media Ethics Code) Rules, 2021, which require platforms to take down posts when ordered to do so by the government, or when required by law.

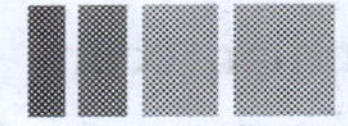

12.10 LET US SUM UP

Globalization has led to integration of economies as well as societies. The unprecedented changes and improvements with the increasing use of Information Technology in the banking and financial services sector has resulted in the toughest competition amongst the various commercial banks and they are now compelled to use the state-of-the-art technology in their services for survival and growth. Banks have a primary moral obligation to ensure against data leaks and data misuse.

As banking transactions are moving from offline to online on various digital platforms, the risks related to data security and privacy are that much more critical. Any lapse in the security can lead to catastrophic consequences and may well lead to failure of the bank. Banks are required to follow "Guidelines on Information Security, Electronic Banking, Technology Risk Management and Cyber Frauds" issued by RBI. Banks also have to ensure that there is no unauthorized use of intellectual property rights.

The IT team of the bank or financial institution in a way becomes the custodian of the information of its customers/dealings/activities. Hence, eventually their work conduct and ethical conduct becomes of paramount importance for the organization. A significant proportion of the customers of banks are still not

adequately well-versed with the importance of cyber security. Banks are making their sincere efforts to educate and bring in awareness among their customers.

Further, with proper Digital Rights Management (DRM) which involves enforcement of a security policy affecting use of digitally-encoded material specified by a content "owner" on computers not in the physical control of the content owner, banks can provide great customer experience to millions of their account holders with minimal cost. In addition, banks will have to develop a framework for data ethics management so that do not lose digital trust *i.e.*, the customers' trust in a digitized banking environment. Legal frameworks for regulating the cyber space activities and data privacy rights are being strengthened in India to protect the digital rights of the Indian citizens.

12.11 KEY WORDS

Operational Efficiency, Online banking, Customer Relationship Management (CRM), Fintech, Regtech, Information Security, Data Ethics, Data Protection Bill, Data Ethics Risk, Technology risk management, Cyber threats, CIA Triad, Cybersecurity Mindset, Human Firewall, DRM, Safe Harbour, Digital India Act, 2023.

12.12 CHECK YOUR PROGRESS

1. Banking Operations in recent years are becoming increasingly customer-focused and, in a way, getting attuned to the ever-growing:
   - (*a*) Regulatory prescriptions
   - (*b*) IT challenges
   - (*c*) Customers' incomes
   - (*d*) Customers' preferences
2. Information Technology (IT) has broadly been used under two different avenues in banking. One is communication and connectivity and other is:
   - (*a*) Digital Rights Management (DRM)
   - (*b*) Business Process Re-engineering (BPR)

(*c*) Intellectual Property Rights (IPR)

(*d*) Data Leak Prevention (DLP)

3. RBI's Committees on Mechanization in the Banking Industry (1984) and on Computerization in Banks (1988) were headed by:

   (*a*) Shri YH Malegam

   (*b*) Dr. C. Rangarajan

   (*c*) Shri WS Saraf

   (*d*) Shri M. Narasimham

4. Intellectual Property Right (IPR) allows its creator/innovator to use the IP for his or her own benefit and -----.

   (*a*) Only allows the government also to use such work

   (*b*) Prohibits any third-party use of such work

   (*c*) Allows anyone else for non-prohibited use

   (*d*) Dilutes the credibility and confidence in business space

5. To prevent or minimize cyber threats, it is recommended that individuals must NOT set their passwords which are:

   (*a*) Simple

   (*b*) Unique

   (*c*) Secret

   (*d*) Complex

6. Reserve Bank of India through its Notification dated June 2, 2016 advised all commercial banks in India to have in place a cyber-security policy with the approval of their Boards. RBI gave a timeframe to the commercial banks to set up such cyber security policy of approximately:

   (*a*) 2 months

   (*b*) 4 months

   (*c*) 8 months

   (*d*) 12 months

7. Two key elements of the Digital Rights Management are:
   (*a*) Access and Protection
   (*b*) Licensing and Enforcement
   (*c*) Fee and Use
   (*d*) Digital Systems and Processes
8. A cybersecurity framework should:
   (*a*) Deter and Protect
   (*b*) Detect, Respond and Protect
   (*c*) Detect, Deter and Respond
   (*d*) Deter, Protect, Detect and Respond

ANSWERS

1. (*d*)	2. (*b*)	3. (*b*)	4. (*b*)	5. (*a*)	6. (*b*)	7. (*b*)	8. (*d*)

12.13 EXERCISE YOUR ETHICS MUSCLE

Case 27: Cyberloafing

Internet access has created a new way to procrastinate at work called cyberloafing or cyberslacking. In cyberloafing, employees use organizational computers, tablets and smart phones for non-productive activities like surfing the Web for personal information, playing games, posting Facebook messages or shopping and chatting online. In one survey, respondents reported spending an average of 51 minutes every workday cyberloafing. Men are more likely to cyberloaf than women.

Many observers consider cyberloafing unethical because it diverts time and attention from organizational tasks and lowers productivity. However, some researchers suggests that cyberslacking can have positive effects. Non-job-related Internet use reduces stress, can stimulate creativity, enhances employees' sense of well-being and helps workers manage their lives so that they can spend more time at work. For example, instead of leaving the office to meet with their children or to run errands, employees can e-mail their kids and conduct banking and other tasks online. Then, too many employees work online when they are at home, more than making up for any time they spend cyberloafing at the office. Rather than trying to outlaw cyberloafing, organizations can regulate and monitor it instead. Some companies create technology use (TU) codes of conduct that spell out organizational policies and guidelines for internet use. Some TU codes urge employees to use the Internet and e-mail responsibly, stating that personal use should not interfere with work productivity. Others contain specific provisions that limit the amount of time spent on non-work-related business or specify times when such activity is forbidden.

Issues to Reflect:

(*a*) Do you cyberloaf? Under what circumstances?

(*b*) Is cyberloafing unethical? Why or why not?

(*c*) What limits, if any should be put on using organizational computers and other electronic devices for personal use?

(*d*) How would you discipline those who violate your TU code?

[(Sources D'Abate (2005). Garrett and Danziger (2008), Griffiths(2010) Henle and Blanchard(2008) Lavoie and Pychyl(2001) Lim and Chen(2012)Mcgill and Baetz(2011) Craig E. Johnson(2016)]

Case 28: Microchip under Skin

More than 50 of the 80 employees at Three Square Market, a technology company in Wisconsin, voluntarily agreed to have the company implant a microchip under their skin between their thumb and index finger. The microchip allowed employees to enter the building by swiping a scanner at the front door or pay for food in the employee cafeteria. Sam Bengston, a software engineer at Three Square, volunteered because "in the next five to ten years, this is going to be normal. I like to jump on the bandwagon with these kinds of things early, just to say that I have it." Others at Three Square were more cautious. "Because it's new, I don't know enough about it yet," said Melissa Timmins, Three Square's marketing director. "I'm a little nervous about implanting something into my body."

Issues to Reflect

(*a*) Is it acceptable for employers to implant microchips into their employees if it is voluntary?

(*b*) What if it is a mandatory condition for employment?

(*c*) How will this technology be used?

(*d*) What are the ethical aspects of implanting microchips in human body?

(*Source:* "Microchip Implants for Employees? One Company Says Yes," The New York Times, July 25, 2017, www.nytimes.com)

Case 29: Privacy in the Digital Era

The right to privacy is foundational for Americans, legally encoded into the Fourth Amendment to the Constitution of the United States. The 1948 United Nations Declaration of Human Rights includes language that acknowledges the right to privacy for people all over the globe. With the dawn of the Internet age, however, privacy has become a hotly contested issue. The revenue model of many technology companies, such as Google and Facebook, relies on gathering data on the private actions of individuals, on the Web and off and providing/selling that data to advertisers to better target potential customers.

Issues to Reflect

(*a*) What should remain private and beyond the reach of technology? What role does privacy play in leading a happy and meaningful life?

(*b*) What have we gained in exchange for our privacy? Are individuals and societies better off now? In what ways?

(*c*) Can companies be trusted to self-police and self-regulate the data they collect and sell? What conflicts of interest are there, and how do these threaten self-regulation?

(*d*) How much should companies disclose about what data they collect and how it is used?

(*e*) Recently, California adopted a law that allows users to opt out of data sharing. The European Union has a similar data privacy law. What are the advantages and disadvantages of such laws?

Case 30: The Peculiar Case of Edward Snowden

In 2013 Edward Snowden leaked a large amount of secret surveillance information, which he had copied from the US National Security Agency (NSA), to newspapers in the United States and the UK. The information released by Snowden included details of alleged mass phone and internet surveillance both in the United States and abroad, by the NSA. In an interview with the Guardian newspaper in June of that year, Snowden said that I can't in good conscience allow the US government to destroy privacy, Internet freedom and basic liberties for people around the world with this massive surveillance machine they're secretly building" (Greenwald, 2013).

Amnesty International has backed Snowden since he released details of the surveillance materials, saying that no one should be prosecuted for exposing human rights violations, which, they claimed, is what indiscriminate mass surveillance of communications amounts to.

Snowden fled to Moscow where, after some delays, he was granted asylum. This right has been extended until 2020 and it is understood that Snowden continues to live in Moscow. Snowden was quoted as saying when he arrived at Moscow's Sheremetyevo airport that: 'I did not seek to enrich myself. I did not seek to sell US secrets. I did not partner with any foreign government to guarantee my safety. 'In 2016 Snowden was awarded the Ossietzky Prize for 'outstanding efforts for freedom of expression'. He still faces possible prosecution in the United States, which could result in an extended prison sentence.

[*Sources:* BBC News USA & Canada (2014) and Greenwald (2013)]

Issues to Reflect:

(*a*) Consider where you believe Snowden's primary duty lay to his employers, to the wider US public interest or to all parties whose data had been subject to surveillance? Provide reasons to support your views.

(*b*) Would your views on his actions change if his disclosures resulted in US security being placed at higher risk as a consequence?

(*c*) Do you believe his motives, which he indicated were not for personal gain, justified his actions?

(*d*) What are the ethical aspects involved the case?

D

WIDER ASPECTS OF ETHICS IN PRACTICE

13 UNIT

Corporate Governance and Ethical Dimensions

13.16 Exercise your Ethics Muscle

Case 31: The Chicago Tylenol Murders

Case 32: Leaving Goldman Sachs

Case 33: The Infamous Story of Satyam: Greed Breeds Fall

13 UNIT

Corporate Governance and Ethical Dimensions

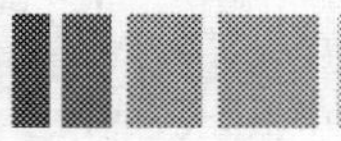

13.1 LEARNING OBJECTIVES

This unit tries to elucidate

- Meaning and significance of corporate governance
- Relationship between ethics and corporate governance by reviewing some scandals in India
- Principles of governance applicable to banking sector and benefits of adhering to them
- International models of corporate governance
- International codes of business conduct
- Initiative in Indian context to improve corporate governance
- Select Scams in India both in Financial and Non-financial sectors
- Some of the RBI initiatives that act as a deterrence to fraudulent behaviour of board and employees, and corporate entities
- What constitutes good corporate governance?

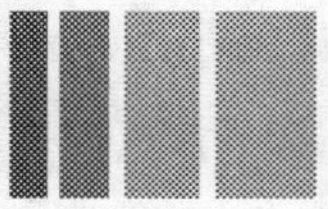

13.2 SIGNIFICANCE OF ETHICS IN CORPORATE GOVERNANCE

Why Ethics?

Let us recall how we studied about the ethics in the introduction chapter of this courseware. Ethics is the moral principles or standards of human behaviour, which help distinguishing between right and wrong. Ethics is also the principles of human conduct or human actions. These actions must serve a purpose, which constitutes part or the whole of moral agent's intention in doing what he or she does.

As we have mentioned in the opening chapter, Thomas Garrett defined ethics as the science of judging specifically human ends and relationship of means with those ends. In some way, it is also the art of controlling means so that they will serve specifically human needs.

What is Corporate Governance?

Joint Stock Corporations of the 20th and 21st Century have understood the need and method for sound monitoring, supervision and direction of the managements of their companies by a body of individuals (called the Board of Directors) who are well-versed with the companies' functioning and are also highly concerned about the companies' reputation and image in the short and long run. This regular oversight and direction of the Board of Directors on the companies' Top managements is expected to ensure desirable output and outcomes, which are appreciated by the stakeholders and would instil confidence of their investments and value their relationships with the companies in various forms, as investors, financiers, suppliers, stockists, distributors, employees, etc.

According to the World Bank, "Corporate Governance (CG) concerns the system by which companies are directed and controlled. It is about having companies, owners and regulators become more accountable, efficient and transparent, which in turn builds trust and confidence. Well-governed companies carry lower financial and non-financial risks and generate higher shareholder returns. They also have better access to external finance and reduce systemic risks due to corporate crises and financial scandals. Reliable financial reporting, timely disclosures, better boards and accountable management also facilitate development of stronger capital markets. They improve a country's ability to mobilize, allocate and monitor investments and help foster jobs and economic growth. Better supervision and monitoring can detect corporate inefficiencies and minimize vulnerability to financial crises".

There is a tendency on the part of the members of the internal management, in the absence of Board's supervision, to remain careless or misuse the funds that are at their disposal. Since the internal management always remains accountable to the Board's questioning both in formal meetings and outside the meetings, the top management is required to maintain the records (including the financial statements) in a transparent manner to satisfy their Board and eventually all the stakeholders of the company.

Relationship between Ethics and Corporate Governance

Small or large scale corporate scandals have their roots in the compromise of ethics particularly by its top managements. The following cursory look at the corporate scandals gives us a clear picture of the role of ethics in proper governance of corporate entities, including banks and financial institutions. The following is a summary of the background and nature of the issues in corporate governance arising out of lack of ethics on the part of the key personnel of the companies:

(*a*) *Enron*

Enron, an American energy company based in Houston, Texas, was formed in 1985 by Kenneth Lay after merging Houston Natural Gas and Inter North. The Company was performing well during the initial years. After some years, key officials of Enron colluded with the audit firm by using accounting loopholes, special purpose entities, and inappropriate financial reporting to conceal billions of dollars in debt from failed deals and projects. When Enron scandal became public, tens of billions of dollars' worth of shareholders' wealth simply eroded in just over a year's time. The exchange traded price of the company's stock went down nose-diving from US$90.75 per share in mid-2000 to less than $1 by the end of November 2001.

(*b*) *Kingfisher Airlines*

Kingfisher Airlines was set up in 2003. Though there is no official statement by the individuals or consortium of creditors, it is believed that of the total of fourteen banks (all excepting 1 are from Public Sector) seems to have lost Rs. 4,300 crores for advancing loans to a poorly governed and eventually grounded Kingfisher Airlines. Wrong operational decisions, improper HR policies, unjustified wage cuts for pilots and ground staff, non-payment of dues to airports for infrastructure, cheque bounce case, probe by the Central Bureau of Investigation case for defaulting to banks, etc. are examples of how a professional company cannot and should not be run by its own promoters by compromising on various principles of governance. It had incurred losses each year, and the earnings per share remained negative each year during 2005-2011. Finally, the Kingfisher Airlines had to stop all its operations when its license was cancelled on 20 October, 2012.

(*c*) *Satyam Computer Services*

On 24th June, 1987 Satyam Computer Services Ltd. (Satyam) (promoted by Mr. B. Rama Raju and Mr. B. Ramalinga Raju) was incorporated as a Private Limited Company for providing Software Development and Consultancy Services. On August 26, 1991 it was converted into a Public Limited Company. The next year, it raised funds through public issue. Satyam initially set up two software technology parks in the twin cities of Secunderabad and Hyderabad. It had also developed a software development center in Bengaluru. Satyam Scandal remains classic example of the corporate governance and fraudulent auditing practices. Worse, the promoters in connivance with auditors and chartered accountants caused fraud with the investors and other stakeholders of the company. For over years, Satyam's employees misrepresented the company's accounts to its board, stock exchanges, regulators, investors and other stakeholders. The Satyam scandal became known to the public at large in 2009 when the Company's founder and Chairman Ramalinga Raju admitted openly that accounts of Satyam were tampered with. His self-declaration revealed a Rs. 7,000 crore accounting fraud in the balance sheets of Satyam took place over the years. In all, 10 persons were found guilty including the Chairman, the MD, CFO, auditor of the internationally renowned audit company, former employees and the chief internal auditor of Satyam.

13.3 PRINCIPLES OF CORPORATE GOVERNANCE: BENEFITS OF GOOD GOVERNANCE

Principles of Corporate Governance

Corporate Governance has two broad facets- one a set of rules and procedures applicable as per the Companies Act, 2013 and the other applicable to the commercial banks and financial institutions. While for non-banking and financial non-companies listed on stock exchanges in India, the set of rules and procedures as specified in the Companies Act become applicable.

While for the commercial banks, the regulator Reserve Bank of India constituted in April, 2002 a Consultative Group of Directors of Banks and Financial Institutions (known as the Dr. Ganguly Group) to review the supervisory role

of Boards of banks and financial institutions and to obtain feedback on the functioning of the Boards *vis-à-vis* compliance, transparency, disclosures, audit committees etc. and make recommendations for making the role of Board of Directors more effective with a view to minimising risks and over-exposure.

The group reviewed existing laws governing banks and financial institutions' boards. It also interacted with various stakeholders to know their views and obtain suggestions, if any. The group also studied international best practices in banking and financial sectors mainly with respect to supervision.

The following are some of major recommendations of the Group:

1. For both public and private sector banks, there needs to be a due diligence of the directors in regard to their suitability for the post by way of qualifications and technical expertise. While carrying out this exercise, Nomination Committee of the Board should be formally involved.
2. While nominating Directors by the Government on the Boards of public sector banks, it needs to follow certain broad "fit and proper" norms for the Directors.
3. A thorough check of antecedents or background verification may be carried out to assess integrity and suitability of person to be nominated on to the Board of banks. Criminal records, civil actions undertaken to pursue personal debts, refusal of admission to or expulsion from professional bodies, sanctions applied by regulators or similar bodies and previous questionable business practices, etc. should be considered.
4. Merit needs to be accorded priority in the appointments or nominations to the Boards. Both for the public and private sector banks, appointment/ nomination of independent/non-executive directors to the Boards of banks should be from a pool of professional and talented people to be prepared and maintained by Reserve Bank of India. The Group suggested that any deviation from this procedure by any bank should be with the prior approval of RBI.
5. The Boards of banks need to be more contemporarily professional by inducting technical and specially qualified individuals. The rationale given

for this was growing complexity of banking and significance of knowledge in banking services.

6. Boards of banks should have representation in the areas such as finance, information technology, human resources development, economics and persons with good track record of experience in managing/advising industrial enterprises.
7. The independent/non-executive directors should raise in the meetings of the Board, critical questions relating to business strategy, including loans & recovery policy, housekeeping and internal control systems, record of exposure to various sectors/industries by way of both credit and investment, risk management systems, internal audit, accounting policy, senior management development, other important aspects of the functioning of the bank and investor relations. The good corporate governance in banks will be sustained by a knowledgeable, skillful and well informed Board of Directors with a proper blend of expertise/professionalism, independence and involvement.
8. In the case of private sector banks where promoter directors may act in unison, the independent/non-executive directors should provide effective checks and balances ensuring that the bank does not build up exposures to entities connected with the promoters or their associates. The independent/non-executive directors should provide effective checks and balances particularly, in widely held and closely controlled banking organisations.
9. Directors on the boards of NBFCs may be permitted to become Independent/non-executive directors on the boards of banks, subject to certain conditions.
10. Every Director should be given a brief on the functioning of the bank, before his appointment/induction, covering various aspects of structure/functioning of the bank.
11. The Board should formulate policies relating to credit dispensation, particularly in regard to exposure to various productive sectors, geographical areas, investments, exposures to sensitive sectors such as capital market, strategies for recovery of loans and status of progress with respect to investments, risk management, etc.

12. The whole-time directors should have sufficiently long tenure to enable them to leave a mark of their leadership and business acumen on the bank's performance.

13. It would be desirable to separate the office of Chairman and Managing Director in respect of large sized public sector banks. This functional separation will bring about more focus on strategy and vision as also the needed thrust in the operational functioning of the top management of the bank.

14. The information furnished to the Board should be wholesome, complete and adequate to take meaningful decisions. A distinction needs to be made between statutory items and strategic issues in order to make the material for directors 'manageable'. The manner in which the Board proceedings are recorded and followed-up in public sector banks leaves much scope for improvement. The reviews dealing with various performance areas could be put-up to the Supervisory Committee of Board and a summary of each such review could be put up to the Main Board. The Board's focus should be devoted more on strategy issues, risk profile, internal control systems, overall performance of the bank, etc.

15. The procedure followed for recording of the minutes of the board meetings in banks and financial institutions should be uniform and formalized. Banks and financial institutions may adopt two methods for recording the proceedings *viz.*, a summary of key observations and a more detailed recording of the proceedings. In every meeting, the board should review the status of the action taken on the points arising from earlier meetings and till action is completed to its satisfaction, the pending items should continue to be put up before the board.

16. All banks should consider appointing qualified Company Secretary as the Secretary to the Board and have a Compliance Officer (reporting to the Secretary) for monitoring and reporting compliance with various regulatory/accounting requirements.

17. There could be a Supervisory Committee of the Board in all banks, be they public or private sector, which will work on collective trust and at the same time, without diluting the overall responsibility of the Board.

Their role and responsibilities could include monitoring of the exposures (credit and investment) review of the adequacy of risk management process & upgradation thereof, internal control systems and ensuring compliance with the statutory/regulatory framework.

18. The Audit Committee should, ideally be constituted with independent/non-executive directors and the Executive Director should only be a permanent invitee. However, in respect of public sector banks, the existing arrangement of including the Executive Director and nominee directors of Government and RBI in the Audit Committee may continue.
19. The Chairman of Audit Committee need not be confined to the Chartered accountant profession but can be a person with knowledge on 'finance' or 'banking' so as to provide directions and guidance to the Audit Committee, since the Committee not only looks at accounting issues, but also the overall management of the bank.
20. It is desirable to have a Nomination Committee for appointing independent/non-executive directors of banks. In the context of a number of public sector banks issuing capital to the public, a Nomination Committee of the Board may be formed for nomination of directors for representing shareholders.
21. With a view to building up credibility among the investor class, a Committee of the Board was suggested by the group to be set up to look into the grievances of investors and shareholders, with the Company Secretary as a nodal point.
22. The formation and operationalization of the Risk Management Committees in pursuance of the guidelines issued by the RBI should be speeded up and their role further strengthened.
23. The banks could be asked to come up with a strategy and plan for implementation of the governance standards recommended and submit progress of implementation, for review after twelve months and thereafter half yearly or annually, as deemed appropriate.

(*Source:* https://www.rbi.org.in/scripts/NotificationUser.aspx?Id=721&Mode=0)

Is Good Corporate Governance Worth Pursuing?

On the importance of corporate governance, Jim Solomon and Aris Solomon in their book (2004) titled Corporate Governance and Accountability, page 2(302 pages) observed as follows: "Policy makers, practitioners and theorists have adopted the general stance that corporate governance reform is worth pursuing supporting such initiatives as splitting the role of chairman/chief executive introducing non-executive directors to boards, curbing excessive executive performance-related remuneration, improving institutional investor relations, increasing the quality and quantity of corporate disclosure, *inter alia*. However, is there really evidence to support these initiatives? Do they really improve the effectiveness of corporations and their accountability? There are certainly those who are opposed to the ongoing process of corporate governance reform. Many company directors oppose the loss of individual decision-making power, which comes from the presence of non-executive directors and independent directors on their boards. They refute the growing pressure to communicate their strategies and policies to their primary institutional investors. They consider that the many initiatives aimed at 'improving' corporate governance in the UK have simply slowed down decision making and added an unnecessary level of bureaucracy and red tape. The Cadbury Report emphasized the importance of avoiding excessive control and recognized that no system of control can completely eliminate the risk of fraud (such as in the case of Maxwell or Satyam) without hindering companies' ability to compete in a free market (Cadbury Report, 1992, p. 12, para. 1.9). This is an important point, because human nature cannot be altered through regulation, checks and balances." Nevertheless, there is a growing perception in the financial markets that good corporate governance is associated with prosperous companies. Numbers of research have provided empirical evidence to support the agenda for corporate governance reform. We shall explore the specific benefits that accrue for good corporate governance in the succeeding heading.

Benefits of Good Corporate Governance

Following are some major benefits one can expect from appropriate corporate governance in the banks:

1. Once suitable banking professionals are identified for the position of top management or nominating on to the Boards of banks, stakeholders get adequate assurance that their banks are in the safe hands.

2. In addition, competence, character or antecedent verification of all top officials and members of the Boards of directors assures that these persons who have got a clean and impeccable track record of their financial and conduct-related matters for a fairly long duration of their careers, it is rare that they suddenly change their very nature once they are entrusted with greater powers. They carry forward in all probability the same values they exhibited in the past during the new stint.
3. Proven merit and selection criterion of picking up persons from the pool of professional and talented people as maintained by Reserve Bank of India would rule out possible negotiations for the coveted banking positions.
4. Appointment of a qualified Company Secretary as the Secretary to the Board a Compliance Officer (reporting to the Secretary) for monitoring and reporting compliance with various regulatory/accounting requirements are expected to bring-in a greater transparency in routine accounts and financial statements of banks.
5. There exists a strong probability that well-governed firms will obtain capital at most competitive rates than banks or firms that have poor corporate-governance practices because investors will require a smaller risk premium for investing in well-governed banks/firms.
6. Grievance mechanism and redressal committee would help sorting out the issues faced by the investors.
7. With sound governance systems in place in banks, it can be expected that these banks not only comply all the requirements of lending and customer services and banking codes, the stakeholders get an assurance that their bank is safe and does not indulge in any opaque activities. Above all, the reputation of the banks is expected to remain high and may even reach newer heights.
8. With good corporate governance in place, it can be expected that profitability of the banks will go up along with growth in market share.

13.4 RBI DISCUSSION PAPER ON 'GOVERNANCE IN COMMERCIAL BANKS IN INDIA'

In view of the growing size and complexity of India's financial system and recent events in a dynamic and rapidly evolving financial landscape, RBI issued a discussion paper in June 2020) to underscore the significance of strengthening governance standards in banks. In the context where management plays the role of an agent of a board and the board in turn plays the role of an agent of shareholders, governance failures have brought to fore the impact of quality of governance on efficiency in allocation of resources, protection of depositors' interest as well as maintaining financial stability. The main points in the discussion paper are as under:

Responsibilities of the Board : The board of a bank has overall responsibility for the bank, including culture, governance framework and approving as well as overseeing management's implementation of the bank's strategic objectives. Directors have responsibilities to the bank's overall interests, regardless of who appoints them.

Culture and Values : A fundamental component of good governance is a culture of reinforcing appropriate norms for responsible and ethical behaviour. These norms are especially critical in terms of a bank's risk awareness, risk-taking behaviour and risk management. To promote a sound culture, the board shall reinforce the "tone at the top" by—

i. playing a lead role in establishing the bank's culture and values; adhering to values that create expectations that all business shall be conducted in a legal and ethical manner.

ii. sustained oversight on adherence to such values by senior management and other employees; ensuring primary responsibility resting with CEO and senior management.

iii. confirming that appropriate steps have been or are being taken to communicate throughout the bank the values, professional standards or code of conduct it sets, together with supporting policies.

iv. an online process by which every employee in the bank spends at least 60 minutes every year reviewing a conduct training manual before signing the code of conduct statement.

v. recognising that changing behaviour cannot always be achieved through "standard" training and requires involvement of senior leaders who champion the effort, develop programs for staff across all areas of the bank, tailored to the bank's circumstances that regularly reinforce what the desired values and conduct mean in practice.

vi. making certain that the CEO and other WTDs are highly visible in championing the desired values and conduct, that they face material consequences if there are persistent or high-profile conduct and value breaches.

vii. confirming that employees, including senior management, are aware that appropriate disciplinary or other actions, including those related to compensation/career progression, will follow unacceptable behaviours including weak management oversight and transgressions including wilful blindness.

viii. implementing a feedback system where the board can systematically assess whether the espoused values are communicated, proactively promoted by management and staff at all levels so that the 'tone at the middle' as well as throughout the bank is consistent with the 'tone at the top'.

ix. putting in place a comprehensive set of indicators based on objective criterion to monitor and assess adherence of individuals, teams at all levels to bank's values, desired conduct.

x. ensuring that assessment of adherence to bank's values and desired conduct is factored in extant performance appraisal system of each employee throughout the bank.

To put all the above into practice the board shall have oversight of

(*i*) Code of conduct or comparable policy, which shall:

- *a.* define acceptable and unacceptable behaviour;
- *b.* explicitly disallow illegal activity, such as financial misreporting, misconduct, economic crime including fraud, breach of sanctions, money laundering, anticompetitive practices, bribery and corruption, or violation of consumer rights; and
- *c.* it shall make clear that employees are expected to conduct themselves ethically, perform their job with skill, due care and diligence in addition to complying with laws, regulations as well as internal policies of the bank.

(*ii*) bank's values which shall recognise critical importance of:

- *a.* timely and frank discussion
- *b.* escalation of problems to higher levels within the organisation.

(*iii*) A whistle-blower policy which shall be well operationalized and widely communicated so that

a. all stakeholders, including employees, shall be encouraged and are able to communicate *bona fide* concerns about illegal, unethical or questionable practices;

b. with adequate procedures and processes that allows *bona fide* concerns to be registered in a confidential manner;

c. with the board taking responsibility for ensuring that those who raise concerns are protected from detrimental treatment or reprisals;

d. with board oversight including approval of how, by whom legitimate material concerns shall be investigated and addressed by an objective independent internal or external body or the board itself. Material concerns shall also be communicated to the Department of Supervision, Reserve Bank of India.

(*iv*) The ultimate responsibility for ensuring accountability for misconduct lies with the board. Therefore, boards shall also oversee compensation system that promote prudent risk-taking behaviour, business practices and identify tools which mitigate / address misconduct (e.g., in year adjustment, malus, claw back arrangement, etc.)

Likewise, the discussion paper has enumerated the responsibilities of the board in the area of recognizing and managing conflict of interest.

1. Conflicts of interest may arise because of various activities/ roles of a bank, or between the interests of a bank or its customers and those of a bank's directors or senior managers. Conflicts of interest may also arise when a bank is part of a broader group. For example, where the bank is part of a group, reporting lines and information flows between bank, its parent and/or other group entities can lead to emergence of conflicts of interest. Where these conflicts cannot be prevented, they shall be properly managed based on permissibility of relationships or transactions under sound policies consistent with existing statutes and provisions prescribed here.
2. Accordingly, the board shall ensure that adequate policies, procedures and measures are implemented to identify actual/potential/perceived conflicts of interest. Thereafter, assess their materiality, decide on mitigating mea-

sures and communicate any material actual/potential/perceived conflicts of interest to the board. The scope of policies, procedures and measures shall include various categories of staff, directors, shareholders, service providers, business partners and other stakeholders as well as legal or natural persons closely linked to the various categories mentioned.

3. The board shall have a formal written 'conflicts of interest' policy and an objective compliance process to ensure implementation of the policy.
4. The board shall ensure that transactions with related parties are reviewed to assess risk. These shall be subject to appropriate restrictions to ensure that resources of the bank are not misappropriated or misapplied.
5. The board shall also oversee and be satisfied with the process by which appropriate public disclosure is made and/or information is provided to supervisors, relating to the bank's policies on actual/potential/perceived conflicts of interest. This shall include information on the bank's approach to disclosing as well as managing actual/potential/perceived conflicts of interest that are not consistent with such policies and conflicts that could arise because of the bank's affiliation or transactions with other entities within the group.
6. As part of overall governance framework, the board is responsible for overseeing a strong risk governance framework. A risk governance framework shall include well defined organisational responsibilities for risk management, typically referred to as 'three lines of defence' *viz.*,
   (*a*) first line of defence - the business line
   (*b*) second line of defence - a risk management function and a compliance function independent from the first line of defence
   (*c*) third line of defence - an internal audit and vigilance function independent from the first and second lines of defence.

   Depending on the bank's nature, size, complexity and risk profile of its activities, specifies of how these three lines of defence are structured can vary. However, regardless of the structure, responsibilities for each line of defence shall be well defined and communicated.
7. Within the above scheme of things, an effective risk governance framework must be operated through:

(*i*) a strong risk culture

(*ii*) a well-developed risk appetite articulated through a RAS

(*iii*) well-defined responsibilities for internal control functions and assurance functions including risk management.

8. The bank's risk appetite shall be developed and conveyed to reinforce a strong risk culture. The risk governance framework shall outline actions to be taken when stated risk limits are breached, including disciplinary actions for excessive risk-taking, escalation procedures and board of director notification.
9. The board shall take an active role in defining the risk appetite, ensuring its alignment with the bank's strategic, capital, financial plans and compensation practices. The bank's risk appetite shall be defined by considering the competitive along with regulatory landscape as well as the bank's long-term interests, risk exposure and ability to manage risk effectively.
10. The bank's risk appetite shall be clearly conveyed through a RAS that can be easily understood by all relevant parties *viz.*, the board itself, senior management, employees and the Reserve Bank. The development of an effective RAS shall be driven by both top-down board leadership and bottom-up management involvement.
11. The board shall approve an approach, oversee the implementation of key policies pertaining to the bank's capital adequacy assessment process including capital raising plans, liquidity plans, compliance policies/obligations and the internal control system.
12. The RAF and risk culture must include a framework for identifying misconduct followed by remedial measures. The process for managing misconduct risk through compensation system must include at minimum, ex-ante process that embed non-financial assessment criteria such as the quality of risk management, degree of compliance with laws and regulations.
13. The board shall ensure that the second and third lines of defence are properly positioned, staffed, resourced to carry out their responsibilities independently, objectively as also effectively. In the board's oversight of the risk governance framework, the board shall regularly review key poli-

cies and controls with senior management. The reviews shall include the heads of second and third lines of defence. These reviews shall identify significant risks, determine areas that need improvement and undertake remedial measures where needed.

14. To achieve desired objective at least one meeting of the board must be exclusively focussed towards fulfilling this responsibility of the board towards 'risk appetite, management and assurance', details of which have been articulated above. (Source: RBI website)

    Based on the suggestions and feedback received on the Discussion Paper, the Reserve Bank issued instructions regarding the Chair and meetings of the Board, composition of certain Committees of the Board, age, tenure and remuneration of Director and appointment of whole-time directors (WTDs) in April 2021. With respect to the other proposals contained in the discussion paper, a Master Direction on Governance will be issued by RBI going forward.

13.5 CORPORATE GOVERNANCE MODELS & RECENT TRENDS

There is no one universal model of corporate governance, be it banking or non-banking corporations. Depending upon the region or culture and context, corporate governance models have some variations. While broad objectives of all these models remain similar and converge, there are some differences between the governance models across regions. Bob Ticker (2012) provides five broad classifications of underlying models of corporate governance across the world. These are:

1. The American rule-based model
2. The UK/Commonwealth principles-based model
3. The continental European two-tier model
4. The Japanese stakeholder-oriented model
5. The Asian family-based model

The US Model

The Anglo-Saxon model of corporate governance is considered with high regard across the world for its thoroughness in the promotion of greater corporate transparencies and the development of a framework where the respective organs of the corporation can work together for the overall interest of shareholders; and with some capacity to take into account the interests of other stakeholders. It is a unitary board model unlike the continental two-tier board model. There exists a predominant representation of outside directors on the board in this model of governance. Governance is regulated by legal statute and rules that are mandatory in nature. There is little flexibility in these rules. Chairman and CEO could be one person in the US listed companies. Shareholders cannot have any control over the board membership. The model was further strengthened and reinforced in the aftermath of the Enron debacle in the US in 2003.

The UK Model

In the United Kingdom, the Corporate Governance Code sets standards of good practice in relation to board leadership and effectiveness, remuneration, accountability and relations with shareholders. In the UK, all companies with a Premium Listing of equity shares must report (as per the Financial Reporting Council directives) in their annual report and accounts on how they have applied the Code, which contains broad principles and more specific provisions. Listed companies are required to report, as part of their annual report and accounts, on how they have applied the main principles of the Code.

Similar to the American Model, company law in UK/Commonwealth Model is based on common law. This is rooted in legislation and extended by case law. As is evident from the description of this model in the above list of 5 models, in the United Kingdom and Commonwealth countries, corporate governance follows a principles-based approach. Companies are required to report having followed specifying governance principles in the codes or explain why they have not followed the laid down principles (if otherwise). UK governance model believes in self-regulation as the theme. While compliance is voluntary, major violations may lead to delisting from stock exchange.

The Continental Model

The two-tier Boards govern the corporate firms in Germany, Netherlands, Austria, Denmark and other European countries like Poland and Croatia. One can broadly describe the corporate governance model in the continental European countries as one that is rule-based. The general characteristic of financial markets is that they are smaller size and are less liquid. Banks have a relatively greater influence over the corporate matters of the firms that are borrowers of these banks. In this structure of governance adopting a two-tier model, there is a formal mechanism worked out for the two boards as Management Board and Supervisory Board. While the members belonging to the Management Board attend meetings of the Supervisory Boards, there is no voting power granted to the members of the Management Boards. Management Board members (as the Top executives of a corporate) present their budgets, strategies, etc. for the comment/advice and approval of the Supervisory Board.

The Japanese Model

Most of the Japanese corporations have close relationships with one main bank. The Japanese corporate governance model has, as a characteristic feature, significant stock of the company held by the affiliated bank or company. The present model is known as *keiretsu* which means grouping of enterprises with inter-locking business relationships. This form of groups of enterprises started playing a major role in the rapid economic progress of the Japanese Economy and industry during the post-World War II. The previous form that existed before the *keiretsu* was known as the *zaibatsu.* Japanese industrial economy prior to the World War II was dominated by four family-controlled vertical monopolies, namely Mitsubishi, Sumitomo, Mitsui and Yasuda.

The governance of Japanese corporations has the spirit of social cohesion in the sense that it encourages lifetime employment, encourage commitment, decision making by consensus, etc. The classical *keiretsu* model of governance follows large size of boards, who are by default the top layers of the management. Representation of outside directors (such as independent directors) is not found. A few of the directors of Japanese Boards under this model can be retired ones having served other companies in the *keiretsu* network of companies, retired from a major bank of the same company or members retired from one of the group companies, etc. A major limitation of the *keiretsu* model is that the tendency for managers to progress to occupy board membership on account of their tenure rather than performance may help some of the mediocre can reach the board. In such scenario, the companies receive far less benefit and lower than desired impact from their association with the boards.

The Asian Model

Corporations located in many of the South-east Asian countries like Malaysia, Singapore, Philippines, Hong Kong, Thailand, etc. are controlled by Chinese

families. Significant percentage of share capital in these companies is held by a few (less than 2 dozens) Chinese families. While notionally the boards of these companies take major policy decisions, in effect these boards have a complete dominance by the select families who exercise the real power by the presence of the head of the family as well as members of these families occupying top management positions. We can describe the corporate governance system in these South-east Asian countries as family-centric and family-controlled, dominant equity of a company is always held by the members of a family, greater importance to amicable method of arriving at decisions and avoiding confrontation approach. Major limitation of this style of governance is that it may lead to corruption, insider-trading, discriminatory treatment to minority shareholders, etc.

Recent trends in Corporate Governance

Over the years, few new common and pressing trends have emerged in the corporate governance models across the geographies. Investors today are more assertive and demanding who feel empowered to demand action and disclosure on a growing number of topics and with failure to meet those demands, more likely than ever to vote against companies and individual directors at annual shareholder meetings. Secondly, higher standards for corporate attention to the climate are being demanded as the materiality of climate change to individual businesses and society writ large is beyond question. As Larry Fink wrote in Blackrock's 2022 letter to CEOs, "most stakeholders now expect companies to play a role in decarbonizing the global economy." Thirdly, enhanced board-effectiveness practices have become the norm as investors and other stakeholders realize that good composition, refreshment and evaluation practices result in improved corporate performance and decreased risk exposure. Fourthly, urgency regarding equity and diversity initiatives both in the enterprise and the boardroom, as evidence mounts that diverse organizations outperform others and stakeholders demand progress without delay.

13.6 THE INSTITUTIONAL FRAMEWORK FOR EFFECTIVE CORPORATE GOVERNANCE

In order to achieving the desired outcomes and benefits of corporate governance, there is a need to have an appropriate and well-crafted institutional framework.

Some of the benefits that are achievable having sound corporate governance practices are:

1. Creates conducive environment that enables incentive to the owners and managers (agents) to achieve objectives which are in the interest of the organization.
2. Minimises corruption, delays, risks and mismanagement.
3. Maintains and enhances reputation of the corporate firm in the industry and society by following best practices besides adhering to all laws, principles and codes and rules laid down by the ministry/exchanges, etc.
4. Share price and market capitalization keeps rising due to the growth in revenues and other positive results.

As discussed above in the corporate governance models across the world, there is no universally-accepted method or structure of governance of corporations. Different regions or countries have developed, over the decades, different institutional structures. We may broadly bifurcate them into institutions developed as formal and non-formal.

Under the formal institutions for ensuring good quality of governance, we can include some of the formal institutions for internal controls-like the management board, supervisory board, audit committee, remuneration committee, corporate social responsibility committee, etc. Also, some corporations may involve workers' councils to represent in the management boards. As far external control is concerned, institutions like the Registrar of Companies require documents to be submitted such as memorandum of association, articles of association, pre-incorporation agreement for appointment of individuals as directors/managing directors, etc. from companies. Competition Commission of India (to oversee whether the Competition Act is adhered to by the companies or not), Ministry of Corporate Affairs (for overseeing the administration of the Companies Act, 2013), Securities and Exchange Board of India (SEBI) for protective, developmental and regulatory functions primarily concerning the exchanges. One of the major roles of SEBI as a regulatory institution is to see that the Directors and other senior members of the listed companies do not resort to insider trading and protection of the minority investors. Institute of Company Secretaries of India is the only recognised professional body created in 1980 by an Act of Parliament to develop and regulation of the profession of Company Secretaries in India. A Company

Secretary is a senior employee of a private or public company who is responsible for its efficient administration, in particular with regard to implementing all compliance matters and statutory and regulatory requirements besides making sure that the Board of Directors' decisions are implemented from time to time. Besides national institutions, other Institutions like the OECD, World Bank, etc. Principles or Codes on governance may be adhered to by companies that have an international presence.

As far the informal institutions are concerned, companies may voluntarily design their own firm-specific (or Group-wide if it is a part of a business group) norms, values, ethos, codes, etc. and may also have some broader social norms or values like environmental-conscious manufacturing, equal-opportunity employment, etc.

While striving to comply with both formal and informal institutional arrangements from time to time, a company or any organisation can achieve the desired outcomes of corporate governance in a seamless manner.

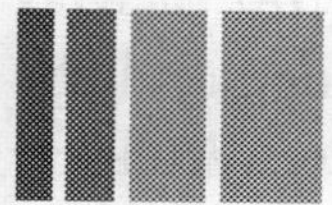

13.7 THE INTERNATIONAL CODES OF BUSINESS CONDUCT

A need for corporate governance code was acutely felt after several incidents of corporate failures in many countries in the world, for e.g.; Maxwell Group, BCCI, Barings Bank can be cited and in USA, MNCs like Enron Power project, WorldCom, Tyco, Global Crossings, Quest, Xerox, Arthur Anderson, etc.

Accordingly, the codes or principles have been drawn up on various aspects of corporate governance, like defining the roles and responsibilities of the board of directors (boards) and stakeholders and setting out guidelines for more effective and improved performance.

Some Renowned Committees and their Salient Features/Recommendations on Corporate Governance

Out of many Committees' reports/recommendations on the issue over the past quarter century for the international corporate world, some select reports and recommendations of the following renowned Committees are given below:

- Cadbury Committee (1992)
- Greenbury Committee (1995)
- Hampel Committee-January (1998)

- LSE Combined Code (1998)
- Blue Ribbon Committee (1999)
- OECD Principles for Corporate Governance (1999 and 2004)
- Myners Committee Report (2001)
- Combined Code of Corporate Governance (2003)
- The UK Corporate Governance Code, 2010 & 2018
- The UK Stewardship Code, 2010 & 2020

It may be mentioned that the reports of the other Committees have not been considered here because their recommendations are found to be almost in line with recommendations of the above mentioned Committees.

The Cadbury Committee Report (1992)

Consequent upon a number of scams and failures in the corporate sector in the late 1980s and the early 1990s, the Cadbury Committee was setup in May 1991 by the Financial Reporting Council, the London Stock Exchange and the accountancy profession to address the financial aspects of corporate governance. The contents of the report are segregated into 3 parts:

(*a*) reviewing the structure and responsibilities of boards of directors and recommending a Code of Best Practice

(*b*) considering the roles of auditors and addressing a number of recommendations to the accountancy profession

(*c*) dealing with the rights and responsibilities of shareholders.

Further, the Code of Best Practice is divided into 4 sections:

1. Board Constitution, Accountability to shareholders.
2. Role of Chairman of the Board.
3. In matters where company's legal and financial advisers may be consulted for necessary clarity. In certain cases, there should be a formal mechanism to seek independent professional advice at the expense of the company through a formal resolution.
4. Directors should undergo some form of internal or external training, in particular for the executive or non-executive directors with no previous board experience.

The Greenbury Committee Report (1995)

In January 1995, the Confederation of British Industry (CBI) organised a committee to study executive pay issues and provide recommendations for governance reform. It recommended setting of Remuneration Committee composing non-executive directors to determine executive remuneration, terminal benefits, etc. It should be published in Annual Report. The chairman of the Committee should attend Annual General Meeting and reply all questions pertaining to executive remuneration, perquisites, etc.

Remuneration policy should be performance-linked and try to attract fresh talents, retain and motivate the existing one.

The Greenbury Committee Recommendations are grouped into three categories:

1. Constitution of the Remuneration Committee
2. Disclosure and approval provisions
3. Remuneration policy

The Hampel Committee on Corporate Governance (1998)

The sponsors of the Hampel Committee were the London Stock Exchange (LSE), the Confederation of British Industry (CBI), the Institute of Directors (IOD), the Consultative Committee of Accountancy Bodies (CCAB), the National Association of Pension Funds (NAPF) and the Association on British Insurers (ABI) to assess the progress of implementation of the Cadbury and Greenbury Committees' recommendations.

Following are the summary of the recommendations of the Hampel Committee:

1. There should be a narrative account of inclusion of the broad principles of corporate governance and also explain the circumstances justifying departure from best practice in its annual report.
2. The majority of non-executive directors should be independent and should be disclosed in the annual report.
3. The board should maintain a sound system of internal control to safeguard shareholders' investment and the company's assets and should report on the company's system for internal control.
4. Each company should establish an Audit Committee of at least three non-executive directors with at least two of them should be independent.

5. The Audit Committee should keep under review the overall financial relationship between the company and its auditors, to ensure a balance between the maintenance of objectivity and value for money.

The Combined Code, Principles of Good Governance and Code of Best Practice, London Stock Exchange (1998)

A Committee was set up by the LSE to:

(*i*) examine the reports and recommendations of Cadbury and Greenbury

(*ii*) suggest to LSE a set of principles of good governance and codes of best practice for the UK companies finally for implementation.

The principles of good governance were spelt out by the Combined Code and then it suggested a Code of Best Practices on these principles. These are in the matters concerning:

(*a*) Directors

(*b*) Directors' remuneration

(*c*) Relations with Shareholders

(*d*) Accountability and Audit

(*e*) Institutional Shareholders

The Committee recommended that the board should meet regularly and take independent professional advice, if necessary, at the company's expense. All directors should bring an independent judgment to bear on issues of strategy, performance, resources, including key appointments and standards of conduct. Every director should receive appropriate training on the first occasion when he or she is appointed to the board of a listed company, and subsequently as necessary. Board should justify a decision to combine the posts of chairman and CEO in one person. The board should include non-executive directors of sufficient caliber and number for their views to carry significant weight in the board's decisions. The directors should annually conduct a review of the effectiveness of the group's system of internal control and should report to the shareholders. The review should cover all controls including financial, operational and compliance controls and risk management.

The Blue-Ribbon Committee Report on Effectiveness of Corporate Audit Committees (1999)

The Blue-Ribbon Committee, co-chaired by John. Whitehead and Ira Millstein was setup in September 1998, by the New York Stock Exchange (NYSE) and the National Association of Securities Dealers (NASD) in response to the concerns expressed by Arthur Levitt, chairman SEC about the financial reporting process.

The Committee submitted their final report on February 08, 1999 announcing the following ten far-reaching recommendations to improve the quality of corporate financial reporting.

1. Revise Definition of Independent Director
2. Require Independent Audit Committee
3. Mandate Minimum Audit Committee Size and Increased Financial Literacy
4. Mandate Written Charter Detailing Responsibilities and Duties
5. Mandate Annual Public Disclosure of Audit Committee Activities
6. Clarify Oversight Responsibility for Outside Auditor's Engagement
7. Mandate Discussion with Outside Auditor Regarding Independence
8. Require Outside Auditor to Discuss Quality of Financial Reporting
9. Require Audit Committee Annual Letter to Shareholders
10. Mandate Interim Review of Quarterly Financial Reporting

It recommended the Audit Committee be composed of solely independent directors. It should be comprised of a minimum of 3 directors, each of who is financially literate or becomes financially literate within a reasonable period of time after appointment. Further, at least 1 member of the Audit Committee should have accounting or related financial management expertise. The Audit Committee Charter shall specify that the outside auditor is ultimately accountable to the board of directors and the Audit Committee. The Audit Committee, as representative of shareholders shall have the ultimate authority and responsibility to propose appointment and replacement of the outside auditor. Audit Committee chairman shall publish a report in the corporate governance report certifying that

(*a*) management has reviewed the audited financial statements with the Audit Committee (*b*) the outside auditors have discussed with the Audit Committee its findings of the accounting principles

(*c*) the members of the Audit Committee have discussed among themselves without management or the outside auditor's presence, the information disclosed to the Audit Committee

(*d*) the Audit Committee believes that the company's financial statements are fairly presented in conformity with Generally Accepted Accounting Principles (GAAP) in all material respects.

OECD Principles on Corporate Governance (1999) and (2004)

Being an inter-governmental organisation of the industrially developed nations of the world, the Organisation for Economic Co-operation and Development (OECD) came out with a set of clearly defined principles, which are useful to all countries irrespective of their stages of development, legal systems, institutional framework and traditions. The aspects covered by OECD in 1999 as well as 2004 are broadly similar.

The main objective of the OECD in drafting these principles was to assist both its member governments as also non-member governments to bring about suitable improvements in their legal, institutional and regulatory framework for facilitating good corporate governance regimes. OECD principles not only incorporate codes to protect interests of the shareholders but also give due importance to safeguarding interests of the stakeholders like employees, creditors, suppliers, customers, environment, etc. as OECD believes that effective co-operation of all the stakeholders is essential for creating wealth for the shareholders and building financially sound corporate entities.

In an exclusive section titled annotations to the OECD principles of corporate governance, the following six major aspects were dealt with in detail:

1. Ensuring the Basis for an Effective Corporate Governance Framework
2. The Rights of Shareholders and Key Ownership Functions
3. The Equitable Treatment of Shareholders
4. The Role of Stakeholders in Corporate Governance
5. Disclosure and Transparency
6. The Responsibilities of the Board

The OECD principles represent the first major international effort in evolving core elements of good corporate governance regimes. However, the OECD Corporate Governance Committee is reviewing the G20/OECD Principles of Corporate Governance. The overall objective of the review is to update the Principles, in light of recent evolutions in capital markets and corporate governance policies and practices. The review was launched in November 2021 and will be completed in 2023.

Myners Committee Report (2001)

Paul Myners Committee was commissioned by the Treasury in March 2000 to review institutional investment in the UK.

The report identified a series of distortions to effective decision-making by the institutions and made a number of proposals to tackle them. One of the proposals was that pension fund trustees voluntarily adopt on a 'comply or explain' basis a series of principles codifying best practice for investment decision-making.

The Committee recommended that:

1. Trustees of Pension Funds should assess the effectiveness of their own contribution to meeting the objectives of the fund as they do that of their advisers and fund managers.
2. The trustees should set out explicitly an overall investment objective for the fund which represents their best judgment of what is necessary to meet the fund's liabilities.
3. Contracts for actuarial services and investment advice should be opened to competition separately. Pension funds should be prepared to pay sufficient fees for each service to attract a broad range of kinds of potential provider.
4. Trustees should not take investment advice on an asset class from an investment consultant who lacks expertise in that asset class.
5. Pension funds should provide fund managers with clarity about the period over which their performance will be judged and hold to that under the terms of the contract, unless clearly abnormal circumstances arise.

Combined Code on Corporate Governance (2003)

The Financial Reporting Council (FRC) of UK announced that this Code supersedes and replaces the Combined Code issued by the Hampel Committee on Corporate Governance in June 1998. It derives itself from a review of the role and effectiveness of non-executive directors by Derek Higgs and a review of audit committees by a Group led by Sir Robert Smith.

Broadly, the Report deals with two segments as far the corporate governance is concerned-companies and institutional shareholders. Further, it provides a detailed section on related guidance and good practice suggestions, which was bifurcated into:

(*a*) guidance on internal control

(*b*) guidance on audit committees

The Code aims to achieve more open and rigorous procedures for the appointment of directors and improved induction and development of non-executive directors (NEDs). It recommends that half of the board members of the Financial Times (FT) 350 companies should be independent NEDs and only NEDs should sit on the audit and remuneration committees. Further, if NEDs serve more than nine years they are no longer considered to be independent. The Code also calls for formal evaluation - of boards, committees and individual directors.

The Code takes a 'comply or explain' approach to encourage best practice in corporate governance. Listed companies have to report on how they have applied the principles in the Code, confirm that they comply with the Code's provisions or provide an explanation of any departures.

The UK Corporate Governance Code, 2010 & 2018

The UK Corporate Governance Code (2010) was issued on 28 May 2010, replacing the Combined Code 2008. It was again reviewed and an updated version was released in 2018 setting out standards of good practice for listed companies on board composition and development, remuneration, shareholder relations, accountability and audit. The code is published by the Financial Reporting Council (FRC). It recommended chairman's responsibility for leading the board, need for directors to devote sufficient time, requirement for non-executive directors (NEDs) to constructively challenge, need for board to have balance of skills and experience, the annual re-election of directors, etc. Measures also include promotion of balance and diversity in relation to the composition of the board, in particular in relation to gender. It also addresses remuneration and how performance related pay for executive directors must have criteria to meet, other than purely financial and must relate to the company's long-terms interests, risks and systems.

The UK Stewardship Code, 2010 & 2020

The UK Stewardship code was published in June 2010 and now its 2020 version is in vogue which sets high stewardship standards for those investing money on behalf of UK savers and pensioners, and those that support them. Stewardship is the responsible allocation, management and oversight of capital to create long-term value for clients and beneficiaries leading to sustainable benefits for the economy, the environment and society. The FRC believes this is complimentary to the UK Corporate Governance Code and should also apply on a 'comply or explain' basis. This entails providing a statement on the institution's website that contains a description on how principles have been applied, disclosure of specific information listed, explanation when the code has not been complied with as some smaller institutions may judge certain elements to be disproportionate, etc. Its aim is to improve long-term returns to shareholders by increasing the quality of strategy, performance and management of risk between institutional investors (such as pension funds, insurance companies and investment trusts) and companies.

Summing up

From the above select international committees on Corporate Governance and their salient recommendations, it can be observed that the corporate governance system in different countries varies as per their practices, culture, ideologies, legal systems, institutional framework, regulatory and macroeconomic circumstances. Moreover, differences are also observed in functioning of the boards - their structures, styles, processes, roles and activities etc. in their companies. However, the expectations and pressures from the stakeholders are gradually bringing further reforms in the corporate governance system through the recommendations of various committees suited to them.

13.8 THE CAUX PRINCIPLES

The Caux Round Table (1994) through an extensive and collaborative process was instrumental for business leaders to come out with a set of principles known as the Caux Round Table Principles (or in short, Caux Principles) for business for carrying out principled leadership.

The Caux Principles stated that these have their roots in two basic ethical ideals: Japanese concept of kyosei and human dignity. Kyosei means living and working together for the common good enabling cooperation and mutual prosperity to coexist with healthy and fair competition. "Human dignity" refers to the sacredness or value of each person as an end, not simply as a mean to the fulfilment of others' purposes or even majority prescription.

Principle 1 - Respect Stakeholders beyond Shareholders

Principle 2 - Contribute to Economic, Social and Environmental Development

Principle 3 - Build Trust by Going beyond the Letter of the Law

Principle 4 - Respect Rules and Conventions

Principle 5 - Support Responsible Globalisation

Principle 6 - Respect the Environment

Principle 7 - Avoid Illicit Activities

Respect Stakeholders beyond Shareholders: This principle prescribes that a responsible business respects the interests of, and acts with honesty and fairness towards, its customers, employees, suppliers, competitors and the broader community. In other words, while shareholders or investors are critical part of the stakeholders, others are no less significant.

Contribute to Economic, Social and Environmental Development: In order that a business remains sustainable, it must ensure that the economy in which it operates remain vibrant, contribute sincerely to social and environmental development of the communities in which it operates.

Build Trust by Going beyond the Letter of the Law: This principle calls for business to work towards achieving the spirit and intent behind the law, besides the letter or mere compliance to the law, which requires conduct that goes beyond minimum legal obligations.

Respect Rules and Conventions: A responsible business respects all local cultures and traditions in the communities in which it operates, consistent with fundamental principles of fairness and equality. Please recall in *Shell & Human Rights Violations in Nigeria,* is exactly the converse of what is prescribed by this principle. Also, all national and international laws and rules must be adhered to in every country a global business operates.

Support Responsible Globalisation: A responsible global business needs to supports open and fair multilateral trade and cooperates with the local governments in all reforms that promote global commerce.

Respect the Environment: A responsible business protects and, where possible, improves the environment and avoids wasteful use of resources. It also ensures that its operations comply with best environmental management practices consistent with meeting the needs of today without compromising the needs of future generations.

Avoid Illicit Activities: A responsible business does not participate in, or condone, corrupt practices, bribery, money laundering or other illicit activities. It also does not participate in or facilitate transactions linked to or supporting terrorist activities, drug trafficking or any other illicit activity.

(*Source:* website: http://www.cauxroundtable.org/index.cfm?menuid=8)

13.9 CORPORATE GOVERNANCE IN INDIA: INITIATIVES AND EMERGING TRENDS

(*a*) *Initiatives*

The Companies Act, 1956 (prior to its amendment in 2013) had some broad provisions, rules and prescriptions as to how companies require to be administered and governed. Some of these included Board size, composition, and functions of board committees, duties, responsibilities and liabilities of directors, appointment, rotation, duties of auditors, auditor's report, corporate governance and compliance under the act, corporate social responsibility, etc.

With effect from the economic liberalization in the early 1990s, the greater interest has been shown by the industry associations in further strengthening corporate governance. The Confederation of Indian Industry (CII) has been at the forefront of the corporate governance movement in India. In April 1998, it released a Task Force report entitled "Desirable Corporate Governance: A Code", which outlined a series of voluntary recommendations regarding best-in-class practices of corporate governance for listed companies.

The Securities and Exchange Board of India (SEBI) set up a committee in 1999 under Shri KM Birla, then member on the SEBI Board, to promote and raise the standards of corporate governance. The recommendations were implemented through Clause 49 of the Listing Agreements, in a phased manner by SEBI. SEBI revised the Clause 49 in April, 2014 consistent with the amendments in Companies Act, 2013.

Report of the SEBI Committee on Corporate Governance headed by Shri NR Narayana Murthy was set up in 2003, (a) to review the performance of corporate governance; and (b) to determine the role of companies in responding to rumour and other price sensitive information circulating in the market, in order to enhance the transparency and integrity of the market.

The Committee divided its recommendations into two categories– mandatory and non-mandatory. Among the mandatory category, the Committee recommended for:

- Strengthening financial responsibilities of the Audit Committee.
- Quality of financial disclosures.
- Bringing out a statement of all transactions with related parties including their bases should be placed before the independent audit committee for formal approval/ratification.
- Procedures should be in place to inform Board members about the risk assessment and minimization procedures, which should be periodically reviewed to ensure that executive management controls risk through means of a properly defined framework.

Recently, the SEBI Committee on corporate governance was formed on June 2, 2017 under the Chairmanship of Mr. Uday Kotak with the aim of improving standards of corporate governance of listed companies in India. The Uday Kotak Committee was specifically asked to address issues like ensuring independence in spirit of Independent Directors, improving safeguards and disclosures pertaining to Related Party Transactions, issues in accounting and auditing practices by listed companies, Improving effectiveness of Board Evaluation Practices, etc.

The major recommendations of Uday Kotak Committee include: separation of the roles of Chairman and Managing Director and Chairman to be limited to a non-executive director. Board minimum size suggested was 6 members with at least one woman member as independent director. As regards the minimum number of board meetings, the Committee suggested to raise it to five a year from existing four. As far as independent directors are concerned, it recommended that at least half of the total board members of a listed company to be independent directors. Updated list of all credit ratings obtained must be available at one place for the benefit of investors and other stakeholders. It also recommended for a risk management and IT committee for Top-500 listed companies to ensure cyber security.

In its Board meeting held end-March 2018, the capital market regulator SEBI accepted several recommendations of the Kotak Committee without any modifications and accepted a few other recommendations with certain modifications as to timelines for implementation, applicability thresholds, among others. Once these become implemented, India would be moving closer to the global best practices in the areas of better disclosures and removal of information asymmetry between managers of a company and its shareholders.

(*b*) *Emerging Trends*

In the Indian corporate landscape, there are several new challenges that are surfacing on a frequent basis. These are posing a real challenge to the internal top managements as well as the supervisory board members. There are no ready reckoner solutions of these challenges, which is making the corporate leadership to devote much of their valuable time to anticipate and handle these challenges in very short time span. Each risk has to be dealt with separately- a sudden change in geopolitical risks, environmental factors, social risks such as agitations and protests by farmers or industry workers, fleet taxi drivers, cyber-attacks, tax-related policy changes, political uncertainties, etc.

These are described as the VUCA (Volatile, Uncertain, Complex, and Ambiguous) (Refer Nathan Bennett and G. James Lemoine, "What VUCA really means for you, Harvard Business Review, Jan-Feb, 2014). There can be two perspectives for the corporate top managements namely to take this dynamically changing business environment to a company's advantage or to treat it as a perennial challenge. As per the regulation 27(2) (listing obligations and disclosure requirements) regulations of SEBI issued during September, 2015, the listed entity shall submit quarterly compliance report on corporate governance in the format specified by the Board from time to time to recognised Stock Exchange(s) within fifteen days from close of the quarter. There are three annexures in prescribed formats in which the listed companies must furnish the information- one on a quarterly basis, one on annual basis and the third on a half yearly basis that can be submitted along with the second quarter report. On 31st May, 2021, SEBI introduced a change in the reporting format by notifying that in order to bring about transparency and to strengthen the disclosures around loans/ guarantees/comfort letters/security provided by the listed entity directly or indirectly to promoter/promoter group entities or any other entity controlled by them, it has been decided to mandate such disclosures on a half yearly basis, in the Compliance Report on Corporate Governance.

In the year 2015, specified listed companies were asked to comply with SEBI (LODR) Regulations, 2015. On 9th May, 2018, recommendations of Kotak Committee to be undertaken, including applicability and constitution of risk management committee for top 500 listed entities from 1st April 2020. On 5th May, 2021, SEBI brought out a few key amendment in SEBI (LODR) regulations emphasizing the need of holistic risk management to improve corporate governance standards of listed companies in India by expanding the requirement of Risk Management Committee from Top 500 to Top 1000 listed entities under Regulation 21. The risk management amendments focused on (a) Applicability for formation of RMC (b) Constitution of RMC (c) Number of meetings and quorum (d) Roles and responsibilities of RMC (e) Power of RMC and (f) Disclosure in annual report about RMC. On 30th June, 2021, the provisions of this Regulation 21 were applicable to top 1000 listed entities determined based on market capitalisation, at the end of the immediate previous financial year. It was also mandated that the Top 1000 listed entities shall confirm in their quarterly filings of Compliance Report on Corporate Governance in lieu of SEBI LODR Regulation 27 whether they have complied with the risk management committee requirements.

In this context, one statement from one of the earlier SEBI Chairman needs mention where he says that "companies (in India) do follow rules

and regulations and if their governance practices are put to test, they will likely stand scrutiny of the law; however, if one delves deeper, one could find that while the letter of the law may have been complied with, the spirit of regulations has not necessarily been embraced wholeheartedly. [Source: sebi.gov.in (speeches section: 4th Annual Corporate Governance Summit on "Gatekeepers of Governance" November 9, 2017)].

The Bombay Stock Exchange and the National Stock Exchange, for example, provide a compliance calendar for the Exchange-listed companies. This is Quarterly/Half Yearly/Annual Compliances under SEBI Listing Regulations, 2015 (LODR or Listing Obligations and Disclosure Requirements).

13.10 CORPORATE SCAMS: ISSUES AND DETERRENTS

Issues

With a view to achieving rapid success, some employees in a few companies or organizations could resort to questionable methods and practices. Top managements and Boards must ever remain vigilant to perceive such developments and take suitable timely actions. If such behaviours are not discouraged and punished, it may bring severe ill repute to the entire organization. There can also be some heavy legal expenses to fight the cases over years and huge fines and penalties may have to be borne by the companies if found guilty.

Some of the wrong and unethical actions by some employees may be found in the banking or financial sector. They can also be witnessed in the non-financial sector and those involving seeking licenses from the government departments. Boards (management and/or supervisory boards) must be keenly studying the applications submitted by their company or organisation for some of the permissions or licenses to a government department. Exemplary punishments including dismissal and filing a criminal case and giving newspaper notice informing the public and industry at large about the unethical and criminal action committed by the employee/s, which would bring in a scare in the minds of those who may wish to play this dangerous game of tarnishing the organization's reputation in the event of their failure and gaining substantial benefits in the form of fast-track promotions if their wrong tricks succeed.

There are some issues in the corporate scams:

i. Are the internal controls adequate or there exist some loopholes?

ii. Is it a case of bribery or general omission or negligence?

iii. Has a scam or scandal resulted in significant financial loss? If so, how can it be recovered with minimal energies and legal and administrative expenses?

iv. Is the reputation of the bank/financial institution eroded? If so, what exemplary actions are taken to punish the guilty?

v. How to deal with the corporate that indulged in financial loss or loss of reputation for a bank?

vi. Have there been additional measures taken to strengthen the internal operational and supervisory control mechanism to avert recurrence of similar scams in future?

Following are some of the instances in Indian context bifurcated into:

(*a*) financial sector

(*b*) non-financial sector

The objective of recalling these recent episodes is to give the readers a perspective as to how the compromise of the ethics and governance can cause harm to the banks, financial or non-financial institutions. At times, companies may have to face embarrassment in a short period, later they may come out clean in the long run if they did not indulge in questionable acts.

A. Financial Sector

(*a*) Money laundering by banks

(*b*) Letters of Understanding Scam

(*c*) Regulatory Non-compliance

(*d*) NBFC Chit Fund Scam

B. Non-financial Sector

(*a*) Conglomerate Debenture Scam

(*b*) 2G Spectrum Auction

(*c*) Corporate Governance at Large Private Corporate Group

A. Financial Sector

(*a*) *Money Laundering by Banks*

During mid-April, 2013, a private electronic channel carried out sting operations in select banks in India and shown the videos to public at large which suggests that some officials of select private banks were involved with the customers in money laundering. With a view to investigate the authenticity as well as to have the faith of customers on India's banking system, the Reserve Bank of India had carried out scrutiny of books of account, internal control, compliance systems and processes of these banks at their offices during April, 2013 itself.

The RBI's scrutiny of these banks revealed violation of certain regulations and instructions issued by the Reserve Bank of India, namely,

- non-adherence to certain aspects of know your customer (KYC) norms and anti-money laundering (AML) guidelines like customer identification procedure, risk categorisation, periodical review of risk profiling of account holders, periodical KYC updation.
- non-adherence of KYC for walk in customers including for sale of third-party products, omission in filing of cash transaction reports (CTRs) in respect of some cash transactions, sale of gold coins for cash beyond Rs. 50,000.
- non-adherence to instructions on monitoring of transactions in customer accounts:
    - non-adherence to instructions on classification of accounts as 'inoperative'/dormant and lapses in monitoring of transactions in dormant accounts.
- non-adherence to instructions which prohibits acceptance of cash above Rs. 50,000 from customers for sale of gold coins and issue of Demand Drafts, etc.
- non-adherence to instructions on the upper limit for remittances under Liberalized Remittance Scheme, upper limit for repatriation of funds from non-resident ordinary (NRO) accounts.
- non-adherence to instructions on import of gold on consignment basis. *(Source: RBI Press Release : 2013-14/95, dated July 15, 2013)*

Reserve Bank of India (RBI) has levied monetary fines on a significant part of the Indian banking sector in 2013 following some violations of norms. Within a span of a week, the RBI imposed penalties first on three private sector banks. Subsequently, 22 other banks (most of which were public sector and a few from private sector) were also levied monetary fines ranging between Rs. 50 lakh to marginally over Rs. 3 crore with average fine amount per non-compliant bank in the range of about Rs. 1.5 crore.

Besides these banks, in case of seven other banks, RBI conducted scrutiny, the regulator found from the written explanations submitted from them that there was either satisfactory or no violation of serious nature was established. Hence, the regulator chose not to levy monetary fines on this set of banks. However, the regulator issued suitable cautionary letters.

RBI did not approve that there was any money laundering that took place in these banks. "The investigation did not reveal any *prima facie* evidence of money laundering. However, any conclusive inference in this regard can be drawn only by an end-to-end investigation of the transactions by tax and enforcement agencies". *(RBI Press Release)*

(*b*) *Letters of Understanding Scam*

Central Bureau of Investigation named 11 persons including a popular diamond merchant, his close relative, and employees working for the merchant's firms, 7 employees of a PSU bank in the case of over Rs. 11,000 crore letter of understanding (LoU) scam.

As part of the international trade facilitation process for its business customers engaged in the foreign trade, banks issue certain documents. These include letters of credit, letters of understanding (LoU) and letters of comfort.

LoU is an undertaking given by a bank by which the given bank allows its customer to raise money from another Indian bank's foreign branch in the form of short-term credit. The loan so obtained by the customer is used to make payment to the customer's offshore suppliers in foreign currency. The overseas bank usually lends to the importer based on the LoU issued by the importer's bank.

A Letter of Comfort is a bank's willingness to support a customer with a short-term loan, if and when required. It is not a letter of commitment. A letter of credit (LC) is a banking instrument by which a bank assures that a buyer's payment to a seller will be received on time and also for the correct amount. After the goods have been shipped, the bank would pay the seller its dues as long as the terms of the LC are met, such as delivery before a certain time or confirmation from the buyer that the goods were received were sound and undamaged. In a situation wherein the buyer is unable to make payment on the purchase, the bank will still be required to pay the full or remaining amount of the purchase.

In case of an Indian PSU bank, a few employees resorted to misuse of the SWIFT (Society for Worldwide Interbank Financial Telecommunication) network and sent messages to other banks bypassing the core banking system. These LoUs were considered genuine by select foreign branches of one offshore private and PSU bank. The PSU bank suddenly realizes that this lead to an unelected financial burden to the tune of over Rs. 11,300 crore besides loss of reputation.

In an extraordinary general meeting (EGM) held on March 16, 2018, the PSU top management assured its shareholders and indirectly banks and public at large that all bona fide letters of understanding will be honoured by the bank.

Reserve Bank of India directed the banks in India to submit detail of LoUs including the amounts outstanding and whether banks had any pre-approved credit limits or set aside enough cash on margin before issuing the guarantees. Banks were directed to furnished details of guarantees issued by them within a week's time for the period 2011 onwards.

While print and electronic media have carried out so much coverage on the matter of the PSU Bank LoU scam, some unfounded news also appears for which the RBI issued a clarification through press release on February 16, 2018. The Press Release states:

> "There have been reports in the media that in the wake of fraud involving a sum of USD 1.77 billion that has surfaced in the PSU bank, the Reserve Bank of India (RBI) has directed PSU bank to meet its commitments under the Letter of Undertaking (LoU) to other

banks. RBI denies having given any such instructions. The fraud in the PSU bank (committed by a few unethical employees) is a case of operational risk arising on account of delinquent behaviour by one or more employees of the bank and failure of internal controls. RBI has already undertaken a supervisory assessment of control systems in the PSU bank and will take appropriate supervisory action".

RBI has decided during mid-March, 2018 to discontinue issuance of LoUs by banks for trade credits for imports into India. Existing LoUs will, however, be honoured.

(c) *Regulatory Non-compliance*

The central bank has a structured, rule-based approach to identify and process the violations by the REs of applicable statutes and rules, regulations, guidelines and orders made, directions issued and conditions imposed thereunder by it, and enforce the same consistently across the Reserve Bank. The objective of enforcement is to ensure compliance by the REs with laws, within the overarching principle of ensuring financial stability, public interest and consumer protection.

Regulatory non-compliances, if any, are viewed quite seriously by the RBI as evident from imposition of penalties aggregating Rs. 31.36 crore on 61 regulated entities/ REs (banks and NBFCs), during the year 2021-22, as per RBI's latest Report on Trend and Progress of Banking in India. Instances of imposition of penalty shot up about three times to 189 in FY22 even as the amount of penalty slapped more than doubled to Rs. 65.32 crore. The major reasons for imposition of monetary penalties included *inter alia*, non-compliance with exposure and IRAC (Income Recognition and Asset Classification) norms, frauds classification and reporting and violation of cyber security framework guidelines. In addition, one large private sector bank was fined for Rs. 10 crores for irregularities in auto loan portfolio while another NBFC was penalized for harassment of borrowers through recovery agents. During the year, the average per instance penalty was the highest for private sector banks (Rs. 29.39 crore on 16 banks) and was the lowest for co-operative banks (Rs. 12.10 crore on 145 co-operative banks). The aggregate amount of monetary penalty on 13 public sector banks was Rs. 17.55 crore.

In the earlier years also, RBI has been imposing penalties on banks due to non-compliances. For example, in one case, penalties were imposed on 14 banks in one go on account of contravention of regulatory norms while dealing with one group. During the July 2019 to June 2020 period, penalties for Rs. 61.15 crore were imposed on 51 regulated entities as against 47 aggregating Rs. 123.86 crore in the year-ago period for non-compliance with/ contravention of its various directions.

Likewise, on February 27, 2018, the Reserve Bank of India has imposed a monetary penalty of Rs. 3 crores on one private sector bank. The RBI has clarified that the penalty was imposed for non-compliance with the directions issued by RBI on Income Recognition and Asset Classification (IRAC) norms. To avoid further speculations on this matter, RBI further stated that "this action is based on deficiencies in regulatory compliance and is not intended to pronounce upon the validity of any transaction or agreement entered into by the bank with its customers". *(Press Release 2017-18/2354 dated March 5, 2018)*

Department of Banking Regulation of the RBI had issued on July 1, 2015 a Master Circular on Prudential norms on Income Recognition, Asset Classification and Provisioning pertaining to Advances.

In response to the recommendations of the Committee on the Financial System (Chairman Shri M. Narasimham; 1997) and aligning India's commercial banking practices with the international practices, Reserve Bank of India gradually introduced prudential norms for income recognition, asset classification and provisioning for the advances portfolio of the banks so as to move towards greater consistency and transparency in the published accounts. The Circular provides clarity on how to treat the income and loans and advances and non-performing assets (NPAs) as under:

The policy of income recognition should be objective and based on record of recovery rather than on any subjective considerations. Likewise, the classification of assets of banks has to be done on the basis of objective criteria which would ensure a uniform and consistent application of the norms. Also, the provisioning should be made on the basis of the classification of assets based on the period for which the asset has remained non-performing and the availability of security and the realizable value thereof. Banks are urged to ensure that while granting loans and advances, realistic repayment schedules may be fixed on the basis of cash flows with borrowers. RBI further defined NPA as "an asset, including a leased asset, becomes non-performing when it ceases to generate income for the bank". It provided seven clear criteria for identifying the non-performing assets, first of which reads "interest and/or instalment of principal remain overdue for a period of more than 90 days in respect of a term loan". Some banks try to violate one or more of these prudential norms with a view to artificially boost their income and suppress the true value of the non-performing assets. By doing so, the exact financial health of a bank does not get reflected to the investors and other stakeholders. However, if the bank gets exposed for wilfully resorting to such wrong deeds or violation out of negligence, it faces monetary fine and loss of reputation, as such matters get covered widely in print and electronic media.

(*d*) *NBFC's Chit fund Scam*

An NBFC of a private Group of companies based in India involved in a financial scandal was a major financial scam and alleged political scandal caused by the collapse of a Ponzi scheme. The Group, a consortium of over 200 private companies, was believed to be running collective investment schemes popularly but incorrectly referred to as chit funds in Eastern India. The Group collected around Rs. 200 to 300 billion (US$4-6 billion) from over 1.7 million depositors before it collapsed in April, 2013.

In West Bengal, Jharkhand, Assam and Chhattisgarh, the group companies began operating variations of collective investment schemes (CIS) involving tourism packages, forward travel and hotel booking timeshare credit transfer, real estate, infrastructure finance and motorcycle manufacturing.

Initially, the frontline companies collected money from the public by issuing secured debentures and redeemable preferential bonds. Under Indian Securities regulations and section 67 of the Indian Companies Act (1956; amended in 2013), a company cannot raise capital from more than 50 people without issuing a proper prospectus and balance sheet. Its accounts must be audited and it must also have explicit permission to operate from the market regulator SEBI.

SEBI first confronted the Group in 2009. The group adapted by opening up to 200 new companies to create more cross-holdings. This created an extremely complex tiered corporate structure to confound SEBI by hampering their ability to consolidate blame. SEBI persisted in its investigation through 2010. The group reacted by changing its methods of raising capital.

Investors were rarely informed about the true nature of their investments. Instead, many were told they would get high returns after a fixed period. With other investors, the investment was fraudulently sold in the form of a *chit fund*. Under the Chit Fund Act (1982), chit funds are regulated by state governments rather than SEBI.

SEBI warned the State Government of West Bengal about the Group's chit fund activities in 2011, again prompting the group to change its methods. This time, it acquired and sold large numbers of shares of various listed companies then embezzled the proceeds of the sale through accounts which as of September, 2014 have not been identified.

Meanwhile, the Group started laundering a large portion of its funds to Dubai, South Africa and Singapore. By 2012, SEBI was able to classify the group's activities as collective investment schemes rather than chit funds—and demanded that it immediately stop operating its investment schemes until it received permission to operate from SEBI. The management of the group did not comply with this ruling and continued to operate until its collapse in April, 2013.

A Ponzi scheme is a fraudulent investment operation where the operator, an individual or organization, pays returns to its investors from new capital paid to the operators by new investors, rather than from profit earned by the operator. Operators of Ponzi schemes usually induce new investors by offering higher returns than other investments, say bank Fixed Deposit which is almost risk-free, in the form of short-term returns that are either abnormally high or unusually consistent in the initial few months to quarters.

In the aftermath of the scandal, the Government of West Bengal, where the Group and most of its investors were based, instituted an inquiry commission to investigate the collapse. The State Government also set up a fund of Rs. 5 billion (US$75 million) to ensure that low-income investors were not bankrupted. The Central Government through the Income-tax

Department and Enforcement Directorate launched a multi-agency probe to investigate the Group scam and similar Ponzi schemes.

In May 2014, the Supreme Court of India, citing inter-state ramifications, possible international money laundering, serious regulatory failures and alleged political nexus, transferred all investigations into the Group Scam and other Ponzi schemes to the Central Bureau of Investigation (CBI). The investigation is still underway and in mid-December, 2017, the Hon'ble Supreme Court ruled that CBI officers involved in the investigation of this Scam cannot be called for grilling to the police station till next hearing.

The Chit Fund Scam involved by one of the companies of the private Group is another example in financial sector as to how some unscrupulous elements can misuse and abuse some of the loopholes in the system to cheat lakhs of poor, daily wage earners and innocent customers through attractive interest rates.

Non-financial Sector

(*a*) Conglomerate Debenture Scam

(*b*) 2G Spectrum Auction

(*c*) Corporate Governance at Large Private Corporate Group

(*a*) Conglomerate's Debentures Scam

In the context of issuance of optionally fully convertible debentures (OFCD) issued by two companies belonging to a large private sector conglomerate, the capital market regulator Securities and Exchange Board of India (SEBI) objected stating that this matter comes under the jurisdiction of SEBI which was not obtained. Therefore, it objected for the OFCD issue. The response from Sahara was that it had sought the approval of the Registrar of Companies and Ministry of Corporate Affairs and as the said bonds were 'hybrid product', it need not seek approval from SEBI for the same.

SEBI had ordered these firms to stop issuing the said bonds and return the amount collected to the investors. After contesting the SEBI decision in various courts since 2009, the Conglomerate finally approached the Supreme Court of India during June, 2012. There was a brief relief to Sahara which obtained a stay order from the Allahabad High Court by

December, 2010 and refused to give any information or to co-operate with SEBI.

The Conglomerate faced a shock when the order of SEBI to refund within 15 days all money collected (Rs. 17,500 crores) through OFCD with 15% interest, was reiterated by the Supreme Court also on August 31, 2012.

After the Conglomerate mentioned that nearly 90% of the amount collected from investors was returned to them, the Supreme Court stated if SEBI did not find the supporting documents claiming the return to the investors, it would be presumed that the money was not returned. If the investors were not found to be genuine, the money owed to the Companies of the Conglomerate would be transferred to the Consolidated Fund of India. A retired judge was appointed to oversee the entire matter of returning the funds. Also, the court empowered SEBI to take suitable actions to recover money from Sahara in case it defaulted.

The conglomerate did submit the documents to the SEBI's headquarters located in Mumbai on the due date. As per details published in the media, these were loaded in 127 Trucks, piled up in 31,000 cartons carrying information of all 30 million subscribers of the OFCD. The regulating body was inundated with 120 tons of documents.

With a view to verify and find out the veracity of the investors who are said to have been returned their monies, SEBI employed persons exclusively for this task and found that barely under 70 of the 20,000 persons responded who were asked to apply for refund. Moreover, it was found that repetition of 3 fictitious names in thousands of the 30 million members reported to be the total by Sahara. The Supreme Court later stated that it was not for SEBI to establish whether the investors were genuine but Sahara requires to prove it.

Given the large amount, Supreme Court gave a relief to the conglomerate to repay the amount in 3 instalments. The first instalment of Rs. 5,120 crores was to be immediately deposited through demand drafts. Further direction was given to deposit the balance amount of Rs. 17,400 crores together with interest @ 15% per annum with SEBI in two instalments. The first instalment amount, of Rs. 10,000 crores, was to be deposited with SEBI within the first week of January, 2013 and balance amount along with interest by first week of February, 2013. After the default was made in the latter instalments, the conglomerate's director was sent to the Tihar Jail. Later in mid-July, 2017, the Supreme Court said that the bail granted to the Director would be cancelled if he fails to provide two post-dated cheques of Rs. 1500 crore and Rs. 552.21 crore by July, 2017.

Thus, conglomerate's episode clearly goes on to establish that how some companies resort to deliberate frauds that the regulators would be ever ready to expose and do justice to the investors.

(*b*) 2G Spectrum Auction: Fair or Unfair?

Indian telecommunication growth over the past 15-20 years period has been phenomenal. More so in the progress and growth rate in the mobile telephony in recent years, India has been the world leader.

A telecom operator wanting to start the service requires to obtain a Unified Access Services (UAS) license from the Department of Telecommunications to operate in one of the 22 circles in the country. Licenses are awarded by auctions. The UAS introduced in end-2003 and its validity is fixed at 20 years that may be extended 10 years in one go per circle. The spectrum auctions have been conducted in India since 1994 with a frequency of once in 3 years or more.

The 2008 auction was accused of serious irregularities including bribes paid to some political leaders to seek favours. In all, 122 licenses were given to telecom companies on the basis of "first-come, first-served" basis. After the case was referred to the Central Bureau of Investigation (CBI), the agency mentioned in its charge sheet that many laws were violated and bribes were paid by some companies to get favours even though they did not fulfil the criteria and therefore would not have deserved license in normal course of scrutiny. The Comptroller and Auditor General of India (CAG) also opined after its audit that licenses were granted to certain in-eligible corporations, those with no experience in the telecom sector and others which hidden relevant information. In the view of the CAG, the difference between the money collected and ought to have been collected had a deficit of Rs. 1,76,000 crore, which was lowered by the CBI in its charge sheet filed on April 02, 2011 at Rs. 30,984.55 crore. Supreme Court scrapped all the 122 licences for 2G spectrum on February 2, 2012.

While passing the order, the Supreme Court ordered three telecommunications companies to pay Rs. 5 crore as fine as they "benefited by a wholly arbitrary and unconstitutional action taken by the DoT for the grant of UAS (Unified Access Service) licences and allocation of spectrum in 2G band and who off-loaded their stakes for many thousand crore in the name of fresh infusion of equity or transfer of equity".

Special CBI Court judge stated that it was 2 senior officials in the then PMO who had "suppressed the most relevant and controversial part" of then Telecom Minister's letter, and the then Telecom Minister "cannot be faulted" for misrepresenting the facts.

In December, 2017, a special CBI court acquitted all 17 persons named in the scam stating that no criminality was involved in the entire episode (2G spectrum allocation). The court found no evidence of alleged kick-backs in the process.

The alleged scam had taken toll on the sector, as many foreign companies had quit India following the outbreak of the scam and the apex court cancelling the licences. It also led to large-scale consolidation in the sector with many companies merging with others.

The Union Government has moved Supreme Court in connection with other inter-related cases with the 2G spectrum case and the Supreme Court decided to examine the status of investigation in the remaining cases linked to the 2G spectrum scam and directed the centre to file a status report in this regard before January 23, 2018. It is, therefore, not an open-and-shut case as it appears at present.

During March, 2018, Hon'ble Supreme Court directed the CBI and Enforcement Directorate to complete their probe into the 2G spectrum allocation cases and other related matters in six months. Hence, the matter is sub-judice and the final outcome will prove the innocence or guilt of the operators or the former political leadership.

At times, though some companies (like in this case of 2G spectrum auction) would face serious problems including allegations of manipulating bureaucrats and ministers for business favours. A great deal of financial and reputation loss may also be seriously eroded. But there would be a final victory in such episodes when the courts acquit them of all these charges, though some pain and anxiety in the matters of alleged compromise on corporate governance need to be undergone. In any case, judicial review process is a must to clear the doubts from the minds of the stakeholders whenever a scam with a *prima facie* suspicion comes to the fore. If proved guilty, such businesses would cause irreparable damage to the stakeholders including the investors.

(*c*) Corporate Governance at a Large Private Group

The evening of 24 October, 2016, when suddenly a Board Meet was convened to replace the Chairman of the Board of a listed private corporate firm headquartered in Mumbai. On the same day of the meeting, the Chairman was briefed about the main agenda of the meeting barely few minutes before the Board meet was to begin in Mumbai. In that informal meeting before the Board meet, the Chairman was informed by the members of the Board that there is a loss of relationship between him and his predecessor and a resolution is moved for the removal of the incumbent Chairman. The Chairman was, however, given an option before the board meeting to resign, which he turned down and attended the meeting of the Board of the listed private corporate firm.

In a press release, the Board shared the resolutions as under:

Resolved that the consent of the Board be and is hereby accorded, to consider and resolve upon, in this meeting of the Board, the following matters which were not included in the agenda circulated for this meeting of the Board:

1. Replacement of Mr. ABC as the Chairman of the Board and from each committee of the Board.
2. Appointment of Mr. XYZ as Additional Director.
3. Election of Mr. XYZ as Interim Chairman of the Board until selection and appointment of a new Chairman of the Board in terms of the Companies Act, 2013 and the Articles of Association of the Company.
4. To take appropriate steps in terms of the Companies Act, 2013 and the Articles of Association of the Company to appoint a new Chairman, including by formation of a Selection Committee com-

prising of: (*i*) Mr. XYZ (Nominee of the Trusts); (*ii*) A (Nominee of Trusts); (*iii*) Mr. V (Nominee of Trusts); (*iv*) Mr. R (Independent Director); and (*v*) Mr. K (Independent Outside Person); and 3 other resolution not totally related to this theme.

Mr. N had joined the board of the listed corporate in October, 2016 and was appointed Chairman in January, 2017.

While during the tenure of over 20 years of Mr. XYZ, revenue growth was higher at 19.2% (compared to 8.5% during ABC's 3-years tenure), in market capitalization, Mr. XYZ's 13.5% versus Mr. ABC's 10.4% does not reflect a great contrast.

Besides the numbers, in terms of emotional matters, it is believed that Mr. ABC has not correctly gauged the freedom given to him as Chairman and tried to bring in major changes in the legacy created by his predecessor. Sale of the Group's UK assets and other decisions like face off with another JV, etc. were seen by many of the veteran employees at the listed corporate as a move that was intended or might eventually would expose his predecessor's decision-making.

According to the former member of the Group Executive Council, Mr. ABC was not given an opportunity to explain his position during the board meeting.

Nevertheless, the technical, legal and ethical issues apart, with a few months left for the completion of the tenure as Chairman of the board for Mr. ABC, such sudden replacement led to a loss of market capitalization of the Group companies to the tune of US$ 7 billion or nearly Rs. 50,000 crore between October 24 and November 08, 2016. Was it so necessary for its top management? The Board may, perhaps, know it better.

Deterrents

The Reserve Bank of India as banking sector regulator in India has directed all the scheduled commercial banks in India, by its circular dated May 7, 2015, to necessarily report the matters involving frauds with the banks.

i. The RBI circular issued the procedure to file complaints with Law Enforcement Agencies.

ii. Banks are required to lodge the complaint with the law enforcement agencies immediately on detection of fraud.

iii. The complaint lodged by the bank with the law enforcement agencies should be drafted properly and invariably be vetted by a legal officer.

iv. No compromise settlement involving a fraudulent borrower is allowed unless the conditions stipulate that the criminal complaint will be continued.

v. In general, the penal provisions as applicable to wilful defaulters would apply to the fraudulent borrower including the promoter director(s) and other whole-time directors of the company insofar as raising of funds from the banking system or from the capital markets by companies with which they are associated is concerned, etc.

vi. In particular, borrowers who have defaulted and have also committed a fraud in the account would be debarred from availing bank finance from Scheduled Commercial Banks, Development Financial Institutions, Government owned NBFCs, Investment Institutions, etc., for a period of five years from the date of full payment of the defrauded amount.

vii. Banks have been categorized for this purpose into two:

(*a*) Private Sector/Foreign Banks

(*b*) Public Sector Banks

In case of Private Sector/Foreign Banks, for fraud amounts of Rs. 1 lakh and above, complaint must be lodged with the state police and for the amounts of Rs. 10,000 and above committed by staff, the complaint also needs to be lodged with the state police. For larger amounts of Rs. 1 crore and above, besides the complaint to be lodged with the state police, it must be lodged with Serious Fraud Investigation Office (SFIO).

For the PSBs, below Rs. 3 crore - state police, Rs. 3 crore and above and up to Rs. 25 crore - CBI (Anti-Corruption Bureau where staff involvement is *prima facie* evident), Economic Offences Wing of the CBI (where staff involvement is *prima facie* not evident). For fraud amounts of more than Rs. 25 crores - CBI (Banking Security and Fraud Cell (BSFC) of the CBI) irrespective of the involvement of a public servant or not.

13.11 WHAT CONSTITUTES GOOD CORPORATE GOVERNANCE: THE NOTION OF ETHICAL GOVERNANCE

So far, the present unit has provided us the meaning of corporate governance, need for the same, how various regions or countries have evolved different governance processes, board of directors and their roles, board meetings and so on. This should not make us believe that good governance involves only rules and procedures and compliance and nothing else. Good corporate governance goes beyond the compliance and forms the broader view of corporate governance that focuses on ethical relationship between a company and broad range of other stakeholders. It can be seen as ethical governance and is based on the satisfaction of all kinds of stakeholders, CSR and ethics. It is about commitment to values, ethical business conduct and exercise of powers in a responsible way *i.e.* while exercising powers always keep the interest of other side (the stakeholders).

Ethical governance involves the top managements of companies not only conceiving good policies and strategies in the interest of its investors, employees and other stakeholders but it also requires that the management should see to it that they themselves and all other stakeholders also necessarily follow principles of ethics and moral values in their actions relating to the company or organisation.

For example, following short cuts in suppressing information should not be followed by the employees and all others like suppliers, distributors, advertisers, applicants as job-seekers, etc. full and complete disclosure of information has to become a routine habit for all the stakeholders. Similarly, no discrimination to be followed by the employees and others while selecting candidates to various positions. It must be purely and solely on a merit basis, subject to the law of the land, such as some positions are to be filled only with the citizens of the same country. All activities of the organisation should be so planned and executed that there is a zero tolerance to unethical behaviours.

Adhering to ethical governance is very tough in itself, as most commercial organisations judge or evaluate the performance of the top management on the basis of the profits (and not the means of achieving the profits). Even when there is a deviation (if not clear violation) of ethics, many a time, the evaluation does not care much about these actions. This is incorrect and if an organisation wants to rise and mature into an ethically governed one, it must adopt such practices which would not only comply with all the legal and other governance norms and codes, but it must also be explaining its stance to all other stakeholders and make them comply as well, failing which the organisation should disassociate itself from such stakeholder/s.

Likewise, care for environment, social causes such as no child labour, utmost care towards public health relating to the ingredients, policy against giving and accepting bribes, recruiting candidates with ethical principles and moral values, and sternly dealing with tainted persons, etc. may be considered example of an ethically governed organisation.

A realistic timeframe may be set by the founders of a new organisation for achieving this goal. Such ethically governed organisation may be achieved rather gradually. As a first step, the top management must not only remain ethical but must seem to be functioning ethically to its own employees. The next step is to transmit the culture across the organisation. Thereafter, it is essential to make sure that all the other stakeholders also embrace ethical principles while dealing with this and other clients.

13.12 CORPORATE GOVERNANCE VERSUS CORPORATE EXCELLENCE

Corporate governance and corporate excellence are closely connected. Corporate excellence is an outcome of good corporate governance. It is difficult to achieve corporate excellence without good governance in long-term as shown in the following figure:

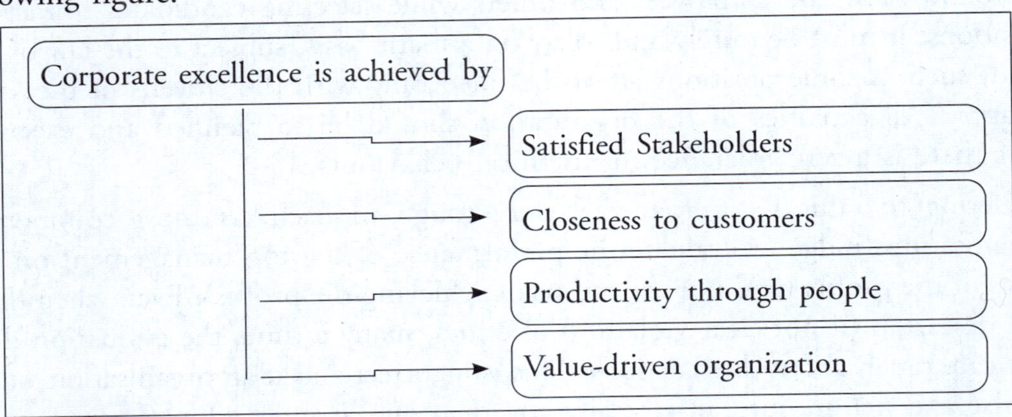

13.13 KEY WORDS

Corporate Governance, Principles of Corporate Governance, Corporate Governance Models, SEBI's Clause 49 of Listing Agreement, Caux Roundtable, Kyosei, Greenbury Committee, Myners Committee, Blue Ribbon Committee, Stewardship Code, OCED Principles of Corporate Governance, The Financial Reporting Council, Corporate scams, Ethical Governance, Corporate Excellence,

13.14 LET US SUM UP

This unit dwells on the relationship between ethics and corporate governance, *i.e.*, the system by which Companies are directed and controlled. Some recent cases of corporate governance which came into the limelight, have been described to underline the impact of poor governance. These include Enron, Kingfisher Airlines and Satyam Computers. The principles and advantages of good corporate governance and the different corporate governance models have been elaborated along with their recent trends and the international codes of business conduct. The Caux principles for conducting business with principle leadership have also been discussed as a part of best corporate governance visions. The unit underscores that corporate excellence is a derivative of good corporate governance which is nothing but ethical governance in essence.

13.15 CHECK YOUR PROGRESS

1. According to the World Bank definition, "Corporate Governance (CG)" concerns the system by which companies are:
   (*a*) Set up and Listed
   (*b*) Funded with the seed capital
   (*c*) Directed and controlled
   (*d*) Wound-up
2. Which of the following about the Board of Directors of the companies is incorrect?
   (*a*) They are well-versed with the companies' functioning

(*b*) They highly concerned about the companies' reputation and image in the short and long-run

(*c*) They are recruited on the basis of a rigorous selection process

(*d*) They carryout regular oversight and direction

3. Enron was:

(*a*) British environment equipment manufacturer based in Birmingham

(*b*) French automobile manufacturer based in Toulouse

(*c*) Australian Banking Corporation based in Canberra

(*d*) An American energy company based in Houston

4. Satyam Computer Services was converted into a Public Limited Company in the year:

(*a*) 1985

(*b*) 1991

(*c*) 1998

(*d*) 2008

5. The US model of corporate governance, which of the following statement is incorrect?

(*a*) Shareholders have no influence on board membership.

(*b*) Positions of the Chairman and CEO can be held by the same person.

(*c*) It is principles-based governance system.

(*d*) It is rules-based governance system.

6. Following recommendations of a committee set up by SEBI in 1999, Clause 49 of the Listing Agreements has been implemented in a phased manner by SEBI. Who headed it?

(*a*) Shri Ratan Tata

(*b*) Shri NR Narayana Murthy

(*c*) Shri Kumar Mangalam Birla

(*d*) Shri Uday Kotak

7. In year 2013, for violation of the Know Your Customer (KYC) norms, RBI imposed monetary fines on how many banks?
   (*a*) 25
   (*b*) 10
   (*c*) 32
   (*d*) 18
8. Letter of Understanding (LoU) is a bank guarantee under which a given bank allows its customer to raise money from which of the following branches of another Indian bank in the form of short-term credit?
   (*a*) Indian branch
   (*b*) Foreign branch
   (*c*) SEZ Branch
   (*d*) Retail branch
9. A Ponzi scheme is a fraudulent investment operation where the operator, an individual or organization, pays returns to its investors from:
   (*a*) Portion of the dividends
   (*b*) New capital paid to the operators by new investors
   (*c*) The profit earned by the operator
   (*d*) Seed capital of the company
10. SEBI Order of 2009 to refund within 15 days all money collected (Rs. 17,500 crore) through OFCD with 15% interest, which was reiterated by the Supreme Court in August 2012. OFDI refers to:
    (*a*) One-time Final Certificate of Deposit
    (*b*) Offshore Financial Convertible Deposit
    (*c*) Onshore Financial Certificate for Drawing
    (*d*) Optionally Fully Convertible Debentures
11. The number of the Caux Principles is:
    (*a*) 10
    (*b*) 8

(*c*) 9

(*d*) 12

12. The UK Stewardship Code 2020 ------.

(*a*) is a part of the UK Code of Corporate Governance

(*b*) has no relationship with the UK Code of Corporate Governance

(*c*) has since been discontinued

(*d*) is complementary to the UK Code of Corporate Governance

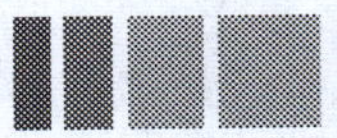

ANSWERS

1. (*c*)	2. (*c*)	3. (*d*)	4. (*b*)	5. (*c*)	6. (*c*)
7. (*a*)	8. (*b*)	9. (*b*)	10. (*d*)	11. (*c*)	12. (*d*)

13.16 EXERCISE YOUR ETHICS MUSCLE

Case 31 : The Chicago Tylenol Murders

In the fall of 1982, Johnson & Johnson faced a public relations nightmare when customers in Cook County, Illinois, began dying eventually, a total of seven people died—after taking over-the-counter, Tylenol-branded acetaminophen capsules. Analysis showed the presence of potassium cyanide, a fatal poison in no way connected with the production of the pill. Johnson & Johnson voluntarily removed all Tylenol products from the U.S. marketplace and offered to pay full retail price for any pills returned to the company. This represented about thirty million bottles of capsules worth more than $100 million. (Significantly, too, Johnson & Johnson decided on this wide-ranging action despite the fact that it and law enforcement realized the cyanide poisoning was limited to Cook County, Illinois.) Because Tylenol was a flagship product bringing in significant revenue, this was an extreme action but one based on the company's ethics, rooted in its corporate credo. Investigation showed that someone had tinkered with the bottles and injected cyanide into the product in stores. Although no one was ever apprehended, the entire drug industry responded, following Johnson & Johnson's lead, by introducing tamper-proof containers that warned consumers not to use the product if the packaging appeared in any way compromised. The strong ethical stance taken by Johnson & Johnson executives resulted in immediate action that reassured the public. When the company eventually returned Tylenol to the market, it introduced it first to clinics, hospitals and physicians' offices, promoting medicine's professional trust in the product. The strategy was successful. Before the poisonings, Tylenol had 37 percent of the market of over-the-counter analgesics. That plunged to 7 percent in fall 1982 but was resurrected to 30 percent by fall 1983. In its corporate credo, Johnson & Johnson identifies multiple stakeholders: users of its products (output), employees (input), employees' families (diffused linkage) and the Government (enabling linkage).

Issues to Reflect

(*a*) What is your opinion about the quality of corporate governance at Johnson & Johnson?

(*b*) Do you believe Johnson & Johnson acted as an enlightened company that shows concern for its stakeholders?

(*c*) U.S. business leaders are often accused of acting on a short-term obsession with profitability at the expense of the long-term interests of their corporation. How could Johnson & Johnson have behaved differently?

(*d*) Which aspects of the Tylenol crisis demonstrate a short-term perspective and the value of a longer-term perspective?

(Source: http://cnx.org/content/col25722/1.3)

Case 32: Leaving Goldman Sachs

Goldman Sachs executive Greg Smith caused a stir on Wall Street when quit the investment firm in 2012. On the day he resigned, Smith detailed the reasons for his departure in an open letter published in the Op-Ed section of the New York Times. He said he could no longer work at the company because its culture had become "toxic." He later wrote a book describing his experiences at Goldman Sachs. Smith had joined Goldman as an intern in 2001, shortly before the 9/11 attacks. The socialization process at the firm was demanding. Interns had to attend weekly open meetings that started at 6 am, not a minute later. Partners and vice-presidents would grill them on their knowledge of Wall Street, financial products and the company's history. Those who tried to fake an answer often ended up in tears. As a sign of their low status, interns had to wear large orange identification tags and sit on folding stools next to traders and sales people. (There never seemed to be enough stools, causing a daily scramble for seating.)

In order to be hired by the firm, interns had to secure "rabbis"- employees who would act as their sponsors. They also had to avoid offending executives while passing the Series 7 exams, which allowed them to trade. Only 40% of the incoming intern class was hired after the summer internship program ended. The lucky survivors joined a fast-paced, highly competitive culture where employees vied for bonuses and promotions through the sale of stocks, bonds, derivatives, foreign currency and other financial products. They were richly rewarded for their efforts. A middle-level executive, for example, could make $250,000 a year.

The pressure to generate sales and profits was tempered by Goldman Sachs's strong emphasis on serving clients. "Our clients come first" is the first of the company's 14 guiding principles. "Culture carriers"-employees who would carry forth the values of the firm-were highly valued. Rabbis encouraged new hires to be truthful and accurate when conducting transactions. Greg rose through the company ranks to become intern supervisor and later head of Goldman Sachs equity derivatives business in Europe, the Middle East and Africa. During this period, the market experienced the dot-com bust, when many technology firms went bankrupt and the financial crisis of 2008-09. Goldman Sachs survived the banking crash by accepting government funds as well as a $5 billion loan from Warren Buffett. These events helped trigger a cultural shift at Goldman Sachs. Many older leaders (those who played an important role in enforcing the firm's values) were replaced. Employees who could develop complex mathematical formulas for making financial trades-called "quants"- were promoted instead of culture carriers. The company began focusing on generating profits, not serving clients. Traders were encouraged to "hunt elephants" by pursuing only those trades that generated a $1 million or more in profit. On occasion the firm would bet against its clients, encouraging them to buy a stock or financial instrument it was trying to sell. Analysts used the term "muppets" to describe customers they thought were dumb or stupid. One company partner summarized the profits-first atmosphere this way. "If I had to choose between my reputation and my P&L, I choose my profit-and-loss. Because I can ultimately recover my reputation, but if I lose a lot of money, I can't recover that."

Goldman Sachs stock sank 3.4% after Greg's letter appeared in the New York Times, wiping out $2.15 billion in value. (The firm made up most of the losses the next day.) CEO Lloyd Blankfein and company president Gary Cohn fired back at Smith. In a memo to employees, the executives said, "The assertions made by [Greg Smith] do not reflect our values, our culture and how the vast majority of people at Goldman Sachs think about the firm and the work it does on behalf of clients." They pointed out that 89 per cent of employees surveyed agreed that the firm supplied outstanding service. The London office (where Smith worked at the end of his career) was named as one of the best places to work in the United Kingdom. Blankfein and Cohn also claimed that Smith never aired his concerns through the company's ethics reporting system.

Issues to Reflect

(*a*) What signs of ethical trouble, if any, were already present at Goldman Sachs when Greg joined?

(*b*) What messages did the socialization process at Goldman Sachs send to interns? Would you like to intern there?

(*c*) Could the cultural shift at Goldman Sachs have been prevented? How?

(*d*) Does Goldman Sachs have an ethical obligation to serve the needs of the clients, or should clients accept the fact that Goldman Sachs might put its own financial interests first?

(*e*) Was it ethical for Greg Smith to blow the whistle on Goldman Sachs by submitting a letter to the New York Times? Why or why not?

(*f*) Do the company CEO and president effectively cast doubt on Smith's description of a toxic culture at Goldman Sachs?

(*g*) What is your assessment of corporate governance practices at Goldman Sachs?

[Source: Internet sites. G. Smith (2012a, March 14). G. Smith (2012b), p. 131. We're committed to our clients. (2012, March 16)]

Case 33: The Infamous Story of Satyam: Greed Breeds Fall

Satyam computers were founded as an information technology services company by Mr. Ramalinga Raju and his brother-in-law in 1987. The company was converted into a public limited company in 1991 and it was listed in the

New York Stock Exchange in 2001. Satyam had nearly 40,000 employees working in India and abroad, with almost 600 global clients. From 2005 to 2008, the company grew steadily, both organically and inorganically. In 2008, the company decided to purchase 51% shares of the Maytas infrastructure development, construction and project management company. The strategic goals of both companies were not aligned. In addition, Mr. Raju did not inform the investors about the bidding process. This led to trust issues between Satyam board members and investors from across the world. Thus, the share-holders of the company requested the Government of India to review this deal. The inquiry revealed that the financial statements showed inflated profits. Moreover, the board members, senior managers and auditors of the company were not aware of the manipulated financial statements. Mr. Raju acknowledged all these allegations including falsifying the accounts and misleading the investors and wrongfully benefit the shareholders. He resigned after confessing manipulating the company's accounts and fudging its cash and bank balances on the balance sheet by almost Rs. 5 crore. He informed that the Maytas company was owned by his son. This incident by the top management changed the image of this organization from a symbol of trust to one of scams and frauds. This was one of the biggest corporate scams that occurred in the corporate history of India involving Rs. 7800 crore. The company is no longer operational in the software industry. Mr Raju was sentenced for 7 years in jail and fined Rs. 5.5 crore. Nine other executives of the company were also given seven years' imprisonment.

Issues to Reflect

1. What was the reason for Mr. Raju's unethical behaviour?
2. What were the shortcomings in the corporate governance practices of Satyam? Analyse the impact of Mr. Raju's behaviour by doing a stake-holder analysis.
3. What kind of ethical infrastructure should companies like Satyam develop to eliminate such incidents?
4. What is the role of checks and balances in corporate governance of a company? Is there a way out to ensure corporate governance if these checks and balances are not working?

14 UNIT

Environmental Ethics

14 UNIT

Environmental Ethics

14.1 LEARNING OBJECTIVES

This unit discusses various aspects relating to environment and its importance to the life of human beings and other creatures on the planet Earth. It attempts to sensitize the readers about:

- Evolution of industrialisation and associated impact on environment.
- Meaning and essence of environmental management.
- Categorization of industries in terms of their levels of pollution using range of pollution index in India.
- How sectoral deployment of bank credit takes place in India?
- Climate risk and sustainable finance.
- Some of major environmental concerns in India.
- Valuing the environment and its benefits.

14.2 BANKING AND ITS ROLE IN ENVIRONMENTAL MANAGEMENT

Industrial Revolution and Role of Electricity

Economies of the world, both advanced and countries of the Third World, remained dependent on primary activities till the mid-18th Century. Agriculture, horticulture, sericulture, mining and quarrying, forestry, plantation, farming, grazing, hunting and gathering, fishing, etc. It is broadly during the phase 1760 to 1840, some revolutionary changes have occurred in the manufacturing process of production in the United Kingdom. Largely, a transition took place in machine-based production (replacing use of human or animal labour), production processes in chemical, iron manufacturing using steam, rail transportation with the use of steam engine (with a maximum speed of 40 km per hour or 25 miles per hour).

The turning point in the industrial revolution during next phase was, of course, use of alternating current (or AC) in place of direct current (or DC). During the 1870s and 1880, DC power systems dominating the manufacturing sector. Scale of manufacturing in these factories in those years was relatively much smaller as we find today. Further, the development of 3-phase supply of power helped further to produce larger outputs in factories and mines initially in the advanced countries of the world.

In India, electricity was first witnessed in late 1870s in Calcutta. Later Mumbai witnessed electricity usage in 1882. With a view to providing electricity in the then existed tramways in the city of Bombay, Bombay Electricity & Tramways (BEST) set up a generating station in 1905 to provide electricity for the tramways.

With a small beginning at the time of independence with India's installed capacity of power at mere 1.36 GW in 1947, the installed capacity grew phenomenally to 416058 Mw by 31st March, 2023. India is the world's third largest producer of electricity and second largest consumer of electricity today. In a span of nearly 150 years when the first use of electricity was witnessed in 1870, recently all villages in India officially became accessible to electricity with Manipur's Leisang village became the last village to be electrified.

In Union Budget 2023-24, the government has allocated US$ 885 million (Rs. 7,327 crore) for the solar power sector including grid, off-grid and PM-KUSUM projects. To meet India's 500 GW renewable energy target and tackle the annual issue of coal demand supply mismatch, the Ministry of Power has identified 81 thermal units which will replace coal with renewable energy generation by 2026. 00% FDI allowed in the power sector has boosted FDI inflow in this sector. Schemes such as Deen Dayal Upadhyay Gram Jyoti Yojana (DDUGJY) and Integrated Power Development Scheme (IPDS) are expected to augment electrification across the country. As per the National Infrastructure Pipeline 2019-2025, energy sector projects accounted for the highest share (24%) out of the total expected capital expenditure of US$ 1.4 trillion (Rs. 111 lakh crore). Total FDI inflow in the power sector reached US$ 16.57 billion between April – December 2022.

Environmental Management

Christopher J. Barrow (2005) in his book titled Environmental Management and Development (published by Routledge) acknowledged that the term environmental management "can refer to a goal or vision, to attempts to steer a process, to the application of a set of tools, to a philosophical exercise seeking to establish new perspectives towards the environment and human societies, and to much more besides. Environmental managers are a diverse group of people including academics, policy-makers, non-governmental organisation (NGO) workers, company employees, civil servants and a wide range of individuals or groups who make decisions about the use of natural resources (such as fishers, farmers and pastoralists). Indeed, environmental management involves all people to some extent because all human activities ultimately have some sort of environmental impact".

At the aggregate level, governments at the national level design some plans as an attempt to make positive impact on the environment by prescribing and ensuring rise in the forest cover, use of the electric vehicles, encouraging mass rapid transport systems, permission to use and increasing the percentage of ethanol mixing in fuels, tougher emission norms, energy-efficient lighting, cables and other gadgets for home use, use of gas in air conditioners and refrigerators (with medium impact from earlier refrigerants using chloro-fluoro-carbons or CFCs to zero-impact by the present R 600-A refrigerant on the protective layer from Sun's UV rays on ozone layer and its depletion), awareness programmes on conservation of energy, etc.

Government Initiatives on Environmental Management

The Government on March 5, 2016 had released a new categorization of industries based on their pollution load. The Ministry stated in its release on Press Information Bureau website that "the new category of White industries which is practically non-polluting will not require Environmental Clearance (EC) and Consent and will help in getting finance from lending institutions. The exercise of "Recategorization" was being carried out for last one year. This is a landmark decision to give a fair picture of the industries".

"Recategorization of industries based on their pollution load is a scientific exercise. The old system of categorization was creating problems for many industries and was not reflecting the pollution of the industries. The new categories will remove this lacuna and will give clear picture to everyone. 25 industrial sectors which were not critically polluting were also earlier categorized as Red. This was creating wrong impression to everyone".

The Ministry of Environment, Forest and Climate Change (MoEFCC) had developed the criteria of categorization of industrial sectors based on the Pollution Index which is a function of the emissions (air pollutants), effluents (water pollutants), hazardous wastes generated and consumption of resources. For this purpose, the references are taken from the Water (Prevention and Control of Pollution) Cess (Amendment) Act, 2003, Standards so far prescribed for various pollutants under Environment (Protection) Act, 1986 and Doon Valley Notification, 1989 issued by MoEFCC. The Pollution Index PI of any industrial sector is a number from 0 to 100 and the increasing value of PI denotes the increasing degree of pollution load from the industrial sector. Based on a series of brain-storming sessions among CPCB, SPCBs and MoEFCC, the following criteria on 'Range of Pollution Index' for the purpose of categorization of industrial sectors is finalized.

- Industrial Sectors having Pollution Index score of 60 and above - Red category
- Industrial Sectors having Pollution Index score of 41 to 59 - Orange category
- Industrial Sectors having Pollution Index score of 21 to 40 - Green category
- Industrial Sectors having Pollution Index score up to 20 - White category

The salient features of the 'Recategorization' exercise are as follows:

- Due importance has been given to relative pollution potential of the industrial sectors based on scientific criteria. Further, wherever possible, splitting of the industrial sectors is also considered based on the use of raw materials, manufacturing process adopted and in-turn pollutants expected to be generated.
- The Red category of industrial sectors would be 60.
- The Orange category of industrial sectors would be 83.
- The Green category of industrial sectors would be 63.

- Newly-introduced White category contains 36 industrial sectors which are practically non-polluting.
- There shall be no necessity of obtaining the consent to operate for White category of industries. An intimation to concerned SPCB/PCC shall suffice.
- No Red category of industries shall normally be permitted in the ecologically fragile area/protected area.

The details of the industries falling under Red, Orange, Green and White categories are presented in tables 1, 2, 3 & 4 respectively (given below).

The newly introduced White category of industries pertains to those industrial sectors which are practically non-polluting, such as Biscuit trays etc. from rolled PVC sheet (using automatic vacuum forming machines), Cotton and woollen hosiery making (Dry process only without any dying/washing operation), Electric lamp (bulb) and CFL manufacturing by assembling only, Scientific and mathematical instrument manufacturing, Solar power generation through photovoltaic cell, wind power and mini hydel power (less than 25 MW).

The purpose of the categorization was to ensure that the industry is established in a manner which is consistent with the environmental objectives. The new criteria will prompt industrial sectors willing to adopt cleaner technologies, ultimately resulting in generation of fewer pollutants. Another feature of the new categorization system lies in facilitating self-assessment by industries as the subjectivity of earlier assessment has been eliminated. This 'Re-categorization' is a part of the efforts, policies and objective of present government to create a clean & transparent working environment in the country and promote the Ease of Doing Business.

Role of Banking on Environment

Banks provide loans to variety of customers ranging between the households, small business, MSME customers, large scale firms, exporters, importers, housing, infrastructure projects, road transportation, tourism, travel, etc.

Banks in India have a mandate not to finance or refinance some environmentally damaging industries. The background for this is provided below, which is in force for close to 35 years now. In the Indian context, however, institutional financing by the banks to such polluting firms was prohibited only in year 2000 through a Gazette Notification. The following content is reproduced by taking from the Ministry of Environment and Forests, GoI. (Source: http://envfor.nic.in/divisions/ic/wssd/doc2/ch2.html)

Montreal Protocol on Substances that deplete the Ozone Layer (to the Vienna Convention for the Protection of the Ozone Layer), 1987.

The Montreal Protocol to the Vienna Convention on substances that deplete the Ozone Layer, came into force in 1989. The protocol set targets for reducing the consumption and production of a range of ozone depleting substances (ODS). In a major innovation, the protocol recognized that all nations should not be treated equally. The agreement acknowledges that certain countries have contributed to ozone depletion more than others. It also recognizes that a nation's obligation to reduce current emissions should reflect its technological and financial ability to do so. Because of this, the agreement sets more stringent standards and accelerated phase-out timetables to countries that have contributed most to ozone depletion (Divan and Rosencranz, 2001).

India acceded to the Montreal Protocol along with its London Amendment in September 1992. The MoEF has established an Ozone Cell and a steering committee on the Montreal Protocol to facilitate implementation of the India Country Program, for phasing out ODS production by 2010.

To meet India's commitments under the Montreal Protocol, the Government of India has also taken certain policy decisions.

Goods required to implement ODS phase-out projects funded by the Multilateral Fund are fully exempt from duties. This benefit has been also extended to new investments with non-ODS technologies.

Commercial banks are prohibited from financing or refinancing investments with ODS technologies.

The Gazette of India on 19 July, 2000 notified rules for regulation of ODS phase-out called the Ozone Depleting Substances (Regulation and Control) Rules, 2000. They were notified under the Environment (Protection) Act, 1986. These rules were drafted by the MoEF following consultations with industries and related government departments.

For the exhaustive list of 242 categories of industries classified as Red (60), Orange (83), Green (63) and White (36), banks in India can follow a method of using the scores indicated by the Environment Ministry. For those select

industries for which the commercial banks are prohibited from financing or refinancing investments with ODS technologies by the Ministry of Environment and Forests, the sanctioning and disbursement authorities in banks must take due care to see that inadvertently the loans are not reached, as they have serious impact on the health and safety of individuals and it is not only undesirable but is contrary to law as well.

What would you do as a banker?

One company's manufacturing facilities contains four very large and very noisy pressing machines. The Chief of the facility has always tried to adhere to the applicable governmental regulations about noise control, but despite the best efforts, it is not possible to completely eliminate the noises unless the company goes for installation fully automated new machinery which is not immediately feasible as the margins are already under strain. The company avails credit facilities from your bank.

Ramesh a long-time worker in the company has been working with these machines since last 10 years. He always wears the prescribed equipment during the work hours. One day he comes to the Chief's office looking very depressed and tells that as per his doctor's opinion he has lost 80% of his hearing in his right ear. The probable reason is the work Ramesh does near the noisy machines.

Sectoral Deployment of Bank Credit

Reserve Bank of India provides data aggregated from all banks in India on a monthly basis. These data give us a broad idea about how the food and non-food credit is deployed by the commercial banks. RBI's press release during end-April, 2018 provides the highlights of deployment of bank credit in India as under, which gives us an idea about the pattern of deployment to non-polluting versus polluting industrial activities as follows:

Credit to industry increased by 0.7 percent in March, 2018 as compared with a contraction of 1.9 percent in March 2017. Credit to major sub-sectors such as 'textiles', 'vehicles, vehicle parts & transport equipment', 'all engineering', 'food processing' and 'rubber, plastic & their products' accelerated. However, credit to 'infrastructure', 'basic metal & metal products', 'cement & cement products', 'chemical & chemical products' and 'petroleum, coal products & nuclear fuels' contracted/declined *(Source: RBI Press Release, April 27, 2018).*

Science and Technology have been revolutionizing the lives of people across the globe. The National Academy of Engineering (US non-profit NGO) through expert vote established 20 most important technological developments of the 20th Century. Electrification, automobile, airplane, etc. are some of the early developments, while the later part of the 20th century of the list includes Highways, Spacecraft, Internet, Imaging Technology, Household Appliances, Laser and Fibre Optics, Nuclear Technology, Material Science, among others.

While commercial banks in India have got the following obligations, a discretion may be used where they have a freehand to channelize the credit to companies.

1. Prohibited for consumption and production of a range of ozone depleting substances (ODS)
2. Priority Sector Lending (with sub-limits)
3. Others (industries and services and a range of non-priority sectors)

In the 'Others' category (above), banks could have their own limited discretion (pre-notified to the customers for their information and as a matter of transparency) and start lending with their own latest updated information of the different technologies that are rated as the best by experts and also ratified by the managements of banks which are the latest in terms of having minimal or no adverse impact on the environment.

By adopting such a process by the end of each financial year, commercial banks may not only comply with the priority sector target and obligation of 40 per cent of Adjusted Net Bank Credit and the rest of the available credit to other sectors, banks may bring in some greater acceptability from the point of view of environmental caring. Such a caring by the significant part of India's financial sector (namely, banking sector) would have a significant positive impact on the environmental quality.

14.3 ENVIRONMENTAL CONCERNS

In the context of India nearing 2023, there are some serious concerns relating to the quality of environment we created for ourselves with a view to achieving rapid industrial, urban and economic progress. Each of the following can be counted

as a serious challenge or concern from the environmental point of view. If not handled well both at the national level with sound and implementable policies and also at micro level with individuals voluntarily realising the importance of preserving environment for their own and their successors' well-being, it may lead to even more severe consequences for the years to come than what India witnessed in recent years. Some of these environmental concerns for India are:

1. Forest Cover
2. Ground Water Depletion
3. Air Pollution
4. Climate Change
5. Loss of Biodiversity

The above concerns are part of the environmental ethics debate not only in India but around the world. These are serious challenges but human values can play a decisive role in encountering them.

14.4 THE VALUE OF NATURE

The term *value* has many connotations. Use value, exchange value, notional value, imputed value, etc. In a typical advanced or less developed country, the consumptive needs of all of us are taken care of by business firms. Our demand in the markets for goods and services are instantly sensed by the business firms and they undertake producing goods and services and take themselves or identify other firms who reach these goods and services to us through market mechanisms. We consume them and want similar goods or other goods to be produced and supplied by the firms and this goes on.

We rarely (but certainly not regularly) think about the impact of our production and consumption of goods on the environment we live-in. Somehow, we are gradually damaging the very nature that is letting us survive on this planet.

Assume that (as this thinking has already been there for at least for a generation now), we "value" the environment and believe that there is a "cost" we have to pay for damaging the environment. Hence, we estimate the cost of damaging environment for each of the good or service we produce, store, distribute, consume, discard, recycle, etc. (besides the capital cost, human cost and other nominal costs) and add this in the price of the good. This at best may minimise reckless or wasteful consumption and throwing away of food or unnecessary long-drives, etc.

We face serious practical challenges in convincing the businesses, buyers and government about incorporating cost of these activities on ecosystem into the pricing of goods and services. The real challenge is how many of us (including the scientists/environmentalists) are aware of all species on the planet, what role they play, what implications would there be with their extinction, etc. In the absence of fool-proof information on these things, even judiciary may direct governments in their countries not to allow such pricing practices. Hence, it is a very difficult idea to implement in practice.

Indirect ways to value environment are seen in media, research articles and symposia. It is estimated that "the economic value of a healthy tree with respect to its oxygen producing capacity is roughly Rs. 23.72 lakh per year". Based on the price of an oxygen cylinder of 300 litre available for sale on a popular e-commerce website in India, one can project that at today's prices a person who takes 550 litres of oxygen in a day owes to the nature or environment Rs. 66 crore. With just Oxygen being valued at the market price, imagine if the sunshine and water (commercial rate, not the yearly cess we pay to the local authority) and so on, the value of the environment becomes extremely high. This is on the premise that land to live on with a proper regulated sunshine and earth's gravity, etc. are given to us by the nature itself which are taken for granted. Imagine how much it costs to train for the research organizations to keep cosmonauts to deal with the zero-gravity situation inside the space laboratories where they require to conduct some experiments.

Hence, in our daily lives, we must remain grateful to nature and this gratefulness has nothing to do with religiosity or any other unscientific belief. It is sheer respect or value that we accord to the environment which is responsible for our birth, survival and growth on this plant. It is our moral obligation to preserve, protect and pass it over to our next generations. The best way to execute it is to remain aware of the environment, respect it through every act of ours and by avoiding the unnecessary and wasteful consumption. United Nations also commemorates 5th June of every year as the 'World Environment Day' since 1973. This day has been set aside by UN to promote worldwide awareness and action for the protection of our environment. In the year 2018, the theme was

'Beat Plastic Pollution' with India being the global host of the 2018 World Environment Day. Likewise in 2021, with the theme of Ecosystem Restoration, Pakistan hosted the day. In 2022, World Environment Day was hosted by Sweden with the campaign slogan "Only One Earth" and the theme of "Living Sustainably in Harmony with Nature". The theme chosen for the current year's World Environmental Day is 'solutions to plastic pollution' and the host is Côte d'Ivoire. Every year the World Environment Day sees participation from 143 countries. The year 2023 will mark the 50th edition of the World Environment Day.

14.5 CLIMATE CHANGE, TRANSITION TO LOW-CARBON ECONOMY AND BANKS: CHALLENGES & OPPORTUNITIES

Banks and financial institutions can play a key role in financing the transition to a low-carbon economy and supporting the national climate commitments. While no entity is immune from climate risks, India is particularly vulnerable to the climate change related physical risks and hence there is a need to be more alive to the urgency of action given its long coastline, high share of fossil fuels in energy systems and relatively high dependence of rural livelihoods on agriculture. Climate trends and events have a direct bearing on the economy and resultantly have an impact on the financial institutions and the financial system. According to a report, the transformation of the global economy needed to achieve net-zero emissions by 2050 would be universal and significant, requiring $9.2 trillion in annual average spending on physical assets, which is $3.5 trillion more than what is being spent today. In the case of India, the Council on Energy, Environment and Water has already estimated that a total investment of US$ 10.1 trillion would be needed to meet the net zero commitments by 2070. This underscores the urgency of efforts for transitioning to a low carbon economy.

Ensuring access to adequate transition finance and supporting technology would be critical in this process. Going forward, there are two key aspects which banks would need to focus on - first, relying on their time-tested expertise in financial intermediation by acting as an effective conduit for channelizing finance to carbon efficient sectors and industries in alignment with national policies and goals and second, improving the management of financial risks in their books which may originate from climate change. Such risks range from the direct physical risks emanating from adverse climate-related events to loss of reputation and legal risks. Obviously, the strategies for mitigating these risks would have to be formulated and all stakeholders would need to play their role in helping the country traverse and transform into a climate-resilient economy.

Challenges for Financial Intermediaries and Banks

Estimating the timing, frequency and severity of climate-related events is a challenging proposition given the uncertainties involved in the process. While significant progress has been achieved globally on developing scenarios and forward-looking approaches for modelling climate risks, the requirement of past data and the unpredictable nature of climate change makes estimation of climate events and their financial impact a challenging endeavour. The work at a global level which is being coordinated by the Financial Stability Board (FSB) and endorsed by the G-20, rests on four building blocks needed for addressing Climate-Related Financial Risks. These four building blocks, *viz.*, Disclosures, Data, Vulnerabilities Analysis and Regulatory and Supervisory Practices and Tools are pre-requisites for a resilient financial system when augmented by informed decision making.

The first building block, an appropriate and adequate disclosure framework, must have three key attributes - first, it should have inter-temporal consistency, second, it should be comparable and the third and most important is that it should be useful for decision making. Climate-related disclosures by firms, that largely contain these attributes, would help policymakers and banks in understanding the enormity of the task ahead in terms of the transition funding requirements. Further, this would help banks understand the level of carbon intensity in the business ventures in case they are to fund them so that they are able to differentiate and appropriately price in such risks. Internationally, a significant body of work has been done on disclosures. The FSB's Task Force on Climate-related Financial Disclosures (TCFD) and the International Sustainability Standards Board (ISSB) under the IFRS Foundation have been leading this work along with other standard setting bodies. In March 2022, the ISSB published Exposure Drafts on its first two proposed standards. The first sets out general sustainability-related disclosure requirements while the other specifies climate-related disclosure requirements. Given the global nature of funding markets and cross-border flows of capital, the idea is to agree upon a common global baseline disclosure requirement which is interoperable among jurisdictions for comparability and consistency. The Reserve Bank, as a part of standard setting bodies has also been contributing and learning from global discussions and experiences. In its recently published Discussion Paper on Climate Risk and Sustainable Finance, RBI has elaborated on how climate-related disclosure is an important source of information for different stakeholders (e.g., customers, depositors, investors, and regulators) of REs to understand relevant risks faced by them and their approach to addressing such issues. For the corporates, beginning from the current financial year FY 2022-23, SEBI has mandated Business Responsibility and Sustainability Reporting (BRSR) for the top 1000 listed companies (by market capitalisation) in India. The disclosures under the BRSR framework would incentivize green financing and help banks and financial institutions in estimating their climate-related exposure to these listed companies. While consistent and comparable disclosures, the first building block, would enable financial institutions make firm level risk assessments.

The second building block, data, is required for making macro level assessment of risks. Like any financial risk, reliable and comprehensive data on climate risk related exposures would aid in making sound policy interventions and undertaking climate scenario analysis and stress testing for the assessment of risks from climate events. While global efforts are underway to create data repositories and provide guidance on collection of data for better comparability; availability of high quality, granular and sufficient data remains a challenge as of now. Availability of granular data also remains crucial for modelling the forward-looking nature of climate events and developing metrics for monitoring climate related financial risks.

The third building block, vulnerabilities analysis, is again a macro level exercise to understand the financial stability risks arising out of climate events and their impact on financial systems. It is focused on analysis and stress testing using various scenarios to help in better assessment of potential pressure points in the financial system and in understanding interlinkages between financial sector and real sector. While the development of climate scenario analysis, stress testing scenarios and analytical tools are still in their infancy, the need for integrating them with regular monitoring exercises and overall financial risk assessment has been well recognized. One particular challenge in modelling climate-related risks is the long time horizon which has to be considered. The climate events may often span across decades, if not centuries and this may make the data collection exercise quite difficult and the outcomes more uncertain.

The fourth and final building block consists of regulatory and supervisory initiatives to facilitate transition. In a way, this is a culmination of the work taken up under the three building blocks discussed above. The regulators may need to fine tune the existing prudential policies to integrate the climate risks into the regulatory frameworks. At the same time, from a supervisory perspective, the expectations may have to be set and communicated to all regulated entities regarding climate-related risks, encompassing organizational strategy, governance, risk management and assurance functions. The global efforts undertaken so far seem to suggest that integrating climate-related risks and capturing them by fine tuning existing prudential frameworks may be possible. The Basel Committee on Banking Supervision (BCBS) has published Principles for the Effective Management and Supervision of Climate-related Financial Risks in June 2022. In October 2022, the Financial Stability Board (FSB) published its Final Report on Supervisory and Regulatory Approaches to Climate-related Risks. Earlier in March 2022, the NGFS published a 'Statement on Nature-related Financial Risks', which acknowledges that failure to account for, mitigate and adapt to nature-related risks could have significant macroeconomic implications and become a source of financial stability risk. While guidance has been made available, regulated entities may need time, resources and capacity to integrate climate related considerations into their decision-making frameworks and customer facing business lines.

Private Sector Initiatives

In the private sector, decarbonisation and digitalisation are emerging as megatrends that could compel sectors and corporates to undertake structural changes and fundamentally alter their traditional business models. It is heartening to note that some of the leading Indian companies in the hard to abate sectors like steel and cement, for example, are working on an ambitious decarbonization agenda aimed at reducing the carbon footprint in their production process. Banks and financial institutions may have to step up their engagement with their corporate customers on ensuring sustainability-focused financing and other support services to help them transition towards a low-carbon economy while reducing their own carbon footprint. The financial sector can channel resources towards green projects/businesses by offering suitable and customized products to businesses.

Over the past three years, the Sustainability Linked Bonds and Sustainability Linked Loans (SLBs and SLLs) market has been a fast-growing segment globally in the sustainable finance market. India too, has seen the introduction of sustainable finance instruments such as sustainability-linked loans. Liberalized External Commercial Borrowings (ECB) norms have also enabled Indian companies to raise offshore finance through green bonds, social bonds, sustainable bonds and sustainability-linked bonds. In line with global trends, the issuance of sustainable debt has risen sharply in India during Calendar Year 2021 taking it to the 2nd place among emerging economies in cumulative Green Bond Issuances. Mechanisms such as blended finance and risk-sharing facilities are also being utilized to finance climate and sustainability-related projects. The above initiatives from the financial sector in India and across the globe make one believe that the private sector is very much alive to the challenges ahead.

Public Sector Initiatives in India

To move the needle towards net zero, progressive decarbonization of all sectors of the economy, including the hard-to-abate ones is a must. This means that banks need to incentivized to provide support in terms of transition finance for businesses and sectors that are not so green, to adopt cleaner technologies, increase energy efficiency and become greener over time. Green finance can play a crucial role in making India's economy resilient to climate change impacts. During the COP26 summit in November 2021, the Hon'ble Prime Minister had announced that by the year 2070, India will achieve the target of net-zero. This would necessitate creating an enabling ecosystem for financing India's transition to a green economy.

In India, both the Government and Reserve Bank of India have been participating in the global discussions on climate risks and have already taken quite a few initiatives in this regard. The climate action is a key governmental priority and it is proposed that as a part of its overall market borrowings in 2022-23, Sovereign Green Bonds (SGBs) will be issued for mobilizing resources for green infrastructure. The proceeds will be deployed in public sector projects which will help in reducing the carbon intensity of the economy. Over time, the SGBs would provide a pricing reference for the private sector entities in India for their INR denominated borrowing for ESG linked debt. Thus, the issuance of SGBs would help in creating an ecosystem which fosters a greater flow of capital into green projects and entities undertaking such projects.

Recognizing the need for concerted efforts in the area, the Reserve Bank has concomitantly set up a Sustainable Finance Group (SFG) within its Department of Regulation in May 2021 to lead the regulatory initiatives in area of climate risk and sustainable finance in the Indian context. A regulatory guidance on climate risk and sustainable finance is expected from RBI in the year 2023. One notable feature for our financial ecosystem is that while rest of the world is still grappling in developing new instruments to funnel funding to green and sustainable companies and projects, India already has a well-accepted incentive-based instrument in the form of Priority Sector. Blended finance involves the use of concessional and catalytic capital to draw in private capital for financing projects with sustainable outcomes as also assist with technology transfer and institutional support, to reduce risk and enhance bankability.

Over the years, the regulators have taken various policy measures to promote and support green finance initiatives through this route. For example, renewable energy projects have been included as a part of Priority Sector Lending (PSL). In 2012, Reserve Bank included loans sanctioned by banks directly to individuals for setting up off-grid solar and other off-grid renewable energy solutions for households and in 2015, the PSL criteria was expanded to bank loans up to a limit of Rs. 15 crore to borrowers for purposes like solar/biomass-based power generators, windmills, micro-hydel plants and for non-conventional energy based public utilities, viz., street lighting systems and remote village electrification. In 2020, this limit for bank loans was doubled to Rs. 30 crore. It is heartening to note that in recent years, leading banks in India have also begun stepping up their exposure to the renewable energy sector.

Enablers for Scaling up Green Finance in India

Banks and financial institutions have always been the backbone of India's economic growth and as the country pivots to sustainable growth, they are taking a lead and accelerating green lending. However, a number of structural changes may be needed in the traditional lending approach, including evaluation and certification of the green credentials of projects to keep up this acceleration. In order to give focused attention to scaling up green finance, banks and financial institutions would have to invest in human resources and capacity building efforts as well as integrate environmental and social risk considerations into their corporate credit appraisal mechanisms.

A taxonomy would also help banks and financial institutions in better assessing the climate risk in their loan portfolio, scaling up green and sustainable finance and mitigating the risk of greenwashing. Another key challenge in scaling up green finance is the availability of a robust ecosystem for third party verification /assurance and impact assessment and the green credentials of businesses and projects. This would also address potential greenwashing concerns and ensure unhindered flow of capital and funding to the entities. The challenge regarding the availability of data and disclosures would also need to be addressed quickly. In this context, the disclosure standards prescribed by SEBI for top 1000 listed entities by market capitalisation is a welcome step. Green finance needs to be scaled up rapidly to meet India's climate targets under the updated Nationally Determined Contribution communicated to the United Nations Framework Convention on Climate Change (UNFCCC) in August 2022. The enhanced ambition requires mobilisation of green finance at a much faster pace. For example, green infrastructure investment trusts could help scale up green finance as also deepen the local bond market.

Climate change may result in physical and transition risks that could have implications for the physical safety and financial soundness of individual regulated entities as well as for the stability of financial system. Thus, there is a need for regulated entities to develop and implement comprehensive frameworks for understanding and assessing the potential impact of climate-related financial risks in their business strategy and operations. Climate risk is the biggest challenge confronting the humanity today and addressing it decisively is the bankers' joint responsibility. Financial sector has a key role to play as it is the sector which finances businesses and can influence their activities. Banks would have their role cut out in handholding the businesses and arranging for the transition finance required by the firms as they try to shift their strategies to make them more sustainable and planet friendly.

The Indian economy is at a stage where it needs to grow rapidly but the challenge is to think of ways to incorporate climate risk and ESG-related considerations into commercial lending and investment decisions while simultaneously balancing the needs of credit expansion, economic growth, and social development. Collective engagement would help build on an early progress and go a long way in addressing the challenges of climate change.

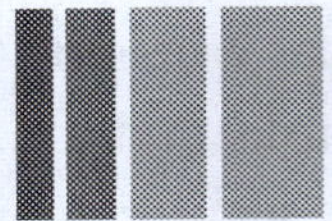

14.6 RBI DISCUSSION PAPER ON CLIMATE RISK & SUSTAINABLE FINANCE

As per the report of the UN's Intergovernmental Panel on Climate Change dated August 9, 2021 the emissions of greenhouse gases (GHGs) from human activities are responsible for ~1.1°C of warming since pre-industrial times. While this change is seemingly small, the current temperatures are unprecedented in comparison to the levels over the past 12,000 years affecting living conditions in many parts of the world. Further, limiting global warming to close to 1.5°C or even 2°C over pre-industrial levels will be "beyond reach" without "immediate, rapid and large-scale reductions" in greenhouse gas emissions. This may have a profound adverse impact on the ecosystem, health, infrastructure and the economy. As per a recent study by CarbonBrief, a 1.5°C - 2°C temperature increase will shave nearly 8-13 percent off the global GDP by 2100. The Global Risks Report5 2022 published by the World Economic Forum presents the results of the latest Global Risks Perception Survey (GRPS) and an analysis of key risks emanating from the current economic, societal, environmental and technological events. According to the Survey, over the next five years, respondents signal societal and environmental risks to be of foremost concern. Over a 10-years horizon, environmental risks are perceived to be the five most critical long-term threats to the world as well as the most potentially damaging to people and planet, with "climate action failure", "extreme weather" and "biodiversity loss" ranking as the top three most severe risks.

Closer home, the latest annual report by the India Meteorological Department (IMD) on the country's climate stated that 2021 was not only the fifth warmest year since 1901, but in the last decade, 2012-2021, was also the warmest on record. Moreover, 11 of the 15 warmest years on record were between 2007 and 2021. The rise in average temperatures could have a cascading effect on extreme weather events, crop patterns and urban disaster management. India recorded 756 instances of natural disasters (landslides, storms, earthquakes, floods, droughts, etc.) since 1900, with a total of 402 and 354 events recorded during 1900-2000 and 2001-2021 respectively, indicating the preponderance of tail events of late.

A report of the Ministry of Earth Sciences, Government of India has concluded that since the middle of the twentieth century, India has witnessed a rise in average temperature; a decrease in monsoon precipitation; a rise in extreme

temperature, droughts and sea levels, as well as increase in the frequency and intensity of severe cyclones. There is compelling scientific evidence that human activities have influenced these changes in regional climate. These developments pose challenges for humanity and warrant an immediate, large-scale and rapid reduction in GHGs.

Concurrently, climate change is increasingly being recognized globally as a source of financial risk for banks. Climate change risk is also ascending the hierarchy of threats to financial stability across advanced and emerging economies alike and consequently, the need for an appropriate framework to identify, assess and manage climate-related risk has become imperative. Accordingly, the RBI has come out with a Discussion Paper on Climate Risk & Sustainable Finance to propose a climate risk management strategy as presented under the following heads:

a. Overview of climate related risk and its unique characteristics as applicable to REs

b. Broad guidance for all REs to have (*i*) appropriate governance (*ii*) strategy to address climate change risks and (*iii*) risk management structure to effectively manage them from a micro-prudential perspective

c. Exploring how forward-looking tools like stress testing and climate scenario analysis can be used to identify and assess vulnerabilities in REs

d. Climate risk related financial disclosure and reporting for REs

e. Capacity Building

f. Voluntary Initiatives

As most of the issues covered under the Discussion Paper have already been explained in the preceding heading 12.5, we have provided above a highly synoptic view of the different areas discussed in the paper.

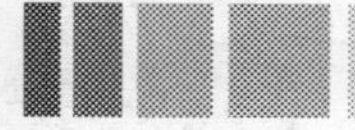

14.7 THE ETHICS OF ENVIRONMENTAL PROTECTION

According to the Stanford Encyclopedia of Philosophy, environmental ethics is the discipline in philosophy that studies the moral relationship of human beings to, and also the value and moral status of, the environment and its non-human contents (Source: https://plato.stanford.edu/entries/ethics-environmental/).

The following two cases lets (a disaster in Uttarakhand and Protecting trees as an integral part of India's culture) discuss about our ethics towards environment.

Uttarakhand Cloudburst 2013: Man-made or Natural Calamity?

India faced one of the worst disasters in June 2013 in Uttarakhand after the 2004 tsunami. In the aftermath of the tragedy, there were several studio discussions on prominent TV channels, lot of news in print media and it made many common people, bureaucrats, pilgrims, politicians and others including environmentalist to seriously think about the root cause of the tragedy. While there is no official confirmation on the toll of people in the tragedy, it is believed that nearly 6,000 persons went missing in the flash floods and who are now presumed to be dead.

During a span of 4 days, June 14-17, the rainfall registered in and around the State of Uttarakhand was close to 4 times the normal monsoon rainfall for the period. Traditionally, four places of Uttarakhand State - Yamunotri, Gangotri, Kedarnath and Badrinath were known as Chhota Char Dham and it is believed in a major religion of India that a visit to these small four abodes gives eternal bliss or moksha to the pilgrims.

Each year, lakhs of people visit these four places from various parts of India and abroad. According to an article published on "The Guardian" website on June 28, 2013, some man-made lapses have aggravated the natural disaster into a much sever catastrophe. The article states "the true causes of the epic tragedy lie in the grievous damage recently wrought on the region's ecology by the runaway growth of tourism, unchecked proliferation of roads, hotels, shops and multi-story housing in ecologically fragile areas, and above all mushrooming hydroelectricity dams that disrupt water balances. Underlying the disaster are multiple governance failures, too.

These man-made factors turned an extreme weather event into a social catastrophe. True, the region experienced heavy rainfall of 340-370 mm within 24 hours on June 16-17, leading to flash floods. But such precipitation isn't unprecedented. Uttarakhand has recorded single-day rainfall in excess of 400 mm several times, including 450 mm in 1995 and 900 mm in 1965. Cloudbursts, floods and rapid swelling of fast-flowing rivers aren't uncommon".

The article states further that "There was local-level governance failure, too. Haphazard, unregulated construction of roads and bridges was allowed on crumbling, landslide-prone ridges and steep slopes, ignoring the region's fragile geology and high earthquake vulnerability. Forests were destroyed on a large scale. Hundreds of buildings were constructed in the flood plains of rivers, their "natural" terrain, which should be no-go areas. Riverbeds were recklessly mined for sand. As construction debris accumulated, land contours and flows of streams and rivers changed.

Indiscriminate building of hydroelectric dams was the worst culprit. These involve drilling huge tunnels in the hills by blasting rocks, placing enormous turbines in the tunnels, destroying soil-binding vegetation to build water channels and other infrastructure, laying transmission lines and carelessly dumping excavated muck. Many dams have been built on the same river so close to one another that they leave no scope for its regeneration".

National Institute of Disaster Management, Ministry of Home Affairs, Government of India brought out a Report called India Disaster Report 2013, under its key recommendations/lessons learnt mentions the following, among other things:

- Flood Plain Zoning Act regulating construction within the flood plain of a river should be implemented strictly.
- Blasting for developmental activities be avoided as it may destabilize the weak rocks in mountainous regions.
- Tourism related development should not be allowed along the river banks.
- The above three points indicate that there were some deviations in the norms while giving permissions in the State.

In December end-2016, the Government of India initiated the Char Dham highway development project, an ambitious initiative to improve connectivity to the Char Dham pilgrimage centres in the Himalayas. The project's main objective is to develop around 900 km of national highways. These highways will be built in Uttarakhand at an approximate cost of Rs. 12,000 crore.

Based on the case let, we should reflect as under:

- Why a commitment to environment has its own merit?
- If the Uttarakhand authorities stuck to the rulebook, could the loss of life of such large scale have been averted besides damage of property?

Protection of Trees: An Integral Part of India's Culture

If one glances through India's history, one finds that the concern and bonding of our ancient Indians towards protecting and worshipping the trees and forests becomes amply clear. Mention of the term "panchavati" (forest home in Ramayana) or "panchavatis" (people managing cluster of five types of trees as part of the village committees) and many of rulers who ruled the country or major parts of the country over centuries before the British conquered India had all gave planting, nurturing and protecting the trees, etc. holds testimony to this. In the early 18th Century, a few hundreds of people in Rajasthan state sacrificed their lives to save a particular variety of tress (khejri) grown in the state.

The Indian Forest Act, 1927 provided powers to all states in India to declare a forest as protected forest. Any person or firm who "fells, girdles, lops or bums any tree or strips off the bark or leaves from or otherwise damages, the same" is punishable with imprisonment or fine or both.

In Uttar Pradesh, a movement called the "Chipko Movement" started about 45 years ago in 1973 to prevent a contractor who was assigned the permit to fell about 300 trees. The initiative came from the local villagers who felt that such a move would severely affect their source of sustenance. During later part of 1970s, Uttar Pradesh, Karnataka, Meghalaya, etc. States have enacted Acts to protect the trees.

While may be heartening to note that there has always been a concern, bonding and love for the Indians for over centuries as discussed above, there has also been a disturbing trend in recent decades. Despite the Union and State governments' efforts, there are some reports in print and electronic media about the so-called timber mafia who became a curse to India's forests. Jammu and Kashmir, parts of Karnataka, Southern Andhra Pradesh, Uttarakhand, etc.

The silver lining is that in Jharkhand, which also has good forest cover but with timber mafia being present, a group of tribal women are seen taking the protection of unauthorised tree harvesting in about 50 hectares.

Hopefully, such movements would also catch-up in other vulnerable parts of India. Leaving the monumental task of protecting the forests and trees of such vast country like ours to only the government with the people remaining indifferent to the acts of illegal harvesting of trees is not going to curb the menace. It is expected that all citizens treat trees and forests in their surroundings truly as part of our national wealth and try to sincerely protect the same for everyone's benefit. By doing so, we can not only feel proud of being part of a great national cause, we also can breathe a clean air, which also has its intrinsic (and market) value.

14.8 OBLIGATIONS TO FUTURE GENERATIONS

History suggests that about 5,00,000 years ago, humans began using fire for heat and cooking. They also gradually developed languages, which are unique to humankind. Linguists from University of California, Berkeley felt that vocal languages must have begun diversifying in our species at least 1,00,000 years ago. We cannot be certain that only human beings have the uniqueness of having language/s and that the other living things on the planet have no such means to communicate among themselves. Ulla Hedeager of the Columbia University writes in an article titled "Is Language Unique to the Human Species?" that "the question whether non-human species in a state of nature have developed a kind of communication similar to that of humans remain open".

As studied in previous units of this courseware that humans have (and are expected to hold) values. Values simply are human ideas that guide their action. We examine and evaluate the manner in which our actions are carried out and not interested in their consequences as such. Each parent all over the world first takes a significant amount of his/her time to coach the offspring the language. This is a wonderful act, which helps the child to read and write later over the years.

Past generations have given us some values and a great world to live. It is our minimum responsibility to pass it on to our next generations. A look at the current race and greed we are engrossed in the present-day context makes us to wonder are we really concerned about our next generations that same way (if not better) than our previous generations must have cared for our well-being.

Each country is competing with the other in terms of producing material wealth by producing goods and services, all of which are not morally justified. They feel it as an achievement if the money value of the output they produce each year simply exceed that of the previous year's output. There is no concern or accounting for that happens on a regular basis on how the rising output has damaged the environment, health of people due to air/water quality, displacement of people due to construction of irrigation dams, highways, railroads, airports, special economic zones, etc.

The rising incomes are making people resorting to consumerism, which is having a serious impact on generating unprecedented urban solid waste and its disposal. Use of electronic gadgets (like toys by kids) and discarding them almost each alternate year is also posing serious environmental threat.

Use of motor cars or other vehicles for personal transportation even when we have public transportation is a growing concern, more so in large cities of India. Purchase and use of air-conditioners, refrigerators, washing machines, dishwashers, ovens, geysers, etc. Travelling to many places in the name of recreation without caring for the effects on the air quality. Use of swimming pools inside villas/ farmhouses, paying a premium to housing societies, residential colleges that provide swimming pools, etc.

On social front, with urbanization parenting has become outsourced to childcare centres. There has been disintegration of the erstwhile joint family system. With both husband and wife engrossed in earning and making their careers more valued in national and global job markets, they are ignoring the basic human value of imparting values in the child. Also, in some cases, the parents are encouraging the child to score more marks in the examinations and learn the art of competing in examinations so that they stand to make more money. It in turn helps them to lead a luxury life. However, stress levels are on the increase and the lifestyles are becoming more prone to unhealthy lives.

It is our basic responsibility (like how our predecessors had felt) towards our next generations by preaching them not to make their lives like that of life-less robots but to thoroughly enjoy their lives by helping the underprivileged sections in the society and be accountable to environment.

14.9 KEY WORDS

Industrial Revolution, Environmental Management, Range of Pollution Index, Ozone Depleting Substances, Value of Nature, Protection of Trees. Climate Risk, Green House Gases(GHGs), United Nations Framework Convention on Climate Change (UNFCCC), Sovereign Green Bonds, Decarbonization.

14.10 LET US SUM UP

This unit elaborates various aspects relating to environment and its importance to the life of human beings and other creatures. It deals with evolution of industrialisation and its associated impact on environment, meaning of environmental management, categorization of Indian industries in terms of their levels of pollution, the manner in which sectoral deployment of bank credit takes place in India and some of major environmental concerns. The unit also elaborates upon the climate risk and green financing as well as the associated challenges and opportunities before banks and the regulatory initiatives in the area.

14.11 CHECK YOUR PROGRESS

1. Industrial Revolution is broadly during the phase in which some revolutionary changes had occurred in the manufacturing process of production in the United Kingdom. It refers to:
   (*a*) 1540-1610
   (*b*) 1910-1950
   (*c*) 1820-1870
   (*d*) 1760-1840
2. Environmental managers refer to a wide range of individuals or groups who primarily make decisions about the -----.
   (*a*) Birds
   (*b*) Use of natural resources
   (*c*) Afforestation
   (*d*) Wellbeing of marine life
3. As per the Government of India, the category of *white industries* are:
   (*a*) Moderately polluting industries and necessarily require Environmental Clearance (EC)

(*b*) Practically non-polluting will not require Environmental Clearance (EC)

(*c*) Industrial Sectors having Pollution Index score of 60 and above

(*d*) Industrial Sectors having Pollution Index score of 41-59

4. The Montreal Protocol on Substances that deplete the Ozone Layer –

(*a*) Would become effective in India from 01 January, 2021

(*b*) Came into force in 1989

(*c*) Came into force in 1981

(*d*) Is not applicable to any industries in India and no timeframe is officially set

5. For investments with ozone depleting substances (ODS) technologies:

(*a*) Commercial banks in India are prohibited from financing or re-financing

(*b*) Commercial banks can charge very high interest rates

(*c*) Commercial banks can have a choice to get the proposals vetted by a foreign environment agency

(*d*) Commercial banks are encouraged to lend at highly concessional interest rates, as it is a national priority

6. Which among the following is NOT an environmental concern before India at present?

(*a*) Ground Water Depletion

(*b*) Decline in tiger population

(*c*) Climate Change

(*d*) Loss of Biodiversity

7. Since 2015, National Air Quality Index in India is calculated and reported on a daily basis in select localities of cities and other places with range of values between ------- classified into 6 categories.

(*a*) 0-100

(*b*) 0 and 500

(*c*) 0-600

(*d*) 1-360

8. The estimated the economic value of a healthy tree with respect to its oxygen capacity is at about Rs. ------- per year

(*a*) 5

(*b*) 24

(*c*) 40

(*d*) 74

ANSWERS

1. (*d*)	2. (*b*)	3. (*b*)	4. (*b*)	5. (*a*)	6. (*b*)	7. (*b*)	8. (*b*)

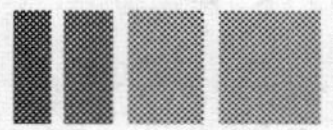

14.12 EXERCISE YOUR ETHICS MUSCLE

Case 34: Environment or Profit?

A global company has approached X Bank to finance a large project to develop an enterprise park and other facilities including one recreational hub in a rural population center. The project will generate many jobs and good amount of trade. As a result, the area will prosper. However, at the same time, the project will destroy a large section of a rainforest and require the relocation of the inhabitants of several nearby villages. There will be an adverse effect on biodiversity. Three banks have already rejected the loan request. Your bank's credit growth has been tardy this year and the said loan looks like a boon helping achieve the business goals and boost profitability. You are heading the loans division of the bank and have to decide whether to lend or not to lend.

Issues to reflect:

(*a*) Is it profitable?

(*b*) Is it legal?

(*c*) Is it fair?

(*d*) Is it right?

(*e*) Is it sustainable?

Pl. add one additional information to the scenario – 'Your CEO is favourably inclined for the loan.'

Issues to reflect:

(*a*) If you say 'Yes' for the loan, it would be good for the bank & your CEO will be happy but would that be an ethical decision?

(*b*) If you decline the loan, credit budget will not be achieved & your bank's profitability will suffer severely. Your CEO will also be unhappy with you. Would that be wise to do so?

(*c*) What is the right thing to do in the situation?

Case 35: The Bhopal Disaster

On December 3, 1984, 40 tons of toxic methyl isocyanate (MIC) gas, a chemical used in pesticides, leaked from a Union Carbide facility in Bhopal, a highly populated city, Bhopal, India. The gas killed at least 3,000 people immediately and thousands later. The gas injured thousands more and created a toxic waste dump in the heart of the city where the 11-acre plant was. More than 5,00,000 people were declared affected by the gas leak and were given an average compensation of $550. In addition, about 7,000 animals were injured, of which about one thousand were killed. The gas leaked from 30-metre-high chimney and this height was not enough to reduce the effects of the discharge. The reason was that the high moisture content (aerosol) in the discharge when evaporating, gave risk to heavy gas which rapidly rank sank to the ground. The chairman of Union Carbide at the time, Warren Anderson, was arrested while he was in India but posted bail and fled India, never to return. He has retired and lives comfortably on Long Island, New York. India had demanded $3.3 billion in damages, but Union Carbon refused to pay that amount. In 1989, Union Carbide agreed to pay a $470 million settlement for damages that were caused to the local residents. Union Carbide abandoned the facility without cleaning up all the toxic material. Hundreds of tons of toxic waste were located within the facility and seeping into the nearby soil and water table. Dow Chemical bought Union Carbide in 2001 and claims no responsibility because it did not cause the leak. A Dow Chemical spokesperson stated, "As there was never any

ownership, there is no responsibility and no liability—for the Bhopal tragedy or its aftermath." Dow argued that the property had been turned over to the Madhya Pradesh State government in June 1998. In 2010, eight former senior officials from Union Carbide India were finally convicted of negligence and were sentenced to two years in jail and fined $2,100. One of the defendants died before the sentencing took place. Some experts in industrial safety believe that the tragedy was preventable and it was due to the negligence on the part of the union carbide corporation and its corporate subsidiary union carbide of India Ltd., which had the responsibility for taking care of the day-to-day operations of the facility. Bhopal gas tragedy was one of the worst industrial disasters in history.

Issues to reflect

1. Examine the case from the aspects of environmental ethics.
2. Why has the U.S. government not extradited former Union Carbide Chairman Warren Anderson to face his charges in India?
3. How would Union Carbide's reaction to the gas leak be different if the plant was located in the United States?
4. Do you think a payment of $550 is fair for the victims of the disaster?
5. Had the tragedy been occurred in 2022, whether the corporate reaction would have been different?

Case 36: Steps to Sustainability

As you say life flows. You stagnate, if not moving. I got posted as an R.M. to one of the RBO's. Nice set up. Great potential. And a trajectory upwards. While going through the monthly reports, particularly, establishment charges, seemed high. And had been growing month on month. Thinking "can these be curtailed". A knock. "Come in", My manger HR. "Sir, a new CM has reported, shall I send him in". "Yes". His name was Rajat. "So Rajat, please have a seat". And then on a cup of coffee I chatted with him. Prior assignment, family, general background. Then I said "Top line is good. Bottom line seems fine. I feel, establishment charges need to be better managed. Work out a strategy, implement, let me know the results, one month from now". Rajat smiled and said, "I would do my best sir".

Month passed. Latest report on my table. Charges down by 15%. Called my secretary. "It appears there is an error. 15% down? Call Rajat. "He is actually waiting for you. I will send him in". She left ushering Rajat in. "Are the figures correct?" I questioned. "Yes, Sir, till the last decimal". He responded, "If that is the case, my congratulations. I'm impressed, How". "Sir", said Rajat "I had my share of experiences, my collation and solution of the same was through "STEPS". S – Share – Resources: A networked printer can be shared. Why buy 2, if one can suffice. T - Technology- Leverage: several reprints can be avoided if a note can be vetted by all concerned in soft form. One print, final print. E- Energy- Conserve: Am I as responsible in conserving the electricity bill of my office as I am at home. P- Paper-Save: A rim lasts twice, if printed both sides. S-Sensitize-Colleagues: I share, how I save, even if I empower one of my colleagues, my contribution is doubled for a sustainable future.

Sir, with this vision I STEPPED. Had meetings. Small groups. In RBO. In Branches. Tried to home in the point. Your efforts will contribute way beyond your official commitments. It's the STEPS we take for a clean and green future, for our kids and us". I congratulated Rajat. Good work. Patted him. He left. Called for another cup of coffee.

A Knock. "Come in" I said. I saw Aristotle standing in front of me." Well, my friend is here. Strange." Exiting from my inner space, beaming ear to ear, I stood up and said "Welcome Sir. Usually you leave a story, today I will tell". When I , Aristotle, smiling, pulled up smart phone down from his tunic. "Well, when here, in your times, I need to keep it, a nice device. Can see my history by googling". He punched some keys. My cell beeped. A WhatsApp message. There was a you tube link. "Please view it" said Aristotle. I did. It was a video by a small girl. A garden. She was speaking to plants, flowers, grass & trees. Thanking them and telling of the small acts that can help protect them. With a surprise I looked at Aristotle. He said "That's Rajat's daughter. Trying to play the role as your green champion. At times, when home, his daughter used to ask "How was your day, papa. What did you do?". Then on dinner he used to explain to her, in simple words how he was meeting his colleagues. Asking them to save paper, electricity etc. "Why papa?" she always asked. And he enjoyed explaining further. His daughter started liking the green conversations. She started, in her own small expressions, writing stories, drawings etc. on the theme of a clean and green world. Hey Dear, the kids now are tech savvy. She

started trying her hands on making a video. Some dummy runs. And uploaded on the you tube. It was decently viewed, recommended and the principal of her school also happened to see it. My friend, today, in the Annual Function at her school, she was felicitated and the video shown to all students".

Looking down to my Apple, I said "Yes, sir, I got your point." I turned my head up. Aristotle was gone.

Master of Ethics. He came to make me realize the twin sides of an ethical value. I intended to control my charges account. A small goal. Yet, this small act could be so big in its manifold dimensions, I had never realized. How many more of my colleagues would have started sharing with their families, their small STEPS. Creating awareness amongst their near and dear ones for a green and sustainable future. Truly, individually, we are one drop. Together, we are an ocean.

I called Rajat. Congratulated again. Taken aback, he asked "Sir, you had already done that." "Well, this one is for your little green champ. Let's go for a cup of coffee." Walking down the stairs, I could sense the sweet music of STEPS. Essence is your ethics is omnipresent. It does not differentiate an office from a home. Good values percolate everywhere.

(Courtesy SBI: this is one of the blogs written under the title" Coffee with Aristotle' by the Bank's then Chief Ethics Officer in 2020)

Issues to Reflect:

(*a*) Did you enjoy reading this blog? Will you do the same in your area of work?

(*b*) What is your opinion about this case-story?

(*c*) Don't you think that we need more green champs like the daughter of Rajat around us?

15 UNIT

Ethics and Globalization

15 UNIT

Ethics and Globalization

15.1 LEARNING OBJECTIVES

This unit will explain the concept of globalization and some of the ethical challenges associated with it including the challenge of ethical diversity. The unit will specifically enable one to understand:

- Role and contribution of Multinational Corporations (MNCs)
- Some of the ethical compromises MNCs are responsible for
- The ethical challenge of diversity
- The role of good governance in globalization
- Global compact & SDGs
- A business case for global ethics

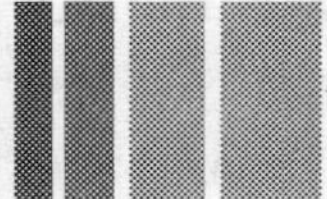

15.2 GLOBALISATION: GROWTH & ROLE OF MULTINATIONAL CORPORATIONS

Globalization is a process that is bringing societies that were previously economically, politically and culturally diverse into convergence. This is being achieved by a combination of interaction and integration among people, companies, and governments worldwide through trade, goods and services, data & technology and the economic resources of capital. It is like the threads of an immense spider web formed over millennia, with the number and reach of these threads increasing over time. It is a multi-dimensional process transforming trade, finance, employment, migration, technology, communications, the environment, social systems, ways of living, cultures and patterns of governance. A World Bank publication defines globalization as 'the growing integration of economies and societies around the world, a complex process integrating not just the economy but culture, technology and governance.'

As a result of globalization, people today inhabit a global society which is knit together by free trade, international travel, immigration, satellite communication systems and the Internet. This process of integration has been super accelerated by the increasing dominance of large global corporations or multi-national corporations (MNCs). This is true in case of all spheres of business including manufacturing, Information Technology, Banking, Insurance and other financial segments. Almost all the businesses in the present global society are carried on by these multinational or transnational corporations, most of which are based in the developed countries. 'Multinational corporations' or MNCs, are business entities that operate in more than one country but face many of the same issues as domestic companies such as maximizing profits, meeting customer demands and adapting to technological change.

In the global society, ethical responsibilities surpass the national boundaries. Decisions about raw materials, manufacturing, outsourcing, farm subsidies, investments, marketing, suppliers, safety standards and energy use made in one country have ramifications for residents of other parts of the world. According to one observer, globalization is "driven by a near-universal push toward trade and capital market liberalization, increasing internationalization of corporate production and distribution strategies and technological change that is fast eroding barriers to the international tradability of goods and services and the mobility of capital, which means a convergence of moral values and in general ethical behaviour" (Zekos 2004, p. 633).

The big winners in globalization are multinational corporations. According to one estimate, 44 of the world's 100 largest economies are corporations. Royal Dutch Shell, for example, has revenues that exceed the gross domestic product of 171 countries. Wal-Mart with over $485 billion in revenue tops the Fortune 500 list with other companies like Berkshire Hathaway, Apple, ExxonMobil, etc. taking other top positions. Banks like Bank of America Corp., Citigroup, Bank of New York Mellon, Sun Trust Banks, etc. also find their place in this list. The multinational enterprise has always been the central figure in the evolution and expansion of globalization. Throughout history, multinational corporations have helped states to exploit their economic resources and become more competitive within the global economy. We all are familiar with the brands like Philips or

Murphy since our childhood. Philips is a Dutch global major and the consumer durables company while Murphy Radio is a British company. These corporations have greatly enhanced social welfare by introducing products and services throughout the world, providing access to worldwide markets, increasing broad access to capital, creating jobs, encouraging local supply chains and transferring advanced technologies. However, empirical data has shown that globalization has exacerbated global inequalities, thereby making the rich become richer and the poor become poorer. In practice, this has meant a concentration of global wealth and power into the hands of the wealthier nations. Some multinationals have pursued free trade at the cost of human rights and environment.

Globalization has also resulted in the increased consumption of non-renewable energy sources, which in turn has increased GHG emissions. Goods are currently travelling to further places, causing an increase in fuel consumption and thereby, GHG emissions for that travel. In addition, the increased demand for products has caused an increase in the number of factories which burn fossil fuels to produce these products, which also increases GHG emissions. Increased GHG results in global warming and ultimately, climate change. The clearing of land for the building of bridges and roads for transportation as well as to accommodate more agricultural and industrial production to meet growing global demand due to globalization has contributed to the global loss of many habitats. In addition, the increase in the number of ships at sea has increased the number of oil spills, which degrade marine habitats. Closely related to habitat destruction is deforestation, more and more tracts of forests are being removed to meet increasing global needs. Deforestation has many widespread environmental implications, including but not limited to contributing to global warming, increased flooding and increased land degradation. The provision of cheap, skilled labour in the developing world puts a lot of persons in the developed world at risk of losing their jobs due to labour outsourcing. Moreover, the need for increased production has resulted in the exploitation of people in sweatshops as well as the use of child labour.

Further, Globalization increases potentiality of global recessions. When many nations' economic systems become interdependent, the likelihood of a global recession increases dramatically-because if one country's economy starts to struggle, this can set off a chain reaction that can affect many other countries simultaneously, causing a worldwide financial crisis as we have recently witnessed after the fall of Silicon Valley and Signature banks in US and Credit Suisse in Switzerland.

However, MNCs are gradually developing geocentric perspective into the very fiber of the business organization to remain competitive in the modern economy. With different socio-economic and political environment, legal framework, institutional set-up, fiscal, monetary and commercial policies, factor endowments, production techniques, nature of products and consumption habits, these companies are not only trying to acclimatize themselves to the existing realities of each of these countries, but also getting prepared to fine-tune their policies and business strategies to the fast-moving changes that occur in these dynamic societies.

The benefits of living in a global economy are also obvious: lower labour costs, higher sales and profits, cheaper goods & services, instant communication to anywhere on earth, increased information flow and cross-cultural contact. At the same time, there is a growing divide between the haves and have-nots. The richest 10% of the global population controls over 855 of the world's assets and income, with the top 10% controlling 46% of the wealth. Four years ago, the Economist published an article under the heading of 'Reinventing Globalization' and used the term 'slowbalisation' to describe the fragile state of international trade and commerce. After the 1990s and 2000s, the pace of economic integration stalled in the 2010s, as firms grappled with the aftershocks of a financial crisis and President Donald Trump's trade war. The flow of goods and capital stagnated. Many bosses postponed big decisions on investing abroad. The juggernaut of globalization faced speed breaker.

However, at present, the situation has improved, as the pandemic and war in Ukraine have triggered a once in a generation reimagining of global capitalism. Everywhere you look, supply chains are being transformed. From the $9trn in inventories, stockpiled as insurance against shortages and inflation, to the fight for workers, as global firms shift from China into Vietnam. After the Berlin war fell in 1989, the lodestar of globalization was efficiency. Companies located production where cost were the lowest, while investors deployed capital where returns were the highest. Governments aspired to treat firms equally, regardless of the nationality and to strike trade deals with democracies and autocracies alike. Over two decades, this gave rise to dazzlingly sophisticated value chains that account for half of all trade. Your car and phone contained components that are better travelled than Phileas Fogg. All these kept prices low for consumers and

helped lift 1bn people out of extreme poverty as the emerging world including China, industrialized.

Ritzer (1993) in his book 'The McDonaldization of Society' took the global success of McDonald's as an example of the growth of a common, worldwide, mass culture. Ritzer argued that the process of McDonaldisation represents the expansion of instrumental rationality–a drive for efficiency, predictability, calculability and control–with no questioning of the ends being sought. A new kind of globalization is taking shape in the world today which focuses on security, not efficiency: which prioritizes doing business with people you can rely on, in countries your government is friendly with. If firms and politicians show will and restraint, the reimagining of the globalization process could change the world economy for the better, keeping the benefits of openness while improving resilience and thereby addressing the ethical questions surrounding the cultural and social aspects of the McDonaldisation, if we may use the term as a metaphor.

15.3 DOING BUSINESS IN A DIVERSE WORLD : GLOBALISATION AND THE ETHICAL CHALLENGE OF DIVERSITY

Globalisation and the Challenge of Ethical Diversity:

The biggest challenge that comes from globalization is the challenge of ethical diversity. Nations, tribes, ethnic groups and religions approach moral dilemmas differently. What members of one group accept as right may rise serious ethical concerns for another. For example, in Germany contracts are highly detailed and strictly enforced. In Egypt, contract spell guidelines for business deals rather than the specific requirements. Egyptians expect to renegotiate and revise contracts, and there is no moral stigma attached to violating a signed agreement. In Mexico, honouring a contract is based on the signer's personal ethics. There is little legal recourse of the contract is violated.

Bribery offers another instance of conflicting moral standards. In South American countries, it is nearly impossible to move goods through customs without making small payment to cut through the red tape. At the other extreme, Malaysia, executes corporate officials who offer and accept bribes. U.S. corporations and foreign firms listed on U.S. stock exchanges are prevented from exchanging money or goods for favours or services under Foreign Corrupt Practices Act,

1977. However, in recognition of the fact that petty bribery is common in some parts of the world, small payments to facilitate travel and business are permitted under the statute. Cultures also clash over the intellectual property rights (which are strictly enforced in the West but not protected in parts of Southeast Asia) and deception (Americans lie to protect their privacy, whereas Mexicans are more likely to lie the protect the group or family).

Coming to Grips with Ethical Diversity

The challenges which arise from the globalization on account of ethical diversity can put unwanted pressures on the ethical decision-making as the workplaces are becoming more globalized. If an organization is just concerned about making or expanding its business and finds the situation as business as usual, it fails to see the possible negative consequences of their choices in a global environment. Experience shows that few leaders encounter the challenge of ethical diversity by behaving as ethical imperialists and by imposing their personal moral standards across the organization despite the fact that the organization is spread around different countries and cultures. Sometimes, they also decide to go for cultural relativism by following local customs in different countries where they have offices.

Whatever may be the case, the managers who are working with a diverse group of workers coming from different cultures need to be more conscious of cross-cultural issues. It would be more successful for leaders to provide standards that are representative of local practices rather than blindly enforcing a set of organizational standards across multinational organizations. However, it is to be kept in mind that just because a culture has adopted a practice doesn't make it right and ethical deliberation is to be employed before making any decision. Cultural diversity has an upside as well that the organizations can gain the benefit of having different perspectives and new insights. However, it needs to be ensured that the organization is mindful of each employee's culture and background and does not exhibit any sort of discrimination by focusing only on the majority group through their policies and standards.

The globalization of economy and the resultant ethical diversity have made it necessary for the bankers to develop 'cross-cultural ethical competence'. At a personal level, this can be done by getting rid of the attitude of ethnocentrism and considering to think in terms of a broader framework of the world as a community or society. As Gudykunst and Kim have explained that it would

be impossible to develop the required cross cultural ethical competence without a conscious effort to avoid ethnocentrism or the view that our customs and values are the standard by which the rest of the world is to be judged. At a managerial level, it is to be appreciated with a pluralistic perspective that what are the value orientations of varying cultural groups and how these patterns influence ethical decision-making in the organization while resolving conflict between competing ethical practices.

Adoption of universal moral principles that govern behaviour in every cultural setting can work like a light house here. In this connection, philosopher and theologian Michael Novak identifies four cardinal virtues essential to encouraging global cooperation: cultural humility, truth, dignity and solidarity. All these qualities have their basis in the personal ethics and, therefore, a strong degree of personal ethics is critical for meeting the challenge of ethical diversity.

Other Ethical Challenges of Globalization

Apart from ethical diversity, other ethical challenges broadly pertain to use of child labour, human rights, environment, rising inequality, safety standards, insensitiveness to local culture, bribery, etc. The following case study gives us some perspective on how the MNCs are indifferent towards the abuse of child labour in the plantations owned by their key suppliers for years.

Child Labour in Chocolate Industry

Multinationals of chocolate industry from Germany, France and Belgium that include Nestle, Mars, Kraft Foods Group (Kraft Heinz), Cargill, ADM and Barry Callebaut are alleged to be involved or are encouraging indirectly child labour and thereby slavery in cocoa plantations from impoverished countries of Africa like Mali, Niger, Burkina Faso, Ivory Coast, Nigeria, Ghana, etc. Despite all these, popular MNCs of the global chocolate industry having their offices in Ivory Coast for decades now, officials from their headquarters reply in a video interview (shot in year 2012 undercover due to risks of being attacked) that they are not simply aware of any such child labour issues, since they do not hire the workers and the cocoa plantations are not owned by the chocolate companies directly. None of these companies' boards has ever asked their CEOs even for any explanation on this issue let alone sacking.

A senior official from International Labour Organization (ILO), Geneva, Switzerland, merely expresses their "helplessness" at the whole issue. Interpol has acknowledged to have rescued over 100 child labourers in one of its recent operations in Africa's cocoa plantations.

In this backdrop, please answer the following questions within the framework of corporate governance:

(*a*) Do MNCs adequately display their commitment to business ethics and exhibit regard to the social values?

(*b*) Simply by outsourcing the supplies of the vital cocoa beans/power to third parties, can the large companies absolve from this crime of encouraging child labour?

(*c*) Can you rate the functioning of the Boards of the above six corporate firms so long as they show healthy top and bottom lines only without any accountability to such grave social issue?

(*d*) By merely displaying some highly appealing codes and convincing sets of principles on the official web sites, do you feel these companies have been showing an utter disregard to the spirit of good governance? Justify your answer.

Shell & Human Rights Violations in Nigeria

Nigeria became politically independent from Britain in 1961. It was believed in the early years of Nigeria becoming an independent country that given rich natural resources, the country would prosper under the self-rule and could turn out to become engine of economic growth for the entire Africa. Since 1958, Royal Dutch Shell, a Multinational Company in the oil, has been having its business interests in this country, when its exploration struck oil reserves in the Ogoni region inhabited with tribal community. There have been allegations that Shell had funded the militant organizations, which was denied by the company.

- Ogoni is a 5-lakh member ethnic group in Nigeria mostly farmers and fishermen. Shell was accused of degrading their lands. The Ogoni was campaigning against Nigeria's military rule and against the Royal Dutch/ Shell. Shell has been pumping oil from Ogoni lands since late 1950s. It extracted US$ 30 bn of oil since then.

- Four Ogoni chiefs who advocated cooperation with the Nigeria's military rule were lynched by a mob of Ogoni. Saro-Wiwa was not present in the attack, but was awarded death penalty.

- In 1995, Military Tribunal in Nigeria (sham trial) ordered execution of noted author and playwright Ken Saro-Wiwa and eight others. Despite international pressure for clemency, execution took place on November 10, 1995.
- This incident made some soul-searching for Shell about social and environmental responsibilities for an MNC. 52-member British Commonwealth suspended Nigeria and warned it would expel if democracy is not restored. EU suspended all aid to Nigeria. Britain banned arms sale to Nigeria. No country had halted purchase of Nigerian oil. US purchases 40% of Nigeria's oil and did not resort to embargo. Shell announced it would "delay" LNG project, as the project might fail if announced soon after the Saro-Wiwa's execution.
- 1996, Center for Constitutional Rights filed a federal lawsuit in US District Court in Manhattan. Shell was accused of being a part of conspiracy that led to execution of Saro-Wiwa. Shell denied all allegations. A resolution for independent external body to monitor Human Right policies, Shell's shareholders rejected by 10 to 1. Shell was also a part of the UN Universal declaration of Human Rights for human rights, and SHE (safety, health and environment).

As per a 76-pages Report published by Platform, a famous London-based NGO published in 2011,

"Shell's close relationship with the Nigerian military exposes the company to charges of complicity in the systematic killing and torture of local residents.

Testimony and contracts seen by Platform (NGO) implicate Shell in regularly assisting armed militants with lucrative payments. In one case from 2010, Shell is alleged to have transferred over $1,59,000 to a group credibly linked to militia violence.

Shell's poor community engagement has provided the "catalyst" for major disruption, including one incident that shut down a third of Shell's daily oil production in August 2011.

In the absence of proper supervision and controls, Shell contractors, including multinationals like Halliburton, Daewoo and Saipem, have replicated many of Shell's mistakes".

Notwithstanding the above-mentioned challenges, globalization has many positive aspects. Yet, it could have been more beneficial, if it were more ethical, as the millennium declaration of the heads of states said, that globalization should work for all the world's people. Former President of Ireland and former United Nations High Commissioner for Human Rights Mary Robinson has formed a platform the Ethical Globalization Initiative, that seeks to integrate human rights norms and standards into a more ethical globalization process and to support local and national human rights using the New Partnership for Africa's Development (NEPAD)as a case study.

15.4 COSMOPOLITANISM: A WAY TO MEET THE CHALLENGES OF GLOBALIZATION

Cosmopolitanism means that all human beings are members of a single community. It is both prescriptive and aspirational, believing that humans can and should be 'world citizens' in a 'universal community'. The idea encompasses different dimensions and avenues of community, such as promoting universal moral standards, establishing global political structures, or developing a platform for mutual cultural expression and tolerance. There is a school of thought that propagates that cosmopolitanism is the best remedy to address the challenge of globalization.

Cosmopolitanism posits a humanistic approach to globalization based on the fundamental premise that every human being has dignity and value regardless of their location, status or background. Thus, it is a moral obligation to have care or empathy for the members of other communities. Kwame Anthony Appiah articulates a cosmopolitan community where individuals from varying locations (physical, economic, etc.) enter into relationships of mutual respect despite their differing beliefs (political, religious, or cultural, etc.). Cosmopolitanism is a highly ethical construct and offers a normative framework for living ethically in a globalized world.

15.5 GLOBALIZATION AND INDIA

Post-globalization, India's rise has certainly been impressive, and warrants the attention that it has commanded. India has been one of the world's best-performing economies for a quarter of a century, lifting millions out of poverty and becoming the world's third-largest economy in PPP terms. India has tripled its defense expenditure over the last decade to become one of the top-ten military spenders. And in stark contrast to Asia's other billion-person emerging power, India has simultaneously cultivated an attractive global image of social and cultural dynamism. Recently, India has overtaken UK in the list of economic rankings of the world. This is evidence that Indian economy is rapidly rising and as RBI has stated that "India is set to be USD 3.7 trillion economy in the year 2023." Morgan Stanley, one of the most influential companies of the world, said last year that three megatrends- global offshoring, digitalization and energy transition — are setting the scene for India's unprecedented economic growth. "We believe India is set to surpass Japan and Germany to become the world's third-largest economy by 2027 and will have the third-largest stock market by the end of this decade. Morgan and Stanley reckon that India's GDP could more than double from $3.5 trillion today to surpass $7.5 trillion by 2031. India's per capita income is projected to rise from $2,000 now to about $5,000 by then.

Post independence, India remained predominantly an inward-looking economy. Due to the bitter experience of the East India Company's entry and subsequently becoming a British colony led our policy-makers to design national economic, investment and trade policies in such a way that it became too hard for the domestic companies to tie-up with foreign counterparts as well as those policies made entry of foreign firms into India almost impossible. This scenario, by and large, continued for about 40 years during 1951 and 1991. However, in the year 1991, globalization started in India with the suggestion of International Monetary Fund (IMF) with the launch of a series of reforms by the Government of India which include sweeping policy changes in industry, trade, banking, insurance, civil aviation, construction, telecommunication, etc. As part of the Industrial Policy announced on July 24, 1991, the Industry Ministry of Government of India announced that "Government have decided to take a series of initiatives in respect of the policies relating to the following areas:

A. Industrial Licensing

B. Foreign Investment

C. Foreign Technology Agreement

D. Public Sector Policy

E. MRTP Act

The much-controlled licensing system was done away with. Some of those which still required licensing included coal and lignite, petroleum and its distillation, brewing of alcoholic drinks, sugar, cigars and other tobacco products, etc. As regards foreign investment, government felt the need to allow liberally foreign direct investments into select priority sectors. These sectors needed besides investments in large amounts latest technology which was not available in India. The Government decided to approve foreign direct investment up to 51% foreign equity in such industries. Government also announced automatic approval of technology agreements relating to high priority industries by doing away delays associated earlier with bureaucratic clearances.

Consequently, there was a massive influx of both foreign capital investment and companies offshoring in India, particularly chemical, pharmaceutical manufacturing and petroleum industries. Advanced kind of technologies and processes helped modernize the Indian industrial sector. India is an agrarian economy, with the majority of the population depended on it. With globalization, the technological capabilities of farmers increased and gave a boost to exports from India. Outsourcing has been a principal result of globalization and has increased because of the increase in the quick forms of communication especially the growth of the IT sector. Many services such as voice-based business processes, accountancy, etc. are being outsourced by companies from advanced countries to India.

Globalization has had a significant impact on Indian society, particularly in terms of social and demographic changes. One of the most significant changes has been the rise of urbanization. As the economy has grown, many people have migrated from rural areas to cities in search of better opportunities. This has led to the growth of cities such as Mumbai, Delhi and Bangalore, which are now home to millions of people. However, urbanization has also brought with it a range of social challenges.

The rapid growth of cities has led to overcrowding, pollution and inadequate infrastructure, such as housing and transportation. In addition, urbanization has contributed to the breakdown of traditional social structures, as people move away from their rural communities and traditional ways of life. Globalization has also had a significant impact on gender relations in India. As more women have entered the workforce, their role in society has changed. Women are now more likely to be educated and employed, which has increased their economic

independence and social status. However, gender inequality remains a significant challenge in India, particularly in rural areas, where women's rights are often neglected.

Globalization has had a significant impact on Indian culture, both positive and negative. On the one hand, the exchange of ideas and cultural practices has enriched Indian culture. For example, the influence of Western music, fashion and cinema has led to the emergence of new cultural forms that are unique to India. On the other hand, globalization has also led to the erosion of traditional cultural practices. As people have migrated to cities and adopted Western lifestyles, traditional practices such as dress, language and religion have been replaced. In addition, the spread of Western media has led to a decline in the popularity of traditional art forms such as classical music and dance.

The literacy level became high and foreign universities started collaborating with different Indian Universities and Indian educational system embraced globalization through Information Technology and other opportunities to evolve education. Globalization promoted new tools and techniques like E-learning, flexible learning, distance education program and overseas training. Government policies like the "New Education Policy" are pushing for a more global education system.

Globalization has a dramatic impact on India's economic conditions and today India has a GDP growth of around 7% per year. Globalization has also led emergence of a new middle class in India with improved purchasing power. This has led to an increase in demand for goods and services such as automobiles, electronics, entertainment, etc., and that has resulted in the multinational corporations targeting the Indian market leading to the establishment of many foreign-owned businesses in the country. Despite the global turmoil as a result of dual shocks emerging from COVID and the Ukraine-Russia war, the long-term growth story of India has remained the only bright spot in the dismal global growth scenario.

According to the World Bank, India's economy is relatively insulated from global spillovers compared to other emerging markets. This is partly because India has a large domestic market and is relatively less exposed to international trade flows. India's economy has been remarkably resilient to the deteriorating external environment and strong macroeconomic fundamentals have placed it in good stead compared to other emerging market economies. During the year

2021-22, FDI inflow have reached an all-time high at almost USD 85 billion. Economic rise is key to global power. That rise in India's case seems almost certain, although with few caveats. Nevertheless, India has assumed the presidency of G20 and Shanghai Cooperation Organization this year. It provides the nation with a unique opportunity to traverse the changing contours of globalization while being one of the strongest voices for the Global south in recent times.

To conclude, although globalization has had a profound effect on Indian society in terms of increased economic growth, more urbanization, demographic changes, cultural practices, access to technology etc., there have also been a few negative consequences such as increased inequality, environmental degradation etc. It is up to policymakers in India to navigate these changes and ensure that the benefits of globalization are distributed fairly across the population.

15.6 GLOBALIZATION, ETHICS & GOOD GOVERNANCE

The increasing influence of international financial institutions is one of the major aspects of globalization. Financial institutions such as the World Bank and the International Monetary Fund (IMF) play a major role in the economic development of developing countries. However, the financial institutions, who have been pressing for good governance, are concerned that despite the significant aid to the developing countries, many of the recipient countries are not achieving expected level of economic development because of poor governance. The World Bank has developed Worldwide Governance Indicators (WGI) to measure good governance. Faced by budget deficits and a scarcity of resources, governments around the world are also under increasing pressure to improve governance. Good governance, however, is possible only when local public services are provided for citizens in an ethical environment. Another school of thought insists on the quality of government for achieving the desired developmental outcomes. Regardless of controversy over the terms being used, the advocates of good governance and the quality of government both assert that public service ethics is a crucial element of governance. Without ethics, the search for good governance is fruitless.

Undoubtedly, globalization has opened up opportunities for development and growth and provided opportunities for multinational corporations to locate their businesses outside their countries, especially in the developing countries, which do not have strict enforcement of laws regulating business, labour and the environment. Furthermore, many developing countries characterized by a high level of corruption allow multinational corporations to bypass laws through the payments of bribes or tax sweeteners. Therefore, as H.A. KHAN explains, one of the major challenges for the developed countries is 'how to enforce laws on the companies, which are located beyond their borders. The challenge for developing countries, by contrast, is to enforce laws without discouraging investment in their countries. There is thus a "race to the bottom" among the developing countries in terms of the enforcement of business, labour and environmental regulations since stricter laws can deter potential investors. Therefore, developing countries must balance economic interest and the protection of labour and environmental interests.' Although labour and environmental degradation can lead to long-term problems, developing countries especially feel the urgency to solve the economic problems of unemployment and poverty. Within this context, the challenge is to establish ethics and accountability frameworks, which could promote quality governance to counteract such systemic issues. Environmentally also, weak enforcement of regulations relating to natural resources and damage to natural resources can have a devastating effect on the welfare of the countries.

Public administrators who have to make a constant stream of decisions involving significant expenditure and affecting a large number of people need ways for ethical decision making that acknowledges the inherent pressures involved in the decision-making during a fluid time of change. In an article 'Grass-Roots Anti-Corruption Drive Puts Heat on Mexican Lawmakers' (published in the New York Times), Semple, K. writes that "corruption is so woven into daily life in Mexico that it has been enshrined in a common saying: *"El que no trans, no avanza"*— "He who doesn't cheat doesn't get ahead". In May 2016, the civil society organizations in Mexico proposed an initiative called *d "3 de 3"*-or "3 out of 3". It required government officials to reveal their assets and potential conflicts of interest and to provide the documentation on the payment of their taxes. The group collected more than 6,30,000 signatures." According to Juan E. Pardinas the Managing Director of the Mexican Institute for Competitiveness, a research group that has helped to lead the citizens' push for the initiative, "The worst problems and challenges faced by Mexico are directly caused or aggravated by corruption".

It is obvious that with the rise of globalization and the attendant challenges, there is a greater need for moral leadership in the world. Moral leadership demands solutions to the severe and complex problems faced by the world: hunger, poverty, terrorism, drug, human trafficking, income inequality, health care, discrimination and environmental degradation. Globalization has led to an understanding and realization of the common problems that people in the world face and which requires cooperation among all the people of the world. Globalization must be considered from the point of an improvement in the quality of life for the people. Though the multinational corporations earlier used to have no clear sense of responsibility to the societies, cultures, and individuals they encountered in the course of their international ventures, but in recent times, after the pandemic, they have clearly understood that if they are involved in the production and distribution of goods and services for a worldwide market, should not only live by and exhibit the principles of ethical principles and good corporate governance practices, but also should be seen practicing them. No corporation that is found to be unethical and wanting in terms of corporate governance will have a future. Good governance, however, bequeaths the moral responsibility of the welfare of the people on the local leadership as well at various levels of public service who are honest in performing the tasks assigned to them for the welfare of the general public rather than benefiting personally from their position of power.

15.7 GLOBAL COMPACT AND INDIA

Global Compact of the United Nations is a voluntary initiative based on CEO commitments to implement universal sustainability principles and to take steps to support UN goals. With the support of business and other stakeholders, the UN Global Compact's governance framework was adopted by then UN Secretary-General Annan on 12 August, 2005.

The UN Global Compact's General Assembly mandate is to "promote responsible business practices and UN values among the global business community and the UN System." It has four segments to interact with one another- Public (General Assembly: government group, group of friends), Private (leaders' summit: Issue platform, working groups), Local (local networks as part of the

annual local network forum) and Global (global compact headquarters: UN Office, Foundation).

Sustainable Development Goals (SDGs): With the goal of achieving a better future for all, all 193 member nations of the United Nations adopted a plan in September 2015, a transformative agenda, the 2030 agenda for sustainable development. This involves ending extreme poverty, fight inequality and injustice, and protect our planet. At the heart of "Agenda 2030" are the 17 Sustainable Development Goals (SDGs) which clearly define the world we want-applying to all nations and leaving no one behind.

Ten Principles of UN Global Compact

The UN Global Compact emphasizes that corporate sustainability begins with company's value system and its approach based on principles. It believes that business must follow their responsibilities towards human rights, labour, environmental and anti-corruption.

Human Rights

1. Businesses should support and respect the protection of internationally proclaimed human rights.
2. Make sure that they are not complicit in human rights abuses.

Labour

Businesses should uphold:

3. the freedom of association and the effective recognition of the right to collective bargaining.
4. the elimination of all forms of forced and compulsory labour.
5. the effective abolition of child labour.
6. the elimination of discrimination in respect of employment and occupation.

Environment

Businesses should:

7. support a precautionary approach to environmental challenges.
8. undertake initiatives to promote greater environmental responsibility.
9. encourage the development and diffusion of environmentally friendly technologies.

Anti-corruption

10. Businesses should work against corruption in all its forms, including extortion and bribery.

    (*Source:* Content is sourced from the website https://www.unglobalcompact.org/take-action)

Progress in India

About 275 local businesses have joined this voluntary movement in India that include small and medium enterprises, companies, academic bodies, foundations, etc.

In the Indian context, a tri-annual news publication titled Nutshell is carried out by Global Compact Network India (GCNI).

Global Compact Society (GCS) was founded in December 2000. It has achieved several milestones over the past 17 years including organizing jointly a conclave in collaboration with Tata Steel and CII in 2005 at Jamshedpur, Asia Pacific Regional Conclave in 2010 at New Delhi. GCS has become Global Compact Network India in July 2011. In December 2016, GCNI partnered with the Government of Assam for advancing Sustainable Development Goals in Assam.

GCNI has carried out three major initiatives so far:

1. Collective Action Project
2. India CEO Forum
3. Women Empowerment Principle

A brief description of these initiatives is given below:

Collective Action Project

In January 2011, GCNI commenced with the Collective Action Project in India. The UNGC Collective Action Project was launched in five countries, Nigeria, South Africa, Brazil, Egypt and India. The Collective Action Project (CAP) India aims to develop a collective action platform, with a unique focus anti-corruption intervention and ethical governance. The project is supported by the Siemens Integrity Initiative Funds.

Project Objectives

- Address the economic implications of corruption
- Explore how leading companies tackle ethical dilemmas concerning environmental sustainability.
- Raise awareness among business executives, government officials and the general public about the value of collective action and corporate sustainability in fighting corruption.
- Facilitate dialogue between the private and public sector and explore good practices in implementing the UNGC principles on Anti-Corruption

The Collective Action Platform in India would provide a road map to increase awareness on anti-corruption strategies among key stakeholders in India including the government, business, international development agencies and think-tanks. The project activities include research study, seminars, workshops and national and stakeholder consultations.

India CEO Forum

The India CEO Forum on Business and Human Rights exists to advance human rights in the business context among Indian Corporates, Companies and Business Houses having operations in India and aboard, and works towards establishing India as a global leader in this critical and valuable area of responsible business. Global Compact Network (GCN) provides vehicle for Indian Companies- Large & SME, Academic institutions and Civil Society organizations to join hands towards strengthening responsible business initiatives in India and internationally.

Women Empowerment Principle

The Women's Empowerment Principles are a set of principles for business offering guidance on how to empower women in the workplace, marketplace and community. They are the result of a collaboration between the United Nations Entity for Gender Equality and the Empowerment of Women (UN Women) and the United Nations Global Compact and are adapted from the Calvert Women's Principles. The development of the Women's Empowerment Principles included an international multi-stakeholder consultation process, which began in March 2009 and culminated in their launch on International Women's Day in March 2010.

Subtitled, 'Equality Means Business', the Principles emphasize the business case for corporate action to promote gender equality and women's empowerment and are informed by real-life business practices and input gathered from across the globe. The Women's Empowerment Principles seek to point the way to best practice by elaborating the gender dimension of corporate responsibility, the UN Global Compact and business' role in sustainable development. In addition to being a useful guide for business, the Principles seek to inform other stakeholders, including Governments, in their engagement with business.

Principle 1: Establish high-level corporate leadership for gender equality.

Principle 2: Treat all women and men fairly at work - respect and support human rights and non-discrimination.

Principle 3: Ensure the health, safety and well-being of all women and men workers.

Principle 4: Promote education, training and professional development for women.

Principle 5: Implement enterprise development, supply chain and marketing practices that empower women.

Principle 6: Promote equality through community initiatives and advocacy.

Principle 7: Measure and publicly report on progress to achieve gender equality.

(*Source:* Content is sourced from the website http://globalcompact.in/)

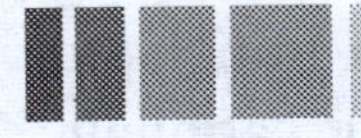

15.8 A BUSINESS CASE FOR GLOBAL ETHICS

Globalization, with its undisputed opportunities and benefits, constitutes a moral challenge. Initiatives such as the Global Compact exemplify a growing insistence that human values should anchor wealth creation. Diverse stakeholders from nations, multinational corporations and small businesses have a diverse set of expectations from their leaders in terms of macro threats, like climate change, resource shortages, pandemic pathogens, financial volatility, economic insecurity, and political instability, and micro threats, like competition, new product roll-out, job relocation, restructuring and the elimination of product lines or business units.

To be effective, leaders need tools and the moral will to move forward to accomplish goals, in a global arena of competing and conflicting value claims.

The existence of different ethical standards and values in different societies and countries raises difficulties for thinking about ethics. If different countries have different customary values that each regard as valid, attempts to define what is good and right are undermined. Although societies may have different ethical practices and values, they all have a universal requirement to have such norms. For example, it is important that all the drivers in a country drive on the right or on the left, if the country wants that road traffic moves in a disciplined manner while minimizing the probabilities of accidents.

The similar situation is in organizations. They all need, for example, ethical standards for their smooth functioning. We can take the example of the treatment of family members working in an organization. In some cultures, they would be seen as an embarrassment and people would feel guilty that they might be seen to be favouring their relatives. In other cultures, it would be expected that family members would be favoured. Yet, in all this variety there is an acceptance that there need to be some standards to help people cope with this particular situation. This allows a universal imperative to underlie ethical diversity.

There are many differences in business and managerial values where value diversity causes no ethical problems. Attitudes to working hours and holidays are an example. Americans generally put more hours into their job than Europeans, and the gap between the two is increasing. Americans also have less entitlement to holidays. The Spanish in contrast to the Americans take two-hour lunch breaks, eat late at night, go to bed late, have lots of public holidays and take extended vacations in July or August. This is often explained by the different cultural values of the Americans and the Europeans. The former value increasing their income over leisure. The Europeans place a premium on leisure. However, some value differences between countries do raise ethical problems. Attitudes towards discrimination at work against certain population groups often differ and they can become points of inter-cultural conflict. For example, the degree to which discrimination against women is accepted varies between countries.

In this connection, Integrative Social Contract Theory (ISCT) developed by Donaldson and Dunfee is helpful. It describes four norms or categories of values. Hyper norms are fundamental human rights or basic prescriptions common to most religions and are acceptable to all cultures and all organizations as values. Second, Consistent norms - these values are more culturally specific than hyper norms, but they are consistent with hyper norms. Third is Moral free space. Moral free space means that conflicting norms may exist within, say, a multinational company and indicates the requirement of flexibility that would be essential for development of any ethical framework to be useful for a multinational corporation. Nepotism might be unacceptable in most western cultures, but acceptable and important in others, for example, in Chinese society.

Fourth are the Illegitimate norms, which are irreconcilable with the hyper norms. ISCT is a pluralist approach, combining the notion of universal norms of behaviour (hyper norms) along with the recognition of important cultural differences (consistent norms and moral free space). In this sense, business ethics in a global context should be viewed more as a story in the process of being written than as a moral code like the Ten Commandments. It can, and should adjust over time – to evolving technology and to the cultural or religious attitudes of particular economic conditions.

The diversity of business values and ethics in different societies and countries does not mean that any ethical position can be justified. There is no debate about the fact that all societies need a system of ethical values and standards that, with more or less effectiveness, creates circumstances in which people feel safe to do business. These values and standards should encourage the trust necessary for people and organizations to work with others or at least provide remedies and sanctions if trust is broken.

In other words, globalization has created an immense need for common ethical norms or of a Global code of ethics that can eliminate differences between countries with regard to the standards of acceptable behaviour. Global code of ethics means an agreement on the rules of conduct for the purpose of justice, respect for human rights and improving the overall performance of countries in their relationship with other countries. To be effective, global ethics should involve the assessment of rules, process and institutions of global society in light of relevant moral mores. All the nations of the world should follow this code in all dealings. The countries that do not follow the code of ethics, can be isolated and barred from any foreign direct investment. Any enforcement of global code of ethics must require a regulatory agency accepted uniformly by the nations of the world.

There could be three approaches to promote global ethical governance. The first approach focuses on the control of corruption by improving transparency and openness. It requires an active media and other avenues for the public to scrutinize the operations and the dealings of the government. The second approach focuses on promoting integrity through education, training and public activism. The education and training curriculum should reflect the ethical principles. The third approach focuses on institution building in combating corruption, but the institutions must have independent power to implement ethics and accountability. For example, an independent audit can help in the process of establishing ethics.

A number of international and non-profit organizations such as Transparency International (TI), the Ethics Resource Center, the Center for Public Integrity, Tiri and most recently, Global Integrity are pushing for Global Ethics. Supranational bodies have also been active including the Organization for Economic Co-operation and Development (OECD), United Nations, World Bank and International Monetary Fund. A number of professional organizations too are emphasizing global ethics, for example, the International Personnel Management Association (IPMA), the International City/County Management Association (ICMA) and the International Chambers of Commerce (ICC) have established ethical principles which they encourage their members to practice. The American Society of Public Administration (ASPA) has come up with eight guidelines to emphasize the following values:

1. **Advance the Public Interest**: Promote the interests of the public and put service to the public above anything.
2. **Uphold the Constitution and the Law**: Obey and respect the constitutions and laws and put efforts to improve the laws and policies to promote the public good.
3. **Promote Democratic Participation**: Encourage public participation in all decision-makings. Promote transparency and openness in all government dealings.
4. **Strengthen Social Equity**: Emphasize the values of equity and inclusiveness. Promote the values of justice and fairness.
5. **Fully Inform and Advise**: Provide full and accurate information to all the people involved in an organization.

6. **Demonstrate Personal Integrity**: Demonstrate a high level of integrity to ensure trust and confidence of the people on the government.
7. **Promote Ethical Organizations**: Promote the organizations with a high standard of ethics and accountability.
8. **Advance Professional Excellence**: Strengthen personal capabilities to act competently.

All these developments of voluntary codes are intended to provide a framework for the global governance of MNCs and world trade however, the application of global ethics will take a collective approach to ensure that matters of ethics remain a priority and awareness is created about the core values and concerns of the profession. The awareness-raising is critical because the corporations may have an ethical responsibility to behave well in their international dealings but it is the individual managers in multinationals, transnationals and international NGOs who exercise that responsibility.

All economies are going through deep and rapid change in a process of transition having not only positive consequences but also causing several interrelated crises: economic recession, energy insecurity, food crisis, demographic challenges, and the overarching climate crisis. In such uncertain times, the nature of ethical governance becomes even more complex, reasserting the need of a global code of ethics which proposes a normative framework not only for the conventional "operational responsibilities" (product safety, social and environmental integrity, responsible supply chain, etc.) but also for the comprehensive "global citizenship responsibilities" which are more socially and ethically oriented.

Overall, it is heartening to see that the global players, including business leaders, social activists, and policymakers in different institutions, have over the years come to appreciate the role of business in society. The "business of business" remains "business," but that business is to compete with integrity to create value by solving problems and meeting customers' demands at a competitive profit on a consistent and sustainable basis. There is a growing realization both in the societies and organizations that global ethics is not only a matter of convenience, but a condition of survival in the modern global society. To sum up in the words of A.C. Fernando- 'If transparency, honesty, fairness, integrity and ethical behaviour alongwith protection of all the stakeholders' interests are

commendable virtues within the country, they are far more preferred outside. The globalization likes and prefers to deal with good and reliable corporations than those whose fairness and integrity are questionable.'

15.9 KEY WORDS

MNC, Ethnocentricity, Geocentricity, Diversity, Child Labour, Human Dignity, Global Compact Network, Worldwide Governance Indicators (WGI), The American Society of Public Administration (ASPA) , Integrative Social Contract Theory (ISCT), Collective Action Project (CAP).

15.10 LET US SUM UP

This unit elaborates on the concept of a global corporation and some of the ethical challenges it is likely to confront while attempting to establish its business in various countries. The unit also deals with the role and contribution of MNCs, and the challenge of cultural diversity they bring in from an ethical perspective. Good governance is a requirement of doing business in a global economy and several International Codes of Business Conduct have been developed in that direction. Various Committees set up for improvement of corporate governance and their recommendations have also been detailed to provide an idea of how the corporate governance has globally evolved over the years. In the end, it has been emphasized that a global ethics is a non-negotiable for the success of globalization in its current version.

15.11 CHECK YOUR PROGRESS

1. Globalization means:

   (*a*) Integration of the trade of countries

   (*b*) Integration of the cultures of countries

   (*c*) Integration of the technology of countries

   (*d*) All of the above

2. Globalization has resulted in:
   (*a*) More advantages than disadvantages
   (*b*) More disadvantages than advantages
   (*c*) Only disadvantages
   (*d*) Difficult to assess
3. The number of Sustainability Development Goals (SDGs) are:
   (*a*) 13
   (*b*) 15
   (*c*) 17
   (*d*) 20
4. The CRT principles aim at:
   (*a*) Promoting a moral capitalism
   (*b*) Promoting global corporate social responsibility
   (*c*) Reducing multilateral trade tensions
   (*d*) All of the above.
5. Ethnocentricity means:
   (*a*) The home country's norms and laws to be dominant
   (*b*) The other country's norms and laws to be dominant
   (*c*) Both of the above
   (*d*) None of the above
6. Global Compact Society (GCS) was founded in December 2000 was renamed as:
   (*a*) India Compact Society
   (*b*) Global Compact Network India
   (*c*) Global Compact Organization
   (*d*) India Global Network Society

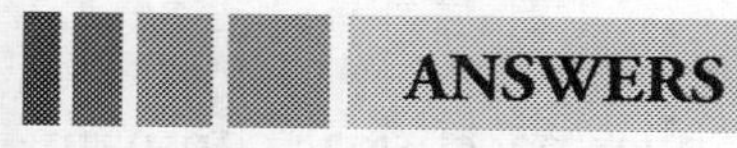

ANSWERS

1. (*d*)	2. (*a*)	3. (*c*)	4. (*d*)	5. (*b*)	6. (*b*)

15.12 EXERCISE YOUR ETHICS MUSCLE

Case 37: The Recommendations

In Italy, it's not what you know but whom you know that is key to getting a job. A recommendation from the right person (a raccomandazione) often gets someone hired, even if the applicant is not the most qualified for the position. The emphasis on connections is blamed for Italy's brain drain, as many outstanding graduates are forced to seek work abroad. You have recently arrived in Italy to manage a small branch office of an international bank. Your best employee asks you to write a letter of recommendation for his daughter who wants a position with one of your major clients. You don't want to offend him and you recognize the importance that Italians place on their families. At the same time, you don't believe his daughter is any more than an average candidate for this position.

Issues to reflect:

(*a*) Would you provide the recommendations for the employee's daughter?

(*b*) If not, then what are your reasons for that decision?

(*c*) Do you see any conflict of values in the situation?

(*d*) What is the right thing to do in the situation?

[While choosing your response, please keep in mind the facts that the request is from your best employee, you are new to the place you need a good team to succeed as a branch manager.]

[*Source:* Associated Press. (2012, September 25). In crisis-hit Europe, nepotism and connection culture stifle youth. The Daily Star (Lebanon)]

Case 38: The Clinical Trials Outsourcing

You are the newly hired research director for a large pharmaceutical company. Like your competitors, your firm is outsourcing clinical drug trials to contract research organizations in such emerging markets as Brazil, Mexico, India, China and South Africa. Clinical trials involve the use of human subjects to test the effectiveness of new medications. Outsourcing drug tests is becoming increasingly popular. Not only are drug companies having a difficult time finding patients in Western countries, but outsourcing can significantly reduce expenses (clinical trials can account for up to 60% of drug development costs) and the time it takes to get a new drug to market, which can take from nine to twelve years on average.

While lower costs and development times boost profitability and stock prices and speed treatment to patients, relying on contract research organizations greatly increases the chances of ethical abuses Your company adheres to the World Medical Association's Declaration of Helsinki, which lays out ethical guidelines for medical testing. According to the declaration, subjects must be fully informed of the risks they face when participating in clinical trials. Trial protocols are to be overseen by ethics committees. Every patient who participates in a research project should have access to the most effective treatment identified in the study after it is over. Participants should never be given an ineffective placebo if it leaves them without adequate treatment.

There is evidence that contract research organization often ignore the Helsinki guidelines. Local review boards, like those in Mexico, are often ineffective and government regulation is lax. Clinical researchers out to reduce their costs may conduct trials without review, test, illegal drugs and misrepresent the nature of the trials to patients. Some subjects in developing nations don't understand the risks even when the dangers are explained to them or they are so desperate to money that they ignore the risk. The best medications may not be given to subjects. Then, distance makes it difficult for drug manufacturers to supervise overseas contractors.

You recognize that while your firm may not be held legally liable for any contract research organization violations, it will be held morally responsible in the court of international opinion.

Issues to reflect:

(*a*) Will you continue to outsource clinical drug trials to developing nations?

(*b*) If so, what steps might you take to endure that your contract research organizations will adhere to Helsinki guidelines?

(*c*) What will you do if your contract research organizations do not adhere to Helsinki guidelines?

(*d*) What are the ethical implications of continuing the outsourcing of clinical drug trials?

[*Source:* Abodor, H (2012), Ethical issues in outsourcing: The case of contract medical research and the global pharmaceutical industry. Journal of Business Ethics, 105, 239-255.]

16 UNIT

Ethical Issues of Corruption, Bribery and White-Collar Crime

16 UNIT

Ethical Issues of Corruption, Bribery and White-Collar Crime

16.1 LEARNING OBJECTIVES

The unit throws light on the meaning of corruption and its characteristics as well as why it is so well spread and has almost become a fact of life. After diagnosing the causes of corruption, the unit describes the negative consequences of corruption and its various manifestations such as bribery, money laundering, corporate corruption, etc. along with the possible measures to effectively control the phenomenon. The unit will also help understand the nature of corporate fraud through the actual examples involving one or two global banks. The importance of FATF guidelines for implementing the AML controls, meaning of bribery and foreign bribery have been highlighted. In the end, a perspective of corruption in the Indian context has been provided. The unit specifically attempts to convey the message that corruption in essence is a moral issue and as we have to tackle it at moral level only for effective control.

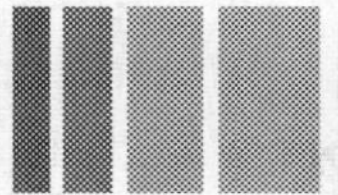

16.2 CORRUPTION: DEFINITION, NATURE, SCOPE & MAGNITUDE

It is generally admitted that corruption is an age-old problem and that all human societies, except the very primitive, are affected by corruption. The ancient Egyptian, Babylonian, Hebrew, Chinese, Greek and Roman civilizations were riddled with the problem of corruption and according to the historian Gibbon, corruption and general moral decay were major factors behind the decline of the Great Roman Empire. Corruption fuelled the French and Russian revolutions, and the Kuomintang regime of China collapsed under its weight.

Definition and Shades of Corruption

Transparency International defines corruption as "the misuse of entrusted power for private gain". The academic literature on corruption uses similar definitions, for example, Ashforth and Anand define corruption as "the misuse of authority for personal, sub-unit and/or organizational gain." United Nations Development Programme (UNDP) refers corruption as to "the misuse of public power, office, or authority for private benefit- through bribery, extortion, influence peddling, nepotism, fraud, speed money or embezzlement". This definition contains seven types of phenomena contained in the concept of corruption: bribery, extortion, influence peddling, nepotism, fraud, speed money and embezzlement. Though all these phenomena are not completely identical in every sense, yet they can be classified under one heading on the ground that a common moral thread runs through all these different types of corruption- the subordination of public interests to private aims involving a violation of the norms of duty and welfare, accompanied by secrecy, betrayal, deception and a callous disregard for any consequence suffered by the public. The corruption *per se* is a distinct moral issue and, in its traditional sense, it also refers to moral impurity. The word itself derives from the Latin for 'to spoil, pollute, abuse or destroy', depending on the context. It broadly describes any deviation from the norm that is considered improper.

Arnold Heidenheimer who is considered as grandfather of comparative corruption studies makes a distinction between what he called 'black', 'white' and 'gray' corruption. Heidenheimer defines 'black corruption' as the activities that most members of society whether rich or poor condemn and want to see punished. 'White corruption' refers to the activities which are formally perceived as corruption, but are more or less tolerated by the society members and they do not want to see the perpetrators penalized. 'Gray corruption' refers to the activities on which there are no consensus of opinion and significant differences of opinion, including ambivalence, prevails among the society members.

Various approaches to Corruption

Another tripartite distinction drawn by Heidenheimer is between public office-centered, market-centered, and public interest-centered approaches to corruption. The first focuses on corruption as behaviour that deviates from what is expected of a public official, and that is explained in terms of the official's desire for

improper personal benefit. Market-centred approaches interpret corruption in terms of public officials treating their positions as a source of private income or business. What they can offer and what they can charge (e.g., how much they can demand as a bribe) depends on the supply of and demand for the good or service they are offering, in short, on the market situation. Finally, the public interest-centered approach focuses on the harm done to the public because of the improper self-serving behaviour of public officials.

The Knapp Commission's early-1970s report on corruption in the New York Police Department uses two very interesting terms- 'grass-eating' and 'meat-eating' corruption. The former refers to the officials who will accept a bribe if offered one, whereas the latter refers to more predatory corruption, in which officials actually solicit bribes. The former approach is also sometimes called reactive corruption, and the latter proactive. Sometimes, a distinction is made between extortive and transactive corruption. In the former, the bribe-taker exerts pressure on someone to give a bribe, which basically equates to meat-eating. In the latter, the two agents (bribe-or favour-taker and bribe-or favour-giver) are more equal; both are basically willing partners, who negotiate a deal.

IFI Anti-Corruption Task Force's Uniform Framework

The harmonized definitions of fraud and corruption by IFI Anti-Corruption Task Force's Uniform Framework provides a common understanding of the illegal practices precisely as we can see below:

- A **corrupt practice** is the offering, giving, receiving, or soliciting, directly or indirectly, anything of value to influence improperly the actions of another party.
- A **fraudulent practice** is any act or omission, including a misrepresentation, that knowingly or recklessly misleads or attempts to mislead, a party to obtain a financial or other benefit or to avoid an obligation.
- A **coercive practice** is impairing or harming or threatening to impair or harm, directly or indirectly, any party or the property of the party to influence improperly the actions of a party.
- A **collusive practice** is an arrangement between two or more parties designed to achieve an improper purpose, including influencing improperly the actions of another party.

The Characteristics of Corruption:

The main features of corruption can be summarised as follows:

(*a*) Corruption always involves more than one person. This need not be the case with stealing, for instance, or embezzlement. The lone operator in corruption is virtually non-existent.

(*b*) Corruption on the whole involves secrecy, except where it has become so rampant and so deeply rooted that some powerful individuals or those under their protection would not bother to hide their activity.

(*c*) Corruption involves an element of mutual obligation and mutual benefit. The obligation or benefit need not always be pecuniary.

(*d*) Those who practise corrupt methods usually attempt to camouflage their activities by resorting to some form of lawful justification. They avoid any open clash with the law.

(*e*) Those who are involved in corruption are those who want definite decisions and those who are able to influence those decisions.

(*f*) Any act of corruption involves deception, usually of the public body or society at large.

(*g*) Any form of corruption is a betrayal of trust.

(*h*) A corrupt act violates the norms of duty and responsibility within the civic order. It is based on the deliberate intent of subordinating common interest to specific interest.

The above list of characteristics of corruption is not exhaustive and could be extended. However, it is sufficient to function as a set of criteria by which the phenomenon of corruption can be classified.

Corruption entails a cause-and-effect relationship. Corruption stimulates further development of greater corruption and this in turn causes an even greater increase in corruption. When extortion becomes widespread in the civil service and is used by policemen on the beat, the clerk at the counter and the nurse at the hospital, it is usually the effect of previous corruption at a higher level. Usually, corruption starts with the group of high officials and well-to-do businessmen and when corruption in this circle has gone on for some time, society will then feel the effect and prices go up. When this happens, the lower levels of government officials take recourse to corruption in an effort to maintain their livelihood.

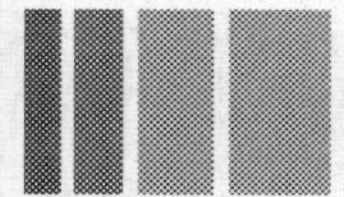

16.3 THE PATHOLOGY OF CORRUPTION: PETTY CORRUPTION AND GRAND CORRUPTION

Let us consider two situations. A Mumbai businessman is visiting Delhi and is travelling from the airport in the company car that has been sent to take him. The road is relatively empty and the car running fast. Suddenly the car is flagged down by one traffic constable who say that it was exceeding the speed limit. The driver steps behind the car for a moment and then returns to his seat. "Have they charged you?" Asks the visitor. No, Sir. He said Rs. 200 now or Rs. 1000 in court next week. I paid. It's cheaper." The visitor reimburses the driver. At the same time, in a small developing country, in the presidential residence, an executive decision is taken. "We must postpone the road building project" says the president, "because the defence needs of the republic are more important. Instead, we shall buy three fighter aircraft. These, I understand, will cost us about \$150m." These two examples indicate two opposite ends of the corruption scale, sometimes described as " petty" and "grand " corruption. The first may put Rs. 200 into the traffic constable back pocket and the second \$15m in the president's offshore bank account.

Grand corruption is practiced by senior officials, government ministers and heads of state and petty corruption is typically the realm of low-paid government officials working in offices like customs, immigration, public utilities, etc. Both form of corruption is equally condemnable. However, it is useful to recognize the different characteristics of the two. Grand corruption, sometimes also called as state capture, is about the distortion of decision-making in matters of economic significance. Firms shaping and affecting formulation of the rules of the game through private payments to public officials and politicians create moral disequilibrium. Procurement policy is driven by personal gain rather than by the aims of usefulness, quality and cost, and may result in construction projects that are a poor use of scarce resources, or the purchase of equipment or goods that are unsuitable or of inferior quality. The national interest may be completely ignored in favour of projects or purchases whose only attraction is that they carry the potential for huge "commissions". Grand corruption is usually international, because of its scale.

Petty corruption or administrative corruption is about 'petty' forms of bribery in connection with the implementation of laws, rules, and regulations. It removes bureaucratic delays – hence the terms "facilitation payment" and "speed money", paying people to do faster what they have already been paid to do. This kind of corruption is likely to be encountered by the ordinary citizen in their everyday lives—while driving or applying for a permit to extend their house. Petty corruption is virtually always domestic, although the payer may not be a citizen or even a resident of the country concerned. Petty corruption is a sort of endemic in many countries.

There is another unfortunate side to the story of corruption. Many financial practices which are corrupt and immoral, but when approved by a government in power are not regarded as corrupt. Switzerland, for example, is generally regarded as a country with little corruption. Yet Switzerland's banking system, under authority from the Swiss Government, provides a haven for massive amounts of ill-gotten and corrupt sources of funds from all over the world. It is only recently that the Swiss Government has begun to tighten controls over the flow of illegal money. A similar situation exists in Singapore.

For several decades, corruption has been increasingly recognized as a significant global problem and an underlying cause of poverty, inequality, terrorism and conflict. Over the last decade in particular, the issue has caught the attention of national regulators, international finance and policy institutions, corporations, activists and the media. Of particular note, the International Consortium of Investigative Journalists (ICIJ) has worked to expose offshore financial structures that facilitate corruption, leading to an ongoing re-examination of the role of the international financial system (including "enablers" such as lawyers and accountants) in facilitating corruption.

Corruption in Private Sector

Corruption is by no means confined to public officials. Individuals in private companies also take bribes to provide goods and services if these are in short supply. The distinction between the bribing of a public official and of a private person is no longer relevant from the payer's point of view. It is as bad to bribe a government officer as to the purchasing manager of a company or indeed, the buyer for a supermarket chain. However, the public-sector official (or even someone performing a quasi-public function within a regulated industry) owes a duty to the public at large as against a private-sector employee who is loyal to his company, its shareholders or its customers. Corruption is ownership

neutral and pervades businesses, the non-profit sector entities, non-governmental organizations, educational institutions and even the hospitals.

What would you advice Mr. X in this situation and why?

Mr. G was working as a senior officer in the excise dept. of a reputed steel company. He belonged to a very reputed and good family. The steel company was reportedly involved in excise evasion of its goods. Excise evasion was resulting in the dealers selling steel which was not excise paid. Mr. G along with his boss were directly involved in this excise evasion. Their thought process being that, they are doing it not for good of their own but for the company. The Government had recently raided few companies practicing excise evasion lying in the vicinity of the steel company. Therefore, Mr. G was under tremendous stress these days. He knew that he would be interrogated if there happens any raid on the company. Mr. G's wife, knowing about the entire situation, advised him to get out of such activity or else quit the company. Mr. G was in dilemma, what should he do?

Causes of Corruption

The constituent elements of occurrence of corruption, which have a pattern of relationships in the causal nexus, are recognized as (*a*) Lack of education (*b*) Poverty (*c*) Absence of severe punitive measures (*d*) Absence of environment conducive to anti-corrupt behaviour (*e*) Structure of government (*f*) The state of society (*g*) Strong red tape (*h*) The weakness of religious and ethical teachings.

How Widespread is Corruption?

Few countries can claim to be absolutely free of corruption. Incidence of corruption varies tremendously from country to country. As corrupt practices are usually hidden and covert the extent of corruption is difficult to measure. A study that compared Hofstede's cultural model and the Transparency International Corruption Perceptions Index found that societies with high power distance (acceptance of unequal power distribution), more collectivistic as opposed to individualistic culture, and an orientation valuing short-term gains over long-term ones were the factors that most clearly drove higher levels of corruption. A more recent study suggests that perceptions of corruption are linked to inequality and perceptions of unfairness. In highly unequal countries, people do not expect fair treatment, so there is a low correlation between perceptions of fairness and corruption. In more equal countries, people are more likely to perceive corruption as due to unfairness.

The most popular measure for a quantitative assessment of corruption is known as the Corruption Perceptions Index (CPI) published by Transparency International (TI). Its latest 2022 report informs that all the countries are failing to control corruption. We will discuss in detail about the TI and its CPI under the heading 'Corruption and Indian Scenario'. However, it focuses on public-sector corruption as perceived by subject-matter experts and is therefore limited in both scope and explanatory power. As the CPI only considers the level of corruption within a country and does not attempt to take account of corrupt payments made by exporters to foreign officials, TI produces another measure of corruption known as the Global Corruption Barometer (GCB). GCB is intended to indicate how and where the ordinary people feel the impact of corruption. This Global Corruption Barometer is a public opinion survey based on responses to questionnaires asked in interviews to a sample population. A third measure is known as the Bribe Payers Index (BPI), which assessees the supply side of corruption and ranks corruption by source country and industry sector is published by Gallup International. The BPI shows that companies from Sweden, Australia and Canada were the least likely to pay bribes and those from Taiwan, South Korea and China were the most likely. Another measure of corruption known as the International Country Risk Guide (ICRG) has been published on a monthly basis since 1980 by PRS Group. Yet, another measure is known as the Opacity Index (OI). This index was produced for the first time in 2001, by the PricewaterhouseCoopers (PwC). The World Bank also brings out a corruption index known as the Control of Corruption Index (CCI). Since the 1990s, the World Bank has been taking an active interest in measuring corruption in the context of 'good governance' as a pre-condition for country-aid and project-aid. The World Bank views good governance and control of corruption as the main strategy for alleviation of poverty. The World Bank seeks to minimize corruption on World Bank funded projects and it also offers all technical assistance to countries in improving governance and controlling corruption.

Gifts and entertainments

The area of accepting entertainment and gifts is very tricky as it is difficult to determine when entertainment and gifts become issues of petty corruption.

Therefore, four criteria can be used in determining the propriety of any gift: frequency, timing, reciprocity and value. There should be extra sensitivity, however, if this coincides with the period of bidding for a major contract. There is a fundamental difference between a gift (even a modest one) given in the hope of winning a contract and a small gift in appreciation of having won a contract. The situation is, of course, eased if the other party gives hospitality or a small present in return. But much the most important consideration is the value of the gift, which should not, in any circumstance, represent more than a tiny fraction of the value of any business completed or under consideration.

16.4 BRIBERY

Bribes are personal payments, gifts or special favours granted improperly to influence the outcome of the decisions. Bribery affects everyone because it leads to perceptions of unfair treatment of some companies and groups at the expense of others and decreases the levels of trust across the groups. Bribery has always been condemned mostly as an unethical act and an anxiety in the acceptance of such gifts has been observed in many countries all over the world since ancient times. In the teachings of Buddhism, bribery is equally condemned as stealing, cheating and killing. Sikhism, Hinduism and Islam all say the same thing. Even the Rig-Veda contains several references to bribery. The Old Testament (Book of exodus) enjoins, "Beware of accepting bribes; they blind even the prudent, and disturb the judgment even of the just."

Much corruption would end today if companies refused to pay bribes to government officials. It would seem that bribes are an additional cost of doing business, so why don't companies just stop paying? The pursuit of profits leads companies to peddle sub-prime mortgages, pollute lakes and rivers and pay bribes. Certainly there are long-term risks from bribery, the possibility of punishment, or the worry that a bribe-taking official will fail to make good on awarding a contract or providing a license. However, the reality is that, for many businesses today, paying bribes has been highly profitable, even over the long-run. In the process, few companies get busted too. For example, Siemens management, might regret paying off procurement officials worldwide to secure contracts for, among other things, hospital equipment supplies in Russia, power generation in Malaysia and subway signalling devices in China. They got caught and paid

US$1.6 billion in fines in 2008. From another angle, despite being caught, the bribes were nonetheless worth it for Siemens, given the profits they made from the many contracts they won as a result.

In some industries and in some locations, it may simply be impossible to get contracts without offering a bribe to sweeten the deal. In Nigeria, for instance, 41 percent of firms expect to make regular "informal payments" to government officials in order to "get things done,". That said, it should not be forgotten that such actions are embedded in a culture of corruption, where expectations and norms for bribe paying are clearly understood by all involved. In such cases, it thus becomes difficult to distinguish perpetrator from victim. However, even in high-corruption environments, every firm doesn't succumb to the culture of paying bribes. But a handful of companies who refuse to pay bribes outright suffer and are frozen out of doing business with the government.

Companies in a corrupt environment face, in effect, a prisoners' dilemma: the rational, profit-maximizing choice is to pay bribes, regardless of what other companies choose to do. If others offer bribes, you need to follow suit to compete on an even footing or else go bankrupt. If other businesses stay honest (the equivalent of remaining silent in the classic prisoners' dilemma), by paying bribes you'll get rich by winning every contract that's put up for bid. This leads to an ever-present temptation to deviate from a no-bribe agreement, making such pacts inherently unstable. It is therefore wrong to expect that businesses will end corruption through collective self-interest and action.

If by increasing enforcement or sanctions it is ensured that companies start seeing bribery as more cost than benefit, a virtuous cycle of stronger enforcement and ever-fewer bribe-paying firms may put into action. The companies that decide to stop paying bribes turn from adversaries into allies in fighting corruption, since they will see themselves as disadvantaged relative to those firms that continue to pay bribes. This's the reason why U.S. companies lobbied for years to have other nations adopt more stringent laws against paying bribes abroad. American firms have been barred from paying bribes to public officials in other countries since 1977 with the passage of the Foreign Corrupt Practices Act (FCPA). The efforts of U.S. firms finally bore fruit in 1997, when the Anti-Bribery Convention was signed by members of the Organization for Economic

Cooperation and Development (OECD), which includes all of the world's richest nations. The convention committed all OECD countries to put in place legislation akin to the FCPA, thereby criminalizing bribery of foreign officials for most companies worldwide. The government's enforcement of the FCPA has increased significantly from 2007 onwards. Since the early 2000s, many other jurisdictions have enacted similar anti-corruption laws, including UK, Canada, Norway, China and Brazil. The UK Bribery Act is notable in being the most extensive in scope—it encompasses commercial bribery and departs from the FCPA in including facilitation payments (small bribes made to speed up or otherwise enable access to government services to which the recipient is entitled) in the scope of regulation.

The Untold Story of Telgi

One of the biggest scams based on the large briberies in the history involving Rs. 4800 crores have been executed by Abdul Karim Telgi alliance Karim Lala. Karim Lala was a daily wage earner of Rs. 30 in the 1980s and he earned a fortune through chicanery and corruption. The man began charting his crime carrier when he got involved in a fake passport case. As he was a novice, he landed in Mumbai crime branch lock-up in 1991 with his very first crime of tempering with the passport. Inside the jail, he received his first tutorial in crime. He came in contact with an expert forger Ram Ratan Soni, who introduced him to fake stamp paper trade. Telgi begun selling fake stamp papers. Tempted by huge profit margins, he acquires 12 machines and recruited several people to run the press. He started printing fake stamp papers, he also manages to acquires stamp paper license set up at mint road, and befriended people in the revenue ministry, registrar of stamps office, and the place where it got printed, Nashik Security Press. His empire rapidly expanded. He began to invest heavily in real estate in a house at Colaba, Mumbai and in movies. Within a short period, he graduated to dealing with seasoned politicians and bureaucrats who later became his errand boys. The kingpin of Rs. 30,000 crores fake stamp paper scam and appointed as many as 300 educated MBAs to sell his fake stamp paper to banks, financial institutions, share companies and earning about Rs. 100 crores a month. His dream run ended in August 2001 and he was arrested for a murder.

(Based on various internet sources)

16.5 FOREIGN BRIBERY

Organization for Economic Cooperation and Development (OECD) is a forum in which governments compare and exchange policy experiences, identify good practices in light of emerging challenges and promote decisions and recommendations to produce better policies for better lives". OECD carried out a publication in 2016 titled *"Foreign Bribery Offence and its Enforcement in Eastern Europe and Central Asia"*. This report studied and analyzed the legislation and enforcement of foreign bribery in Eastern Europe and Central Asia. The report covers 25 countries that participated in OECD's Anti-Corruption Network for Eastern Europe and Central Asia (ACN).

The report first defines what foreign bribery is. In essence, foreign bribery is bribery of a foreign official. It then observes that foreign bribery has increasingly become an important topic in the expanded world economy. Several international instruments now require state parties to criminalize bribery of foreign government officials, including the following:

- 1997 OECD Convention on Combating Bribery of Foreign Public Officials in International Business Transactions.
- 1999 Council of Europe Criminal Law Convention on Corruption.
- 2003 United Nations Convention against Corruption.

The OECD Report mentions that "foreign bribery is an extremely difficult crime to investigate and prosecute. Like other forms of corruption, foreign bribery is a covert act that often remains hidden. Foreign bribery is especially difficult to detect because the individuals, companies and officials involved are across borders. In addition, funds used to provide foreign bribes may be channeled through offshore bank accounts or delivered to third parties (often in different jurisdictions). Thus, foreign bribery may involve actors not only from the country of the company that provides a bribe and the country of the official who receives the bribe, but also from third countries where consultants, agents or shell companies are located. Furthermore, documents regarding the bribery may be in a variety of languages. A jurisdiction that wishes to investigate or prosecute a foreign bribery case is often reliant upon the good graces of other countries in providing necessary mutual legal assistance, extraditing defendants, or assisting in obtaining documents or the assistance of witnesses".

The OECD Working Group on Bribery is leading the global efforts to fight a key source of corruption from the bribery of foreign public officials in international business transactions. It is custodian of the OECD Convention on Combating Bribery of Foreign Public Officials in International Business Transactions. The launch of the 2021 Anti-Bribery Recommendations is a major achievement for the Working Group in this regard to update and expand on the provisions of the earlier 2009 Recommendations. These changes will ensure that standards continue to reflect good practices, trends and challenges that have emerged in the global anti-corruption landscape. Key revisions relate to strengthening enforcement, addressing the demand side of foreign bribery, enhancing international co-operation, introducing the use of non-trial resolutions, incentivizing compliance and providing comprehensive protection for reporting persons. To ensure a fully collaborative effort, the Working Group continues to engage with major emerging economies. The Group also continues to raise awareness through its regional initiatives in Africa, the Asia-Pacific, Eastern Europe and Central Asia, Latin America and the Caribbean, and the Middle East and North Africa about the negative impacts of corruption on sustainable growth. The 2021 Anti-Bribery Recommendation complements the convention with the following key elements:

- A holistic approach to fighting foreign bribery through new measures to increase awareness-raising and training of, as well as detection by, key government agencies, including foreign representations, financial intelligence units, tax authorities and official development assistance agencies.
- Provisions for improved enforcement of foreign bribery laws, including through proactive detection and investigation of foreign bribery, more effective international co-operation among law enforcement authorities and co-operation in multi-jurisdictional cases.

Can Corruption be Challenged in the Consumer Forum?

Consumers often find getting their work done in government-owned institutions without paying bribe. And hospitals are no exception. If the patients are to be looked after well you need to look after the ward boy, aaya and doctors well. If you refuse to pay, you run the danger of being denied medical treatment. In such a case, can you approach the Consumer Forum?

Perhaps for the first time in the history of Consumer Protection Act (CPA), a case has been reported wherein a patient was denied surgery because he did not pay Rs. 20,000 as bribe to the doctor. The patient Mallikarjun Laxman Babre of Maharashtra, was taken to the operation theatre (OT) on the appointed day. It is alleged by the patient that the doctor demanded money which he did not give. Immediately the doctor removed the patient from the OT. However, the patient was given some injections. The patient approached another doctor in a private hospital who said that the injections and treatment given by the ESI hospital doctor was not wrong and advised the patient to undergo operation immediately. On this basis, the patient filed a complaint in the District Consumer Forum and claimed compensation on the basis of deficiency in service.

The doctor denied having asked for money. He explained to the forum that the complainant was to be operated upon on a particular day, but was postponed due to prior commitments. Besides, the surgeon was of the view that operation was not necessary. Hence, he was treated with injections and was discharged. The doctor said there was no case of deficiency.

The Forum found that there was no deficiency in service as the patient was treated with medicines, X-Ray etc. Secondly as the patient failed to prove the allegation of corruption against doctor, it was not sustainable. The Forum dismissed the complaint. But while doing so it directed the superior officers to hold an inquiry against the doctor and inform the same to the Forum. It also ordered that hospital reimburse the expenses incurred by the patient for the operation.

The doctor approached the Bombay High Court by way of a petition against the order of the District Forum. The HC set aside the order of the Forum. It said that the Forum has no authority to order an administrative enquiry. It is for the state government to do so. Besides, when there was no deficiency in service, the Forum could not have ordered reimbursement of expenses incurred by the patient.

What would you recommend?

(*Source:* Times of India, September 20, 2003)

16.6 CORPORATE CORRUPTION: THE WHITE-COLLAR CRIME AND ITS NATURE

Corporate Fraud continues to be one of highest criminal pursuits globally. It causes significant financial losses to investors and immeasurable damage to the economy. Corporate fraud mainly takes place through the following modes:

- Falsification of financial information
- False accounting entries and/or misrepresentations of financial condition
- Fraudulent trades designed to inflate profits or hide losses
- Illicit transactions designed to evade regulatory oversight
- Self-dealing by corporate insiders
- Insider trading (trading based on material, non-public information)
- Kickbacks
- Fraud in connection with an otherwise legitimately operated mutual hedge fund
- Certain market timing schemes
- Falsification of net asset values

White-collar criminals inflict far more damage on society than all street crimes combined. To give the flavour of corporate fraud, we shall try to look at few fraud cases involving global banks. For example, last year, Credit Suisse & Credit Suisse Securities (Europe) Limited pleaded guilty to conspiracy to commit Wire Fraud in a fraudulent Mozambique loan case.

> Credit Suisse Group AG, a global financial institution headquartered in Switzerland and Credit Suisse Securities (Europe) Limited (CSSEL), its subsidiary in the United Kingdom (together, Credit Suisse), have admitted to defrauding U.S. and international investors in the financing of an $850 million loan for a tuna fishing project in Mozambique and have been assessed more than $547 million in penalties, fines and disgorgement as part of coordinated resolutions with criminal and civil authorities in the United States and the United Kingdom. Among other things, Credit Suisse Group AG, CSSEL, and their co-conspirators deceived investors by hiding information about the risk that loan proceeds were used for illegal purposes in connection with the restructuring of the loan.

[Text from US DoJ Website (February 5, 2022): Link: https://www.justice.gov/opa/pr/credit-suisse-resolves-fraudulent-mozambique-loan-case547-million-coordinated-global 140]

Similarly, Deutsche Bank have been found to be involved in a number of unethical issues:

> Deutsche Bank lent money and traded currencies for the well-known sex offender Jeffrey Epstein up to May 2019, long after Epstein's 2008 guilty plea in Florida to soliciting prostitution from underage girls, according to news reports. Epstein and his businesses had dozens of accounts through the private-banking division. From 2013 to 2018, "Epstein, his related entities and his associates" had opened over forty accounts with Deutsche Bank. According to The New York Times, Deutsche Bank managers overruled compliance officers who raised concerns about Epstein's reputation. The bank found suspicious transactions in which Epstein moved money out of the United States, The Times reported. On 7 July 2020, the New York Department of Financial Services (DFS) imposed a $150 million penalty on Deutsche Bank, in connection with Epstein. The bank had "ignored red flags on Epstein".

Text from Wikipedia 11 (February 5, 2022) Fine for Business with Jeffrey Epstein, on 2020 1 June, 2018]

The criminal cartel charges were laid by the Commonwealth Director of Public Prosecutions Australia against ANZ Bank, its group treasurer Rick Moscati, along with Deutsche Bank, Citigroup and a number of individuals. On 20 July 2018, Deutsche Bank agreed to pay nearly $75 million to settle charges in this case. In July 2019, U.S. prosecutors investigated Deutsche Bank's role in a multibillion-dollar fraud scandal involving the 1 Malaysia Development Ber had or 1MDB. Deutsche Bank helped raise $1.2 billion for the 1MDB in 2014. As of May 2021, Malaysia sued Deutsche Bank to recover billions in alleged losses from a corruption scandal at the fund. Further, in January 2021, Deutsche Bank agreed to pay a U.S. fine of more than $130 million for a scheme to conceal bribes to foreign officials in countries such as Saudi Arabia and China, and the city of Abu Dhabi, between 2008 and 2017 and a commodities case where it spoofed precious metals futures. In another case involving Danske Bank, Deutsche Bank's US arm was found to be involved in money laundering.

Danske Bank Money-Laundering Scandal

On 19 November 2018, a whistle-blower of the Danske Bank stated that a large European bank was involved in helping Danske process $150 billion in suspect funds. Although the whistle-blower, Howard Wilkinson, did not name Deutsche Bank directly, another inside source claimed the institute in question was Deutsche Bank's U.S. unit. In 2020 it became known that the U.S. arm of Deutsche Bank processed more than $150 billion of the $230 billion dirty money through New York, for which it was fined 150 million $. After a raid in 2019, Frankfurt-based prosecutors imposed a fine of $15.8 million in 2020 for DB's failure on more than 600 occasions to promptly report suspicious transactions.

In short, corporate malfeasance is a compelling problem with significant effects on society, but the same is unlikely to be prosecuted fully and deterred due to business-friendly statutes and case settlements that protect companies from serious consequences of wrongdoing. We have given examples of banks here but the malady is limited just not only to banks but corporates have also been frequently found to be involved in the corporate frauds. For example, we can take case of Kobe steel as shown in the box:

Kobe Steel data falsification

Car, train and aircraft makers are investigating whether they have used sub-standard materials made by Kobe steel after the company admitted falsifying quality data, dating back as long as a decade, regarding the strength and durability of products delivered to more than 500 companies. Kobe Steel's shares fell close to 38% and about $1.8bn has been wiped off the company's market value. Kobe's president, Hiroya Kawasaki said "The credibility of Kobe Steel has plunged to zero. We will make efforts to regain trust as soon as possible." Dozens of employees are alleged to have been involved in the fabrication of the data.

It is difficult to believe that the Kobe's management wasn't aware that the certificates were being falsified.

16.7 CORRUPTION, MONEY LAUNDERING AND FINANCIAL ACTION TASK FORCE

Money laundering is intrinsically linked to corruption. It is the process of concealing the illicit gains that were generated from criminal activities. By successfully laundering the proceeds of a corruption offence through a trail of money and make them appear to have come from legitimate sources, the illicit gains may be enjoyed without fear of being confiscated. Money laundering thus allows criminals to hide and accumulate wealth, avoid prosecution, evade taxes, increase profits through reinvestment and fund further criminal activity. Simply, money laundering can be defined as turning "dirty" money into "clean" money. There are three steps in the money laundering process-placement, layering and integration. Placement represents the initial entry of the criminal's proceeds into the financial system. Layering is the most complex and often entails the international movement of funds. Layering separates the criminal's proceeds from their original source and creates a complex audit trail through a series of financial transactions. And integration occurs when the criminal's proceeds are returned to the criminal from what appear to be legitimate sources.

Money laundering is very serious form of corruption that can undermine the integrity and stability of financial institutions and systems, discourage foreign investment and distort international capital flows. Criminals who engage in money laundering derive their proceeds through complex financial crimes, human trafficking, International and domestic public corruption, narcotics trafficking & terrorism. The conduits used for these activities are financial institutions, International trade, Precious metals, Real estate, Third-party service providers and Virtual currency etc.

Combating Money-laundering

To combat money laundering, the Financial Action Task Force (FATF), an inter-governmental policymaking body and global financial crime watchdog, has developed a methodology and set of recommendations to be complied with by all countries. During the course of the FATF mutual evaluation process which assesses countries' compliance with the FATF Recommendations, the FATF considers how effectively AML/CFT measures are implemented in a country by considering the number of investigations, prosecutions and convictions for money laundering, and the amount of property confiscated in relation to money laundering or underlying predicate offences, including corruption and bribery. FATF also considers whether the country can demonstrate that it has a solid framework of measures to prevent and combat corruption through respect for transparency, good governance principles, high ethical and professional requirements, and established a reasonably efficient court system to ensure that judicial decisions are properly enforced. These elements are important because significant weaknesses or shortcomings in these areas may impede effective implementation of the FATF Recommendations.

Private sector institutions are an attractive venue for laundering the proceeds of corruption, particularly if they are owned or infiltrated by corrupt persons or have implemented weak AML/CFT measures. Effective implementation of the FATF Recommendations helps to protect designated financial institutions (such as banks, securities firms, insurance companies, foreign exchange dealers and money remitters) and other designated businesses and professions by requiring that their owners, controllers and employees are properly vetted, and they have adequate systems in place to comply with AML/CFT requirements. Persons holding a significant controlling interest or management function in a designated private sector institution must be vetted.

In the case of financial institutions, such vetting should use "fit and proper" criteria for directors and managers. This helps to prevent corrupt persons and other criminals from gaining control over a financial institution. Designated private sector institutions must screen employees to ensure high standards. This helps to prevent corrupt persons from infiltrating or otherwise criminally abusing a financial service provider. Designated private sector institutions must implement internal control systems and audit functions to ensure compliance with AML/CFT measures. This helps such institutions to detect when they are being abused by criminals and corrupt persons.

Designated private sector institutions must be subject to adequate supervision and monitoring by supervisory authorities with sufficient supervisory, inspection and sanctioning powers to ensure compliance with AML/CFT measures. Designated private sector institutions must conduct ongoing due diligence on all business relationships to ensure that the transactions being conducted are consistent with their knowledge of the customer, business and risk profile and where necessary, the source of funds with special attention to any complex, unusual or large transactions or unusual patterns of transactions, that have no apparent or visible economic or lawful purpose. This enables the detection of unusual or suspicious activity that might be related to corruption and which must be reported to the authorities for further analysis and investigation.

By effectively implementing the FATF Recommendations, a proper culture of compliance with AML/CFT standards can be created with an environment in which it is more difficult for corruption to thrive undetected and unpunished.

16.8 COMBATING CORRUPTION THROUGH ETHICS PROMOTION

Corporates tend to treat corruption as a risk that should be tackled *via* internal controls and make anti-corruption programs the responsibility of the compliance and legal departments. The dominant corporate approach is to treat corruption risk as a version of the principal-agent problem (meaning that employees who pay bribes violate their fiduciary duty to the corporate "principal") that can be eliminated with the right processes. The regulatory climate means that "zero tolerance" is the only appropriate public position for companies to take on the issue. It is logical and unsurprising that companies that have implemented anti-corruption programs lean heavily on audits, due-diligence checks and other documentary processes that demonstrate efforts to reduce corruption exposure.

However, as several studies mention, not all corrupt acts can be characterized as principal-agent problems. Several studies have shown the many scenarios where individual employees can participate in unethical behaviour for prosocial reasons, with the belief that they will support their boss, their organization or both. These studies find a positive social relationships and higher levels of identification with the organization may unintentionally encourage unethical behaviour designed to benefit the organization. This involves "neutralization," a process which masks the moral content of an unethical action or otherwise causes it to be overlooked. Organizational identification can also lead employees to ignore the victims of the firm's unethical behaviour, focus on the perceived wrongs victims commit and maintain a higher loyalty to the organizational group than wider society.

The issue is that a compliance-led approach does not adequately address either the individual or group psychology of corruption. Preventative policies and

processes are necessary, but not sufficient. Corruption risk touches almost every aspect of a multinational company's business and has consequences across back and front office functions. Senior leadership commitment to anti-corruption and legal compliance and ethical norms more broadly, is rightly understood to be a critical factor in anti-corruption. However, the dominant approach is to view anti-corruption efforts as a regulatory cost and make it the compliance department's responsibility, while giving this department limited or no independence from the C Suite. The tensions that result from that approach have been recognized and have resulted in a recent push to give Chief Compliance Officers a direct reporting line to the Board of Directors. Making a business case for anti-corruption may also be critical in creating organizational buy-in, even if it shouldn't be necessary. Corruption may appear to be efficient or beneficial, but this is probably not true in the long-term or when examining sophisticated analyses of the impacts.

Corruption has a dynamic relationship with the bureaucratic environment in which a company operates. Once bribery is on the table, the cost of bribes usually increases, as do the number of procedural barriers that can only be cleared *via* bribes, and the number of individuals seeking bribes. Ultimately, this leads to higher costs and more harassment than operating with integrity. There is also the potential for reputational damage and the threat of exposing past bribery as leverage against the company. Risking criminal penalties only to participate in conduct that typically has the opposite of the intended result, just isn't a good business proposition. This remains widely misunderstood, in line with the perception that "greasing a few wheels" may be necessary in certain business environments.

A common element of anti-corruption efforts is a "zero-tolerance" or "clean-hands" policy approach. While zero tolerance is a just aim, ensuring such an approach is successful requires consideration of the psychological and socio cultural influences in the environment that affect individual decisions. For example, youth raised in corrupt environments are highly accepting of corruption, and few have ethical objections to actions like bribery. Regulatory investigations are still a low-likelihood/high-impact event. At the same time, regulation has become more aggressive in the United States and regulators tend to reward examples of aggressive enforcement inside companies.

Corruption is not an easy issue to tackle. Corrupt practices are so pervasive in business and society, it is impossible for governments or companies to completely eliminate the risk of corruption. There will always be grey areas and borderline cases. However, if systemic efforts are made to change the perception of corruption being a low-risk, high-profit enterprise to that of a high-risk, low-profit peril, the problem may be mitigated to a great extent. This evidence on the importance of culture and group dynamics to anti-corruption efforts has refocused regulators on "cultures of compliance" and "conduct risk."

Key Elements of an Effective Anti-Corruption Program

Taking into account the guidance given by international regulators including the US Department of Justice, and the UK Ministry of Justice who have written extensive guidance on the key elements of an anti-corruption program, consistent across jurisdictions, an effective anti-corruption program may comprise the following elements:

- A commitment for the task of national progress from both the public and the bureaucracy to fight the societal corruption.
- Rule of law, Efficient administration and effective governance so as to avoid the creation of sources for corruption.
- Vigorous political leadership &Institutions designed to serve the common-weal.
- Fortifying a merit based public service with high moral and intellectual standards.
- Commitment from senior management of companies and a clearly articulated policy against corruption.
- Code of conduct and compliance policies and procedures.
- Risk assessment; Third-party due diligence and payments.
- A strong whistle-blowing mechanism and investigations.
- A strong civil society and an educated public.
- Training and continuing advice.
- Rigorous oversight, autonomy, and resources; strong accountability mechanisms; incentives and disciplinary measures.
- Strengthening role of the educational institutions for moral education.

The design of the program is important as it should focus both on a commitment to anti-corruption *via* "tone at the top," as well as on policies, procedures, and processes, along with culture, norms-or human behaviour. The best-practice framework whether for the country or an organization should be holistic. We should understand that no organization or social system is corruption-proof. Dishonourable behaviour is often easy because it pays, and getting caught is improbable. Such behaviour is often driven by greed. The battle should be fought at a mindset level by working on fortifying the ethical bearings of the people in organizations or in the public service and simultaneously by removing a main incentive for engaging in corrupt activities by depriving the perpetrators and others from the benefit of such crimes. For doing so, countries must have effective laws and procedures to freeze, seize and confiscate stolen assets, the proceeds of corruption and laundered property, while also protecting the rights of *bona fide* third parties. The United States has successfully shown the path by introducing the 1977 Foreign Corrupt Practices Act (FCPA) by which it became as criminal for an American citizen to bribe a foreign public official as to bribe an official in the United States with strict penalty provisions. FCPA has substantially improved the behaviour of corporate America.

The most important factor in the dynamics of corruption control is the moral and intellectual stature of leaders of the society and organizations. Liu Ann, grandson of the first Han emperor, around 122 B.C. aptly described the decisive influence of rulers in the promotion of rectitude values, or vices. 'The power to achieve success or failure,' it says, 'lies with the ruler. If the measuring-line is true, then the wood will be straight. In the same way if the ruler is sincere and upright, then honest officials will serve in his government and scoundrels will go into hiding."In this context, it is imperative to ensure that the public service is a merit-based cadre with absolute probity of conduct and commitment to deter and detect corruption.

From an organizational point, when implementing a program to address or prevent corruption, it is also advisable to implement all parts of the program simultaneously, affecting all levels and roles in the organization at once. This reduces the appearance of corruption as common, and instead signals unified (and fair) commitment to ethical behaviour. Ultimately corruption results from the choices individuals make, balancing both their values and needs.

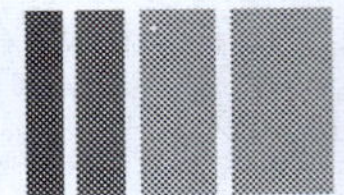

16.9 CULTURE, ETHICAL LEADERSHIP, ORGANIZATIONAL FACTORS & CORRUPTION

Corrupt actions may require action by an individual, but the influences on the individual are varied and strong. Culture, leaders and the nature of the organization can be key influencers of individual corrupt behaviour. Identifying and mitigating these influences will be critical for successfully attenuating corrupt activities through ethics promotion.

Psychological contracts between employee and employer may be a strong driver of actual behaviour. Unethical leadership is associated with increased crimes of obedience, but this relationship is dampened by individual moral awareness. This may show an organizational need to select and train moral awareness and moral development, particularly among leaders, but also to help employees raise concerns and resist managerial pressure. The importance of unspoken psychological contracts is further clarified by research findings that the contract can create feelings of shame and guilt when an employee feels that failure to participate in corruption is a disruption/violation of the agreement. Activating or guiding these self-conscious emotions to align with ethical pursuits such as feeling more guilt about corruption than organizational non-compliance, may be an important lever in the reduction of corrupt behaviours.

With employees subject to positive and negative organizational pressures regarding ethics and corruption, their own moral awareness and courage may be the only saving grace. So, it follows that anti-corruption training can improve their ability to reject justifications for corruption. The conversion of pressures into behaviour are governed in large part by the employees ability to think morally and act in accord with moral values. It is also likely effective to manage the sources of pressure on individual employees. Corruption can be seen as "degeneration of a legitimate value". By designing and implementing appropriate training programmed around this theme, individual responsibility and methods of sense-making can be altered to encourage corruption. Because moral behaviour develops in the context of relationships, even well-intentioned and morally engaged individuals can become corrupt, either when there is moral ambiguity or they succumb to instrumental pressures. Importance of cognitive factors in corruption should also not be overlooked. The assumption that individuals are rational actors simply responding to available rewards and punishments has failed to adequately explain corrupt behaviour. For potential punishments to be impactful, they need to be salient (and therefore front of mind) and the likelihood (or perceptions of likelihood) of corrupt behaviour leading to detection/punishment must be relatively high. When the possibility of getting caught seems distant and unlikely, risk-aversion may not be strong enough to prevent corrupt actions. This can be remedied in part with improved information flows about the costs of corruption, rewarding ethical behaviour and providing frameworks for high-quality organizational decision-making. Ethical training programmes should incorporate all these elements for obtaining the positive outcomes. Corrupt behaviour is often intuitive and unintentional as well. This means that when corruption is commonplace, or decisions are made under time pressure, there may be no evaluation of the decision's ethics at all. Accountability mechanisms, transparency and codes of conduct can be helpful in this regard.

Developing Moral Competence

Corruption, in its broadest sense, is the lack of integrity-whether intellectual, moral or financial. When integrity fails, society collapses. The prevalence of systemic corruption weakens the will to fight corruption. This weakening of the will manifests itself in various forms, such as resignation to the climate of corruption and attempts to relate it to preceding institutional and cultural norms. To say that corruption all pervasive and nothing can be done to eradicate it is a self-defeating statement. Poor health is worldwide, but no one says that treating it is a bad idea. Likewise, saying that corruption is culturally determined and therefore incurable is wrong. Corruption researchers have suggested that cultures universally condemn corruption, but may see differences in the presence of corruption due to other factors. It is likely that in some places corrupt behaviours are necessary for survival, and so people participate despite viewing it as unethical, or they justify the behaviour in their mind, all without changing their larger view that corruption is generally wrong.

Moral competence can be a potent weapon against corruption with a proper understanding of the culture and environment in which the corruption takes place. This is an often-overlooked factor along with the epistemic trespassing (failing to identify the limits of one's skills). Individuals with greater moral commitment, regardless of demographics and personal characteristics, may be less likely to give in to corruption. Those who are uncompromising with respect to their integrity are less likely to accept bribes, while those with more honesty/humility are less likely to give bribes. To garner such moral support, ethical training programme should be framed in a way that appeals to large numbers of people and generate their buy-in. For example, ethics can be rooted in environmentalism, which many people support. Then, corruption should be viewed in gradations along a continuum, rather than all or nothing. Usually only some percentage of people participate in corruption, even when it seems to be the norm. Similarly, each person could participate in corruption rarely, or frequently and engage in minor or major forms of corruption. Further, efforts should be made to identify and appeal to the types of stakeholders the organization relies on (indifferent, absentee, ethical, pragmatic). Being ethical can please many of them while only a few might be lost to less ethical competitors.

In brief, the beginning and end of wrongdoing starts with each person. It is important to be aware of the types of circumstances likely to disorient one's moral compass and the rationalizations used to excuse dubious behaviour and address them at the individual as well as collective levels through robust ethical, awareness creation interventions.

16.10 THE INDIAN SCENARIO OF CORRUPTION

Indian society faces the biggest challenge of tackling and handling corruption. Though governmental regulation and social awareness are there, this menace is still continuing without any cure due to our diversity in culture, social set up, religion and certain other historical and political reason.

Corruption takes place both in public and private sector enterprises. In the public sectors undertakings, business executives encourage corruption due to the influence of politicians. In private sector, most of the entrepreneurs and business organization try to help political leaders during election time and the other critical junctures in order to obtain their favour when they are in power.

While there are some laws aimed at preventing corruption by public sector agencies and public sector businesses, the Prevention of Corruption Act, 1988 was enacted for this specific purpose. The Law Commission in its 166th Report observed that "The Prevention of Corruption Act has totally failed in checking corruption. In spite of the fact that India is rated as one of the most corrupt

countries in the world, the number of prosecutions and more so the number of convictions are ridiculously low". During July 2018, both houses of Parliament have passed a Bill seeking to amend the various provisions of PC Act, 1988. The amendments pertain to making the bribe-giving as punishable offence, redefine the criminal misconduct and introduces a time limit for trial of cases, among others.

Serious Fraud Investigation Office (SFIO) has also been set up under the Ministry of Corporate Affairs with the expertise of persons from multiple related fields like accountancy, forensic audit, law, information technology, investigation, company law, capital market and taxation in detecting and prosecuting or recommending for prosecution of white-collar crimes/frauds. Suitable changes have been brought in to the Companies Act, 2013.

The Institute of Company Secretaries of India (ICSI) has brought out a Code called the "Corporate Antibribery Code" released on October 4, 2017. It is a voluntary set of prescriptions to the corporate firms. In Chapter 2 of the Code, ICSI states the objective as "to ensure that neither the company nor any of its employees, directors or authorized representatives indulge in bribery in any of their actions taken for and on behalf of the company in the course of economic, financial or commercial activities of any kind".

The Code defines the scope applicable to the company and its—

(*a*) Board of Directors

(*b*) Employees (full-time or part-time or employed through any third party contract)

(*c*) Agents, Associates, Consultants, Advisors, Representatives and Intermediaries

(*d*) Contractors, Sub-contractors and Suppliers of goods and/services

With the introduction of this Code, this was hoped that the menace of giving and accepting bribes in Indian private companies (including foreign bribery) would show a decline in coming years. However, no empirical evidence to that effect is seen till date. What is needed in this regard is the operationalization of the tenets of the Code through day today procedures and systems. In addition, professionalism must be the watch word for Indian corporates to reinvent themselves. In the Indian context, the records of the company like the TATA and TVS Group that have maintained standards of integrity over the years show that it is possible to have successful business enterprise while maintaining high standards of ethics.

Rankings on Corruption

Transparency International India (TII) is a leading non-political, independent, non-governmental anti-corruption organization of India. TII has extensive expertise and understanding of issues of corruption in India. This organisation raises awareness about corruption, advocates legal and policy reforms at national and state levels; designs practical tools for institutions, individuals and companies wishing to combat corruption and acts as a leading centre of anti-corruption expertise in India.

According to the data released by TII in its latest 2022 report, various regions and countries are having different scores in case of perceived corruption. The Report reveals a serious trend that for the year 2022 that, "the majority of countries are failing to stop corruption. " The global CPI average remains unchanged for over a decade at just 43 out of 100. Despite concerted efforts and hard-won gains by some, 155 countries have made no significant progress against corruption or have declined since 2012. At the top of the CPI, countries in Western Europe and the European Union continue to wrestle with transparency and accountability matters in their response to Covid-19, threatening the region's clean image. In parts of Asia Pacific, the Americas, Eastern Europe and Central Asia, increasing restrictions on accountability measures and basic civil freedoms allow corruption to go unchecked. Even historically high-performing countries are showing a sign of decline. The methodology adopted by this organization is as follows:

The index, which ranks 180 countries and territories by their perceived levels of public sector corruption according to experts and business people, uses a scale of 0 to 100, where 0 is highly corrupt and 100 is very clean. This year, the index found that more than two-thirds of countries score below 50, while 26 countries have fallen to their lowest scores yet. Unfortunately, compared to recent years, this poor performance is nothing new.

As far the TII findings are concerned for 2022, Denmark, Finland and New Zealand and rank highest with scores of 90, 87 and 87 respectively. South Sudan, Syria and Somalia rank lowest with scores of 13, 13 and 12 respectively.

India stands at 85th rank with a score of 40. In 2021 as well, India was at 85th ranking. India's rank improved by one place to 85 in 2021 from 86th in 2020. Except for Bhutan, all of India's neighbours are ranked below it. Pakistan dropped 16 spots in the index and was ranked at 140. Although the situation is lot better than 2013 when the country was ranked 94, India has a long way to go to tackle this perverse phenomenon.

According to another TI survey, in wider Asian region, India has one of the highest incidences of bribery and use of personal connections to access key public services such as health and education. According to the same survey, state services particularly courts, police, revenue department and hospitals are the most corrupt bodies. However, given the magnitude and pernicious nature of corruption affecting every aspect of society and economy, the Indian state has been making concerted efforts to reduce corruption India and has made significant progress too. A serious attempt at this was made in 1963, when the then Nehru government set up the Santhanam Committee following the Mundhra Corruption Scandal. The Santhanam Committee minutely detected many key sources of corruption within the state, including red-tapism and administrative control.

A notable outcome of this Committee was the setting up of the Central Vigilance Commission as an apex anti-corruption body. In addition, the government established the Comptroller and Auditor General of India in 1971 to audit the public finances of key institutions and to prevent incidences of corrupt practices. This apart, offices of Lokayukta or civil commissioners were set up at the state-level to tackle corrupt practices. The first office of Lokayukta was set up in 1966. Following this, a number of Indian states have set up their own Lokayuktas. The most notable example of Lokayukta has been the case of Karnataka. For instance, in 2011, Karnataka Lokayukta indicted the then chief minister B.S. Yeddyurappa in illegal mining graft cases. He was forced to step down from the position of chief minister. Yet, what has done more to the anti-corruption crusade is the enactment of the Right to Information (RTI) legislation in 2005. As per the RTI Act, government authorities are legally required to respond to requests on information regarding government activities. The RTI Act has emerged as a key instrument against corruption. For example, an RTI application by two activists, Simpreet Singh and Yogacharya Anand, in

2008 brought to public knowledge the major kickbacks in allocation of flats in Adarsh Housing, a society that was constructed for survivors of the 1999 Kargil war. Similarly, the scams relating to the Commonwealth Games were also unearthed by an RTI applicant.

When India started its globalization process, economic reforms led to the ending of licensing for industrial activities and the abolition of import quotas, thereby, removing many corrupt practices linked license permit raj. The rent seeking behaviour took on many new innovative forms and continued in several key sectors, particularly minerals, natural resources, and services. For example, the opaque and arbitrary allocation of coal blocks and the telecom spectrum (infamously called 2G).

In short, fighting corruption requires bold structural reforms and a comprehensive refinement of existing laws. A closer examination of the accountability in our public services is also necessary. Accountability is the soul of good governance. The major reason for lack of accountability is the lack of transparency. Transparency is the best guarantee that no malpractices occur the greater the transparency, the greater the accountability as far as the decision making is concerned. In addition, there is a need to urgently repair India's broken criminal justice system, which, in many ways, acts as the real mothership of corruption. Cases taking years and decades to be resolved, including big-ticket scandals, encourage impunity and reinforce corrupt behaviour. Similarly, it is widely known that most corruption or kickbacks are linked to opaque political funding (evident in the current practice of allowing opaque electoral bonds) in India. In short, without major improvement in campaign finance reforms, particularly transparency, disclosures and accountability, it would be impossible to cut the roots of grafts in key sectors of the economy and society.

Nonetheless, the anti-bribery and anti-corruption landscape in India both in the public and private sectors has seen rapid constructive changes in the recent past and we expect this trend to continue and help India emerge as a cleaner country. Here, we should remember the eternal call of the Kathopanishad which Vivekanand used to invoke, " Arise, Awake and not stop till the goal is not reached."

16.11 KEY WORDS

White Corruption, Black corruption, Gray corruption, Petty Corruption, Grand Corruption, Extortive Corruption, Transactive Corruption, Predatory Corruption, Coercive Practice, Collusive Practice, FCPA 1977, Money Laundering, FATF Recommendations, Layering, Serious Fraud Investigation Office, Fit and Proper, Transparency International, Corruption Perception Index.

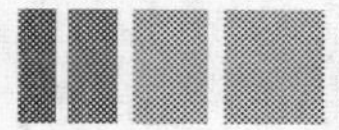

16.12 LET US SUM UP

Corruption is not a static phenomenon. It feeds on itself and keeps on spreading and eating into the vitals of the system. It violates the public trust and erodes the social capital in both of its forms - grand corruption and petty corruption. Bribery, another manifestation of corruption, distorts the economic equilibrium. Foreign bribery, though attracting significant regulatory attention globally, is still taking place as a cost of doing business. Public sector corruption has high visibility but it is chicken-feed compared to corporate corruption which is widespread as is seen in the wrongdoings of few global banks as penalized by the regulators. Continuous promotion of ethical awareness across the organizations and societies and exemplary punishments for the violators are the two methods which can mitigate the corruption risk in the long run. The corruption is still prevalent in India despite the all-round efforts made by the government and other regulatory agencies and needs systemic interventions to reduce opacity in the election funding process to make any significant headway towards the goal of a "Corruption-Free India".

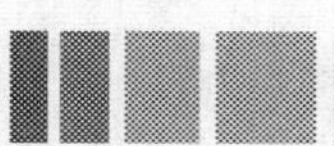

16.13 CHECK YOUR PROGRESS

1. The following is a leading non-political, independent, non-governmental anti-corruption organization of India.

   (*a*) Corruption-Free India

   (*b*) Clean India

   (*c*) Transparency International India

   (*d*) Honest India

2. As per the Transparency International India for the year 2022, the two countries perceived to be least corrupt are ------.
   (*a*) Britain and France
   (*b*) Sweden and Norway
   (*c*) USA and China
   (*d*) New Zealand and Denmark
3. As per the Transparency International India for the year 2022, which of the following two countries are perceived to be the most corrupt ones?
   (*a*) Kazakhstan and Turkmenistan
   (*b*) Sri Lanka and Bangladesh
   (*c*) Pakistan and Iran
   (*d*) Syria, South Sudan
4. Prevention of Corruption Act, 1988 covers:
   (*a*) Public Sector Employees
   (*b*) Private Sector Employees
   (*c*) Both Public & Private Sector Employees
   (*d*) Only Civil Servants
5. Financial Action Task Force (FATF) is a:
   (*a*) US-controlled Body
   (*b*) Europe- controlled Body
   (*c*) Controlled by G-20
   (*d*) Global Independent Body
6. Corruption is a:
   (*a*) Social Issue
   (*b*) Economic Issue
   (*c*) Moral Issue
   (*d*) All of the Above

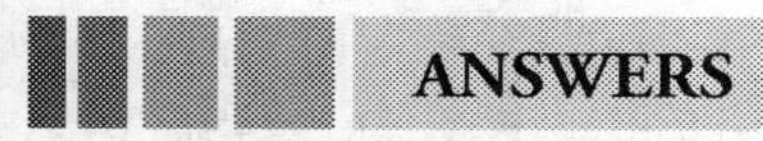

ANSWERS

1. (*c*)	2. (*d*)	3. (*d*)	4. (*a*)	5. (*d*).	6. (*d*)

16.14 EXERCISE YOUR ETHICS MUSCLE

Case 39: A Bribe to Save Lives?

An Airplane manufacturer has spent a great deal of money developing a new airplane. As a result, the company badly needs cash. If it does not procure some large orders soon, it will have to close down some part of its operations. Doing that will put several thousand workers out of job. The result will be disastrous not only for the workers and their families but also for the town in which they live. The President of the company has been trying to woo the government of a foreign country in a large purchase. He learns that one of the key ministers in charge of making final decision about the deal is heavily in debt because of gambling. He quietly contacts that minister and offers him 25 lakhs in cash if he awards the contracts for five planes to his firm. The money is paid and the contract is awarded.

Issues to Reflect

(*a*) What are the ethical aspects inherent in the above situation? Pl list out.

(*b*) Had the president not managed the contract, thousands of workers would have lost their jobs. Therefore, it was urgent to procure the contract irrespective of the means used. Do you agree?

(*c*) A bribe solved both problems of the company's operational viability and probable job losses in huge numbers. There is nothing ethically wrong here . What do you think?

(*d*) Was it prudent on the part of the manufacturer to develop a new airplane without adequate financial resources?

Case 40: Hire Me & Get Your Competitor's Plans

Mr. Ashok Mitra is HR Head in a manufacturing firm. The firm is in a tight spot and undergoing a transformation to adapt to the changing industry dynamics. In this rapidly evolving environment, Mr. Ashok is thinking of hiring a few young, energetic domain experts who would help transition the dynamic situation successfully. As such, the firm organizes a walk-in interview for new recruitments. One of the candidates, Narayan Salve is well qualified as well as experienced in the similar field. He has just left one of the competitor's companies. During the interview, he gives the hints that he would be happy to share all the competitors' plans and policies. What should Ashok do?

Issues to Reflect

(*a*) Narayan is a good choice and can vitally help the firm by sharing the competitor's plans & policies. Do you agree?

(*b*) If Narayan is selected, what would you think of the Ashok Mitra's ethical standards?

(*c*) Is Narayan wrong in hinting that he would be sharing his previous employer's confidential information?

(*d*) What would be the ethically correct course of action in the situation and why?

Case 41: How to Retain Your Market Share Ethically?

X Chemicals Limited (XCL) is a market leader. It supplies chemicals in Maharashtra, Tamil Nadu, Andhra Pradesh and Kerala. This company has been supplying its products in these states for more than 30 years and enjoys a kind of monopoly. Their major portion of sales is towards Government supply. Recently the company started losing its market share of government supply to their competitor. When the company made enquiries to know the reasons for this sudden reduction in market share, they found that the competitors were offering bribes to obtain big orders of government supply. XCL is known in the market for its ethical practices and providing good services to its customers. The company always cared for its stakeholders such as employees, small contractors, distributors and customers. XCL is losing customers and is not in a position to diversify the target market. XCL is now in a dilemma how to control corrupt practices of the competitors and retain its share of the government sector without compromising its ethical practices.

Issues to Reflect

(*a*) What are the various ethical aspects involved in the case, directly and indirectly?

(*b*) Do you think that XCL can meet the challenge ethically? If yes, then how?

(*c*) Discuss the different options available to XCL to tide over the crisis? Should XCL not try to survive the competition by changing its marketing approach?

(*d*) What is your personal opinion on the adage Honesty Always Pays ?

Case 42: Pseudo-Ethics

Mr. X was working in Delhi in a Central police force; on a deputation. During a holiday in his home-town, a classmate of Mr. X invited him over to his place for tea. A Deputy Commissioner of Police (DCP), a common friend, Mr. Y was the other invitee. Since it was raining, they had an extended tea session. When the rain stopped, Mr. X and Y both took leave of the host to return home. Y requested X to drop him home as he had sent his vehicle away. X had parked his old Premier Padmini car on the road. As he opened the door, he noticed that some burglar had broken into the car and had stolen the tape-recorder fitted in it. The rains had given the thief a good cover. X was aghast. Addressing the DCP, X said, "Look, both of us are senior police officers. Is it not ironical that X should be a victim of a theft, and that too in your jurisdiction, when both of us were socializing?"

The DCP, who was visibly embarrassed, muttered. "I am sorry about this theft. Please lodge a complaint. We will do our best to recover what was stolen." X said, "My friend, you are as much aware as I am that there is no chance of recovering my stereo system. Why do you want me to lodge a complaint and add this to the long list of undetected case in your town? Even if you do succeed, do you think I will come all the way from Delhi to depose in the court, spending more money on my travel than what the lost stereo cost?" X started the car, telling the DCP to forget the incident.

X dropped the DCP off and returned home. An hour later, the phone rang. The assistant commissioner of police (Crime) was the caller. He spoke. "Sir, I am sorry to learn that your car stereo was stolen. Even though you have decided not to lodge a complaint, we shall leave no stone unturned to retrieve what was stolen." X wished him good luck.

The next morning an Assistant Sub-Inspector (ASI) and a Head Constable (HC) from the Crime Branch came home. Giving X a smart salute, the ASI said, "Sir, we caught a notorious burglar an hour ago. He had a number of car stereos with him. Our ACP asked us to show you the stereo systems and to find out if any of them belongs to you. The HC opened a gunny sack and took out three car stereos. X looked at them and said that none of them was mine. With great disappointment the duo went back. That evening, the ACP himself came home. He spoke. "Sir, we have cracked your case. Our team picked up an inter-state criminal when he was disposing of some stolen goods. They found your car stereo in his possession." The ACP opened his briefcase and placed on X's table a lovely Sony car stereo. X looked at him and said, "Friend, I am sorry to disappoint you. My car is an old Premier Padmini and my stereo was made locally. This is a Sony and does not belong to me."

The ACP was startled. Recovering his composure soon, he said, "Sir, I knew that this did not belong to you. But I am certain that it is a stolen stereo system. The owner of this stereo system has preferred not to lodge a complaint and in this vast city there is no chance of locating him. We both know that your set was lost. If you do not accept this piece as yours, it will get consigned to the Lost Property Room and become junk in six months. No one will be happy if that happens."So saying, he got his driver to fit the 'Sony' stereo system in X's car. X was a mute spectator.

(Source Courtesy: Business Ethics by C.S.V. Murthy)

Issues to Reflect :

(*a*) Do you find that X is ethical in his act? Comment.

(*b*) Did the ACP's logic prevail over X's conscience? Discuss.

(*c*) If you were X, how you have reacted in this context considering the question of logic over conscience?

(*d*) Make an ethical assessment of the case.

17

UNIT

Ethics: A Holistic Approach

17

17 UNIT

Ethics: A Holistic Approach

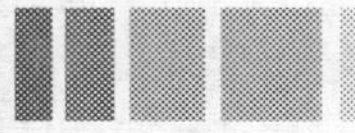

17.1 LEARNING OBJECTIVES

In this unit, we will understand some of the factors that influence development of ethical norms. We will also understand the various aspects of generational impact on ethics and the different types of generations that are observed today.

17.2 SOURCES OF ETHICAL NORMS

Society evolves over time and so would culture, of which values and ethics are integral parts. There is a need to understand the major changes which have a potential to affect and modify the thinking patterns of persons in the society over the decades or generations. These changes have a bearing on their behaviour, attitudes in organizations and outside and towards work.

Let us try to understand how values and ethics are internalized by persons in a typical context. It would become clearer subsequently as to how the ethics are likely to vary between the generations.

Sources of Ethical norms: Ethical norms are ways of behaving that are considered normal within a particular culture, group or society. Norms are more specific than values. Honesty is a value but the rules defining what is honest behaviour in a particular situation are norms.

Ethical norms are the expectation of a proper behaviour and not the requirement of it as such. They essentially represent the standards of desirable behaviour by reference to which a behaviour is judged and approved or disapproved. They may be prescriptive (encouraging positive behaviour; for example, "be honest") or proscriptive (discouraging negative behaviour; for example; "do not cheat".) They can also be formal and informal, visible or invisible, or explicit or implicit. As norms reflect a consensus pattern of behaviours and internalized values, they are learned through socialization and enforced through negative or positive sanctions. Ethical norms function like a glue and contribute to maintain social order. Let us see some of the major factors that shape-up ethical norms to get formed or undergo a change:

(*a*) Family

(*b*) Religion

(*c*) School & teachers

(*d*) Friends

(*e*) Co-employees

(*f*) Profession

(*g*) Employer

(*h*) Law

(*i*) Society

Family: The most important source of ethical norms is one's family, particularly the parents. The beliefs that the family members have about right and wrong, or good and bad deeply influence a child while growing up. A person first observes the daily behaviour of his or her family members (parents, grandparents and other elders in a nuclear or joint family, as the case may be) and forms a viewpoint on the core values and morals. A few of them are integrity, credibility, truthfulness, responsibility, fairness, respect for elders, dignity, etc. Family not only occupies a strategic and sensitive position in the ethical upbringing of children, but it also helps them establish their ethical or moral identity through dialogic interactions during this early period. Family-based businesses are a great example for their success (although beyond first three generations, many family businesses fail world over) in this context as how their family values help influencing the employees and the workplace. Some families set a wrong example on a person from the very childhood on account of the poor value system, which makes the children to take many of the things as acceptable.

Religion: The second most important source of formation of ethical norms is the religion. The religion of the family in which one is born contributes to forming and shaping of one's values. Ethical norms are acquired by a child through the religious inclinations of his or her parents and grandparents during the formative years. When a child goes to temple or mosque or church or any

other religious place with parents, such visits help to understand what sorts of behaviours are acceptable and what actions are deemed unacceptable. All religions which have been embraced by humankind over thousands of years preach ideals, ethics and moral values that are universal in nature such as truth, forgiveness, harmlessness, respecting all human beings, hope, compassion, etc. To take an example, all religions contain in their religious texts some version of the Golden Rule: "Do unto others as you would wish them do unto you". In other words, we should treat others the way we would want to be treated. This is the basic ethic that guides all religions. Thus, religion prescribes what is right and wrong and society subscribes to such norms.

Schools/Teachers: The third vital source of transmission and promotion of the ethical norms are schools and teachers. Home is the first place, while schools and teachers are the second place where moral socialization of children or students takes place. Teachers are a role model for the students. Their actions convey more than the word. As students spend a large amount of time in schools, they closely observe the behaviours of their teachers and try to imitate these behaviours in the school and afterwards. In the process, students come to imbibe, learn and assimilate the same behaviours in themselves knowingly or unknowingly. Thus, teachers exercise a huge impact on the personality of a student in the formative years and in order to develop a desirable character in the students, they are expected to set a standard of ethical behaviours before the student. They can foster various moral qualities to the students through both curricular and co-curricular activities. Otherwise too, apart from the parents, school teachers are the most influential adults in the life of the children right from the stage of the pre-school years. As such, it is the core professional responsibility of teachers that they should act as mentors or moral exemplars of the students and contribute not only in teaching them, but also in shaping up their ethical bearings through moral education.

Friends: Exposure to a group of close friends has its own positive or adverse effect on an individual in firming up the moral value and ethics. Some statements or disclosures by the friends is taken on its face value and children in the formative age of their personality form strong opinions that are hard to change as they grow-up into adults. At times, simply for quick recognition or gaining popularity in a group, youngsters might lie something and other/s might believe in it and would like to follow the same unsuspectingly, which may make the followers to face troubles in future. Alternatively, good values (such as hard-work, straightforwardness, perseverance, etc.) may build strong zeal and encourage and eventually contribute some children to become highly successful in the studies, careers and even in life.

Co-employees: Great organizations are differentiated from the ordinary ones not merely on account of their financial and business-related achievements but also on their value systems. Those organizations that have shown enough care in selecting employees in the formative years after they were founded, those individual employees by virtue of their personal values and conduct influence the other employees. This would lead to a chain reaction and one day the entire organization transforms itself into a value-driven organization ensuring not merely desirable business results but results in the much-needed goodwill and reputation.

Profession: Several professions like law, teaching and research, banking and insurance, auditing, medicine, journalism, information technology, armed forces, bureaucracy, etc. require highest ethical standards. Knowingly, a professional cannot be expected to compromise on some values of honesty and integrity, confidentiality, empathy, lawful behaviour, loyalty, etc. Those persons who follow these make the profession a revered one. Society exhibits a great respect while it deals with persons engaged in such great services which have immense contribution to the well-being of the people at large.

Employer: Employers have an influence on the ethics of the employees and other stakeholders. As was covered earlier in this book in the context of ethical leadership, moral, amoral and immoral leadership styles have different influences on the employees in adopting different ethical principles. The moral leadership, which not only follows highest ethical standards personally but strongly supports and defends their subordinates and equally strongly ensures unethical employees are given deserving punishment, promote ethical conduct among all the employees. Vice versa is true in case of immoral leadership, while amoral leadership leaves the "choice" of being ethical to the employees themselves.

Law: This source of ethical norms is different than the others. By definition, law mandates or prohibits certain activities that are considered by society at large as unethical or immoral. In all countries that respect the rule of law, law makers (like the members of parliament in India) formulate and make laws that are

made as Acts. These Acts are then enforced by law (subject to technical scrutiny for their legality and constitutional validity). Once notified, all these laws must be followed by the concerned, failing which there will be fines/penalties or even imprisonment depending upon the seriousness of the offence. For example, theft is morally wrong. The law also proscribes it as a punishable activity. However, the law makes it just not only morally wrong, but legally wrong as well. In this way, law is a system of rules enforced through penalties for anyone who violates the rules. This creates a deterrent effect in the mind of the people and they shun any unethical behaviour that breaks the law.

Society: It is an old saying that it takes a village to raise a child. The same can be said about the contribution of society in inculcating the ethical norms in an individual. Every society has its own beliefs, customs, shared values, rules and standards of living which are transmitted to its members over the years and largely guide their actions and reactions. This ethical transmission takes place in the course of social interactions or through family and friends or at religious places which not only help ingraining the collective beliefs and values but also in strengthening the same through reiterated experiences. Society tells people how they should behave. It promotes self-discipline among the people who try to behave in a manner commensurable to the expected standards. If someone doesn't align with the societal expectations, he or she may have to face sanctions in the form of social isolation, etc. However, what society tells is not always fair or right. Sometimes a society places emphasis on a particular behaviour that may stem from history, religion, a tradition or a commonly held belief but may not be right or morally correct. For example, few societies regard honour killing as an accepted behaviour believing that the victim has brought dishonour upon the family name or prestige or caste. However, honour killing as it denies the right to life and personal liberty is neither fair nor legal. It is often the result of strongly misogynistic views towards women and the position of women in society and total disregard towards the value of compassion, tolerance, diversity and empathy. It may be noted that ethics is always in the context of a particular form of societal organization whether it is a group of people or a particular community or a society or culture.

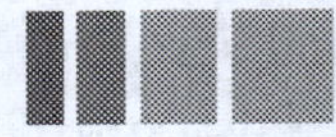

17.3 GENERATIONAL DIFFERENCE IN ETHICS

All persons are born during a phase of broadly 30 years, which constitutes a generation. In this 30-years span, children born witness common significant events (be it wars, famines, influence of great spiritual or political leaders, fruits of science and technology, economic or political order like world turning towards globalization or democracy, so on), grow up and mature into adults and become parents.

Organisations (both in the banking or financial sector or non-financial sectors) function with persons of varying ages. The Boards of Directors, top internal management generally comprise of persons who have significant number of experiences in the same functional area or related or relevant sectors. For example, a Board member on a steel manufacturing company can be from the fields of law, audit, public relations, etc. Middle-management personnel can be in their mid-30s or early 40s, however they are younger to the members occupying the external or internal leadership positions. New recruits will be mostly in mid-20s or nearing the age of 30 with high academic and professional qualifications at the entry and with no or minimal work experience or exposure. The organisation must function with these three categories of employees who are distinct groups inside the same organisation.

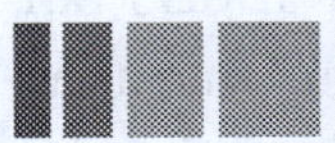

17.4 GEN X, GEN Y OR MILLENNIALS

There is a manner presently in which the generations are commonly described or labelled for the past, present and future generations. The Gen-X, Gen-Y or the Millennials.

One thing that is clear about the labelling of generations as X, Y (sometimes called the Millennial/s) is that there are no universally acceptable dates for them.

Gen-X refers to persons who are born roughly between 1961 and 1983 (some define those born during 1965-1980). The inference we can draw is that these persons of Gen X, if employed, would just be on the verge of their retirement from active working or would be just gaining maturity in job and aspiring to scale up the organizational hierarchy. Gen-Y or the Millennials refers to those who are born after 1980. (Source: http://www.pewsocialtrends.org/2014/03/07/millennials-in-adulthood/sdt-next-america-03-07-2014-0-06/).

Understanding Differences between the Generations: While many of us can form personal views or opinions on the characteristics of persons belonging to a certain age group or a Generation, for a greater acceptability, there needs to be a proper research survey and the responses to scientifically formed questions need to be analysed before forming some inference on characteristics of each of the generations.

National Business Ethics Survey (NBES) has been carrying out survey reports of employees working in corporate firms based in the United States of America almost for a quarter century now since 1994.

The Ethics Research Centre (ERC) is a non-profit organisation (NPO) working for almost a century now since 1922 by carrying out independent research and advancement of high ethical standards in public and private institutions which are committed to strong ethical culture.

NBES and ERC have carried out a survey in 2011 and published these results. The NBES Survey classified the generations into 4 categories:

- Baby Boomers: born between 1946-1964
- Gen X: Born during 1965-1982
- Gen Y or Millennial: Born during 1981-2000

Major findings of the Survey were:

1. Millennial segment appears to observe fewer boundaries than previous generations and are more flexible about when and how to apply them.
2. Their flexibility might make Millennials more likely to engage in or tolerate behaviour that many consider unacceptable.
3. Gen X'ers are less likely to turn to formal systems and corporate standards to help with their ethics questions, but still do so more than Boomers and Traditionalists.
4. Baby Boomers are more likely to listen to management and take cues from company leaders on ethics matters. (Source: NBES Survey, pp: 8-9)

Millennials also prefer constant feedback from their seniors. Seniors should be open in communicating with their millennial staff regarding ethical behaviour to improve the overall standards of behaviour.

As far the Indian scenario is concerned, the events and the development of the economy and businesses are somewhat different as compared to the United States, which has been always a developed country.

Tammy Erickson (2009) carried a gist of the differences between the generations in the two countries - United States of America and India in his article "Generational Differences between India and the US" published by the Harvard Business Review (HBR March 01, 2009).

(Source: https://hbr.org/2009/02/global-generations-focus-on-in).

The article considers Generation X as people born during 1961-79 and Generation Y during 1980 and 1995. The events that have a bearing on the Generation Y are summarized by Erickson in the above HBR article as follows:

"In India, the late 1990's and 2000's saw the development of a large middle-class and increased demand for and production of many consumer goods - in many ways, a situation reminiscent of the U.S. Traditionalists' experience with a rapidly expanding pie. The Indian economy grew under liberalization and reform policies, the country was stable and prosperous and political power changed hands without incident. India became a prestigious educational powerhouse and respected source of IT talent. By 2008, 34 Indian companies were listed in Forbes Global 2000 ranking".

The characteristics of Generation Y are summarized by Erickson as follows:

1. Y's in India share the generation's global sense of immediacy, coupled with the excitement of being part of the country's first wave of broad economic opportunity.
2. As a result, young employees in India tend to share the rapid tempo of U.S. Y's ambitions, but with a greater emphasis on financial reward as a desired outcome.
3. They have come of age in an exciting, dynamic country with significant economic opportunity.
4. Most are entrepreneurial and business savvy, as well as technologically capable and connected.
5. Their mental model is heavily influenced by India's rich, complex democracy - they easily accept diversity of opinion - as well as by the Western

heritage of laws and customs left from the old days of British rule, making them strongly suited for global interaction.

Of late, one more category namely Generation Z or Post-Millennials or Zoomers has been recognised. They are also called as iGeneration or Centennials. The demographers describe Generation Z as those born between 1995-2014. This generation precedes Generation Alpha and is the successor to Generation Y. The main characteristics of this generation, largely consisting of the children of Gen Y, are independence, compassion, open-mindedness, low loyalty and digital nativity. This is a highly entrepreneurial generation which is progressive, ambitious, incredibly competitive but less focused and seek out constant feedback. To remain motivated, they also look for diversity, individuality and creativity in their organizations. It is thought that this generation is more open to ethical inculcation and exhibit a higher degree of ethical sensitivity.

Few demographers are of the view that Generation Z is of those born between 1995-2010 and not between 1995-2014. Those born after 2010 are called Alpha generation. This generation is the most highly educated generation in the history and has heightened awareness of social issues like sustainability, climate, inequality, nutrition, gender diversity, and race. They possessability to establish large companies at a very young age and are relatively materialistic. One unique characteristic of this generation is that they feel a deep responsibility to reverse the damage of the past generations.

Thus, there are obvious differences in attitudes towards ethical issues among the various generational cohorts. This inconsistency results into a good deal of variability in the effectiveness of the measures deployed to improve workplace ethics. Even so, the encouraging finding for the banks is that Millennials and post-Millennials show high inclination and active involvement to be ethically proactive in response to the ethics initiatives. They are going to form a major part of the banking workforce in days to come.

17.5 ETHICS MANUAL

In order to set an example, RBI has brought out for its own employees an Ethics Manual in 2013 by defining the purpose, vision, mission, quality policy, etc. Each individual scheduled commercial banks also need to develop brief and easily comprehensible ethics manual for all its employees, which may be periodically updated and made accessible to them at all times so that in case of any ethical dilemma, they may refer to it. Although there is no one universal format for the Ethics Manual world over for the banking sector or other non-banking entities, yet there can be some common aspects that can be found across the organisations that are highly committed for making them ethically-bound. Some of the points discussed in section 11.2 may also appear in the Ethics Manual.

I. Defining the Purpose

II. Vision/Mission

III. Our Personality

IV. Our Values

V. Our Assurance

VI. Employees' Commitment to
- (*a*) Law
- (*b*) Government
- (*c*) Regulator
- (*d*) Customers regarding
  - ◆ Courtesy
  - ◆ Service Quality
- (*e*) Public At large

VII. Employees' Commitment to Bank
- (*a*) Protect, Preserve and Defend Bank's reputation
- (*b*) Retain confidential or sensitive Information
- (*c*) Integrity
- (*d*) Fairness
- (*e*) Avoidance and/or Managing Conflicts of Interest
- (*f*) Social Media Protocols

VIII. Commitment to Community
- (*a*) Corporate Social Responsibility
  - ◆ Activities Currently Covered

- Possible New Areas (with the written Approval of Designated Top Management)

(*b*) Promoting Art

(*c*) Promoting Talent among youngsters

(*d*) Basic Financial Literacy

IX. Commitment to Environment

X. Employee Rights

Bank may inform and educate all employees in the training itself about all applicable Laws/regulations which makes his employment a career with enough security. Employees should be free of all kinds of apprehensions that they may be terminated at the will of the employer in an unfair manner. Enough assurance may be provided during the probation period itself about their rights.

XI. Professional Rules and Ethical Principles

(*a*) Professional Rules

(*b*) Ethical Principles

XII. Defining the Procedure

i. Who can file application for violation of Ethics/Professional Principle/s? Which are not to be considered (like matters which are *subjudice*)

ii. Time limitation (from the date of an incident/observation, application must be submitted within a specified time limit)

iii. Complete details to be furnished

iv. Preliminary Scrutiny/Escalation procedure. If rejected, applicant should be informed in writing the reason for rejection within a stipulated timeframe.

v. The Ethics Committee (Chief Ethics Officer and other members with high ethical record or least controversial members of management)

vi. Process to be followed by the Ethics Committee

vii. Actions from Ethics Committee (may not find *prima facie* evidence or may refer to the Board of Directors) *viii.* Decisions may be communicated in writing to complainant and accused within a timeframe even no evidence of ethics violation was found

ix. Decisions taken by the Board on matters of ethics cases referred to it within a timeframe (twice or at least once a year)

XIII. Internal Record System

There needs to be an internal record system of Zone/Division/Branch-wise cases filed, disposed, dismissed along with reasons. These can be used (by masking specific details) to provide training the younger staff with no prior banking experience at the stage of induction so as to capitalize the entire time and efforts of the top managements in creating the ethical organisation as a mission.

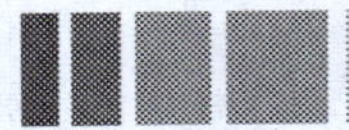

17.6 BUSINESS CYCLES & ETHICS

Business Cycles

A progressive country's output rises over time with some trend rate of growth say 5-6 percent per annum. But this increase is not uniform across all years over a phase like 20 years or more. Fluctuations in the real economic growth measured by real GDP over a long period can be analyzed in terms of a *business cycle*. This cycle has four phases. These phases are:

- Expansion or Boom
- Recession
- Depression
- Recovery

The business cycle is the periodic but irregular up-and-down movements in economic activity, measured by fluctuations in real GDP and other macroeconomic variables. A business cycle is not a regular, predictable or repeating phenomenon like the swinging of the pendulum of a clock. Its timing is random and to a large degree, unpredictable.

Business cycle theory matters simply because many people believe business cycles exist. This has not been a permanent belief. In the 19th Century, business cycles were not thought of as cycles at all but rather as spells of "crises" interrupting

the smooth development of the economy. In later years, economists and non-economists alike began believing in the regularity of such crises, analyzing how they were spaced apart and associated with changing economic structures.

Business cycles are witnessed commonly in capitalistic economies. Such economies are largely handled by a small group of capitalists whose investment is vital for the country's output and its growth. When the economy has higher aggregate demand, there exists a widespread optimism amongst the capitalists who continue making higher and higher investments. Sooner the economy starts moving towards a boom. However, the investments in the recent past would have created the capacities in the existing firms to such large level that currently all that is produced and supplied by the business firms cannot be sold easily. This makes some capitalists to hold back the investment plans either partly or fully. This move would cause a decline in the demand for the goods and services for all the firms. This makes the capitalists to review and downwardly adjust their future investment plans. The economy produces less and the growth slows down. The previous phase of boom now takes a down turn, called the recession.

During recession, the governments spend money through public investments and also provide incentives that encourage the individuals to spend more. These would eventually revive the economy from a depression.

Naturally, not every economic cycle operates on the same yardstick. The following classification, originally conjured up by Schumpeter (1939), defines a few of them by their duration (trough to trough or peak to peak).

The business cycle or economic cycle refers to the fluctuations of economic activity about its long-term growth trend. The cycle involves shifts over time between periods of relatively rapid growth of output (recovery and prosperity), and periods of relative stagnation or decline (contraction or recession). These fluctuations are often measured using the real gross domestic product. Despite being named cycles, these fluctuations in economic growth and decline do not follow a purely mechanical or predictable periodic pattern.

- Seasonal cycles - within a year
- Kitchin cycles - 3 years
- Juglar cycles - 9-10 years

- Kuznets cycles - 15-20 years
- Kondratiev cycles - 48-60 years

Long protracted recession is called depression. Recession is often defined as contraction in the GDP growth for at least two consecutive quarters. Boom represents the highest point of economic activity before a downturn. The low point of economic activity prior to the recovery is known as trough.

Movements in US real GDP since 1920s till 2004 could be identified with the phases of several business cycles. For instance, the initial decline between 1929 and 1933 was known as The Great Depression, the period of 1942 to 1945 boom and recession occurred during 1973-1975, 1981-1982 and 1990-91 and 2001.

Long-duration business cycles are not in vogue in recent past, as the citizens and business leaders have become more vocal and media have been exerting greater pressure on the governments (even in the so-called capitalistic countries) to intervene decisively to revive the economies if they are hit by severe recessions.

When the output is growing more quickly than normal trend rate of growth, the phase is known as expansion. Conversely, when the output grows slower than the normal growth, the phase is called recession.

Peak and trough are beginning and ending of recession. Expansion and recession are difficult to predict due to irregular length and severity. They have global and local impacts affecting various industries and regions. Expansions and recessions are marked by fall and rise in unemployment. Industries of durable goods are impacted by recessions and expansions whereas non-durable goods and services are less sensitive to short-term economic fluctuations. Before one realizes the recessionary phase, one would have already witnessed a decline in the rate of inflation.

Characteristics of Business Cycles

- Fluctuations of aggregate economic activity.
- Expansion/Boom and Contraction/Recession.
- Peak and Trough: They are the turning Points of the business cycle.
- Co-movements of many macro variables over the business cycle.
- Business Cycles are Recurrent but not periodic.

Four phases of business cycles

A boom is a rise which lasts until the peak is reached; a recession is the drop or downturn from the peak back to the mean (or average or trend growth rate); a depression is the slide from the mean down to the trough; a recovery is the rise from the trough back up to the mean. From the mean, we then move up into another boom and thus the beginning of another four-phase cycle. In a sense, any cycle of whatever duration can be described as going through these four phases - otherwise the fluctuations cannot really be described as "cycles".

Relationship between Business Cycles and Ethics

- During recovery of the economy, corporate firms and other businesses face higher demand for their products and services, which make them borrow heavy loans from the banking sector.
- Due to internal and external shocks, economies might face slower growth leading to recessional conditions.
- Banks may not do appropriate credit appraisals and take risk measures taking into account projected growth rates and business cycle movements.
- Some of the decisions to liberally fund the expansion of the corporate and business sectors may prove incorrect resulting in non-performing assets problem and its accumulation.
- Genuine defaulters need to be differentiated from the wilful defaulters.
- Basic understanding of business cycles helps banking personnel in appraisal and disbursement departments. It helps to evaluate credit proposals with a realistic view based on the laid down ethical principles and norms of the banks. For instance, a client may be optimistic in the projected annual sales of his entity. However, a sudden turn in business cycle may adversely impact his expectations and dampen his repayment capacity.

In an essay 'A Theory of the Ethical Business Cycle', Ian Maitland suggests that the ethics of business is congruent with business cycles. He argues that business ethics deteriorates during boom times and improves during recessions. He makes a valid point in the sense that it is human nature to not ask questions about why things are going well and to become introspective when things fall apart. (Source: Is Business Ethics Getting Better? A Historical Perspective by Joanne B. Ciulla)

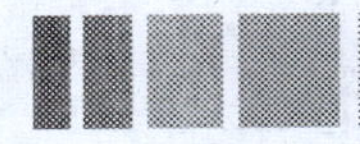

17.7 ACCOUNTABILITY

The term Accountability derives from the Latin word 'accompare' which means to account. The word 'accompare' is a prefixed form of Latin 'computare' (to calculate) which takes its origin from 'putare' or 'to reckon'. Greg Bust in his book 'Accountability' tells us that account-giving has its roots in record keeping activities related to governance and money lending systems first developed in Ancient Israel, Babylon, Egypt, Greece, and later, Rome. In this sense, accountability is concerned within the past, settling up accounts and takes the form of a contract, a commitment, a personal promise. Accountability is critical for all organizations because, after all, every business is a people business and accountability works as a support system for success.

Accountability is an elusive concept and may have more than one meaning depending upon the context in which it is used. A simple definition of accountability is taking or being assigned, responsibility for something that you have done, or something you are supposed to do. It is mainly concerned about the definition of a certain type of conduct and how it is assessed. Boven (2010) describes accountability as a synonym to good governance.

The activities of an organization have the potential to impact on all aspects of society and this drives the need for organization to demonstrate good ethical and moral behaviour and accountability.

There are two aspects that need to be clearly differentiated, responsibility and accountability. All individuals employed in various capacities are responsible for the bank's overall performance. While different departments are entrusted with specific tasks, their role is considered fulfilled once they complete the tasks within the stipulated timeframe and in a prescribed manner. In the quality standards' terminology, a process is performed by several members of whom someone is a process owner.

Accountability differs from responsibility in the sense that responsibility can be shared while accountability cannot. Responsibility is one's duty to respond to the assigned tasks appropriately. Multiple people can be responsible for achieving a specific outcome. However, being accountable not only means being responsible for something but also ultimately being answerable for your actions. As Tom Moore explains, "Accountability is not task-focused but result focused. Whereas

responsibility is an ongoing duty to complete the task, accountability happens after completing the task. To be accountable, one is obligated and answerable for the results of one's or other's actions. Being account table often means that the person(s) is likely to face the consequences from some authority if the result does not meet the expectations. To cite an example, we can take the case of Enron scandal that led to the bankruptcy of the Enron Corporation. Members of the executive board were indicted for their illegal and unethical actions. CEO Kenneth Lay was of the people indicted. Lay insisted that Enron's collapse was due to a conspiracy waged by short sellers, rogue executives and the news media -implying that while he could be held accountable as the CEO and leader of the organization, he was not in any way responsible for the fraud in the company. However, a jury found Lay guilty on six counts of conspiracy and fraud, making the CEO responsible as well as accountable for the downfall of the company. (Source for this example: diffen.com)

Usually, a person who supervises and monitors the tasks of all other departments and divisions remains the one who the owners expect to give explanation or reasoning for a lapse in the functioning of an organisation. In fact, accountability is in every organisation where there is delegation of power and more so in the banks who deals with public funds. In banks, where a large number of people are employed to do specific tasks and vested with various level of powers, it is unavoidable that they should be held accountable for their actions or decisions. However, if the delegated actions have remained within the framework of the prescribed guidelines or norms, there arises no question of accountability of whatsoever nature. Mere ethical deviation, not amounting to a breach of law or rule, may go unpunished. At best, there can be a reprimanding by a senior official and an advice not to repeat the act by explaining to the person concerned as to why such an act is seen within the framework of a workplace, such as a bank or financial institution for example, as an unethical deed. Here again, it is to be remembered that the purpose of looking into the accountability aspect of an action is to safeguard the interests of the organisation in the long-term and with this perspective every mistake need not attract punishment of even the mildest nature.

17.8 ACCOUNTABILITY IN THE PUBLIC SECTOR BANKS

The present system of accountability in the public sector banks has evolved over the years stemming from the concern to establish as to which of the rules or instructions or practices were overlooked by an individual in the discharge of his or her responsibilities in a particular post or role. The aim of the accountability exercise has always ideally been to shield the genuine business decisions of the employees and thereby ensuring that the initiative and prompt decision-making do not get discouraged amongst them. However, during the course of time, the term 'accountability' has taken on a negative connotation and more so amongst the bankers since their dealings are entirely financial in nature. Many instances and practices of fixing accountability in public sector banks have been found to be inconsistent with the corporate goals of these commercial organization. While leadership of the banks keeps on emphasizing aggressive marketing and innovative approach to succeed in a competitive market, the accountability exercises within the banks have often tended to be a drag and a discouraging factor in taking business-related decisions. This creates a feeling amongst the officers that there should be no room for error in one's work and makes them wary of taking business decisions as they are apprehensive that, if any of the commercial decisions taken by them, despite being *bona fide*, turn bad and fail to meet the acceptable parameters, they will have to face the scrutiny of probes and vigilance enquiries in future. This inhibition makes them extremely cautious and risk-averse in asmuchas the credit decisions are concerned and adversely affects the growth of the banks. The banks are commercial organizations where decisions are taken on the basis of available data and each decision contains some element of fair banking risks. In the process, there is a possibility for genuine errors of judgment/ decisions taken on purely commercial considerations and in good faith after following the procedures. Such errors and judgments are to be examined with an absolute professional approach. While there is agreement all around that the cases involving lack of integrity need to be dealt with severely, the practices followed for determining whether a given cases has 'vigilance angle' or not seem to need more clarity to eliminate the subjectivity.

The negative perception is compounded by the fact of an independent statutory watchdog- the Central Vigilance Commission (CVC) monitors the vigilance

function and implements the measures for maintenance of integrity and probity in PSBs. Moreover, as the officials in the public sector banks are treated as public servants, they are subject to the provisions of Prevention of Corruption Act, 2018 and any failed credit decision which is in the range of Rs. 3 crore and above and has an element of fraud is to be reported to the Central Bureau of Investigation.

This perception existed in the minds of bankers notwithstanding the fact that the vigilance administration in public sector banks aspires not to be a restraining factor for business growth rather a constructive tool for achieving organizational excellence by ensuring that the officers dealing with the public funds feel responsible as well as accountable while dealing with the public funds. An excerpt from the **Vigilance Manual** published by the **Central Vigilance Commission** may shed some light on the fallacy associated with the vigilance function while highlighting its positive role in accelerating the growth of quality business-

> 'The raison d'etre of vigilance activity in banks is not to reduce but to enhance the level of managerial efficiency and effectiveness in the organization. In banking, risk taking forms an inalienable part of business. Therefore, every loss caused to the bank, either in pecuniary or non-pecuniary terms, need not necessarily become the subject matter of vigilance enquiry. A distinction has to be drawn between a business loss which has arisen as a consequence of a *bona fide* commercial decision, and an extra ordinary loss which has occurred due to any *mala fide*, motivated or reckless performance of duties. While the former has to be accepted as a normal part of business and ignored from the vigilance point of view, the latter has to be viewed adversely and dealt with under the extant disciplinary procedures.'

To illustrate, a loan can turn bad due to a number of reasons like change in market conditions, change in law, inefficient management, natural calamities etc. which are beyond the control of the officials dealing with the particular loan in a bank. In this situation, there should be no case for accountability. At the same time, there may be reasons attributable to the staff who handled the advance and who by negligence/omission/commission/collusion failed to protect the interests of the bank. In this situation, the accountability could be for acts of inadvertence or deliberate omission and commission as the case may be. A meaningful reading of the excerpt brings out in categorical terms that the CVC's guidance is for an accountability process that is positive in its approach and intends to support the banks for achieving a sustainable growth. Otherwise also, as stated in the earlier section, the purpose of conducting the accountability exercise *per se* is to protect the larger interests of the bank. To that end, the first step that ought to be taken should be to identify the areas where the rules and procedures designed to protect the interests of the bank are not being followed. As a follow up of such identification, the bank should take necessary corrective steps by way of strengthening any knowledge gaps or by way of augmenting the resources or by any other action to create an environment which could be conducive for better observance of rules and procedures for ethically attaining the business goals. Punishing people should be the secondary step. The intention of punishment should be:

1. To instill a sense of guilt and resultant repentance on the part of the official who committed the lapses, so that, in future, he/she will conduct himself in a more responsible fashion, and
2. To convey a message to the rest of the staff in the organization that they should not conduct themselves in a way detrimental to the interests of the bank as otherwise they also might have to suffer similar unpleasant consequences.

In this context, following a few instances of the arrest of senior bank executives by the law enforcement agencies, the Government, in order to assure the bankers that adequate measures shall be taken to protect *bona fide* commercial decisions and a distinction would be made between genuine commercial failures and culpability, incorporated one Section 17A in the Prevention of Corruption Act. This section mandates that prior permission from the organization is required before initiating an investigation against a public servant if the issue is relatable to any recommendation made or decision taken by him in the discharge of his official functions/duties. In order to standardize and operationalize the procedures of the prior approval process under Section 17A of PC Act effectively, the Government has also laid down an Standard Operating Procedures (SOP) for the purpose.

Further, the Finance Ministry asked the public sector banks to adopt a uniform Staff Accountability Framework for Non-Performing Asset (NPAs) up to Rs. 50 crore based on the guidelines issued by them. This was done to introduce a standardization in the processes of staff accountability exercises being conducted

by different banks in respect of all accounts that turn into NPA. These guidelines have been implemented with effect from April 1, 2022 with the main objective that the new norms would provide protection for the *bona fide* actions of bank officials while also call them to the books for any wrong doing or in action on their part. The guidelines emphasize that the staff accountability exercise is to be carried out in the light of circumstances prevailing at the time the events occurred and not with the benefit of hind sight and isolating the specific causes (internal or external) for the loss should form an important element of the process.

Bolstering the morale of bankers becomes vital in the backdrop of slow credit off take as a growing economy depends heavily on bank credit. Therefore, eradication of fear in taking business decisions was an urgent imperative and the amendment in PC Act has truly contributed towards that direction by saving the honest bankers from the agony of undergoing unnecessary probes and inquiries. Nonetheless, as the PSBs will have to live with the vigilance oversight for the foreseeable future, subject to supervisory jurisdiction of CVC, and this being so, it is essential for the bank management to convey to the staff the importance and efficacy of putting their faith in the internal set up of revised accountability in the banks. It is also necessary to stress that accountability and business development are complimentary to each other and not mutually exclusive. Healthy accountability process enables sound growth of business.

17.9 SUPPORTIVE ACCOUNTABILITY: AN ACCOUNTABILITY MODEL TO DRIVE HIGH PERFORMANCE IN PSBs

Sylvia Melena in her book "Supportive Accountability – How to Inspire People and Improve Performance" proposes a powerful framework for positive accountability around the centerpiece of supportive accountability, which blends supportive supervision and accountability to engage employees and ignite strong performances. This framework has four constituents as under:

1. **Unsupportive Accountability** is characterized by high levels of accountability and low levels of support. In extreme cases of this approach, a high degree of accountability is applied but the emotional and material support that employees need to be successful is not provided. In this scenario, it is difficult to achieve the organizational goals.

2. **Supportive Unaccountability** is demonstrated by high levels of support and low levels of accountability. In this approach, there is a high degree of supportive unaccountability to keep employees happy but it tends to lead to permissiveness in adherence to the prescribed rules and regulations. In this case, organizational goals are achieved but in a short-term only and not in a sustainable way.
3. **Total Avoidance** is the absence of both support and accountability. This is a hands-off approach, where the organization relinquishes its responsibility to lead, guide, inspire and hold the employees accountable for meeting the organizational goals. Achievement of organizational goals may happen sometimes and sometimes not.
4. **Supportive Accountability** is the most effective of the four performance management styles. It's exemplified by a high level of supportiveness complemented by a high level of accountability. Organizations gauge each situation and provide the right amount of support and accountability based on the needs of the individual employee, the facts involved, environmental conditions and other factors. The organization not only achieves its goals but also grows sustainably.

The above framework is based on seven elements of strong performance management – expectations, monitoring, feedback, support, recognition, documentation and accountability. Expectations give direction and focus. Monitoring is the act of measuring, observing and reviewing performance. It focuses employees on what matters. Performance feedback lets employees know whether or not they are on target in meeting expectations, goals and objectives. To perform at their best, employee needs support. Support comes in many forms, including tools, equipment, guidance, training, access to information and more. Employee recognition lets employee know that their contributions towards the goals of organization are acknowledged and appreciated. Adequate documentation is critical in the accountability management process. It serves as evidence for whether one has met one's responsibility in discharging duties. Accountability makes employees to hold themselves accountable for meeting performance goals and objectives. Accountability again has a sub-framework of the four P's that can help promote accountability. This framework consists of principles:

1. **People** – People are the most important resources of a bank or any other organization. They need to feel safe, valued and cared about if accountability is to be promoted.
2. **Purpose** – Accountability starts with purpose. In Supportive Accountability Model, the goal of accountability isn't to punish, but rather to create a supportive work environment where employees can thrive and drive performance.
3. **Performance** – Accountability promotes performance. Effective supervisors manage performance with a balanced approach of support and accountability to move the dial in the right direction. They achieve and sustain great performance by simultaneously creating a great work environment and continuously focusing on performance.
4. **Progression** – Progression is the act of moving forward through continuous improvement until the desired performance outcomes are achieved. For accountability to advance performance, use progression.

Justice Potter Stewart noted that ethics is knowing the difference between what you have. The supportive accountability model adopts the most ethical approach towards the management of accountability in an organization. Both in the letter as well as the spirit, it is in alignment with the progressive discipline process which is used to correct behaviours and improve performance and promoting a work environment where employees are happy, perform better and are committed to the success of the bank. Every bank has a defined discipline process which is progressive in nature and aspires to improve performance or behaviour of employee by first resorting to the softer measures. However, in some serious cases, it becomes unavoidable to use the progressive levels of demonstrative corrections for maintaining the organizational order. What values should guide the behaviour of public servants in future and how these values might be operationalized in practice? Public servants are firstly expected to behave in 'responsible' way. This means that they take up their role as a public servant seriously and be aware of the consequences of their behaviour. Secondly, they should be transparent in their actions and decisions. Thirdly, they should follow integrity in their conduct meaning that the general interest and not the personal interest should determine their behaviour.

17.10 DOES ACCOUNTABILITY FOSTER ETHICAL BEHAVIOUR?

If we look at both accountability and ethics in behavioural terms within the institutional context, they are mutually inclusive from an outcome perspective. The presence of accountability mechanisms requiring 'answerability' in banks or other organizations *suo motu* helps fostering standards of responsible behaviours and professional integrity amongst the employees. Simple commitment to conduct one self responsibly or ethically is not sufficient to ensure that the spirit of the commitment will be carried out in actual practice or in high stake situations. Accountability in the form of external constraints and controls is necessary to render the decisions and behaviour of the officials more responsible whether in the public sector or otherwise, not merely from administrative aspects but morally as well. Ethical behaviour requires the presence of effective accountability mechanisms in all their various forms.

Several studies have been done to examine the effectiveness of the accountability. Ethics relationships and it is found that accountability impacts on the ethical standards of the employees/officials in an organization. While accountability is a kind of institutional forms of oversight in an organization ethical behaviour is associated with the individuals. Both accountability and ethical behaviour are organizational mechanisms design to obtain the desired outcomes for the organizational development and growth. Accountability as a process creates a situated pressure for account–giving behaviour on the organizational actors. Norms and standards of behaviour are followed as responses to the pressures created by accountability mechanisms and helps nurturing of ethical behaviours.

Historically, the turn accountability has distinctly angelicin and feudalistic routes and has only recently emerged has universal standards of governance. An individual is accountable to the extent that their exist and expectation within the organization that they would provide an explanation for any act regarded as worthy of account-giving. Accountability-as-Answerability is an important element for creating and sustaining cooperative organizational systems. In an environment where standards and rules are ambiguous or unstable, it would be reasonable to assume that a consistent adherence to some higher standards of personal conduct (e.g. to be trustworthy, honest, caring, etc.) would provide some protection from the whims off accountability as attribution (Source: Accountability and Ethics "reconsidering the relationship", by Melvin J. Dubnick). Ethics is an essence of professionalism as well efficiency in the workplace. They represent the character and standards that lead to behaviours and activities of individual. According to Davis, ethics are in morally accepted standards of behaviours and actions desired by every member of your organization in other fellows. It is also defined as a just or right moral of the behaviours among parties, something constituting good or bad conduct of the individuals, as a criterion to differentiate between good and bad, right and wrong and something that awareness about what we should do or should not do. They have impact on the ethical judgments made by the individuals having the legal and moral acceptance by the community. Hence, the organizational ethics can be observed in a form which controls the behaviours and action of the members of the organization. Moreover, thus ethics claims a legitimacy which is quite powerful and limits the behaviours and actions of individuals and holds them accountable for their doings. In the contemporary past, organizations have raised accountability in terms of ethics which make employees follow the highest standards regarding ethics. Accountability is an effective mechanism to control the conduct of the behaviours of individuals and employees within the societies and organizations respectively (Syial and Xin 2020). This connects the business ethics and accountability to determine the way individuals react to the dilemmas of ethics. Accountability represent the perception to defend and justify the conduct and behaviour of audience (employees) having rewards and sanctioning authority which are subject to the evaluation by the employees. Hence, accountability is based on certain rules and regulations, the way of evaluation of acts and behaviours, approaches of control in the organization set up, and the predefined expectations. Accountability has been well described from the lens of agency theory which argues that utility and effectiveness of individual depend on the level of essential in active restriction that hold them accountable. The employees who have certain constrains which stop them from actions and behaviours having the possibility of making them accountable are less liable to get involved in such behaviours and action against ethics. While the employees who are not bound with such restriction may get involved in such behaviours and acts which might be against the ethics of organization.

In banking ethics and accountability go hand in hand. Ethics and accountability are interconnected and should be seen in a corelated perspective to increase the understanding of both. Any variation in one leads towards another. A list of ethical responsibilities is not enough to create ethical responsibility in practice in the bank. If an employee perform beyond the established norms is liable to be held accountable for that (Source: Ethics and Accountability by Saeed Siyal). While accountability checks abuse of power, corruption, fraud, makes system more responsive and stops arbitrary and unauthorized exercise of authority. It also brings in risk aversion and develops status quoist attitude in fear of scrutiny. In a different context, Amartya Sen has aptly stated that "We don't need a democracy, we need an accountable democracy."

17.11 CHOOSING TO BE ETHICAL

As can be seen from all the Modules and Units covered in this courseware so far, there are several obligations and responsibilities in the career of a banker. With growing competition in media and the globalization and the connected world we are living in the 21st Century today, banks have multiple and complex situations to face. On one hand, they need to compete internally with others in their segment or across the banking system. Customers and clients are now well-informed in the Internet era about the costs of funds to a bank, bank's credit-deposit ratios, profit margins of banks, employee - strengths and top management remuneration, etc. On the other hand, simultaneously, more and more regulatory pressure for greater compliance is getting built up on the commercial banks in India. It is in the area of service quality standards, provisioning, disclosure of the asset quality, non-performing assets, reporting of frauds, etc. the objective of the strengthening regulation is to improve the Indian banking system and make it reach on par with the most credible banking industries of the world.

Making employees realize and adhere to their individual ethics, professional ethics, developing an ethical environment and an entire organization to follow ethical principles as a habit, in the midst of rapid improvements in technology, is really a tough challenge before the current top managements and boards of the banks and financial institutions.

As individuals, it is our capacity for self-accountability that keeps us functioning ethically and responsibly. Self-accountability is the cornerstone of ethics. It is who you are sand what you do when none is watching. As Ben Benjamin says that when you have a well-developed sense of self-accountability, you are honest with yourself, and are answerable and responsible for what you say and do. You have

the ability to look beyond the immediate moment to consider the consequences and know that if you are willing to pay them. You have personal ethics.

Personal ethics is precursor to the professional ethics, since we are not likely to be more ethical in our professional life than in our personal life. As the saying goes, " no matter where you go, there you are" in other words, if we are dishonest in our personal life, we are likely to be dishonest in our business affairs. (Ben Benjamin in Ethics and Self-Accountability from massagetoday.com) accountability has a positive effect on ethical competence. It's a significant positive predictor of ethical climate in an organization.

Despite the fact that an employee may have been influenced from a variety of sources for the ethical norms, which as mentioned in the earlier part of this Unit, but these are mere expectations from an individual or group of persons for a proper or acceptable behaviour and not necessarily a requirement. Though family, friends, co-employees, religion, etc. may have influenced the behaviour of a person (particularly at workplace), the employee as individual holds the sole accountability for lapses, if any, that are in contravention to an ethical code or a law. Therefore, as an employee, we should never lose sight of the fact that we all possess an innate capacity for moral growth. Learning to be an ethical person is an end-less process. We should also understand that environment and other factors, no doubt, influence our behaviour to a certain extent, yet we can always choose to place value on being ethical and make persistent efforts to shape our character on the desired lines.

It is generally seen that we all often go with the flow and put very little thought or conscious effort into determining how we respond to our daily decisions, however being ethical at work requires that we should always be mindful of the ethical dimensions that are embedded in our everyday activities. As L.E. Sekreka writes in the book, "Ethics is a Daily Deal" – ethics is about choosing to be morally aware and applying this moral awareness to your daily life. In ascertaining the ethical elements within a situation, both challenges and opportunities, a person has committed to being a moral agent, looking for the ethical features of decisions and choosing to address them with prudential judgment. The reality, however, is that many of us go through our day without a careful consideration of the ethical elements embedded in many of our choices. If you have a desire to be ethical, it is essential that you are rigorously honest with yourself about your motives and intentions as you make decisions.

Aristotle has explained that none of your moral virtues or character arise by nature. He goes on to say that neither by nature, nor contrary to it, do the virtues arise within us, rather we perfect them through our habits of use. Are you willing to develop the necessary skills to be more ethical? Perhaps one of the most exiting revolutions about being human is that we have a choice in how we steer our thoughts and behaviour. That means we can actually choose how our nature is manifest. Overtime, many of us develop patterns, habits that are incorporated into our daily actions repeatedly. Rather than maintain a conscious mind fullness of why we act in a certain way, we can become define by unattended familiar thoughts and behaviour. We fall into the comfort or ease of their own automaticity. it is easy to lose sight of the fact that there are opportunities for new ways of thinking and being throughout our day. As humans, we have a ongoing capacity to learn and change. But to tap into this capacity, we must choose to do so.

Being ethical implies that you have learned how to be honest with yourselves about who you really are. This in tales looking into your own behaviour, inclinations and practices, and striving to do better on and on basis. It is essential that people continually strive to ensure that the values they say they hold are demonstrated in their daily choices and actions. Thus, the ethical soundness within a person's identity is lifelong aspirations and daily chore. Your integrity is developed through conscious awareness, ongoing efforts to put your best ethical self forward. Because character is vulnerable to temptations and sometimes blind to automatic responses that can become ingrain over time, we all need to take stalk of our own behaviour, to look within, committing to self-direct reflection, discovery and improvement. The old days "you cannot teach an old dog new tricks" is inaccurate. Although our brain circuitry is laid out by a time, we are an adult, most of us have cognitive dexterity – the power, ability and capacity to change. Given the ability for cognitive and behavioural dexterity you can learn to be your own role model. You may not see yourself as a person with moral strength. However, if you begin to engage, you're in actions that demonstrate virtues (best ethical self), you essentially role-play your way in to a revised identity, fostering a new way of being. Responsibilities is about creating an internal process for building and sustaining a habit of ethical awareness and the desire and willingness to do the right thing. This translates into paying attention into how, where and when you can assume the responsibility

for doing good and avoiding unethical missteps. Such efforts require looking for an attending to the ethical elements of a situation – before taking action. To do this, one has to be mindful of the presence and recognize that once ethicality can improve or regress. The fact of the matter is that being ethical is not always easy. Being ethical at work takes work. The effort pays well in many forms, but not necessarily immediately. It requires a commitment to exercise your moral strength even when you may not be certain of a particular return. To own and develop your own ethical identity requires taking the bull by the horns and owing responsibilities for your decisions and actions. It is all about "just doing the right things". When individual begins to exercise their character strengths in achieving their personal and professional goals, ethics become inculcate into how business is actually conducted.

We can close this chapter with the words of ethics asks us to think mindfully, and challenges emotions by asking why we feel the way we do and if that feeling is fair. It demands that we not only feel but think through the situation. Ethics, then, is about creating strength (to turn a phrase, "right makes might"). It is not primarily about staying out of trouble, although avoiding misdoing is often a beneficial side effect of worthy behaviour. A person need not be an angel or a hero to behave ethically. The only moral requirement is to do good and avoid doing evil. Ethics does not demand sainthood, just ordinary decency, a readiness to wrestle with fundamental issues in human relations and to learn enough to make informed decisions. Put another way the right to do and what is right to do (Caccese, 1997, 10)

17.12 THE WAY FORWARD

In the Indian and global contexts, there are adequate number of the Ethical Codes, Corporate Governance Codes, Rules from the regulators, Laws, directions from select enforcement agencies and Government authorities in the context of acceptable behaviour at work. There is also substantial literature that is available both in the form of books, research reports, and wide range of material available on the Internet relating to cases of financial misbehaviour, inquiry and reports, appeals, court verdicts, and action taken reports by banks/financial institutions, regulatory bodies and concerned department/ministry of the governments all across the globe.

The fact of the matter is that the ethical behaviour has not yet been imbibed by the entire fraternity of the financial sector. The reasons could be many. Materialistic behaviour, greed, negligence, pressures from the unscrupulous borrowers, lack of involvement in work or inadequate diligence and above all the lack of fear that the career will be damaged if the employee is caught and faces punishment.

There are two ways in which employees may be persuaded to remain ethical in their career and life. First is through the efforts by the top managements in the form of training the personnel at the stage of induction and orienting them towards ethical conduct. Also, there might be some motivational sessions by the outside experts who themselves have been known for their impeccable track records as non-pliable employees all through their careers (whether received any awards or may have remained as unsung heroes). This may also have some positive impact. Besides, there can be some reward and recognition system for those who have remained ethical in their duties rather than merely treating it as a job they have been paid for. Preparing an Ethics Manual is also another way in which organisations may influence their employees.

The other approach is to bring in the trust factor in the organisation and make employees feel (notionally) the owner of the organisations they have been employed at. This brings in a sense of belongingness and pride, and they resist automatically thinking anything against the interest of the organisation. There can be serious efforts needed in making the employees to believe that they are the owners of their organisation. Instead of questioning everything, they should be give a free hand within the framework of the banking rules and laws. Employees can be asked to explain only when there is an apparent wilful deviation from the set rules. Likewise, unjustified targets on the employees is also one of the sources of the unethical behaviour. The Top managements, with a view to get better appreciation from their boards and also with a view to get higher rewards for themselves, may not be justified in pushing their subordinates to do aggressive sale of financial products. The quality of credit appraisal is bound to suffer in that scenario. Blaming select subordinates for rise in NPAs and taking action against them for poor recovery of loans is not a practice that ensures ethical functioning.

The Boards need to be focusing more on the possible risks and the measures to mitigate them on a constant basis. Rather than always questioning the top

internal managements for their lapses or deficiencies, a proper mentoring of the top management by the members of boards of the banks may also go a long way in retaining committed and highly experienced bankers at the top for their entire appointed term.

As noted in the beginning sections of this Unit that there are different generations of employees who are found at the workplace in banks or other non-banking organisations at various layers. They have grown in their childhood under different circumstances and are influenced by various events that are unique for a given generation. Hence, it is desirable that the top managements spend some time in understanding the perspectives and views of the present generations (the Generation Y or Millennials) and not to simply direct them to embrace what has been developed as a set of ethics prepared generally or solely by the senior managements of banks, which may not be totally convincing.

Nevertheless, having a formal operational framework for ethics for each bank in the form of a Code of Ethics will give adequate clarity for all the employees as to which are acceptable and encouraged behaviours and which are not, which itself takes care of much proportion of the dilemmas that might arise in the minds of many while dealing with non-routine tasks in a new role.

17.13 KEY WORDS

Sources of Ethical norms, Prescriptive, Proscriptive, Generational differences in Ethics, Zoomers, Generation Z, Generation Alpha, Formal systems, Ethics manual, Basel guidelines, Business Cycles, Accountability, Responsibility, Supportive Accountability, Total Avoidance, Statutory Watchdog, Central Vigilance Commission, Section 17A PC Act, 1988.

17.14 LET US SUM UP

In this unit, factors that influence development of ethical norms have been discussed. Also, various aspects of generational impact on ethics, such Gen X, Gen Y or Millennials and Post-Millennials, etc. and the different types of generations that are observed today have been elaborated. Focus has also been made on Business Cycles and their effect on ethics. The unit further deliberates on the concept of accountability, its negative connotation in public sector banks and its relationship with ethics. A model of Supportive Accountability has also been proposed to leverage the accountability mechanism for improving the performance irrespective of the ownership structure of commercial banks. The unit, being the last chapter of the courseware, summarizes the message of the book and urges the individual bankers for choosing to be ethical in their personal as well as professional lives, while, as the way forward, also suggesting measures for creating an ethical infrastructure in the banks for enabling the employees to be ethical in their daily activities.

17.15 CHECK YOUR PROGRESS

1. Ethics are:
   (*a*) External
   (*b*) Internal
   (*c*) Both external and internal
   (*d*) Neither external nor internal
2. Between the two-morals and ethics, the one that is relatively flexible is:
   (*a*) Ethics
   (*b*) Morals
   (*c*) Both are equally flexible
   (*d*) Both are equally inflexible
3. Of the following sources of ethical norms, find the wrong one:
   (*a*) Religion
   (*b*) Family and friends
   (*c*) Law enforcement agencies
   (*d*) Co-employees
4. Mr. Suraj Singh was born on January 01, 1979. In the terminology of generations, we can say he is:
   (*a*) Traditional
   (*b*) Gen X

(*c*) Gen Y/millennial

(*d*) Boomer

5. Ms. Alka Nair was born on 31 December, 1983. She belongs to which generation?

   (*a*) Traditional

   (*b*) Gen X

   (*c*) Gen Y/millennials

   (*d*) Boomer

6. As per a study by Tammy Erickson (2009) comparing generations between the US and India, which generation of India is found to share the generation's global sense of immediacy, coupled with the excitement of being part of the country's first wave of broad economic opportunity?

   (*a*) Traditional

   (*b*) Gen X

   (*c*) Gen Y/millennials

   (*d*) Boomer

7. Which of the following is NOT part of Manual for ethics?

   (*a*) Vision/Mission

   (*b*) Employees' Commitment to Bank

   (*c*) Commitment to Community

   (*d*) Investment in selling bank's stock

8. Which of the following is the most desirable kind of accountability in banks ?

   (*a*) Total avoidance

   (*b*) Unsupportive accountability

   (*c*) Supportive accountability

   (*d*) Supportive unaccountability

9. Which of the following is a business cycles of less than a year duration?
   (*a*) Seasonal cycles
   (*b*) Kitchin cycles
   (*c*) Juglar cycles
   (*d*) Kuznets cycles

ANSWERS

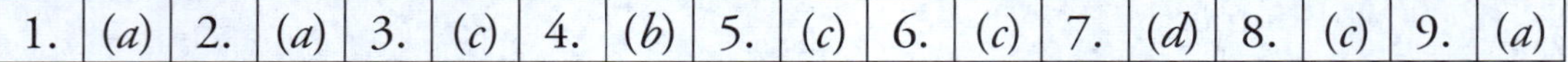

1.	(*a*)	2.	(*a*)	3.	(*c*)	4.	(*b*)	5.	(*c*)	6.	(*c*)	7.	(*d*)	8.	(*c*)	9.	(*a*)

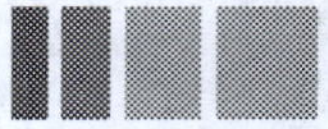

17.16 EXERCISE YOUR ETHICS MUSCLE

Case 43 : Using Smartphones in Office

You are working in a public sector bank in a senior position reporting to a Deputy General Manager (DGM). You oversee the work of 24 employees. Of them, 10 are in the age of 24-27 years and others are either in their late 30s or early 40s. Your boss has asked you to prepare some guidelines for use of smartphones during the workhours so that an office order for the purpose be issued and acknowledged by all employees. He is unhappy to see that most of the younger employees spend a lot of time on their smartphones during workhours. He is 54 years old and finds it unethical to use the smartphones during the office time whether for personal work or visiting the social media sites. Productivity of the department is good. Young employees do spend time on their mobiles but always complete the given work within time. Smartphones have not slowed down their work.

This is a tricky matter. You don't exactly relish the task given to you. At the same time, you are eager to prove yourself in front of your boss as you are due for your next promotion within a few months.

Issues to Reflect

(*a*) What are the issues at play in this situation both from the viewpoint of individual ethics and organizational ethics ?

(*b*) Do you agree with the view of the DGM that there should be some restrictions on the use of smartphones during office hours?

(*c*) What would be the best course of action to resolve the situation?

(*d*) What do you think? Is it possible to stop the use of smartphones altogether in the offices in today's time?

Case 44: Staff Accountability in a Loan case

M/s Rama was incorporated on 05.08.2008. The company was closely held Public Ltd. engaged in trading of ago product, cleaning chemicals & other FMCG products. Company was having reputed client base like Emami, Adani Wilmar Ltd. HUL etc. and also international presence in Asian, African & Middle East market. At the time of submission of the proposal, company was banking under consortium arrangement. Considering the growth opportunities and business expansion, management decided for expansion of business for which they required enhanced working capital. As such company decided to induct new banks in the existing consortium to tie up the fresh limits. The proposal was appraised by a PSB based on the lead bank approved note for enhancement of limit and fund-based limit of Rs. 20 crore & NFB of Rs. 40 crore was sanctioned to the company by the Credit Approval Committee headed by a General Manager. The credit limits were disbursed.

As the they could not receive payments from their buyers due to gap in demand and supply, the Company's account came into stress. Thereafter all the LCs which were opened by the bank devolved. Subsequently, the account turned NPA. The officials who did the credit appraisal at the branch and zone levels were found to be erring and disciplinary action taken against them including the GM who headed the sanctioning committee. Final outstanding in the account at the time becoming NPA was Rs. 46.50 crore.

Vigilance overtone was perceived on the basis of following lapses:

(*i*) Pre-sanction appraisal not conducted properly. The account was in SMA-2 category with other banks at the time of considering credit facilities. Due Diligence, as prescribed not done.

(*ii*) CR from other bank showed adverse features.

(*iii*) Despite these adverse features, the credit facility was disbursed and Bank was exposed to significant risk by approval of credit limits of Rs. 60 crores.

(*iv*) Margin money at the rate of 20% was required for ILC limit. Entire margin was debited to CC account and FDRs prepared towards margin in account.

(*v*) Stock statement and DP from Lead Bank not received and drawings were allowed without valid DP.

Issues to Reflect:

(*a*) Do you agree with the view that the concerned officials committed irregularities by sanctioning the credit facilities to M/s Rama?

(*b*) If yes, then what was the nature of the irregularities? Was it intentional or just a case of normal business judgment going wrong?

(*c*) How will you classify the nature of staff accountability here in terms of the staff accountability model proposed in this module under heading 15.9?

(*d*) Examine the case from the view point of the organizational ethics. Can business growth be achieved by strictly following the prescribed rules?

Case 45: Good Always Comes Back

Tomorrow is Sunday. Nice time to catch up with sleep. Wake late in morning. Have a nice coffee. Read newspaper. As I was getting ready for office, got a WhatsApp message. One of my batch mates posted overseas as a Branch Head, was in India with family. Home travel. He was returning back. Had a connecting flight from the city. Couple of hours to spare. Messaged him, "Let's meet tomorrow." The time was set, as well as the venue. A coffee shop in a mall. Next day, hugging each other, as meeting after such a long time, families settled and engrossed in an animated conversation. I asked my friend "So, how's life out there". "It's an altogether different experience professionally, socially and culturally". He then started delving on his experiences there and the cup, he was about to take another sip, got put it down. Silent. He was staring across the window of the restaurant. I sipped and waited.

Looking at me he said "You know. We needed to hire an assistant for my branch as one of the local staff had put down papers. As per the policy there, we were required to hire only a local as a replacement. We followed the set recruitment process. We got several applications which we shortlisted. Finally, for the interview, we called 15 shortlisted applicants. The day before interview,

I got a call from one of my top branch credit clients. He told me one of the employees in his company has also applied for the post. Since the employee's current role in the company is vital, he should not be selected. And his company would be requiring a good enhancement in limits this time. They already had a lot of confirmed orders. Though the company had in principle approval from two other local banks for fresh limits, he shall prefer to get enhanced limits from us. Then he hung up.

My branch was short on credit targets. Next day the interviews. The outcome was, the very employee of my client ranked best. The result will be declared when I report back to the Branch. What you would do if in my shoes. And yes, my promotion is also due this year." "Can I have some time to think over, I said as we parted." Back home, after enjoying my live news TV channels, dinner done, before going to bed, gazing the half-moon from my balcony, I felt the moon becoming fuller and closing on me. This time with an Aristotle face, I heard the moon conversing with me. May be, the great Aristotle was playing Armstrong today. Before I could even start." Choose the best option. Not for you. But for your organization. It is, paying it forward. **Short-term individual goals should never compromise the long-term organizational goals**. And my gut feeling is, your client will also, in bottom of heart appreciate, that his Bank, looks not for short-term petty gains, but a long-term engagement."

As I stared at the moon, hoping it coming further near it receded. It was again half. No sign of Aristotle. I went inside. Before sleeping, called my friend. Repeated the conversation from my side, first person, hung up and went to bed. A hectic week was underway.

After a few days, I got a WhatsApp call. It was the same friend. "Hi there. How's life." I asked. "Good. Hope same there." And then he continued, "On my return, first thing I did was to sign the appointment letter of the selected candidate. My client was upset, called me. "We will close our limits with you" and hung up. I was taken aback. The day felt unusually long. Every call, every mail gave me goose bumps. Instructions to close off the limits! With a heavy heart, I closed the branch in the evening. Was driving home when got a call from the new employee. "Sir, there is an important client issue to be sorted. Can you come to the branch?" It seemed like a nail hammered to my head. So finally, the instructions to close off the limits have come. I turned back and reached the branch. He was waiting there. Opened the branch and asked,

"What is the emergency."

"Sir, I got call from my ex-employer. He said that he was calling me because he knew that the branch was closed. He has made a request to make urgent outward remittance to one of his overseas suppliers for a consignment. If the payment is not made today, he will lose on a good discount which will cost him significantly in monitory terms." We checked the mail for the relevant payment instructions and documentation. It was there. The payment was processed. I closed the branch again. Reached home. Was settling for dinner, got a message. It was from the customer- can I call you. So, this wily fellow, made me slog today and now maybe he will give closure instructions. I called him. "My apologies. I was rude to you. That is the reason I chose to call my ex-employee rather than you. I was wrong when I said don't select my employee. Well, he was vital for me, but I am proud to say, he proved vital for me even after leaving me because of your decision of not compromising on merit. I will be sending formal request for additional credit requirements tomorrow." And he hung up. I looked outside the window. In disbelief. Full moon was there, with a face of smiling Aristotle.

Issues to reflect:

(*a*) What ethical learnings do you see from the incident mentioned above?

(*b*) Is choosing to be ethical very difficult?

(*c*) Do you think the narrator took an unnecessary risk by selecting the said employee even after the phone call from his valued client?

(*d*) How do you evaluate the narrator on the scale of personal ethics?

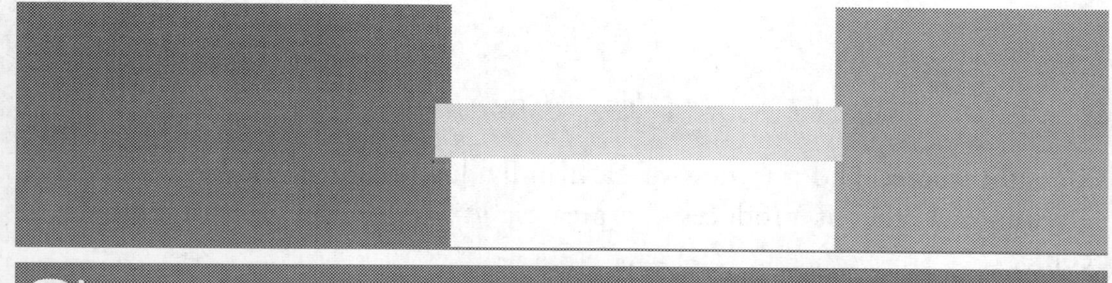

Glossary

This glossary defines technical or special terms used in this book. Students may use it as a quick and handy reference for terms that may be unfamiliar without having to refer to the specific chapter(s) where they are used. It also can be a very helpful aid in studying for examinations and for writing term papers where precise meanings are needed.

A

Accountability: Answering to someone (such as the chief executive or supervisor) for something (such as a decision, a program, or a mistake); hierarchical authority and performance appraisals are two ways by which the public managers are held accountable in public service.

Administrative discretion: The scope for decision making within a limited range of options that are permissible under law and agency rules, regulations, policies, and procedures; often involves deciding which broad rule applies and how a particular case fits the rule.

Accounting: The definition of the accounting in any business book is the process by which any business keeps track of its financial activities by recording its debits and credits and balancing its accounts. This offers a system of rules and principles which govern the format and content of financial statements.

Accounting fraud: Inaccurate information in a corporation's financial reports, in which companies provide important information on which investors and others base decisions involving millions of dollars.

Act deontologists hold that actions are the proper basis to judge morality or ethicalness.

Active bribery: When the person who promises or gives the bribe commits the offense.

Act utilitarians: The rightness of each individual action must be evaluated to determine whether it produces the greatest utility for the greatest number of people.

Affective(feeling): Means an evaluative framework guided by hedonism. One behaves in ways that increase pleasure and decrease pain. Hedonism is the doctrine that tells happiness is the highest good.

Ahimsa: The Buddhist principle of avoiding harm. It implies an attitude of non-violence and respect towards all living things. Altruism A belief that people ought to act in an unselfish manner for the good of others without regard for rewards.

Anonymity: A person's wish to be free from external surveillance.

Applied Ethics: The study of how ethical theories are put into practice.

Aristotle's ethics: A theory based on the concept of virtue. Virtue ethics asks, what kind of person should we be? Moral character rather than right action is fundamental in this ethical tradition which originated with the ancient Greeks and received its fullest expression in Aristotle's Nicomache an Ethics. The role of ethics according to Aristotle is to enable us to lead successful, rewarding lives-the kind of lives that we would call "the good life."

B

Backdoors: In case the original entry point (Front door) has been detected, having a few hidden ways back makes re-entry easy-and difficult to detect.

Beliefs: The beliefs in an ethical code are standards of thought. These are the ways that the senior executives in the organization want others to think. The intention is to encourage ways of thinking and patterns of attitudes that will pave way towards the wanted behaviour. It is expressed in a positive form in an ethical Code "Our first intention to serve our customer is...." is an example of a positive belief that commonly appears in code of ethics.

Big data: Large volumes of structured and unstructured data that need to be transmitted at very high speeds.

Bribe is a payment made with an intention to corrupt. Bribes are personal payments, gifts, or special favours granted improperly to influence the outcome of decision.

Bribery is one of the most common and controversial issues that global companies face. It is universally condemned and no government in the world legally permits bribery of its own officials.

Business ethics: The conduct by which companies and their agents abide by the law and respect the rights of their stakeholders, particularly their customers, clients, employees, and the surrounding community and environment Business ethics is the evaluation of business activities and behaviour as right or wrong. Ethical conduct conforms with what society, as a whole considers right behaviour.

Business Cycle: Also known as trade cycle, it refers to an alternate expansion and contraction of overall business activity in a wave-like rhythmic cycle, in a capitalist economy. The four phases of the business cycles are recovery, prosperity, recession and depression.

C

Capitalism is an economic system combining the 'private ownership productive enterprises with 'competition between them in the pursuit of profit'.

Carbon Footprint: The amount of carbon dioxide and other carbon compounds released by the consumption of fossil fuels.

Categorical Imperative: Kant's unconditional precept that we must "act only according to that maxim whereby you can, at the same time, will that it should become a universal law"; to act on the basis of good will rather than purely self-interested motives and never treat others as means toward an end without consideration of them as ends in themselves.

Caux Roundtable: Principles for business articulate a worldwide vision for ethical and responsible corporate behaviour. They serve as a foundation for ethiocal action for business leaders across globe.

Churning: It is excessive or inappropriate trading for a client's account by a broker who has control over the account with the intent to generate commissions rather than to benefit the client.

Confucianism: Practices and teachings of Confucius.

Clause 49: It is a clause in the Listing Agreement (LA) of stock exchanges with companies that want to be listed with the former. Stock exchanges endeavour to bring in corporate governance standards among companies, by the introduction of

Clause 49 in the LA before the latter are listed. Clause 49 requires companies to comply with SEBI's stipulations with reference to corporate governance practices such as Board composition, inclusion of independent directors, whistle-blower policy, disclosure norms, etc.

Code of Ethics are statements of values and principles which define the purpose of the company; seeks to clarify the ethics of an organization. The first step in developing an ethics programme. A code of ethics is a statement of the norms and beliefs of an organization.

Codes of Conduct are statements of rules (comprised of a list of rules). It says, 'This is what you must not do or you must do.'

Code of Conduct: A statement laying down guidelines regarding the ethical principles and acceptable behaviour expected of a professional organization or company. For example, the Market Research Society has a professional code of conduct; utility companies have customer charters.

Code of Ethics: A written system of standards for ethical conduct. A code of ethics lays down the ethical behaviour that must be followed by employees.

Cognitive dissonance: The discomfort or distress people feel when their beliefs are inconsistent or conflicting; needing to resolve this, people reassess the information or discount one of the beliefs.

Collusion: Collusion is a secret agreement to deceive. Producers of an industry reduce competition among themselves to raise their profits. They fix the price themselves with a clear mutual understanding. This understanding among different firms is called collusion.

Corporate Citizen: A corporate is likened to a resident of a country, and is presumed to have rights and obligations towards the nation. Therefore, if a corporation performs the duties and carries out its obligations to different stakeholders in a civil society like a true citizen, it is called an ideal corporate citizen.

Corporate Credos: Corporate credos are defined as broad general statements of corporate commitments, as for instance, the credo of Johnson & Johnson.

Commercial Bribe is a consideration given or offered to an employee by a person outside the bank with the understanding that when the employee transacts

business for his bank, the employee will deal favourably with that person or with that person's firm.

Compensatory Justice and Retributive Justice are concerned with correcting wrongs. Generally compensating the victims is the just way of correcting wrongs in private dealings such as losses resulting from accidents and the failure to fulfil contracts; whereas retribution that is, punishment-is the just response to criminal acts, such as assault or theft.

Computer Abuse: It is the commission of acts involving a computer that may not be illegal but are considered unethical.

Computer ethics refer to standards of moral conduct demonstrated in computer related matters.

Consequentialism: An ethical theory in which actions are judged solely by their consequences without regard to character, motivation, or absolute principles of good and evil and separate from their capacity to produce happiness and pleasure.

Conduct: The character of a man is expressed in terms of his conduct. Conduct of a person is a series of actions, which when taken together is termed as 'good' or 'bad': 'right' or 'wrong': 'moral' or 'immoral (meaning is eating his own food as---- example: immoral is steal and eat the food).

Conflicts of interest arises when an employee or officer of bank is engaged in carrying out a task on behalf of the bank and the employee/ officer has private interest in the outcome of the task. This is a situation in which one relationship or obligation places one in direct conflict with an existing relationship or obligation.

Consumer Financial Protection Bureau (CFPB): A government agency within the Federal Reserve that oversees financial products and services.

Corporate Governance: The system by which business corporations are directed and controlled.

Consumerism: A lifestyle characterized by the acquisition of goods and service.

Copyright protection comes into existence from the moment the work is fixed in a tangible expression. Copyright registration is not mandatory.

Corporate Ethics. The conduct of a corporate with all the stakeholders.

Corporate Social Responsibility: The practice in which a business views itself within a broader context, as a member of society with certain implicit social obligations and responsibility for its own effects on environmental and social well-being.

Corrective Advertising: The company must publicly correct a false impression created by past advertising. So, a second remedy is sometimes applied known as corrective advertising.

Corruption: A form of dishonesty or criminal offense which is undertaken by a person or an organization which is entrusted in a position of authority in order to acquire illicit benefits or abuse of power for one's personal gain.

Culture: A particular set of attitudes, beliefs, and practices that characterize a group of individuals.

Cybercrime: Criminal activity done using computers and the Internet.

Cyberspace: A virtual location where information is stored, ideas are described, and communication takes place in and through an electronic network of linked systems

D

Data Diddling: It involves performing unauthorized modifications to data stored within the computer system.

Deception is the act of deceiving. Sales people have to explain all the relevant information truthfully in an understandable, non-misleading way.

Deceptive advertising: An advertisement that makes false or misleading claims about the company's own product or its competitor's product, withholds relevant information, or creates unreasonable expectations; generally illegal in most countries.

Denial of service is becoming a common networking prank. By hammering a website's equipment with too many requests for information, an attacker can effectively log the system showing performance or even crashing the site. This method of overloading computers is used sometimes to cover up an attack.

Deontology: A normative ethical theory suggesting that an ethical decision requires us to observe only the rights and duties we owe to others, and, in the context of business, act on the basis of a primary motive to do what is right by all stakeholders. Deontology reflects important features of our moral common

sense, but it usually breaks down as a guide to conflict when lists of rules differ or when rules conflict.

Descriptive ethics: An approach to ethics that deals with what people do rather than what people should do.

Digital Right Management (DRM): A powerful long-term solution to this widespread devaluation of intellectual property, now being explored within the international standards community, is the coordinated use of a Digital Right Management (DRM) strategy.

Dilemma: A dilemma is a situation that requires a choice between equal balanced arguments or a predicament that seemingly defies a satisfactory solution.

Distributive justice arises mostly in the evaluation of our social, political and economic institutions, where the benefits and burdens of engaging cooperative activities must be spread over a group.

Diversity Dividend: The financial benefit of improved performance resulting from a diverse workforce.

E

Ecoterian philosophy: Deals with harm minimization compassion respect for other living beings. Eco-friendly and humanistic development.

Ethical egoism: An ethical doctrine that individual self-interest is the paramount focus of moral concern. Psychological egoism maintains that we are all primarily motivated by seeking our own interests. Ethical egoism makes the normative claim that individuals should seek their own self-interest.

Embezzlement is the fraudulent appropriation of another's property by the person to whom it was entrusted.

Environment: The living and non-living surroundings, natural or human-made, which make life on earth possible. Environmental issues include, *inter alia* impacts of processes, products and services on air, water, land, biodiversity and human health.

Environmental Audit: An investigation of processes and procedures of a company or site with respect to its compliance with applicable laws, regulations and impacts on environmental conditions.

Environmental Impact assessment: An assessment of the impacts on the natural or human environment of a proposed project or development, usually performed by an environmental consultant.

Environmental Management System (EMS): It is a tool that provides an organization with a method to manage systematically its environment activities, products and services and helps it achieve its environmental obligations and performance goals. It can also refer to the combination of arrangements for assessing, monitoring and recording a company's environmental impact.

Epicurean means a follower of Epicures (341-270 BC), a Greek follower who taught that pleasure was the chief good.

Epistemology is the theory and study of the nature and limits of knowledge.

Ethical Algorithm: Analyzing situations from ethical perspectives constitutes an ethical algorithm which can increase our sense of certainty about decisions and ultimately provide a defendable decision-making process.

Ethical consumerism: Should be about using our purchasing power to make the world a better place feeling pure will not help the worlds pure.

Ethical egoists: Supporters of ethical egoism who believe people promote their own good and do whatever is in their best interest.

Ethical Dilemma: A situation in which there is no obvious right or wrong decision, but rather a right or right answer.

Ethical Reasoning: Looking at the information available to us in resolving an ethical dilemma, and drawing conclusions based on that information in relation to our own ethical standards.

Ethics: The manner by which we try to live our lives according to a standard of "right" or "wrong" behaviour—in both how we think and behave toward others and how we would like them to think and behave toward us.

Ethical Audit: An audit that assessee's business structures, procedures, systems and policies. It measures the extent to which the activities of a business complies with the standards it has publicly declared.

Ethical climate: An unspoken understanding among employees of what is and is not acceptable behaviour based on the expected standards or norms used for ethical decision making.

Ethical Decision: Ethical decision helps in identifying business problems and works out the best way of resolving them.

Ethical Decision-making Model: A model that helps to identify business problems and works out the best way of resolving the problems. Ethical Intensity: It is defined as the degree of importance given to an ethical issue.

Ethics Officer: A senior executive responsible for monitoring the ethical performance of the organization both internally and externally.

External Whistle-Blowing: An employee discovering corporate misconduct and choosing to bring it to the attention of law enforcement agencies and/or the media.

Ethical Relativism: A view that ethics depends entirely upon context.

Ethical Responsibilities: Are additional behaviour and activities that are not necessarily codified into law but nevertheless are expected of business by society's members.

Ethical Rules: Are guides to moral behaviour. For example, all societies have ethical rules forbidding, lying, stealing, deceiving and harming others similar to the other ethical rules that approve of honesty, keeping promises, helping others and respecting the right of others. These are the basic rules of behaviour which are of much use for the preservation and continuation of organized life.

Extortion: Extortion is engaging in a commercial extortion if the employee demands a consideration as a condition for dealing favourably with the work he is doing on behalf of bank.

Eudemonia: The happiness or human flourishing that results from virtuous activity; it is more than contentment or satisfaction.

F

Fair value: The fair value of a fixed asset is represented by the cost of replacing it with an asset which would give the same service. Because of inflation, an asset fair value is usually greater than to its net book value.

Firewalls: Firewall is a device or program that stops people accessing a computer without permission while it is connected to the Internet.

Fiduciary duty: A very high level of legal responsibility owed by those who manage someone else's money, which includes the duties of care and loyalty.

Foreign Corrupt Practices Act: An amendment to the Securities and Exchange Act of 1934; its main purpose is to make it illegal for companies and their managers to influence or bribe foreign officials with monetary payments or rewards of any kind in an attempt to get or keep business opportunities outside the United States the buying or selling of stocks, bonds or other investments.

G

General Data Protection Regulation (GDPR): A European law regulating the processing of personal information of European Union residents by an individual, a company or an organization.

The Golden Rule: Do not do unto others, what you would not have others do unto you (or your loved ones). Do not do something to others which you want others not to do to you. Kant's categorical imperative in a deontological theory suggests that individuals should be willing to have their actions become universal laws, that would apply equally to themselves as to all others.

Golden Mean: The term comes from Aristotelian virtue ethics. It means the aim of ethical behaviour-a value between excess and deficiency.

Globalization: The expansion of international trade to a point where national markets have been overtaken by regional trade blocs (Latin America, Europe, Africa), leading eventually to a global marketplace.

Governance is control or direction for the purpose of conducting business.

Grease payments: 'Facilitating payments' made to expedite the performance of routine governmental action.

Green Product: A product that is claimed by its manufacturers as not causing damage to the environment, especially a new product or formulation that is being launched to replace one that is said to cause environmental damage.

Greenhouse Effect: If is an effect occurring in the atmosphere because of the presence of certain gases known as greenhouse gases that absorb infrared radiation.

Green Washing: Carrying out superficial CSR efforts that merely cover up systemic ethics problems for the sake of public relations.

H

Hacker: An individual who circumvents computer security (*via* a modem or some other communication device) and breaks into a computer system. It can also be defined to mean a person who hacks into other people's computer systems without permission in order to steal information or to carry out something illegal. The term "hacker" originally referred to computer professionals who solved complex computer problems. Today the term "Hacker" (or 'cracker' a term used in computer circles) has a negative meaning.

Hacktivist: A hacktivist is an individual who performs the act of hacking or breaking into a computer system for a political reason.

Hedonism: The idea that pleasure is the ultimate good, or the best moral end involves the greatest balance of pleasure over pain.

Honesty: Refers to truthfulness or trustworthiness

Hostile work environment: Three criteria must be met: the conduct was unwelcome; the conduct was severe, pervasive, and regarded by the claimant as so hostile or offensive as to alter his or her conditions of employment; and the conduct was such that a reasonable person would find it hostile or offensive

Human rights: Defined by the United Nations as an inherent dignity with equal and inalienable rights and the foundation of freedom, justice, and peace in the world.

I

Integrity: The adherence to a code of moral values implying trustworthiness and incorruptibility because there is unity between what we say and what we do.

Insider Trading is the act of buying and selling a company's stock on the basis of 'inside' information about the company. 'Insider' information about a company is confidential or proprietary information about a company that is not available for the general public outside the company, but which would have a material significant impact on the price of the company's stock.

Instrumental Approach: The perspective that the only obligation of a corporation is to maximize profits for its shareholders in providing goods and services that meet the needs of its customers.

Instrumental Value: The quality by which the pursuit of one value is a good way to reach another value. For example, money is valued for what it can buy rather than for itself.

Internal Whistle-Blowing: An employee discovering corporate misconduct and bringing it to the attention of his or her supervisor, who then follows established procedures to address the misconduct within the organization.

Intrinsic Value: The quality by which a value is a good thing in itself and is pursued for its own sake, whether anything comes from that pursuit or not.

Intellectual Property (IP): A creation of the mind, is an asset, and as such it can be bought, sold, licensed, exchanged or gratuitously given away like any other form of property.

J

Justice : An ethical approach that emphasizes whether the distribution of benefits and burdens among people are fair, according to some agreed-upon rule. This philosophy is used in making ethical decisions to ensure the equal distribution of burdens and benefits. These principles include a belief that people should be treated equally, that rules should be applied consistently and that people who harm others should be held responsible and make restitution.

K

Kantianism is an ethic of duty. Non-consequentialism in ethics is an approach that is labelled 'deontological' (for duty in Greek). Its definitive formulation is provided by the German philosopher Immanuel Kant (1724-1804).

Kohlberg's Model of Cognitive Moral Development (CMD): Theory in which people make different decisions in similar ethical situations because they are in different moral development stages.

Kyoto Protocol: An international treaty meant to curb global greenhouse gas emissions by having countries voluntarily reduce national outputs.

L

Larceny is the legal term in England and Ireland for stealing or theft.

Limited Liability: A business owner's protection against loss of personal assets, granted with corporate status.

Logic Bombs: It is a routine that causes parts of the computer system to become inoperative or to malfunction as soon as the routine is executed.

Long-term social responsiveness is as necessary for an enterprise as long-term planning. The extent to which an enterprise has such an ability over the long-term will primarily be a result of the short-term actions which are (1) Pro-active or (ii) Reactive.

M

Malicious Applets: Tiny programmes, sometimes written in the popular Java computer language, that misuse computer's resources, modify files on the hard disk, send take e-mail, or steal passwords.

Managerial Ethics: The moral principles employees in managerial positions follow to guide their actions and behaviours. This is a major factor affecting how socially responsive an enterprise will be in the long-term.

Marketing consists of the performance of business activities that direct the flow of goods and services from producer or manufacturer to consumer or user.

Marketing ethics: Marketing ethics relate to application of moral standards of behaviour while marketing products to consumers.

Meta Ethics: It is the study of the origin and meaning of ethical concepts.

Metaphysics: It deals with the question whether the moral values exist independently of humans or whether they are simply human conventions.

Moral dilemma: Two or more morals in conflict with one another moral intensity.

Moral philosophy is a set of principles setting forth what is believed to be the right way to behave.

Moral reasoning is a more intentional form of decision making where the actor considers the basis for and implications of the decision before acting.

Morals are one's personal guiding principles. Moral implies conformity with the generally accepted standards of goodness or rightness in conduct or character. It is generally used to describe who people are, e.g. a moral person.

Moral agency: The self-awareness, freedom, and ability to make choices based on one's perception of right and wrong.

Motivation is the act of simulating someone to take a desired course of action to push the right button to get a desired reaction. It includes a stimulus and desired results.

N

NAFTA: The implementation of the multilateral international trade agreement which addresses the mean issues of multinational trade, environment protection, intellectual property and employment.

Norms are expectations of proper behaviour, not requirements for that behaviour, a major difference between a norm and law. Each individual within the society has a set of norms beliefs, and values that together form his or her moral standards.

Normative Ethical theories: A group of philosophical theories that describe how people ought to behave on the basis of reason.

Non-consequentialism: Regard for certain behaviours as inherently right, and the determination of this rightness focuses on the individual actor, not on society.

Normative approaches: How organizational decision makers should approach an issue.

Normative myopia: When managers overlook or stifle the importance of core values in their business decisions.

O

Organizational Culture: The values, beliefs, and norms that all the employees of that organization share.

Organizational Integrity: A characteristic of publicly committing to the highest professional standards and sticking to that commitment.

P

Password Crackers: Software that can guess passwords.

Pluralists: Often referred to as non-hedonists, take the opposite position that no one thing is intrinsically good.

Power distance dimension: The power inequality between superiors and subordinates

Proactive Ethical Policies: Policies that result when the company develops a clear sense of what it stands for as an ethical organization.

Predictive analytics: Using values or algorithms to provide data-backed decision options.

Primary stakeholders: Those whose continued association and resources are absolutely necessary for a firm's survival.

Principles: Specific and pervasive boundaries for behaviour that should not be violated.

Procedural justice: Considers the processes and activities that produce a particular outcome.

Professionalism: Attitude or behaviour, or both, that calls on the values of excellence, quality, competence, and merit.

Privacy: The dictionary meaning of privacy is freedom from intrusion or public attention.

Privacy, right to: The right against unsanctioned violation of being left alone by the government, corporations, or individuals; an example of a sanctioned action in the United States is a search warrant or a court order.

R

Rule Deontologists: Argue that general rules should be followed to decide which action is best.

Rational economics: Based on the assumption that people are predictable and will maximize the utility of their choices relative to their needs and wants.

Realism: The view that an external world exists independent of our perceptions.

Reciprocity: An interchange of giving and receiving in social relationships.

S

Salami Slicing: This technique works on the assumption that if small quantities of money are shaved from a lot of balances that are not closely checked, and these shavings are combined in a central account which would swell to a large amount over time.

Sarbanes-Oxley Act: U.S. law enacted in 2002 that greatly expanded the powers of the SEC to regulate information disclosure in the financial markets and the accountability of an organization's senior leadership regarding the accuracy of this disclosure. The most far reaching change in organizational control and accounting regulations since the Securities and Exchange Act of 1934, which made securities fraud a criminal offence.

Sexual Harassment is defined as an unwanted conduct of a sexual nature or other behaviours based on sex that affects the dignity of men and women at work. This includes uninvited and unwelcome physical, verbal or non-verbal conduct.

Social Engineering: A tactic used to gain access to the computer system by talking unsuspecting company employees out of variable information such as passwords.

Social Responsibility is the implied, enforced, or felt obligation of managers. opting in their official capacity, to serve or protect the interests of groups other than themselves.

Social Responsibility of Business: The view that stakeholders are not the means to the end (profit) but are ends in and of themselves as human being.

Software Piracy refers to the unauthorized copying or use of programs.

Spoofing is faking an E-mail address or web page to trick users into passing e.g. critical information like password or credit card number.

Stakeholders are groups who are vital to the survival and success of the corporation.

Stakeholder model of corporate governance: A broader view of the purpose of business that considers stakeholder welfare in tandem with corporate needs and interests.

Stakeholder orientation: The degree to which a firm understands and addresses stakeholder demands.

Stewardship: To protect the value of an asset, community, or interest over time; to care for the public's interests, along with future choices and opportunities.

Sustainability: A long-term approach to the interaction between business activity and societal impact on the environment and other stakeholders.

Sustainable Development: Development that meets the needs of the present without compromising the ability of future generations to meet their own needs; ensuring a better quality of life for everyone, now and for generations to come.

T

Teleological word is derived from the Greek word Telos (means end), Teleological ethics focuses on the end results and then relating the end results to the process of achieving the autonomy of the individual.

The Trojan Horse Technique: The name Trojan horse in Greek mythology represents a large wooden horse left by the Greeks upon their pretended retreat of the siege of Troy. The Trojans, thinking it was a sacrifice to Athena, let the horse into the city gates.

Trade Secrets: Big corporations attempt to protect themselves against the loss of trade secrets and to utilise what they can learn about their competitors. It is a known fact that information is a vital thing which provides all companies to have many advantages over competitors who lack it.

Tragedy of Commons: An economy theory highlighting the human tendency to use as much of a free natural resource as wanted without regard for others' needs or for long-term environmental effects or issues.

Transparency: Openness in business operation.

Triple Bottom-line: A measure that accounts for an organization's results in terms of its effects on people, planet, and profits.

U

Universal Values: Ethical principles that apply everywhere despite differences in time, geography, and culture.

United Nations Global Compact: A set of 10 principles that promote human rights, sustainability, and the eradication of corruption.

Utilitarian thinking is on the concept of utility maximisation (utility means capacity in actions to have good results; also means usefulness); leads to Egotism (win as much as you can) concept.

Utilitarianism: A normative theory of ethics suggesting that an ethical act is the one whose consequences create the greatest good for the greatest number of people. It is a powerful and widely accepted ethical theory that has specific relevance to problems in business.

V

Values are a general term referring to those things which people regards good, bad, right, wrong, desirable. justifiable. etc. We can speak of 'truth values' ('true' or 'false'), and of value judgments which are statements about what is valued, sound, deplorable, skilled, etc. It is useful to distinguish between technical prudential and moral values. In short, these are enduring beliefs and ideals that are socially enforced.

Values Orientation: A control system that strives to develop shared values value statement. A declaration of an organization's top priorities that serves the general public and also addresses distinct groups such as stakeholders.

Value Dilemma: Two or more beliefs/ ideals in conflict with one another.

Values-based ethics culture: Relies on an explicit mission statement that defines the core values of the firm and how the customers and employees should be treated.

Virtue Ethics: An ethical system based on the exercise of certain virtues (loyalty, honour, courage) emphasizing the formation of character.

Virtues are acquired traits. Mere feelings like hanger, are not virtues according to Aristotle Honesty on the other hand cannot consist in telling the truth once is rather trail of a person who tells the truth as a general practice. A virtue is also something we actually practice. Honesty involves habitually telling the truth. It is not knowing how to tell the truth.

Virtue Theory: A normative theory that focuses on proper conduct guided by the training we received growing up.

W

Whistle blowing: The disclosure outside routine channels of wrongdoing in an organization or agency, usually by a member; often associated with public disclosure through media revelations.

White-collar Crime: Crimes perpetrated by non-violent business criminals.

Wire Tapping: The practice of connecting a listening device to a telephone line to monitor conversations secretly. A kind of eavesdropping by setting up a special transmission path to divert the flow of data.

Further Reading: A Few Good Books on Ethics You Must Read

1. **Defining Moments: When Managers Must Choose Between Right and Right**. Joseph L. Badaracco. Harvard Business School Press 1997
2. **Why Should Anyone Be Led by You? What it Takes to be an Authentic Leader.** Rob Goffee and Gareth Jones. Harvard Business School Press 2006
3. **Good to Great; Why Some Organizations Make the Leap and Others Don't**. Jim Collins. Random House Business Books 2001
4. **Justice:** What's the Right Thing to Do. Michael J. Sandel. Allen Lane 2009
5. **Conversations on Ethics**. Alex Voorhoeve. Oxford University Press 2009
6. **Giving Voice to Values: How to Speak Your Mind When You Know What's Right**. Mary C. Gentile. Yale University Press 2010
7. **A Question of Trust: The Crucial Nature of Trust in Business, Work and Life and How to Build it.** Sally Bibb and Jeremy Kourdi .Cyan Books and Marshall Cavendish 2006
8. **The CEO and the Monk.** Robert B. Cattell, Kenny Moore, Ken Rifkin. John Wiley and Sons 2004
9. **Business Ethics:** C.S.V. Murthy. Himalaya Publishing House 2016
10. **Public service: Individual and Institutional Responsibilities.** James S. Bowan & Jonathan P. West. Sage Publications, 2015
11. **Meeting the Ethical Challenges of Leadership**: **Casting Light or Shadow**. Craig E. Johnson. Sage publications, 2018
12. **Business Ethics and Corporate Governance**: A.C. Fernando. Pearson India, 2016

13. **Ethics in Finance**. John K Boatright. Wiley Blackwell, 2014

14. **Business Ethics**: Concepts and Cases. Manuel G. Velasquez 2014

15. **This is Business Ethics**: An Introduction. Tobey Scharding. Wiley Blackwell. 2018

References

[Several internet websites on ethics such as https://www.justice.gov; https://www.scu.edu › ethics; ethics.org; https://www.ibe.org.uk; www.ethicsandbusiness.org/strategy, www.globalethics.org/bds/ reading etc. and other a number of general websites including the RBI and other regulators websites as well as articles from Economic Times, Mint, Times of India and Deccan Herald etc.]

1. D. Ariely : Predictably Irrational: The Hidden Forces That Shape Our Decisions. (Rev. ed.). New York: HarperCollins, 2009
2. William G. Shepherd, Richard D. Irwin: Public Policies Towards Business, Inc. Illinois, 1975.
3. Thomas M. Garrett : Business Ethics, , The Times of India Press, Bombay, 1970.
4. Richard T. DeGeorge and Joseph A. Picler: Donald P. Robin. R. Eric Reidenbach: Business Ethics, , Prentice Hall. Englewood Cliffs, New Jersey 07632, 1989.
5. Ethics, Free Enterprises and Public Policy, Oxford University Press, New York, 1978.
6. Stephen J. Caroll, Martin J. Gannon: Ethical Dimensions of International Management, Safe Publications. London.
7. S. Manikutti. Being Ethical. IIM Ahmedabad. Random House 2014
8. Cees Van Dam and Land Stallaert, Martinus Nijoff: Trends in Business Ethics. Special Sciences division, Boston, 1978.
9. Rogene A. Buchholz: Fundamental Concepts and Problems in Business Ethics, , Prentice Hall, Englewood Cliffs, New Jersey.
10. Theophand A. Mathias : Corporate Ethics. Allied Publishers Ltd., New Delhi.

11. Newman S. Perry: Business, Government and Society, Jr. Prentice Hall, Englewood Cliffs, New Jersey 07632.
12. Thomas R. Piper, Mary C. Gentile, Sharon Dalo Parks: Can Ethics be taught? Harvard Business School, Boston, 1993.
13. John Donaldson: Key Issues in Business Ethics, Academic Press, London, 1989.
14. Norman E. Bowie and Ronald F. Duska: Business Ethics Prentice Hall, Englewood Cliffs. New Jersey, 1982.
15. James J. Lynch: Managing the Integrity Factor. IFS International Limited, UK, 1994.
16. Edward Freeman: Business Ethics, R Oxford University Press, New York, 1991.
17. Kann Paul: Business Environment and Business Ethics, Ballenger Publishing Company, Cambridge, 1987.
18. Ethics in Organization, Coopers & Lybrand, 1997.
19. David Murray: The Ethics of Management, Larae Tone Hosmer; Universal Book Stall, New Delhi.
20. Ronald M. Green: The Ethical Manager, Macmillan College Publishing Company, New York, 1993.
21. Dr. Subash Sharma, Ethics and Human Values in Management: Indian Ethos and Indian Management, 1998.
22. Brain Harvey: Business Ethics (A European Approach)., Prentice Hall, New York, 1994.
23. Robert K. Mueller: The Innovation Ethics, American Management Association, 1971.
24. Joseph A. Petnick, John F. Quinn: Management Ethics, 1993 Response Book, Sage Publications Inc. New Delhi.
25. Frank K. Sonnenberg: Managing with a Conscience., McGraw Hill Inc. New York, 1994.
26. John Donaldson. Ethics in Organizations, David Murray, Coopers and Lybrand. 1997, London.

27. Business Ethic, A European Case Book. UK Academic Press, Harcourt Brace Jovanovch Publishers, 1992.
28. George D. Chryssides and John H. Kaler, An Introduction to Business Ethics. Chapman and Hall. London, 1993.
29. Bartley A. Brennan. The legal environment of business. Nancy Cavicek.
30. Hindu, Feb.8. 1999. R. Krishna Kumar, Nov.16. 1997. Sudha S Narayan (courtesy: Savita Prabhakar).
31. E.P. Samuel Abideen and K.P. Muralidharan : Ethical and Social issues in Advertising,
32. R.P. Banerjee: Ethics in Business and Management [Concepts-Western and Indian; Cases (National and International) 2003 Edition. Himalaya Publishing House, Mumbai.
33. Manuel G Velasquez. Business Ethics (concepts and cases-5th Edition) by Pearson Education, Asia, 2002, New Delhi.
34. John R Boatright, Ethics and the conduct of Business, Fourth Edition by Pearson Education (Singapore) Pvt. Ltd., Delhi, 2003.
35. Laura P. Hartman: Perspectives in Business Ethics-Second Edition by Tata McGraw Hill Publications, New Delhi written by, 2003 Edition.
36. S.A. Sherlekar :Ethics and Management. Himalaya Publishing House, Mumbai, 1999.
37. George A. Steiner and John F. Steiner, Business, Government and Society, McGraw Hill International.
38. Kautilya's Arthasastra by Penguin.
39. S.K. Chakraborty. Ethics in Management Vedantic Perspective: Oxford University Press.
40. M.K. Gandhi, My Experiments with Truth, Navajeevan Publishing House, Ahmedabad.
41. Subash Sharma, Management in New Age. Western Windows. Eastern Doors, New Age International Publishing. New Delhi.
42. R.C. Sekhar: Ethical choices in Business, 4th Edition, Response Books, 1999.

43. Dr. (Mrs.) Rituparna: A Study in Business Ethics Raj 2003 Edition Himalaya Publishing House, Mumbai.
44. Joseph M. Juran: Juran's Quality Hand Book. 5th edition McGraw-Hill, 2000, Information Edition.
45. New Leaders, Daniel Goleman, 1st edition Little Brown Publish USA, 2002.
46. Arthur Dobrin, Ethics for Everyone: How to Increase Your Moral Intelligence (New York: Wiley, 2002), pp. 31–32
47. Joseph L. Badaracco Jr., Defining Moments: When Managers Must Choose between Right and Right (Cambridge, MA: Harvard Business School Press, 1997), pp. 41–42.
48. Saul W. Gellerman, "Why 'Good' Managers Make Bad Ethical Choices," Harvard Business Review, July– August 1986
49. P. Kotler, "Is Marketing Ethics an Oxymoron?" Marketing Management, November–December 2004, pp. 30–35.
50. M. R. Vickers, "Business Ethics and the HR Role: Past, Present, and Future," Human Resource Planning 28, No. 1 (2005).
51. Curtis C. Verschoor, "Ethical Culture: Most Important Barrier to Ethical Misconduct," Strategic Finance 87, No. 6 (December 2005), p. 19
52. Walter J. Salmon, "Crisis Prevention: How to Gear Up Your Board," Harvard Business Review, January– February 1993.
53. International Finance Corp., World Bank Group, "The Irresistible Case for Corporate Governance," September 2005, www.gcgf.org/.
54. Ronald Berenbeim, "Giving Ethics Operational Meaning in Corporate Governance," Executive Speeches 19, No. 5 (April–May 2005), p. 19.
55. "Corporate Governance Mom: Nell Minow," The Economist, April 10, 2003. 12. Cadbury Report, "The Financial Aspects of Corporate Governance," December 1992.
56. Yilmaz Argüden, "Measuring the Effectiveness of Corporate Governance," INSEAD Knowledge, April 16, 2010
57. Richard T. DeGeorge, Business Ethics, 5th ed. (Upper Saddle River, NJ: Prentice-Hall, 1999).

58. Mark Taylor, "$73 Million . . . and Counting?" Modern Healthcare 49 (December 5, 2005), p. 18.

59. Neil Weinberg, "The Dark Side of Whistleblowing," Forbes 175, No. 5 (March 14, 2005), p. 90.

60. Richard C. Warren, "Whistleblowing: Subversion or Corporate Citizenship?" (review), Journal of Occupational and Organizational Psychology 71, No. 4 (December 1998), p. 372;

61. Ann Hayes Peterson, "Inside the WorldCom Fraud," Credit Union Magazine 71, No. 8 (August 2005), p. 15.

62. Laura M. Franze, "Corporate Compliance: The Whistleblower Provisions of the Sarbanes-Oxley Act of 2002," Insights: The Corporate & Securities Law Advisor 16 (December 2002), p. 12.

63. Peter Rost, The Whistleblower: Confessions of a Healthcare Hitman (Brooklyn, NY: Soft Skull Press, 2006).

64. Barry, V. (1978). Personal and social ethics: Moral problems with integrated theory. Belmont, CA: Wadsworth.

65. Bazerman, M. H. (1986). Management in managerial decision making. New York, NY: Wiley.

66. Bazerman, M. H. (2014). The power of noticing: What the best leaders see. New York, NY: Simon & Schuster.

67. Bazerman, M. H., & Tenbrunsel, A. E. (2011). Blind spots: Why we fail to do what's right and what to do about it. Princeton, NJ: Princeton University Press.

68. Bird, F. B. (1996). The muted conscience: Moral silence and the practice of ethics in business. Westport, CT

69. Qyorum, Birkinshaw, P. (2006). Transparency as a human right. In C. Hood & D. Heald (Eds.), Transparency: The key to better governance? (pp. 47-57). Oxford, England: Oxford University Press.

70. Blasi, A. (1984). Moral identity: Its role in moral functioning. In W. M. Kurtines & J. L. Gewirtz (Eds.), Morality, moral behaviour, and moral development (pp. 128-139). New York, NY: Wiley

71. Brown, M. T. (2005). Corporate integrity: Rethinking organizational ethics and leadership. Cambridge, England: Cambridge University Press.

72. Brown, R. (1995). Prejudice: Its social psychology. Oxford, England: Blackwell.

73. Brown, R. P. (2003). Measuring individual differences in the tendency to forgive: Construct validity and links with depression. Personality and Social Psychology Bulletin, 29, 759-771.

74. Adam, Paul J. 1963. Dealing with conflicts of interest. Management Review 52:50-53

75. Hurst R.: Code of Ethics. New York. Anderson, 1954. Ethical values in administration. Personnel Administration 17:1-12.

76. Andriacco, Dan. 1988. Ethics: The new fad in business circles spawns new business. The Birmingham News (July 9), p. B12

77. Richard T. DeGeorge. Business Ethics: Macmillan Publishing Co., New York, 1990, 3rd edition

78. Alan R. Malachowski, Business Ethics—Critical Perspective on Business and Management: Taylor & Francis, London, 2001

79. Manuel G. Velasquez: Business Ethics—Concepts and Cases: Pearson Education, Indian Br., Delhi, 2002, 5th edition 4. The Concept of Law: H.L.A. Hart, Oxford University Press, London, 1961

80. Alex C. Michales: A Pragmatic Approach to Business Ethics: Sage Publications, 1995

81. Alan Donagan: The Theory of Morality: University of Chicago Press, Chicago, 1977.

82. S.J. Wirtenberger: Morality and Business: Loyola University Press, Chicago, 1962.

83. Ethical Theory and Business: (Eds.), Prentice Hall, New Jersey, 1979

84. Tom L. Beauchamp and N.E. Bowie: Thomas A. Klein: Social Costs and Benefits of Business: Prentice Hall, New Jersey, 1977

85. Peter Singer: Practical Ethics: Cambridge University Press, London, 1993

86. Ackerman, Robert. The Social Challenge to Business. Cambridge, MA: Harvard University Press, 1975.

87. Albrecht, Karl. Corporate Radar: Tracking the Forces That Are Shaping Your Business. New York: American Management Association, 2000.

88. Barth, Regine, and Franziska Wolff (eds.). Corporate Social Responsibility in Europe—Rhetoric and Realities. Cheltenham, UK: Edward Elgar Publishing, 2009.

89. Bhagwati, Jagdish. In Defense of Globalization. New York: Oxford University Press, 2007. Bowen, Howard R. Responsibilities of the Businessman. New York: Harper, 1953.

90. Andrew W. Ghilliyar: Business Ethics Now. 2018: McGraw Hill Education

91. Data Ethics - The New Competitive Advantage: Gry Hasselbalch & Pernille Tranberg ApS / Spintype.com, 2016

92. Chris Moon & Clive Bonny : Business ethics: Facing up to the Issues: The Economist in association with Profile Books Limited. 2008

93. Lipman-Blumen, J. (2005). The allure of toxic leaders: Why we follow destructive bosses and corrupt politicians-and how we can survive them. Oxford, England: Oxford University Press.

94. Lisman, C. D. (1996). The curricular integration of ethics: Theory and practice. Westport, CT: Praeger.

95. Mathews, M. C. (1990). Codes of ethics: Organizational behaviour and misbehaviour. In W. C. Frederick & L. E. Preston (Eds.), Business ethics: Research issues and empirical studies (pp. 99-122). Greenwich, CT: JAI Press.

96. Pearson, G. (1995). Integrity in organizations: An alternative business ethic. London, England: McGraw-Hill

97. Price, T. L. (2006). Understanding ethical failures in leadership. Cambridge, England: Cambridge University Press. Provis, C. (2010).

98. Virtuous decision making for business ethics journal of Business Ethics, 91, 3-6.

99. Sturm, R. E. (2017). Decreasing unethical decisions: The role of morality-based individual differences. Journal of Business Ethics, 142, 37-57.

100. Sucher, S. J. (2008). The moral leader: Challenges, tools, and insights. London, England: Routledge.

101. Trevino, L. K., & Nelson, K. A. (2004). Managing business ethics: Straight talk about how to do it right (3rd ed.). Hoboken, NJ: Wiley.

102. Trevino, L. K., & Weaver, G. R. (2001). Organizational justice and ethics program "follow-through": Influences on employees' harmful and helpful behaviour. Business Ethics Quarterly, 11, 651-671.

103. Trevino, L. K., & Weaver, G. R. (2003). Managing ethics in business organizations: Social scientific perspectives. Stanford, CA: Stanford University Press.

104. Trevino, L. K., & Weaver, G. R. (2001). Organizational justice and ethics program "follow-through": Influences on employees' harmful and helpful behaviour. Business Ethics Quarterly, 11, 651-671. Trevino, L. K., & Weaver, G. R. (2003). Managing ethics in business organizations: Social scientific perspectives. Stanford, CA: Stanford University Press.

105. Yukl, G. (2013). Leadership in organizations (8th ed.). Upper Saddle River, NJ: Prentice-Hall.

106. Yukl, G., Falbe, C. M., & Yount, J. (1993). Patterns of influence behaviours for managers. Group and Organization Management, 18.